Lecture Notes in Computer Scienc

T0238089

Commenced Publication in 1973
Founding and Former Series Editors:
Gerhard Goos, Juris Hartmanis, and Jan van Leeuwen

Giancarlo Mauri   Gheorghe Păun
Mario J. Pérez-Jiménez
Grzegorz Rozenberg   Arto Salomaa (Eds.)

Membrane Computing

5th International Workshop, WMC 2004
Milan, Italy, June 14-16, 2004
Revised Selected and Invited Papers

 Springer

Volume Editors

Giancarlo Mauri
E-mail: mauri@disco.unimib.it

Gheorghe Păun
E-mail: gpaun@us.es

Mario J. Pérez-Jiménez
E-mail: marper@us.es

Grzegorz Rozenberg
E-mail: rozenberg@liacs.nl

Arto Salomaa
E-mail: asalomaa@cs.utu.fi

Library of Congress Control Number: 2005921095

CR Subject Classification (1998): F.1, F.4, I.6, J.3

ISSN 0302-9743
ISBN 3-540-25080-8 Springer Berlin Heidelberg New York

Springer is a part of Springer Science+Business Media

springeronline.com

© Springer-Verlag Berlin Heidelberg 2005
Printed in Germany

Typesetting: Camera-ready by author, data conversion by Scientific Publishing Services, Chennai, India
Printed on acid-free paper   SPIN: 11399940   06/3142   5 4 3 2 1 0

Preface

This volume is based on papers presented at the **5th Workshop on Membrane Computing, WMC5**, which took place in Milan, Italy, in the period June 14–16, 2004, as a satellite event of DNA10 (10th International Workshop on DNA-Based Computing). The first three workshops were organized in Curtea de Argeş, Romania – they took place in August 2000 (with the proceedings published in *Lecture Notes in Computer Science*, volume 2235), in August 2001 (with a selection of papers published as a special issue of *Fundamenta Informaticae*, volume 49, numbers 1–3, 2002), and in August 2002 (with the proceedings published in *Lecture Notes in Computer Science*, volume 2597). The fourth workshop took place in Tarragona, Spain, in July 2003 (the proceedings appeared as volume 2933 of *Lecture Notes in Computer Science*).

Like the previous two meetings, also WMC5 was an official workshop of the Molecular Computing Network (MolCoNet) funded by the EU Commission in the Fifth Framework program Information Society Technologies (project number IST-2001-32008). The preproceedings of WMC5 were published as a MolCoNet report, and they were available during the workshop.

This volume contains only a selection of the papers from the preproceedings. Moreover, the selected papers were significantly modified/improved according to the really vivid discussions that took place during the workshop – all the selected papers were additionally refereed. The papers in the volume cover all the main directions of research in membrane computing, ranging from topics in mathematics and theoretical computer science, to applications in biology, linguistics, and computer graphics. Research related to the computing power and the complexity classes, new classes of P systems, fuzzy approaches, reversibility and energy accounting, and to many other topics is presented. Unlike the previous workshops, the WMC5 scientific program included invited lectures, by leading researchers in membrane computing, and in the general area of natural computing – almost all of these invited talks are represented in the volume. Altogether, the volume is a faithful illustration of the current state of research in membrane computing (a good source of information about this fast-emerging area of natural computing is the webpage `http://psystems.disco.unimib.it`).

The workshop was organized by the Computer Science Department of the University of Milano-Bicocca, under the auspices of the European Molecular Computing Consortium (EMCC). The program committee consisted of Giancarlo Mauri (Milan, Italy), Gheorghe Păun (Bucharest, Romania, and Seville, Spain), Mario J. Pérez-Jiménez (Seville, Spain), Grzegorz Rozenberg (Leiden, The Netherlands, and Boulder, Colorado, USA), and Arto Salomaa (Turku, Finland).

The editors are indebted to the participants of WMC5 and in particular to the contributors to this volume. Special thanks go to Springer for the efficient cooperation in the timely production of this volume.

November 2004

Giancarlo Mauri
Gheorghe Păun
Mario J. Pérez-Jiménez
Grzegorz Rozenberg
Arto Salomaa

Table of Contents

Invited Lectures

λP Systems and Typed λ-Calculus
Loïc Colson, Nataša Jonoska, Maurice Margenstern 1

P Automata
Erzsébet Csuhaj-Varjú 19

Asynchronous P Systems and P Systems Working in the Sequential
Mode
Rudolf Freund 36

Evolution and Oscillation in P Systems: Applications to Biological
Phenomena
Vincenzo Manca, Luca Bianco, Federico Fontana 63

An Approach to Computational Complexity in Membrane Computing
Mario J. Pérez-Jiménez 85

LMNtal: A Language Model with Links and Membranes
Kazunori Ueda, Norio Kato 110

Regular Presentations

Executable Specifications of P Systems
Oana Andrei, Gabriel Ciobanu, Dorel Lucanu 126

On the Efficiency of P Systems with Active Membranes and Two
Polarizations
Artiom Alhazov, Rudolf Freund 146

Communicative P Systems with Minimal Cooperation
*Artiom Alhazov, Maurice Margenstern, Vladimir Rogozhin,
Yurii Rogozhin, Sergey Verlan* 161

Ultimately Confluent Rewriting Systems. Parallel Multiset–Rewriting
with Permitting or Forbidding Contexts
Artiom Alhazov, Dragoş Sburlan 178

Unstable P Systems: Applications to Linguistics
Gemma Bel Enguix 190

A P System Description of the Sodium-Potassium Pump
Daniela Besozzi, Gabriel Ciobanu 210

Inhibiting/De-inhibiting Rules in P Systems
Matteo Cavaliere, Mihai Ionescu, Tseren-Onolt Ishdorj 224

Time–Independent P Systems
Matteo Cavaliere, Dragoş Sburlan 239

On Two-Dimensional Mesh Networks and Their Simulation with P
Systems
Rodica Ceterchi, Mario J. Pérez-Jiménez 259

Exploring Computation Trees Associated with P Systems
Andrés Cordón-Franco, Miguel A. Gutiérrez-Naranjo,
Mario J. Pérez-Jiménez, Agustín Riscos-Núñez 278

Approximating Non-discrete P Systems
Andrés Cordón-Franco, Fernando Sancho-Caparrini 287

Reducing the Size of Extended Gemmating P Systems
Erzsébet Csuhaj-Varjú, György Vaszil 296

P Systems Generating Trees
Rudolf Freund, Marion Oswald, Andrei Păun 309

On Descriptive Complexity of P Systems
Miguel A. Gutiérrez-Naranjo, Mario J. Pérez-Jiménez,
Agustín Riscos-Núñez 320

P Systems with Symport/Antiport: The Traces of RBCs
Shankara Narayanan Krishna 331

Conservative Computations in Energy–Based P Systems
Alberto Leporati, Claudio Zandron, Giancarlo Mauri 344

General Multi-fuzzy Sets and Fuzzy Membrane Systems
Adam Obtułowicz 359

Trading Polarization for Bi-stable Catalysts in P Systems with Active
Membranes
Mario J. Pérez-Jiménez, Francisco José Romero-Campero 373

Modelling Dynamic Organization of Biology-Inspired Multi-agent
Systems with Communicating X-Machines and Population P Systems
  Ioanna Stamatopoulou, Marian Gheorghe, Petros Kefalas 389

On the Size of P Systems with Minimal Symport/Antiport
  György Vaszil 404

Author Index 415

λP Systems and Typed λ-Calculus

Loïc Colson[1], Nataša Jonoska[2,*],
and Maurice Margenstern[1,**]

[1] LITA, EA 3097, Université de Metz, UFR MIM
Île du Saulcy, 57045 Metz, Cédex, France
{colson, margens}@sciences.univ-metz.fr
[2] Department of Mathematics, University of South-Florida,
4202 E. Fowler Ave., PHY 114
Tampa, FL 33620-5700, USA
jonoska@math.usf.edu

Abstract. In this extended abstract, we recast first the implementation
of tree operations in P systems with λP systems and simulation of pure
λ-calculus as proposed in [6]. Further, we indicate a similar way to implement Gödel's *T*-systems. This provides a family of P systems with each
system implementing a family of total recursive functions. The union
of the implemented functions coincides with the set of provably total
recursive functions in Peano arithmetic.

1 Introduction

P systems are now well known as a distributed parallel computing paradigm. In
these systems, multisets of symbol-objects are processed in the compartments
defined by a predetermined hierarchy of membranes. These objects evolve by
means of rewriting-like rules applied in a maximally parallel (all objects that can
evolve, do evolve) nondeterministic (the objects to be processed and the rules to
be applied are chosen in a random way) manner. For a detailed exposition on P
systems we refer the reader to the book [11].

Initially, the membrane structure of a P system was fixed such that only
the evolution of the objects was considered as essential part of the computation.
Soon after, it became clear that the active role of the membrane structure carries
a very powerful benefit as well as it is naturally occurring. The first observation
about the power of the active membranes was introduced in [10] where it was
shown that if membrane division and membrane dissolution is allowed in the
system, then **NP**-complete problems can be solved in polynomial time. Many
authors improved on this result by considering different variants of P systems
with active membranes (see, for example, [9, 13, 15]). However, in each of these

* Partially supported by NSF Grants CCF #0432009 and EIA#0086015, and by
NATO grant PST. CLG. 976912.
** Partially supported by the European project *MolCoNet* IST-2001-32008.

G. Mauri et al. (Eds.): WMC5 2004, LNCS 3365, pp. 1–18, 2005.

cases the evolving membrane structure is used to facilitate the computation and the membrane structure itself is not considered an essential part of the final product. In [3] authors define P systems that generate rectangular grids of membranes (that are not nested) such that the objects inside membranes represent rectangular picture languages. Labels for membranes appear from the initial definitions but most of the time their rôle is simply to differentiate the membranes and to locate them.

In [6], a new type of P systems was introduced where the membrane structure (i.e., its tree structure) is an essential part of the computation and the objects are used as facilitators. This system, called λP in [6], presented a new type of P systems where the membranes are used in an active way such that they are treated as objects, and the objects inside the membranes are treated as catalysts for the reactions. The P systems with active membranes use the creation of membranes, however λP systems go further: they not only create membranes, but they allow membranes to be inserted into other membranes, possibly in the innermost ones in the tree of the whole membrane structure. The main idea for λP systems came from (a) [2] where membranes in the P system are using different channels and as such could be considered as having different labels, and (b) [14] where the labeling of the membranes is used to identify them, but the structure of the whole system is of an essential importance. The membranes in λP systems have labels (the labeling is not injective) and according to these labels the membranes act in different ways after being subjected to the set of general rules. Hence, the labels can be considered in some sense as "different states" of the membrane channels such that in some cases they can be "open to objects only", in some cases are "open for other membranes", and in some cases are "closed". The rules do not allow relabeling of the membranes, but relabeling is intrinsically included by dissolving and then creating new membranes. The computation in λP systems uses labeled membranes and the final configuration is the result of the computation.

In [6], the λP systems are illustrated through a system that simulates β-reductions in pure λ-calculus expressions. As λ-calculus has Turing-complete power of computation, λP systems have the same equivalent computational power. It is also shown in [6] that 3SAT and hence other **NP**-complete problems can be solved in polynomial time by λP systems (though in the process of computation, there is an exponential expansion of the number of membranes involved).

In this paper, we go one step further and one step back. The step further is the simulation of **typed** λ-calculus. This amounts to inforce the rôle of the membrane labelling. Here, labels have a complex structure as they encode **types** and they control the computation in a more strong way than in [6]. By modelling a special kind of typed λ-calculus, namely Gödel's T system, we go one step back: we loose Turing-complete power of computation. With this construction we obtain functions whose computation always completes, they are **total** recursive functions, and all functions needed for practical purposes are obtained.

In fact, the set of functions computed by Gödel's T system is the set of all partial recursive functions which are provably total in Peano arithmetic.

This will be obtained by a hierarchy of functions. Each class of the hierarchy is attached to a fixed **recursor** (see below for the definition of this notion).

Due to space considerations, this extended abstract provides only guidelines for this implementation and details are omitted.

2 λP Systems

We refer the reader to [11, 12] for an introduction to P systems and we assume some general knowledge for this computational model. All membranes in a λP system have a label from a predetermined alphabet of labels Λ. The set of objects that can appear in the membranes is denoted with $\mathcal{O}$. The membrane structure is represented as a tree with the skin being the root. If a membrane with label α is an inner membrane of β such that there is no inner membrane of β that contains α, then α is an immediate child of β. We write $C(\beta) = \{\alpha_1, \ldots, \alpha_k\}$ to represent that all immediate children of β are $\alpha_1, \ldots, \alpha_k$.

A membrane with label α is denoted with $[^\alpha]$ and the label is denoted with $\textcircled{\alpha}$. The circle around α is used to indicate that α is a label of a membrane visible from outside. In a membrane, the labels of all immediate inner membranes (immediate children) are visible (detectable). All rules can use the objects currently in the membrane and have contextual dependence on the labels of the inner membranes. Three basic types of operations with membranes (tree structure) are performed.

$$(a) \quad \textcircled{\alpha} \rightarrow [^\alpha]_{in[^\beta]}, \qquad (\textcircled{\alpha} \rightarrow [^\alpha]_{out[^\beta]})$$

$$(b) \quad \textcircled{\alpha} \rightarrow [^\alpha]_{in^*[^\beta]}, \qquad (\textcircled{\alpha} \rightarrow [^\alpha]_{out^*[^\beta]})$$

$$(c) \quad \textcircled{\alpha} \rightarrow [^\beta[^\alpha]]$$

The first operation takes a membrane and all its structure and includes it in a membrane at the same level. This tree operation is performed such that if α and β are children of ρ, i.e., $\alpha, \beta \in C(\rho)$, then α and all its subtree is removed as a child from ρ and is added to $C(\beta)$ as a child to β (see Figure 1 (a)).

The operation (b) takes the membrane α with all its structure and includes this structure inside the innermost membranes of β (see Figure 1 (b)). As a tree operation, if α and β are children of ρ, i.e., $\alpha, \beta \in C(\rho)$, then the operation removes α and its subtree as a child of ρ and adds it to the leaves of β. If the target β is not indicated, then membrane α becomes a subtree of all leaves of its parent ρ. Both of these operations have a variation (in parenthesis) which gives opposite operations to the trees. When the membrane α and its subtree is not removed, it is indicated by the appearance of $[^\alpha]$ on the right hand side of the rule.

The third type of rules (c) surrounds the membrane α with a membrane β. The tree structure in this case changes such that if α is a child of ρ, then after

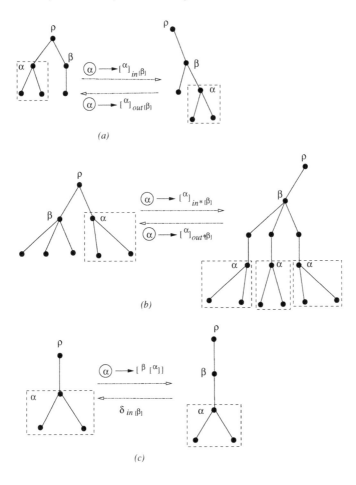

Fig. 1. The change of the tree structure by λP operations. The subtree that is moved by the operation is included in a dashed box

the operation of type (c), ρ has a child β which has a child α (see Figure 1 (c)). The reverse of the process (removing β as a child from $C(\rho)$) is obtained by introducing a special symbol δ in membrane β. The presence of this symbol removes the current membrane, but does not change the rest of the structure of that membrane. We assume that the set of objects (denoted with $\mathcal{O}$) always contains this symbol δ. Another special symbol that removes a membrane together with all its substructure (i.e., removes a whole subtree in the tree structure) is δ^*. We assume that $\delta^* \in \mathcal{O}$.

In addition to the standard targets of objects in P systems, $\{in, out, stay\}$, we add two additional targets $\{in^*, out^*\}$. These operations are similar to the ones for the membranes. The target in^* denotes that the object is sent to the innermost membranes of the substructure of the membrane where it currently belongs, and the target out^* indicates that the object is sent to the skin. The standard target $in_\#$, where $\#$ is the number of the membrane, is substituted with $in_{[\alpha]}$ where $[\alpha]$ is a membrane labeled α. There may be several such membranes, and in that case the object is sent to all membranes with the indicated label.

Definition 1. *A λP rule is a rule of the form* $X_1, \ldots, X_s \rightarrow Y^1_{tar_{Z_1}}, \ldots, Y^t_{tar_{Z_t}}$ *where*

- $X_i \in \mathcal{O}$, *or* $X_i = \boxed{Z}$, *for* $Z \in \Lambda$,
- $Y^j \in \mathcal{O}$, *or* $Y^j = [^Z]$, *or* $Y^j = [^Z[^U]]$, *for* $Z, U \in \Lambda$,
- $tar \in \{in, in^*, out, out^*, stay\}$, $Z_i \in \Lambda$.

From now on, in order to simplify the notation, the target *stay* will be omitted.

Definition 2. *A λP system is a construct*

$$\Pi = (\Lambda \cup \mathcal{O}, \mu(V), R, f),$$

where Λ is an alphabet of the labels of the membranes, $\mathcal{O}$ is the alphabet of objects, μ is the initial tree of a membrane structure with nodes V, R is the set of λP rules, and $f : V \rightarrow \Lambda$.

Execution of the Rules. The set of rules is fixed for the whole system. The presence of objects and labels of membranes trigger the evolution. All rules that can be applied are applied (note that the rules may depend on the labels of the inner membranes and as such are contextual). Objects in the membranes are acting as catalysts, that is, the presence of an object within a context of a given membrane label triggers all membranes with that label to take part in the application of the rule. As is standard for P systems, all objects that take part in the operation (i.e., are on the left hand side of the rule) and do not appear on the right hand side of the same rule, are considered to be destroyed in the process. A weak priority is imposed such that all rules that do not depend on the context of membrane labels are applied first.

Computation. The λP system stops evolving when none of the rules can be applied. The result of the computation is the final membrane configuration. A formal definition follows. As in the standard definition of a configuration of a P system the membrane tree structure is indicated with square brackets (see [11, 12]). Let μ be the initial tree representing a membrane structure of a λP system Π. The **initial configuration** of Π is denoted with $\mathcal{C}_0 = [^S \mathcal{O}_S [^{Y_1} \mathcal{O}_{Y_1}] \cdots [^{Y_k} \mathcal{O}_{Y_k}]]$ where $[^S]$ is the skin (i.e., the root of μ) and $[^{Y_i}]$ are membrane structures corresponding to the subtrees of μ with roots in the set of immediate children $C(S)$ of the root S ($i = 1, ..., k$). The sets $\mathcal{O}_S, \mathcal{O}_{Y_i}$ denote the set of objects in each of the membranes. We write

$$\mathcal{C}_i \rightarrow_R \mathcal{C}_{i+1}$$

if by applying all λP rules from R in parallel as described above one changes the configuration $\mathcal{C}_i$ into $\mathcal{C}_{i+1}$. A **computation of the λP system** Π is a sequence: $\mathcal{C}(\Pi) = \mathcal{C}_0, \mathcal{C}_1, \ldots$ such that $\mathcal{C}_i \rightarrow_R \mathcal{C}_{i+1}$ for all i. The computation is finite if there is j such that $\mathcal{C}_j = \mathcal{C}_{j+1}$. In this case we say that $\mathcal{C}_j$ is a **final configuration**. We say that the *result* of the λP system is the final configuration. The result for Π is denoted with $\mathcal{F}(\Pi)$.

In the sections that follow we concentrate on specific λP systems which can be used to simulate pure λ-calculus in parallel and further the Gödel T system.

3   Simulating Pure λ-Calculus

Pure λ-calculus was created by Alonso CHURCH in the early 1930's We refer the reader to [1, 8] for an introduction and for references. We recall a very short definition and basic properties of pure λ-calculus.

3.1   Pure λ-Calculus

This formal system consists of a countable number of **symbols**. Three of them, 'λ', '(' and ')' can be seen as punctuation symbols while the remaining ones are called **variables** which are usually denoted by individual letters with possible indices: a, b, x, y_1, ..., y_k.

λ-terms are defined by induction, as follows:

Definition 3. *(i) A variable x is a λ-term being denoted by x; x is **free** in this term;*

*(ii) if M is a λ-term and if x is a variable, $\lambda x\, M$ is a λ-term, and all occurrences of x are **bound** in $\lambda x\, M$; we say that these occurrences of x are **controlled** by this λ and that M is the **scope** of this λ; $\lambda x\, M$ is called the **abstraction** of M with respect to x;*

*(iii) if M and N are λ-terms, then $(M)\, N$ is a λ-term; this term is called the **application** of M to N; the free occurrences of x in M and N are still free in $(M)\, N$.*

This notation of λ-terms is taken from [8]. It has the property that it needs exactly the symbols which we indicated to define the λ-terms. We note that our definition is a variation of the traditional notation $(M\ N)$ for the application that uses an additional symbol: the blank, used as a separator in the application.

A **sub-term** U of a λ-term M is a λ-term which, as a word, is a factor of M.

The notion of computation for λ-terms is defined through β-reductions. We say that a λ-term of the form $(\lambda x\, M)\, N$ is a **redex** and that its **reduction** is the term $M\, [x := N]$ which is obtained from M by replacing all free occurrences of x in M by N. This restriction is due to the following natural requirement: if N contains a variable which is free before the reduction, the variable must remain free after the reduction. We denote the reduction by $(\lambda x\, M)\, N \Rightarrow M\, [x := N]$.

When a λ-term contains no redex, we say that it is in **normal form**. The goal of a computation is to transform a λ-term into a λ-term which is in normal form and, by definition, this normal form is called the result of the computation. In order to do so, we apply successively the β-reduction until we arrive to a term without a redex.

For a λ-term M, we denote with $\mathcal{N}(M)$ the normal form obtained by performing β-reductions to M.

Example 1. Consider the following λ-term:

$$((\lambda x\, \lambda y\, (x)\, y)\, a)\, b.$$

This term represents the application of $\lambda x\, \lambda y\, (x)\, y$ to two arguments: first a, then b. Notice that in pure λ-calculus, $\lambda x\, \lambda y\, (x)\, y$ is defined as the representation of number 1, see [1, 8]. The reduction goes as follows:

$$((\lambda x\, \lambda y\, (x)\, y)\, a)\, b \Rightarrow (\lambda y\, (a)\, y)\, b \Rightarrow (a)\, b$$

In this computation in two steps, there is no choice in the order of reduction of the redexes. In general, this may not be the case. Assume that a is an abstract term, e.g., $\lambda z P$. Then, we have

$$((\lambda x\, \lambda y\, (x)\, y)\, \lambda z\, P)\, b \Rightarrow (\lambda y\, (\lambda z\, P)\, y)\, b$$

and, at this point, there are two redexes at the same stage of the computation (λy-term and λz-subterm) and so there are two possible paths for the continuation of the computation.

Note that a term may have several subterms which are redexes and these redexes, as in the above example, can be nested.

The rules of λ-calculus do not fix the choice and the computation can be executed by any order, even in parallel if it is possible when the redexes are independent. Fortunately, the Church-Rosser theorem (see [1] for instance) indicates that this is not a problem. The theorem says that any path of the computation which leads to a normal term leads to the same normal term. In this case, this normal term is called the **result** of the computation. A path of computations which leads to the result is called a **terminating path**.

Continuing Example 1, if we reduce the leftmost redex first, we have:

$$((\lambda x\, \lambda y\, (x)\, y)\, \lambda z\, P)\, b \Rightarrow (\lambda y\, (\lambda z\, P)\, y)\, b \Rightarrow (\lambda z\, P)\, b \Rightarrow P[z := b]$$

Otherwise, by reducing the λz-subterm first, we have:

$$((\lambda x\, \lambda y\, (x)\, y)\, \lambda z\, P)\, b \Rightarrow (\lambda y\, (\lambda z\, P)\, y)\, b \Rightarrow (\lambda y\, P[z := y])\, b$$
$$\Rightarrow P[z := b]$$

as we assumed that y does not appear in P and is free in the λ-term $(\lambda z\, P)\, y$.

This computation is very simple. For more complex terms, it may be a real question whether the computation terminates. The theorem of Church-Rosser says that if there are terminating paths they all lead to the same result. But in general, a terminating path may not exist. If there is a terminating path, by reducing the leftmost redex in a λ-term, the sequence of reductions leads to the normal form, see for example [8]. This result is called the theorem of the **leftmost reduction strategy**.

Pure λ-calculus is computationally equivalent to the Turing machines, see for instance [1]. The λP simulation of a general λ-term is described in the next subsection.

3.2   The Simulation of General Terms; The System Π

When the terms contain several occurrences of the same variable, it is necessary to rename variables in different copies of the same λ-term during the reduction. This is required since in the reduction of $(\lambda x\, M)\, N$, if N contains a free variable y, this y must be free in $M[x := N]$.

This is usually solved by the introduction of an equivalence relation on λ-terms, called α-conversion [1, 8]. The variables of a λ-term are called **separated** when the occurrences of a given variable are all free or all bound. The two λ-terms U and V are said α-equivalent if there is a bijection φ from the set of variables of U to the set of variables of V such that replacing each occurrence of a variable x of U in U by $\varphi(x)$ we obtain V. Performing such a bijection is called **renaming** the variables.

Renaming of the variables during the computation is an essential feature of pure λ-calculus, see for example [1, 8]. Representing λ-terms by **binary trees** is one way to solve this. The representation is as follows:

- a variable is represented by a **leaf**

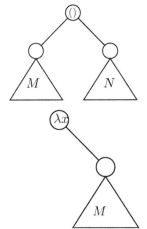

- the term $(M)\, N$ is represented by:

- the term $\lambda x\, M$ is represented by:

Notice that this tree representation of a λ-term shows why λP systems are able to simulate λ-calculus. However, the link between the λ-node and the occurrences of the corresponding variable further down the tree cannot be directly implemented in λP systems without employing renaming of the variables. This is due to the fact that objects within one membrane can only "see" the label of the immediate children membranes and not deeper in the tree. A solution to this problem was given in [6].

The solution consists of implementing a 'primitive' renaming by appending numbers, i.e., 'indices' to variables which indicate when the renaming is to be performed. The general description of λP systems uses unary representation of numbers by objects as a way to implement indices.

When a redex $(\lambda x \; M) \, N$ is reduced, we *freeze* the argument N in order to prevent later substitutions of the variables. During the further steps of the computation, the variables of N remain frozen, as long as N does not come to the functional position inside a parenthesis. We solve this by putting a 'freezing membrane' labelled by F around the term to be frozen. Then, in context of F, to all variable-labeled membranes an object representing a "red light" r is added. This r may increase the number of r's that are already in the membrane. When a freeezing F-membrane comes in a functional position, a signal, an object representing a "green light" g is sent to all variable-labeled membranes contained in F which erases exactly one r in these membranes and this former F-membrane is dissolved. Accordingly, the number of r's in a variable-labeled membrane is exactly the number of F-membranes which contain it. This is implementation of De Bruijn solution for automatic renaming based on integers, see [4].

It is not difficult to check that this mechanism simulates a correct renaming and we obtain an exact simulation of the leftmost reduction strategy of a general λ-term. As observed in [6], we can extend this λP system such that a parallel reduction to several terms with several arguments is possible.

3.3 Representing General λ-Terms with Membranes

Alphabets for the λP System Π. Assume that X_Φ is the set of variables that appear in the λ-term Φ. The set of objects for the λP system Π is

$$\mathcal{O} = \{\delta, \delta^*\} \cup \{B, S, d, d', \eta, \nu, \sigma, \eta', \nu', r, g\} \cup \{s_x, c_x \,|\, x \in X_\Phi\}.$$

The set of membrane labels is the following:

$$\Lambda = \{(), P, F\} \cup \{x, \lambda_x \,|\, x \in X_\Phi\}.$$

Initial Configurations for Π. In order to keep the same representation pattern of membrane structures corresponding to all λ-terms from initial to the final normal form, we admit both 'red light' r's and/or 'green light' g's in the variable labeled membranes. This comes from the observation that in a λ-term M the appearance of x may be bound **and** unbound. However, for the initial configuration, we may assume that the λ-term which we translate has separated variables. Accordingly, we have the following definition.

Definition 4. *For each λ-term α in which the variables are separated, we define a membrane structure μ_α inductively,*

(i) For a variable x we have the membrane $[^x s_x]$.

(ii) If M is a λ-term represented by a membrane system $M_{[\,]}$, then the λ-term $\lambda_x M$ is represented by the membrane system $[^{\lambda_x} \bar{M}_{[\,]}]$ such that $\bar{M}_{[\,]}$ is obtained from $M_{[\,]}$ by adding the object g in all membranes $[^x]$ representing a free appearance of x in M.

(iii) If M is represented by a membrane system $M_{[]}$ and N with a membrane system $N_{[]}$, then the λ-term $(M)N$ is represented by the membrane system $[^{()}M_{[]}[^{P}N_{[]}]]$.

The membrane structure μ_α that corresponds to the λ-term α with membrane representation $\alpha_{[]}$ is $\mu_\alpha = \left[\alpha_{[]}\right]$.

Notation. When $\mathcal{A}$ is a set of λ-terms, we write $\mathcal{A}_{[]}$ for the set of membrane representations of $\alpha_{[]}$ for $\alpha \in \mathcal{A}$, and we write $\mu_\mathcal{A} = \left[\mathcal{A}_{[]}\right]$. For the λ-term α we denote by $\mathcal{N}(\alpha)$ the normal form for α obtained at the end of computation.

Rules for the λP System *Π*. In this paper we clarify the set of rules from [6] by including rules 1.1 to 1.7 which assures simultaneous unfreezing of the membranes and reduction of one "red light" in the leaf membranes. This simultaneous unfreezing and red light reduction was not specified in [6] and hence in certain cases the rules in [6] do not simulate correct reduction.

The reduction of one "red' light" when "unfreezing" is simulated with rules 8.1–8.3 which are executed with priority since they have no contextual dependence from membrane labels.

Rules 1. Search for the first reduction position. Due to the protection membrane P specified with the initial configuration, this reduction is determined to be the leftmost. In the process of this search a freezing membrane may be found that require unfreezing.

    rule 1.1. $B, \left(()\right) \to S_{\text{in }[()]}$

                (B is the beginning of the reduction; it explores the parenthesis becoming S: possibly substitution)

    rule 1.2. $B, \left(\lambda x\right) \to B_{\text{in }[\lambda x]}$

                (B meets a λ-labeled membrane: go on further)

    rule 1.3. $B, \left(F\right) \to \delta_{\text{in }[^F]}, \eta'_{\text{in}* \; [^F]}, B$

                (B meets a freezed membrane: unfreeze once by sending η' to reduce the number of r's (rules 81.-8.3) and go further)

    rule 1.4. $S, \left(F\right) \to \delta_{\text{in }[^F]}, \eta'_{\text{in}* \; [^F]}, S$

                (S meets a freezed membrane: it destroys the F-membrane and a signal is sent to reduce the red signals by one, S is kept to proceed further)

    rule 1.5. $S, \left(\lambda x\right), \left(P\right) \to \eta$

                (begin reduction: prepare for separation of the arguments)

    rule 1.6. $S, \left(x\right)\left(P\right) \to B$

                (S meets a variable: go further with B)

    rule 1.7. $S, \left(()\right)\left(P\right) \to B$

                (S meets a parenthesis: go further with B)

Rules 2. Identify the arguments and the variables for the substitution.

  rule 2.1. $\eta,(P) \rightarrow [^{()} [^P]], \nu$

  (include each argument in an additional membrane $[^{()}]$)

  rule 2.2. $\nu,(\lambda x) \rightarrow [^{\lambda x}]_{\text{in} [^{()}]}, \sigma_{\text{in} [^{()}]}, \delta,$ $(x \in X_\Phi)$

  (include all functional terms into the membrane with the arguments, destroy the current membrane, send the starting symbol σ to each of the membranes with arguments)

  rule 2.3. $\sigma,(\lambda x), (P) \rightarrow d, c_{x \text{in}^*}[^{\lambda x}], [^P]_{\text{in}^*}[^{\lambda x}], \delta_{\text{in}}[^{\lambda x}],$ $(x \in X_\Phi)$

  (for each function in the membrane of a given argument, prepare to destroy the current membrane, search for the current variable into all most-inner membranes, send the argument in the innermost membranes, destroy λx)

Rules 3. Destroy the argument.

  rule 3. $d, (P) \rightarrow \delta, \delta^*_{\text{in} [^P]}$

  (destroy the argument, destroy the current membrane $[^{()}]$)

Rules 4. Stop the substitution process if it is not allowed.

  rule 4.1 $(P) s_y, c_x \rightarrow s_y, B_{\text{out}^*}, \delta^*_{\text{in} [^P]}$ $(x, y \in X_\Phi, x \neq y)$

  (if the right variable is not found, destroy the argument, and send the beginning symbol B to the skin)

  rule 4.2 $(P), r, s_y, c_x \rightarrow s_y, r, B_{\text{out}^*}, \delta^*_{\text{in} [^P]}$ $(x, y \in X_\Phi, x = y$ or $x \neq y)$

  (whatever the variable is, if there is a 'red light' signal, destroy the argument, and send the beginning symbol B to the skin)

Rules 5. Perform the substitution if allowed by freezing the argument first.

  rule 5.1 $(P) s_x, c_x, g \rightarrow [^F [^P]], g$ $(x \in X_\Phi)$

  (if there is a 'green light' and if the variable is found, create the membrane inside which further substitutions must be frozen)

  rule 5.2 $(F), g \rightarrow \delta, r_{\text{in}^* [^F]}, d'_{\text{in} [^F]}$

  (when F is present, send inside all innermost membranes of $[^F]$, an additional 'red light' in order to stop further substitution, destroy the current variable membrane and prepare to destroy the protection of the argument)

  rule 5.3 $d', (P) \rightarrow \delta_{\text{in} [^P]}$

  (destroy the protection)

Priority rules.

  rule 6. $B, B \rightarrow B$

  (assure one beginning symbol)

rule 7. $\nu, \nu \quad \to \nu$

(assure one substitution indicator when multiple arguments are identified)

rule 8.1 $\eta', r \quad \to \nu'$

rule 8.2 $s_x, \nu' \quad \to g, s_x$

rule 8.3 $r, g \quad \to r$

(rule 8.1 kills one r; rule 8.2 generates one g, the 'green light'; if there are no more r's, then the g produced by rule 8.2 remains, and the substitution is allowed).

Denote by $\Pi(\mathcal{A})$ the λP system of type Π that has an initial configuration $\mu_{\mathcal{A}}$ for a set of λ-terms $\mathcal{A}$. We see that the computational power of λP systems of type Π is equivalent to the computational power of a universal Turing machine. We have the following.

Theorem 1. *Let α be a general λ-term. Then $\mathcal{F}(\Pi(\alpha)) = \mu_{\mathcal{N}(\alpha)}$, i.e., the λP system $\Pi(\alpha)$ simulates the reduction steps of the term α.*

Proof. The proof follows from the construction of Π and the initial membrane configuration μ_α. $\square$

Since λ-calculus is computationally equivalent to any universal Turing machine we have:

Corollary 1. *The λP systems can simulate the computation of a universal Turing machine.*

4 λP Systems and Gödel's T-System

As indicated in the introduction, λP systems can simulate typed λ-calculus. Only the guidelines of such an implementation are included here by first considering typed λ-calculus and then the Gödel's T-system.

4.1   Typed λ-Calculus

A **typed** λ-calculus is a system of computation which, append to λ-terms an additional information which is called the **type** of the term. Types over λ-terms are defined inductively. We are given a set of types $\mathcal{T}$ which obeys the following rules: σ, τ are in $\mathcal{T}$, $\sigma \to \tau$ is also in $\mathcal{T}$. Type $\sigma \to \tau$ has to be interpreted as the type of λ-terms which represents the functions which transforms λ-terms of type σ into λ-terms of type τ. As we shall need the notion a bit later, we define a **subtype** of τ to be such a factor σ of τ that, considered as a word, σ is also a type.

By definition, a set of variables for each type in $\mathcal{T}$ is given. If x is a variable and σ a type, we denote by $x : \sigma$ the fact that x has type τ. This relation is also denoted x^σ and, in this latter case, we say that x is decorated by σ.

Next, we inductively define the type of more complex λ-terms by induction on their structure by using the following two rules:

- if $x : \sigma$ and $M : \tau$, then $\lambda x\, M : \sigma \to \tau$;
- if $U : \sigma \to \tau$ and $V : \sigma$, then $(U)\, V : \tau$.

We call typed λ-calculus any subset of pure λ-terms which can be typed according to the above rules with types in $\mathcal{T}$. A λ-term M of λ-calculus is called **typable** if there is such a set $\mathcal{T}$ of types that it is possible to type M according to the above rules, starting from the variables of M, appropriately typed with $\mathcal{T}$.

As the pure λ-calculus has a computational power which is equivalent to universal Turing macine, it is undecidable to know whether the sucessive β-reductions of a given term of the pure λ-calculus leads to a term in normal form or not. However, it is decidable to know whether a given term of the pure λ-calculus is or not typable. A lot of terms of pure λ-terms are known to be not typable. As an example, $(x)\, x$ cannot be typed: the type of x should satisfy the type equation $\sigma = \sigma \to \sigma$, which is impossible. As a consequence, typed λ-calculi cannot contain fixed-points. This induces a serious restriction on the power of computation of typed λ-calculuses. In particular, if we take the simplest typing indicated above, the corresponding typed λ-calculus can only compute polynomial functions, which was first shown by Turing, see [16].

Before turning to the solution which was found out by Gödel in the late fifties of last century, let us notice that we can simulate typed λ-calculus by P systems. It is enough to introduce **typed** labels subjected to observe the type axioms indicated above. This means that a label $\boxed{\lambda x}$ will be replaced by label $\boxed{\lambda x : \sigma \to \tau}$ where $x : \sigma$ and τ is the type of the body of the considered λ-term. Similarly, a label $\boxed{()}$ will be replaced by label $\boxed{() : \tau}$, where the considered parenthesis contains a term of type $\alpha \to \tau$ in functional position and a term of type α as the argument. At last, a label $\boxed{x}$ will be replaced by label $\boxed{x : \sigma}$, where σ is the type of x. Of course, we assume that the P systems are given by correctly typed terms. Under this assumption, as the reduction keeps invariant the type of a redex, it is clear that this labelling remains untouched during any computation.

4.2   Gödel's *T*-System

As mentioned above, Gödel provided us in the late fifties of the previous century a typed λ-calculus able to simulate any total recursive functions which is provable in Peano arithmetic, see [5]. Notice that this set is not the set of all total functions, as this was first shown in [7]. Indeed, the set of parial recursive functions which are provably total in Peano arithmetic is recursively enumerable while the set of total recursive functions is not. Recall that $\{e\}$, the partial recursive function with number e, is provably total in Peano arithmetic if and only if in this theory there is a proof of the sentence $\forall x\, \{e\}(x)\!\downarrow$, where $\{e\}(x)\!\downarrow$ means that the computation of function $\{e\}$ on x terminates. And so, from this, we easily derive the recursive enumerability of partial recursive functions which are provably total in Peano arithmetic.

T-system is a typed λ-calculus which is constructed as follows:

The set of types satisfies the axioms of Subsection 4.1, and it contains a type **0** which is called type of the **integers**.

Besides variables of all types, as usual, T-system also contains a **constant** term denoted **0** of type **0**, i.e., we have **0**:**0**. Term **0** is called **zero**. T-system also contains a constant term **S** called **successor** which is of type **0** → **0**. We may interpret **0** as integer zero and **S** as the function which associates $n+1$ to integer n.

We define **integers** in T-system as the following terms:

– **0** is an integer;
– if N is an integer, (**S**) N is also an integer.

And so, the integers in T-sytems are terms **0**, (**S**) **0**, (**S**) (**S**) **0**, and so on.

Next, for each type $s \in \mathcal{T}$, there is a constant term $\mathbf{R}_s$ called **recursor** of type s such that:

– $\mathbf{R}_s$ is of type $\mathbf{0} \to (s \to \mathbf{0} \to s) \to s \to s$;
– $(((\mathbf{R}_s) \, \mathbf{0}) \, \mathbf{Step}) \, \mathbf{Base} = \mathbf{Base}$;
– $(((\mathbf{R}_s) \, (\mathbf{S}) \, n) \, \mathbf{Step}) \, \mathbf{Base} = ((\mathbf{Step}) \, (((\mathbf{R}_s) \, n) \, \mathbf{Step}) \, \mathbf{Base}) \, n$.

Indeed, $\mathbf{R}_s$ defines a recursion. It has three arguments: the first one is an integer and the second is a function of two arguments and the third is a term of type s. The first argument is called the **recursion parameter**. The second argument is called the **step function** and the third argument is called the **base case**. When the recursion parameter is **0**, we get the base case. When the recursion parameter is positive, it is then of the form (**S**) n for some integer n, then we apply the step function to the previous value of the recursor and to n which is the previous value of the recursion parameter.

It is well known that $\mathbf{R_0}$ defines exactly primitive recursive functions. Next, $\mathbf{R_{0 \to 0}}$ contains Ackermann function which is known to be non primitive recursive. It is also known that the hierarchy of functions defined by the set of functions which are defined by all $\mathbf{R}_s$ with s being a type of a finite subset of $\mathcal{T}$ defines an infinite hierarchy. It is also known that the union of the members of the hierarchy is the set of partial recursive functions which are provably total in Peano arithmetic.

4.3   Implementing T-System in λP Systems

The basic idea consists in using the frame of [6] to implement P systems by using a translation of T-system terms into pure λ-calculus.

Pure λ-calculus Translation of P system. Consider the developement of a recursor term $(((\mathbf{R}_s) \, (\mathbf{S}) \, (\mathbf{S}) \, (\mathbf{S}) \, n) \, \mathbf{Step}) \, \mathbf{Base}$. We get:

$(((\mathbf{R}_s) \, (\mathbf{S}) \, (\mathbf{S}) \, (\mathbf{S}) \, n) \, \mathbf{Step}) \, \mathbf{Base}$
$= ((\mathbf{Step}) \, (((\mathbf{R}_s) \, (\mathbf{S}) \, (\mathbf{S}) \, n) \, \mathbf{Step}) \, \mathbf{Base}) \, (\mathbf{S}) \, (\mathbf{S}) \, n$
$= ((\mathbf{Step}) \, ((\mathbf{Step}) \, (((\mathbf{R}_s) \, (\mathbf{S}) \, n) \, \mathbf{Step}) \, \mathbf{Base}) \, (\mathbf{S}) \, n) \, (\mathbf{S}) \, (\mathbf{S}) \, n$
$= ((\mathbf{Step}) \, ((\mathbf{Step}) \, ((\mathbf{Step}) \, (((\mathbf{R}_s) \, n) \, \mathbf{Step}) \, \mathbf{Base}) \, n) \, (\mathbf{S}) \, n) \, (\mathbf{S}) \, (\mathbf{S}) \, n$

Consider now the formation of couples in pure λ-calculus. We define $<U,V>$ to be the term $\lambda x\,((x)\,U)\,V$. It is not difficult to see that we can extract U and V from $<U,V>$ using the following terms which are the first and second projection: $\pi_1 == \lambda x\,\lambda y\,x$ and $\pi_2 == \lambda x\,\lambda y\,y$. Indeed, $(<U,V>)\,\pi_1 \Rightarrow U$ and $(<U,V>)\,\pi_2 \Rightarrow V$.

Consider the term $c_n = <(((\mathbf{R}_s)\,n)\,\mathbf{Step})\,\mathbf{Base}, n>$. Then:
$$c_{n+1} = <(((\mathbf{R}_s)\,(\mathbf{S})\,n)\,\mathbf{Step})\,\mathbf{Base}, (\mathbf{S})\,n)>$$
$$= <((\mathbf{Step})\,(((\mathbf{R}_s)\,n)\,\mathbf{Step})\,\mathbf{Base}, n)\,n, (\mathbf{S})\,n)>$$
$$= <((\mathbf{Step})\,(c_n)\,\pi_1)\,(c_n)\,\pi_2, (\mathbf{S})\,(c_n)\,\pi_2>.$$

And so,
$$c_{n+1} = <((\mathbf{Step})\,(c_n)\,\pi_1)\,(c_n)\,\pi_2, (\mathbf{S})\,(c_n)\,\pi_2> = (\mathbf{L})\,c_n.$$

From this, using classical arguments, we infer that
$$c_n = ((\overline{n})\,\mathbf{L})\, <\mathbf{Base}, 0>,$$
where $\overline{n}$ is the integer of Church corresponding to integer n. Church integers are a way to represent non-negative integers in pure λ-calculus. They are defined by the following induction axioms:

- $\lambda x\,\lambda y\,y$ is an integer of Church, namely the representation of 0;
- if $\overline{n}$ represents n, then $n{+}1$ is represented by $\lambda x\,\lambda y\,(x)\,((\overline{n})\,x)\,y$.

And so $\overline{1} = \lambda x\,\lambda y\,(x)\,y$, $\overline{2} = \lambda x\,\lambda y\,(x)\,(x)\,y$, $\overline{3} = \lambda x\,\lambda y\,(x)\,(x)\,(x)\,y$, and so forth. Notice that $((\overline{1})\,x)\,y = (x)\,y$, $((\overline{2})\,x)\,y = (x)\,(x)\,y$, $((\overline{3})\,x)\,y = (x)\,(x)\,(x)\,y$ and so on.

As a consequence, a representation of $(((\mathbf{R}_s)\,n)\,\mathbf{Step})\,\mathbf{Base}$ in pure λ-calculus is given by: $(((\mathbf{R}_s)\,n)\,\mathbf{Step})\,\mathbf{Base} = (((\overline{n})\,\mathbf{L})\,<\mathbf{Base}, 0>)\,\pi_1$.

At this point, there is a problem: how to transform integers in T-system into the corresponding integers of Church? We have to find the simplest type for Church integers which are typable: it is not difficult to see that $\overline{0} : \tau \to (\sigma \to \sigma)$ and next: $\overline{1} : (\sigma \to \tau) \to (\sigma \to \tau)$, $\overline{2} : (\sigma \to \sigma) \to (\sigma \to \sigma)$. The simplest solution is $\sigma = \mathbf{0}$ and so, by induction on n, we can see that we obtain that $\overline{n} : (\mathbf{0} \to \mathbf{0}) \to (\mathbf{0} \to \mathbf{0})$. Define $\mathbf{N} == (\mathbf{0} \to \mathbf{0}) \to (\mathbf{0} \to \mathbf{0})$. The translation requires that we have $\mathbf{R_N}$ at our disposal. Then the translation can be performed by: $\overline{n} = (((\mathbf{R_N})\,n)\,\mathbf{Step})\,\mathbf{0}$ where $\mathbf{Step} == \lambda x\,\lambda a\,\lambda b\,(a)\,((x)\,a)\,b$.

And so, to translate the recursors we need to translate the integers, which also requires a recursor.

Implementation of T-System by P Systems. In order to break the above circle, we perform the translation of Gödel integers directly into Church integers by the λP system under consideration. At this point, notice that the translation of types requires special symbols and so, as an explicit P system has only finitely many symbols, a P system can handle only a certain type of recursors, namely the recursors $\mathbf{R}_\sigma$ for all σ which are subtypes of a fixed type τ.

This shows that the considered implementation defines a family of P systems which are indexed by the types of recursors and a family is attached to a type σ: it simulates the functions which are definable by this recursor and by all the other recursors which can be defined by the subtypes of σ.

Now we indicate the main guidelines for this implementation.

We use the same frame as was used for λ-calculus, appending types to the labels of membranes as we already mentioned. The input of a P system Π of family σ where σ is a possible type for a recursor in T-system is a term V of T-system defined by a recursor of type σ. Term V may be considered of the form $(\ldots((((\mathbf{R}_\sigma)\, n)\, \mathbf{Step})\, Base)\, m_1)\ldots)\, m_k$ where n, m_1, ..., m_k are Gödel integers. In the new frame, we need only to introduce a new type of membranes labelled by both $\mathbf{R}$ and the indication of the type of the recursor which this membrane implements.

An object traverses the representation of term V in Π and proceeds to the translation of each term, according to its label. Integers are identified by their label $\mathbf{0}$ and recursors by the label $\mathbf{R}$ which is introduced for this purpose. The type part of the label of $\mathbf{R}$ indicates the type of the recursor which this label represents. The order of the terms in a recursor facilitates the translation as far as the recursion parameter is the active membrane inside the membrane which represents the application where the recursor is involved. The object carries the set B of possible types for resursors of the family in order to compare it with the label of each recursor it will meet. If the label matches with a type contained in B, the translation is performed. If not, another object stops the computation. In order to simplify things, we may assume that V is not only a correct term of T-system but it also does not contain a recursor of type higher than type σ which delimits the considered family of P systems.

When the object completed the traversal, it sends back another object in order to start the computation. This sending back mechanism follows the same idea already implemented in [6].

When the pure λ-calculus computation stops, another translation mechanism which converts Church integers into their representation in Gödel's T-system starts. As any term in T-system represents a **total** recursive function, we know that the computation of the translation of V in pure λ-calculus will eventually stop. Hence the leftmost reduction strategy which is implemented in λP systems also garantees the termination of the computation. This backward translation is the same as the direct translation. It is simply processed by a different object.

5   Conclusion

In Section 3 we show that λP systems have the power of Turing machines whereas in Section 4, we implemented a fine tuning of the set of labels that allows to restrict the scope of simulation and to obtain typed λ-calculus. This tuning is fine enough that the power of computation is not restricted too much, i.e., we obtain Gödel T-system.

This was done by first introducing more complex labels for the membranes, i.e., types of the membranes. Also a new kind of membrane, "the recursor", was introduced which through translation mechanism transforms the representation of a T-system term into an enconding in λP systems. After the computation is completed, another translation mechanism transforms the result in the same format as the input.

With this mechanism, we have an infinite hierarchy of infinite families of P systems representing terms whose computations always complete. Hence, a **secure** computation within P systems is obtained. As is known, the recursive functions, provably total in Peano arithmetics, contain all functions needed for practical purposes. Thus we have a secure and powerful enough P system. This frame may be a starting point for applications.

The first step towards an applicable implementation is developing a control mechanism which filters the input of the λP system in order to garantee that the input is actually a term of T-system. This part is already known to implementors of functional languages where structures much richer than T-systems are handled.

Finally, we have given a solution for secure and powerful P systems within framework of λP systems. We believe that other such systems may appear within both P systems computing by objects as well as in λP systems computing by membrane structure. We hope some of them will find their way to practical applications.

References

1. H.P. Barendregt, *The Lambda Calculus: Its Syntax and Semantics*, North Holland, Amsterdam, 1984.
2. D. Besozzi, I.I. Ardelean, G. Mauri, The potential of P systems for modeling the activity of mechanosensitive channels in E. Coli, *Preproceedings of the Fourth Workshop on Membrane Computing* (A. Alhazov, C. Martín-Vide, Gh. Păun *Editors*), Report GRLMC 28/03, Universitat Rovira i Virgili, Tarragona, Spain, 2003, 84–102.
3. R. Ceterchi, R. Gramatovici, N. Jonoska, K.G. Subramanian, Tissue-like P systems for picture generation, *Fundamenta Informaticae*, **56** (2003), 311–328.
4. N.G. De Brujin, Lambda calculus notation with nameless dummies, a tool for automatic formula manipulation, with application to the Church-Rosser theorem, *Indagationes Mathematicae*, **34** (1972), 381–392.
5. K. Gödel, Über Eine Bischer Noch Nicht Benützte Erweiterung des Finiten Standpunktes, *Dialectica*, **12** (1958), 280–287. (On a hitherto unexploited extension of the finitary standpoint, *Journal of Philosophical Logic*, **9** (1980) – English translation).
6. N. Jonoska, M. Margenstern, Tree operations in P systems and λ-calculus, *Fundamenta Informaticae*, **59**, 1 (2004), 67–90.
7. G. Kreisel. On the interpretation of nonfinitist proofs, Part I, II., *Journal of Symbolic Logic*, **16,17** (1952, 1953).
8. J.L. Krivine, *Lambda-Calculus, Types and Models*, Ellis Horwood, 1993.
9. A. Păun, On P systems with membrane division, in *Unconventional Models of Computation* (I. Antoniou, C.S. Calude, M.J. Dinneen, eds.), Springer-Verlag, London, 2000, 187–201.
10. Gh. Păun, P systems with active membranes: Attacking NP-complete problems, *J. Automata, Languages and Combinatorics*, **6**, 1 (2001), 75–90.
11. Gh. Păun, *Membrane Computing: An Introduction*, Springer, Berlin, Heidelberg, 2002.

12. Gh. Păun, G. Rozenberg, A guide to membrane computing, *Theoretical Computer Science*, **287** (2002), 73–100.

13. M.J. Pérez-Jiménez, A. Romero-Jiménez, F. Sancho-Caparrini, Solving VALID-ITY problem by active membranes with input, *Brainstorming Week on Membrane Computing*, Tarragona, February 5-11, 2003, in Report GRMLC 26/03, Universitat Rovira i Virgili, Tarragona, Spain, 279–290.

14. V. Rogozhin, E. Boian, Simulation of mobile ambients by P systems, *Preproceedings of the Fourth Workshop on Membrane Computing* (A. Alhazov, C. Martn-Vide, Gh. Păun *Editors*), Report GRMLC 28/03, Universitat Rovira i Virgili, Tarragona, Spain, 2003, 404–427.

15. P. Sosík, Solving a PSPACE-complete problem by P systems with active membranes, *Brainstorming Week on Membrane Computing*, Tarragona, February 5-11, 2003, in Report GRMLC 26/03, Universitat Rovira i Virgili, Tarragona, Spain, 305–312.

16. A.M. Turing, Computability and lambda-definability, *Journal of Symbolic Logic*, **2** (1937), 153–163.

P Automata*

Erzsébet Csuhaj-Varjú

Computer and Automation Research Institute,
Hungarian Academy of Sciences,
Kende utca 13-17, 1111 Budapest, Hungary
csuhaj@sztaki.hu

Abstract. In this paper we discuss P automata, i.e., accepting P systems, using in most cases only communication rules. We briefly describe the most important variants of these systems and report on their important properties, with special emphasis on their computational power and size. We also propose some new topics and problems for future research.

1 Introduction

Membrane systems are computing devices abstracted from the functioning of the living cells. This and similar sentences can be found in hundreds of publications about models, results, and ideas in a recent area of molecular computing, the theory of membrane systems or P systems. The research field has been launched by Gheorghe Păun in 1998 [19], with the inspiration to construct a framework which provides effective and powerful computational tools that can also be used for studying and simulating natural processes. Since 1998, the fruitful idea has been extensively and intensively explored, the theory of *membrane systems* or *P systems* has proved to be a successful and promising field in the area of unconventional models of computation. Several variants of the basic notion, demonstrating the power of the framework, have been introduced and investigated; the interested reader is referred to [20, 21, 24] for basic information, and to the book [23] for a summary of the achievements and open problems in the area. The reader is also advised to consult the P systems web page where a lot of down-loadable papers and important information can be found [25].

The main component of a P system is a *membrane structure* consisting of membranes hierarchically embedded in the outermost *skin membrane*. Each membrane encloses a *region* containing a *multiset of objects* and *possibly other membranes*. Each region has an associated set of operators acting on the objects contained by the region. These operators can be of different types, they can modify the multisets of objects in the regions but also can provide the possibility of transferring the objects from one region to another one. The first type of these operations, where usually both the change and the communication of

---

* Research supported in part by project "MolCoNet" IST-2001-32008 and the Hungarian Scientific Research Fund (OTKA) Grant No. T 042529.

G. Mauri et al. (Eds.): WMC5 2004, LNCS 3365, pp. 19–35, 2005.

the object are allowed, are the so-called *evolution rules*, which can be *applied* in *parallel* across all membranes or in a rather *sequential manner*. The rules to be applied are chosen nondeterministically, that is, if an object can evolve according to more than one evolution rule at the same time, than any of the rules can be chosen. The second type of rules, providing only the possibility of *transportation* of objects, are called *communication rules*.

At any moment of time, the membrane system can be described by its *configuration* which consists of the actual membrane structure and the contents of the regions. (We note that some of the variants of P systems allow to dynamically change the membrane structure.) In this sense, membrane systems can be considered as *computing devices*: starting from an initial configuration, the system evolves by passing from one configuration to another one, thus realizing a computation. If the system halts, that is, no rule can be applied anymore, the computation is successful. For more details about the different variants of these constructs the reader is referred to [23, 25]. However, we can also consider that the sequence of configurations describes the behavior of the P system, thus membrane systems can be investigated from systems theoretic aspects as well.

Considering the P systems briefly described above, the reader can observe that these constructs *restrict their functioning to the membranes and to the contents of the regions*: the system is not in interaction or communication with its surrounding environment, with the outside world. However, since P systems attempt to model living cells and the cell communicates with its biological environment, it would be reasonable to take also this aspect into account. Thus, *studying variants of P systems, where the system is in communication (in interaction) with its environment* can be considered as a well-motivated area of research in membrane systems theory. Communication can be interpreted in several manners. One possibility is the case where the *environment* represents an *infinite (or finite) supply of objects* from which individual objects or *multisets of objects* can be or must be *imported by the skin membrane in the system* under the functioning of the membrane system. The reader can observe that these P systems can be considered as *automata* or *accepting systems* (P automata or accepting P systems), since the configuration of the membrane system *changes* due to both the *imported objects* and the *actual state of the system* and its *input* (the sequence of imported multisets of objects) can be distinguished as *accepted* or *rejected* input.

Although the idea of defining accepting variants of P systems is reasonable, the theory of P automata or accepting P systems was explicitly inspired by two problems raised by Gheorghe Păun. The first, from [22], is the following. "What about the possibility of considering a class of P systems, meant to compute, where no rule for objects evolution appears, but only rules governing object communication from a region to another one". The second one is Problem $Q32$ in [23]: "What about using P systems as accepting devices?"

Motivated by these questions, the *first variant of P automata* was introduced in [5], and realized a *purely communicating, accepting P system*. (See also [6].) Almost at the same time, a closely related notion, the *analyzing P system* was defined in [9], formulating another concept of an accepting P system. Both systems are *computationally complete*, that is, as powerful as Turing machines, thus prove that not only generating but accepting P systems are sufficiently powerful tools for computation. Since that time, several variants of P automata have been introduced and studied. For more information the reader is referred to the excellent summary in [17] and for further details to the articles referred in the on-line bibliography [25]. Although all of these models are accepting P systems, they *differ* from each other in several features: *in the way of defining the acceptance of the input, in the way of communication with the environment, in the types of communication rules used by the regions, in the way of functioning of the membrane system (whether or not it has evolution rules), and whether or not the membrane structure changes under the computation.*

In the following, without the aim of completeness and with providing only some basic formal definitions – the details can be found in the corresponding articles – we briefly recall some models and discuss their computational power and size properties. We also propose some new topics and problems for future research.

2   P Automata: The Formal Concept

In order to provide the reader with sufficient formal details to understand the concept and to follow the discussion of the models, we present the notion of a *P automaton*. We give the definition in a generalized manner ([4]): most of the variants that have been studied so far can be obtained as special cases or (slightly) modified versions of the given notion.

We assume that the reader is familiar with formal language theory and with the basics of membrane computing; the interested reader can find detailed information on the theory of P systems in the monograph [23] and on the P systems web page [25].

We first recall the notions and the notations we use. Let V be an alphabet, let V^* be the set of all words over V, and let $V^+ = V^* - \{\varepsilon\}$ where ε denotes the empty word. We denote the length of a word $w \in V^*$ by $|w|$, and the number of occurrences of a symbol $a \in V$ in w by $|w|_a$. The set of natural numbers is denoted by $\mathbb{N}$.

Let U be a set – the universe – of objects. A multiset is a pair $M = (V, f)$, where V is an arbitrary (not necessarily finite) set of objects from U and $f : U \to \mathbb{N}$ is a mapping which assigns to each object its multiplicity, such that, if $a \notin V$ then $f(a) = 0$. The support of $M = (V, f)$ is the set $supp(M) = \{a \in V \mid f(a) \geq 1\}$. If $supp(M)$ is a finite set, then M is called a finite multiset. The set of all finite multisets over the set V is denoted by V°.

The number of objects in a finite multiset $M = (V, f)$, the cardinality of M, is defined by $card(M) = \Sigma_{a \in V} f(a)$. We say that $a \in M = (V, f)$ if $a \in supp(M)$, and $M_1 = (V_1, f_1) \subseteq M_2 = (V_2, f_2)$ if $supp(M_1) \subseteq supp(M_2)$ and for all $a \in V_1$, $f_1(a) \leq f_2(a)$. The union of two multisets is defined as $(M_1 \cup M_2) = (V_1 \cup V_2, f')$ where for all $a \in V_1 \cup V_2$, $f'(a) = f_1(a) + f_2(a)$. For $M_2 \subseteq M_1$ the difference

$(M_1 - M_2) = (V_1, f'')$ where $f''(a) = f_1(a) - f_2(a)$ for all $a \in V_1$, and the intersection of two multisets is $(M_1 \cap M_2) = (V_1 \cap V_2, f''')$ where for $a \in V_1 \cap V_2$, $f'''(a) = min(f_1(a), f_2(a))$, $min(x, y)$ denoting the minimum of $x, y \in \mathbb{N}$. We say that M is empty, denoted by ϵ, if its support is empty, $supp(M) = \emptyset$.

A multiset M over the finite set of objects V can be represented as a string w over the alphabet V with $|w|_a = f(a)$, $a \in V$, and with ε representing the empty multiset ϵ.

In the following we identify the finite multiset of objects $M = (V, f)$ with the word w over V representing M, thus we write $w \in V^\circ$.

A *P system* is a *structure of hierarchically embedded membranes*, each having a *label* and enclosing a *region* containing a *multiset of objects* and possibly other membranes. The out-most membrane which is unique and usually labeled with 1, is called the *skin membrane*.

The membrane structure is denoted by a sequence of matching parentheses where the matching pairs have the same label as the membranes they represent. If $x \in \{[_i,]_i \mid 1 \le i \le n\}^*$ is such a string of matching parentheses of length $2n$, denoting a structure where membrane i contains membrane j, then $x = x_1 [_i x_2 [_j x_3]_j x_4]_i x_5$ for some $x_k \in \{[_l,]_l \mid 1 \le l \le n, l \neq i, j\}^*$, $1 \le k \le 5$. If membrane i contains membrane j, and there is no other membrane, k, such that k contains j and i contains k (x_2 and x_4 above are strings of matching parentheses themselves), then we say that membrane i is the *parent membrane* of j, denoted by $i = parent(j)$, and at the same time, membrane j is one of the *child membranes* of i.

The *contents of a region* is the multiset of objects which is contained by the corresponding membrane excluding those objects which are contained by its child membranes.

The *evolution* (the change) of the contents of the regions of a P system is described by *rules associated to the regions*. Applying the rules *synchronously* in each region, the system performs a computation by *passing from one configuration to another one*. These rules can be of different types. We define here two basic types of communication rules: the *symport rules* and the *antiport rules*.

A *symport rule* is of the form (x, in) or (x, out), $x \in V^\circ$. If such a rule is present in a region i, then the objects of the multiset x must enter from the parent region or must leave to the parent region, $parent(i)$. An *antiport rule* is of the form $(x, in; y, out)$, $x, y \in V^\circ$. In this case, objects of x enter from the parent region and at the same step, objects of y leave to the parent region. All types of these rules might be equipped with a *promoter* or *inhibitor* multiset, denoted as $(x, in)|_Z, (x, out)|_Z$, or $(x, in; y, out)|_Z, x, y \in V^\circ, Z \in \{z, \neg z \mid z \in V^\circ\}$, in which case they can only be applied if region i contains the objects of multiset z, or, if $Z = \neg z$, then region i must not contain the elements of z.

The rules can be applied in the *maximally parallel* or in the *sequential* manner. When they are applied in the sequential manner, one rule is applied in each region in each derivation step, when they are applied in the parallel manner, as many rules are applied in each region as possible.

The *end of the computation* is defined by *halting*. A P system halts when no more rules can be applied in any of the regions. In the case of P automata, however, we consider *predefined accepting configurations* called *final states*, by associating a finite set of multisets to each region. The P automaton *accepts the input sequence* when the contents of each region coincides with one element of these previously given finite sets of multisets.

The result of the computation in a P system can also be given in several ways, see [23] for more details. In the case of *P automata, the result of the computation is an accepted multiset sequence*, the sequence of multisets entering the skin membrane during a successful computation, that is, a computation leading to a final state.

Now we give the formal definition of a P automaton.

Definition 1. A *P automaton* with n membranes is defined as

$$\Gamma = (V, \mu, (w_1, P_1, F_1), \ldots, (w_n, P_n, F_n)),$$

where $n \geq 1$, μ is a membrane structure of n membranes with label 1 being assigned to the skin membrane, and for all $i, 1 \leq i \leq n$,

- $w_i \in V^\circ$ is the initial contents (state) of region i, that is, it is the finite multiset of all objects contained by region i,
- P_i is a finite set of communication rules associated to membrane i; they can be symport rules or antiport rules, with or without promoters or inhibitors, as above, and
- $F_i \subseteq V^\circ$ is a finite set of finite multisets over V called the set of final states of region i; if $F_i = \emptyset$, then all the states of membrane i are considered to be final.

To simplify the notations, we denote symport and antiport rules with or without promoters/inhibitors as $(x, in; y, out)|_Z$, $x, y \in V^\circ$, $Z \in \{z, \neg z \mid z \in V^\circ\}$ where we also allow x, y, z to be the empty string. If $y = \varepsilon$ or $x = \varepsilon$, then the notation above denotes the symport rule $(x, in)|_Z$ or $(y, out)|_Z$, respectively, and, if $Z = \varepsilon$, then the rules above are without promoters or inhibitors.

The n-tuple of finite multisets of objects present in the n regions of the P automaton Γ describes a *configuration* of Γ; $(w_1, \ldots, w_n) \in (V^\circ)^n$ is the *initial configuration*.

The P automaton changes its configuration by *transitions*.

Definition 2. The *transition mapping* of a P automaton is a partial mapping $\delta_X : V^\circ \times (V^\circ)^n \to 2^{(V^\circ)^n}$, with $X \in \{seq, par\}$ for sequential or for parallel rule application. These mappings are defined implicitly by the rules of the rule sets P_i, $1 \leq i \leq n$. For a configuration $(u_1, \ldots, u_n)$,

$$(u'_1, \ldots, u'_n) \in \delta_X(u, (u_1, \ldots, u_n))$$

holds, that is, while reading the input $u \in V^\circ$ the automaton may enter the new configuration $(u'_1, \ldots, u'_n) \in (V^\circ)^n$, if there exist rules as follows.

- If $X = seq$, then for all $i, 1 \leq i \leq n$, there is a rule $(x_i, in; y_i, out)|_{Z_i} \in P_i$ with $z \subseteq u_i$ for $Z_i = z \in V^\circ$, and $z \cap u_i = \epsilon$ for $Z_i = \neg z, z \in V^\circ$, satisfying the conditions below, or
- if $X = par$, then for all $i, 1 \leq i \leq n$, there is a multiset of rules $R_i = \{\{r_{i,1}, \ldots, r_{i,m_i}\}\}$, where $r_{i,j} = (x_{i,j}, in; y_{i,j}, out)|_{Z_{i,j}} \in P_i$ with $z \subseteq u_i$ for $Z_{i,j} = z \in V^\circ$, and $z \cap u_i = \epsilon$ for $Z_{i,j} = \neg z, z \in V^\circ$, $1 \leq j \leq m_i$, satisfying the conditions below, where x_i, y_i denote the multisets $\bigcup_{1 \leq j \leq m_i} x_{i,j}$ and $\bigcup_{1 \leq j \leq m_i} y_{i,j}$, respectively. Furthermore, there is no $r \in P_j$, for any j, $1 \leq j \leq n$, such that the rule multisets R_i' with $R_i' = R_i$ for $i \neq j$ and $R_j' = \{\{r\}\} \cup R_j$, also satisfy the conditions.

The conditions are given as

1. $x_1 = u$, and
2. $\bigcup_{parent(j)=i} x_j \cup y_i \subseteq u_i$, $1 \leq i \leq n$,

and then the new configuration is obtained by

$$u_i' = u_i \cup x_i - y_i \cup \bigcup_{parent(j)=i} y_j - \bigcup_{parent(j)=i} x_j, \ 1 \leq i \leq n.$$

We define the *sequence of multisets of objects accepted by the P automaton* as an input sequence which is consumed by the skin membrane while the system reaches a final state, a configuration where for all j with $F_j \neq \emptyset$, the contents $u_j \in V^\circ$ of membrane j is "final", i.e., $u_j \in F_j$.

Note that in the case of parallel rule application, the set of multisets which may enter the system in one step is not necessarily bounded, thus, this type of P automata may work with strings over infinite alphabets. Since we study languages over finite alphabets, we apply a mapping to produce a finite set of symbols from a possibly infinite set of multisets, and we assume that it is computable by a linear space bounded Turing machine.

Definition 3. Let us extend δ_X to $\bar{\delta}_X, X \in \{seq, par\}$, a function mapping $(V^\circ)^*$, that is, the sequences of finite multisets over V, and $(V^\circ)^n$, the configurations of Γ, to new configurations. We define $\bar{\delta}_X$ as

1. $\bar{\delta}_X(v, (u_1, \ldots, u_n)) = \delta_X(v, (u_1, \ldots, u_n))$, $v, u_i \in V^\circ$, $1 \leq i \leq n$, and
2. $\bar{\delta}_X((v_1)\ldots(v_{s+1}), (u_1, \ldots, u_n)) = \bigcup \delta_X(v_{s+1}, (u_1', \ldots, u_n'))$
   for all $(u_1', \ldots, u_n') \in \bar{\delta}_X((v_1)\ldots(v_s), (u_1, \ldots, u_n))$, $v_j, u_i, u_i' \in V^\circ$, $1 \leq i \leq n$, $1 \leq j \leq s+1$.

Note that we use brackets in the multiset sequence $(v_1)\ldots(v_{s+1}) \in (V^\circ)^*$ in order to distinguish it from the multiset $v_1 \cup \ldots \cup v_{s+1} \in V^\circ$.

Definition 4. Let Γ be a P automaton as above with initial configuration $(w_1, \ldots, w_n)$ and let Σ be a finite alphabet. The *language accepted by Γ* (the language of Γ) with a mapping f in the sequential way of rule application, denoted by $L_{seq}(\Gamma, f)$, or in the maximal parallel way of rule application, $L_{par}(\Gamma, f)$, is

$$L_X(\Gamma, f) = \{f(v_1) \ldots f(v_s) \in \Sigma^* \mid$$
$$(u_1, \ldots, u_n) \in \bar{\delta}_X((v_1) \ldots (v_s), (w_1, \ldots, w_n))$$
$$\text{with } u_j \in F_j \text{ for all } j \text{ with } F_j \neq \emptyset, \ 1 \leq j \leq n, \ 1 \leq s\},$$

for $X \in \{seq, par\}$, and for a linear space computable mapping $f : V^\circ \longrightarrow \Sigma \cup \{\varepsilon\}$ with $f(x) = \varepsilon$ if and only if $x = \epsilon$.

We illustrate the notion by an example.

Example 1. Let

$$\Gamma = (\{S_1, S_2, S_3, a, b, c\}, [_1 \ [_2 \ [_3 \ ]_3 \ ]_2 \ ]_1 (S_1, P_1, \{d\}), (S_2, P_2, \{S_1 S_2\}), (S_3, P_3, \emptyset),$$

with

$$P_1 = \{(a, in)|_{S_1}, \ (a, in)|_a, \ (b, in)|_a, \ (b, in)|_b, \ (c, in)|_b, \ (c, in)|_c,$$
$$(d, in)|_c, \ (\varepsilon, in)|_d\},$$
$$P_2 = \{(S_1, in)|_{S_2}, \ (a, in)|_{S_1}, \ (b, in)|_{S_1}, \ (c, in)|_{S_1}, \ (\varepsilon, in)|_c\},$$
$$P_3 = \{(\varepsilon, in)|_{S_3}, \ (abc, in)|_{S_3}\}.$$

Then, for $f(x) = x$, for $x \in \{a, b, c\}$, the P automaton accepts words of the form $a^n b^n c^n$, $n \geq 1$, with sequential application of rules and with only symport rules with promoters. Thus, the language accepted by Γ is a well-known non-context-free context-sensitive language. This can be easily seen by analyzing the sequence of transitions of Γ.

3   P Automata: Power and Size

As we mentioned in the Introduction, the first variant of P automata was introduced in [5], as a purely communicating accepting P system with one-way (top-down) communication. It is called a *one-way P automaton*, for short. This variant is a P automaton with only symport rules with promoters and functioning in the sequential mode. Although the model is rather restricted, these systems are very powerful computational tools:

In [5] it was shown that *any recursively enumerable language can be obtained as a mapping of the language of a one-way P automaton*, with seven membranes.

To prove the result, a well-known technique from membrane computing was applied, the simulation of the two-counter machines by P systems. The result was improved in [8] as follows:

One-way P automata are able to compute any recursively enumerable language, even having only two membranes and with promoters and moved multisets of size (of number of elements) of two.

While the above result proved to be important and interesting, the question, what about the exact characterization of the language classes accepted by P automata remained open. Although the original model allowed only symport rules with promoters to use, and in a sequential manner, it was reasonable to *extend the formalism to systems with symport and antiport rules and with or without promoters and inhibitors.* Moreover, it also appeared to be natural to consider not only the sequential, but the *maximally parallel* use of communication rules as well. (See [4] for the details.)

The answer to the previously mentioned question was given in [4], where the classes of languages of P automata, with the above extensions of the one-way P automaton, were characterized.

It was shown that *if the rules of the P automata are applied sequentially, then the accepted language class is strictly included in the class of languages accepted by one-way Turing machines with a logarithmically bounded workspace, while if the rules are applied in the maximal parallel manner, then the class of context-sensitive languages is determined.*

In the sequential case, the number of different multisets that may ever enter the system is finite which means that there is a natural one-to-one correspondence between these multisets and the symbols of a finite alphabet. This is not necessarily so when the rules are applied in the maximal parallel way. In this case P automata can be considered as devices accepting finite strings over an infinite alphabet. However, the case of infinite alphabets was not studied in the above paper, instead a mapping that maps the infinite set of different multisets to a finite alphabet was used (mapping f, Definition 4), thus it was possible to speak of languages accepted by P automata using the rules in the sequential or in the maximal parallel manner, the languages being in both cases over a finite alphabet. We note that the case of *infinite alphabets would be of particular interest for future research.*

Actually, *problems concerning P automata* form a broad area for future research. Particularly interesting research topics are the *descriptional (mainly size) complexity aspects* of these constructs, especially the cases when *all significant parameters* (the number of membranes in the systems, the number of rules associated to the regions, etc.) are bounded (at the same time). Analogously, notions for describing *communication complexity of P automata* would be worth developing and studying. Finding proper conditions for communication or different types of communication rules based on *quantitative properties* of the contents of the regions are also challenging problems. *Probabilistic and stochastic* P automata and their behaviour can also be in the focus of future interest. Since P automata represent systems being in interaction with its environment, system theoretic aspects of these constructs form an important part of their study. Thus, concepts for P automata theory as *tolerance, robustness, stability, equilibrium, periodical or aperiodical state transition sequence* should be developed and investigated in the future.

In the following, without the aim of completeness, we present some important models that have been introduced so far and briefly discuss their computational power and size properties.

4   Variants of P Automata

P automata or accepting P systems have raised immediate interest, several variants have been introduced, with the aim of formulating a concept which is more proper for modelling natural processes and at the same time sufficient and suitable for computation. This aim is attempted to be obtained by modifying the main ingredients and features of P automata: the way of defining acceptance, the notion of the accepted language, the way of communication, the definition of the communication rules or possibly evolution rules, and the way of the functioning of the system. In the following, without the aim of completeness, we discuss some of these models and open problems related with them.

4.1   Acceptance and Language

The first variant of P automata, the one-way P automaton used *final configurations* for determining *acceptance*. However, *accepting computation* can also be defined by *halting*, thus exactly in the same way as the original concept of defining successful computations is defined for membrane systems.

Analyzing P systems with antiport rules, introduced in [9], define acceptance in this way. The concept of an analyzing P system with antiport rules was published just after, almost at the same time as the one-way P automaton. According to this idea, the membranes of the P system have antiport rules as communication rules without any promoter or inhibitor. Starting from an initial configuration, which is given by the membrane structure and the initial multisets in the regions, the P system performs computation steps, by applying its rules in a maximal parallel way. The skin membrane communicates with the outside world, with the environment, where *symbols* as objects can be found. *A sequence of computation steps is successful, if and only if the system halts after a while.* Then, the *analyzed string* is the sequence of terminal symbols that were taken from the environment. If more than one terminal symbol is taken from the environment in one step, then any permutation of these symbols is considered as a valid subword of the input string. Notice that analyzing P systems with antiport rules are P automata where both the acceptance of the input and the accepted language is defined in a different way from that of the generalized notion of a P automaton given in Section 2.

As it was shown in [9], *analyzing P systems with antiport rules compute any recursively enumerable language, only in one membrane using antiport rules with radius* $(1, 2)$ *or* $(2, 1)$.

(The radius of an antiport rule $(x, in; y, out)$ is $(|x|, |y|)$.

Furthermore, the *computational completeness of these constructs* was demonstrated also in that case, where the multiset over the set of terminal symbols is initially put into a specified membrane together with possibly some other, nonterminal symbols (for so-called *initial analyzing P systems with antiport rules*).

Another variant of P automata, with also a well-founded motivation from systems theory, is the so-called ω-*P automata* [12]. This variant (with so-called membrane channels and antiport rules) was introduced to simulate the functioning of ω-Turing machines, that is, actions of Turing machines on *infinite words*. To formulate the proper notion, special efforts and considerations have to be made, since in usual P systems successful computations are defined by halting and the *failing computations are defined by non-halting* (with failure symbols with rules for allowing infinite computations). In the case of *infinite words to be analyzed, failing computations have to stop*.

The authors proved that *for any well-known variant of acceptance mode of ω-Turing machines one can construct an ω-P automaton with two membranes which simulates the computations of the corresponding ω-Turing machine*.

These types of P automata are of *particular interest*, since assuming a P automaton as a system being in interaction with its environment, we also should consider communication processes (functioning) not limited in time.

According to the basic definitions, the *accepted language* of a P automaton corresponds to a sequence of input multisets that is *observed* by an observer and recorded as the description of the behaviour of the system. But, the *behaviour* of the P automata can also be characterized in another manner: a description or observation of the *sequence of state transitions* in these systems would be of particular interest as well. What about P automata with *periodical or aperiodical behaviour*, with respect to its state transitions? The reader can notice that to answer these questions new concepts and notions should also be developed.

4.2   Communication

One of the main features of P automata is the *way of communication* and the *type of the used communication rules*. There have been several models introduced for investigating the role of the changes in these characteristics.

A concept developed from the original variant, from the one-way P automaton [5] was introduced in [15], called *P automaton with states*, where each membrane has a state from a given finite set, and the communication rules are of the form $(py, in)|_{qx}$, where p, q are states and x, y are multisets of symbols. The rule means the following: for $x, y \neq \varepsilon$, if x is contained in region i which is in state q and y is contained in its parent region, then the objects of y must leave the parent region and enter region i and then the state of the region i is changed for p. (The reader can notice that these rules are modified versions of symport rules.) If $x = \varepsilon$, then the region i must be empty, if $y = \varepsilon$, then no object is requested from the parent region. The notion was also motivated by tissue-like P systems, and unlike the sequential application of the rules of one-way P automata, the authors consider a maximal mode application of rules (given for tissue P systems).

It was shown that *these constructs describe the recursively enumerable sets of vectors of natural numbers*.

Improvements of the results of [15] were presented in [8], namely the authors proved that the result can be *extended to languages, moreover, to obtain computational completeness it is sufficient to consider only rules of restricted forms*.

Another model, with constraints concerning the communication, and strongly motivated by natural processes taking place in cells, is the so-called *P automa-*

ton with membrane channels. (See [17, 18] for details.) In this case, the sets of communication rules of the regions are of the following forms: $\langle P; x, out; y, in \rangle$, the so-called activating rules, and $\langle b, out; Q \rangle$ or $\langle b, in; Q \rangle$, the so-called prohibiting rules. (P, Q, x, and y are finite multisets of objects (symbols), and b is an object (a symbol).) Starting from the initial configuration, the system passes configurations by using its rules in a nondeterministic, maximally parallel manner, where the activating rules and the prohibiting rules are meant the following: Let $x = x_1 \ldots x_m$ and $y = y_1 \ldots y_k$, where x_i, y_j are symbols for $1 \leq i \leq m$, $1 \leq j \leq k$. Then, an activating rule $\langle P; x, out; y, in \rangle$ means that by the activator multiset P an output channel for each symbol x_i is activated, and for each y_j an input channel is activated. Then, each activated channel allows the transport of one object x_i and y_j, provided that no prohibitor multiset Q is active by a prohibiting rule, respectively. (This means that the multiset Q cannot be found in the corresponding region.) For this model, the acceptance is defined by final states and the accepted language is defined in the same way as for analyzing P systems with antiport rules.

A system that uses only activating rules is called *P automata with activated membrane channels.* This model is a computational complete device:

It was shown that P automata with membrane channels are able to recognize any recursively enumerable set, in one membrane with singleton activators and prohibitors.

A similar result was obtained about so-called *initial P automata with activated membrane channels.* (Roughly speaking, in the case of an initial P automaton with membrane channels, the multiset to be analyzed is initially put into the skin membrane possibly together with some other objects (symbols).)

It was shown that *any recursively enumerable set of (vectors) of non-negative integers can be accepted by an initial P automaton with activated membrane channels, in one membrane using only singleton activators and prohibitors.*

Continuing the investigations of the role of conditions associated with the constituents of P automata, the notion of (initial) *P automata with conditional communication rules associated with the membranes* was introduced and studied. (See [17], and [10] for background information.) The rules of these constructs are of the form $(P_{in}, Q_{in}; P_{out}, Q_{out}; y, in; x, out)$, which means that the transporting of the multiset x outside the membrane and the transporting of multiset y inside the membrane is possible if and only if the promoting multisets P_{in} and P_{out} are present in the respective regions, while the inhibiting multisets Q_{in} and Q_{out}, respectively, cannot be found in them. The objects forming the multisets P_{in} and P_{out} cannot be part of the multisets x and y, respectively.

As it was expected, *these variants of P automata proved to be computationally complete, with even one membrane and singleton promoters, inhibitors, and singleton objects transported through the skin membrane.*

The reader can observe that the above variants of P automata attempt to find in some sense *minimal conditions* for communication that still provide the computational completeness of the model but easier to handle or more economical in description. It appears that P automata with rather simple conditions for communication and rather bounded size properties are as powerful as Turing machines. However, the question what about accepting P systems where *all of the important size parameters are bounded (at the same time)* remains open. Analogously, an interesting problem is to formulate conditions for communications based on *quantitative properties of the contents of the regions.* Namely, what about those P automata, where communication takes place if the contents of the regions satisfy some quantitative properties, for example, the number of objects a is more than the number of objects b in the region. Similarly, we can introduce and study *communication by request*: communication does not take place at every step of the computation, but only if some predefined conditions for the contents of the region hold. Notice that this concept would introduce asynchrony in the functioning of the P automata.

A common feature of the above models is that the *environment is supposed to be an infinite supply of objects.* But, this assumption is in some sense artificial, usually only a *finite collection of input objects* is available for a natural system.

A model corresponding to the latter concept was introduced and discussed in [13, 14], called *restricted communicating P system.* In this case, the objects taken from the environment can only be those which were present in the system at the initialization, and later were sent out from the system. Such system consists of an alphabet of objects V including a distinguished object o, and a membrane structure μ with $m \geq n$ membranes, such that n of them are distinguished as input membranes. Initially, the regions may contain multisets of objects, whereas the objects o may only be put into the input membranes.

The regions of the system has special evolution rules, which are of the form $a \to a_\tau$, or $ab \to a_{\tau_1} b_{\tau_2}$, or $ab \to a_{\tau_1} b_{\tau_2} c_{come}$. Letters a, b, and c denote objects, while $\tau, \tau_1, \tau_2 \in \{here, out\} \cup \{in_j \mid 1 \leq j \leq n\}$. For an object being in membrane k, out means that it is transported out from the region to the surrounding region, in_j means that it is transported to membrane j in, provided that j is directly contained in membrane k. The subscript $here$ refers to that the object must stay in the same region. Evolution rules of the third type can be used only in the skin membrane, with the meaning that an object c is transported in from the environment. (Remember, that this is only possible if a c had already been sent out from the membrane system.) Thus, the number of objects in the P system and its environment together remains the same during the computation.

It was shown that *these constructs are equivalent in computational power to two-way multihead finite automata over bounded languages.*

Moreover, it was also proved that *the number of membranes in these P systems induces an infinite hierarchy according to the recognized language classes with respect to inclusion.* We should note that this type of P automata is particularly interesting, since in this case the system has a bounded environment, more precisely, its actual environment consists of those objects which are temporarily or forever non-activated (they are sent out, are not in the membrane system).

Restricted communicating P systems or P automata with a *bounded environment* can be of particular interest for further study. What about those systems where some of the objects that were sent out from the system might be lost?

What about those P automata which have an *environment consisting of a finite number of objects that can dynamically change at any step of the functioning.* (For example, the environment is "generated" by some computational mechanism at any moment of the functioning of P the system.)

An interesting research area can be the study of accepting P systems with *objects associated with so-called life-time*: after some steps, the object would disappear from the system or would never be allowed to be communicated. Similarly, we can ask about the role of associating time factors to the conditions for communication: the *conditions may dynamically change in time.*

4.3   Evolution and Communication

Although the concept of P automata was formulated to develop a concept for purely communicating, accepting P systems, if we consider P systems as models of evolving (dynamically changing) systems interacting with their environments, P automata with both communication and evolution rules are of a particular interest. *Evolution-communication P automata*, where both communication and evolution rules (the latter without the possibility of the transportation of objects) are allowed to use [1] are good examples for such models.

Important related variants of accepting P systems are the so-called *catalytic P automata* or *P automata with catalysts* [11, 7]. Catalytic P systems were introduced already in [20]; these are membrane systems with special objects called catalysts, which are used in the evolution rules. In these systems, the evolution rules are of the forms $a \rightarrow v$ or $ca \rightarrow cv$, where c is a catalyst, a is an object which is not catalyst, and v is a string from $((V \setminus C) \times \{here, out, in\})^*$. ($V$ is the set of objects and C is a proper subset of V, the set of catalysts.) In these systems the transition between two configurations is governed by the evolution rules, done in parallel, that is, any object which can be a subject of evolution, must evolve according to a local rule. The transportation of the objects is realized through the targets added to the evolution rules, namely, *in, out, here.* Catalytic systems have been in the focus of interest since the beginning of P systems theory. For the case of P automata with catalysts particularly important and interesting results were obtained in [7].

It has been shown that only one membrane and two catalysts are sufficient to obtain the computational completeness.

An open field for research in the theory of P automata is the study of the *role of possible evolution and its relation to communication in the model.* Are there P automata with both types of rules more efficient than the others based on only communication rules? What are the properties of these systems which are different from the properties of the generic variants of P automata?

4.4   Structure and Functioning

The basic variants of P automata and the models discussed above have so-called *static* membrane structure, that is, the their membrane structure does not change under the functioning of the system. However, this condition is rather strict, the structure of natural systems may vary under functioning.

An interesting and well-motivated concept is introduced in [2, 3], where the so-called *active P automata* is defined. In this case, unlike the previously defined variants of P automata, the construct computes with the structure of the membrane system, using operations like *membrane creation, division, and dissolution*. Briefly, in an active P automaton the accepting computation starts with one membrane which contains the string to be accepted and some other information. The computation follows according to the input string and during the evolution membranes can be created or dissolved. The computation ends, when all input symbols are consumed and also some termination condition is fulfilled. The authors demonstrate how to apply these constructs in natural language processing, in parsing.

As in the previous case, we would like to mention that these and similar variants of P automata, where the *membrane structure can dynamically change under functioning* is of particular interest, since it brings the concept closer to natural systems.

Moreover, the notion of P automata would be worth introducing for constructs with non-standard membrane structures as *tissue P systems* and comparing the properties of these models to those of the generic variants. (For the notion of a tissue P system, see [16].)

The previous models demonstrated that the different variants of P automata are – almost in any case – computationally complete computational devices, and this power can be obtained even with systems with a bounded size. Although it is an important issue to determine the computational power of accepting P systems, we should also pay attention to the *characteristics of the way of their functioning* as well. Among these properties, *determinism* plays an outstanding role. However, while it is easy to formulate a concept describing determinism, for example, for context-free grammars, this is not the case for sophisticated constructs with sophisticated behavior as P automata. A successful attempt has been made in [17], where so-called k-*determinism* (a "weak" type of determinism) was introduced and interpreted, based on the computation tree in P automata. This means, by [17], that for "every run starting from an initial configuration, if at any moment going at most k steps further for an arbitrary choice of productions to be applied, it can be decided (i.e., syntactically checked) which might be a reasonable continuation that possibly may lead to successful acceptance."

It was shown that for every recursively enumerable set of vectors of natural numbers there exists a 2-deterministic initial analyzing P system with antiport rules with radius $(2, 1)$ or $(1, 2)$.

The notion of k-determinism, and the notion of determinism at all, raises several further interesting research topics for the future. Investigations in the *determinism* of P automata is certainly of among the most interesting topics, and a lot of new results in the area are expected in the future.

5   Topics for Future Research

Investigations in the theory of P automata are expected to be continued in different directions, as we mentioned above. Although we have made several proposals, we summarize the ideas we find most important. Firstly, P automata can be considered as a construct attempting to build a *bridge between automata theory and membrane systems theory*, thus similarities and differences between the two fields are certainly of interest. But, as we mentioned in the Introduction, P automata or accepting P systems are models of *dynamically changing systems which are in communication (interaction) with their environments* as well. According to this approach, the *behavior* of the P automaton is of special interest – with the behavior interpreted as the set of accepted (consumed) multiset sequences, but also can be defined as the sequence of its states following each other. The following question immediately arises: is there any difference between the so-called *input-driven behavior* of the system, where some multiset of objects must enter the system from outside at any moment of time, and between the so-called *state-driven behavior* of the system, where the P automaton requests multisets of symbols from outside at any computational step, that is, the communication between the P automaton and its environment is driven by the current state of the P automaton? (This question, that is, the difference between the two interpretations of the notion of a P automaton was asked by György Vaszil.) Continuing this line of considerations, we can ask what about those variants of P automata, which communicate with their environment only by *dynamically emerging request*, that is, not in each computation step, but if it is necessary. This aspect would lead to studying *asynchronous systems*. Another possibility is to assume communication as a tool for leading to *equilibrium* in the state of the system. To do this, for example, we can pre-define some constraints that the regions should satisfy (this would mean a balanced situation), and then we can study which amount and which type of communication with the outside world are necessary to satisfy these conditions. Moreover, we can study the *robustness* or the *tolerance* of the P system, that is, how much and which kind of changes are caused in the behavior of the system (in the sequence of its configurations) taking different amount of multisets imported or to be imported from outside into account. In most of the models, an infinite supply of objects is supposed to be found in the environment. The question, what about systems with *finite, but dynamically changing (evolving) supplies of objects* would also be interesting.

References

1. Alhazov, A.: Minimizing Evolution-Communication P Systems and EC P Automata. In: Cavaliere, M., Martín-Vide, C., Păun, Gh. (eds): Brainstorming Week on Membrane Computing, Technical Report 26/03 of the Research Group on Mathematical Linguistics, Rovira i Virgili University, Tarragona, Spain, 2003, 23–31.

2. Bel-Enguix, G., Gramatovici, R.: Active P Automata and Natural Language Processing. In: Alhazov, A., Martín-Vide, C., Păun, Gh. (eds.): Workshop on Membrane Computing, WMC-2003, Tarragona, July 17-22, 2003. Technical Report 28/03 of the Research Group on Mathematical Linguistics, Rovira i Virgili University, Tarragona, Spain, 2003, 61–71.
3. Bel-Enguix, G., Gramatovici, R.: Parsing with Active P Automata. In: Martín-Vide, C., Mauri, G., Păun, Gh., Rozenberg, G., Salomaa, A. (eds.): Membrane Computing. International Workshop WMC 2003. Lecture Notes in Computer Science, Vol. 2933. Springer, Berlin, 2004, 203–217.
4. Csuhaj-Varjú, E., Ibarra, O.H., Vaszil, Gy.: On the Computational Complexity of P Automata. Ferretti, C., Mauri, G., Zandron, C. (eds.): Preliminary Proceedings of DNA10. Tenth International Meeting on DNA Computing. June 7-10, 2004, Milan. University of Milano-Bicocca, Italy, 2004, 97–106.
5. Csuhaj-Varjú, E., Vaszil, Gy.: P Automata. Păun, Gh., Zandron, C. (eds.): Pre-Proceedings of the Workshop on Membrane Computing WMC-CdeA 2002, Curtea de Argeş, Romania, August 19-23, 2002. Pub. No. 1 of MolCoNet-IST-2001-32008, 2002, 177–192.
6. Csuhaj-Varjú, E., Vaszil, Gy.: P Automata. Păun, Gh., Rozenberg, G., Salomaa, A., Zandron, C. (eds.): Membrane Computing. Lecture Notes in Computer Science, Vol. 2597. Springer, Berlin, 2003, 219–233.
7. Freund, R., Kari, L., Oswald, M., Sosik, P.: Computationally Universal P Systems without Priorities: Two Catalysts Are Sufficient. Theoretical Computer Science, to appear.
8. Freund, R., Martín-Vide, C., Obtułowicz, A., Păun, Gh.: On Three Classes of Automata-like P Systems. In: Ésik, Z., Fülöp, Z. (eds.): Developments in Language Theory. 7th International Conference, DLT 2003, Szeged, Hungary, July 2003. Proceedings. Lecture Notes in Computer Science, Vol. 2710. Springer, Berlin, 2003, 292–303.
9. Freund, R., Oswald, M.: A Short Note on Analysing P Systems. Bulletin of the EATCS, **78** (October 2002), 231–236.
10. Freund, R., Oswald, M.: P Systems with Conditional Communication Rules Assigned to Membranes. In: Alhazov, A., Martín-Vide, C., Păun, Gh. (eds.): Workshop on Membrane Computing, WMC-2003, Tarragona, July 17-22, 2003. Technical Report 28/03 of the Research Group on Mathematical Linguistics, Rovira i Virgili University, Tarragona, Spain, 2003, 231–240.
11. Freund, R., Oswald, M., Sosik, P.: Reducing the Number of Catalysts Needed in Computationally Universal Systems without Priorities. In: Csuhaj-Varjú, E., Kintala, C., Wotschke, D., Vaszil, Gy. (eds.): Fifth International Worskhop Descriptional Complexity of Formal Systems. MTA SZTAKI, Budapest, 2003, 102–113.
12. Freund, R., Oswald, M., Staiger, L.: ω-P Automata with communication rules. In: Martín-Vide, C., Mauri, G., Păun, Gh., Rozenberg, G., Salomaa, A. (eds.): Membrane Computing. International Workshop WMC 2003. Lecture Notes in Computer Science, Vol. 2933. Springer, Berlin, 2004, 203–217.
13. Ibarra, O.H.: The Number of Membranes Matters. In: Martín-Vide, C., Mauri, G., Păun, Gh., Rozenberg, G., Salomaa, A. (eds.): Membrane Computing. International Workshop WMC 2003. Lecture Notes in Computer Science, Vol. 2933. Springer, Berlin, 2004, 218–231.
14. Ibarra, O.H.: On the Computational Complexity of Membrane Systems. To appear in Theoretical Computer Science.
15. Madhu, M., Krithivasan, K.: On a Class of P Automata. *Intern. J. Computer Math.*, **80**, 9 (2003), 1111–1120.

16. Martín-Vide, C., Păun, Gh., Pazos, J., Rodrígez-Patón: Tissue P Systems. Theoretical Computer Science, **296**, 2 (2003), 295–326.
17. Oswald, M.: P Automata. PhD dissertation, Technical University of Vienna, 2003.
18. Oswald, M., Freund, R.: P Automata with Membrane Channels. In: Sugisaka, M., Tanaka, H. (eds): Proc. of the Eight Int. Symp. on Artificial Life and Robotics, Beppu, Japan, 2003, 275–278.
19. Păun, Gh.: Computing with Membranes. TUCS Report 208, Turku Centre for Computer Science, 1998.
20. Păun, Gh.: Computing with Membranes. An Introduction. Bulletin of the EATCS, **67** (1999), 139–152.
21. Păun, Gh.: Computing with Membranes. Journal of Computer and System Sciences, **61**, 1 (2000), 108–143.
22. Păun, Gh.: Computing with Membranes (P Systems): Twenty six research topics. CDMTCS Technical Report 119, Univ. of Auckland, 2000.
23. Păun, Gh.: Membrane Computing. An Introduction. Springer Verlag, Berlin-Heidelberg, 2002.
24. Păun, Gh., Rozenberg, G.: A Guide to Membrane Computing. Theoretical Computer Science, **287** (2002), 73–100.
25. The P systems web page at http://psystems.disco.unimib.it.

Asynchronous P Systems and P Systems Working in the Sequential Mode

Rudolf Freund

Faculty of Informatics,
Vienna University of Technology,
Favoritenstr. 9, A-1040 Wien, Austria
rudi@emcc.at

Abstract. In the area of P systems, applying the rules in a maximally parallel way is one of the most common features of many models introduced so far. Whereas the idea of membranes as well as many operations and rules used in membrane systems have a concrete biological background, the universal clock assumed to control the parallel application of rules is unrealistic, but on the other hand relevant for many interesting theoretical results, especially when proving computational completeness and solving computationally hard problems. Based on a quite general definition of tissue P systems, we investigate several models of P systems and compare their computational power in the classic case (i.e., applying the rules in the maximally parallel mode) and in the case of applying the rules in an asynchronous way (i.e., an arbitrary number of rules may be applied in one derivation step) or in the sequential mode (i.e., exactly one rule is applied in one derivation step). Moreover, we also recall some results for (tissue) P systems working in an asynchronous or sequential mode already in the original definition. Finally, we also raise several questions for future research in this subarea of (tissue) P systems working in the asynchronous mode and (tissue) P systems working in the sequential mode.

1 Introduction

When in 1998 Gheorghe Păun in [20] introduced membrane systems (which soon afterwards were called P systems), the way of applying the evolution rules in a maximally parallel way was one of the intrinsic features of this new model. Although biological processes in living organisms happen in parallel, they are not synchronized by a universal clock as assumed in the original model of membrane systems, instead many processes involve several objects in parallel, but the processes themselves are carried out in an asynchronous way, which feature formally can be captured by letting these processes happen in an unsynchronized or even sequential manner.

Many variants of P systems have been investigated so far (see [21] for a comprehensive overview as well as [23] for the actual state of research). We here consider several of these models of P systems, and we assume the reader to be

G. Mauri et al. (Eds.): WMC5 2004, LNCS 3365, pp. 36–62, 2005.
© Springer-Verlag Berlin Heidelberg 2005

familiar with the original definitions and explanations given for these models, as going into more details would go far beyond the scope of an overview article as this one is intended to be.

Already in his first papers on P systems, the author investigated generalized models of membrane systems with sequential application of (quite complex) rules (*generalized P systems*, e.g., see [10], [11], [12]). We will not recall the complex definitions of these systems, as they also used a kind of bounded parallel application of rules, i.e., when applying a complex rule to several objects, the simple rules working together in this complex rule themselves may be consumed, whereas other simple rules become applicable afterwards. Yet the complex rules were applied in a sequential way and in that way were already examples for sequential P systems. Most recently, some new results on P systems working in the sequential mode were elaborated in [7] (*P systems operating in sequential mode*).

In order to show some common features of various more recent models, in the third section we will define a general model of *tissue P systems* using states for the communication channels between the cells (compare with the model introduced in [16]) and priorities on the rules used in these channels as well as with energy assigned to the cell membranes. On the other hand, this general model is only meant for static membrane structures (although we could deal with deletion of elementary membranes), not for dynamic ones (especially, we do not consider membrane division or generation). As long as no dynamic membrane features as membrane division and membrane generation are involved, the graph structure representing the channels between the cells in a tissue P system is just a generalization of the tree structure of the membranes in a classic P system, hence many results known from literature only for classic tree structures of membranes can be directly carried over or at least quite easily be adapted for this general case of tissue P systems.

Based on the general model of tissue P systems defined in the third section, we then consider several variants of P systems and tissue P systems known from literature, redefine them in the sense of the general model, and investigate their generative power when applying the rules in the maximally parallel mode as well as in the sequential or asynchronous mode.

In the fourth section, we consider *P systems with symbol objects* and report on some first results on asynchronous P systems already mentioned in [21] and establish a result for P systems working in the sequential mode as well. Then we consider the model of *tissue(-like) P systems with channel states* as defined in [16] which formed the background for definition of the general model of tissue P systems defined in the third section; we show that one-cell tissue P systems with channel states and antiport rules working in the sequential mode (i.e., one-cell tissue P systems with antiport rules working in the sequential mode) characterize the Parikh sets of languages generated by matrix grammars without appearance checking; a similar characterization of these languages was also obtained in [18] by showing that *P systems with antiport rules working in the sequential mode* characterize the sets of numbers recognized by partially blind counter automata.

When using antiport rules transporting symbol objects between the cells and between cells and the environment, respectively, as well as maximal parallelism, we already reach computational completeness with only one membrane (see [15]). *(Tissue) P systems with unit rules and energy assigned to (cell) membranes* are another example for (tissue) P systems working in the sequential mode (see [14]); for obtaining computational completeness, we need a priority relation on the rules, and these P systems can be constructed in such a way that the same result is obtained for all three derivation modes, i.e., not only for the sequential mode, but also for the asynchronous mode and even for the maximally parallel mode. By (tissue) P systems with unit rules and energy assigned to (cell) membranes without priorities we only obtain a characterization of the Parikh sets of languages generated by matrix grammars without appearance checking.

In the fifth section, we deal with string objects. We first consider *gemmating P systems* (see [3], [2], [1], and [6]); the rules used there specify on which end of the current string a rule has to be applied; computational completeness can be obtained with the corresponding model of gemmating (tissue) P systems working in any of the three derivation modes, i.e., not only in the maximally parallel, but as well in the asynchronous and in the sequential mode. (Tissue) *P systems with splicing rules or cutting/recombination rules* by definition are working in an asynchronous (or even sequential) way and reach computational completeness with only one cell (again taking advantage of the fact that one can make the rules working at the ends of the strings). Finally, we investigate the generative power of *(tissue) P systems working in the sequential mode* (on strings); when using priorities, we obtain universality, without priorities we obtain a characterization of languages generated by matrix grammars without appearance checking.

A short summary of the models of (tissue) P systems and of the results, especially for (tissue) P systems working in the asynchronous and in the sequential mode, exhibited in sections four and five as well as an outlook to future research conclude the paper.

2   Prerequisites

In this section, we give some preliminary definitions, consider basic facts of register machines, and then define a general notion for grammars, graph-controlled grammars, and matrix grammars; moreover, we consider two normal forms for matrix grammars working on strings.

2.1   Preliminary Definitions

The set of non-negative integers is denoted by $\mathbf{N}$. An *alphabet* V is a finite non-empty set of abstract *symbols*. Given V, the free monoid generated by V under the operation of concatenation is denoted by V^*; the *empty string* is denoted by λ, and $V^* - \{\lambda\}$ is denoted by V^+. By $|x|$ we denote the length of the string x over V.

Let $\{a_1, ..., a_n\}$ be an arbitrary alphabet; the number of occurrences of a symbol a_i in x is denoted by $|x|_{a_i}$; the *Parikh vector* associated with x with respect to $a_1, ..., a_n$ is $\left(|x|_{a_1}, ..., |x|_{a_n}\right)$. The *Parikh image* of a language L over $\{a_1, ..., a_n\}$ is the set of all Parikh vectors of strings in L. For a family of languages FL, the family of Parikh images of languages in FL is denoted by $PsFL$. A (finite) multiset $\langle m_1, a_1 \rangle ... \langle m_n, a_n \rangle$ with $m_i \in \mathbf{N}$, $1 \leq i \leq n$, is represented as any string x the Parikh vector of which with respect to $a_1, ..., a_n$ is $(m_1, ..., m_n)$.

In the following we will not distinguish between a vector $(m_1, ..., m_n)$, its representation by a multiset $\langle m_1, a_1 \rangle ... \langle m_n, a_n \rangle$ or its representation by a string x with Parikh vector $\left(|x|_{a_1}, ..., |x|_{a_n}\right) = (m_1, ..., m_n)$.

For more notions as well as basic results from the theory of formal languages, the reader is referred to [8] and [24].

2.2 Register Machines

A *register machine* is a construct $M = (n, R, l_0, l_h)$, where n is the number of registers, R is a finite set of instructions injectively labelled with elements from a given set $lab(M)$, l_0 is the initial/start label, and l_h is the final label.

The instructions are of the following forms:

- $l_1 : (add(r), l_2, l_3)$
  Add 1 to the contents of register r and proceed to the instruction (labelled with) l_2 or l_3. (We say that we have an ADD instruction.)
- $l_1 : (sub(r), l_2, l_3)$
  If register r is not empty, then subtract 1 from its contents and go to instruction l_2, otherwise proceed to instruction l_3. (We say that we have a SUB instruction.)
- $l_h : halt$
  Stop the machine. The final label l_h is only assigned to this instruction.

Without loss of generality, one can assume that in each ADD instruction $l_1 : (add(r), l_2, l_3)$ and in each SUB instruction $l_1 : (sub(r), l_2, l_3)$ the labels l_1, l_2, l_3 are mutually distinct.

The following result already follows from the results proved in [19]:

Proposition 1. *Let $L \subseteq \mathbf{N}^\beta$ be a recursively enumerable set of (vectors of) non-negative integers. Then L can be generated by a register machine with at most $\beta + 2$ registers; moreover, at the beginning of a computation, all registers are empty; the results of a halting computation appear in the first β registers.*

2.3 Grammars

As we deal with various types of objects and grammars in the following, we first introduce a general model of a grammar:

A *grammar* G is a construct $(O, O_T, P, \Longrightarrow_G, w)$, where:

- O is the set of *objects*;
- $O_T \subseteq O$ is the set of *terminal* objects;
- P is a finite set of *productions*;

- $\Longrightarrow_G \subseteq O \times O$ is the *derivation relation* of G induced by the productions in P;
- $w \in O$ is the *axiom*.

The derivation relation $\Longrightarrow_G$ is obtained as the union of all $\Longrightarrow_p \subseteq O \times O$, i.e., $\Longrightarrow_G := \bigcup_{p \in P} \Longrightarrow_p$, where each $\Longrightarrow_p$ is a relation that we assume at least to be recursive. The reflexive and transitive closure of $\Longrightarrow_G$ is denoted by $\Longrightarrow_G^*$. The *language generated by* G is the set of all terminal objects (we also assume $v \in O_T$ to be decidable for every $v \in O$) derivable from the axiom, i.e.,

$$L(G) = \{v \in O_T \mid w \Longrightarrow_G^* v\}.$$

Depending on the components of G, especially with respect to different types of productions, we consider different types of grammars. The family of languages generated by grammars of type X is denoted by $\mathcal{L}(X)$.

String Grammars. Usually, a string grammar is defined as a construct (N, T, P, S), where:

- N is the alphabet of *non-terminal symbols*;
- T is the alphabet of *terminal* symbols, $N \cap T = \emptyset$;
- P is a finite set of *productions* of the form $u \to v$ with $u \in V^+$ and $v \in V^*$, where $V := N \cup T$;
- $S \in N$ is the *start symbol*.

In the general notation defined above, a string grammar now is represented as $(V^*, T^*, P, \Longrightarrow_G, S)$ where the derivation relation for $u \to v \in P$ is defined as usual by $xuy \Longrightarrow_{u \to v} xvy$ for all $x, y \in V^*$, thus yielding the well-known derivation relation $\Longrightarrow_G$ for the string grammar G.

As special types of string grammars we consider string grammars with arbitrary productions, context-free productions of the form $A \to v$ with $A \in N$ and $v \in V^*$, and λ-free context-free productions of the form $A \to v$ with $A \in N$ and $v \in V^+$, the corresponding types of grammars denoted by $ENUM$, CF, and $CF_{-\lambda}$, thus yielding the families of languages $\mathcal{L}(ENUM)$, i.e., the family of recursively enumerable languages, as well as $\mathcal{L}(CF)$ and $\mathcal{L}(CF_{-\lambda})$, i.e., the families of context-free and λ-free context-free languages, respectively.

2.4   Graph-Controlled Grammars

A *graph-controlled grammar* G_C of type X is a construct

$$(O, O_T, P, \Longrightarrow_G, w, R, L_{in}, L_{fin}),$$

where $G = (O, O_T, P, \Longrightarrow_G, w)$ is a grammar of type X, R is a finite set of rules r of the form $(l(r) : p(l(r)), \sigma(l(r)), \varphi(l(r)))$, where $l(r) \in Lab(G_C)$, $Lab(G_C)$ being a set of labels associated (in a one-to-one manner) with the rules r in R, $p(l(r)) \in P$, $\sigma(l(r)) \subseteq Lab(G_C)$ is the *success field* of the rule

r, and $\varphi\left(l\left(r\right)\right) \subseteq Lab\left(G_C\right)$ is the *failure field* of the rule r; $L_{in} \subseteq Lab\left(G_C\right)$ is the set of initial labels, and $L_{fin} \subseteq Lab\left(G_C\right)$ is the set of final labels. For $r = \left(l\left(r\right) : p\left(l\left(r\right)\right), \sigma\left(l\left(r\right)\right), \varphi\left(l\left(r\right)\right)\right)$ and $v, u \in O$ we define $\left(v, l\left(r\right)\right) \Longrightarrow_{G_C} \left(u, k\right)$ if and only if

- **either** $p\left(l\left(r\right)\right)$ is applicable to v, $v \Longrightarrow_{p(l(r))} u$, and $k \in \sigma\left(l\left(r\right)\right)$,
- **or** $p\left(l\left(r\right)\right)$ is not applicable to v, $u = v$, and $k \in \varphi\left(l\left(r\right)\right)$.

The language generated by G_C is

$$L\left(G_C\right) = \{v \in O_T \mid \left(w_0, l_0\right) \Longrightarrow_{G_C} \left(w_1, l_1\right) \ldots \Longrightarrow_{G_C} \left(w_k, l_k\right), \ k \geq 1,$$
$$w_j \in O \ \text{and} \ l_j \in Lab\left(G_C\right) \ \text{for} \ 0 \leq j \leq k,$$
$$w_0 = w, \ w_k = v, \ l_0 \in L_{in}, \ l_k \in L_{fin}\}.$$

The graph-controlled grammar G_C is said to be of type GC_{ac}; it is said to be of type GC – to be *without appearance checking (without* ac$)$ – if $\varphi\left(l\right) = \emptyset$ for all $l \in Lab\left(G_C\right)$. The corresponding families of languages are denoted by $\mathcal{L}\left(X{-}GC_{ac}\right)$ and $\mathcal{L}\left(X{-}GC\right)$, respectively.

2.5 Matrix Grammars

A *matrix grammar with appearance checking (with* ac for short$)$ G_M of type X is a construct

$$\left(O, O_T, P, \Longrightarrow_G, w, M, F\right),$$

where $G = \left(O, O_T, P, \Longrightarrow_G, w\right)$ is a grammar of type X, M is a finite set of finite sequences of productions (an element of M is called a *matrix*), and $F \subseteq P$. For a matrix $m_i = \left[m_{i,1}, \ldots, m_{i,n_i}\right]$ in M and $v, u \in O$ we define $v \Longrightarrow_{m_i} u$ if and only if there are $w_0, w_1, \ldots, w_{n_i} \in O$ such that $w_0 = v$, $w_{n_i} = u$, and for each $j, 1 \leq j \leq n_i$,

- **either** $w_{j-1} \Longrightarrow_{m_{i,j}} w_j$ according to $\Longrightarrow_G$,
- **or** $m_{i,j}$ is not applicable to w_{j-1} according to $\Longrightarrow_G$, $w_j = w_{j-1}$, $m_{i,j} \in F$.

The language generated by G_M is

$$L\left(G_M\right) = \{v \in O_T \mid w \Longrightarrow_{m_{i_1}} w_1 \ldots \Longrightarrow_{m_{i_k}} w_k, \ w_k = v,$$
$$w_j \in O, \ m_{i_j} \in M \ \text{for} \ 1 \leq j \leq k, k \geq 1\}.$$

The matrix grammar G_M is said to be of type MAT_{ac}; it is said to be of type MAT – to be *without appearance checking (without* ac$)$ – if $F = \emptyset$. The corresponding families of languages are denoted by $\mathcal{L}\left(X{-}MAT_{ac}\right)$ and $\mathcal{L}\left(X{-}MAT\right)$, respectively.

We should like to mention that according to the definitions given in [8], when applying the last matrix, the derivation may already end before the sequence of this matrix has been exhausted.

Lemma 2. *For any arbitrary type X,*

$$\mathcal{L}\left(X{-}MAT\right) \subseteq \mathcal{L}\left(X{-}GC\right) \text{ and } \mathcal{L}\left(X{-}MAT_{\mathsf{ac}}\right) \subseteq \mathcal{L}\left(X{-}GC_{\mathsf{ac}}\right).$$

Proof. Consider a matrix grammar $G_M = (O, O_T, P, \Longrightarrow_G, w, M, F)$ of arbitrary type X with

$$M = \{[m_{i,1}, ..., m_{i,n_i}] \mid 1 \le i \le n, n_i, n \ge 1\};$$

then we construct the graph-controlled grammar $G_C = (O, O_T, P, \Longrightarrow_G, w, R, L_{in}, L_{fin})$ with

$$
\begin{aligned}
Lab &= \{(i,j) \mid 1 \le i \le n, 1 \le j \le n_i\}, \\
L_{in} &= \{(i,1) \mid 1 \le i \le n\}, \\
L_{fin} &= Lab, \\
R &= \{((i,j) : m_{i,j}, \{(i,j+1)\}, \{(i,j+1)\} \circ \chi\,(m_{i,j}, F)) \mid \\
& \quad 1 \le i \le n, 1 \le j \le n_i\} \\
& \cup \{((i,n_i) : m_{i,n_i}, \{(k,1) \mid 1 \le k \le n\}, \\
& \quad \{(k,1) \mid 1 \le k \le n\} \circ \chi\,(m_{i,n_i}, F)) \mid 1 \le i \le n\},
\end{aligned}
$$

where Lab is the set of labels in G_C and the notation $X \circ \chi\,(a, Y)$ for two sets X and Y stands for X if $a \in Y$ and the empty set otherwise. The matrices of G_M are simulated by suitable sequences in the graph-controlled grammar G_C; the given construction obviously yields $L\,(G_C) = L\,(G_M)$; moreover, all failure fields in G_C are empty if and only if F is empty, i.e., if G_M is a matrix grammar without ac, then G_C is a graph-controlled grammar without ac, too; this observation completes the proof.   □

2.6   Normal Forms for Matrix Grammars

For matrix grammars without appearance checking of string type CF, we have the following special normal form: $G_M = ((N \cup T)^*, T^*, P, \Longrightarrow_G, S, M)$ (where N and T are the sets of terminal and non-terminal symbols, respectively, S is the start symbol, and M is the set of matrices) is said to be in the *f-binary normal form*, if $N = N_1 \cup N_2 \cup \{S, f\}$, with these three sets being mutually disjoint, and the matrices in M are in one of the following forms:

1. $[S \to XA]$, with $X \in N_1, A \in N_2$,
2. $[X \to Y, A \to x]$, with $X, Y \in N_1$, $A \in N_2$, $x \in (N_2 \cup T)^*$, $|x| \le 2$,
3. $[X \to f, A \to x]$, with $X \in N_1$, $A \in N_2$, and $x \in T^*$, $|x| \le 2$,
4. $[f \to \lambda]$.

Moreover, there is only one matrix of type 1 and only one matrix of type 4, which is only used in the last step of a derivation yielding a terminal result.

The following lemma is an immediate consequence of the binary normal form established in [8] for matrix grammars of type CF (see [16]):

Lemma 3. *For every matrix grammars without ac of string type CF, we can effectively construct a matrix grammar in f-binary normal form.*

A matrix grammar $G_M = ((N'' \cup T)^*, T^*, P, \Longrightarrow_G, w, M, F)$ of string types CF and $CF_{-\lambda}$, respectively, is said to be in *activator normal form* (anf for short) if $N'' = N' \times L \cup N \cup \{H\}$ for two disjoint sets N' and L with $N' = N \cup T (\cup \{\lambda\})$, $H \notin N$ is a trap symbol (i.e., H cannot evolve any more), $w \in N \times L$, $F \subseteq \{X \to H \mid X \in N\}$, and every matrix in M is of one of the following forms:

1. $[(X, r) \to (Y, s) Y_1...Y_k]$, $X \in N$, $Y \in N'$, $Y_1, ..., Y_k \in N \cup T$ for $1 \le i \le k$, $k \ge 0$, $r, s \in L$;
2. $[X \to (X, r), (Y, r) \to Y]$, $X \in N$, $Y \in N'$, $r \in L$;
3. $[(a, r) \to a]$, $a \in T (\cup \{\lambda\})$, $r \in L$;
4. $[X \to H, (Y, r) \to (Y, s)]$, $X \in N$, $Y \in N' - \{X\}$, $r, s \in L$.

The rules of type 4 only appear in the case of a matrix grammar with ac, i.e., if $F \ne \emptyset$. Moreover, the notation $(\cup \{\lambda\})$ indicates that we have to take the empty string λ into account only for the case of type CF.

Lemma 4. *For any matrix grammar without/with* ac *of type* X, *we can effectively construct an equivalent matrix grammar without/with* ac *in* anf *of the same type, for any* $X \in \{CF, CF_{-\lambda}\}$.

Proof. Given any matrix grammar G_M without/with ac of type X, the main idea is to construct the corresponding graph-controlled grammar G_C according to Lemma 2 and then to simulate G_C by a matrix grammar G'_M without/with ac in anf of the same type X. The set L in G_C then corresponds to the set of labels of the control graph of G_C, i.e., we keep track of the current label r in G_C by the second component in the activated symbol (X, r). Matrices of type 1 simulate the corresponding successful applications of productions in G_C, whereas matrices of type 4 simulate the failure case. Matrices of type 3 are to be used in the last step of a derivation in G'_M, and matrices of type 2 allow the activator, i.e., the current label, to move around within the underlying string. Following these explanations, we now construct G'_M from G_M via G_C:

Let $G_M = ((N \cup T)^*, T^*, P, \Longrightarrow_G, w, M, F)$ be a matrix grammar of string type X, $X \in \{CF, CF_{-\lambda}\}$, and let

$$G_C = ((N \cup T)^*, T^*, P, \Longrightarrow_G, w, R, L_{in}, L_{fin})$$

be the corresponding graph-controlled grammar as constructed in the proof of Lemma 2. Then we construct the equivalent matrix grammar G'_M without/with ac of type X in anf as follows:

$$G'_M = ((N'' \cup T)^*, T^*, P \cup \{S \to S\}, \Longrightarrow_G, w, M', F'),$$
$$N'' = N' \times L \cup N \cup \{H\},$$
$$N' = N \cup T (\cup \{\lambda\}),$$
$$L = Lab \cup \{0\}, 0 \notin Lab,$$
$$w = (S, 0),$$
$$F' = \{X \to H \mid X \in N\},$$

and M contains the following matrices:

1. $[(X,r) \rightarrow (Y,s)Y_1...Y_k]$, $(r : p(r), \sigma(r), \varphi(r)) \in R$, $p(r) = X \rightarrow YY_1...Y_k$,
   $X \in N$, $Y \in N'$, $Y_1, ..., Y_k \in N \cup T$ for $1 \leq i \leq k$, $k \geq 0$, $r, s \in Lab$, $s \in \sigma(r)$;
2. $[X \rightarrow (X,r), (Y,r) \rightarrow Y]$, $X \in N$, $Y \in N'$, $r \in Lab$;
3. $[(a,r) \rightarrow a]$, $a \in T (\cup \{\lambda\})$, $r \in Lab$;
4. $[X \rightarrow H, (Y,r) \rightarrow (Y,s)]$, $(r : p(r), \sigma(r), \varphi(r)) \in R$, $p(r) = X \rightarrow Y_1...Y_k$,
   $X \in N$, $Y \in N' - \{X\}$, $Y_1, ..., Y_k \in N \cup T$ for $1 \leq i \leq k$, $k \geq 0$, $r, s \in Lab$,
   $s \in \varphi(r)$, $H \notin N$ is the trap symbol;
5. $[(S,0) \rightarrow (S,i)]$, $i \in L_{in}$; using these initial matrices, we can start from an
   arbitrary initial label in L_{in}.

Observing that $L_{fin} = Lab$ we see that every terminal string derivable in
G_C belongs to $L(G_C)$ and therefore the construction elaborated above yields
$L(G_M) = L(G_C) = L(G'_M)$. As can be immediately seen from the construction
given above and the proof of Lemma 2, the rules of type 4 only appear in the
case of the original grammar G_M being a matrix grammar with ac, i.e., if $F \neq \emptyset$.
Moreover, λ-rules of the form $[(a,r) \rightarrow \lambda]$ indicated by the notation $\cup \{\lambda\}$ only
occur in the case of type CF. These observations complete the proof.   □

3   A General Model of Tissue P Systems

The reader is assumed to be familiar with the main ingredients and variants of
the basic models of P systems and tissue P systems; we especially refer to [21]
and the original papers cited there. In this section we define the general model
of tissue P systems we are going to use for representing the different models of
(tissue) P systems considered in this paper.

A *tissue P system* (of degree $m \geq 1$) *with channel states, priorities on the
channel rules, and energy assigned to cell membranes* is a construct

$$\Pi = \left(m, O, T, K, O_\infty, W, E, ch, \left(s_{(i,j)}, R_{(i,j)}, \rho_{(i,j)}\right)_{(i,j) \in ch}, i_0 \right),$$

where:

- m is the number of *cells* assumed to be labelled with $1, 2, \ldots, m$;
- O is the alphabet of *objects*;
- $T \subseteq O$ is the alphabet of *terminal* objects;
- K is the alphabet of *states* (not necessarily disjoint from O);
- O_∞ consists of $m + 1$ sets of objects indicating those objects from O that
  are present in arbitrarily many copies in the environment and the m cells;
- W consists of $m+1$ strings over $O-O_\infty$ representing the *initial finite multiset*
  of objects present in the environment and the m cells of the system;
- $E \subseteq N^m$ are m numbers indicating the *initial energy values* assigned to the
  cell membranes of the m cells;
- $ch \subseteq \{(i,j) \mid i,j \in \{0,1,2,\ldots,m\}, (i,j) \neq (0,0)\}$ is the set of *links* (called
  synapses in [16]; in the following, we will use the term *channels*) between
  two cells or a cell and the environment (indicated by 0);

- $s_{(i,j)}$ is the *initial state* of the channel $(i,j) \in ch$;
- $R_{(i,j)}$ is a finite set of *rules*, associated with the channel $(i,j) \in ch$, of the form (s, r, s'), for some $s, s' \in K$ and r being a rule which involves objects in the cells i and j and yields new objects in these cells and also involves and possibly changes the energies assigned to these cells i and j; the rules also have to obey to a *priority relation* $\rho_{(i,j)}$, i.e., a rule from $R_{(i,j)}$ can only be applied if no other rule of higher priority could be applied, too;
- $i_0 \in \{0, 1, 2, \dots, m\}$ is the *output* cell (0 means that the output is to be found in the environment).

A rule of the form $(s, r, s') \in R_{(i,j)}$ changes the state of the channel between the cells i and j from s to s', it can only be applied if the current state is s. In contrast to the definition of tissue P systems with channel states in [16] where one rule had to be used in each channel for which a rule could be used, we here will consider the maximally parallel, the asynchronous, and the sequential derivation mode. Moreover, the channels in this general model are directed, i.e., we distinguish between $R_{(i,j)}$ and $R_{(j,i)}$.

The computation starts with the configuration specified by W, E, and $(s_{(i,j)})_{(i,j) \in ch}$. In the sequential derivation mode, only one rule in one channel is applied in one derivation step (in each time unit); in the maximally parallel derivation mode, as many rules as possible – which do not cause conflicts with respect to changing states – are used in parallel in every channel; in the asynchronous derivation mode, arbitrarily many rules – which do not cause conflicts with respect to changing states – are applied in parallel in arbitrary channels. The results of a computation are described either by the multiplicity of symbol objects from T or by the string objects over T present in cell i_0 in a halting configuration or by the terminal strings appearing in cell i_0 during an arbitrary computation (we will usually restrict ourselves to these variants).

4   (Tissue) P Systems Working on Symbol Objects

In this section we consider several models of (tissue) P systems working on symbol objects. We first recall some results for the original model of P systems as introduced in [20]. Then we exhibit a result from [16] saying that one-cell tissue P systems with channel states and antiport rules (i.e., asynchronous one-cell tissue P systems with antiport rules) characterize the (Parikh sets of) languages generated by matrix grammars without appearance checking. Moreover, we recall the optimal result (with respect to the number of membranes and the weight of the rules) for P systems with antiport rules for the case of applying rules in the maximally parallel way (e.g., see [15]) as well as mention the result proved in [18] showing that when applying rules in an asynchronous way, only the generative power of partially blind counter automata can be obtained. Finally, we consider (tissue) P systems with unit rules and energy assigned to (cell) membranes, which work in the sequential mode; for obtaining computational completeness, a priority relation on the rules is needed, whereas without priorities we obtain a characterization of Parikh sets of languages generated by matrix grammars without appearance checking.

4.1   The Classic Model

For the classic model of P systems, we refer to the original article [20] and the detailed explanations given in [21]. As shown in [13], *P systems with catalysts (but without priorities)* are able to generate any arbitrary recursively enumerable set of numbers with only two catalysts in only one membrane provided we impose the condition of maximal parallelism and collect the results of halting computations. On the other hand, one of the first results dealing with P systems working in the asynchronous mode (see [21], Subsection 3.4.5) says that *asynchronous P systems with catalysts (but without priorities)* can only generate regular sets of numbers. The notion asynchronous means that we do not enforce maximal parallelism, but instead allow an arbitrary number of rules to happen in parallel. Obviously, for P systems without priorities this is equivalent with just letting them work in the sequential mode, i.e., by just performing one rule in one derivation step; for P systems with priorities this observation would not be true any more, because the outcome of performing one rule might affect the applicability of another rule.

Therefore, let us consider *P systems with catalysts (but without priorities) working in the sequential mode* in more detail; by the result proved in [21], Subsection 3.4.5, these P systems can only generate regular sets of numbers. In fact, as only one rule is carried out in one derivation step, the catalysts can simply be omitted! Hence, what remains is a P system working in the sequential mode with context-free rules carrying targets of the form $a \rightarrow \lambda$ or $a \rightarrow b_1 (t_1) ... b_k (t_k)$, where $a, b_1, ..., b_k$ are symbols and $t_1, ..., t_k$ are targets of the form *here* (let the symbol in the current membrane), *out* (move the symbol out to the surrounding membrane), or in_j (move the symbol into the inner membrane labelled by j).

Obviously, the Parikh sets of context-free languages therefore can be generated in only one membrane by such P systems (without priorities, without catalysts) working in the sequential mode. On the other hand, also with an arbitrary number of membranes only Parikh sets of context-free languages can be generated: In the simulating context-free grammar, we use the non-terminal symbols (a, i) with $a \in O$ and i being the label of the membrane where the copy of the object a is present. Hence, a rule $a \rightarrow b_1 (t_1) ... b_k (t_k)$ in membrane i is simulated by the corresponding context-free production $(a, i) \rightarrow (b_1, m_1) ... (b_k, m_k)$ such that, for $1 \leq l \leq k$, $m_l = i$ for $t_l = here$, $m_l = j$ for $t_l = out$ and j being the label of the membrane surrounding membrane i, and $m_l = j$ for $t_l = in_j$ and j being the label of the membrane j inside membrane i; $a \rightarrow \lambda$ in membrane i is simulated by $(a, i) \rightarrow \lambda$. Moreover, we also add the production $(a, i) \rightarrow \lambda$ for all symbols a such that there is no rule with a on the left-hand side in membrane $i \neq i_0$ and $(a, i_0) \rightarrow a$ for $a \in T$ if there is no rule with a on the left-hand side in the output membrane i_0; non-terminal symbols (a, i_0) with $a \notin T$ for which there is no rule with a on the left-hand side in the output membrane i_0 (which means that the computation in the P system will not yield a result because the symbol a cannot be eliminated any more from the output membrane) cannot be derived any more. We leave the further details of this proof to the reader.

In the setting of this paper, we consider the following variant of tissue P systems working in the sequential mode:

A *tissue P system* (of degree $m \geq 1$) *working in the sequential mode* is a construct

$$\Pi = \left(m, O, T, W, ch, \left(R_{(i,j)}\right)_{(i,j)\in ch}, i_0\right),$$

where:

- m is the number of *cells* assumed to be labelled with $1, 2, \ldots, m$;
- O is the alphabet of *objects*;
- $T \subseteq O$ is the alphabet of *terminal* objects;
- W consists of m strings over O representing the *initial finite multiset* of objects present in the m cells of the system;
- $ch \subseteq \{(i,j) \mid i, j \in \{1, 2, \ldots, m\}\}$ is the set of *channels*;
- $R_{(i,j)}$ is a finite set of *rules*, associated with the channel $(i,j) \in ch$, of the form (a, v) with $a \in O$ and v being a multiset over O; $(a, v) \in R_{(i,j)}$ removes a copy of the symbol a from cell i and adds the multiset v to the contents of cell j;
- $i_0 \in \{1, 2, \ldots, m\}$ is the *output* cell.

The computation starts with the configuration specified by W; in each time unit, one rule is used in one channel. The results of a computation are described by the multiplicity of symbol objects from T present in cell i_0 in a halting configuration (yet only if no non-terminal symbol is present in i_0 at that time).

Following the explanations exhibited above for P systems (without priorities, without catalysts) working in the sequential mode, we can easily show the following result:

Theorem 5. *Tissue P systems working in the sequential mode characterize the sets of Parikh vectors generated by context-free grammars (i.e., the regular sets of vectors of non-negative integers).*

Proof. Given a context-free grammar $G = (N, T, P, S)$ (without loss of generality we may assume G to be reduced, i.e., for each $X \in N$ there exist $u, v \in (N \cup T)^*$ and $w \in T^*$ such that $S \Longrightarrow_G^* uXv \Longrightarrow_G^* w$) we immediately get $L(G) = L(\Pi)$ for the tissue P system working in the sequential mode Π with

$$\Pi = \left(1, N \cup T, T, (S), \{(1,1)\}, R_{(1,1)}, 1\right),$$
$$R_{(1,1)} = \{(X, v) \mid X \to v \in P\}.$$

On the other hand, let

$$\Pi = \left(m, O, T, (w_1, \ldots, w_m), ch, \left(R_{(i,j)}\right)_{(i,j)\in ch}, i_0\right)$$

be a tissue P system working in the sequential mode. Then we construct the context-free grammar $G = (N, T, P, S)$ with

$$N = \{(a,i) \mid a \in O, 1 \le i \le m\} \cup \{S\},$$
$$P = \{S \to h_1(w_1)...h_m(w_m)\}$$
$$\cup \{(a,i) \to h_j(v) \mid (a,v) \in R_{(i,j)}, (i,j) \in ch\}$$
$$\cup \{(a,i) \to \lambda \mid a \in O, 1 \le i \le m, i \ne i_0,$$
$$\text{there exist no } j, v \text{ such that } (a,v) \in R_{(i,j)}\}$$
$$\cup \{(a,i_0) \to a \mid a \in T \text{ and}$$
$$\text{there exist no } j, v \text{ such that } (a,v) \in R_{(i_0,j)}\},$$

where, for $1 \le i \le m$, $h_i : O^* \to (O \times \{i\})^*$ is the homomorphism defined by $h_i(a) = (a,i)$ for $a \in O$. Due to the explanations already given in the first part of this subsection, we immediately infer $L(\Pi) = L(G)$. $\square$

At the end of this subsection, we should like to mention that a similar result like that stated in Theorem 5 also holds true for tissue P systems working in the asynchronous mode.

4.2   Tissue P Systems with Channel States and Antiport Rules

The background for the definition of the general model of tissue P systems defined in the third section was the model of tissue(-like) P systems with channel states as defined in [16]. One main difference between the two models is that there for each set $\{i,j\}$ of cell labels i, j only for one channel (i,j) or (j,i) a set of rules was defined. We now consider our general model of *tissue P systems with channel states and antiport rules* (but without energy assigned to cell membranes and without priorities on the rules, therefore we omit specifying these ingredients E and $\rho_{(i,j)}$): A rule of the form $(s, x/y, s') \in R_{(i,j)}$ is interpreted as an antiport rule for the ordered pair (i,j) of cells, acting only if the channel (i,j) has the state s; the application of the rule means moving the objects specified by x from cell i (from the environment, if $i = 0$) to cell j, at the same time moving the objects specified by y in the opposite direction, as well as changing the state of the channel from s to s'. (The rules with one of x, y empty are, in fact, symport rules, but we do not explicitly consider this distinction here, as it is not relevant for what follows.) The weight of an antiport rule x/y is the maximum of the lengths of x and y. If, at the end of a halting computation, the contents of the final cell labelled by i_0 consists only of terminal symbols, then the (vector of) numbers represented by the copies of terminal symbols constitutes the result of this successful computation in the tissue P system with channel states and antiport rules.

Based on the results proved in [16] for tissue P systems with channel states and antiport rules we now exhibit a characterization of Parikh sets of matrix languages:

Theorem 6. *Any Parikh set of a language that can be generated by a matrix grammar without appearance checking can be generated by a tissue P system with only one cell, only one channel state and antiport rules of weight at most two working in the sequential mode.*

Proof. Consider a matrix grammar $G = (N_1 \cup N_2 \cup \{S, f\}, T, S, M)$ in the f-binary normal form and construct the tissue P system with channel states and antiport rules (working in the sequential mode)

$$\Pi = \left(1, O, T, \{s\}, (O, \emptyset), (\lambda, X_0 A_0), \{(1,0)\}, \left(s, R_{(1,0)}\right), 1\right),$$
$$O = N_1 \cup \{f\} \cup N_2 \cup T \cup \{\langle Y, \alpha\beta \rangle \mid Y \in N_1 \cup \{f\}, \alpha, \beta \in N_2 \cup T\},$$
$$R_{(1,0)} = \{(s, XA/Yx, s) \mid (X \rightarrow Y, A \rightarrow x) \in M$$
$$X \in N_1, Y \in N_1 \cup \{f\}, A \in N_2, x \in N_2 \cup T \cup \{\lambda\}\}$$
$$\cup \{(s, XA/Y \langle Y, \alpha_1 \alpha_2 \rangle, s), (s, \langle Y, \alpha_1 \alpha_2 \rangle / \alpha_1 \alpha_2, s) \mid$$
$$(X \rightarrow Y, A \rightarrow \alpha_1 \alpha_2) \in M,$$
$$X \in N_1, \ Y \in N_1 \cup \{f\}, A \in N_2, \alpha_1, \alpha_2 \in N_2 \cup T\}$$
$$\cup \{(s, \alpha/\alpha, s) \mid \alpha \in N_1 \cup N_2\} \cup \{(s, f/\lambda, s)\},$$

where $(S \rightarrow X_0 A_0)$ is the initial matrix of M.

The state plays no rôle, the matrices of M are simulated by the antiport rules. As long as at least one non-terminal symbol from $N_1 \cup N_2$ is present, the computation must continue. By halting computations, Π (in cell 1) obviously generates exactly the same set of vectors of non-negative integers as G.   □

As it is easy to see, the tissue P system with channel states and antiport rules constructed in the preceding proof generates the same set of vectors of non-negative integers even when working in the asynchronous mode or in the maximally parallel way.

For tissue P systems with only one cell also the converse of the preceding theorem holds true as was shown in [16], i.e., any Parikh set of a language that can be generated by a one-cell tissue P system with channel states and antiport rules working in the sequential mode can be generated by a matrix grammar without appearance checking (we here omit the proof which could be an adequate adaptation of the proof given in [16]).

4.3   P Systems with Antiport Rules

The preceding results have shown that with (tissue) P systems with antiport rules and only one cell working in the sequential mode we can only get Parikh sets of matrix languages. With imposing the condition of maximal parallelism, we obtain full computational power. The proof of the following theorem follows the proof given in [15]; for the representation of the P system we take a similar model as before in the proof of Theorem 6, but we omit the state and when applying the rules have in mind the condition of maximal parallelism:

Theorem 7. *Any Parikh set of a recursively enumerable language can be generated by a P system working in the maximally parallel mode with only one cell (membrane) and antiport rules of weight two.*

Proof. For a given register machine $M = (n, R, l_0, l_h)$ we consider $lab(M)$ to be the set of instruction labels and the alphabet $U = \{a_1, \ldots, a_m\}$ (the symbol a_i is associated with register i and the contents of this register will be represented by the multiplicity of object a_i in the P system we are going to construct); we now construct the P system

$$\Pi = \left(1, O, T, (O, \emptyset), (\lambda, l_0), \{(1, 0)\}, R_{(1,0)}, 1\right),$$
$$O = U \cup \{l, l', l'', l''', l^{iv} \mid l \in lab(M)\},$$
$$R_{(1,0)} = \{l_1/l_2 a_r, l_1/l_3 a_r \mid l_1 : (add(r), l_2, l_3) \in R\}$$
$$\cup \{l_1/l'_1 l''_1, l'_1 a_r/l'''_1, l''_1/l^{iv}_1, l^{iv}_1 l'''_1/l_2, l^{iv}_1 l'_1/l_3 \mid$$
$$l_1 : (sub(r), l_2, l_3) \in R\}.$$

We start with l_0 present in the system, and then we simulate M : Each add-instruction $l_1 : (add(r), l_2, l_3)$ of M is simulated by a rule $l_1/l_2 a_r$ or $l_1/l_3 a_r$ in Π, while a subtract-instruction $l_1 : (sub(r), l_2, l_3) \in R$ is simulated as follows. The available object l_1 is sent out, in exchange of l'_1 and l''_1. The first object checks whether the register is non-empty, and in the affirmative case it exits the system (together with a copy of a_r) and is replaced by l'''_1; if no copy of a_r is available, then l'_1 remains in the system and waits. The object l''_1 checks what the other object has done, allowing it a step for acting (this is the step when the antiport rule l''_1/l^{iv}_1 is used). The object l^{iv}_1 will find inside either one of the objects l'_1 (if the register r was empty) or l'''_1 (if the register r was not empty), and in each case the next object to be introduced in the system, l_3 or l_2, respectively, is the correct label to be used in the program of M. Hence, halting computations in the P system Π generate the same numbers as M. □

In the case of *P systems with antiport rules working in the sequential mode*, we obtain a characterization of the family languages generated by partially blind counter automata (see [18]), i.e., the same characterization as by Parikh sets of matrix languages.

4.4   (Tissue) P Systems with Unit Rules and Energy Assigned to (Cell) Membranes

In [14], P systems with unit rules and energy assigned to (cell) membranes were introduced as a model of P systems working in the sequential mode; adapting the definitions given there, we get the following definition (we omit the states and O_∞, because all symbols are assumed to occur in a finite number only; moreover, we only consider a restricted variant with cells only communicating via the environment):

A *tissue P system with unit rules and energy assigned to cells (of degree m)* is a construct

$$\Pi = \left(m, O, T, W, E, ch, \left(R_{(i,j)}, \rho_{(i,j)}\right)_{(i,j) \in ch}\right),$$

with $ch = \{(0, i), (i, 0) \mid 1 \leq i \leq m\}$ and the rules in the sets $R_{(i,j)}$ being of the form $(a, b, \Delta e)$ with $a, b \in O$ and $|\Delta e|$ being the amount of energy that - for $\Delta e \geq 0$ - is added to or - for $\Delta e < 0$ - is subtracted from e_i, respectively (the energy assigned to cell i) by the application of the rule which in addition moves an object a from the environment to cell i or from cell i to the environment thereby changing a to b. Observe that negative values for the energy assigned to a cell are not allowed. We restrict ourselves to a general priority relation ρ on the rules saying that the rules with maximal value for $|\Delta e|$ have to be applied.

In contrast to other models, the output values have nothing to do with the objects in some specific cell, but are constituted by the energy values assigned to the cells at the end of a halting computation.

The following theorem is an immediate consequence of the corresponding proof given in [14]:

Theorem 8. *Let $L \subseteq \mathbf{N}^\beta$ be a recursively enumerable set of vectors of non-negative integers. Then L can be generated by a tissue P system with unit rules and energy assigned to cells with (at most) $\beta + 2$ cells (working in the sequential mode).*

Proof. Consider a register machine $M = (m, P, 1, n)$ generating L with m registers, where $m = \beta + 2$, and $lab\,(M)$ being the set of instruction labels; the output values from M are expected to be in registers 1 to β at the end of a successful computation; moreover, without loss of generality, we may assume that at the beginning of a computation all the registers contain zero (see Lemma 1).

We construct the tissue P system (working in the sequential mode)

$$
\begin{aligned}
\Pi &= \left(m, O, \{p_n\}, W, E, ch, \left(R_{(i,j)}, \rho\right)_{(i,j) \in ch}\right), \\
O &= \{p_j, \widetilde{p}_j \,|\, 1 \le j \le n, j \in lab\,(M)\}, \\
W &= (p_1, \lambda, ..., \lambda), \\
E &= (0, ..., 0), \\
ch &= \{(0, i), (i, 0) \mid 1 \le i \le m\}, \\
R_{(0,i)} &= \{(p_j, \widetilde{p}_j, 0) \mid j : (add\,(i), k, l) \in P\} \\
&\quad \cup \{(p_j, \widetilde{p}_j, 0) \mid j : (sub\,(i), k, l) \in P\}, \\
&\qquad \text{for } 1 \le i \le m, \\
R_{(i,0)} &= \{(\widetilde{p}_j, p_k, 1), (\widetilde{p}_j, p_l, 1) \mid j : (add\,(i), k, l) \in P\} \\
&\quad \cup \{(\widetilde{p}_j, p_k, -1), (\widetilde{p}_j, p_l, 0) \mid j : (sub\,(i), k, l) \in P\}, \\
&\qquad \text{for } 1 \le i \le m.
\end{aligned}
$$

The contents of register i, $1 \le i \le m$, is represented by the energy value e_i of membrane i.

The sets of rules R_i depend on the instructions of P; in more detail, the simulation works as follows:

1. Each add-instruction $j : (add\,(i), k, l) \in P$, $1 \le i \le m$ is simulated in two steps by using the rules $(p_j, \widetilde{p}_j, 0)$ and $(\widetilde{p}_j, p_k, 1), (\widetilde{p}_j, p_l, 1)$.
2. Each conditional subtract-instruction $j : (sub\,(i), k, l) \in P$ is simulated in two steps by the rules $(p_j, \widetilde{p}_j, 0)$ as well as $(\widetilde{p}_j, p_k, -1)$ or $(\widetilde{p}_j, p_l, 0)$.
   The condition of priority guarantees that $(\widetilde{p}_j, p_k, -1)$ is applied as long as e_i has a positive value. Only if in the current configuration $e_i = 0$, i.e., register i is empty, the rule $(\widetilde{p}_j, p_l, 0)$ can be used.

It follows from the description given above that after each simulation of an instruction each energy value e_i of cell i equals the contents of register i,

$1 \leq i \leq m$. Hence, after having simulated the halt instruction labelled by n and halting the system by just doing nothing with the halting symbol p_n anymore, the energy values $e_1, \ldots, e_m$ equal the output of the program P. The only object remaining within the system is the final label p_n in the environment.   □

As can be seen from the construction given in the preceding proof, the same result can be obtained when we let the tissue P system with unit rules and energy assigned to cells work in the asynchronous or even in the maximally parallel mode (as there is only one object moving around in the system at any moment).

Without priorities, we only get a characterization of Parikh sets of languages generated by matrix grammars without ac (see the corresponding proofs in [14]). Here we only give the corresponding proof for showing that Parikh sets of languages generated by matrix grammars without ac can be generated by a tissue P system with unit rules and energy assigned to cells without priorities working in the sequential mode:

Theorem 9. *Let L be the Parikh set of a language generated by a matrix grammar without ac (i.e., let $L \in Ps\mathcal{L}(CF-MAT)$). Then L can be generated by a tissue P system with unit rules and energy assigned to cells without priorities working in the sequential mode.*

Proof. Let $G_M = ((N \cup T)^*, T^*, P, \Longrightarrow_G, w, M, F)$ be a matrix grammar without ac of type CF with every matrix being of the form $m_i = (m_{i,1}, \ldots, m_{i,n_i})$, $1 \leq i \leq n$, where $m_{i,j} = A_{i,j} \rightarrow w_{i,j,1} \ldots w_{i,j,n_{i,j}}$. Without loss of generality, we may assume that $n_{i,j} \leq 2$. Then we construct a tissue P system Π with unit rules and energy assigned to cells that simulates G_M as follows:

For all elements B_i in $N \cup T$ we take a membrane labelled by i, $1 \leq i \leq m$, where $m = card(N \cup T)$ and $m' = card(T)$; moreover, we define a bijective function $index : \{1, \ldots, m\} \rightarrow N \cup T$ such that the terminal symbols have the indices 1 to m' and the start symbol S has the label m. Initially, every cell has the energy value 0, i.e., $e_j = 0$ for $1 \leq j \leq m$.

Before starting the simulation of the matrices, we begin with p_0 in the environment and first make an additional step in order to get $e_m = 1$ as well as to have a non-deterministic choice for m_i by taking the rules $(p_0, \widetilde{p_0}, 1) \in R_{0,m}$ as well as $(\widetilde{p_0}, p_{i,1,0}, 0) \in R_{m,0}$ for every i with $1 \leq i \leq n$.

For the simulation of $m_{i,j}$, $1 \leq j \leq n_i$, $1 \leq i \leq n$, we have to take the following rules:

1. $(p_{i,j,0}, \widetilde{p_{i,j,0}}, 0) \in R_{0,index(A_{i,j})}$ and $(\widetilde{p_{i,j,0}}, \alpha_{i,j}, -1) \in R_{index(A_{i,j}),0}$ with
   - $\alpha_{i,j} \in \{p_{k,1,0} | 1 \leq k \leq n\}$ for $w_{i,j} = \lambda$ and $j = n_i$,
   - $\alpha_{i,j} = p_{i,j+1,0}$ for $w_{i,j} = \lambda$ and $j < n_i$,
   - $\alpha_{i,j} = p_{i,j,1}$ otherwise.
2. $(p_{i,j,1}, \widetilde{p_{i,j,1}}, 1) \in R_{0,index(w_{i,j,1})}$ and $(\widetilde{p_{i,j,1}}, \beta_{i,j}, 0) \in R_{index(w_{i,j,1}),0}$ with
   - $\beta_{i,j} \in \{p_{k,1,0} | 1 \leq k \leq n\}$ for $|w_{i,j}| = 1$ and $j = n_i$,
   - $\beta_{i,j} = p_{i,j+1,0}$ for $|w_{i,j}| = 1$ and $j < n_i$,
   - $\beta_{i,j} = p_{i,j,2}$ for $|w_{i,j}| = 2$.

3. $(p_{i,j,2}, \widetilde{p_{i,j,2}}, 1) \in R_{0,index(w_{i,j,2})}$ and $(\widetilde{p_{i,j,2}}, \gamma_{i,j}, 0) \in R_{index(w_{i,j,2}),0}$ with
   - $\gamma_{i,j} \in \{p_{k,1,0} | 1 \le k \le n\}$ for $j = n_i$,
   - $\gamma_{i,j} = p_{i,j+1,0}$ for $j < n_i$.

At some moment during the simulation of a derivation in the matrix grammar G_M by Π, we non-deterministically have to guess whether the current sentential form is already terminal (in order to be able to halt the computation in Π); for this purpose, we take the following rules:

1. $(\widetilde{p_{i,j},0}, p_f, 0) \in R_{index(A_{i,j}),0}$ can always be applied directly after having applied $(p_{i,j,0}, \widetilde{p_{i,j},0}, 0) \in R_{0,index(A_{i,j})}$; it allows us to finish the computation with the final object p_f if the current sentential form is terminal (i.e., $e_j = 0$ for $m' + 1 \le j \le m$).
2. $(p_f, \widetilde{p_f}, -1) \in R_{0,j}$ and $(\widetilde{p_f}, \#, 0) \in R_{j,0}$ for $m' + 1 \le j \le m$ are used if the current sentential form has not been terminal (which means $e_j \ne 0$ for some j with $m' + 1 \le j \le m$) when introducing p_f; in that case we ensure that the system Π does not halt by entering an infinite loop with the trap symbol $\#$ using the following rules:
   $(\#, \#, 0) \in R_{0,m}$ and $(\#, \#, 0) \in R_{m,0}$.

If p_f cannot enter any of the cells $m' + 1 \le j \le m$ this means that no non-terminal symbol occurs any more in the current sentential form of the simulated derivation in G_M, hence, it is correct to halt and thus to get the result stored in the values of e_j, $1 \le j \le m$, which by construction represents the corresponding result obtained by the simulated derivation in G_M.   □

5   (Tissue) P Systems Working on String Objects

In this section we consider (tissue) P systems working on string objects. First we investigate gemmating P systems (see [3], [2], [1], and [6]) and show that we obtain computational completeness when working in any of the derivation modes (i.e., in the maximally parallel mode, in the asynchronous mode, and in the sequential mode). A similar result holds true for (tissue) P systems with splicing or cutting/recombination rules (see [9]). Finally, we consider (tissue) P systems working in the sequential mode (on strings); when using priorities on the rules, we obtain universality, whereas without priorities we get a characterization of languages generated by matrix grammars without appearance checking (see [17]).

5.1   Gemmating P Systems

The model of gemmating P systems first was examined in [3] and is abstracted from the way bigger substances like proteins are moved across cell membranes by means of vesicles, i.e., some string objects can be transported in a mobile membrane to a target membrane and then being fused with it. For more detailed explanations we refer to [3], [2], and [1]. We only define a restricted variant of the general model considered there:

An (*extended*) *gemmating P system* is a construct

$$\Pi = (V, T, \mu, M_1, ..., M_n, D_1, ..., D_n),$$

where:

- V is an alphabet,
- $T \subseteq V$ is the terminal alphabet,
- $\mu = [_0[_1 \ ]_1...[_n \ ]_n]_0$ is a membrane structure of depth 2 and degree $n + 1$,
- M_i, $1 \leq i \leq n$, are finite multisets of strings over V,
- D_i, $1 \leq i \leq n$, are sets of *pre-dynamic evolution rules* associated with membrane i, i.e., sets of mutation rules of the form $a \rightarrow v$ with $a \in V$ and $v \in V^* \{@_j\} \cup \{@_j\} V^*$ where $@_j \notin V$, $0 \leq j \leq n$ and $i \neq j$. (Note that the special symbol $@_j$ can only appear on either end of the string.)

Starting from an initial configuration consisting of μ and M_i, $1 \leq i \leq n$, in membrane i, the system proceeds from one configuration to the next one by non-deterministically applying the rules in the sets D_i, $1 \leq i \leq n$, in a maximally parallel way: A string can only be rewritten by one rule per step and the resulting strings then are transported by mobile membranes to the membranes specified by the target indications given by $@_j$, i.e., in sum, applying the rule $a \rightarrow u@_j$ (resp., $a \rightarrow @_j u$) in membrane i, $i \neq j$, to a string wa (resp., aw) means removing this string from membrane i and instead adding the string wu (uw) in membrane j in case $j \geq 1$, whereas for $j = 0$ this means that the string is sent out of the system. The *language generated by the (extended) gemmating P system* is considered to be the set of terminal strings that have been sent out of the system during a halting computation.

In the general model defined above, an extended gemmating P system can be represented as an *extended gemmating tissue P system*

$$\Pi = \left(m, V^*, T^*, W, ch, \left(R_{(i,j)}\right)_{(i,j) \in ch}, 0\right),$$

where we have omitted O_∞, because $(O_\infty)_i = \emptyset$, $1 \leq i \leq m$, as well as E, because we do not use energies assigned to the cell membranes, and we also omitted K, $s_{(i,j)}$ and $\rho_{(i,j)}$, because we do not need states (in fact, we use only one steady state) and we do not need priorities on the rules either.

A rule $a \rightarrow u@_j$ (resp., $a \rightarrow @_j u$) in D_i in the extended gemmating P system now means putting the rule $a \rightarrow u@$ (resp., $a \rightarrow @u$) into $R_{(i,j)}$ in the gemmating tissue P system. As results of computations in gemmating tissue P systems we take the terminal strings appearing in the environment at any derivation step.

The main result for extended gemmating P systems proved in [6] immediately infers the following result for extended gemmating tissue P systems:

Proposition 10. *For every recursively enumerable string language L there exists an extended gemmating tissue P system Π with (at most) three cells such that $L(\Pi) = L$.*

In contrast to the original definition of gemmating P systems, we do not need maximal parallelism; instead, throughout any computation, we may consider exactly one string in the system, and when this string is sent out (contributing to the generated language if and only if it consists of terminal symbols), the computation halts in any case. If we start with an arbitrary number of axioms w_0, then each copy may evolve according to the rules given in the proof, and we may take each terminal string sent out during any computation (halting or non-halting) as the result of a successful computation in the extended gemmating tissue P system. The derivation of different strings may happen in a completely unsynchronized way, and we even may assume that in one derivation step of the gemmating tissue P systems several strings are affected by (possibly different) rules in parallel. In sum, all three derivation modes (maximally parallel, asynchronous, sequential) yield universality.

5.2 (Tissue) P Systems with Splicing or Cutting/Recombination Rules

P systems with splicing or cutting/recombination rules were considered in [9], see there for detailed definitions and explanations. Expressed in the general model used in this paper, we deal with (tissue) P systems using splicing or cutting/recombination rules as the rules used in the channels. For obtaining computational completeness, we do not need states, energy assigned to membranes or priorities on the rules, and moreover, only one cell is needed. The proofs given in [9] can directly be expressed in the notions of this article, hence, we do not repeat the extensive definitions and proofs given there and state the following result without proof:

Proposition 11. *For every recursively enumerable string language L there exists a one-cell tissue P system with splicing or cutting/recombination rules generating L.*

We should like to stress the fact that the derivation of an arbitrary number of initial strings (the axioms are available in an unbounded number) happens in a completely unsynchronized way; in fact, we could even assume that several strings are affected even in a parallel manner (but without enforcing maximal parallelism), hence, similar results are obtained for *one-cell tissue P system with splicing or cutting/recombination rules working in the sequential mode, in the asynchronous mode,* as well as *in the maximally parallel mode.*

5.3 (Tissue) P Systems Working in the Sequential Mode

In this subsection, we investigate the generative power of (tissue) P systems working in the sequential mode based on the results proved for *matrix grammars without/with* ac *in* anf. When using priorities, we obtain universality, without priorities we obtain a characterization of languages generated by matrix grammars without appearance checking (also see [17]).

A tissue P system (of degree $m \geq 1$) *of string type X working in the sequential mode with priorities* is a construct

$$\Pi = \left(m, V^*, T^*, W, ch, \left(R_{(i,j)}, \rho_{(i,j)} \right)_{(i,j) \in ch} \right),$$

where:

- m is the number of *cells* assumed to be labelled with $1, 2, \ldots, m$;
- V is an alphabet; $V = N \cup T$; N is the alphabet of non-terminal symbols;
- $T \subseteq V$ is the alphabet of *terminal* symbols;
- W consists of arbitrary initial finite multisets of strings over V in the m cells;
- $ch \subseteq \{(i,j) \mid i, j \in \{1, 2, \ldots, m\}\}$ is the set of *channels*;
- $R_{(i,j)}$ is a finite set of *string productions of type X*, associated with the channel $(i,j) \in ch$, of the form (u,v) with $u \in V^*$ and $v \in V^+$; $(u,v) \in R_{(i,j)}$ removes a copy of a string containing the substring u, replaces this substring by v and adds a copy of the resulting string to the contents of cell j;
- $\rho_{(i,j)}$ is a priority relation on the rules in $R_{(i,j)}$, i.e., a rule from $R_{(i,j)}$ can only be applied if no other rule from $R_{(i,j)}$ according to $\rho_{(i,j)}$ could be applied.

A derivation in Π works as follows: we start with the axioms from W in the m cells. In the sequential derivation mode, exactly one string from a cell i is taken, modified by a rule $(u,v) \in R_{(i,j)}$ observing the priority relation $\rho_{(i,j)}$, and the resulting string is added in cell j. All terminal strings from T^* ever appearing at any step in any membrane contribute to the language $L(\Pi)$ generated in the sequential derivation mode by Π. The family of languages generated by tissue P systems of degree $m \geq 1$ of string type X working in the sequential mode with priorities is denoted by $\mathcal{L}(X-sP_m(pri))$. If all priority relations $\rho_{(i,j)}$ in Π are empty, we call it a *tissue P system of degree $m \geq 1$ of string type X working in the sequential mode without priorities* and denote the corresponding family of languages by $\mathcal{L}(X-sP_m)$.

We can also consider the systems defined above to work in the asynchronous or in the maximally parallel derivation mode. As all the strings in the system evolve independently from each other without influencing the behaviour of the system (e.g., we do not use channel states that might be changed when a channel is used) and we collect the terminal results at any stage of the derivation (i.e., we do not only consider halting computations), the resulting languages do not depend on the derivation mode, i.e., all three derivation modes yield the same language.

Theorem 12. For any $X \in \{CF, CF_{-\lambda}\}$, $\mathcal{L}(X-MAT) = \mathcal{L}(X-sP_3)$.

Proof. Let the string language $L \in \mathcal{L}(X-MAT)$ be given by a matrix grammar G'_M without ac in anf of type X according to Lemma 4, i.e.,

$$G'_M = \left((N'' \cup T)^*, T^*, P', \Longrightarrow_G, w, M'\right),$$
$$N'' = N' \times L \cup N,$$
$$N' = N \cup T (\cup \{\lambda\}).$$

Then we construct the corresponding tissue P system Π of type X without priorities as follows:

$$\Pi = \left(3, V^*, T^*, W, ch, \left(R_{(i,j)}\right)_{(i,j) \in ch}\right),$$
$$W = (w, \lambda, \lambda),$$
$$ch = \{(1,1), (1,2), (2,1), (2,3), (3,2)\},$$
$$V = N' \times L \cup N' \times L \times L \cup \tilde{N}' \times L \times L \cup N \cup T;$$

the matrices $[(X, r) \to (Y, s) Y_1...Y_k]$ and $[(a, r) \to a]$ can be simulated directly in the first cell, whereas for moving the activator to another position, i.e., for simulating a matrix $[X \to (X, r), (Y, r) \to Y]$, we also need the other two cells to synchronize the change:

$$R_{(1,1)} = \{(X, r) \to (Y, s) Y_1...Y_k \mid$$
$$[(X, r) \to (Y, s) Y_1...Y_k] \in M'\}$$
$$\cup \{(a, r) \to a \mid [(a, r) \to a] \in M'\},$$
$$R_{(1,2)} = \{X \to (X, r, r) \mid [(X \to (X, r), (Y, r) \to Y)] \in M'\},$$
$$R_{(2,1)} = \{(X, r, 0) \to (X, r) \mid [X \to (X, r), (Y, r) \to Y] \in M'\},$$
$$R_{(2,3)} = \{(Y, r) \to (\bar{Y}, r, r), (\bar{Y}, r, i) \to (\bar{Y}, r, i - 1) \mid$$
$$[X \to (X, r), (Y, r) \to Y] \in M', 1 \leq i \leq r\},$$
$$R_{(3,2)} = \{(X, r, i) \to (X, r, i - 1), (\bar{Y}, r, 0) \to Y \mid$$
$$[X \to (X, r), (Y, r) \to Y] \in M', 1 \leq i \leq r\}.$$

The idea with the indices for synchronizing the derivation of two variables has already been used quite often in the area of P systems; hence, we immediately conclude $L(\Pi) = (G'_M)$.

For the inverse inclusion $\supseteq$, i.e., for simulating a given tissue P system Π of type X without priorities, we construct a graph-controlled grammar without ac of the corresponding type where the node in the control graph indicates the cell i where the underlying string currently can be found (we can restrict ourselves to consider one string as $\mathcal{L}(X{-}MAT)$ is closed under union) and carries one production from $R_{i,j}$ leading from cell i to cell j; whereas the edges from cell i go to all nodes representing cell j.

Hence, given a tissue P system of type X

$$\Pi = \left(m, V^*, T^*, (w, \lambda, ..., \lambda), ch, \left(R_{(i,j)}\right)_{(i,j) \in ch}\right),$$

we construct the corresponding graph-controlled grammar G_C without ac of type X as follows: Let

$$R_{(i,j)} = \{p_{i,j,k} \mid 1 \leq k \leq n_{i,j}\} \text{ for some } n_{i,j} \geq 0$$

and let $\Longrightarrow_G$ be the usual derivation relation for context-free string grammars; then

$$G_C = (V^*, T^*, P, \Longrightarrow_G, w, R, L_{in}, L_{fin}),$$
$$P = \bigcup_{(i,j) \in ch} R_{(i,j)},$$
$$Lab = \{(i, j, k) \mid 1 \leq k \leq n_{i,j}, (i, j) \in ch\},$$
$$R = \{((i, j, k) : p_{i,j,k}, \{(j, l, m) \mid l, m \geq 1 \text{ and } (j, l, m) \in Lab\}, \emptyset) \mid$$
$$(i, j, k) \in Lab\}$$
$$L_{in} = \{(1, j, k) \mid (1, j, k) \in Lab\},$$
$$L_{fin} = Lab.$$

Obviously, $L(G_C) = L(\Pi)$.

As a technical detail, it should be mentioned that one could even take $L_{in} = Lab$ (in that way, G_C becomes what is usually known from the literature as a programmed grammar).

According to the proof of Lemma 4, from G_C now a matrix grammar G_M without ac and even in anf of type X can be constructed in such a way that $L(G_M) = L(G_C) = L(\Pi)$, which observation completes the proof. □

When using priorities, we only need two cells to characterize $\mathcal{L}(X-MAT_{ac})$, $X \in \{CF, CF_{-\lambda}\}$:

Theorem 13. For any $X \in \{CF, CF_{-\lambda}\}$, $\mathcal{L}(X-MAT_{ac}) = \mathcal{L}(X-sP_2(pri))$.

Proof. For proving the inclusion $\mathcal{L}(X-MAT_{ac}) \subseteq \mathcal{L}(X-sP_2(pri))$, let us first consider the P system Π of type X without priorities constructed for a matrix grammar without ac of type X in anf as constructed in the proof of Theorem 12. When using priorities, we may omit the third cell and include the rules from $R_{(3,2)}$ into $R_{(1,2)}$ and from $R_{(2,3)}$ into $R_{(2,1)}$; moreover, for every rule $X \to (X, r, r)$ we add $\alpha \to H$ in $R_{(1,2)}$ (where H is the trap symbol) for every non-terminal symbol α of the form (Y, s, j) and $(\bar{Y}, s, j)$ as a rule of higher priority (in $\rho_{(1,2)}$). For every matrix $[X \to H, (Y, r) \to (Y, s)]$ including appearance checking we add these two rules in $R_{(1,2)}$ as well as the priority

$$X \to H > (Y, r) \to (Y, s)$$

to $\rho_{(1,2)}$. The details of this construction as well as the proof of the inverse inclusion are rather obvious and therefore omitted. □

As $\mathcal{L}(CF-MAT_{ac}) = \mathcal{L}(ENUM)$ (see [8]), we even obtain a characterization of recursively enumerable string languages by tissue P systems with priorities using context-free string productions in only two membranes:

Corollary 14. $\mathcal{L}(CF-sP_2(pri)) = \mathcal{L}(CF-MAT_{ac}) = \mathcal{L}(ENUM)$.

Observe that this result is already optimal with respect to the number of cells for P systems of type CF with priorities being able to generate any arbitrary recursively enumerable string language, as $\mathcal{L}(CF-sP_1(pri))$ only corresponds with the family of string languages generated by ordered grammars, which family is strictly included in $\mathcal{L}(ENUM)$, e.g., see [8].

As elaborated in [17], similar results as those exhibited in Theorems 12 and 13 for families of string languages also hold true for the corresponding families of d-dimensional array languages.

6   Summary and Future Research

Within the big variety of (tissue) P systems, we could only investigate a small number for the case of applying rules not in the maximally parallel way, but instead in a sequential or asynchronous way. A strict interpretation of the sequential way of applying rules says that in each step exactly one rule is applied and the next rule can only be applied after finishing the previous step. In a more natural sense, an asynchronous way of applying rules allows for the application of an arbitrary number of rules in parallel, but does not enforce maximality. In many cases, there is no real difference between strict sequential and asynchronous application of rules, hence, the notion *asynchronous P system* or *asynchronous tissue P system* in fact will cover a lot of models of P systems and tissue P systems, respectively, where the rules are not applied in a maximally parallel way.

The feature of applying rules in a maximally parallel way seems to be essential for obtaining universal computational power in many cases, at least when dealing with symbol objects: *P systems with catalysts* are able to generate any arbitrary recursively enumerable set of numbers with only two catalysts in only one membrane (see [13]), whereas *asynchronous P systems with catalysts* can only generate regular sets of numbers (see [21], subsection 3.4.5). *Tissue P systems with channel states and antiport rules* with only one cell work in the sequential mode and thus only allow for a characterization of Parikh sets of languages generated by matrix grammars without appearance checking. P systems with antiport rules are computationally complete with only one membrane (e.g., see [15]), and, due to the cooperative nature of these rules, *asynchronous P systems with antiport rules* can generate any set of numbers which can be obtained by partially blind counter automata (see [18]). *(Tissue) P systems with unit rules and energy assigned to (cell) membranes* are another example for (tissue) P systems working in the sequential mode (see [14]); for obtaining computational completeness, we need a priority relation on the rules. In sum, we made the observation that for most models of (tissue) P systems working on symbol objects considered in the literature of membrane systems so far, the feature of applying the rules in a maximally parallel way is essential for obtaining computational completeness or else some other powerful feature has to be used (e.g., priorities), which somehow is not too surprising, because in most proofs to be found in literature this feature is needed for capturing the feature of appearance checking when simulating matrix grammars or the feature of checking the contents of a register for zero when simulating register machines.

When dealing with string objects, some small additional ingredients allow to obtain computational completeness even with (tissue) P systems working in the asynchronous or sequential mode: For example, *extended gemmating P systems* (see [3], [2], [1], [6]) specify on which end of the current string a rule has to be applied and in that way computational completeness even is obtained with the corresponding model of (tissue) P systems working in the asynchronous or in the sequential mode. *(Tissue) P systems with splicing rules or cutting/recombination* rules are also working in an asynchronous or sequential way and reach computational completeness with only one cell (again taking advantage of the fact that one can make the rules working at the ends of the strings). *(Tissue) P systems working in the sequential mode* on strings gain computational completeness when using priorities, whereas without priorities we obtain a characterization of the languages generated by matrix grammars without appearance checking.

Many topics remain for future research, for example, we have not investigated the accepting variants of P systems (*P automata*) considered in this paper. Moreover, many other models of (tissue) P systems not considered in this article (e.g., one may simply consider some variants of the big variety of remaining models of membrane systems described in the book of Gheorghe Păun, [21]) deserve to be investigated for the case of asynchronous or sequential application of rules, too. In addition, other new variants, already from the beginning omitting the feature of a universal clock and relying on an asynchronous way for the application of rules (e.g., see [4]), promise interesting new results and applications for the future.

Finally, even more variants of derivation modes should be investigated, too: Like in the case of grammar systems (see [5]), we may also consider the following sequential derivation modes:

- $*$: perform an arbitrary number of steps;
- $= k, \geq k, \leq k$: perform exactly k, at least k, at most k steps, $k \geq 1$;
- t: perform as many steps as possible.

These modes may either be considered as overall conditions considering applications in any membrane or cell or channel between two cells; on the other hand, we may also restrict the application of rules according to these conditions to only one membrane, one cell or one channel between two cells.

As overall condition, the t-mode simply yields halting computations in a (tissue) P system working in the sequential mode, whereas the $*$-mode corresponds to the sequential derivation mode.

The modes $*, = k, \geq k, \leq k, t$ can also be considered for the parallel derivation mode, and again we may consider these conditions for the whole system or only one membrane, one cell or one channel. The $= 1$-mode in the parallel case corresponds with the sequential derivation mode. The t-mode in the parallel case corresponds with the maximally parallel derivation mode, and the $*$-mode in the parallel case corresponds with the asynchronous derivation mode.

All these variants of parallel and sequential derivation modes deserve thorough investigations in the future.

Acknowledgements

The author acknowledges many interesting and inspiring discussions with many colleagues working in the area of membrane systems as well as Marion Oswald's help in preparing this article; moreover, he acknowledges IST-2001-32008 project "MolCoNet".

References

1. D. Besozzi, E. Csuhaj-Varjú, G. Mauri, C. Zandron: Size and power of extended gemmating P systems. In: [22] (2004), 92–101.
2. D. Besozzi, G. Mauri, Gh. Păun, C. Zandron: Gemmating P systems: collapsing hierarchies. *Theoretical Computer Science* **296**, 2 (2003), 253–267.
3. D. Besozzi, C. Zandron, G. Mauri, N. Sabadini: P systems with gemmation of mobile membranes. In: A. Restivo, S. Ronchi Della Rocca, L. Roversi (eds.): Proc. of the 7th Italian Conf. of Theoretical Computer Science 2001, *Lecture Notes in Computer Science* **2202**, Springer-Verlag, Berlin, 2001, 136–153.
4. M. Cavaliere, D. Sburlan: Time-Independent P Systems. *This volume.*
5. E. Csuhaj-Varjú, J. Dassow, J. Kelemen, Gh. Păun: *Grammar Systems: A Grammatical Approach to Distribution and Cooperation.* Gordon and Breach, London, 1994.
6. E. Csuhaj-Varjú, Gy. Vaszil: Reducing the size of extended gemmating P systems. *This volume.*
7. Z. Dang, O.H. Ibarra: On P systems operating in sequential mode. In: L. Ilie, D. Wotschke (eds.): *Pre-proceedings of the Workshop Descriptional Complexity of Formal Systems (DCFS) 2004.* Report No. **619**, Univ. of Western Ontario, London, Canada, 2004, 164–177.
8. J. Dassow, Gh. Păun: *Regulated Rewriting in Formal Language Theory.* Springer-Verlag, Berlin, 1989.
9. R. Freund, F. Freund, M. Margenstern, M. Oswald, Yu. Rogozhin, S. Verlan: P systems with cutting/recombination rules assigned to membranes. In: C. Martín-Vide, G. Mauri, Gh. Păun, G. Rozenberg, A. Salomaa (eds.): Membrane Computing, International Workshop, WMC 2003, Tarragona, Spain, July 17-22, 2003, *Lecture Notes in Computer Science* **2933**, Springer-Verlag, Berlin, 2004, 191–202.
10. R. Freund: Generalized P systems. In: G. Ciobanu, Gh. Păun Gh.(eds.): *Proceedings Fundamentals of Computation Theory, Lecture Notes in Computer Science* **1684**, Springer-Verlag, Berlin, 1999, 281–292.
11. R. Freund, F. Freund: Molecular computing with generalized homogeneous P-systems. In: A. Condon, G. Rozenberg (eds.): *DNA Based Computers*, Proceedings DNA 6, Leiden, 2000, 113–125.
12. R. Freund: Sequential P-systems. *Romanian Journal of Information Science and Technology*, **4**, 1-2 (2001), 77–88.
13. R. Freund, L. Kari, M. Oswald, P. Sosík: Computationally universal P systems without priorities: Two catalysts are sufficient. To appear in *Theoretical Computer Science.*
14. R. Freund, A. Leporati, M. Oswald, C. Zandron: Sequential P systems with unit rules and energy assigned to membranes. In: [22] (2004), 168–182.
15. R. Freund, Gh. Păun: Deterministic P systems. *Submitted*, 2004.
16. R. Freund, Gh. Păun, M.J. Pérez Jiménez: Tissue-like P systems with channel states. In: [22] (2004), 206–223.
17. R. Freund: P systems working in the sequential mode on arrays and strings. To appear in *Proceedings Developments in Language Theory 2004.*
18. P. Frisco: About P systems with symport/antiport. In: [22] (2004), 224–236.
19. M.L. Minsky: *Computation: Finite and Infinite Machines.* Prentice Hall, Englewood Cliffs, New Jersey, USA, 1967.
20. Gh. Păun: Computing with membranes. *Journal of Computer and System Sciences* **61**, 1 (2000), 108–143, and TUCS Research Report 208 (1998) (http://www.tucs.fi).

21. Gh. Păun: *Membrane Computing: An Introduction.* Springer-Verlag, Berlin, 2002.
22. Gh. Păun, A. Riscos Nuñez, A. Romero Jiménez, F. Sancho Caparrini (eds.): *Second Braainstorming Week on Membrane Computing*, Sevilla, Spain, Febr. 2004, Dept. of Computer Sciences and Artificial Intelligence, Univ. of Sevilla Tech. Report 01/2004.
23. The P Systems Web Page: `http://psystems.disco.unimib.it/`
24. A. Salomaa, G. Rozenberg (eds.): *Handbook of Formal Languages.* Springer-Verlag, Berlin, 1997.

Evolution and Oscillation in P Systems: Applications to Biological Phenomena

Vincenzo Manca, Luca Bianco, and Federico Fontana

University of Verona,
Department of Computer Science,
strada Le Grazie, 15
37134 Verona, Italy
vincenzo.manca@univr.it
http://www.sci.univr/~manca

Abstract. Some computational aspects and behavioral patterns of P systems are considered, emphasizing dynamical properties that turn useful in characterizing the behavior of biological and biochemical systems. A framework called state transition dynamics is outlined in which general dynamical concepts are formulated in completely discrete terms. A metabolic algorithm is defined which computes the evolution of P systems modeling important phenomena of biological interest once provided with the information on the initial state and reactivity parameters, or growing factors. Relationships existing between P systems and discrete linear systems are investigated. Finally, exploratory considerations are addressed about the possible use of P systems in characterizing the oscillatory behavior of biological regulatory networks described by metabolic graphs.

1 Introduction

In 1998 *P systems* were presented as a new model of computation [14]. Before their advent, some classes of rewriting systems had already shown the ability of expressing specific biological phenomena [22, 9, 10]. P systems move a step further: they have clear structural analogies with the cell, in particular they model several features of the biological membranes (for this reason they are often referred to as *membrane systems*). Moreover, the transitions happening in these systems recall certain evolution processes that take place in a living cell.

From a formal viewpoint, P systems satisfy a result of universality even in their basic definition [14]. In this sense they have all the computational power needed to capture a biomolecular process—provided that we are able to arrange it into an algorithmic procedure. In addition to this, the similarities existing between P systems and (at least some aspects of) biological cells might suggest that P systems are also able to represent the same process in a meaningful way, that is, not only to compute it as any universal machine would do, but also to provide potential insight on the biological mechanisms determining and controlling the process via the observation of the transitions of the system.

G. Mauri et al. (Eds.): WMC5 2004, LNCS 3365, pp. 63–84, 2005.

However, this is true only to some extent. Modeling specific biological activities inside a P system is not an easy task. A lot of alternative constructs derived from the basic definition of P system have been proposed, sometimes capturing crucial aspects of the biology of cells such as *thickness, polarity, catalysts, inhibitors, promoters, carriers, porters (symport-antiport), priority, division, replication, creation, dissolution, resources*, and *energy* [15, 17, 16, 12, 5, 1]. In other cases, powerful paradigms were imported from other formal systems having biological implications too, such as *splicing* and object-structuring (in form of strings) [15]. All these alternative constructs exhibit properties of universality, hence by all means they represent a first, necessary attempt to get P systems closer to the world of bio-molecules meanwhile preserving their computational power.

Nevertheless there are some aspects, that are crucial in almost any study of biomolecular processes, that the traditional formulations of P systems do not develop in a sufficient way from a biological point of view.

The halting of a P system tells that a computation has terminated successfully, but the terminal state is not a primary object of investigation in many biomolecular realities. Rather, we would shift the focus on the computation during its "life", in an aim to observe the living organism while surviving in the environment and, possibly, to influence his life cycle when some bio-chemical indicators tell that his physiological activity is altered (possibly harmfully). In other words, biological systems do not compute states, but rather stable behavioral pattern that satisfy some "enjoyable" conditions, and life cycles are combined and organized in very complex forms. This means that considering all the forms of periodicity in the framework of P systems is of key importance if we want to apply P systems to modeling biological processes [1]. Moreover, life, in its adaptation and evolution strategies, explores behavior spaces in a range between simple cycles and chaotic behavioral magmas where space in lost in time and *vice versa*. Therefore, chaos is very important as limit border that life try to approximate to (with the risk of falling in its destructive abyss) because "at edge of chaos" is available the dynamical richness necessary for adaptation and evolution [10].

Biomolecular mechanisms are the result of many individual local reactions, each one of those being formed by processes whose extension is limited in time and space. These processes interact with each other by means of specific communication strategies, in a way that they finally exhibit a (sometimes surprising) overall co-ordination. In this sense, and despite this co-ordination, biomolecular processes are by all means *asynchronous*.

P systems, in their classical formulation, are intended to "consume" the available resources in a maximally parallel way during the rewriting of symbols. Holding this property, then all the symbols that are present in the system at a given configuration become potential resources: they are consumed as many as possible, and new symbols are produced in consequence of that action. In other words, maximal parallelism constrains the system to consume all the available resources during a transition. Moreover, their evolution is synchronous, i.e., a global clock triggers the production of new symbols inside all membranes. This limits their versatility in modeling biological asynchronous phenomena.

In this paper we focus on some theoretical and practical issues especially oriented to biomolecular computing. First, we consider a perspective (still in progress for many aspects) according to which P systems are cast in a discrete dynamical framework. In this perspective, we will characterize classical dynamical concepts in terms of *state transition dynamics* [11].

Next, we propose to observe rewriting rules in membranes from a different viewpoint. Membranes are intended to host "symbolic reactions", and rules apply according to some reaction parameters and substance concentration, as it normally happens in biochemical phenomena. We define a *metabolic algorithm* for computing the evolution of (deterministic) P systems when some initial state and some reaction parameters are given, such as reactivities or growing factors. This algorithm is applied to known bio-chemical oscillatory phenomena, and put in relation with differential equations.

The similarities arising between the symbolic and quantitative approach pursued by P systems and differential equation systems, respectively, stimulate the discovery of relationships existing between P systems and some widely used, simple but powerful systems of equations expressing differential problems in the discrete time, called *discrete linear systems*. Such relationships are addressed before the conclusion, where some extra considerations are made on the possibility to reproduce the behavior of biological networks expressed in terms of *metabolic graphs*: in the description of these graphs (networks) the emphasis is on the oscillatory rather than temporal behavior, so that specific mathematical tools based on a model description in the frequency domain are proposed.

2   State Transition Dynamics

One classic approach to discrete system modelling consists in first analyzing a continuous phenomenon, then producing a discrete model of it according to a given discretization method, and finally running a simulation, provided that the discrete model respects certain stability conditions.

There are cases in which a discrete model of a continuous phenomenon generates errors, but such errors can be arbitrarily reduced or, equivalently, the precision is proportional to the granularity with which the continuous phenomenon is reproduced by the discrete model. Sometimes the information needed to describe a physical phenomenon is *inherently* discrete in a way that the resulting discrete model reproduces the reality almost directly (think, for instance, to DNA replication). In this last case having a method that could compute the dynamics of the system directly from its discrete representation would be a great advantage with respect to many aspects.

The *state transition dynamics* formalism considers a system defined in a discrete domain, assuming discrete values. It studies properties such as orbits and trajectories, periodicity, eventual periodicity and divergence, fixed points, attractors and recurrence [4, 6, 3], aimed at defining analogous concepts in the context of systems discrete in space and in time, with no metric or topological structure. It is surprising that, even assuming a very weak mathematical structure, many concepts can be defined formally in such a way that interesting facts can be deduced on the structure of attractors, on deterministic *chaos*, and on its relationship with nondeterminism [11].

To give an idea of the characterization given by state transition dynamics, here we report the most important definitions. For more details, discussions and mathematical developments we refer to [11] where we started a general approach to discrete systems dynamics that is under development.

Definition 1. *A state transition dynamics is a pair* (S, q) *where* S *is a set of states and* q *is a function from* S *into its power set,*

$$q : S \rightarrow \mathcal{P}(S).$$

By calling *quasi state* any subset X of S, and extending the application of q over quasi states, i.e.,

$$q(X) = \bigcup_{x \in X} q(x),$$

then we map quasi states into quasi states by means of q to form *orbits*, and characterize specific *trajectories* along these orbits by means of the following definitions.

Definition 2. *An* X-orbit *is a sequence* $\{X_i\}_{i \in \mathbf{N}}$ *of quasi states such that*

$$\begin{aligned} X_0 &= X, \\ X_i &\subseteq q(X_{i-1}) \, , \, i > 0. \end{aligned} \tag{1}$$

A X-orbit *is complete when the previous inclusion is replaced by an equality. When* x *is a state, we write simply* x-orbit *instead of* $\{x\}$-orbit.

An s-trajectory *is a function* $\xi : \mathbf{N} \rightarrow S$ *such that*

$$\begin{aligned} \xi(0) &= s, \\ \xi(i) &\in q\big(\xi(i-1)\big) \, , \, i > 0. \end{aligned} \tag{2}$$

By denoting with q^i the composition of q repeated i times and $q^*(s) = \bigcup_{i \in \mathbf{N}} q^i(s)$, we refer as *flights* and *blackholes* to the following special trajectories:

Definition 3. *An* s-trajectory *is an* s-flight *if it is an injective function on* $\mathbf{N}$. *An* s-flight *is an* s-blackhole *if* $q^*(s) \subseteq \xi(\mathbf{N})$ *(where* ξ *is extended to sets).*

When S is made of symbolic values then the relation $y \in q(x)$ induced by q between two states, x and y, is conveniently expressed using the notation typical to rewriting systems: $x \rightarrow y$. Note that we can easily introduce non terminating computations as long as q is total.

It is clear that the notion of dynamical system defined above is nondeterministic, because any state can transform into a set of possible states—though, an equivalently expressive deterministic system where states are the quasi states of the original system can be figured out. The nondeterministic aspect is essential for the modeling of many phenomena.

We now give a characterization of the evolution in these systems.

Definition 4. *An X-orbit is* periodic *if $q^n(X) = X$ for some $n > 0$. An orbit is* eventually periodic *if $q^{n+k}(X) = q^k(X)$ for some $k, n > 0$. In this case k is called the* transient *and n the* period.

Definition 5. *An X-orbit is $\Omega(f(n))$-divergent with respect to a function $\mu : S \to \mathbf{N}$, called Ljapounov function, if $\mu(q^n(X))$ has order $\Omega(f(n))$. A similar definition holds for the order of divergence $O(f(n))$.*

Definition 6. *A state s is a* fixed point *if the transition relation transforms it into itself, that is, $q(s) = \{s\}$.*

Periodicity and eventual periodicity are properties with a strong computational significance. It can be shown that, in a suitable computational framework where every machine finds a counterpart in a corresponding state transition dynamics, the periodicity decision problem turns out to be computationally equivalent to the termination problem [11]:

Proposition 1 *Given a computationally universal class of machines, then the (eventual) periodicity of the related dynamical systems is not decidable.*

Affine to periodicity (but weaker) is recurrence:

Definition 7. *A state x is* recurrent *if $x \in q^n(x)$ for some $n > 0$. A state x is* eternally recurrent *if $\forall n > 0 : y \in q^n(x) \Rightarrow \exists m > 0 : x \in q^m(y)$.*

A system dynamics is ultimately characterized by its *attractors*, that in very first approximation can be seen as quasi states in which the system must fall in the end. First of all, we say that an orbit is *included* in another orbit if the former sequence is contained in the latter sequence, and we say *eventually included* if it is included in the other orbit except for a finite number of quasi states.

We call *basin* a set $B \subseteq S$ such that $q(x)$ is included in B for every state $x \in B$. Inside a basin we possibly find an *attracting set* A, i.e., a subset which eventually includes the complete x-orbit of every state $x \in B$. If A is minimal under set inclusion, i.e., no subsets (even made of a single state) can be removed from A otherwise causing the lost of the attracting property, then our attracting set is an attractor.

A complete characterization of attractors requires more definitions than those reported in this paper [11]. In particular, here we have only outlined the so-called *unavoidable* attracting sets that can have three different types:

1. *periodic attractors*, that is, periodic orbits (fixed point attractors are a special case);
2. *eternally recurrent blackholes*;
3. *complex attractors*, that is, a combination of the two previous cases.

Many concepts in formal language theory can be revisited in the framework of state transition dynamics. For example, languages generated by grammars or recognized by automata are special cases of attractors. But next issues, that are crucial in the development of state transition dynamics, are: i) the extension of its focus on more complex dynamical phenomena such as the forms and degrees of chaos, intermittency, dissipation, resonance; ii) the search for dynamical parameters useful in the qualitative analysis of dynamical patterns. In fact, both cellular automata and Kauffman networks enlighten that the relationship between the transition function and the state structure strongly determines dynamically relevant qualities [20, 21]. We put forward that several parameters that are identified in those contexts, such as *connectivity, channeling, majority, input entropy, and Derrida plot*, could inspire some analogues in P systems. The approach we present in the next section will give some hints in this direction. In fact, the metabolic viewpoint will cast P systems in the framework of dynamical networks to which both cellular automata and Kauffman networks belong.

3   Metabolic Algorithm and Oscillatory Phenomena

Our proposed algorithm is inspired by a chemical reading of the rewriting rules. Due to the biological implications of this type of reading, we called the algorithm *metabolic*.

The re-interpretation of the rewriting rules in the light of chemical reactions is not new: several researchers have applied rewriting systems to contexts different from the purely abstract one, giving alternative meanings to the rules [18, 19]. In P systems every rule can be seen as a binary relation between strings, mapping the leftward argument into the rightward one. For instance, a rule $r : AB \rightarrow CD$ containing symbols defined over an alphabet V states that every occurrence of the object $A \in V$ in the system, once paired with $B \in V$, can be substituted by the pair of objects $CD \in V^*$.

If we look at r as a *chemical reaction*, now the leftward objects A and B have the role of *reactants* whereas those on the right are *products*. Following this chemical interpretation, we propose to look at rules as descriptors of the changes in concentration of the reactants into products. In other words, r says that a number of objects of type A and B transforms into objects of type B and C. In this way we deal with populations rather than single objects.

This interpretation needs the introduction of some definitions. Consider a P system on an alphabet $V = \{A, B, C, \ldots\}$, provided with a nonempty set R of rewriting rules. Every rule $r : \alpha \rightarrow \beta$, with $\alpha, \beta \in V^*$, is associated to a *reactivity coefficient* k_r whose role will be made clear in the following.

For each membrane M we give a maximum number of objects $|M|$ that cannot be overcome. From here we agree to define a conventional *molarity unit*:

$$\mu = \nu \, |M|,$$

where ν is a molarity factor ($\nu = 0.01$ in our experiments). We denote with $|X|$ the number of elements of type X in M, and define the quantity

$$||X|| = \frac{|X|}{\mu} \tag{3}$$

as the number of *moles* of X inside M. This molar formulation for the quantities involved in a reaction leads to the α-*molar concentration*, defined as the product of the moles of every object in a string $\alpha = \alpha_1 \ldots \alpha_{|\alpha|}$:

$$||\alpha|| = \prod_{i=1}^{|\alpha|} ||\alpha_i||. \tag{4}$$

It is now possible to describe an algorithm that translates the rewriting rules into a set of equations defining the *molar variation*, $\Delta||X||$, of every element X in consequence of the application of the rules.

A rule $r : \alpha \to \beta \in R$ acts on the leftward (i.e., reactant) and rightward (i.e., product) objects: the leftward part of r diminishes the concentration of the reactants, whereas the rightward part increases the concentration of the products. Hence, the changes in the amount for an element X in M due to r are equal to the *stoichiometric coefficient*:

$$|\beta|_X - |\alpha|_X,$$

where $|\gamma|_S$ indicates the number of occurrences of S contained in γ.

In chemical terms, r affects the concentration of every element appearing in it by a similar contribution, depending on the concentration of all the reactants at the instant of application. The term $||\alpha||$ takes this aspect into account, according to equation (4). Thus, we can compute the effect $\Delta_r||X||$ of a rule $r : \alpha \to \beta$ on the concentration of X, as

$$\Delta_r||X|| = k_r\,||\alpha||\,(|\beta|_X - |\alpha|_X), \tag{5}$$

where k_r is the *reactivity coefficient* of the rule.

In general an object is involved in more than one rule. In order to compute the overall molar variation of an object X we have to take the contributions of all rules into account. This is made by summing up their effects on the concentration of X:

$$\Delta||X|| = \sum_{r \in R} \Delta_r||X||, \tag{6}$$

where R is the set of rules in our P system.

Hence, after the application of a set of rules our algorithm updates the number of moles of an object X according to the following assignment:

$$||X|| := ||X|| + \Delta||X||. \tag{7}$$

The multiplicity of X is updated accordingly:

$$|X| := |X| + \mu\Delta||X||. \tag{8}$$

Let us now see a concrete example of this translation from rewriting rules to *metabolic equations*. Consider the following set of rules:

$$\begin{aligned} r1 &: AC &\to AB, \\ r2 &: BC &\to A, \\ r3 &: BBB &\to BC, \end{aligned} \tag{9}$$

each of them associated to a coefficient, respectively k_{r1}, k_{r2}, and k_{r3}. We want to calculate the variation in the multiplicity of every object in the system caused by the rules.

If we apply equation (6) to each object, then we obtain the following system of metabolic equations:

$$
\begin{aligned}
\Delta\|A\| &= 0 \cdot k_{r1}\|AC\| +1 \cdot k_{r2}\|BC\| +0 \cdot k_{r3}\|BBB\|, \\
\Delta\|B\| &= +1 \cdot k_{r1}\|AC\| -1 \cdot k_{r2}\|BC\| -2 \cdot k_{r3}\|BBB\|, \\
\Delta\|C\| &= -1 \cdot k_{r1}\|AC\| -1 \cdot k_{r2}\|BC\| +1 \cdot k_{r3}\|BBB\|,
\end{aligned}
\tag{10}
$$

where k_{r1}, k_{r2}, and k_{r3} can be read as "rates" of application of $r1$, $r2$ and $r3$, respectively. As we can see from (10), where all contributions (including null ones) are represented, it is always possible to figure out an equation for every object of the P system from the correspondent set of rewriting rules. Each of these equations gives the molar variation of the related element as time elapses.

By applying equation (3) we can figure out the finite *differentials* associated to the system (10):

$$
\begin{aligned}
\Delta a &= +\mu \cdot \tfrac{k_{r2}}{\mu^2} \cdot bc, \\
\Delta b &= +\mu \cdot \tfrac{k_{r1}}{\mu^2} \cdot ac -\mu \cdot \tfrac{k_{r2}}{\mu^2} \cdot bc -2\mu \cdot \tfrac{k_{r3}}{\mu^3} \cdot b^3, \\
\Delta c &= -\mu \cdot \tfrac{k_{r1}}{\mu^2} \cdot ac -\mu \cdot \tfrac{k_{r2}}{\mu^2} \cdot bc +\mu \cdot \tfrac{k_{r3}}{\mu^3} \cdot b^3,
\end{aligned}
\tag{11}
$$

in which we have denoted numbers of elements with a, b, c instead of $|A|, |B|, |C|$, respectively. Note that the correspondence between rewriting rules and differential equations is not bi-directional: in general there is no unique way to translate a system of differentials into a set of rewriting rules, whereas the other way round holds.

We want to emphasize an important fact about the coefficients k_r. In the molar formulation of rewriting rules they are called *reactivities*, and their role is to weight each rule's action. The reactivity of a rule takes many aspects into account: i) chemical and physical aspects of the reaction environment (pressure, temperature, PH level, catalyst activity, ...), ii) reaction speed (increasing or decreasing speed corresponds to a finer or coarser observation granularity), iii) proper features of single reactions that should account for the following aspects:

- rule activation percentage;
- synchronization and parallelism degree;
- reactants and energy partition.

If we consider all the interconnections existing between the points introduced in the previous list, then it is easy to understand that the tuning of reactivity factors is very important. We think that this aspect needs further investigation, and our future work will proceed along this line.

As previously seen, the multiplicity of X is updated according to (7) after each system transition. Unfortunately it might happen that a rule is applied too many times with respect to the reactant allowance, due to a wrong choice of the reactivity coefficients. In other words, the system in principle can consume more reactants than those which are available at a given configuration. This violates the Principle of Mass Conservation.

To account for this, we add in our model a set of constraints that force the system to respect the Principle of Mass Conservation. One possible algorithm is the following: for every object X, before calculating its molar variation $\Delta||X||$ check if the amount $|X|$ becomes negative; if so, then stop the computation, else go on. Another possible work-around to a violation of the previously discussed constraints is to decrease each of the values of the reactivity parameters by a certain rate and, then, check again.

To clarify these ideas it is useful to calculate this set of constraints on a concrete example. Consider a P system with the set of rules (9) previously discussed; in order not to use more reactants than those available, we add the above constraints we to each reactant. In the example seen before these constraints become:

$$\begin{aligned} &\mathbf{C}_{|A|} : k_{r1}||AC|| < |A|, \\ &\mathbf{C}_{|B|} : k_{r2}||BC|| + k_{r3}||BBB|| < |B|, \\ &\mathbf{C}_{|C|} : k_{r1}||AC|| + k_{r2}||BC|| < |C|, \end{aligned} \qquad (12)$$

where $\mathbf{C}_{|A|}$, $\mathbf{C}_{|B|}$ and $\mathbf{C}_{|C|}$, respectively, denote the constraints on the corresponding objects.

We want to stress that someone could think that the constraint on an object X can be equivalently calculated *after* the updating of $|X|$, by simply checking that it never assumes negative values. Once more, this is the wrong approach. In fact, even if the balance of positive and negative contributions results in an admissible variation, no one is able in this way to prevent that the amount of X consumed by all the reactions (those including it among their reactants) during a transition exceeds its real amount.

Once a constraint violation is discovered there are several ways to react. This investigation is still in progress. There are some open questions in our model, and our future work will try to give an answer to them. One of such questions deals with the temporal variation of the reactivity parameters, as independent functions in the system: we think that setting these parameters free to vary along time would have a strong impact on the system behavior, enabling it to simulate more complex reactions.

We would like to end this brief treatment outlining some of the results we get by this model implemented in a simulator *Psim*, developed in Java with an xml representation of membrane structure [2].

The first dynamical system we intend to model is a well known chemical oscillator called *Brusselator*; it is a simplified model of the Belousov-Zhabotinsky reaction [13, 7, 19]. When certain reactants like sulphuric acid, malonic acid, ferroin and bromate are combined together, in presence of a cerium catalyst, the chemical compound obtained, after a period of inactivity, starts a series of sudden oscillations in color ranging from red to blue. This chemical reaction could be described by the following rewriting rules:

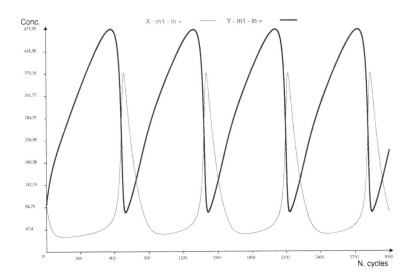

Fig. 1. Oscillations of Belousov-Zhabotinsky reaction model simulated by *Psim* with parameters $k_1 = 0.9$, $k_2 = 0.7$, $k_3 = 0.36$, $k_4 = 0.36$, $k_5 = 0.1$, $k_6 = 0.15$ and $\mu = 1000$ ($|M| = 100000$). Parameters could be rewritten in terms of k_1 in this way: $k_2 = 0.78 \cdot k_1$, $k_3 = 0.4 \cdot k_1$ and $k_4 = 0.4 \cdot k_1$

$$
\begin{aligned}
r_1 &: A &&\to X, \\
r_2 &: BX &&\to YD, \\
r_3 &: XXY &&\to XXX, \\
r_4 &: X &&\to C.
\end{aligned}
\tag{13}
$$

It is usually made the assumption that the system described in this way inputs continuously reactants A and B from the outside environment; for this reason, in order to implement the reaction into our simulator, two rules have to be added at the set of rules (13):

$$
\begin{aligned}
r_5 &: \lambda \to A, \\
r_6 &: \lambda \to B,
\end{aligned}
\tag{14}
$$

that are two generative rules which introduce some amount of objects A and B into the system.

It turns out that the oscillating behavior of the chemical reaction is mirrored, in the abstract system outlined by the rewriting rules, in the oscillations of the amounts of objects X and Y. We have translated this extended set of rules into our xml input file and fed it to the simulator: the trend of X and Y is visible in Figure 1, where it is possible to appreciate the perfect oscillating behavior of the system's limit cycle. Accordingly with the assumptions made in [18] initially all objects have multiplicity equal to zero. Note that it is possible to relate all reactivity coefficients to their maximum value, as in Figure 1 k_1. This relationship is emphasized in Figure 1.

The second dynamic system we intend to investigate is a very basic predator-prey model, described, among others, in [7]. It is constituted by only two objects evolving over time: preys X and predators Y. We make the following four simplifying assumptions:

- preys grow up following a Malthusian model;
- preys' growing rate is reduced proportionally to predators' number;
- predators extinguish exponentially in absence of preys because they are predators' only sustenance;
- preys' presence make predators' growing rate increase proportionally to their number.

Under these assumptions this predator-prey model could be described by the well known Lotka-Volterra differential equations, where now $x = ||X||$ and $y = ||Y||$:

$$\begin{aligned} x' &= ax - dxy, \\ y' &= exy - by, \end{aligned} \tag{15}$$

extended by the initial conditions that $x_0 > 0$ and $y_0 > 0$.
Starting from these differential equations we have translated them into the following rewriting rules:

$$\begin{aligned} r1: \; & X \;\; \rightarrow \;\; XX, \\ r2: \; & XY \rightarrow \;\; YY, \\ r3: \; & Y \;\; \rightarrow \;\; \lambda, \end{aligned} \tag{16}$$

with the following assignments:

$$a = k_{r1}; \;\; d = \frac{k_{r2}}{\mu}; \;\; b = k_{r3}; \;\; e = \frac{k_{r2}}{\mu}$$

where k_{ri} and μ have the usual meaning and are input parameters of our model; in this way we get the metabolic equations:

$$\begin{aligned} \Delta ||X|| &= \;\;\; k_{r1} \cdot ||X|| - k_{r2} \cdot ||XY|| \\ \Delta ||Y|| &= - \, k_{r2} \cdot ||XY|| \;\; - k_{r3} \cdot ||Y|| \end{aligned} \tag{17}$$

Note that again all these rules and objects could be contained into a system with just one membrane.

We tested the system described so far starting with an initial amount of 100 preys and 20 predators. The simulation, as we can see from Figure 2, confirmed the oscillating behavior of the number of preys and predators in the predator-pray model described by the Lotka-Volterra system of equations.

The last model we discuss in this paragraph is that of an infective disease that spreads through a population and that could cause infected people's death or permanent immunity to the infection.

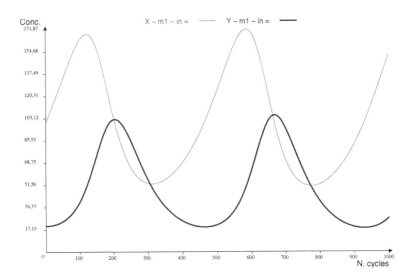

Fig. 2. Oscillations of the predator-prey model simulated by *Psim* with $k_1 = 0.01$, $k_2 = 0.02$, $k_3 = 0.02$ and $\mu = 100$ ($|M| = 10000$)

We make the simplifying assumption that the population is closed (e.g., it is made by a certain amount of people and where no births, immigration or emigration are allowed). The population of this dynamical system is partitioned into three different categories (objects of our system): healthy people C, ill people G, and immune people K. When an healthy person meets an ill one he becomes ill, with a probability depending on the reaction rate of the rule; an ill person has two possibilities: he could die, and could otherwise become immune forever to the infection. On the other hand, an healthy individual could keep his state until he gets no contact with an ill one. This pattern is common to many contagious phenomena, and could model also some forms of prion propagation that are the biomolecular basis of various infectious diseases of the nervous system (as bovine spongiform encephalopathy and Creutzfeldt-Jakob disease).

The behavior just described could be expressed with the following set of rules:

$$
\begin{aligned}
r_1 &: CG \rightarrow GG, \\
r_2 &: G \;\;\rightarrow K, \\
r_3 &: G \;\;\rightarrow \lambda,
\end{aligned}
\tag{18}
$$

in which all the symbols have the meaning previously discussed. The simulation of such a system with our tool has outlined results in agreement with literature. In particular, it has put into evidence the existence of a threshold of activation for the epidemic: on the one hand, if the initial healthy population is below a certain amount, the epidemic does not start and so ill people decrease in number until its complete vanishing. On the other hand, whenever the initial healthy population is beyond that threshold the epidemic activates and the number of ill people grows up until reaching its maximum and then drops again to zero thus vanishing.

Due to our choice of the parameters, as indicated in Figure 3 and 4, it turns out that the threshold we talked about is near 2570; we find accordingly two kinds of behaviors depending of the initial amount of healthy people: in Figure 3 is depicted the case in which the epidemic doesn't activate because of the number of initial healthy people being 2000 and thus under the threshold. On the other hand, in Figure 4 the initial amount of healthy people is 7000 and the epidemic does its course reaching its maximum and then vanishing. In both cases the initial number of ill people is fixed to 300.

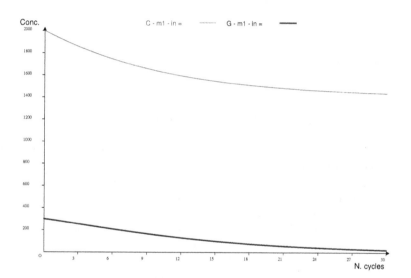

Fig. 3. Not active epidemic model simulated by *Psim* with $k_1 = 0.3$, $k_2 = 0.1$, $k_3 = 0.12$ and $\mu = 3500$

We end the section stressing once more the fact that all the examples discussed here, in spite of their extreme interest, are very simple from a topological viewpoint but their study has been very useful in order to evaluate the effectiveness of the metabolic algorithm proposed. Our work will, from now on, concentrate on the simulation of more elaborate systems.

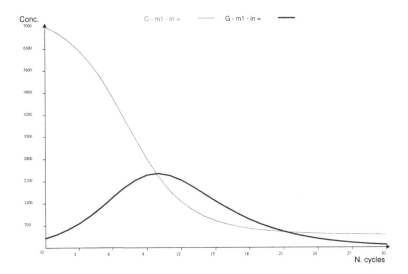

Fig. 4. Active epidemic model simulated by *Psim* with $k_1 = 0.3$, $k_2 = 0.1$, $k_3 = 0.12$ and $\mu = 3500$

4   Relationships with Linear Systems

As opposite to State Transition Dynamics, the traditional linear paradigm results in systems that are extremely simple from a formal point of view; meanwhile a lot of theoretical results exist about such systems that are useful in practice [8]. For these two reasons linear systems have found plenty of practical applications in system modeling and control, even of nonlinear phenomena.

Here we want to show that P systems can represent linear systems. Although this fact is implied by universality, nevertheless it is interesting to see how this representation can be given. We will make use of no peculiar and/or advanced properties to derive a linear restriction of P systems. In other words, we do not want to define any novel or complicate kind of construct to characterize a weaker family of P systems as those reproducing linear systems.

In its traditional formulation a *discrete linear* (DLI) system transforms, at a temporal step n, an N-dimensional state vector $\boldsymbol{v}$ according to a linear (matrix) transformation in a way that a new state will hold at the following time step. In the meantime, an output vector is produced as a linear combination of the actual state itself. It is well known by theory that for a stable system this output consists of (however many) damped sinusoids.

Coherently with the classic notion of P system here we do not consider the existence of an external input—though, this aspect is likely to be object of future research in conjunction with formulations of P systems that are capable of accepting an input from the external environment [1]. Indeed, the external input is a crucial aspect in linear systems theory, and more in general in the modeling of real phenomena, as a factor that excites initially quiet systems and forces their evolution along time.

Apart from the input, the core structure (and, hence, the overall behavior, or *free evolution*) of a linear system depends on the structure of the transition matrix A, sized $N \times N$. Thus, we can completely characterize a free-evolving linear system by the following set of equations holding at time step n:

$$\begin{cases} v(n+1) = Av(n), \\ u(n) \quad = Cv(n), \end{cases} \tag{19}$$

in which the upper formula expresses the state transition, whereas the lower formula is responsible of the system output. Let $v(0)$ be the initial state.

P systems cannot associate real numbers to symbols directly, as it happens for linear systems. We, then, restrict our numerical domain to rational numbers in a way that A and C can be respectively approximated by two matrices containing only rational numbers, with the desired precision. Now we collect all the matrix elements and, for each matrix, we compute the least common factor of such elements, k_A and k_C respectively. Similarly, we compute the least common factor k_v of the initial state elements. In this way we can move to a slightly different system:

$$\begin{cases} \tilde{v}(n+1) = \tilde{A}\tilde{v}(n), \\ \tilde{u}(n) \quad = \tilde{C}\tilde{v}(n), \end{cases} \tag{20}$$

in which $\tilde{A} = k_A A$, $\tilde{C} = k_C C$, and $\tilde{v}(0) = k_v v(0)$. In other words we multiply both the transition and output matrix by their respective least common factors, in a way that the matrices resulting from this operation, $\tilde{A}$ and $\tilde{C}$, respectively, contain only signed integers. Likewise we define $k_v(0)$ as a modified initial state made of only integer values. These three rescalings lead to a modified linear system evolving within the domain of signed integers.

Since we are interested in studying the dynamic evolution of populations, then we can restrict our analysis to linear systems whose state is positive or null. The formal complications needed to account for negative values are left to further research: at the moment $\tilde{A}$ and $\tilde{C}$ are made of positive numbers, and the modified initial state is positive as well.

Let us define a P system using symbols describing the state, $x_1, x_2, \ldots, x_N$, and z, and the output: $y_1, y_2, \ldots, y_N$ (output symbols are defined to add clarity to the treatment although they are not strictly necessary):

$$V = \{x_1, x_2, \ldots, x_N, y_1, y_2, \ldots, y_N, z\},$$
$$T = \{y_1, y_2, \ldots, y_N\}.$$

Let this system contain N membranes inside the skin:

$$\mu = [_{skin} [_1 \,]_1 \, [_2 \,]_2 \, \cdots \, [_N \,]_N \,]_{skin}.$$

The inner membrane labeled with j will contain the value of the j-th element of $\tilde{v}(n+1)$, in terms of multiplicity of objects z contained in the membrane itself.

In the beginning, the initial state is encoded in the skin membrane as the following multiset of symbols:

$$w_{\text{skin}} = x_1^{\tilde{v}_1(0)}\, x_2^{\tilde{v}_2(0)}\, \cdots\, x_N^{\tilde{v}_N(0)},$$

where $\tilde{v}_i(n)$ denotes the value of the i-th element of the state vector $\tilde{v}$ at time step n. Any other membrane is set to be initially empty: $w_1 = \ldots = w_N = \emptyset$.

A single-step evolution of the linear system is resolved in one transition of the corresponding P system involving both the symbols in the skin and in every inner membrane:

1. Every symbol x_j located inside the skin is distributed, once turned into z, into the i-th inner membrane with the multiplicity given by $a_{ij} \in \tilde{A}$, for every $i = 1, \ldots, N$. In the meantime the same symbol, once turned into y_i, is sent out of the system with a multiplicity given by $c_{ij} \in \tilde{C}$, again for each $i = 1, \ldots, N$. This happens for every component so that in the end we write

$$x_j \rightarrow z_{\text{in}_1}^{a_{1j}} \cdots z_{\text{in}_N}^{a_{Nj}}\, y_{1\,\text{out}}^{c_{1j}} \cdots y_{N\,\text{out}}^{c_{Nj}}, \quad j = 1, \ldots, N. \tag{21}$$

Thus, (21) stores symbols z accounting for the new state in the inner membranes, meanwhile produces symbols $y_1, \ldots, y_N$ accounting for the system output.

2. Every inner membrane sends its symbols back to the skin, once properly renamed—say, every symbol z in the i-th membrane is sent out as x_i. These symbols form the new state and, at the end of the transition, they are ready to take part in the next one-step evolution of the linear system.

Finally, the P system output must be converted back to the original linear system output. This is made by clearing out, at temporal step n, the factors k_A, k_C and k_v from the multiplicity value of every output symbol y_i, here denoted with $|y_i|$:

$$u(n) = \frac{1}{k_A^n k_C k_v^{n+1}}\, \big|\, |y_1|\, |y_2|\, \cdots\, |y_N|\, \big|^T \tag{22}$$

in which T denotes transposition.

Although both $\tilde{v}(n+1)$ and $\tilde{u}(n)$ are linear combinations of $\tilde{v}(n)$, nevertheless we must note that the computation of the output is performed by a procedure that differs from the one used for evolving the state. In fact, the latter makes use of membranes in which to store the new state, whereas the former sends the result directly out of the skin hence avoiding the use of additional membranes. Indeed, inner membranes can be even avoided in the production of the new state provided that additional symbols, $z_1, \ldots, z_N$, are added to the P system to keep trace of it. In this case (21) is rewritten as

$$x_j \rightarrow z_1^{a_{1j}} \cdots z_N^{a_{Nj}}\, y_{1\,\text{out}}^{c_{1j}} \cdots y_{N\,\text{out}}^{c_{Nj}}, \quad j = 1, \ldots, N, \tag{23}$$

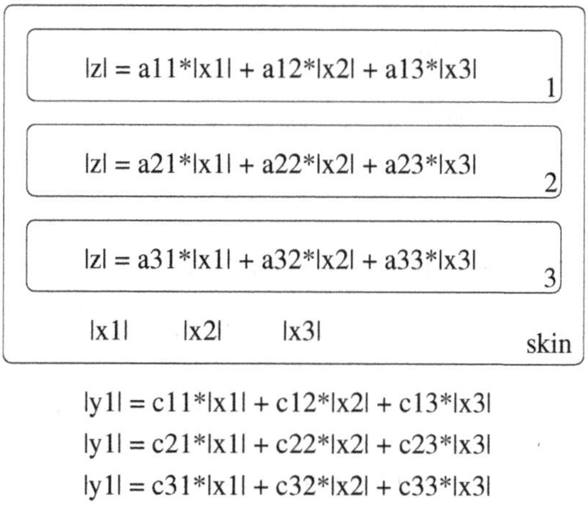

$$|z| = a11*|x1| + a12*|x2| + a13*|x3|$$
$$\boxed{1}$$

$$|z| = a21*|x1| + a22*|x2| + a23*|x3|$$
$$\boxed{2}$$

$$|z| = a31*|x1| + a32*|x2| + a33*|x3|$$
$$\boxed{3}$$

$$|x1| \qquad |x2| \qquad |x3| \qquad\qquad \text{skin}$$

$$|y1| = c11*|x1| + c12*|x2| + c13*|x3|$$
$$|y1| = c21*|x1| + c22*|x2| + c23*|x3|$$
$$|y1| = c31*|x1| + c32*|x2| + c33*|x3|$$

Fig. 5. Graphic representation of the P system proposed in the example. Module operators give the multiplicity of the respective surrounded symbols

meanwhile (again for each j) further rules of the type $z_j \to x_j$ update the state in parallel, by transforming the (previous) new state in the actual state of the system.

We think that the existence of inner membranes, as expressed by (21), puts more emphasis on the system's structural properties and paves the way for strategies aimed at characterizing linearity in P systems containing multiple nested membranes.

As an example, suppose to have

$$A = \begin{vmatrix} 1 & 1/2 & 0 \\ 0 & 1 & 0 \\ 1 & 1/3 & 1 \end{vmatrix} \quad C = \begin{vmatrix} 1 & 0 & 0 \\ 0 & 1 & 0 \\ 1 & 0 & 1 \end{vmatrix}, \quad v(0) = \begin{vmatrix} 0 \\ 1 \\ 0 \end{vmatrix}.$$

First, we compute $k_A = 6$, $k_C = 1$ and $k_v = 1$ in a way that

$$\tilde{A} = \begin{vmatrix} 6 & 3 & 0 \\ 0 & 6 & 0 \\ 6 & 2 & 6 \end{vmatrix}, \quad \tilde{C} = C, \quad \tilde{v}(0) = v(0).$$

Then, provided $V, T, \mu, w_{\text{skin}}, w_1, \ldots, w_N$ as above, the rule set is the following:

$$R_{\text{skin}} = \{ x_1 \to z_{\text{in}_1}^6 \, z_{\text{in}_3}^6 \, y_{1\,\text{out}} \, y_{3\,\text{out}},$$
$$x_2 \to z_{\text{in}_1}^3 \, z_{\text{in}_2}^6 \, z_{\text{in}_3}^2 \, y_{2\,\text{out}},$$
$$x_3 \to z_{\text{in}_3}^6 \, y_{3\,\text{out}} \},$$
$$R_1 = \{ z \to x_{1\,\text{out}} \},$$
$$R_2 = \{ z \to x_{2\,\text{out}} \},$$
$$R_3 = \{ z \to x_{3\,\text{out}} \}.$$

Figure 5 can help the reader in decoding the process.

The absence of further elements in the construct such as, for example, priorities on the rules, proves that such a construct is not universal, as it had to be expected. Despite this, the symbols which are read out of the skin give, at each temporal step n, the linear system solution once it is computed as $\boldsymbol{u}(n) = (1/6^n)\big| |y_1| \, |y_2| \, \ldots \, |y_N| \big|^T$ according to (22).

5   Conclusion and Future Research Directions

Let us call MA the metabolic algorithm. If E is a system of metabolic equations derived from a set of rewriting rules, then $MA(E, \mu)$ is the dynamics we get with a molarity unit μ. Let us call $[E]_\mu$ the "molar normalization" of equations E which is obtained by replacing every reactivity parameter k in E by $k/\mu^{(t-1)}$ where t is the degree of reactant monomial associated to k. Finally, let us call by $d(E)$ the differential form of equations E which is obtained by replacing in E the Δ finite difference operator by the differential operator d/dt, and the molar quantities by absolute quantities, that is, by putting $\mu = 1$. If $Euler$ is the Euler's approximation method for solving differential equations, the following proposition is easily proved.

Proposition 2. $MA(E, \mu) = Euler(d([E]_\mu))$.

It is very interesting that, in the case of oscillatory phenomena that we studied, especially in the Brusselator reported in [13], we get the following experimental result where $Runge\text{–}Kutta$ is a very common and reliable integration method.

Proposition 3. $MA(E, \mu) = Runge\text{–}Kutta(d([E]))$.

This result shows the relevance of molar normalization. We plan to develop further experimental and theoretical work for a better understanding of this phenomenon and for improving our metabolic algorithm by means of a more systematic and adaptive use of molar normalization. However, it is important

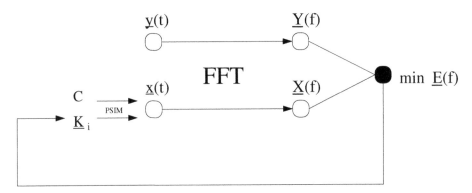

Fig. 6. Schematic of our resolution strategy of the inverse oscillating problem

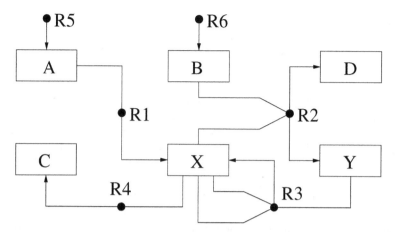

Fig. 7. The neuron-like structure of Brusselator Metabolic Graph

that this metabolic approach seems to be a basis for a reliable direct discrete tool for computing the behavior of P systems. The next step is the extension of this dynamic approach to more complex membrane topologies, and to situations where reaction parameters change in time under the influence of external factors.

Now let us express the rewriting rules of Brusselator with the graph given in Fig. 7. This formulation suggests us a new perspective in P system analysis. First, we could extend this representation to any membrane structure by a suitable use of labels. In this way any membrane system becomes a dynamical network, that is a graph where at each time nodes have a state that depend on the state of other nodes of the graph (nodes and arcs can be added and removed in time). In other words, a membrane system is always related to a sort of "neuron-like" membrane structure, according to Păun's terminology. It is easy to discover that a dynamics associated to some rewriting rules can present oscillatory phenomena only if the relative metabolic graph has (some form) of cycles. But in general finding parameters that ensure some kind of oscillations is not a simple task. In the case of the Brusselator graph, the search space is a vector space of twelve dimensions (six for initial concentrations and six for reactivities). The *Inverse Oscillation Problem* can be stated in the following way: *Given a metabolic graph, find initial concentrations and reactivity parameters that ensure an oscillation of quantities of some given types.*

We are currently working on a strategy of solution of the inverse oscillation problem[1]. As suggested by the name of the problem, we are mainly interested in dynamic oscillating behaviors. The initial data typically consist in a metabolic graph, that provides relations on the system constituents, and in a set of oscil-

---

[1] In fact the proposed strategy deals with a simplified instance of the problem, in which we know, even roughly, the initial concentrations and moreover we need initial estimates of the reactivity parameters. In this way the solution of the Brusselator's inverse oscillation problem lies within a six-dimensional vector space rather than a twelve one.

lating functions, usually obtained by experiments, that we intend to reproduce. Our goal is to define an automatic procedure that, in the same initial conditions (mainly in terms of reactivity coefficients) realizes the desired oscillating system behavior.

Starting from a periodic signal, in the time domain, we can describe its behavior in a more compact way by analyzing its dual representation in the frequency domain. Let $y(t)$ be the signal to be reproduced and let us denote with $x(t)$ the signal obtained from the simulation. The simulated signal will depend on the reactivity coefficients $k_1, \ldots, k_N$, whose values are our subject of investigation. For this reason, from now on we will denote the simulated signal x as $x(k_1, \ldots, k_N, t)$, where N is the number of unknown reactivity coefficients.

Note that we have to consider a pair of signals y_i, x_i for each one of the different kind of objects present in the system. Let's denote with m the number of different types of elements populating the system under investigation and with n the number of discrete-time samples forming our signals. According to the previous observation we have to deal with a couple of matrices $\underline{y}(t)$ and $\underline{x}(k_1, \ldots, k_N, t)$, sharing the same dimension, that is, $m \times n$.

Our approach starts from the observation that a periodic signal (e.g., a sinusoidal function) is described in a compact way in the frequency domain by means of the *Fourier Transform* operator (e.g. a sine in time becomes an impulse in frequency). This translation from time to frequency domain is implemented very efficiently, thanks to fast implementations of the Fourier Transform, known as *Fast Fourier Transform* or FFT [8].

For the previously described reasons we suggest to perform a Fourier Transform on our signals, $\underline{y}(t)$ and $\underline{x}(k_1, \ldots, k_N, t)$, and this lead to their dual representations $\underline{Y}(f)$ and $\underline{X}(k_1, \ldots, k_N, f)$, where the symbol f reminds that Y and X belong to the frequency domain. The target of our investigation is the minimization of the norm:

$$\underline{E}(f) = ||\underline{Y}(f) - \underline{X}(k_1, \ldots, k_N, f)||, \tag{24}$$

that is, to calculate

$$\min_{\underline{K}} ||\underline{Y}(f) - \underline{X}(f)|| = \min_{\underline{K}} \underline{E}(f), \tag{25}$$

where we have defined the norm $||M||$ of a matrix M as the maximum value of the norms of all rows of M.

In order to minimize the distance function $\underline{E}$ we can use several minimization algorithms. The important thing to point out here is that the translation to the frequency domain can be performed very efficiently by FFT algorithms, and the minimization procedure is in general carried out in a more efficient way in frequency rather than in the time domain; this efficiency is gained when $\underline{E}(f)$ turns out to be an $m' \times n'$ matrix where $m' = m$ and $n' < n$, as it happens when the maximum number of pure oscillatory behaviors under investigation (chosen to be equal to $n'/2 - 1$) is likely to be smaller than the number n of temporal samples included in the analysis window of every signal $y_1, \ldots, y_m$.

Note also that, in general, the solution obtained in the frequency domain may result in a phase-shifted time signal, but this is not limiting our point because our interest focuses on the periodical trend of the system as a whole.

In Figure 6 our approach is depicted in a schematic way. The inputs of the method are:

- $\underline{C}$, the initial concentrations of all objects;
- $\underline{K_0}$, initial estimates of reactivities;
- $\underline{y}(t)$, the matrix of signals that we want to reproduce;
- the metabolic graph (not depicted in figure), necessary to describe all relationships between objects populating the system.

Starting from objects' relationships described by the metabolic graph, and by using $\underline{K_0}$ and $\underline{C}$, an implementation of the metabolic algorithm provides the simulated behavior $\underline{x}(t)$. The FFT block translates our signals $\underline{y}(t)$ and $\underline{x}(t)$ in their frequency duals $\underline{Y}(f)$ and $\underline{X}(f)$. We perform a minimization algorithm on $\underline{Y}(f)$ and $\underline{X}(f)$ in order to adjust the vector K_0 into another one, say K_1, on which the metabolic algorithm is applied again and again until the distance between $\underline{Y}(f)$ and $\underline{X}(f)$ falls below a certain threshold τ. If this happens at the iteration cycle $i + 1$ then K_i contains the result, otherwise it's desirable to specify a maximum number of cycles after that the procedure terminates without convergence.

Another research topic, related the inverse oscillation problem, is the finding of parameters, possibly defined on the metabolic graphs of P systems, that could have some dynamical relevance. Many of them are suggested by parameters introduced for cellular automata and Kauffman networks, but a lot of experimental work and theoretical analysis has to be developed along this direction.

References

1. F. Bernardini and V. Manca. Dynamical aspects of P systems. *BioSystems*, 70:85–93, 2002.
2. L. Bianco, F. Fontana, G. Franco, and V. Manca. P systems for biological dynamics. In G. Ciobanu, G. Păun, M.J. Pérez-Jiménez, eds., *Applications of Membrane Computing*, Springer-Verlag, Berlin, 2005, to appear.
3. C. Bonanno and V. Manca. Discrete dynamics in biological models. *Romanian J. of Inform. Sc. and Tech.*, 5(1–2):45–67, 2002.
4. R.L. Devaney. *Introduction to Chaotic Dynamical Systems*. Addison-Wesley, 1989.
5. R. Freund. Energy-controlled P systems. In G. Păun and C. Zandron, editors, *Proc. Int. Workshop WMC-CdeA 2002*, number 2597 in Lecture Notes in Computer Science, pages 247–260, Curtea de Arges, Romania, August 2002. Springer.
6. R. C. Hilborn. *Chaos and Nonlinear Dynamics*. Oxford University Press, 2000.
7. D.S. Jones and B.D. Sleeman. *Differential Equations and Mathematical Biology*. Chapman & Hall/CRC, London, 2003.
8. T. Kailath. *Linear Systems*. Prentice-Hall, Englewood Cliffs, 1980.
9. S.A. Kauffman. *The Origins of Order*. Oxford University Press, New York, NY, 1993.

10. C.G. Langton. Computation at the edge of chaos: phase transitions and emergent computation, *Physica D*, **42**, 12, 1990.
11. V. Manca, G. Franco, and G. Scollo. State transition dynamics: basic concepts and molecular computing perspectives. In M. Gheorghe, ed., *Molecular Computational Models: Unconventional Approaches*, Idea Group Inc., 2004.
12. C. Martin-Vide, G. Păun, and G. Rozenberg. Membrane systems with carriers. *Theoretical Computer Science*, 270:779–796, 2002.
13. G. Nicolis and I. Prigogine. *Exploring Complexity, An Introduction.* Freeman and Company, San Francisco, 1989.
14. G. Păun. Computing with membranes. *J. Comput. System Sci.*, 61(1):108–143, 2000.
15. G. Păun *Membrane Computing - An Introduction.* Springer-Verlag, Berlin, 2002.
16. G. Păun and G. Rozenberg. A guide to membrane computing. *Theoretical Computer Science*, 287:73–100, 2002.
17. G. Păun, Y. Suzuki, and H. Tanaka. P systems with energy accounting. *Int. J. Computer Math.*, 78(3):343–364, 2001.
18. Y. Suzuki and H. Tanaka. Chemical oscillation in symbolic chemical systems and its behavioral pattern. In Y. Bar-Yam, editor, *Proc. International Conference on Complex Systems*, pages 0–7, New England Complex Systems Institute, 1997.
19. Y. Suzuki, H. Tanaka. Abstract rewriting systems on multisets and their application for modelling complex behaviours, in G. Paun, M. Cavaliere, and C. Martin-Vide eds., *Brainstorming Week on Membrane Computing, Tarragona, February 5-11 2003*, Tarragona, Feb 5-11 2003.
20. A. Wuensche. Discrete dynamical networks and their Attractor Basins, online journal *Complexity International*, 1998.
21. A. Wuensche. Basins of attraction in network dynamics: A conceptual framework for biomolecular networks, in G. Schlosser and G.P. Wagner, eds., *Modularity in Development and Evolution*, Chicago University Press, 2003.
22. S. Wolfram. *Theory and Application of Cellular Automata*, Addison-Wesley, 1986.

An Approach to Computational Complexity in Membrane Computing

Mario J. Pérez-Jiménez

Research Group on Natural Computing,
Department of Computer Science and Artificial Intelligence,
University of Sevilla
Avda. Reina Mercedes s/n, 41012 Sevilla, Spain
Mario.Perez@cs.us.es

Abstract. In this paper we present a theory of computational complexity in the framework of membrane computing. Polynomial complexity classes in recognizer membrane systems and capturing the *classical* deterministic and non-deterministic modes of computation, are introduced. In this context, a characterization of the relation $\mathbf{P} = \mathbf{NP}$ is described.

1   Introduction

The necessity to define in a satisfactory way what means a *definite method* for solving mathematical problems was studied by A. Turing who investigated how such methods should be applied *mechanically*, and, moreover, he formalized the task of performing such methods in terms of the operations of a *machine* able to read and write symbols on a tape divided into parts called cells (simulating how a person can solve a problem with paper and pencil manipulating symbols).

The *theory of computation* deals with the *mechanical solvability* of problems, that is, searching solutions that can be described by a finite sequence of elementary processes or instructions. The first goal in the theory of computation is general problem solving; that is, to develop principles and special methods that are able to solve any problem from a certain class of questions.

A *computational model* tries to capture those aspects of mechanical solutions of problems that are relevant to these solutions, including their inherent limitations. In some sense, we can think that computational models design machines according to certain necessity.

From a practical point of view, the goal of computation theory is to take real–life problems and try to solve them through a method capable of being simulated by a machine when we use a suitable language to communicate that problem to the machine (a language is a system of signs used to communicate information between different parties).

Abstract machines are formal computing devices that we use to investigate properties of real computing devices. Computable languages are a special type of formal languages that can be processed by abstract machines that represent computers.

G. Mauri et al. (Eds.): WMC5 2004, LNCS 3365, pp. 85–109, 2005.
© Springer-Verlag Berlin Heidelberg 2005

If we have a mechanically solvable problem and we have a specific algorithm solving it that can be implemented in a real machine, then it is very important to know how much computational resources (time or memory) are required for a given instance, in order to recognize the limitations of the real device.

One of the main goals of the *theory of computational complexity* is the study of the efficiency of algorithms and their data structures through the analysis of the resources required for solving problems (that is, according to their intrinsic computational difficulty). This theory provides a classification of the *abstract problems* that allows us to detect their inherent complexity from the computational solutions point of view.

Of course, such a classification demands a precise and formal definition of the concept of *abstract problem* and the model to be considered.

The following parameters are used to specify a *complexity class* within a general computational framework:

- First: the *model* of computation, D (in our case, recognizer P systems).
- Second: the *mode* of computation, M (in our case, non-deterministic and parallel).
- Third: the resource, r, that we wish to bound (usually time and space).
- Finally, we must specify an upper *bound* of the resources, f (a total recursive function from natural numbers to natural numbers).

Then, a complexity class is defined as the set of all languages decided by the device D operating in mode M and such that for any input string, u, D expends at most $f(|u|)$ units of the resource r, to accept or reject u.

Many interesting problems of the real world are presumably intractable and hence it is not possible to execute algorithmic solutions in an electronic computer when we deal with instances of those problems whose size is large. The theoretical limitations of the Turing machines in terms of computational power are also practical limitations to the digital computers.

Natural Computing is a new computing area inspired by nature, using concepts, principles and mechanisms underlying natural systems. *Evolutionary Algorithms* use different concepts from biology. *Neural Networks* are inspired in the structures of the brain and nervous system. *DNA Computing* is based on the computational properties of DNA molecules and on the capacity to handle them. *Membrane Computing* is inspired by the structure and functioning of living cells.

These two last models of computation provide unconventional devices with an attractive property (*computational efficiency*), they are able to create an exponential workspace in polynomial time (and, in some sense, trading space for time).

Can some unconventional devices be used to solve presumably intractable problems in a feasible time? The answer is affirmative at least from a theoretical point of view.

In this paper we provide a systematic and formal framework for the design of polynomial solutions to hard problems, and to classify them according to their polynomial solvability by cell–like membrane systems. Complexity classes in the framework of membrane computing and their relationships with the problems they contain, are the main subjects of this paper.

The paper is structured as follows. The next section is devoted to describe in an informal way the deterministic and non-deterministic mode of computation in a computing model. In Sections 3, 4, and 5 combinatorial optimization problems and decision problems are introduced, and a relationship between them from a complexity point of view is showed. The **P** versus **NP** problem is presented in Section 6, and in Section 12 a characterization of that problem is obtained. In Section 7 weakly and strongly **NP**–complete problems are studied. Sections 8 and 9 are devoted to present the general framework (recognizer membrane systems) within a theory of computational complexity developed here. Deterministic and non-deterministic polynomial complexity classes in membrane systems are introduced in Sections 10 and 11. Finally, we study the P systems with the capability to construct an exponential workspace in polynomial time, and the polynomial complexity classes associated with them.

2   Determinism Versus Non-determinism

A model of computation is properly given when we formally define the concept of mechanical procedure (*algorithm*). For that, it is necessary to syntactically define it, and determine precisely how such procedures can be executed (the semantic of the model).

The devices (systems or machines) modelling mechanical procedures can be represented through *configurations* (containing a complete description of the current state of the device). These configurations can evolve according to the semantic of the model. Formally, the semantic defines the concept of *transitions* from a configuration of the system to a next configuration; that is, the semantic of the model specifies what means *next configuration* of a given configuration. A configuration which has no next configuration is called a *halting configuration*.

A *computation* or execution of a device of a model is a sequence (finite or infinite) of configurations such that each configuration (except the first) is obtained from the previous one by a (step of) transition of the system. That is, a computation starts with an *initial configuration* of the system, and then it proceeds step by step, and halts when reaches a halting configuration (and then the result is encoded in this configuration).

When we use the devices of a model of computation to solve certain kind of problems on strings (in particular to *recognize* a language), it is necessary to define what means to *accept* or *reject* a string. In this case it is possible to consider two *modes of computation* in a computing model.

– The *deterministic mode* is characterized by the following fact: each configuration has *at most* one next configuration. In a deterministic device, given a current configuration, the next configuration of the system is uniquely determined, if any.

– The *non-deterministic mode* verifies the following property: each non halting configuration hast *at least* a next configuration. In a non-deterministic device several next configurations can be reached from a current configuration.

The computation of deterministic devices can be viewed as a tree with only one branch, whereas the computation of a non-deterministic device can be viewed as a tree having many possible branches. The root of the tree corresponds to the beginning of the computation, and every node in the tree corresponds to a point of the computation at which the machine has eventually multiple choices. Each branch of this tree determines one computation of the system.

Next we define what means to accept or reject a string by a deterministic or non-deterministic device (whose answers are only *yes* or *no*).

– A deterministic device M *accepts* (respectively, *rejects*) a string a if the answer of M on input a is *yes* (respectively, *no*).
– A non-deterministic device M *accepts* a string a if there exists a computation of M with input a such that the answer is *yes*.

Let us note the difference between the definition of acceptance by deterministic and non-deterministic devices. An input string a is accepted by a deterministic machine M, if *the* computation of M on input a halts and answers *yes*. A non-deterministic machine M accepts a string a if there exists *some* computation of M on input a answering *yes*; that is, there exists a sequence of non-deterministic choices that answers *yes*. In this case, it is possible that we accept a string but that there exists another computation with the same input that either halts and answers *no*, or does not halt.

Thus, a deterministic device can (mechanically) reject a string, but this is not the case in non-deterministic machines. How can we decide (in a mechanical way) whether there exists a non halting computation?

Non-deterministic Turing machines are like existential quantifiers: they accept an input string if there exists an accepting path in the corresponding computation tree. In some sense, we can affirm that non-deterministic devices do not properly capture the intuitive idea underlying the concept of algorithm, because the result of such a machine on an input (that is, the output of a computation) is not reliable, since the answer of the device is not always the same.

non-determinism can be considered as a generalization of determinism (the computation may branch at each configuration), and it can be viewed as a kind of parallel computation where several "processes" can be run simultaneously.

3   Combinatorial Optimization Problems

Roughly speaking, when we deal with *combinatorial optimization problems* we wish to find the *best* solution (according to a given criterion) among a class of possible (candidate or feasible) solutions. That is, in this kind of problems there can be many possible solutions, each one has associated a value (a positive rational number), and we aim to find a solution with the optimal (minimum or maximum) value.

For example, a *vertex cover* of an undirected graph is a set of vertices such that any edge of the graph has, at least, an endpoint in that set. Then, we may want to find one of the smallest vertex covers among all possible vertex covers in the input graph. This is the combinatorial optimization problem called *Minimum Vertex Cover Problem*. The main ingredients in this problem are the following: (a) the collection of all undirected graphs, (b) the finite set of all vertex covers associated with a given undirected graph, and (c) the cardinality of each vertex cover of a given undirected graph.

We can formalize these ideas in the following definition.

Definition 1. *A combinatorial optimization problem, X, is a tuple (I_X, s_X, f_X) where:*

- I_X *is a language over a finite alphabet.*
- s_X *is a function whose domain is I_X and, for each $a \in I_X$, the set $s_X(a)$ is finite.*
- f_X *is a function (the objective function) that assigns to each instance $a \in I_X$ and each $c_a \in s_X(a)$ a positive rational number $f_X(a, c_a)$.*

The elements of I_X are called *instances* of the problem X. For each instance $a \in I_X$, the elements of the finite set $s_X(a)$ are called *candidate* (or *feasible*) *solutions* associated with the instance a of the problem. For each instance $a \in I_X$ and each $c_a \in s_X(a)$, the positive rational number $f_X(a, c_a)$ is called *solution value* for c_a. The function f_X provides the criterion to determine the *best* solution.

For example, the *Minimum Vertex Cover* problem is a combinatorial optimization problem such that I_X is the set of all undirected graphs, and for each undirected graph G, $s_X(G)$ is the set of all vertex covers of G; that is, each vertex cover of the graph is a candidate solution for the problem. The objective function f_X is defined as follows: for each undirected graph G and each vertex cover C of G, $f_X(G, C)$ is the cardinality of C.

Definition 2. *Let $X = (I_X, s_X, f_X)$ be a combinatorial optimization problem. An optimal solution for an instance $a \in I_X$ is a candidate solution $c \in s_X(a)$ associated with this instance such that,*

- *either for all $c' \in s_X(a)$ we have $f_X(a, c) \leq f_X(a, c')$ (and then we say that c is a minimal solution for a),*
- *either for all $c' \in s_X(a)$ we have $f_X(a, c) \geq f_X(a, c')$ (and then we say that c is a maximal solution for a).*

A *minimization* (respectively, *maximization*) *problem* is a combinatorial optimization problem such that each optimal solution is a minimal (respectively, maximal) solution.

That is, an optimization problem seeks the best of all possible candidate solutions, according to a simple cost criterion given by the objective function. For example, the *Minimum Vertex Cover* problem is a minimization problem because a minimal solution associated with an undirected graph G, provides one of the smallest vertex covers of G.

An *approximation computational device*, $\mathcal{D}$, for a combinatorial optimization problem, X, provides a candidate solution $c \in s_X(a)$ for each instance $a \in I_X$. If the provided solution is always optimal, then $\mathcal{D}$ is called an *optimization computational device* for X.

For instance, an approximation machine for the *Minimum Vertex Cover* problem needs only find some vertex cover associated with each undirected graph, whereas an optimization machine must always find a vertex cover with the least cardinality associated with each undirected graph.

Having in mind that until now polynomial time optimization algorithms have not be found for many presumably intractable problems (it is believed that this kind of solutions can never be found), it is convenient to find an approximation algorithm running in polynomial time and such that, for all problem instances the candidate solution given by the algorithm is *close*, in a sense, to an optimal solution.

4   Decision Problems

An important class of combinatorial optimization problems is the class of decision problems, that is, problems that require either an *yes* or a *no* answer.

Definition 3. *A decision problem, X, is a pair (I_X, θ_X) such that I_X is a language over a finite alphabet (whose elements are called instances) and θ_X is a total boolean function (that is, a predicate) over I_X.*

Therefore, a decision problem $X = (I_X, \theta_X)$ can be viewed as a combinatorial optimization problem $X = (I_X, s_X, f_X)$ where for each instance $a \in I_X$ we have the following:

- $s_X(a) = \{\theta_X(a)\}$ (the only possible candidate solution associated with instance a is 0 or 1, depending on the answer of the problem to a).
- $f_X(a, \theta_X(a)) = 1$.

Thus, each decision problem can be considered as a minimization (or maximization) problem.

There exists a natural correspondence between languages and decision problems in the following way. Each language L, over an alphabet Σ, has a decision problem, X_L, associated with it as follows: $I_{X_L} = \Sigma^*$, and $\theta_{X_L} = \{(x, 1) \mid x \in L\} \cup \{(x, 0) \mid x \notin L\}$; reciprocally, given a decision problem $X = (I_X, \theta_X)$, the language L_X over the alphabet of I_X corresponding to it is defined as follows: $L_X = \{a \in I_X \mid \theta_X(a) = 1\}$.

Usually, NP-completeness has been studied in the framework of decision problems. Many abstract problems are not decision problems, but combinatorial optimization problems, in which some value must be optimized (minimized or maximized). In order to apply the theory of NP-completeness to combinatorial optimization problems, we must consider them as decision problems.

We can transform any combinatorial optimization problem into a roughly equivalent decision problem by supplying a target/threshold value for the quantity to be optimized, and asking the question whether this value can be attained. Next we give two examples.

1. The *Minimum Vertex Cover Problem.*
   Optimization version: Given an undirected graph G, find the cardinality of a *minimal* set of a vertex cover of G.
   Decision version: Given an undirected graph G, and *a positive integer k*, determine whether or not G has a vertex cover of size *at most k*.
2. The *Common Algorithmic Problem* [10].
   Optimization version: given a finite set S and a family F of subsets of S, find the cardinality of a *maximal* subset of S which does not include any set belonging to F.
   Decision version: given a finite set S, a family F of subsets of S, and a positive integer k, we are asked whether there is a subset A of S such that the cardinality of A is *at least k*, and which does not include any set belonging to F.

If a combinatorial optimization problem can be *quickly* solved, then its decision version can be quickly solved as well (because we only need to compare the solution value with a threshold value). Similarly, if we can make clear that a decision problem is hard, we also make clear that its associated combinatorial optimization problem is hard.

For example, let A be a polynomial time algorithm for the optimization version of the Minimum Vertex Cover problem. Then we consider the following polynomial time algorithm for the decision version of the Minimum Vertex Cover problem: given an undirected graph G, and a positive integer k, if $k < A(G)$ (here $A(G)$ is the cardinality of a smallest vertex cover of G), then answer *no*; otherwise, the answer is *yes*.

Reciprocally, let B be a polynomial time algorithm for the decision version of the Minimum Vertex Cover problem. Then we consider the following polynomial time algorithm for the optimization version of the Minimum Vertex Cover problem: given an undirected graph G, repeatedly while $k \le$ number of vertices of G (starting from $k = 0$, and in the next step considering $k + 1$) we execute the algorithm A on input (G, k), until we reach a first *yes* answer, and then the result is k.

5   Solving Decision Problems

Recall that, in a natural way, each decision problems has associated a language over a finite alphabet. Next, we define the solvability of decision problems through the recognition of languages associated with them.

In order to specify the concept of solvability we work with an universal computing model: Turing machines.

Let M be a Turing machine such that the result of any halting computation is *yes* or *no*. Let L be a language over an alphabet Σ.

If M is a *deterministic* device (with Σ as working alphabet), then we say that M *recognizes* or *decides* L whenever, for any string a over Σ, if $a \in L$, then the answer of M on input a is *yes* (that is, M accepts a), and the answer is *no* otherwise (that is, M reject a).

If M is a *non-deterministic* Turing machine, then we say that M *recognizes* or *decides* L if the following is true: for any string a over Σ, $a \in L$ if and only if there exists a computation of M with input a such that the answer is *yes*. That is, an input string a is accepted by M if there is *an* accepting computation of M on input a. But now we do not have a mechanical criterion to reject an input string.

Recall that any deterministic Turing machine with multiple tapes can be simulated by a deterministic Turing machine with one tape with a polynomial loss of efficiency, whereas the simulation of non-determinism through determinism involves an exponential loss of efficiency.

In the context of computation theory, we consider a problem X to be solved when we have a *general* (definite) *method* (described in a model of computation) that works for any instance of the problem. From a practical point of view, such methods only run over a finite set of instances whose sizes depend on the available resources.

We say that a Turing machine M solves a decision problem X if M *recognizes* the language associated with X; that is, for any instance a of the problem: (1) in the deterministic case, the machine (with input a) output *yes* if the answer of the problem is *yes*, and the output is *no* otherwise; (2) in the non-deterministic case, some computation of the machine (with input a) output *yes* if the answer of the problem is *yes*.

Due to the fact that we represent the instances of abstract problems as strings we can consider their size in a natural manner: the size of an instance is the length of the string. Then, how do the resources required to execute a method increase according to the size of the instance? This is a relevant question in computational complexity theory.

6   The P Versus NP Problem

In order to solve an abstract problem by a computational device, problem instances must be represented (encoded) in an adequate way that the device understands.

Given a problem it is possible to use different *reasonable* encoding schemes to represent the instances (we do not attempt to define *reasonable*, however informally we say that *reasonable* means [8] to codify instances in a concise manner, without irrelevant information, and the numbers occurring in them should be represented in binary, or any fixed base other than 1). It is easy to prove that the input sizes that different reasonable encoding schemes determine differ, at most, polynomially from one another.

Recall that complexity classes provide a way to group decision problems of similar computational complexity.

P is the class of all decision problems solvable (or languages recognized) by some deterministic Turing machine in a time bounded by a polynomial on the size of the input. Having in mind that all *reasonable* deterministic computational models are polynomially equivalent (that is, any one of them can simulate another with only a polynomial loss of efficiency), this class is the same for all models of computation that are polynomially equivalent to the deterministic Turing machine with one tape. Moreover, informally speaking, **P** corresponds to the class of problems having a *feasible* algorithm that gives an answer in a *reasonable* time; that is, problems that are realistically solvable on a machine (even for large instances of the problem).

NP is the class of all decision problems solvable in a polynomial time by non-deterministic Turing machines; that is, for every accepted input there exists at least one accepting computation taking an amount of steps bounded by a polynomial on the length of the input. This class is invariant for all reasonable non-deterministic computational models because all of them are polynomially equivalent.

Every deterministic Turing machine can be considered as a non-deterministic one, so we have $\mathbf{P} \subseteq \mathbf{NP}$. In terms of the previously defined classes, the **P** *versus* **NP** problem can be expressed as follows: is it verified the relation $\mathbf{NP} \subseteq \mathbf{P}$? That is, the **P** versus **NP** problem is the problem of determining whether every language recognized by some non-deterministic Turing machine in polynomial time is also can be recognized by some deterministic Turing machine in polynomial time.

The $\mathbf{P} \overset{?}{=} \mathbf{NP}$ question is one of the outstanding open problems in theoretical computer science. The relevance of this question is not only the inherent pleasure of solving a mathematical problem, but in this case an answer to it would provide information of high economical interest. On the one hand, a negative answer to this question would confirm that the majority of current cryptographic systems are secure from a practical point of view. On the other hand, a positive answer would not only show the uncertainty about the secureness of these systems, but also this kind of answer is expected to come together with a general procedure provides a deterministic algorithm solving most of **NP**-complete problem in polynomial time (furthermore, mathematics would be *transformed* because real computers will be able to find a formal proof of any theorem which has a proof of reasonable length).

In the last years several computing models using powerful tools from nature have been developed (because of this, they are known as *bio-inspired* models) and several solutions in polynomial time to problems from the class **NP** have been presented, making use of non-determinism and/or of an exponential amount of space. This is the reason why a practical implementation of such models (in biological, electronic, or other mediums) could provide a significant advance in the resolution of **NP**-complete problems.

7 Strongly NP–Complete Problems

The *Subset Sum* problem is the following: given a finite set A, a weight function, $w : A \to \mathbf{N}$, and a constant $k \in \mathbf{N}$, determine whether or not there exists a subset $B \subseteq A$ such that $w(B) = k$.

It is well known that *Subset Sum* can be solved in time $O(n \cdot k)$, using a dynamic programming algorithm. Hence, that algorithm is polynomial in the number of input items n and the magnitude of the items k. But such a algorithm is not a polynomial algorithm because its time bound is not a polynomial function on the size of the input (that is, of the order $\Omega(n \cdot \log k)$). Then we say that such a algorithm is *pseudo-polynomial*, and that the problem can be solved in *pseudo-polynomial time*. Nevertheless if we represent the input in *unary* form then that algorithm becomes a polynomial algorithm.

Definition 4. *An algorithm that solves a problem X will be called a pseudo-polynomial time algorithm for X if its running time would be polynomial if all input numbers associated with each instance were expressed in unary notation.*

The *Knapsack* and *Partition* problems are also **NP**–complete problems that can be solved by a pseudo-polynomial time algorithm.

Often, problems which can be solved in pseudo-polynomial time are also called *weakly **NP**–complete* problems. The existence of a pseudo-polynomial time algorithm for a given **NP**–complete problem illustrate that the problem is not so *intractable* after all.

Thus it is important to determine whether a problem is weakly **NP**–complete, or whether it has the following stronger property.

Definition 5. *A problem is said to be **NP**–complete in the strong sense if the variant of it in which any instance of size n is restricted to contain integers of size at most $p(n)$, where p is a polynomial, remains **NP**–complete.*

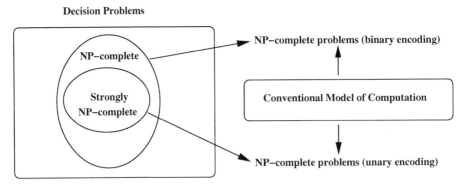

Fig. 1. NP–Completeness and codification of instances

That is, the strongly **NP**–complete problems remains **NP**–complete even if all numbers in the input are written in unary notation.

For example, the decision version of the *Minimum Vertex Cover* problem is a strongly **NP**–complete problem since the numbers in the input (an undirected graph) are bounded by a polynomial in the number of vertices (input size).

Other strongly **NP**–complete problems are the following: *3–Partition*, *Sat*, *Clique*, *HPP* (Hamiltonian Path Problem), *TSP* (Travelling Salesman Problem), and *Bin Packing*.

What happens if a strongly **NP**–complete problem can be solved by a pseudo-polynomial time algorithm? Let X be such a problem. Then the variant Y of it in which all input numbers of X are written in unary notation is also **NP**–complete. Moreover, if A is a pseudo-polynomial time algorithm solving X, then it is also a polynomial time algorithm that solves Y. Hence, **P=NP**.

Theorem 1. *The following propositions are equivalent:*

1. **P = NP**.
2. Every strongly **NP**–*complete problem can be solved by a pseudo-polynomial time algorithm.*
3. There exists a strongly **NP**–*complete problem that can be solved by a pseudo-polynomial time algorithm.*

Thus, to prove **P=NP** suffices to find a strongly **NP**–complete problem solvable in pseudo-polynomial time. Recall that the concept of solvability above mentioned is formally associated with deterministic Turing machines.

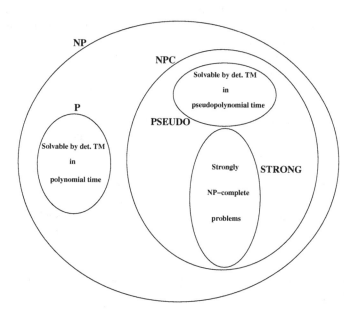

Fig. 2. Kinds of NP–complete problems

However, P systems take multisets as input and handle them through computations. Hence the inputs in P systems are provided in *unary*, so it is necessary to analyze with more details when it is said that a problem is polynomial-time solvable in the framework of membrane computing (particularly, concerning the size of the problem instances).

In this context we can say that polynomial solutions to **NP**–complete problems in the framework of membrane computing, can be considered, in a sense, as *pseudo-polynomial* solutions in the classical sense.

8   Recognizer Membrane Systems

Membrane computing is a recent branch of natural computing initiated in [23]. It has been developed basically from a theoretical point of view.

Membrane systems – usually called P systems – are distributed parallel computing models inspired by the structure and functioning of living cells.

Membrane systems have several *syntactic* ingredients: a *membrane structure* consisting of a hierarchical arrangements of membranes embedded in a *skin* membrane, and delimiting *regions* or compartments where multisets of *objects* and sets (eventually empty) of (evolution) *rules* are placed.

Also, P systems have two main *semantic* ingredients: their inherent *parallelism* and *non-determinism*. The objects inside the membranes can evolve according to given rules in a synchronous (in the sense that a global clock is assumed), parallel, and non-deterministic manner.

Can this parallelism and non-determinism be used to solve hard problems in a feasible time? The answer is affirmative, but we must point out two considerations. On the one hand, we have to deal with the non-determinism in such a way that the solutions obtained from these devices are algorithmic solutions in the classic sense; that is, the answers of the computations of the system must be reliable. On the other hand, the drastic decrease of the execution time from an exponential to a polynomial one is not achieved for free, but by the use of an exponential workspace (in the form of membranes or string–objects), although this space is created in polynomial (often linear) time.

In this paper we use membrane computing as a framework to attack the resolution of decision problems. In order to solve this kind of problems and having in mind the relationship between the solvability of a problem and the recognition of the language associated with it, we consider P systems as *recognizer languages* devices.

Moreover, for technical reasons we only work with devices such that all computations halt, and such that the result (*yes* or *no* answer, because we deal with recognition of strings) is collected in the environment (and in the last step of the computation).

All these restrictions make more difficult the process of designing families of recognizer P systems to solve decision problems.

Definition 6. *A recognizer P system is a P system with external output such that:*

1. *The working alphabet contains two distinguished elements* yes *and* no.
2. *All computations halt.*
3. *If C is a computation of the system, then either object* yes *or object* no *(but not both) must have been released into the environment, and only in the last step of the computation.*

In recognizer P systems, we say that a computation $\mathcal{C}$ is an *accepting computation* (respectively, *rejecting computation*) if the object *yes* (respectively, *no*) appears in the environment associated with the corresponding halting configuration of $\mathcal{C}$. Hence, these devices send to the environment an accepting or rejecting answer, in the end of their computations.

If we want these kind of systems to properly solve decision problems and capture the true algorithmic concept, it is necessary to require a condition of *confluence*; that is, the system must always give the same answer. In order to accept or reject a string it should be enough to read the answer of *any* computation of the system. In this manner, an observer outside the system can identify the exact moment when the system halts, and know the answer.

Since P systems work in a non-deterministic manner, we need to adapt the usual definition of acceptance in non-deterministic Turing machines.

9   Soundness and Completeness

In order to assure that a family of recognizer P systems solves a decision problem, two main properties must to be proved: for each instance of the problem,

(a) if *there exists an* accepting computation of the membrane system processing it, answering *yes*, then the problem also answer *yes* for that instance (*soundness*);
(b) if the problem answers *yes*, then *any* computation of the system processing that instance, answer *yes* (*completeness*).

If we demand that the family of membrane systems is sound and complete, then it satisfies a condition of *confluence*: every computation of a system from the family has the same output.

Next, we formalize these ideas in the following definition.

Definition 7. *Let* $X = (I_X, \theta_X)$ *be a decision problem. Let* $\mathbf{\Pi} = (\Pi(w))_{w \in I_X}$ *be a family of recognizer membrane systems without input.*

- *We say that the family* $\mathbf{\Pi}$ *is sound with regard to* X *if the following is true: for each instance of the problem* $w \in I_X$, *if there exists an accepting computation of* $\Pi(w)$, *then* $\theta_X(w) = 1$.
- *We say that the family* $\mathbf{\Pi}$ *is complete with regard to* X *if the following is true: for each instance of the problem* $w \in I_X$, *if* $\theta_X(w) = 1$, *then every computation of* $\Pi(w)$ *is an accepting computation.*

The soundness property means that if we obtain an *acceptance response* of the system (associated with an instance) through some computation, then the answer of the problem (for that instance) is *yes*. The completeness property means that if we obtain an *affirmative* response to the problem, then any computation of the system must be an accepting one.

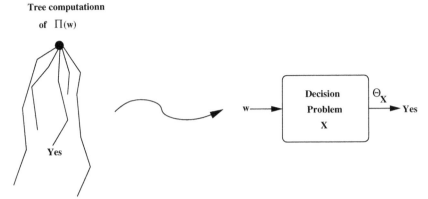

Fig. 3. Soundness of a family of P systems without input

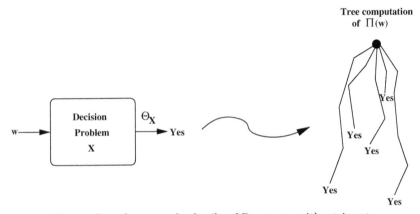

Fig. 4. Completeness of a family of P systems without input

These concepts can be extended to families of recognizer P systems *with input membrane* in a natural way, but in this case a P system belonging to the family can process several instances of the problem provided that an appropriate input, depending on the instance, is supplied to the system.

Definition 8. *Let* $X = (I_X, \theta_X)$ *be a decision problem. Let* $\mathbf{\Pi} = (\Pi(n))_{n \in \mathbf{N}}$ *be a family of recognizer membrane systems with input. A polynomial encoding of* X *in* $\mathbf{\Pi}$ *is a pair* (cod, s) *of polynomial time computable functions over* I_X *such that for each instance* $w \in I_X$, $s(w)$ *is a natural number and* $cod(w)$ *is an input multiset of the system* $\Pi(s(w))$.

Definition 9. *Let* $X = (I_X, \theta_X)$ *be a decision problem. Let* $\mathbf{\Pi} = (\Pi(n))_{n \in \mathbf{N}}$ *be a family of recognizer membrane systems with input. Let* (cod, s) *be a polynomial encoding of* X *in* $\mathbf{\Pi}$.

- *We say that the family* $\mathbf{\Pi}$ *is sound with regard to* (X, cod, s) *if the following is true: for each instance of the problem* $w \in I_X$, *if there exists an accepting computation of* $\Pi(s(w))$ *with input* $cod(w)$, *then* $\theta_X(w) = 1$.
- *We say that the family* $\mathbf{\Pi}$ *is complete with regard to* (X, cod, s) *if the following is true: for each instance of the problem* $u \in I_X$, *if* $\theta_X(u) = 1$ *then every computation of* $\Pi(s(u))$ *with input* $cod(u)$ *is an accepting computation.*

The soundness property means that if given an instance we obtain an *acceptance response* of the system associated with it (and individualized by the appropriate input multiset) through some computation, then the answer of the problem (for that instance) is *yes*. The completeness property means that if we obtain an *affirmative* response to the problem, then any computation of the system associated with it (and individualized by the appropriate input multiset) must be an accepting one.

10   Polynomial Complexity Classes in Membrane Systems

Next, we consider different complexity classes in the framework of recognizer membrane systems.

10.1   Recognizer Membrane Systems Without Input

The first results about *solvability* of **NP**–complete problems in polynomial time (even linear) by membrane systems were given by Gh. Păun [25], C. Zandron et al. [43], S.N. Krishna et al. [12], and A. Obtulowicz [16] in the framework of P systems that lack an input membrane. Thus, the constructive proofs of such results design *one* system for *each* instance of the problem.

In this context, next we define polynomial complexity classes in recognizer membrane systems without input. In order to solve a decision problem we need, then, to associate with each instance of the problem a system which decides the instance. We impose these systems to be *confluent* in the following sense: an instance of the problem will have a positive answer if and only if *every* (or, equivalently, there exists a) computation of the corresponding system is an accepting computation.

We also demand that *every* computation is bounded, in execution time, by a polynomial function. This is because we do not only want to obtain the same answer, independently of the chosen computation, but that all the computations consume, at most, the same amount of resources (in time).

Definition 10. *Let* $\mathcal{R}$ *be a class of recognizer P systems without input membrane. A decision problem* $X = (I_X, \theta_X)$ *is solvable in polynomial time by a family* $\mathbf{\Pi} = (\Pi(w))_{w \in I_X}$, *of P systems of type* $\mathcal{R}$, *and we denote it by* $X \in \mathbf{PMC}^*_{\mathcal{R}}$, *if the following is true:*

- *The family* $\mathbf{\Pi}$ *is polynomially uniform by Turing machines; that is, there exists a deterministic Turing machine working in polynomial time which constructs the system* $\Pi(w)$ *from the instance* $w \in I_X$.

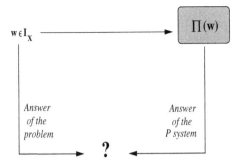

Fig. 5. Complexity class for membrane systems without input

– *The family* **Π** *is polynomially bounded; that is, there exists a polynomial function $p(n)$ such that for each $w \in I_X$, all computations of $\Pi(w)$ halt in at most $p(|w|)$ steps.*
– *The family* **Π** *is sound and complete with regard to X.*

Note that in this complexity class we consider two different tasks: the first one is the construction of the family, which we require to be done in polynomial time (sequential time by deterministic Turing machines). The second one is the execution of the systems of the family, in which we imposed that the total number of steps performed by their computations are bounded by the function g (parallel time by non-deterministic membrane systems).

As a direct consequence of working with recognizer membrane systems is the fact that these complexity classes are closed under complement.

Moreover, the complexity classes are closed under polynomial time reduction, in the classical sense. Recall that if $X = (I_X, \theta_X)$ and $Y = (I_Y, \theta_Y)$ are decision problems, then we say that X is reducible to Y in polynomial time if there exists a polynomial time function f from I_X to I_Y verifying the following condition: for each $w \in I_X$ we have $\theta_X(w) = 1$ if and only if $\theta_Y(f(w)) = 1$.

Proposition 1. *Let $\mathcal{R}$ be a class of recognizer P systems without input membrane. Let X and Y be two decision problems such that X is reducible to Y in polynomial time. If $Y \in \mathbf{PMC}^*_{\mathcal{R}}$, then $X \in \mathbf{PMC}^*_{\mathcal{R}}$.*

The *Hamiltonian Path Problem* can be solved in *quadratic time* by a family $\mathcal{R}$ of recognizer P systems without input in an uniform way (see [26]). Then $\mathbf{NP} \subseteq \mathbf{PMC}^*_{\mathcal{R}}$.

10.2   Recognizer Membrane Systems with Input

A computation of a Turing machine starts when the machine is in the initial state and we "write" a string in the input tape of the machine. Then, the machine starts to compute according to the transition function. In the definitions of basic P systems that have been initially considered, there is no membrane in which we can "introduce" input objects before allowing the system to begin to work. However, it is easy to consider input membranes in this kind of devices.

In this section we deal with recognizer membrane systems *with an input membrane* and we propose to solve hard problems in an *uniform* way in the following sense: all instances of a decision problem that have the same *size* (according to a prefixed polynomial time computable criterion) are processed by the same system, to which an appropriate input, that depends on the specific instance, is supplied.

Now, we formalize these ideas in the following definition.

Definition 11. *Let $X = (I_X, \theta_X)$ be a decision problem. We say that X is solvable in polynomial time by a family of recognizer membrane systems* with *input $\Pi = (\Pi(n))_{n \in \mathbf{N}}$, and we denote it by $X \in \mathbf{PMC}_\mathcal{R}$, if the following is true:*

- *The family Π is polynomially uniform by Turing machines; that is, there exists a deterministic Turing machine that constructs in polynomial time the system $\Pi(n)$ from $n \in \mathbf{N}$.*
- *There exists a polynomial encoding (cod, s) of X in Π such that:*
  - *The family Π is polynomially bounded with regard (X, cod, s); that is, there exists a polynomial function $p(n)$ such that for each $w \in I_X$ every computation of the system $\Pi(s(w))$ with input $cod(w)$ is halting and, moreover, it performs at most $p(|w|)$ steps.*
  - *The family Π is sound and complete with regard to (X, cod, s).*

Note that in the above definition and in order to decide about an instance, w, of a decision problem, first of all we need to compute the natural number $s(w)$, obtain the input multiset $cod(w)$, and construct the system $\Pi(s(w))$. This is properly a *pre-computation stage*, running in polynomial time expressed by a number of *sequential steps* in the framework of the Turing machines. After that, we execute the system $\Pi(s(w))$ with input $cod(w)$. This is properly the *computation stage*, also running in polynomial time, but now it is described by a number of *parallel steps*, in the framework of membrane computing.

As mentioned above, these complexity classes are closed under complement.

Moreover, these complexity classes are closed under polynomial time reduction, in the classical sense.

Proposition 2. *Let $\mathcal{R}$ be a class of recognizer P systems with input membrane. Let X and Y be two decision problems such that X is reducible to Y in polynomial time. If $Y \in \mathbf{PMC}_\mathcal{R}$, then $X \in \mathbf{PMC}_\mathcal{R}$.*

The *Satisfiability Problem* can be solved in linear time by a family $\mathcal{R}$ of recognizer P systems with input (see [36]). Then $\mathbf{NP} \subseteq \mathbf{PMC}_\mathcal{R}$.

11   (Non-deterministic) Polynomial Complexity Classes in Membrane Systems

According to the usual manner of considering acceptance by non-deterministic Turing machines, we can consider non-deterministic complexity classes in P systems without requiring them to be confluent, that is, *characterizing* the acceptance of an input string by the existence of an accepting computation.

Definition 12. *Let $\mathcal{R}$ be a class of recognizer P systems without input mem-brane. A decision problem $X = (I_X, \theta_X)$ is non-deterministically solvable in polynomial time by a family $\boldsymbol{\Pi} = (\Pi(w))_{w \in I_X}$, of P systems of type $\mathcal{R}$, and we denote it by $X \in \mathbf{NPMC}^*_{\mathcal{R}}$, if the following is true:*

- *The family $\boldsymbol{\Pi}$ is polynomially uniform by Turing machines.*
- *The family $\boldsymbol{\Pi}$ is polynomially bounded.*
- *The family $\boldsymbol{\Pi}$ is sound and complete with regard to X, in the following sense: for each instance $w \in I_X$ of the problem, $\theta_X(w) = 1$ if and only if there exists an accepting computation of $\Pi(w)$.*

Note that in this definition, in contrast to the corresponding definition for de-terministic complexity classes, we only demand that for each instance w with affirmative answer there exists at least *one* accepting computation of the system $\Pi(w)$, instead of demanding *every* computation of the system to be an accepting one.

Again, this class is closed under polynomial time reduction, but notice that it does not have to be closed under complement.

Let us denote by $\mathcal{T}$ the class of recognizer *transition* P systems (see [23]). In [36] we construct a family of recognizer transition P systems solving *HPP* (in the directed version with two distinguished nodes) in *linear time*, in a non-deterministic manner. That is, we have the following:

Proposition 3. *$HPP \in \mathbf{NPMC}^*_{\mathcal{T}}$, and $\mathbf{NP} \subseteq \mathbf{NPMC}^*_{\mathcal{T}}$.*

In a similar way we can define non-deterministic complexity classes for rec-ognizer membrane systems with input.

Definition 13. *Let $X = (I_X, \theta_X)$ be a decision problem. We say that X is non-deterministically solvable in polynomial time by a family of recognizer membrane systems with input $\boldsymbol{\Pi} = (\Pi(n))_{n \in \mathbf{N}}$, and we denote it by $X \in \mathbf{NPMC}_{\mathcal{R}}$, if the following is true:*

- *The family $\boldsymbol{\Pi}$ is polynomially uniform by Turing machines.*
- *There exists a polynomial encoding (cod, s) of X in $\boldsymbol{\Pi}$ such that:*
  - *The family $\boldsymbol{\Pi}$ is polynomially bounded with regard to (X, cod, s).*
  - *The family $\boldsymbol{\Pi}$ is sound and complete with regard to (X, cod, s), but now in the following sense: for each instance $w \in I_X$ of the problem, $\theta_X(w) = 1$ if and only if there exists an accepting computation of $\Pi(s(w))$ with input $cod(w)$.*

This class is closed under polynomial time reduction, but it does not have to be closed under complement.

In [36] we construct a family of recognizer transition P systems solving *SAT* in *constant time*, in a non-deterministic manner. That is, we have the following:

Proposition 4. *$SAT \in \mathbf{NPMC}_{\mathcal{T}}$, and $\mathbf{NP} \subseteq \mathbf{NPMC}_{\mathcal{T}}$.*

12 Characterizing the P ≠ NP Relation Through P Systems

In this section we show how it is possible to attack the **P** versus **NP** problem within the framework of membrane computing.

We consider deterministic Turing machines as language decision devices. That is, the machines halt over any string on the input alphabet, with the halting state being equal to the accepting state, in the case that the string belongs to the decided language, and with that state equal to the rejecting state, in the case that the string does not belong to that language.

It is possible to associate with a Turing machine a decision problem, which will permit us to say when such a machine is simulated by a family of P systems.

Definition 14. *Let TM be a Turing machine with input alphabet Σ_{TM}. The decision problem associated with TM is the problem $X_{TM} = (I, \theta)$, where $I = \Sigma_{TM}^*$, and for every $w \in \Sigma_{TM}^*$, $\theta(w) = 1$ if and only if TM accepts w.*

Obviously, the decision problem X_{TM} is solvable by the Turing machine TM.

Definition 15. *We say that a Turing machine TM is simulated in polynomial time by a family of recognizer P systems if $X_{TM} \in \mathbf{PMC}_{\mathcal{R}}$.*

In P systems, evolution rules, communication rules and rules involving dissolution are called *basic rules*. That is, by applying this kind of rules the size of the structure of membranes does not increase. Hence, it is not possible to construct an exponential working space in polynomial time using only basic rules in a P system.

In Chapter 9 of [40], and following the ideas from [41], we state that every deterministic Turing machine can be simulated in polynomial time by a family of systems of the class $\mathcal{R}$.

Proposition 5. *Let TM be a deterministic Turing machine working in polynomial time. Then TM can be simulated in polynomial time by a family of recognizer P systems using only basic rules.*

In [38], we proved the following result that can be considered as a reciprocal of the above proposition.

Proposition 6. *If a decision problem is solvable in polynomial time by a family of recognizer P systems (using only basic rules), then there exists a Turing machine solving it in polynomial time.*

From the above propositions, we establish characterizations of the **P** ≠ **NP** relation by means of the polynomial time unsolvability of **NP**–complete problems by families of recognizer P systems.

Theorem 2. *The following conditions are equivalent:*

(1) $\mathbf{P} \neq \mathbf{NP}$.
(2) There exists an $\mathbf{NP}$*–complete decision problem unsolvable in polynomial time by a family of of recognizer P systems using only basic rules.*
(3) Each $\mathbf{NP}$*–complete decision problem is unsolvable in polynomial time by a family of of recognizer P systems using only basic rules.*

From the constructive proof given in [38], we can deduce the following nice result characterizing the class $\mathbf{P}$.

Proposition 7. *Let* $\mathcal{T}$ *the class of recognizer transition P systems. Then* $\mathbf{P} = \mathbf{PMC}_{\mathcal{T}}$.

13   P Systems with Active Membranes

P systems with membrane division were introduced in [25], and in this variant the number of membranes can increase exponentially in polynomial time.

Next, we define P systems with active membranes using 2-division for elementary membranes, with polarizations, but without cooperation and without priorities (and without permitting the change of membrane labels by means of any rule).

Definition 16. *A P system with active membranes using 2-division for elementary membranes is a tuple* $\Pi = (\Sigma, H, \mu, \mathcal{M}_1, \ldots, \mathcal{M}_m, R)$, *where:*

1. *$m \geq 1$, is the initial degree of the system;*
2. *Σ is an alphabet of symbol-objects;*
3. *H is a finite set of labels for membranes;*
4. *μ is a membrane structure, of m membranes, labelled (not necessarily in a one-to-one manner) with elements of H;*
5. *$\mathcal{M}_1, \ldots, \mathcal{M}_m$ are strings over Σ, describing the initial multisets of objects placed in the m regions of μ;*
6. *R is a finite set of evolution rules, of the following forms:*
    (a) $[a \rightarrow \omega]_h^\alpha$ for $h \in H, \alpha \in \{+, -, 0\}$, $a \in \Sigma, \omega \in \Sigma^*$: This is an object evolution rule, associated with a membrane labelled with h and depending on the polarity of that membrane, but not directly involving the membrane.
    (b) $a [\ ]_h^{\alpha_1} \rightarrow [b]_h^{\alpha_2}$ for $h \in H$, $\alpha_1, \alpha_2 \in \{+, -, 0\}$, $a, b \in \Sigma$: An object from the region immediately outside a membrane labelled with h is introduced in this membrane, possibly transformed into another object, and, simultaneously, the polarity of the membrane can be changed.
    (c) $[a]_h^{\alpha_1} \rightarrow b [\ ]_h^{\alpha_2}$ for $h \in H$, $\alpha_1, \alpha_2 \in \{+, -, 0\}$, $a, b \in \Sigma$: An object is sent out from membrane labelled with h to the region immediately outside, possibly transformed into another object, and, simultaneously, the polarity of the membrane can be changed.
    (d) $[a]_h^\alpha \rightarrow b$ for $h \in H$, $\alpha \in \{+, -, 0\}$, $a, b \in \Sigma$: A membrane labelled with h is dissolved in reaction with an object. The skin is never dissolved.

(e) $[a]_h^{\alpha_1} \rightarrow [b]_h^{\alpha_2} [c]_h^{\alpha_3}$ *for* $h \in H$, $\alpha_1, \alpha_2, \alpha_3 \in \{+, -, 0\}$, $a, b, c \in \Sigma$: *An elementary membrane can be divided into two membranes with the same label, possibly transforming some objects and their polarities.*

These rules are applied according to the following principles:

- All the rules are applied in parallel and in a maximal manner. In one step, one object of a membrane can be used by only one rule (chosen in a non-deterministic way), but any object which can evolve by one rule of any form, must evolve.
- If a membrane is dissolved, its content (multiset and internal membranes) is left free in the surrounding region.
- If at the same time a membrane labelled by h is divided by a rule of type (e) and there are objects in this membrane which evolve by means of rules of type (a), then we suppose that first the evolution rules of type (a) are used, and then the division is produced. Of course, this process takes only one step.
- The rules associated with membranes labelled by h are used for all copies of this membrane. At one step, a membrane can be the subject of *only one* rule of types (b)-(e).

Note that these P systems have some important properties:

- They use three electrical charges.
- The polarization of a membrane can be modified by the application of a rule.
- The label of a membrane cannot be modified by the application of a rule.
- They do not use cooperation neither priorities.

Let us denote by $\mathcal{AM}$ the class of recognizer P systems with active membranes using 2-division for elementary membranes.
In this class of recognizer membrane systems:

- Some weakly **NP**–complete problems are solvable in polynomial time: for example, *Knapsack* ([31]), *Subset Sum* ([30]), *Partition* ([9]) $\in$ **PMC**$_{\mathcal{AM}}$.
- Some strongly **NP**–complete problems are solvable in polynomial time: for example, the following problems *SAT* ([36]), *Clique* ([3]), *Bin Packing* ([33]), *CAP* ([34]) belong to the complexity classes **PMC**$_{\mathcal{AM}}$.

Recall that polynomial time solutions to strongly **NP**–complete problems by recognizer membrane systems, can be considered as pseudo-polynomial solutions in the classical sense.

Having in mind that the complexity class **PMC**$_{\mathcal{AM}}$ is closed under complement and polynomial time reductions we have the following result.

Proposition 8. NP $\subseteq$ **PMC**$_{\mathcal{AM}}$, *and* **co-NP** $\subseteq$ **PMC**$_{\mathcal{AM}}$.

P. Sosik in [42] provides a semi–uniform efficient solution to *QBF* (satisfiability of quantified propositional formulas), a well known **PSPACE**–complete problem, in the framework of P systems with active membranes but using 2–division for non–elementary membranes. Hence we have the following result.

Proposition 9. *Let* $\mathcal{AM}^*$ *be the class of recognizer P systems with active membranes using 2-division for non–elementary membranes. Then,* **PSPACE** $\subseteq$ **PMC**$^*_{\mathcal{AM}^*}$.

This result shows that the complexity classes **PMC**$_{\mathcal{AM}}$ and **PMC**$^*_{\mathcal{AM}^*}$ are not precise enough to describe classical complexity classes below **NP**. Therefore, it is challenging to investigate weaker variants of P systems with active membranes able to characterize classical complexity classes (especially, the classes **NP** and **PSPACE**).

In [4], universality has been achieved removing the polarization of membranes from P systems with active membranes but allowing the change of membrane labels by means of communication rules and membrane division rules. Moreover, in this framework it is possible to solve **NP**–complete problems (e.g., the *SAT* problem) in linear time.

Several efficient solutions to **NP**–complete problems have been obtained within the following variants of membrane systems with active membranes:

- P systems using 2–division for elementary membranes, without cooperation, without priorities, without label changing, but using only two electrical charges ([1], [39]).
- P systems using 2–division for elementary membranes, without cooperation, without priorities, without changing of membrane labels, without polarizations, but using bi–stable catalysts ([32]).
- P systems without polarizations, without cooperation, without priorities, without label changing, without division, but using three types of membrane rules: separation, merging, and release ([19]).
- P systems with separation rules instead of division rules, in two different cases: in the first, using polarizations and separation rules; and in the second one, without polarizations, without change of membrane labels but using separation rules with change of membrane labels ([20]).

It is easy to obtain solutions to **NP**–complete problems through P systems with active membranes using 2-division for elementary membranes, without polarizations, without priorities, without label changing possibilities, but using cooperation (or trading cooperation by priority).

But, what happens if we consider only recognizer P systems with active membranes using 2-division for elementary membranes, without polarizations, without cooperation, without priority, and without changing of membrane labels? Let $\mathcal{AM}^0$ be the class of recognizer P systems of this kind.

What is exactly the class of decision problems solvable in polynomial time by families of systems belonging to $\mathcal{AM}^0$? Is the relation **P** = **PMC**$_{\mathcal{AM}^0}$ true?

Another interesting questions about the relationship between classical and cellular complexity classes are the following ones:

Question 1: Is there a classical complexity class $\mathcal{C}$, such that $\mathcal{C}$ = **PMC**$_{\mathcal{AM}}$?
Question 2: Given a classical complexity class $\mathcal{C}$, determine a (minimal in a descriptive sense) class of recognizer P systems $\mathcal{F}$ such that $\mathcal{C}$ = **PMC**$_{\mathcal{F}}$?

14   Conclusions

In this paper, some polynomial complexity classes in recognizer membrane systems, without or with input, and capturing the "classical" deterministic and nondeterministic modes of computation, have been introduced.

The complexity classes corresponding to membrane systems without input (respectively, with input) provide the general framework to design solutions to decision problems in a *semi–uniform* (respectively, *uniform*) way.

In this context we have proven that membrane computing offers a new way to attack the **P** versus **NP** problem.

The convenience of characterizing classical complexity classes through these new classes is an interesting topic in order to study the minimal ingredients required, from membrane systems point of view, to obtain certain *computational efficiency*.

Acknowledgement

The author wish to acknowledge the support of the project TIC2002-04220-C03-01 of the Ministerio de Ciencia y Tecnología of Spain, cofinanced by FEDER funds.

References

1. A. Alhazov, R. Freund, Gh. Păun, P systems with active membranes and two polarizations. *Proceedings of the Second Brainstorming Week on Membrane Computing* (Gh. Păun, A. Riscos, A. Romero, F. Sancho, eds.), Report RGNC 01/04, 2004, 20–35.
2. A. Alhazov, T.-O. Ishdorj, Membrane operations in P systems with active membranes. *Proceedings of the Second Brainstorming Week on Membrane Computing* (Gh. Păun, A. Riscos, A. Romero, F. Sancho, eds.), Report RGNC 01/04, 2004, 37–52.
3. A. Alhazov, C. Martín–Vide, L. Pan, Solving graph problems by P systems with restricted elementary active membranes. *Aspects of Molecular Computing* (N. Jonoska, Gh. Păun, G. Rozenberg, eds.), Lecture Notes in Computer Science, 2950 (2004), 1–22.
4. A. Alhazov, L. Pan, Gh. Păun, Trading polarizations for labels in P systems with active membranes. *Acta Informatica*, to appear.
5. J. Castellanos, Gh. Păun, A. Rodríguez–Patón, P systems with worm–objects. *IEEE 7th International Conference on String Processing and Information Retrieval, SPIRE 2000*, La Coruña, Spain, 64–74.
6. A. Cordón–Franco, M.A. Gutiérrez–Naranjo, M.J. Pérez–Jiménez, F. Sancho–Caparrini, Implementing in Prolog an effective cellular solution for the Knapsack problem. *Membrane Computing* (C. Martín-Vide, Gh. Păun, G. Rozenberg, A. Salomaa, eds.), Lecture Notes in Computer Science, 2933 (2004), 140-152.
7. E. Czeiler, Self–activating P systems. *Membrane Computing* (Gh. Păun, G. Rozenberg, A, Salomaa, C. Zandron, eds.), Lecture Notes in Computer Science, 2597 (2003), 234–246.
8. M.R. Garey, D.S. Johnson, *Computers and Intractability. A Guide to the Theory of NP-Completeness.* W.H. Freeman and Company, New York, 1979.

9. M.A. Gutiérrez–Naranjo, M.J. Pérez–Jiménez, A. Riscos–Núñez, A fast P system for finding a balanced 2-partition. *Soft Computing*, in press.

10. T. Head, M. Yamamura, S. Gal, Aqueous computing: writing on molecules. *Proceedings of the Congress on Evolutionary Computation 1999*, IEEE Service Center, Piscataway, NJ, 1999, 1006–1010.

11. M. Ito, C. Martín–Vide, Gh. Păun, Characterization of Parikh sets of ET0L languages in terms of P systems. In *Words, Semigroups, and Transducers* (M. Ito, Gh. Păun, S. Yu, eds.), World Scientific, Singapore, 2001, 239–254.

12. S.N. Krishna, R. Rama, A variant of P systems with active membranes: Solving NP–complete problems. *Romanian Journal of Information Science and Technology*, 2, 4 (1999), 357–367.

13. S.N. Krishna, R. Rama, P systems with replicated rewriting. *Journal of Automata, Languages and Combinatorics*, 6, 1 (2001), 345–350.

14. S.N. Krishna, R. Rama, Breaking DES using P systems. *Theoretical Computer Science*, 299, 1-3 (2003), 495–508.

15. M. Madhu, K. Kristhivasan, P systems with membrane creation: Universality and efficiency. *Proceedings Third International Conference on Universal, Machines and Computations*, Chisinau, Moldova, 2001 (M. Margenstern, Y. Rogozhin, eds.), Lecture Notes in Computer Science, 2055 (2001), 276–287.

16. A. Obtulowicz, Deterministic P systems for solving SAT problem. *Romanian Journal of Information Science and Technology*, 4, 1–2 (2001), 551–558.

17. A. Obtulowicz, On P systems with active membranes: Solving the Integer Factorization problem in a polynomial time. In *Multiset Processing. Mathematical, Computer Science, and Molecular Computing Points of View* (C.S. Calude, Gh. Păun, G. Rozenberg, A. Salomaa, eds.), Lecture Notes in Computer Science, 2235 (2001), 267–285.

18. A. Obtulowicz, Note on some recursively family of P systems with active membranes. Submitted, 2004.

19. L. Pan, A. Alhazov, T.-O. Ishdorj, Further remarks on P systems with active membranes, separation, merging, and release rules. *Proceedings of the Second Brainstorming Week on Membrane Computing* (Gh. Păun, A. Riscos, A. Romero, F. Sancho, eds.), Report RGNC 01/04, 2004, 316–324.

20. L. Pan, T.-O. Ishdorj, P systems with active membranes and separation rules. *Journal of Universal Computer Science*, 10, 5 (2004), 630–649.

21. L. Pan, C. Martín–Vide, C. Solving multiset 0–1 knapsack problem by P systems with input and active membranes. *Proceedings of the Second Brainstorming Week on Membrane Computing* (Gh. Păun, A. Riscos, A. Romero, F. Sancho, eds.), Report RGNC 01/04, 2004, 342–353.

22. A. Păun, On P systems with membrane division. In *Unconventional Models of Computation* (I. Antoniou, C.S. Calude, M.J. Dinneen, eds.), Springer, London, 2000, 187–201.

23. Gh. Păun, Computing with membranes, *Journal of Computer and System Sciences*, 61, 1 (2000), 108–143, and *Turku Center for Computer Science-TUCS Report* Nr. 208, 1998.

24. Gh. Păun, Computing with membranes: Attacking **NP**–complete problems. In *Unconventional Models of Computation* (I. Antoniou, C.S. Calude, M.J. Dinneen, eds.), 2000, 94–115.

25. Gh. Păun, P systems with active membranes: Attacking **NP**–complete problems. *Journal of Automata, Languages and Combinatorics*, 6, 1 (2001), 75–90.

26. Gh. Păun, *Membrane Computing. An Introduction*, Springer-Verlag, Berlin, 2002.

27. Gh. Păun, M.J. Pérez–Jiménez, A. Riscos–Núñez, P systems with tables of rules. *Theory is Forever. Essays Dedicated to Arto Salomaa on the Ocassion of His 70th Birthday* (J. Karhumaki, H. Maurer, Gh. Păun, G. Rozenberg, eds.), Lecture Notes in Computer Science, 3113 (2004), 235-249.

28. Gh. Păun, G. Rozenberg, A guide to membrane computing. *Theoretical Computer Science*, 287 (2002), 73–100.

29. Gh. Păun, Y. Suzuki, H. Tanaka, T. Yokomori, On the power of membrane division in P systems. *Theoretical Computer Science*, 324, 1 (2004), 61–85.

30. M.J. Pérez–Jiménez, A. Riscos–Núñez, Solving the Subset-Sum problem by P systems with active membranes. *New Generation Computing*, in press.

31. M.J. Pérez–Jiménez, A. Riscos–Núñez, A linear time solution to the Knapsack problem using active membranes. *Membrane Computing* (C. Martín-Vide, Gh. Păun, G. Rozenberg, A. Salomaa, eds.). Lecture Notes in Computer Science, 2933 (2004), 250–268.

32. M.J. Pérez–Jiménez, F.J. Romero-Campero, Trading polarizations for bi-stable catalysts in P systems with active membranes. In this volume.

33. M.J. Pérez–Jiménez, F.J. Romero-Campero, An efficient family of P systems for packing items into bins. *Journal of Universal Computer Science*, 10, 5 (2004), 650–670.

34. M.J. Pérez–Jiménez, F.J. Romero-Campero, Attacking the Common Algorithmic problem by recognizer P systems. *Pre-proceedings of the Machines, Computations and Universality, MCU'2004 (abstracts)*, September 21-26, 2004, Sankt Petesburg, p. 27.

35. M.J. Pérez–Jiménez, A. Romero-Jiménez, F. Sancho-Caparrini, *Teoría de la Complejidad en Modelos de Computación con Membranas*, Ed. Kronos, Sevilla, 2002.

36. M.J. Pérez–Jiménez, A. Romero–Jiménez, F. Sancho–Caparrini, Complexity classes in models of cellular computing with membranes. *Natural Computing*, 2, 3 (2003), 265–285.

37. M.J. Pérez–Jiménez, A. Romero–Jiménez, F. Sancho–Caparrini, Solving VALIDITY problem by active membranes with input. *Proceedings of the Brainstorming Week on Membrane Computing* (M. Cavaliere, C. Martín-Vide, Gh. Păun, eds.), Report GRLMC 26/03, 2003, 279–290.

38. M.J. Pérez–Jiménez, A. Romero–Jiménez, F. Sancho–Caparrini, The P versus NP problem through cellular computing with membranes. *Aspects of Molecular Computing. Essays Dedicated to Tom Head on the Ocassion of His 70th Birthday* (N. Jonoska, Gh. Păun, G. Rozenberg, eds.), Lecture Notes in Computer Science, 2950 (2004), 338–352.

39. A. Riscos-Núñez, *Programación celular: Resolución eficiente de problemas numéricos **NP**-completos*. PhD. Thesis, University of Seville, Spain, 2004.

40. A. Romero-Jiménez, *Complexity and Universality in Cellular Computing Models*, PhD. Thesis, University of Seville, Spain, 2003.

41. A. Romero-Jiménez, M.J. Pérez–Jiménez, Simulating Turing machines by P systems with external output. *Fundamenta Informaticae*, 49, 1-3 (2002), 273–287.

42. P. Sosik, The computational power of cell division. *Natural Computing*, 2, 3 (2003), 287–298.

43. C. Zandron, C. Ferreti, G. Mauri, Solving NP-complete problems using P systems with active membranes. In *Unconventional Models of Computation, UMC'2K* (I. Antoniou, C. Calude, M.J. Dinneen, eds.), Springer-Verlag, Berlin, 2000, 289–301.

44. C. Zandron, G. Mauri, C. Ferreti, Universality and normal forms on membrane systems. *Proceedings International Workshop on Grammar Systems, 2000* (R. Freund, A. Kelemenova, eds.), Bad Ischl, Austria, July 2000, 61–74.

LMNtal: A Language Model with Links and Membranes

Kazunori Ueda[1,2] and Norio Kato[1]

[1] Dept. of Computer Science, Waseda University,
3-4-1, Okubo, Shinjuku-ku, Tokyo 169-8555, Japan
{ueda, n-kato}@ueda.info.waseda.ac.jp
[2] CREST, Japan Science and Technology Corporation

Abstract. *LMNtal* (pronounced *"elemental"*) is a simple language model based on graph rewriting that uses logical variables to represent links and membranes to represent hierarchies. The two major goals of LMNtal are (i) to unify various computational models based on multiset rewriting and (ii) to serve as the basis of a truly general-purpose language covering various platforms ranging from wide-area to embedded computation. Another important contribution of the model is that it greatly facilitates programming with dynamic data structures.

1 Introduction

This work is motivated by two "grand challenges" in computational formalisms and programming languages. One is to have a computational model that unifies various paradigms of computation, especially those of concurrent computation and computation based on multiset rewriting. The other is to design and implement a programming language that covers a variety of computational platforms which are now developing towards both wide-area computation and nanoscale computation. As the first step towards these ends, this paper proposes a language model LMNtal (pronounced *"elemental"*) whose design goals are as follows:

1. *Simple* — to serve as a computational model as well as the basis of a practical programming language (hence a language *model*).
2. *Unifying and scalable* — to unify and reconcile various programming concepts. For instance, LMNtal treats
   (a) processes, messages, and data uniformly,
   (b) dynamic process structures and dynamic data structures uniformly, and
   (c) synchronous and asynchronous communication uniformly.
   Also, through such uniformity and resource-consciousness implied by (a) and (b) above, LMNtal is intended to be *scalable*, that is, be applicable to computational platforms of various physical scales.
3. *Easy to understand* — since we often use figures to explain and understand concurrent computation and programming with dynamic data structures, the language is designed so that computation can be viewed as diagram transformation.

G. Mauri et al. (Eds.): WMC5 2004, LNCS 3365, pp. 110–125, 2005.

4. *Fast* — optimizing compilation techniques are an important subject of the project, though this paper will focus on basic concepts.

We briefly describe the design background of LMNtal. The first author designed Guarded Horn Clauses (GHC) [14] in mid 1980's, a concurrent language that made use of the power of logical variables to feature channel mobility. Various type systems such as mode and linearity systems were later designed for GHC [15]. A lot of implementation efforts and techniques have been accumulated over the past two decades. Concurrent logic programming was generalized to concurrent constraint programming that allowed data domains other than finite trees, and a concurrent constraint language Janus [13] chose multisets (a.k.a. bags) as an important data domain. Another important generalization was Constraint Handling Rules (CHR) [8] that allowed multisets of atomic formulae in clause heads. CHR was designed as a language for defining constraint solvers, but at the same time it is one of the most powerful multiset rewriting languages.

Given these two extensions, a natural question arises as to whether (the multiset aspect of) the two extensions can be unified or embedded into each other. LMNtal was designed partly as a solution to this question. The language design was first published in [16]. It was then reviewed and revised through intensive discussions, receiving feedback from the implementation effort that ran in parallel. This paper reflects the latest design published in [17].

2   Overview of LMNtal and Related Work

The "four elements" of LMNtal are *logical links, multisets, nested nodes, and transformation* — hence the name LMNtal. This section elaborates these four elements, touching on related work.

1. **Logical links** — Structures of communicating processes can be represented as graphs in which nodes represent processes and links represent communication channels. Likewise, dynamic data structures can be represented using nodes and links. LMNtal treats them uniformly, that is, links represent both one-to-one communication channels between logically neighboring processes and logical neighborhood relations between data cells.

   Two major mechanisms in concurrency formalisms are name-based communication (as in the π-calculus) and constraint-based communication using logical, single-assignment variables (as in concurrent constraint programming [15]). Of these, links of LMNtal are closer to communication using logical variables in that (i) a message sent through a link changes the identity of the link and (ii) links are always private (i.e., third processes cannot access them). The first point is the key difference between LMNtal and the π-calculus. However, LMNtal links are different also from links of concurrent logic/constraint programming and CHR in that LMNtal has no notion of *instantiating* a link variable to a value.

LMNtal links are non-directional like chemical bonds. However, if links are always followed in a fixed direction to reach partners, the direction could be represented and "reconstructed" using appropriate type systems.

2. **Multisets of nested nodes** — There have been many diverse proposals of computational models equipped with the notion of multisets, early examples of which include Petri Nets and Production Systems. Concurrent processes naturally form multisets; Gamma [2] and Chemical Abstract Machines [3] are two typical computational models based on multiset rewriting; languages based on Linear Logic [10] take advantage of the fact that the both sides of a sequent are multisets; Linda's tuple spaces are multisets of tuples.

   However, not all of them feature multisets as first-class citizens; many of the programming languages featuring multisets (e.g., Gamma, Linda, CHR) incorporate them in a way different from other data structures. The advantage of having multisets as first-class citizens is that it gives us greater expressive power such as the nesting and the mobility of multisets.

   LMNtal features multiset hierarchies and encapsulation by allowing a multiset of nodes enclosed by a membrane to be viewed as a single node. Hierarchical multisets can be found in the ambient calculus [4], the P-system [12], the bigraphical model [11], as well as in the fields of knowledge representation [6].

   Hierarchization of multisets plays many important rôles, for instance in (i) logical management of computation (e.g., user processes running under administrative processes), (ii) physical management of computation (e.g., region-based memory management), and (iii) localization of computation (i.e., reaction rules placed at a certain "place" of the hierarchy of membranes can act only on processes at that place).

3. **Transformation** — LMNtal has a rewrite-rule-based syntax. There has been a lot of work on graph grammars transformation [1], including hierarchical graph transformation [5], but LMNtal's emphasis is on its design from the programming language point of view. The key design issue has been the proper treatment of free links in the presence of membrane structures.

   Rewrite rules specify reaction between elements of a multiset, but reaction between interlinked elements can be much more efficient (in finding partners) than reaction between unlinked elements.

LMNtal features both channel mobility and process mobility. In other words, it allows dynamic reconfiguration of process structures as well as the migration of nested computation.

3   Syntax of LMNtal

3.1   Links and Names

First of all, we presuppose two syntactic categories:

- *Links* (or *link variables*), denoted by X. In the concrete syntax, links are denoted by identifiers starting with capital letters.

$$
\begin{array}{lll}
P ::= & \mathbf{0} & \text{(null)} \\
 & |\quad p(X_1, \ldots, X_m) & (m \geq 0) \text{ (atom)} \\
 & |\quad P, P & \text{(molecule)} \\
 & |\quad \{P\} & \text{(cell) } \dagger \\
 & |\quad T :\text{-} T & \text{(rule)} \\[4pt]
T ::= & \mathbf{0} & \text{(null)} \\
 & |\quad p(X_1, \ldots, X_m) & (m \geq 0) \text{ (atom)} \\
 & |\quad T, T & \text{(molecule)} \\
 & |\quad \{T\} & \text{(cell) } \dagger \\
 & |\quad T :\text{-} T & \text{(rule)} \\
 & |\quad @p & \text{(rule context) } \dagger \\
 & |\quad \$p[X_1, \ldots, X_m \,|\, A] & \text{(process context) } \dagger \\
 & |\quad p(*X_1, \ldots, *X_m) & (m > 0) \text{ (aggregate) } \dagger \\[4pt]
A ::= & [] & \text{(empty) } \dagger \\
 & |\quad *X & \text{(bundle) } \dagger
\end{array}
$$

Fig. 1. Syntax of LMNtal (Lines with daggers (†) are not in Flat LMNtal)

- *Names* (including numbers), denoted by p. In the concrete syntax, names are denoted by identifiers different from links. The name "=" is the only reserved name in LMNtal.

3.2   Syntax

The two major syntactic categories of LMNtal are processes and process templates. The former is the subject of the language that evolves with program execution. The latter is used in reaction rules and can express *local contexts* of processes, namely contexts within particular cells.

The syntax of LMNtal is given in Figure 1. As usual, parentheses ( ) are used to resolve syntactic ambiguities. Commas for molecules connect tighter than the ":-" for rules. P and T have several syntactic conditions, as will be detailed in this section. The part of a process not included in any rule is called the *non-rule part* of the process. Cells can be arbitrarily nested. The part of a cell $\{P\}$ or $\{T\}$ not contained in nested cells is called the *toplevel* of $\{P\}$ or $\{T\}$, respectively.

We can think of a subset of LMNtal, *Flat LMNtal*, that does not allow cell hierarchies. The syntax of Flat LMNtal does not feature the lines with daggers (†).

The rest of this section explains processes, rules and process templates in more detail.

Processes. A process P must observe the following *link condition*:

Link Condition: Each link in the non-rule part of P can occur *at most twice*.

A link occurring only once in the non-rule part of P is called a *free link* of P. Each of the other links occurring in P is called a *local link* of P. A *closed process* is a process containing no free links.

Intuitively, **0** is an empty process; $p(X_1, \ldots, X_m)$ is an atom with m ordered links; P, P is parallel composition (or multiset union); $\{P\}$ is a process enclosed with the *membrane* $\{\ \}$; and $T :\text{-} T$ is a rewrite rule for processes.

An atom $X = Y$, called a *connector*, connects one side of the link X and one side of the link Y.

Note that the link condition never prevents us from composing two processes P_1 and P_2. When each of P_1 and P_2 satisfies the link condition but the composition P_1, P_2 does not, there must be a link occurring twice in one and at least once in the other. Since the former is a local link, we can always α-convert it to a fresh link (Section 4.1) to restore the link condition. The links used in rules are not considered in the link condition because they are understood to be local to the rules.

Rules and Process Templates. Rules have the form $T :\text{-} T$, where the T's are called *process templates*. The first and the second T are called the left-hand side (LHS) and the right-hand side (RHS), respectively.

Process templates have three additional constructs, namely *rule contexts*, *process contexts*, and *aggregates*. *Contexts* in LMNtal refer to the rest of the entities in the innermost surrounding membrane. Rule contexts are to represent multisets of rules, while process contexts are to represent multisets of cells and atoms.

A process context consists of a name $\$p$ and an argument $[X_1, \ldots, X_m | A]$. The argument of a LHS process context specifies the set of free links that the context must have. X_i denotes a specific link if it occurs elsewhere in the LHS and an arbitrary free link if it does not occur in the LHS. The final component A is called a *residual*. A residual of the form $*V$ receives the bundle of zero or more free links other than $X_1, \ldots, X_m$, and a residual $[]$ means that there should be no free links other than $X_1, \ldots, X_m$.

An aggregate represents a multiset of atoms with the same name, whose multiplicity coincides with the number of links represented by the argument bundles.

The precise semantics of all these additional contexts will be given in Section 4.

Rules have several syntactic side conditions. Firstly, process contexts and rule contexts in a rule must observe the following:

LHS Conditions:

1. A rule cannot occur in the LHS of a rule.
2. Aggregates cannot occur in the LHS of a rule.
3. Rule contexts and process contexts occurring in the LHS of a rule must occur within a cell.

Note that the first condition disallows the decomposition of rules. The third condition means that rule contexts and process contexts deal only with local contexts delimited by membranes.

Secondly, rules must satisfy the following *occurrence conditions* on links and other syntactic constructs:

Occurrence Conditions:

1. A link and a bundle occurring in a rule must occur exactly twice in the rule.
2. Links occurring in the argument of a process context must be pairwise distinct.
3. Bundles occurring in the LHS of a rule must be pairwise distinct.
4. A rule context and a process context occurring in a rule must occur exactly once in the LHS and must not occur in another rule occurring inside the rule.
5. The toplevel of each cell occurring in the LHS of a rule may have at most one process context and at most one rule context.

Condition 1 implies that a rule cannot have free links. Condition 2 is imposed because the links specify the *set* of free links to be owned by a process matching the process context. Condition 3 is imposed because a bundle in the LHS of a rule is to receive, rather than compare, a set of free links of the matching process. The "must occur once" condition in Condition 4 means that a rule context or a process context must receive a multiset of rules or a process upon application of the rule, and the "exactly once" condition means that they cannot be used to compare two contexts. Note that rule contexts and process contexts may occur more than once in the RHS of a rule. Condition 5 is to ensure that the values received by rule contexts and process contexts are uniquely determined.

In what concerns the links occurring in a rule L :- R, those occurring only in L are consumed links; those occurring only in R are links generated by the rule, and those occurring once in L and once in R are inherited links.

Finally, we introduce several *consistency conditions*:

Consistency Conditions:

1. The residuals of the process contexts with the same name in a rule must be either all empty ([]) or all bundles.
2. The arity m of the process contexts with the same name in a rule must coincide.
3. The process contexts having the same bundle must have the same name.
4. For each aggregate $p(*X_1, \ldots, *X_m)$ $(m > 0)$ in a rule, there must be a process context name q and each $*X_i$ must occur as the residual of a process context with the name q in the rule.

For example, the rule

```
{exch,$a[X,Y|[]]} :- {$a[Y,X|[]]}
```

satisfies Consistency Conditions 1 and 2 (Conditions 3 and 4 hold vacuously) and says that when a cell contains an atom exch and exactly two free links at its toplevel, the two free links are crossed and the atom exch is erased.

The rule

```
{kill,$a[|*X]} :- killed(*X)
```

satisfies Consistency Conditions 3 and 4 (the other conditions hold vacuously) and says that when a cell contains an atom kill at its toplevel, the cell is erased and each link crossing the membrane is terminated by a unary atom killed.

The above conditions do not allow dynamic composition of rules, but do allow (i) statically determined rules to be spawned dynamically and (ii) the set of rules inside a cell to be copied and migrated to another cell. Thus LMNtal enables the cell-wise compilation of the set of rules while providing certain higher-order features.

4   Operational Semantics

We first define structural congruence ($\equiv$) and then the reduction relation ($\longrightarrow$) on processes.

4.1   Structural Congruence

We define the relation $\equiv$ on processes as the minimal equivalence relation satisfying the rules shown in Figure 2. Two processes related by $\equiv$ are essentially the same and are convertible to each other in zero steps. Here, $[Y/X]$ is a *link substitution* that replaces X with Y.

(E1)–(E3) are the characterization of molecules as multisets. (E4) allows the renaming (α-conversion) of local names. Note that the link Y cannot occur free

---

(E1)	$\mathbf{0}, P \equiv P$	
(E2)	$P, Q \equiv Q, P$	
(E3)	$P, (Q, R) \equiv (P, Q), R$	
(E4)	$P \equiv P[Y/X]$	if X is a local link of P
(E5)	$P \equiv P' \Rightarrow P, Q \equiv P', Q$	
(E6)	$P \equiv P' \Rightarrow \{P\} \equiv \{P'\}$	
(E7)	$X = X \equiv \mathbf{0}$	
(E8)	$X = Y \equiv Y = X$	
(E9)	$X = Y, P \equiv P[Y/X]$	if P is an atom and X occurs in P
(E10)	$\{X = Y, P\} \equiv X = Y, \{P\}$	if exactly one of X and Y is a free link of P

Fig. 2. Structural congruence on LMNtal processes

$$(\text{R1}) \ \frac{P \longrightarrow P'}{P, Q \longrightarrow P', Q} \qquad (\text{R2}) \ \frac{P \longrightarrow P'}{\{P\} \longrightarrow \{P'\}} \qquad (\text{R3}) \ \frac{Q \equiv P \quad P \longrightarrow P' \quad P' \equiv Q'}{Q \longrightarrow Q'}$$

$$(\text{R4}) \quad \{X = Y, P\} \longrightarrow X = Y, \{P\} \quad (X \text{ and } Y \text{ are distinct and don't occur in } P)$$

$$(\text{R5}) \quad X = Y, \{P\} \longrightarrow \{X = Y, P\} \quad (X \text{ and } Y \text{ occur in the non-rule part of } P)$$

$$(\text{R6}) \quad T\theta, (T :- U) \longrightarrow U\theta, (T :- U)$$

Fig. 3. Reduction relation on LMNtal processes

in P for the link condition on $P[Y/X]$ to hold. (E5)–(E6) are structural rules that make $\equiv$ a congruence. (E7)–(E10) are concerned with connectors. (E7) says that a self-absorbed loop is equivalent to **0**, while (E8) expresses the symmetry of =. (E9) is an absorption law of =, which says that a connector can be absorbed by another atom (which can again be a connector). Because of the symmetry of $\equiv$, (E9) says that an atom can emit a connector as well. (E10) says that a connector can be moved across a membrane boundary as long as it does not change the number of free links of the membrane.

4.2   Reduction Relation

Computation proceeds by rewriting processes using rules collocated in the same "place" of the nested membrane structure.

We define the reduction relation $\longrightarrow$ on processes as the minimal relation satisfying the rules in Figure 3. Note that the right-hand side of $\longrightarrow$ must observe the link condition of processes.

Of the six rules, (R1)–(R3) are structural rules. (R1) says that reductions can proceed concurrently based on local reducibility conditions. Fine-grained concurrency of LMNtal originates from this rule. (R2) says that computation within a cell can proceed independently of the exterior of the cell. For a cell to evolve autonomously, it must contain its own set of rules. Computation of a cell containing no rules will be controlled by rules outside the cell. (R3) incorporates structural congruence into the reduction relation.

(R4) and (R5) deal with the interaction between connectors and membranes. (R4) says that, when a connector in a cell connects two links both coming from outside, the cell can expel the connector. (R5) says that, when a connector connects two links both entering the same cell, the connector itself can enter that cell.

(R6) is the key rule of LMNtal. The substitution θ is to represent what process (or multiset of rules) has been received by each process context (or rule context), respectively, and what multiset of atoms each aggregate represents. In Flat LMNtal, θ becomes unnecessary and (R6) is simplified to

$$(\text{R6}') \quad T, (T :- U) \longrightarrow U, (T :- U).$$

(R6′) describes the reaction between a process and a rule not separated by membranes.

Matching between a process and the LHS of a rule under (R6′) should generally be done by α-converting the rule using (E4) and (R3). The whole resulting process, namely $U, (T :\text{-} U)$ and its surrounding context, should observe the link condition, but this can always be achieved by α-converting $T :\text{-} U$ before use so that the local links in U won't cause name crashes with the context.

The substitution θ in (R6) is represented as a finite set of *substitution elements* of the form β_i/α_i (meaning that α_i is replaced by β_i), and should satisfy the following three conditions. In the third condition, we assume that the occurrences of the process context name $\$p$ in the RHS U are uniquely numbered, and that the function v is a one-to-one mapping from link names and natural numbers to link names.

1. The domain of θ is the set of all rule contexts, process contexts and aggregates occurring in the LHS T or in the non-rule part of the RHS U.
2. For each rule context $@p$ in T, θ must contain $P/@p$, where P is a sequence of rules.
3. For each process context $\$p[X_1,\ldots,X_m\,|\,A]$ in T, the following (i)–(iii) hold, where P is a process whose free links are $\{X_1,\ldots,X_{m+n}\}$ (if $A = [\,]$, then $n = 0$; otherwise $n \geq 0$), whose local links are $\{Z_1,\ldots,Z_\ell\}$, and which has no rules outside cells.

   (i) If $A = [\,]$, then
      (a) $P/\$p[X_1,\ldots,X_m] \in \theta$
      (b) For $\$p[Y_1,\ldots,Y_m]$ with the number h in the RHS U,

      $$P[v(Z_1,h)/Z_1,\ldots,v(Z_\ell,h)/Z_\ell,Y_1/X_1,\ldots,Y_m/X_m]$$
      $$/\,\$p[Y_1,\ldots,Y_m] \in \theta$$

   (ii) If $A = *V$, then
      (a) $P/\$p[X_1,\ldots,X_m\,|\,*V] \in \theta$
      (b) $v(V,i) = X_{m+i}$ for $1 \leq i \leq n$
      (c) For $\$p[Y_1,\ldots,Y_m\,|\,*W]$ with the number h in the RHS U,

      $$P[v(Z_1,h)/Z_1,\ldots,v(Z_\ell,h)/Z_\ell,Y_1/X_1,\ldots,Y_m/X_m,$$
      $$v(W,1)/X_{m+1},\ldots,v(W,n)/X_{m+n}]$$
      $$/\,\$p[Y_1,\ldots,Y_m\,|\,*W] \in \theta$$

      (d) For each $q(*V_1,\ldots,*V_k)$ in the non-rule part of U such that some V_i is V,

      $$(\,q(v(V_1,1),\ldots,v(V_k,1)),\,\ldots,q(v(V_1,n),\ldots,v(V_k,n))\,)$$
      $$/\,q(*V_1,\ldots,*V_k) \in \theta$$

   (iii) a free link of T occurring in an atom (i.e., not in process contexts) doesn't occur in P.

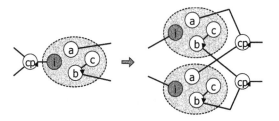

Fig. 4. Cell copying using process contexts and aggregates

Suppose the LHS of a rule contains a process context $p[X_1,\ldots,X_m|*V]$. When the RHS contains a process context of the same name, say $\$p[Y_1,\ldots,Y_m|*W]$, a process isomorphic to the process matched by the corresponding process context in the LHS is created. Its free links corresponding to $X_1,\ldots,X_m$ are connected to $Y_1,\ldots,Y_m$, respectively, and the free links corresponding to $*V$ are connected to the links represented by $*W$.

An aggregate $p(*V_1,\ldots,*V_m)$ represents as many copies of the m-ary atom p as the number of links denoted by the bundle $*V_i$. Each $*V_i$ must have the same origin with respect to the process context name (Consistency Condition 4); in other words, the other occurrences of the $*V_i$'s must all appear in process contexts with the same name. Occurrence Condition 4 implies that exactly one of $*V_1,\ldots,*V_m$ occurs in the LHS of a rule.

Let us give two examples. The LHS of the rule

$$\text{kill(S), \{i(S),\$p[|*P]\} :- killed(*P)}$$

can reduce the process

$$\text{kill(S), \{i(S),a(X),b(Y,Z),c(Z,U)\},}$$

by letting $\$p[|*P]$ receive $a(X),b(Y,Z),c(Z)$, and the process is reduced to

$$\text{killed(X), killed(Y).}$$

In this example, the membrane is used to delimit the process structure to be controlled, and the tag i( ) is attached to the message channel from outside the cell. The above rule says that, when a kill message is sent through the channel, the target cell is deleted and each free link owned by the cell is terminated by an atom killed.

Next, consider the process

$$\text{cp(S,S1,S2), \{i(S),a(X),b(Y,Z),c(Z)\}}$$

and the rule

$$\text{cp(S,S1,S2), \{i(S),\$p[|*P]\} :-}$$
$$\text{\{i(S1),\$p[|*P1]\}, \{i(S2),\$p[|*P2]\}, cp(*P,*P1,*P2) .}$$

Then the process is reduced to

```
{i(S1),a(X1),b(Y1,Z1),c(Z1)}, {i(S2),a(X2),b(Y2,Z2),c(Z2)},
cp(X,X1,X2), cp(Y,Y1,Y2) .
```

In short, the `cp` message makes two copies of the target cell and connects the free links of the copied cells and the original free links using ternary `cp` atoms (Figure 4).

5   Program Examples

5.1   Concatenating Lists

The skeleton of a linear list can be represented, using element processes c(ons) and a terminal process n(il), as $c(A_1, X_1, X_0), \ldots, c(A_n, X_n, X_{n-1}), n(X_n)$. Here, A_i is the link to the ith element and X_0 is the link to the whole list (from somebody else). This corresponds to a list formed by the constraints $X_0 = c(A_1, X_1), \ldots, X_{n-1} = c(A_n, X_n), X_n = n$ in (constraint) logic programming languages, except that the LMNtal list is a resource rather than a value. Two lists can be concatenated using the following two rules:

```
append(X0,Y,Z0), c(A,X,X0) :- c(A,Z,Z0), append(X,Y,Z)
    append(X0,Y,Z0), n(X0) :- Y=Z0
```

Figure 5 shows a graphical representation of the append program and its execution.

The above program has clear correspondence with **append** in GHC:

```
append(X0,Y,Z0) :- X0=c(A,X) | Z0=c(A,Z), append(X,Y,Z).
append(X0,Y,Z0) :- X0=n | Y=Z0.
```

but LMNtal has eliminated syntactic distinction between processes and data.

The above program resembles **append** in Interaction Nets [9]. Indeed, Lafont writes "our rules are clearly reminiscent of clauses in *logic programming*, especially in the use of variables (see the example of difference-lists), and our proposal could be related to PARLOG or GHC" [9]. LMNtal generalizes Interaction Nets by removing the restriction to binary interaction and allowing hierarchical processes.

5.2   Stream Merging

As in logic programming, streams can be represented as lists of messages, and n-to-1 communication by stream merging can be programmed as follows:

```
{i(X0),o(Y0),$p[|*Z]}, c(A,X,X0) :-
            c(A,Y,Y0), {i(X),o(Y),$p[|*Z]}
```

Here, the membrane { } of the left-hand side records n (≥ 1) input streams with the name i and one output stream with the name o. The process context

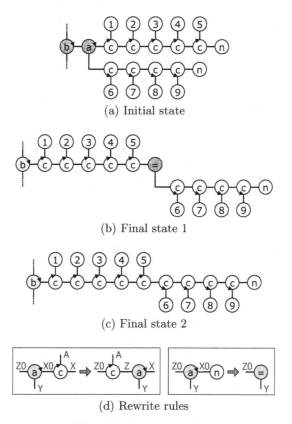

(a) Initial state

(b) Final state 1

(c) Final state 2

(d) Rewrite rules

Fig. 5. List concatenation

$p[|*Z]$ is to match the rest of the input streams and pass them to the RHS. Figure 6 shows a redex to which the above rewrite rule is applicable and the result of reduction.

5.3   Process Migration

Consider two cells that share a communication link. Suppose they run independently using individual sets of reaction rules most of the time but sometimes migrate processes to each other through the link. The rule for migration is given in an upper layer.

It is the rôle of the upper layer to determine the protocol of process migration, while the cells "hook" processes to be migrated on the communication link according to the protocol. Here we assume that the innermost cell containing $g(S, D)$ is to be migrated by the upper layer, where S and D are the source and the destination sides of the communication link, respectively (Figure 7).

```
{$s[S0|*S], @s, {g(S0,D0),$m[|*M],@m}}, {$d[D0|*D], @d} :-
        {$s[S|*S], @s}, {{s(S,D),$m[|*M],@m}, $d[D|*D], @d}
```

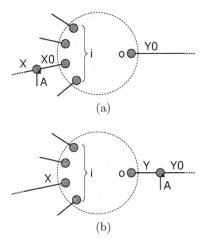

(a)

(b)

Fig. 6. Multiway stream merging

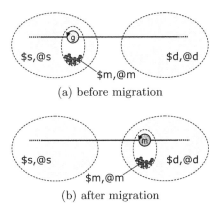

(a) before migration

(b) after migration

Fig. 7. Process migration

When @m is non-empty, the rule acts as active process migration; otherwise it acts as data migration. Note that the communication link between the source and the destination processes changes after migration. This is an important characteristic of logical links. The membrane delimiting migrated resources can be removed at the destination site.

5.4   Cyclic Data Structures

Most declarative languages handle lists and trees elegantly but cyclic data structures awkwardly. This is not the case with LMNtal. In LMNtal, a bidirectional circular buffer with n elements can be represented as

$$\mathbf{b}(S, X_n, X_0), \mathbf{n}(A_1, X_0, X_1), \ldots, \mathbf{n}(A_n, X_{n-1}, X_n),$$

where $\mathbf{b}$ is a header process, the A_i's are links to the elements, and S is the link from the client process. Operations on the buffer are sent through S as messages

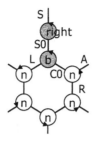

Fig. 8. Cyclic data structures

such as **left**, **right** and **put** (Figure 8). The reaction rules between messages and the buffer can be defined as follows:

```
left(S,S0), n(A,L,C0), b(S0,C0,R)  :- b(S,L,C), n(A,C,R)
right(S,S0), b(S0,L,C0), n(A,C0,R)  :- n(A,L,C), b(S,C,R)
          put(A,S,S0), b(S0,L,R)  :- n(A,L,C), b(S,C,R)
  . . .
```

Shape Types [7] are another attempt to facilitate manipulation of dynamic data structures. Interestingly, Shape Types took a dual approach, namely they used variables to represent graph nodes and names to represent links.

6   Concluding Remarks

We have presented a concise language model LMNtal, which has logical links, multisets, nested nodes (membranes), and transformation as its "big four" elements. LMNtal was inspired by communication using logical variables, and its principal goal as a concurrent programming language has been to unify processes, messages, and data. There are many languages and computation models that support multisets and/or graph rewriting, but LMNtal is unique in the design of link handling in the presence of membrane hierarchies.

CHR is another multiset rewriting language that features logical variables. While Flat LMNtal can be thought of as a linear fragment of CHR, LMNtal and CHR have many differences in the use of logical variables, control of reactions, intended applications, and so on. It is a challenging research topic to embed CHR into LMNtal.

Both P systems and LMNtal feature membrane hierarchies and rewrite rules local to membranes. One apparent difference between P systems and LMNtal is that LMNtal features logical links as another key construct. We can think of a fragment of LMNtal that allows only nullary atoms (atoms without links). This fragment is somewhat close to P systems, but one important design criteria of LMNtal has been that computation inside a cell cannot affect its environment, that is, a cell cannot export any process by itself. Instead, a cell communicates with its environment by spawning (within the cell) particular processes that can be recognized and handled by the rules in the environment.

We have released a prototype implementation in Java[1]. It features

- a construct for detecting inactive cells,
- built-in number types,
- the notion of type constraints for typechecking and comparison of numbers and symbols, and
- foreign language interface,

in addition to most of the constructs described in this paper.

Many things remain to be done. The most important issue in the language design is to equip it with useful type systems. We believe that many useful properties, for instance, shapes formed by processes and links, the directionality of links (i.e., whether links can be implemented as unidirectional pointers), and properties about free links of cells, can be guaranteed statically using type systems. Challenging topics in our implementation project include compact representation of processes and links, optimizing compilation of reaction rules, and parallel and distributed implementation. Since LMNtal is intended to unify various existing computational models, relating LMNtal to them by embedding them into LMNtal is another important research subject. When the embeddings are simple enough, LMNtal will be able to act as a common implementation language of various models of computation.

Last but not least, we should accumulate applications. Some interesting applications other than ordinary concurrent computation are graph algorithms, multi-agent systems, Web services, and programming by self-organization.

Acknowledgments

Discussions with the members of the programming language research group at Waseda University helped the development of the ideas described here. This work is partially supported by Grant-In-Aid for Scientific Research ((B)(2) 16300009, Priority Areas (C)(2)13324050 and (B)(2)14085205), MEXT and JSPS.

References

1. M. Andries et al., Graph Transformation for Specification and Programming. *Sci. Comput. Program.*, Vol. 34, No. 1 (1999), pp. 1–54.
2. J.-P. Banâtre, D. Le Métayer, Programming by Multiset Transformation. *Commun. ACM*, Vol. 35, No. 1 (1993), pp. 98–111.
3. G. Berry, G. Boudol, The Chemical Abstract Machine. In *Proc. POPL'90*, ACM, pp. 81–94.
4. L. Cardelli, A.D. Gordon, Mobile Ambients, in *Foundations of Software Science and Computational Structures*, Nivat, M. (ed.), LNCS 1378, Springer-Verlag, 1998, pp. 140–155.
5. F. Drewes, B. Hoffmann, D. Plump, Hierarchical Graph Transformation. *J. Comput. Syst. Sci.*, Vol. 64, No. 2 (2002), pp. 249–283.

---

[1] http://www.ueda.info.waseda.ac.jp/lmntal/

6. G. Engels, A. Schürr, Encapsulated Hierarchical Graphs, Graph Types, and Meta Types. *Electronic Notes in Theor. Comput. Sci.*, Vol. 1 (1995), pp. 75–84.
7. P. Fradet, D. Le Métayer, Shape Types. In *Proc. POPL'97*, ACM, 1997, pp. 27–39.
8. T. Frühwirth, Theory and Practice of Constraint Handling Rules. *J. Logic Programming*, Vol. 37, No. 1–3 (1998), pp. 95–138.
9. Y. Lafont, Interaction Nets. In *Proc. POPL'90*, ACM, pp. 95–108.
10. D. Miller, Overview of Linear Logic Programming, to appear in *Linear Logic in Computer Science*, Ehrhard, T., Girard, J.-Y., Ruet, P. and Scott, P. (eds.), Cambridge University Press.
11. R. Milner, Bigraphical Reactive Systems. In *Proc. CONCUR 2001*, LNCS 2154, Springer, 2001, pp. 16–35.
12. Gh. Păun, Computing with Membranes. *J. Comput. Syst. Sci.*, Vol. 61, No. 1 (2000), pp. 108–143.
13. V.A. Saraswat, K. Kahn, J. Levy, Janus: A Step Towards Distributed Constraint Programming. In *Proc. 1990 North American Conf. on Logic Programming*, MIT Press, 1990, pp. 431–446.
14. K. Ueda, Concurrent Logic/Constraint Programming: The Next 10 Years. In *The Logic Programming Paradigm: A 25-Year Perspective*, K.R. Apt, V.K. Marek, M. Truszczynski, D.S. Warren (eds.), Springer-Verlag, 1999, pp. 53–71.
15. K. Ueda, Resource-Passing Concurrent Programming. In *Proc. TACS 2001*, LNCS 2215, Springer, 2001, pp. 95–126.
16. K. Ueda, M. Kato, Programming with Logical Links: Design of the LMNtal Language. In *Proc. Third Asian Workshop on Programming Languages and Systems (APLAS 2002)*, 2002, pp. 115–126.
17. K. Ueda, M. Kato, The Language Model LMNtal. *Computer Software*, Vol. 21, No. 2 (2004), pp. 44-61 (in Japanese).

Executable Specifications of P Systems

Oana Andrei, Gabriel Ciobanu, and Dorel Lucanu

"A.I.Cuza" University of Iaşi, Faculty of Computer Science,
Iaşi, Romania
{oandrei, gabriel, dlucanu}@info.uaic.ro

Abstract. This paper presents a natural algebraic specification for the
P systems. The specification is executable in Maude, a software system supporting rewriting and equational logic. We define the P system
maximal parallel evolution as a specific rewriting strategy in Maude. By
extending the Maude rewriting semantics with this strategy, we provide
an operational semantics of the P systems. We present few examples of
specifying and executing simple P systems, describing how target indications, dissolving and priorities are handled. Moreover, the Maude system
allows the verification of various properties of the P systems expressed
as linear temporal logic formulas by using a model checker.

1 Introduction

Membrane computing is a branch of natural computing which studies distributed
and parallel computing models abstracted from the living cell structure and functioning. Membrane computing is based on *membrane systems* or *P systems*, a
new class of computing devices introduced in [8]. The approach is based on hierarchical systems: finite cell-structures consisting of membranes embedded in
a main membrane. The membranes determine regions where objects and evolution rules can be placed. The objects evolve according to the rules associated
with each region. A computation starts from an initial configuration of the system, and terminates when no further rule can be applied. The P systems are
inspired by biological systems, but they are based on the theory of automata
and formal languages. Since their introduction, many results of universality for
the P systems were proved, and several problems were solved with the help
of formal languages. The field is very active; new properties are discovered, as
well as connections with already known concepts. It is desirable to find more
connections with the applied computer science, including implementations and
executable specifications. A sequential software simulator of membrane systems
is presented in [1], and a parallel simulator is presented in [2].

This paper presents a natural specification for P systems. Such a specification is executable by using the sequential rewriting software tool called Maude.
Forced to execute parallel steps on a sequential machine, we give an algorithmic description of the "nondeterministic maximal parallel" evolution in the P
systems. Using the facilities provided by reflection, we define this specific strategy of controlling the rewriting process at the meta-level. This strategy leads

G. Mauri et al. (Eds.): WMC5 2004, LNCS 3365, pp. 126–145, 2005.

to an operational semantics of the P systems based on the rewriting semantics of Maude. We can verify the properties of the P systems expressed as linear temporal logic formulas by using the model checker implemented in Maude.

The paper is organized as follows. Section 2 briefly presents the P systems, as well as the mathematical specification system called Maude. We emphasize on the power given by reflection in Maude. Section 3 presents the specifications of the P systems in Maude, as well as their operational semantics. Two examples of specifications and their executions are described in Section 4. Model checking some temporal properties of the P systems is discussed in Section 5.

2   P Systems and Maude

A detailed description of the P systems can be found in [9]. A *P system* consists of several membranes that do not intersect, and a *skin membrane*, surrounding them all. The membranes delimit *regions*, and contain multisets of *objects*, as well as *evolution rules*. Only rules in a region delimited by a membrane act on the objects in that region. Moreover, the rules can contain target indications, specifying the membrane where objects are sent after applying the rule. The objects can pass through membranes, in two directions: they can be sent *out* of the membrane which delimits a region from outside, or can be sent *in* one of the membranes which delimit a region from inside, precisely identified by its label. In a step, the objects can pass only through a membrane. The membranes can be *dissolved*. When such an action takes place, all the objects of the dissolved membrane remain free in the membrane placed immediately outside, but the evolution rules of the dissolved membranes are lost. The skin membrane is never dissolved. The application of evolution rules is done in parallel, and it is eventually regulated by *priority* relationships between rules.

We can identify a membrane structure with a tree (with skin as its root), or a string of correctly matching parentheses, placed in a unique pair of matching parentheses; each pair of matching parentheses corresponds to a membrane. Graphically, a membrane structure is represented by a Venn diagram in which two sets can be either disjoint, or one the subset of the other. The membranes are labelled in a one-to-one manner. A membrane without any other membrane inside is said to be *elementary*. The space outside the skin membrane is called the *outer region*.   More formally, a P system is a structure
$\Pi = (O, \mu, w_1, \ldots, w_m, R_1, \ldots, R_m, i_o)$, where:

(i) O is an alphabet of objects;
(ii) μ is a membrane structure consisting of labelled membranes;
(iii) w_i are multisets over O associated with the regions defined by μ;
(iv) R_i are finite sets of evolution rules over O associated with the membranes, of typical form $ab \rightarrow a(c, in_2)(c, out)$;
(v) i_0 is either a number between 1 and m specifying the *output* membrane of Π, or it is equal to 0 indicating that the output is the outer region.

These are the general P systems; many other variants and classes were introduced.

In order to relate the P systems to Maude, we express a membrane as a structure $M = (R_M, w_M)$, and its evolution rules as rewriting rules. We consider the following maximal parallel application of rules: in a transition step, the rules of each membrane are used against its resources such that no more rules can be applied. Considering an *elementary membrane* $M = (R_M, w_M)$, where R_M is the finite set of evolution rules and w_M is the initial multiset, a computation step transition is defined as a rewriting rule by

$$\frac{x_1 \to y_1, \ldots, x_n \to y_n \in R_M, z \text{ is } R_M\text{-irreducible}}{x_1 \ldots x_n z \Rightarrow y_1 \ldots y_n z} \tag{1}$$

A multiset z is R_M-irreducible whenever there does not exist rules in R_M applicable to z.

A *composite membrane* is a membrane with the structure provided by the membranes $M_1, \ldots, M_k$ located inside it. It is denoted by $(M_1, \ldots, M_k, R_M, init)$, where each $M_i (1 \leq i \leq k)$ is an elementary or a composite membrane. R_M represents the finite set of evolution rules of M, and $init$ is its initial configuration of form $(w, (w_1, \ldots, w_k))$, where w_i is the multiset associated with the membrane M_i. A computational step of a composite membrane is defined as a rewriting rule by

$$\frac{w \Rightarrow w', w_1 \Rightarrow w'_1, \ldots, w_n \Rightarrow w'_n}{(w, (w_1, \ldots, w_k)) \Rightarrow (w', (w'_1, \ldots, w'_k))} \tag{2}$$

In this way, the objects of the membranes are the subject of local evolution rules that evolve simultaneously. A sequence of computation steps represents a computation. A computation is successful if this sequence is finite, namely there is no rule applicable to the objects present in the last configuration. In a final configuration, the result of a successful computation is the total number of objects present in the membrane considered as the output membrane. If no internal membrane is specified as an output, we consider the skin to be the output membrane.

Maude is a software system developed around the Maude language. Core Maude is the Maude interpreter implemented in C++; it provides the Maude's basic functionality. Full Maude is an extension written in Maude itself, allowing combination of various Maude modules to build more complex modules. Maude can be used for many applications with competitive performance and advantages over the conventional code. The current Maude implementation can execute syntactic rewriting with speeds from half a million to several million rewrites per second, depending on the particular application and machine. It is able to work well with multisets having millions of elements.

The Maude system is available free of charge, under the terms of the GNU General Public License, at the Maude home page http://maude.cs.uiuc.edu. Many useful materials are available, and Maude binaries are provided for selected architectures and operating systems, together with installation instructions. We have used the version 2.1 of Maude, under Linux.

Maude is essentially a mathematical language. The OBJ theory and languages [7] have influenced the Maude design and philosophy. The basic programming statements are equations, membership assertions, and rules. Their rewriting semantics is given by the fact that instances of the left hand side pattern are replaced by corresponding instances of the righthand side. A Maude program containing only equations and membership assertions is called a *functional module*. The equations are used as rules (equational rewriting), and the replacement of equals for equals is performed only from left to right. A Maude program containing both equations and rules is called a *system module*. Rules are not equations, they are local transition rules in a possibly concurrent system. Unlike for equations, there is no assumption that all rewriting sequences will lead to the same final result, and for some systems there may not be any final states. The functional modules define a functional sublanguage of Maude, and the system modules extend the purely functional semantics of equations to the concurrent rewriting semantics of rules.

If we consider, for example, a membrane system in which we have the objects floating in a *soup* (that is, a multiset of objects), then the objects can interact in this soup, and can work locally according to specific rewriting rules. These rules are the local transition rules of the system, and they can be applied concurrently to different membranes of the system. The rewriting performed for membranes is a multiset rewriting. In Maude this is specified in the equational part of the program (system module) by declaring that the multiset union operator satisfies the associativity and commutativity equations, and has also an identity. This is done simply by using attributes, and this information is used to generate a multiset matching algorithm. Further expressiveness is gained by various features as equational pattern matching, user-definable syntax and data, generic types and modules, support for objects, reflection.

Regarding both expressiveness and performance, we can mention the *evaluation strategies* and use of *reflection property*. Evaluation strategies control the positions in which equations can be applied, giving the user the possibility of indicating which arguments to evaluate before simplifying a given operator with the equations. Reflective computations allow the link between meta-level and the object level, whenever possible. A typical meta-level computation may perform efficiently millions of rewrites at the object level, paying a reasonable linear cost in changing the representations from the meta-level to the object level and back, only at the beginning and at the end of the computation.

A Maude program can be seen as a logical theory, and a Maude computation as a logical deduction using the axioms specified in the program. The foundations of Maude is given by membership equational logic and rewriting logic. A functional module specifies a theory in membership equational logic. Mathematically, we can view such a theory as a pair $(\Sigma, E \cup A)$, where Σ is the signature and specifies the type structure, E is the collection of equations and memberships declared in the functional module, and A is the collection of equational attributes (e.g., assoc, comm) declared for different operators.

Similarly, a system module specifies a rewriting theory, that is, a theory in rewriting logic. A *signature* in rewriting logic is an equational theory (Σ, E), where Σ is an equational signature and E is a set of Σ-equations and it describes a particular structure for the state of a system (for instance, for string rewriting systems E consists of the associativity axiom, for multiset rewriting systems E consists of the associativity and commutativity axioms, and for term rewriting systems E is empty). A *sentence* over the signature (Σ, E) is an expression of the form $(\forall X)[t]_E \rightarrow [t']_E$, where t and t' are $\Sigma(X)$-terms, and $[t]_E$ denotes the equivalence class of t modulo the equations E. A sentence describes the possible transitions from the states described by $[t]$ to the corresponding states described by $[t']$. If $X = \{x_1, \ldots, x_n\}$, then we denote a sentence by $[t(\overline{x})]_E \rightarrow [t'(\overline{x})]_E$, where $\overline{x}$ is the sequence $x_1, \ldots, x_n$. If E and X are understood from the context, we simply write $[t(\overline{x})] \rightarrow [t'(\overline{x})]$ or $[t] \rightarrow [t']$. A *rewriting specification* $\mathcal{R}$ is a 4-tuple $\mathcal{R} = (\Sigma, E, L, R)$ where (Σ, E) is a rewriting logic signature, L is a set whose elements are called *labels*, and R is a set of labelled rewriting rules (sentences) written as $r : [t(\overline{x})]_E \rightarrow [t'(\overline{x})]_E$. The inference rules of rewriting logic allow to deduce general (concurrent) transitions which are possible in a system satisfying $\mathcal{R}$. We say that $\mathcal{R}$ *entails the sentence* $[t] \rightarrow [t']$ and write $\mathcal{R} \vdash [t] \rightarrow [t']$ iff $[t] \rightarrow [t']$ can be obtained by finite application of the following *inference rules*:

(1) *Reflexivity*. For each $\Sigma(X)$ term t,

$$\overline{[t] \rightarrow [t]}$$

(2) *Congruence*. For each operation symbol $f \in \Sigma$,

$$\frac{[t_1] \rightarrow [t'_1], \ldots, [t_n] \rightarrow [t'_n]}{[f(t_1, \ldots, t_n)] \rightarrow [f(t'_1, \ldots, t'_n)]}$$

(3) *Unconditional replace*. For each $r : [t(\overline{x})] \rightarrow [t'(\overline{x})]$ in R,

$$\frac{[u_1] \rightarrow [v_1], \ldots, [u_n] \rightarrow [v_n]}{[t(\overline{u}/\overline{x})] \rightarrow [t(\overline{v}/\overline{x})]}$$

(4) *Transitivity*.

$$\frac{[t_1] \rightarrow [t_2], [t_2] \rightarrow [t_3]}{[t_1] \rightarrow [t_3]}$$

The general theory of the rewriting logic allows *conditional sentences* and *conditional rewriting rules*. The interested reader is invited to read, e.g., [3].

Rewriting logic is *reflective*, i.e. there is a (finitely presented) *universal rewriting specification* $\mathcal{U}$ such that for any (finitely presented) rewriting specification $\mathcal{R}$ (including $\mathcal{U}$ itself), we have the following equivalence:

$$\mathcal{R} \vdash [t] \rightarrow [t'] \text{ iff } \mathcal{U} \vdash \langle \overline{\mathcal{R}}, \overline{t} \rangle \rightarrow \langle \overline{\mathcal{R}}, \overline{t'} \rangle,$$

where $\overline{\mathcal{R}}$ and $\overline{t}$ are terms representing $\mathcal{R}$ and t as data elements of $\mathcal{U}$. Since $\mathcal{U}$ is representable in itself, it is possible to achieve a "reflective tower" with an arbitrary number of reflection levels:

$$\mathcal{R} \vdash [t] \rightarrow [t'] \text{ iff } \mathcal{U} \vdash \langle \overline{\mathcal{R}}, \overline{t} \rangle \rightarrow \langle \overline{\mathcal{R}}, \overline{t'} \rangle \text{ iff } \mathcal{U} \vdash \langle \overline{\mathcal{U}}, \overline{\langle \overline{\mathcal{R}}, \overline{t} \rangle} \rangle \rightarrow \langle \overline{\mathcal{U}}, \overline{\langle \overline{\mathcal{R}}, \overline{t'} \rangle} \rangle \ldots$$

This interesting and powerful concept is supported by Maude through a built-in module called META-LEVEL. This module has sorts Term and Module such that the representation $\bar{t}$ of a term t is of sort Term and the representation $\overline{SP}$ of a specification SP is of sort Module. There are also functions like metaReduce($\overline{SP}, \bar{t}$) which returns the representation of the reduced form of a term t using the equations in the module SP.

META-LEVEL module can be extended by the user to specify strategies of controlling the rewriting process. We use META-LEVEL in order to define the "maximal parallel rewriting" strategy. Forced to execute parallel steps on a sequential machine, we provide an algorithmic description (given by maxParRew) of the rather ambiguous "nondeterministic and maximal parallel" application of the evolution rules in a P system. For our sequential thinking, such a clarifying and conceptual description of the P systems is helpful, and it could become a useful framework for further investigations. Using maxParRew as a transition step between meta-level configurations, we then provide an operational semantics of the P systems.

3   P Systems Specifications and Semantics

A P system Π is naturally represented as a collection of Maude modules, each membrane M_i of Π corresponding to a module denoted also by M_i.

We consider a sort Obj is for object names, and its subsort Output is for results. Since we wish to pass the alphabet of objects as a parameter, we use a theory OBJ defining the "type" of the parameter:

```
(fth OBJ is
  sorts Obj Output .
  subsort Output < Obj .
endfth)
```

In order to cope with the membrane dissolving, and the priority relationship between rules, we add new sorts, namely Dissolve and Priority that are subsorts of the sort Ingredient. For the target indications, we consider the sort Target, two operations for sending objects *out* of the membrane or *in* a specified membrane, such that a pair composed of a multiset of object and a target represents also an element of sort Ingredient. We add a sort Soup for the multisets of ingredients, and a sort Config for the states of a P system. These sorts and their operations are defined by the following functional module:

```
(fmod CONFIG(X :: OBJ) is
  pr QID .
  sorts Dissolve Priority Target Ingredient .
  sorts Soup Config .
  subsort Priority < Ingredient .
  subsort Dissolve < Ingredient .
  subsort X@Obj < Ingredient .
  subsort Ingredient < Soup .
  op empty : -> Soup .
```

```
op delta : -> Dissolve .
op __ : Soup Soup -> Soup [assoc comm id: empty] .

vars P1 P2 : Priority .
vars S1 S2 : Soup .
vars I1 I2 : Ingredient .

op _<_ : Priority Priority -> Bool .
op _<_ : Soup Soup -> Bool .
ceq I1 S1 < I2 S2 = S1 < S2 if not (I1 :: Priority or I2 :: Priority) .
ceq I1 S1 < P2 S2 = S1 < P2 S2 if not (I1 :: Priority) .
ceq P1 S1 < I2 S2 = P1 S1 < S2 if not (I2 :: Priority) .

op out : -> Target .
op in : Qid -> Target .
op '(_',_') : X@Obj Target -> Ingredient .

op <_|_> : Qid Soup -> Config .
op <_|_;_> : Qid Soup  Config -> Config .
op _',_ : Config Config -> Config [assoc comm] .
endfm)
```

The subsort relation Ingredient < Soup says that each ingredient defines a particular multiset. The operation _ _ is required to satisfy the structural laws of associativity, commutativity, and it has an identity empty. The operation _`,_ is required to satisfy only the structural laws of associativity and commutativity. For the declaration of the operators (_,_) and _,_ we write '(_`,_`) and _`,_, respectively, according to the syntax constraints imposed by Maude. An expression of the form $\langle M \mid S \rangle$ represents a configuration corresponding to an elementary membrane M with its multiset S, and an expression of the form $\langle M \mid S; C_1, \ldots, C_n \rangle$ represents a configuration corresponding to a composite membrane M in state S and with the component i having the configuration C_i.

A membrane can be described by a system module of the form:

```
(mod M is
  inc CONFIG(⟨ objects-of-M⟩) .
  op init : -> Soup .
  eq init = ⟨init-soup⟩ .
  rl ['M] : ℓ_1  => r_1 .
  ...
  rl ['M] : ℓ_k  => r_k .
endm)
```

The Maude semantics of the module M is not the same with the P system semantics. Therefore we must associate with M the appropriate semantics based on the maximal parallel rewrite relation. We use the facilities provided by reflection in Maude, defining this semantics at the meta-level in a module named COMPS. For the elementary membranes, a computation step between configurations is defined as:

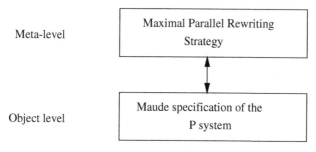

Meta-level

Maximal Parallel Rewriting
Strategy

Object level

Maude specification of the
P system

Fig. 1. Rewriting strategy is defined at the meta-level

$$\frac{S \Rightarrow S'}{\langle M \mid S \rangle \Rightarrow \langle M \mid S' \rangle} \tag{3}$$

where $S \Rightarrow S'$ is defined in (1). $S \Rightarrow S'$ is not the rewriting defined by M, but they are strongly related:

$$S \Rightarrow S' \text{ iff } S \xrightarrow{+}_{R_M} S' \text{ s.t. } maxParCons(R_M, S, S')$$

where $\xrightarrow{+}_{R_M}$ is the rewriting defined by R_M, and $maxParCons(R_M, S, S')$ represents the constraints defining the maximal parallel rewriting strategy over R_M. More precisely, we have:

1. if $S = S'$, then $maxParCons(R_M, S, S)$ holds iff S is R_M-irreducible;
2. if $S \neq S'$, then $maxParCons(R_M, S, S')$ holds iff there exists $S_1, S'_1, \ell \to r \in R_M$ such that $S = \ell\, S_1$, $S' = r\, S'_1$, the rule $\ell \to r$ has maximal priority in R_M, and $maxParCons(R'_M, S_1, S'_1)$, where R'_M contains the rules from R_M that do not have a lower priority than the priority of the chosen rule.

Since $maxParCons$ has the set of rules of the module M as parameter, it follows that it can be decided only at meta-level. The transition between configurations for composite membrane is defined as:

$$\frac{S \Rightarrow S', C_1 \Rightarrow C'_1, \ldots, C_k \Rightarrow C'_k}{\langle M \mid S; C_1, \ldots, C_k \rangle \Rightarrow \langle M \mid S'; C'_1, \ldots, C'_k \rangle} \tag{4}$$

A computation is a sequence of transitions steps $C_0 \Rightarrow C_1 \Rightarrow C_2 \Rightarrow \ldots \Rightarrow C_n \Rightarrow \ldots$, where C_0 is the initial configuration. The result of a successful computation is extracted from the final configuration; for instance, the result could be the total number of objects present in the output membrane.

We present the Maude implementation of the computation for P systems. As we have seen above, a computation step is depending on the rewriting rules included in the Maude description of the P system, and therefore it must be defined at the meta-level (see Figure 1).

The meta-level is needed for two main reasons:

1. to locate the set of rules corresponding to a certain membrane in the structured Maude specification of a composite P system;

2. to describe the maximal parallel application of the located rules as a rewriting strategy.

The maximal parallel rewriting strategy corresponding to a computation step of an elementary membrane M_i is given by

$$\text{maxParRewS} : \text{RuleSet} \times \text{Term} \to \text{Term}$$

and it is defined by the following rewriting rules:

$[r1] : maxParRewS(R, S) \to maxParRewS(filter(R), \ell \to r, S)$
        if $(\ell \to r)$ is a rule in R applicable to S, having maximal priority
$[r2] : maxParRewS(R, \ell \to r, S) \to r\ maxParRewS(R, S_1)$
        if $S == \ell\, S_1$
$[r3] : maxParRewS(R, S) \to S$ if S is R-irreducible

The first rule nondeterministically chooses from the set R an evolution rule that verifies its condition. The filter operator removes from a rule set the rules that have a lower priority than a given priority, in our case the one of the chosen rule. The second rule applies the chosen evolution rule over the soup represented by S, and applies maxParRewS over the remaining non-processed soup. The third one is applied at the end of the strategy, and it does not modify an irreducible soup. The first two rules above are implemented in Maude at the meta-level as follows:

```
crl maxParRewS(RS, T) =>
   (if (MP :: MatchPair)
    then if hasMaxPriority(RS, rl X => Y [label(Q)] ., T)
         then maxParRewS(filter(getPriority(Y), RS),
                           (rl  X =>  Y [label(Q)] .), MP, T)
         else maxParRewS(RS2, T) fi
    else maxParRewS(RS2, T) fi)
  if (rl X => Y [label(Q)] .) RS2 := RS /\
     MP := metaXmatch(m, X, T, nil, 0, unbounded, 0) .
crl maxParRewS((rl X => Y [label(Q)] .), T) =>
   (if (MP :: MatchPair)
    then '__[removePriority(Y), maxParRewS((rl X => Y [label(Q)] .),
                               toTerm(getContext(MP)))]
    else T fi)
  if MP := metaXmatch(m, X, T, nil, 0, unbounded, 0) .

crl maxParRewS(RS, R, MP, T) =>
    '__[removePriority(Y), maxParRewS(RS, toTerm(getContext(MP)))]
  if (rl  X =>  Y [label(Q)] .) := R .
```

where := is the matching operator, and :: is the membership predicate. The function metaXmatch(m, X, T, nil, 0, unbounded, 0), used in the conditional part of the first rule, computes the first matching (if any) of X and T in the module m, without condition (nil), and without boundary in choosing the depth in the term where the application of the rule takes place. In our case, the resulting MP has the sort MatchPair iff the left hand side of the rule is a subterm of T, therefore the rule is applicable to T, and in that case MP is a pair consisting of the empty substitution (the lefthand side has no variables), and its context. The function getContext(MP) extracts the context from MP. Since we are working over multisets, the subterm to be processed by maxParRewS is the context after removing the placeholder [_], operation done by the function toTerm. The data structure MP help us to implement more efficiently the rules [r1] and [r2]. The function removePriority removes the priority ingredient from a soup, in this case from the righthand side of the chosen rule, and getPriority extracts the priority ingredient, if any. The priority ingredients help the rewriting process to choose at any moment an evolution rule with maximal priority with respect to a partial order $<$ over the sort Priority. This is realized with the help of a predicate $hasMaxPriority(R, \ell \to r, S)$ which returns true iff there is no higher priority rule than $\ell \to r$ in the set R which can be applied to the multiset S. The definition of this predicate is:

$$hasMaxPriority(\emptyset, \ell \to r, S) = \text{true}$$

$$hasMaxPriority(\{\ell' \to r'\}, \ell \to r, S) = \begin{cases} \text{false} & \text{if } r < r' \wedge \ell' \to r' \\ & \text{is applicable to } S \\ \text{true} & \text{otherwise} \end{cases}$$

$$hasMaxPriority(R \cup \{\ell' \to r'\}, \ell \to r, S) =$$
$$= \begin{cases} \text{false} & \text{if } r < r' \wedge \ell' \to r' \text{ is applicable to } S \\ hasMaxPriority(R, \ell \to r, S) & \text{otherwise} \end{cases}$$

The corresponding operator is given by

```
op hasMaxPriority : RuleSet Rule Term -> Bool .
```

We interpret the priority in a *strong* sense as described in [8]: if a rule with a higher priority is used, then no rule of a lower priority can be used, even if the two rules do not compete for objects. We can imagine that each rule "consumes" not only objects, but also energy: if a rule of a higher priority is used, then no energy remains available for rules of a lower priority. In order to use this interpretation we add the operator filter.

The computation for composite membranes is given by

$$\text{maxParRew} : \text{Term} \to \text{Term}$$

The definition of $maxParRew$ is:

[r4] : $maxParRew(\langle M \mid S \rangle) \to \langle M \mid maxParRewS(rules(M), S) \rangle$

[r5] : $maxParRew(\langle M \mid S; C \rangle) \to \langle M \mid maxParRewS(rules(M), S); maxParRew(C) \rangle$

[r6] : $maxParRew(C_1, C_2) \to maxParRew(C_1), maxParRew(C_2)$

and its Maude implementation at the meta-level is:

```
crl maxParRew('<_|_>[X , Y]) =>
   '<_|_>[X, maxParRewS(getQRls(getRls(m), X), Y)]
   if sameKind(m, getType(metaReduce(m, Y)), 'Soup) .
rl maxParRew('_',_[X , Y]) => '_',_[maxParRew(X), maxParRew(Y)] .
rl maxParRew('<_|_;_>[X , Y, Z]) =>
   '<_|_;_>[X, maxParRewS(getQRls(getRls(m), X), Y), maxParRew(Z)] .
```

The function getRls(m) returns the set of rules included in a Maude module m, and getQRls(R, X) selects the subset of rules corresponding to the submodule identified by X. In our case, m represents the module specifying a (composite) P system Π at meta-level, and X is the meta-level representation of a membrane label in Π.

The invocation of maxParRew could be given by the rewriting rule $X \to$ maxParRew(X). In order to avoid infinite rewriting of the form

$$X \to \text{maxParRew}(X) \to \text{maxParRew}(\text{maxParRew}(X)) \to \cdots$$

we use two auxiliary operations

$$\text{rwf} : \text{Term} \to \text{Term}$$
$$\text{intermediate} : \text{Term} \to \text{Term}$$

The corresponding definitions are:

$$[\text{r7}] : rwf(X) \to intermediate(maxParRew(X))$$
$$\text{if } X \text{ does not contain dissolving ingredients}$$
$$[\text{r8}] : intermediate(X) \to rwf(moveToTarget(X))$$
$$\text{if } X \text{ is not intermediate}$$

The Maude implementation is given by the rules

```
crl rwf(X) => intermediate(maxParRew(X))
    if (not hasDissolve(X)) .
crl intermediate(X) => rwf(moveToTarget(getTerm(metaReduce(m, X))))
    if (not isIntermediate(X)) .
```

The predicate isIntermediate verifies if a term has an intermediate form, that is if at least one of its subterms contains the operator maxParRew or maxParRewS. During the intermediate form, a maximal parallel step is executed. After a maximal parallel step and before another one, the target indications are processed, and the condition for the rule [r7] prevents the beginning of a new rewriting step if there are unprocessed dissolving ingredients occurred at the previous step. The function metaReduce(m,X) returns a data structure including the normal form of X with respect to the equations of the module m; in our case m represents the module specifying the P system at meta-level. getTerm selects the normal form of X from the data structure returned by metaReduce. The operation moveToTarget deals with the pairs formed by objects and a target, sending

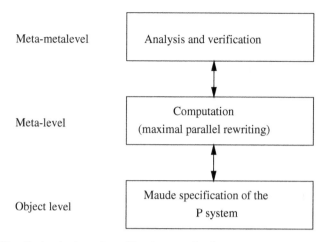

Fig. 2. Analysis and verification can be done at meta-metalevel

the objects *out* of the current membrane, or *in* a specified membrane. An object sent out of the skin membrane is deleted from the system.

For each $\delta \in$ Dissolve we add the following "dissolving" rules:

$$\langle M_i \mid S_i; \langle M_j \mid S_j\delta\rangle, C\rangle \to \langle M_i \mid S_iS_j; C\rangle$$
$$\langle M_i \mid S_i; \langle M_j \mid S_j\delta; C_1\rangle, C_2\rangle) \to \langle M_i \mid S_iS_j; C_1, C_2\rangle$$

Note that if S_j contains more δ objects, then all these objects must be removed; this will be done by a function called clean(). We give as example the Maude implementation of the first rule:

```
crl '<_|_;_>[X, Y, '<_|_>[U, V] ] =>
    '<_|_>[X , '__[Y, clean(toTerm(getContext(MP)))]]
    if MP := metaXmatch(m, 'delta.Dissolve, V, nil, 0, unbounded, 0) /\
       MP :: MatchPair .
```

We can use the Maude commands like rew to verify local properties concerning the behavior of a P system. Sometimes we need more than that. For instance, we have to extract the result from a configuration. This can be done using meta-commands like getTerm, metaRewrite and metaSearch. Therefore we need to work at the meta-metalevel (Figure 2). This will be exemplified in the next section.

4   Examples of P System Specifications

In this section we consider two simple P systems examples, and then describe and execute their Maude specification.

Example 1: We consider a P system generating symbols b and c with the properties that the number of c's is double of the number of b's, and the total number of b's and c's is a multiple of 6.

$$\Pi_{\bar{I}}(O, \mu, w_1, w_2, R_1, R_2, i_o),$$
$$O = \{a, b, c\},$$
$$\mu = [_1[_2\ ]_2]_1,$$
$$w_1 = a^2,$$
$$w_2 = \lambda,$$
$$R_1 = \{a \rightarrow a(b, in_2)(c, in_2)^2,\ a^2 \rightarrow (a, out)^2\},$$
$$R_2 = \emptyset,$$
$$i_o = 2.$$

The initial configuration is:

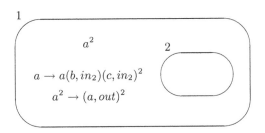

The alphabet of objects is specified by

```
(fmod ABC is
  sorts Obj Output .
  subsort Output < Obj .
  ops a b c : -> Obj .
  mb b : Output .
  mb c : Output .
endfm)
```

The two membership assertions `mb` are used to declare `b` and `c` of subsort `Output`. The alphabet is passed to the generic module `CONFIG` using a morphism declared as:

```
(view OBJ-TO-ABC from OBJ to ABC is
   sort Obj to Obj .
   sort Output to Output .
endv)
```

Each membrane is specified in Maude by an independent system module.

```
(mod M2 is
  inc CONFIG(OBJ-TO-ABC) .

  op init2 : -> Soup .
  eq init2 = empty .
endm)
```

```
(mod SKIN is
  inc CONFIG(OBJ-TO-ABC) .

  op init1 : -> Soup .
  eq init1 = a a .
  rl ['SKIN] : a => a (b, in('M2)) (c c, in('M2)) .
  rl ['SKIN] : a a => (a, out) (a, out) .
endm)
```

The Maude specification of a P system is a system module importing the modules corresponding to the component membranes, and defining the initial configuration. We do not need to write the rules in the initial configuration of the system because we can get them easily through the label of each membrane. Therefore the initial configuration contains the objects of each membrane, together with the label of the membrane, and the structure of the system. The module describing Π_1 is:

```
(mod PSYS is
  inc M2 + SKIN   .
  op initConf : -> Config .
  eq initConf = < 'SKIN | init1 ; < 'M2 | init2 > > .
endm)
```

We can use various Maude commands in order to make software experiments with the P system specification. For instance, we use the command **rew** to see the result of maximal parallel rewriting after a fixed number the steps:

```
Maude> (rew [11] rwf(getTerm(metaReduce(up(PSYS), up(PSYS, initConf)))) .)
result Term :
  rwf('<_|_;_>['''SKIN.Qid,'__['a.Obj,'a.Obj],'<_|_>[''M2.Qid,'__['b.Output,
    'b.Output,'c.Output,'c.Output,'c.Output,'c.Output]]])
```

We should note that the number of rewriting steps in Maude is not the same with the number of computation steps of the P systems. However the rewriting process could be restricted by the configuration size. The function #(X) recursively counts the number of the objects in the term X, ignoring the other ingredients.

```
  crl rwf(X) => intermediate(maxParRew(X))
      if (not hasDissolve(X)) /\
         (#(X) < maxSize) .
  crl rwf(X) => idle if #(X) >= maxSize .
```

We use the meta-level function **metaSearch** to help us finding all the states of the P system that are not intermediate, states for which the system has completed a maximal parallel rewriting step; **metaSearch** is used at meta-metalevel. We define the operator **offRwf** in a module METACOMPS in order to remove the top operator **rwf** from a term. In METACOMPS, **rwf** has the meta-representation 'rwf[_].

```
(mod METACOMPS is
  including META-LEVEL(COMPS) .
  vars T T1 : Term .
  op offRwf : Term -> Term .
  ceq offRwf(T) = T1 if 'rwf[T1] := T .
  eq offRwf(T) = T [owise] .
endm)
```

After application of `metaSearch` and `offRwf`, we can apply twice the command `down` that takes us to the object level. The command `down` is used to move between two successive levels of the reflection tower. For instance, `down COMPS` : interprets the result returned by `red` in the module `COMPS`.

```
Maude> (down PSYS : down COMPS : red offRwf(getTerm(metaSearch(up(COMPS),
up(COMPS, rwf(getTerm(metaReduce(up(PSYS), up(PSYS, initConf)))))),
'rwf['T:Term],nil, '+, unbounded, 4))) .)
rewrites: 61862 in 1071ms cpu (1071ms real) (57715 rewrites/second)
result Config :
  < 'SKIN | empty ; < 'M2 | b b b b c c c c c c c c > >
```

Example 2: We consider now an example of a P system with dissolving and priorities ingredients; it is taken from [9], page 71. This P system Π_2 is generating (in its halting configurations) values of the form n^2 for $n \geq 1$.

$$\Pi_2 = (O, \mu, w_1, w_2, w_3, (R_1, \rho_1), (R_2, \rho_2), (R_3, \rho_3), 1),$$
$$O = \{a, b, d, e, f\},$$
$$\mu = [_1[_2[_3 \ ]_3]_2]_1,$$
$$w_1 = \lambda, R_1 = \emptyset, \ \rho_1 = \emptyset,$$
$$w_2 = \lambda, R_2 = \{b \to d, \ d \to de, \ r_1 : ff \to f, \ r_2 : f \to \delta\}, \ \rho_2 = \{(r_1, r_2)\},$$
$$w_3 = af, R_3 = \{a \to ab, a \to b\delta, f \to ff\}, \ \rho_3 = \emptyset,$$

The initial configuration is given in Figure 3.

Since no object is free in membranes 1 and 2, the only possibility to start is by using the rules of membrane 3 together with its free objects a and f. Using the rules $a \to ab$ and $f \to ff$ in parallel for the available occurrences of a and f, after $n \geq 1$ steps we get n occurrences of b and 2^n occurrences of f. At any moment we can use $a \to b\delta$ instead of $a \to ab$, and consequently we get $n + 1$ occurrences of b and 2^{n+1} occurrences of f, followed by the process of dissolving membrane 3. Region 3 disappears, its rules are lost, and its objects move to region 2. The obtained configuration is

$$[_1 \ [_2 \ b^{n+1} f^{2^{n+1}}, \ b \to d, \ d \to de, \ r_1 : ff \to f, \ r_2 : f \to \delta, \ r_1 > r_2, \ ]_2 \ ]_1.$$

According to the priority relation, the rule $ff \to f$ is used as much as possible. In one step b^{n+1} are transformed in d^{n+1}, while the number of f occurrences is divided by two. Then, in the next step, $n+1$ occurrences of e are produced, and the number of f occurrences is divided again by two. At each step, further $n+1$ occurrences of e are produced. Finally, after $n + 1$ steps (n steps when the rule

$ff \rightarrow f$ is used, and one when using the rule $f \rightarrow \delta$), membrane 2 is dissolved, its rules are removed, and its objects move to the skin region. The number of the objects e is the square of the number of d. Consequently, Π_2 generates values of the form n^2, for $n \geq 1$.

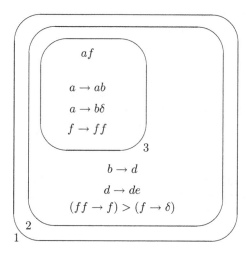

Fig. 3. The initial configuration of a P system generating n^2

The alphabet of objects is specified in Maude by

```
(fmod OBJN2 is
  sorts Obj Output .
  subsort Output < Obj .
  ops a b d f e : -> Obj .
  mb d : Output .
  mb e : Output .
endfm)
```

Membrane 2 contains both dissolving and priority ingredients:

```
(mod M2 is
  inc CONFIG(OBJ-TO-OBJN2) .
  ops p1 p2 : -> Priority .
  eq (p1 < p2) = true .
  op init2 : -> Soup .
  eq init2 = empty .
  rl ['M2] : b => d .
  rl ['M2] : d => d e  .
  rl ['M2] : f f => f p2 .
  rl ['M2] : f => delta p1 .
endm)
```

The priority set ρ_2 is modelled by the constants p1 and p2 together with the equation stating the priority order. The structure of the P system Π_2 is given by:

```
(mod PSYS is
  inc M3 + M2 + SKIN .
  op initConf : -> Config .
  eq initConf = < 'SKIN | init1 ; (< 'M2 | init2 ; < 'M3 | init3 > >) > .
endm)
```

Here we have an example showing how the dissolving rules work:

```
Maude> (down PSYS : down COMPS : red offRwf(getTerm(metaSearch(up(COMPS),
up(COMPS, rwf(getTerm(metaReduce(up(PSYS), up(PSYS, initConf)))))),
'rwf['T:Term],nil, '+, unbounded, 9))) .)
rewrites: 3853155 in 102572ms cpu (102877ms real) (37565 rewrites/second)
result Config :
  < 'SKIN | empty ; < 'M2 | d d e e f > >
Maude> (down PSYS : down COMPS : red offRwf(getTerm(metaSearch(up(COMPS),
up(COMPS, rwf(getTerm(metaReduce(up(PSYS), up(PSYS, initConf)))))),
'rwf['T:Term],nil, '+, unbounded, 13))) .)
rewrites: 12585081 in 333343ms cpu (337463ms real) (37754 rewrites/second)
result Config :
  < 'SKIN | d d e e e >
```

For more details and a complete Maude implementation of the P systems see http://www.info.uaic.ro/rewps.

5   Model Checking P Systems

Maude has a collection of formal tools supporting different forms of logical reasoning to verify program properties, including a model checker to verify temporal properties of finite-state system modules. Therefore, once we have a Maude description of the membrane systems, we may use the Maude implementation of Linear Temporal Logic (LTL) to verify various properties expressed in LTL [6]. The LTL model checker provides a powerful tool to detect subtle errors and to verify some desired temporal properties.

LTL was designed for expressing the temporal ordering of events. In computer science, temporal logics keep track of the systems states, changes of the variable values, and the order in which they occur. Intuitively, the system state is a snapshot of the system's execution. In this snapshot, every variable has some value. A particular execution of the system is represented by a sequence of system states, and obviously, time progresses during the execution, but there is no keeping track of how long the system is in any particular state. In LTL, formulas are evaluated with respect to a particular execution and a particular state in that execution. Time is totally ordered, usually bounded in the past and unbounded in the future. LTL formulas allows boolean connectives and modalities together with the operators **X** expressing "in the next state", and **U** expressing that one property holds until another holds (Until). These formulas are evaluated on individual executions (computation paths). The modal path operators are $\Diamond$ and $\Box$; $\Diamond$ expressing "at some future time", and $\Box$ expressing "at all future times". They are also found as the letters **F** and **G**. More information on LTL, and its link to Maude can be found in [6].

In order to apply the model checker, the space of the reachable states of the P system must be finite. Unfortunately, this requirement is not fulfilled by almost all the P systems. Therefore we have to consider a finite subspace of reachable states. An example is the subspace including the states with the size less than, or equal to, a given `maxSize`. The size of a state is computed by the function `#(X)` which counts the number of the objects that occur in X. In this sense, we modify the rule for `rwf`:

```
crl rwf(X) => intermediate(maxParRew(X))
    if (not hasDissolve(X)) /\
        (#(X) < maxSize) .
```

In order to avoid deadlock situation, we add a stutter extension rule along with a state `idle` that is always executable and has no effect, defined as a constant operation of sort `Term`. The system reaches this state in the next step when the size of the current state is greater than `maxSize`:

```
op idle : -> Term .
crl rwf(X) => idle if #(X) >= maxSize.
rl idle => idle .
```

We exemplify the use of LTL model checker by verifying three atomic propositions: `isConfig`, satisfied by a term iff it is not intermediate; `isMultipleOf6`, satisfied by a configuration iff the number of objects b and objects c is a multiple of 6; and `isDouble`, satisfied by a configuration iff the number of objects c is double the number of the objects b in it:

```
(mod 2B4C-PREDS is
  including COMPS .
  including SATISFACTION .
  subsort Term < State .
  ops isConfig isMultipleOf6 isDouble : -> Prop .
  var T : Term .
  ceq T |= isConfig = true if not isIntermediate(T) .
  ceq rwf(T) |= isMultipleOf6 = true if  (#(T, 'c) + #(T, 'b)) rem 6 == 0 .
  ceq rwf(T) |= isDouble = true if #(T, 'c) == 2 * #(T, 'b) .
endm)
```

`SATISFACTION` is a built-in module which includes the specifications for the atomic linear temporal formulas and the satisfaction relation between states and propositions. For the P systems, the states correspond to the configurations and these are represented at the meta-level by terms. We define the initial state against which we wish to check the temporal formulas $\Box$(`isConfig` $\rightarrow$ `isMultipleOf6`) and $\Box$(`isConfig` $\rightarrow$ `isDouble`):

```
(mod PROOF is
  including 2B4C-PREDS .
  including MODEL-CHECKER .
  including LTL-SIMPLIFIER .

  op init : -> Term .
  eq init = rwf(getTerm(metaReduce(m, up(PSYS, initConf)))) .
endm)
```

The temporal formulas are verified by using the **red** command:

```
red modelCheck(init, [](isConfig -> isMultipleOf6) ) .
red modelCheck(init, [](isConfig -> isDouble) ) .
```

and Maude supplies the following output:

```
Maude> (red modelCheck(init, [] (isConfig -> isMultipleOf6)) .)
rewrites: 34448 in 669ms cpu (774ms real) (51422 rewrites/second)
reduce in PROOF :
  modelCheck(init,[](isConfig -> isMultipleOf6))
result Bool :
  true

Maude> (red modelCheck(init, [] (isConfig -> isDouble)) .)
rewrites: 34429 in 576ms cpu (576ms real) (59677 rewrites/second)
reduce in PROOF :
  modelCheck(init,[](isConfig -> isDouble))
result Bool :
  true
```

6   Conclusion

The contributions of this paper consist in providing executable specifications of the P systems, using a complex software system based on rewriting. Moreover, it is presented for the first time the use of a software verification tool able to automatically check properties of a P system. The approach fully exploits the reflection property of the rewriting logic, property which allows a meta-level implementation of the P systems operational semantics. It is also presented an algorithmic description of the nondeterministic maximal parallel evolution rules in the P systems.

The paper does not present the rich theoretical worlds of the P systems and rewriting logic, respectively. It rather concentrates on fruitful bridge between these two worlds, emphasizing the use of Maude as a complex tool able to execute specifications of the P systems, and then to verify the desired properties of the specified P system. Since this is the first paper describing executable specifications for the P systems, we have used two simple examples.

References

1. G. Ciobanu, D. Paraschiv. P System Software Simulator. *Fundamenta Informaticae* vol. 49, 61–66, 2002.
2. G. Ciobanu, W. Guo. P Systems Running on a Cluster of Computers. In Gh. Păun, G.Rozenberg, A.Salomaa (Eds.): *Membrane Computing*, LNCS vol. 2933, Springer, 123–139, 2004.
3. M. Clavel, F. Durán, S. Eker, P. Lincoln, N. Martí-Oliet, J. Meseguer, J.F. Quesada. Maude: Specification and Programming in Rewriting Logic. *Theoretical Computer Science*, vol. 285(2), 187–243, 2002.
4. M. Clavel, F. Durán, S. Eker, P. Lincoln, N. Martí-Oliet, J. Meseguer, C .Talcott. *Maude Manual* (Version 2.1). http://maude.cs.uiuc.edu, 2004.
5. F. Durán and J. Meseguer. Structured theories and institutions. In M. Hofmann, G. Rosolini, and D. Pavlovic, editors, *Procs. of the 8th Conference on Category Theory and Computer Science (CTCS'99)*, volume 29 of *ENTCS*. Elsevier, 1999.
6. S. Eker, J. Meseguer, and A. Sridharanarayanan. The Maude LTL Model Checker and Its Implementation. In T. Ball, S.K. Rajamani (Eds.): *Model Checking Software: 10th SPIN Workshop*, LNCS vol. 2648, Springer, 230–234, 2003.
7. J. Goguen, T. Winkler, J. Meseguer, K. Futatsugi, J.-P. Jouannaud. Introducing OBJ. In *Software Engineering with OBJ: Algebraic Specification in Action*, 3–167, Kluwer, 2000.
8. Gh. Păun. Computing with membranes. *Journal of Computer and System Sciences* vol. 61, 108–143, 2000.
9. Gh. Păun. *Computing with Membranes: An Introduction*, Springer, 2002.

On the Efficiency of P Systems with Active Membranes and Two Polarizations

Artiom Alhazov[1,2] and Rudolf Freund[3]

[1] Research Group on Mathematical Linguistics,
Rovira i Virgili University,
Pl. Imperial Tàrraco 1, 43005 Tarragona, Spain
artiome.alhazov@estudiants.urv.es

[2] Institute of Mathematics and Computer Science,
Academy of Sciences of Moldova,
Str. Academiei 5, Chişinău, MD 2028, Moldova
artiom@math.md

[3] Faculty of Informatics,
Vienna University of Technology,
Favoritenstr. 9, A-1040 Wien, Austria
rudi@emcc.at

Abstract. We present an algorithm for deterministically deciding SAT in linear time by P systems with active membranes using only two polarizations and rules of types (a), (c), and (e). Moreover, various restrictions on the general form of the rules are considered: global, non-renaming, independent of the polarization, preserving it, changing it, producing two membranes with different polarizations, having exactly one or two objects in (each membrane of) the right-hand side, thus improving results from [1]. Several problems related to different combinations of these restrictions are formulated, too.

1 Introduction

Membrane systems are biologically motivated theoretical models of distributed and parallel computing. The most interesting questions probably are completeness (solving every solvable problem) and efficiency (solving a hard problem in feasible time). We here address the latter problem, i.e., we shall give an algorithm how to decide SAT in linear time using only two polarizations in P systems with active membranes.

The question of removing the polarizations (charges $+, -, 0$ associated with the membranes) from P systems with active membranes without diminishing their computing power or their efficiency in solving computationally hard problems in a feasible time was formulated several times and was recently considered in various contexts (with the polarizations replaced by various other features, such as label changing – see, e.g., [2], [3]). Here, following [1], we present another way for improving previous results: the number of polarizations can be decreased to two, without introducing new features.

G. Mauri et al. (Eds.): WMC5 2004, LNCS 3365, pp. 146–160, 2005.
© Springer-Verlag Berlin Heidelberg 2005

There are numerous results of solving such (mostly NP-complete) problems as SAT, HPP, Validity, Subset-Sum, Knapsack, Vertex Cover, Clique, QBF-SAT by P systems with active membranes with three polarizations (e.g., see [2], [3], [4], [5], [9], [10], [12], [13], [14], [16], [17], [18], [20], [21]). The ability of the systems to act depending on the membrane polarizations and to change them is a powerful control feature, the use of which is not necessary if one pays the price of changing membrane labels. Another result is solving SAT in a semi-uniform manner, without polarizations and without changing labels, but also using membrane dissolution and non-elementary membrane division. Here we show that two polarizations are enough even when restricting the types of rules to (a), (c), and (e). It remains as an open question whether polarizations can be completely removed, and we *conjecture* that the answer is negative.

Moreover, we consider a few restrictions on the general form of the rules, under which it is still possible to solve SAT. The motivations of considering these restrictions are of three kinds: bringing the construction closer to biological cells (making it as "realistic" as possible); building a normal form (as restrictive as possible), for the possible future direct simulation results; and finding out which aspects of active membranes are essential for the efficiency of P systems.

2   Prerequisites

The reader is assumed to be familiar with basic elements of formal language theory. For an alphabet V, by V^* we denote the free monoid generated by V under the operation of concatenation; the *empty string* is denoted by λ, and $V^* - \{\lambda\}$ is denoted by V^+. By $\mathbf{N}$ we denote the set of positive integers, and $\mathbf{N}_0 := \mathbf{N} \cup \{0\}$ is the set of non-negative integers. In the following we will not distinguish between a vector $(y_1, ..., y_\beta) \in \mathbf{N}_0^\beta$, its representation by a multiset or its representation by a string with Parikh vector $(y_1, ..., y_\beta)$. For more notions as well as basic results from the theory of formal languages, the reader is referred to [6] and [19].

We also assume the reader to be familiar with the basic elements of membrane computing, e.g., from [15] (comprehensive details can be found at http://psystems.disco.unimib.it), in particular, with P systems with active membranes.

For the sake of completeness, we recall the definition of P systems with active membranes for the case when only rules of types (a) to (e) are used; in a more general way, as in the original definition, we allow the polarizations to be arbitrary non-negative integers.

A *P system system with active membranes* (of degree $m \geq 1$) is a construct of the form

$$\Pi = (O, E, \mu, w_1, \cdots, w_m, e_1, \cdots, e_m, R),$$

where O is the alphabet of objects, $E = \{0, \cdots, n-1\}$ with $n \geq 1$ is the set of electrical charges (polarizations), μ is the membrane structure (with m membranes, bijectively labelled with $1, 2, \cdots, m$; by H we denote the set of labels $\{1, 2, \cdots, m\}$), $w_1, \cdots, w_m$ are strings over O indicating the multisets of objects at the beginning present in the m regions of μ, $e_1, \cdots, e_m$ are the polarizations at the beginning assigned to the membranes $1, \cdots, m$, and R is a finite set of rules of the following forms:

(a) $[\, a \rightarrow v \,]_h^i$, $a \in O$, $v \in O^*$, $h \in H$, $i \in E$
   (evolution rules, used in parallel in the region of membrane h, provided that the polarization of the membrane is i);

(b) $a[\ ]_h^i \rightarrow [\, b \,]_h^j$, $a, b \in O$, $h \in H$, $i, j \in E$
   (communication rules, sending an object into a membrane, possibly changing the polarization of the membrane);

(c) $[\, a \,]_h^i \rightarrow [\ ]_h^j b$, $a, b \in O$, $h \in H$, $i, j \in E$
   (communication rules, sending an object out of a membrane, possibly changing the polarization of the membrane);

(d) $[\, a \,]_h^i \rightarrow b$, $a, b \in O$, $h \in H$, $i \in E$
   (membrane dissolution rules; in reaction with an object, the membrane is dissolved);

(e) $[\, a \,]_h^i \rightarrow [\, b \,]_h^j [\, c \,]_h^k$, $a, b, c \in O$, $h \in H$, $i, j, k \in E$
   (division rules for elementary membranes; in reaction with an object, the membrane is divided into two membranes with the same label, possibly of different polarizations, and the object specified in the rule is replaced in the two new membranes by possibly new objects).

The rules of types (b), (c), (d), and (e) are considered as involving the membrane, hence, we assume at most one of such a rule to be used for each membrane in a given step; the use of rules is maximally parallel, with the rules chosen in a non-deterministic manner.

An output is associated with a halting computation – and only with halting computations – in the form of the objects sent into the environment during the computation. When using a P system Π for decision problems, we also specify an input membrane i_0, where the input to be analysed is put in addition to the axiom multiset w_{i_0}; in sum, we then write

$$\Pi = (O, E, \mu, w_1, \cdots, w_m, e_1, \cdots, e_m, R, i_0).$$

3   Solving SAT in Linear Time

Throughout this section we use the following notation for instances of the SAT problem.

We consider a propositional formula in conjunctive normal form:

$$\beta = C_1 \wedge \cdots \wedge C_m,$$
$$C_i = y_{i,1} \vee \cdots \vee y_{i,l_i}, \ 1 \leq i \leq m, \ \text{where}$$
$$y_{i,k} \in \{x_j, \neg x_j \mid 1 \leq j \leq n\}, \ 1 \leq i \leq m, 1 \leq k \leq l_i,$$

i.e., n is the number of variables and m is the number of clauses, hence, to β the size (n, m) is associated. For arbitrary $(n, m) \in \mathbf{N}^2$, we denote the family of SAT problems of size (n, m) by SAT(n, m).

3.1   Using Global Rules

As it was shown in [1], $\mathtt{SAT}(n, m)$ can be decided in linear time (linear with respect to n and m, i.e., the algorithm has time complexity $O(n + m)$) by a uniform family of P systems with two polarizations, only using rules of types (a), (c), and (e). Throughout this section we will always restrict ourselves to restricted variants of these types of rules.

We first recall the theorem from [1], giving the construction of the proof and short explanations as well as repeating the example that illustrates the corresponding construction.

Theorem 1. $\mathtt{SAT}(n, m)$ *can be deterministically decided in linear time (linear with respect to n and m) by a uniform family of P systems with active membranes with two polarizations and global rules of types (a), (c), and (e).*

Proof. An instance β of the $\mathtt{SAT}(n, m)$ problem as described above is encoded as a multiset over

$$V(n, m) = \{x_{i,j,j}, x'_{i,j,j} \mid 1 \leq i \leq m, 1 \leq j \leq n\}.$$

The object $x_{i,j,j}$ $(x'_{i,j,j})$ represents the variable x_j appearing in the clause C_i without (with) negation. Thus, the input multiset is

$$w = \{x_{i,j,j} \mid x_j \in \{y_{i,k} \mid 1 \leq k \leq l_i\}, 1 \leq i \leq m, 1 \leq j \leq n\}$$
$$\cup \{x'_{i,j,j} \mid \neg x_j \in \{y_{i,k} \mid 1 \leq k \leq l_i\}, 1 \leq i \leq m, 1 \leq j \leq n\},$$

which is placed into membrane 2 in addition to the initial symbol d_0 in the P system $\Pi(n, m)$ we will construct for any given $(n, m) \in \mathbf{N}^2$:

$$\Pi(n, m) = (O(n, m), \{0, 1\}, [_1 \; [_2 \;]_2 \;]_1, t_0, d_0, 0, 0, R, 2),$$
$$O(n, m) = \{x_{i,j,k}, x'_{i,j,k} \mid 1 \leq i \leq m, 0 \leq k \leq j \leq n\} \cup \{z, o, \mathtt{yes}, \mathtt{no}\}$$
$$\cup \{c_{i,j} \mid 0 \leq i \leq m, 0 \leq j \leq n\} \cup \{c_i \mid 0 \leq i \leq m\}$$
$$\cup \{d_i \mid 0 \leq i \leq n + 1\} \cup \{e_i \mid 0 \leq i \leq m + 1\}$$
$$\cup \{t_h \mid 0 \leq h \leq n + 2m + 4\};$$

R contains the following rules (grouped by sub-tasks; see [1] for more explanations and details):

Global Control in Skin Membrane

- $[\, t_h \rightarrow t_{h+1} \,]^0$, $0 \leq h \leq n + 2m + 2$.

Generation Phase

- $[\, d_j \,]^e \rightarrow [\, d_{j+1} \,]^0 [\, d_{j+1} \,]^1$, $e \in \{0, 1\}$, $0 \leq j < n - 1$;
- $[\, x_{i,j,k} \rightarrow x_{i,j,k-1} \,]^e$,
  $[\, x'_{i,j,k} \rightarrow x'_{i,j,k-1} \,]^e$, $e \in \{0, 1\}$, $1 \leq i \leq m, 1 \leq k \leq j \leq n$;

- $[\, x_{i,j,0} \to \lambda \,]^0$,
  $[\, x_{i,j,0} \to c_{i,j} \,]^1$,
  $[\, x'_{i,j,0} \to c_{i,j} \,]^0$,
  $[\, x'_{i,j,0} \to \lambda \,]^1$, $1 \le i \le m$, $1 \le j \le n$;
- $[\, c_{i,j} \to c_{i,j+1} \,]^e$, $e \in \{0,1\}$, $1 \le i \le m$, $1 \le j < n$;
- $[\, d_n \to d_{n+1}z \,]^1$,
  $[\, d_n \to d_{n+1} \,]^0$.

During each of the first n steps, every elementary membrane is duplicated, in order to examine all possible truth assignments to the variables $x_1, \cdots, x_n$.

In step j of the generation phase, one of the membranes resulting from the application of the rule

$$[\, d_j \,]^e \to [\, d_{j+1} \,]^0 [\, d_{j+1} \,]^1$$

gets polarization 0, corresponding to assigning the truth value **false** to x_j (and in this case the clauses where $\neg x_j$ appears are satisfied), and the other membrane gets polarization 1, corresponding to assigning the truth value **true** to x_j (and in this case those clauses where x_j appears without negation are satisfied). Due to the application of the rules

$$[\, x_{i,j,0} \to \lambda \,]^0, [\, x_{i,j,0} \to c_{i,j} \,]^1, [\, x'_{i,j,0} \to c_{i,j} \,]^0, [\, x'_{i,j,0} \to \lambda \,]^1,$$

only those variables "survive" which correspond to the correct truth assignment at the moment the last index has reached the ground level 0.

After the end of this first phase of the algorithm, 2^n elementary membranes (each of them with label 2) have been produced, each of them containing d_{n+1} and objects $c_{i,n}$ for all clauses C_i that are satisfied. Every membrane with polarization 1 also contains an object z. This procedure described so far in total takes $n + 1$ step.

Transition Phase

- $[\, z \,]^1 \to [\ ]^0 o$;
- $[\, d_{n+1} \to e_1 \,]^e$, $e \in \{0,1\}$;
- $[\, c_{i,n} \to c_i \,]^e$, $e \in \{0,1\}$, $1 \le i \le m$.

By the application of the rule $[\, z \,]^1 \to [\ ]^0 o$ the polarization of the membranes polarized by 1 is reset to zero again by passing through the surrounding membrane, thereby also yielding the "garbage" symbol o within the skin membrane. After this single step of the transition phase all the elementary membranes now have the polarization 0 and contain e_1 as well as c_i for every satisfied clause C_i.

Checking Phase

- $[\, c_1 \,]^0 \to [\ ]^1 o$;
- $[\, e_i \to e_{i+1}z \,]^0$, $1 \le i < m$;
- $[\, c_1 \to \lambda \,]^1$;
- $[\, c_i \to c_{i-1} \,]^1$, $2 \le i \le m$;

$$- [\, e_m \to e_{m+1} \,]^0;$$
$$- [\, e_{m+1} \,]^1 \to [\, \ ]^1 \ \text{yes}.$$

All clauses are satisfied if and only if all objects $c_1, \cdots, c_m$ are present in some membrane, and at the end all objects c_i, $1 \leq i \leq m$, have been sent out into the skin membrane. While checking the last clause, no object z (for resetting the polarization of the membrane as this is done in the preceding steps) is produced from e_m by applying the rule $[\, e_m \to e_{m+1} \,]^0$, hence, e_{m+1} will be present in a membrane with polarization 1 thus allowing for the application of the rule

$$[\, e_{m+1} \,]^1 \to [\, \ ]^1 \ \text{yes}$$

indicating that the corresponding elementary membrane represented a solution of the given satisfiability problem. In total, this phase takes $2m$ steps.

Output Phase

$$- [\, \text{yes} \,]^0 \to [\, \ ]^1 \ \text{yes};$$
$$- [\, t_{n+2m+3} \,]^0 \to [\, \ ]^1 \ \text{no}.$$

Every elementary membrane which after the first $n+1$ steps had represented a solution of the given satisfiability problem, after $n+1+1+2m$ steps has sent a copy of **yes** into the skin membrane, and in the next step one of these copies exits into the environment by using the rule

$$[\, \text{yes} \,]^0 \to [\, \ ]^1 \ \text{yes}$$

thus giving the positive result **yes** and changing the skin polarization to 1 in order to prevent further output. If, on the other hand, the given satisfiability problem has no solution, after $n + 2m + 3$ steps the polarization of the skin membrane will still be 0, hence, the rule

$$[\, t_{n+2m+3} \,]^0 \to [\, \ ]^1 \ \text{no}$$

sends out the correct answer **no**.   □

The construction elaborated above is illustrated by an example, see Figure 1.

It is worth noticing that the rules are *global*: the same set of rules is valid for all membranes, i.e., in the rules, the labels of the membranes can be omitted. We also note that in this construction already elaborated in [1], the membrane division rules do not depend on the polarization (which therefore can be omitted in the meaning of "applicable for any membrane"), and the contents of membranes after division is identical, but the polarizations are different. Finally, every rule of type (c) changes the polarization (the superscript $\neg$ will be used to denote this variant).

Thus, all rules used are even of the following restricted forms (where the interpretation of the subscripts g, $g1$, and $g2$ is explained in the subsequent subsection; the superscript $\neg$ indicates that the polarization is changed):

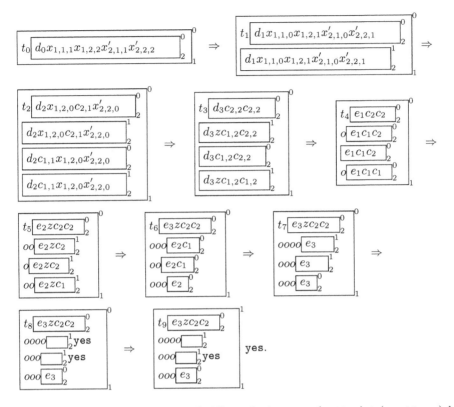

Fig. 1. Evolution of a P system deciding whether $\gamma = (x_1 \vee x_2) \wedge (\neg x_1 \vee \neg x_2)$ has solutions

(a_g) $[\ a \to v\ ]^i$,
(c_{g1}) $[\ a\ ]^i \to [\ \ ]^{\neg}\ b$,
(e_{g2}) $[\ a\ ] \to [\ b\ ]^0[\ b\ ]^1$,
       where $a, b \in O$, $v \in O^*$, $h \in H$, $i \in \{0, 1\}$.

According to the explanations given above, we now have even proved a stronger result than that already shown in [1].

3.2   Using Rules of a Specific "Normal Form"

In this subsection we now consider the following forms (particular cases) of the types (a), (c), (e) of rules (where $a, b, c \in O$, $h \in H$, $i \in \{0, 1\}$):

(a_{gb}) $[\ a \to bc\ ]^i$ (global split rule),
(a_{gu}) $[\ a \to b\ ]^i_h$ (rename only),
(c_{np1}) $[\ a\ ]_h \to [\ \ ]^{\neg}_h\ a$ (exit only, polarization switched),
(c_{gp1}) $[\ a\ ] \to [\ \ ]^{\neg}\ b$ (global exit rule, polarization switched),
(c_{gny}) $[\ \text{yes}\ ]^0 \to [\ \ ]^1\ \text{yes}$ (a special rule for ejecting the result),

(e_{gp0}) [a] $\rightarrow$ [b][c] (global polarizationless division rule),
(e_{gp2}) [a] $\rightarrow$ [b]^0[c]^1 (global polarization-independent division rule,
  producing membranes of different polarizations).

In the subscripts of the rules, we write g if the rule is global (does not depend on the label of the membrane), n if the rule is not-renaming (the object(s) in (each membrane of) the right-hand side is(are) the same as the object in the left-hand side), p if the rule does not depend on the polarization, 0 if the rule preserves it, 1 if the rule changes it, 2 if the rule produces two membranes with different polarizations, and b (u) if the number of the objects in (each membrane of) the right-hand side is two (one, respectively). Finally, y is used if the rule acts on the object **yes**.

The main idea of the possible restrictions is the following: to try to make rules of types (c) and (e) independent of the polarization by remembering the needed value in a corresponding object, and then decoding it by generating copies of z if needed (using such an approach, the computation slows down by a constant factor). In the same time, other restrictions are put on the general form of the rules, leading to the following theorem:

Theorem 2. $\mathrm{SAT}(n, m)$ *can be deterministically decided in linear time (linear with respect to nm, i.e., the algorithm has time complexity $O(nm)$) by a uniform family of P systems with active membranes with two polarizations and rules of the forms (a_{gb}), (c_{np1}), (c_{gny}), and (e_{gp0}).*

Proof. An instance β of the $\mathrm{SAT}(n, m)$ problem as described above is encoded as a multiset over

$$V(n, m) = \{x_{i,j,j,0}, x'_{i,j,j,0} \mid 1 \leq i \leq m, 1 \leq j \leq n\}.$$

The object $x_{i,j,j,0}$ represents the variable x_j appearing in the clause C_i without negation, and the object $x'_{i,j,j,0}$ represents the variable x_j appearing in the clause C_i with negation. Thus, the input multiset is

$$w = \{x_{i,j,j,0} \mid x_j \in \{y_{i,k} \mid 1 \leq k \leq l_i\}, 1 \leq i \leq m, 1 \leq j \leq n\}$$
$$\cup \{x'_{i,j,j,0} \mid \neg x_j \in \{y_{i,k} \mid 1 \leq k \leq l_i\}, 1 \leq i \leq m, 1 \leq j \leq n\},$$

which has to be put into membrane 2 in addition to the initial symbol $d_{0,0}$ in the P system $\Pi(n, m)$ defined below:

$$\Pi(n, m) = (O(n, m), \{0, 1\}, [_1 \ [_2 \ ]_2 \ ]_1, t_0, d_{0,0}, 0, 0, R, 2),$$
$$O(n, m) = \{x_{i,j,k,l}, x'_{i,j,k,l} \mid 1 \leq i \leq m, 0 \leq k \leq j \leq n, 0 \leq l \leq 3\}$$
$$\cup \{z, o, \mathbf{yes}, \mathbf{no}\}$$
$$\cup \{c_{i,j,l} \mid 0 \leq i \leq m, 0 \leq j \leq n, 0 \leq l \leq 3\}$$
$$\cup \{c_{i,l} \mid 0 \leq i \leq m, 0 \leq l \leq 2\}$$
$$\cup \{d_{j,l}, d'_{j,l} \mid 0 \leq j \leq n, 0 \leq l \leq 3\}$$
$$\cup \{e_{i,l} \mid 0 \leq i \leq m + 1, 0 \leq l \leq 2\}$$
$$\cup \{t_h \mid 0 \leq h \leq 2mn + 4n + 3m + 4\};$$

Let us briefly describe the meaning of the objects: objects $x_{i,j,k,l}, x'_{i,j,k,l}$ encode the instance of the problem, objects $c_{i,j,l}, c_{i,l}$ represent clauses satisfied, objects $d_{j,l}, d'_{j,l}$ control the generation phase, objects $e_{i,l}$ control the checking phase, objects t_h produce the negative answer in case no positive answer is given. Object z is used to change the polarization of the membrane, object o is a "garbage" object, and finally yes and no are the possible results. The subscript l is used to switch between different states within cycles of the generation or the checking phase.

R contains the following rules (we also give explanations for the use of these rules):

Global Control in Skin Membrane

- $[\, t_h \rightarrow t_{h+1}o \,]^0, \, 0 \leq h \leq 2mn + 4n + 3m + 3.$

The control variables t_h only occur in exactly one copy in the skin membrane. As we shall see at the end of the description of the whole algorithm, after $2mn + 4n + 3m + 3$ derivation steps in the corresponding P system $\Pi(n, m)$ the answer yes appears outside the skin membrane if the given satisfiability problem has a solution, whereas in the case that no solution exists, one step later the answer no appears in the environment.

The main task of the algorithm is accomplished in the generation phase of the algorithm where for each possible truth assignment to the n variables one elementary membrane is generated which after $n + 1$ steps will contain all the information needed to decide whether it represents a solution of the given problem or not:

Generation Phase

- $[\, d_{j,0} \,] \rightarrow [\, d_{j,1} \,][\, d'_{j,1} \,], \, 0 \leq j \leq n - 1;$
- $[\, d_{j,1} \rightarrow d_{j,2}o \,]^0,$
  $[\, d'_{j,1} \rightarrow d'_{j,2}z \,]^0, \, 0 \leq j \leq n - 1;$
- $[\, d_{j,2} \rightarrow d_{j,3}o \,]^0,$
  $[\, d'_{j,2} \rightarrow d_{j,3}z \,]^0, \, 0 \leq j \leq n - 1;$
- $[\, d_{j,3} \rightarrow d_{j+1,0}o \,]^e, \, e \in \{0,1\}, \, 0 \leq j \leq n - 1;$
- $[\, z \,]_2 \rightarrow [\, \,]_2^{-} \, z.$

There are n cycles, each taking four steps and duplicating every elementary membrane in order to examine all possible truth assignments to the variables $x_1, \cdots, x_n$. Symbols $d_{j,1}$ ($d'_{j,1}$) correspond to the value false (true) of x_j, respectively. In the case of the value true, the membrane polarization changes (using object z) to 1 two steps after the division, and then it is restored to 0.

- $[\, x_{i,j,k,l} \rightarrow x_{i,j,k,l+1}o \,]^0,$
  $[\, x'_{i,j,k,l} \rightarrow x'_{i,j,k,l+1}o \,]^0, \, 1 \leq i \leq m, \, 0 \leq k \leq j \leq n, \, 0 \leq l \leq 2;$
- $[\, x_{i,j,k,3} \rightarrow x_{i,j,k-1,0}o \,]^e,$
  $[\, x'_{i,j,k,3} \rightarrow x'_{i,j,k-1,0}o \,]^e, \, e \in \{0,1\}, \, 1 \leq i \leq m, \, 1 < k \leq j \leq n;$

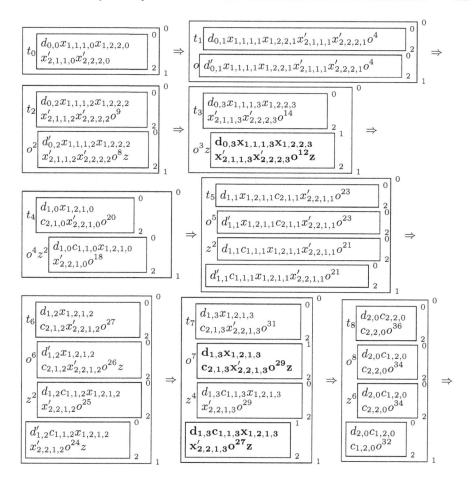

Fig. 2. Generation phase

$- [x_{i,j,1,3} \rightarrow oo]^0,$
$\quad [x_{i,j,1,3} \rightarrow c_{i,j,0}o]^1,$
$\quad [x'_{i,j,1,3} \rightarrow c_{i,j,0}o]^0,$
$\quad [x'_{i,j,1,3} \rightarrow oo]^1, 1 \leq i \leq m, 1 \leq j \leq n;$
$- [c_{i,j,l} \rightarrow c_{i,j,l+1}o]^0, 0 \leq l \leq 2,$
$\quad [c_{i,j,3} \rightarrow c_{i,j+1,0}o]^e, e \in \{0,1\}, 1 \leq i \leq m, 1 \leq j < n.$

Now let us consider step $4j - 1$ of the generation phase: Two steps after the application of the rule

$$[d_{j,0}] \rightarrow [d_{j,1}][d'_{j,1}],$$

one of the resulting membranes carries polarization 0, corresponding to assigning the truth value `false` to x_j (and in this case the clauses where $\neg x_j$ appears are satisfied), and the other membrane carries polarization 1, corresponding to assigning the truth value `true` to x_j (and in this case those clauses where x_j

appears without negation are satisfied). Most important for the correct answer to the decision problem is the application of the rules

$$[\ x_{i,j,1,3} \rightarrow oo\ ]^0, \ [\ x_{i,j,1,3} \rightarrow c_{i,j,0}o\ ]^1, \ [\ x'_{i,j,1,3} \rightarrow c_{i,j,0}o\ ]^0, \ [\ x'_{i,j,1,3} \rightarrow oo\ ]^1,$$

which in the corresponding step of the derivation act according to the truth value assigned to x_j in the underlying elementary membrane, i.e., only those variables "survive" which correspond to the correct truth assignment at the moment the last index has reached the ground level 0.

After the end of this first phase of the algorithm, 2^n elementary membranes (each of them with label 2) have been produced, each of them containing $d_{n,0}$ and objects $c_{i,n,0}$ for all clauses C_i that are satisfied. This procedure described so far in total takes $4n$ steps.

Transition Phase

$$- \ [\ d_{n,0} \rightarrow e_{1,0}\ ]^0,$$
$$[\ c_{i,n,0} \rightarrow c_{i,0}\ ]^0, \ 1 \leq i \leq m.$$

After this single step of the transition phase, all the elementary membranes now have the polarization 0 and contain $e_{1,0}$ as well as $c_{i,0}$ for each satisfied clause C_i.

Checking Phase

$$- \ [\ c_{1,0} \rightarrow zz\ ]^0,$$
$$- \ [\ c_{i,0} \rightarrow c_{i,1}o\ ]^1,$$
$$[\ c_{i,1} \rightarrow c_{i,2}o\ ]^0,$$
$$[\ c_{i,2} \rightarrow c_{i,1}o\ ]^1,$$
$$[\ c_{i,2} \rightarrow c_{i-1,0}o\ ]^0, \ 1 < i \leq m;$$
$$- \ [\ e_{i,0} \rightarrow e_{i,1}o\ ]^1,$$
$$[\ e_{i,1} \rightarrow e_{i,2}o\ ]^0,$$
$$[\ e_{i,2} \rightarrow e_{i,1}o\ ]^1,$$
$$[\ e_{i,2} \rightarrow e_{i+1,0}o\ ]^0, \ 1 \leq i \leq m.$$

All clauses are satisfied in some membrane labelled by 2 if and only if all objects $c_1, \cdots, c_m$ are present in this membrane. In each cycle i, $1 \leq i \leq m$, there are $k_i \leq n$ sub-cycles, each activated and closed again by symbols z that were generated from a symbol $c_{1,0}$ at the beginning of the cycle; going out, a symbol z always changes the polarization. Thus, if at the beginning of some cycle $c_{1,0}$ is not present, then the objects in the corresponding membrane do not evolve any more.

Otherwise, $k_i > 0$ copies of $c_{1,0}$ lead to $2k_i$ steps of changing the polarization between 0 and 1. Finally, the polarization becomes 0 and remains so, and then the objects $e_{i,2}$ and $c_{i,2}$ "notice" this and the next cycle may begin. The whole cycle takes $2k_i + 3$ steps.

If all clauses are satisfied, then finally the membrane will only contain object $e_{m+1,0}$. In total, this phase takes at most $m(2n + 3) = 2mn + 3m$ steps.

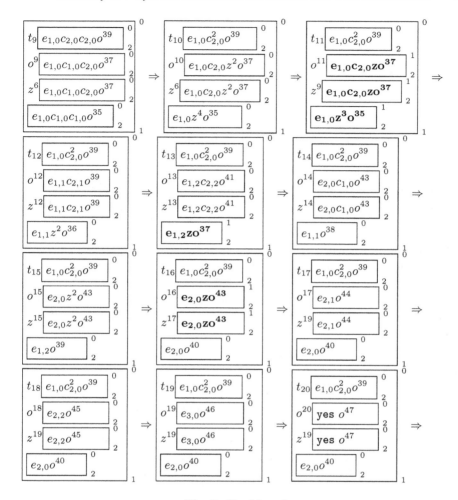

Fig. 3. Checking phase

Output Phase

- $[e_{m+1,0} \to \textbf{yes } o]^0$,
  $[\textbf{yes }]^0 \to [\ ]^1 \textbf{yes};$
- $[t_{2mn+4n+3m+4} \to \textbf{no } o]^0$,
  $[\textbf{no }] \to [\ ]^- \textbf{no}.$

Every elementary membrane which after the first $4n$ steps had represented a solution of the given satisfiability problem, after at most $(4n) + 1 + (3m + 2mn) + 3 = 2mn + 4n + 3m + 4$ steps has sent a copy of **yes** into the skin membrane, and, when the first copy of **yes** arrives in the skin, one copy of these copies exits into the environment, thus giving the positive result **yes** and changing the skin polarization to 1 in order to prevent further output. If, on the other hand, the given satisfiability problem has no solution, after $2mn + 4n + 3m + 4$ steps the

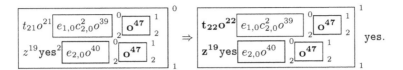

Fig. 4. Output phase

polarization of the skin membrane still will be 0, hence, the object **no** is produced and sent out as the correct answer.

Due to the explanations given above, one can easily verify that in any case the given algorithm will correctly decide a given satisfiability problem in n variables and m clauses in at most $2mn + 4n + 3m + 5$ steps, i.e., the algorithm has time complexity $O(nm)$. This observation completes the proof.   □

We illustrate the construction given in Theorem 2 by an example: Figures 2, 3, and 4 show the evolution of the P system deciding whether $\gamma = (x_1 \vee x_2) \wedge (\neg x_1 \vee \neg x_2)$ has solutions.

The objects are written in boldface if the corresponding membrane has polarization 1. The input of the system is $x_{1,1,1,0} x_{1,2,2,0} x'_{2,1,1,0} x'_{2,2,2,0}$ in membrane 2, and the output of the system is **yes**. The computation takes 22 steps.

3.3   Remarks and Other Variants

Some definitions of decisional P systems require that the result is ejected into the environment only in the last step of the computation. Our construction can be easily adjusted to fulfill this property by remembering, in the objects $e_{i,j}$, also the number l of times the number of steps the membrane had polarization 1 during the checking phase, and then "keeping them busy" for $2(mn - l)$ steps. Then, all elementary membranes with positive answers will stop evolving at the same time by sending **yes** into the skin, and those with negative answers will stop evolving earlier.

In the construction given above, the time for giving a positive answer is actually bounded by $2K + 4n + 3m + 4$, where K is the number of occurrences of the variables in β. Thus, if the size of the problem is given as (n, m, K), then (adjusting the counter in the skin) the time can be made at most $2K + 4n + 3m + 5$.

On the other hand, we do not believe that the rule sending object **yes** into the skin can be made independent of the polarization; otherwise, multiple answers are given and the halting time is no longer polynomial. This can easily be avoided for the price of using membrane dissolution (rules of type (d_{gp})) and one more membrane: a copy of the "witness" of the positive result dissolves the middle membrane, releasing a unique object **yes** into the skin, otherwise object **no** is ejected to the skin, as it was done in the proof of Theorem 9 in [3].

Finally, we mention alternative variants of restrictions.

Using the generation phase similar to that from the proof of Theorem 1 and making relevant adjustments to the global control, one can quite easily replace the rules of type (e_{gp0}) by rules of type (e_{gp2}).

By replacing the rule $[\ z\ ]_2 \to [\ ]_2^\neg\ z$ by $[\ z\ ] \to [\ ]^\neg\ o$, one can remove type (c_{np1}) for the price of introducing type (c_{gp1}).

Corollary 3. *For* $\mathbf{t} \in \{n, g\}$ *and* $\mathbf{k} \in \{0, 2\}$, $\mathtt{SAT}(n, m)$ *can be decided in linear time (linear with respect to* nm*) by a uniform family of P systems with active membranes with two polarizations and rules of the forms* (a_{gb}), $(c_{\mathbf{t}p1})$, *and* $(e_{gp\mathbf{k}})$.

4   Conclusions

In Theorem 2 we have given an algorithm for deciding the NP-complete decision problem $\mathtt{SAT}(n, m)$ by a uniform family of P systems with active membranes in linear time (linear with respect to nm) with only two polarizations and rules of types (a), (c), and (e), of specific restrictive types. Various other restrictions are summarized in Corollary 3, and the discussion is given in Subsection 3.3.

The question remains whether further or other restrictions, respectively, of the general form of these rules are possible. For instance, can the problem be solved using only rules of types (a), (c_{p0}), (e) (the rules of type (c) do not depend on the polarization and preserve it)? What about using only types (a_p), (c), (e) (the rules of type (a) do not depend on the polarization)?

Another interesting question is to study systems with rules of types (a_u), (b), (c), (d), (e); such systems can only increase the number of objects via membrane division. What is their generative power? Are they efficient?

Acknowledgements

This paper was initiated during the Brainstorming Week on Membrane Computing taking place in Sevilla during the first week of February, 2004 (see [1] for more details).

The first author is supported by the project TIC2002-04220-C03-02 of the Research Group on Mathematical Linguistics, Tarragona. The first author also acknowledges the Moldovan Research and Development Association (MRDA) and the U.S. Civilian Research and Development Foundation (CRDF), Award No. MM2-3034. Both authors acknowledge IST-2001-32008 project "MolCoNet".

References

1. A. Alhazov, R. Freund, Gh. Păun: P systems with active membranes and two polarizations. In: Gh. Păun, A. Riscos-Núñez, A. Romero-Jiménez, F. Sancho-Caparrini (eds.): *Second Brainstorming Week on Membrane Computing*, TR 01/2004, University of Seville, Seville (2004), 20–36.
2. A. Alhazov, L. Pan: Polarizationless P systems with active membranes. *Grammars*, **7**, 1 (2004).
3. A. Alhazov, L. Pan, Gh. Păun: Trading polarizations for labels in P systems with active membranes. *Acta Informaticae*, accepted (2003).

4. A. Alhazov, C. Martín-Vide, L. Pan: Solving graph problems by P systems with restricted elementary active nembranes. In: N. Jonoska, Gh. Păun, G. Rozenberg (eds.): *Aspects of Molecular Computing, Lecture Notes in COmputer Science*, **2950** Festschrift, Springer, 2004, 1–22.

5. A. Alhazov, C. Martín-Vide, L. Pan: Solving a PSPACE-complete problem by P systems with restricted active membranes. *Fundamenta Informaticae*, **58**, 2 (2003), 67–77.

6. Dassow, J., Păun, Gh.: *Regulated Rewriting in Formal Language Theory*. Springer, Berlin, 1989.

7. R. Freund, C. Martín-Vide, Gh. Păun: From regulated rewriting to computing with membranes: collapsing hierarchies, *Theoretical Computer Science*, **312** (2004), 143–188.

8. R. Freund, Gh. Păun: Deterministic P systems. *Submitted* (2004).

9. M.A. Gutierrez-Narajano, M.J. Pérez-Jiménez, A. Riscos-Núñez: Solving numerical NP-complete problems using P systems with active membranes: the partition problem and beyond. *EMCC Workshop,* Vienna, 2003.

10. S. N. Krishna, R. Rama: A variant of P systems with active membranes: solving NP-complete problems. *Romanian J. of Information Science and Technology*, **2**, 4 (1999), 357–367.

11. M. Madhu, K. Krithivasan: Improved results about the universality of P systems. *Bulletin of the EATCS*, **76** (February 2002), 162–168.

12. A. Obtułowicz: Deterministic P systems for solving SAT problem. *Romanian J. of Information Science and Technology*, **4**, 1-2 (2001), 195–202.

13. A. Obtułowicz: On P systems with active membranes solving integer factorizing problem in a polynomial time. In: C.S. Calude, Gh. Păun, G. Rozenberg, A. Salomaa (eds.): *Multiset Processing. Mathematical, Computer Science, and Molecular Computing Points of View. Lecture Notes in Computer Science* **2235**, Springer, 2001, 267–286.

14. A. Păun: On P systems with global rules. In: N. Jonoska, N.C. Seeman (eds.): *Proc. 7th Intern. Meeting on DNA Based Computers*. Tampa, 2001, 43–52.

15. Gh. Păun: *Computing with Membranes: An Introduction*. Springer, Berlin, 2002.

16. Gh. Paun: Computing with Membranes - A Variant: P systems with polarized membranes. *Intern. J. of Foundations of Computer Science*, **11**, 1 (2000), 167–182.

17. M. Pérez-Jiménez, A. Romero Jiménez, F. Sancho Caparrini: *Teoria de la complejidad en modelos de computacion celular con membranas*. Kronos Editorial, Seville, 2002.

18. M. J. Pérez Jiménez, A. Romero Jiménez, F. Sancho Caparrini: Solving VALIDITY problem by active membranes with input. In: M. Cavaliere, C. Martín-Vide, Gh. Păun (eds.): Rovira i Virgili Univ. Tech. Rep. **26/03**, *Proc. Brainstorming Week on Membrane Computing*, Tarragona, 2003, 279–290.

19. A. Salomaa, G. Rozenberg (eds.): *Handbook of Formal Languages*. Springer, Berlin, 1997.

20. P. Sosík: Solving a PSPACE-complete problem by P systems with active membranes. In: M. Cavaliere, C. Martín-Vide, Gh. Păun (eds.): Rovira i Virgili Univ. Tech. Rep. **26/03**, *Proc. Brainstorming Week on Membrane Computing*, Tarragona, 2003, 305–312.

21. Cl. Zandron, Cl. Ferretti, G. Mauri: Solving NP-complete problems using P systems with active membranes. In: I. Antoniou, C.S. Calude, M.J. Dinneen (eds.): *Unconventional Models of Computation*. Springer, London, 2000, 289–301.

Communicative P Systems with Minimal Cooperation

Artiom Alhazov[1,2], Maurice Margenstern[3], Vladimir Rogozhin[4],
Yurii Rogozhin[1], and Sergey Verlan[3]

[1] Institute of Mathematics and Computer Science,
Academy of Sciences of Moldova, Chişinău, Moldova
{artiom, rogozhin}@math.md
[2] Research Group on Mathematical Linguistics,
Rovira i Virgili University, Tarragona, Spain
artiome.alhazov@estudiants.urv.es
[3] LITA, Université de Metz, France
{margens, verlan}@sciences.univ-metz.fr
[4] State University of Moldova, Chişinău, Moldova
rv@math.md

Abstract. We prove that two classes of communicative P systems with 3 membranes and with minimal cooperation, namely P systems with symport/antiport rules of size 1 and and P systems with symport rules of size 2, are computationally complete: they generate all recursively enumerable sets of vectors of nonnegative integers. The result of computation is obtained in the elementary membrane.

1 Introduction

P systems were introduced by Gheorghe Păun in [12] as distributed parallel computing devices of biochemical inspiration. The original definition is quite general and many different variants of P systems were proposed; we refer to [15] for a comprehensive bibliography. One of these variants, P systems with *symport/antiport*, was introduced in [11]. This variant uses one of the most important features of membrane systems: the communication. This operation is so powerful, that it suffices by itself for a big computational power. These systems have two types of rules: symport rules, when several objects go together from one membrane to another, and antiport rules, when several objects from two membranes are exchanged. In spite of the simple definition, using such operations we can compute all Turing computable sets of numbers [11]. This result was several times improved with respect to the number of used membranes and/or the size of symport/antiport rules ([4], [6], [9], [13], [2], [8], [14]).

Rather unexpectedly, *minimal symport/antiport* P systems, *i.e.*, systems where symport rules move only one object and antiport rules move only two objects across the same membrane in different directions, are universal. The proof of this result may be found in [1] and the corresponding system has 9 membranes.

G. Mauri et al. (Eds.): WMC5 2004, LNCS 3365, pp. 161–177, 2005.
© Springer-Verlag Berlin Heidelberg 2005

This result was improved first by reducing the number of membranes to six [7], five [2], four [5, 8], and at last G. Vaszil [14] showed that three membranes are sufficient to generate all recursively enumerable sets of numbers (but his proof had one disadvantage: the output membrane contains 5 additional symbols). In this paper we give another proof of the last result which was obtained independently. We also remark that in our proof the output membrane does not contain superfluous symbols.

Minimally cooperative symport P systems, *i.e.*, P systems only having symport rules and only moving one or two objects, are universal with four membranes [6]. In this paper we improve that result down to three membranes.

Our proofs of both results are based on a simulation of counter automata (or register machines [10]), see also [3], which was also used in [1], [4], [7], and [2].

The question about universality of P systems with minimal symport/antiport (symport) rules with 1 and 2 membranes is still open.

2   Basic Notions

A non-deterministic *counter automaton* is a 5-tuple $M = (Q, q_0, q_f, C, P)$, where

- Q is a finite set of states,
- $q_0 \in Q$ is the initial state,
- $q_f \in Q$ is the final state,
- C is a finite set of counters,
- P is a finite set of instructions of the following form:
  1. $(q_i \to q_l, c_k+)$, with $q_i, q_l \in Q$, $q_i \neq q_f$, $c_k \in C$ increment instruction). This instruction increments counter c_k by 1 and changes the state of the system from q_i to q_l.
  2. $(q_i \to q_l, c_k-)$, with $q_i, q_l \in Q$, $q_i \neq q_f$, $c_k \in C$ decrement instruction). If the value of counter c_k is greater than zero, then this instruction decrements it by 1 and changes the state of the system from q_i to q_l. Otherwise (when the value of c_k is zero) the computation is blocked in state q_i.
  3. $(q_i \to q_l, c_k = 0)$, with $q_i, q_l \in Q$, $q_i \neq q_f$, $c_k \in C$ (zero test instruction). If the value of counter c_k is zero, then this instruction changes the state of the system from q_i to q_l. Otherwise (the value of c_k is greater than zero) the computation is blocked in state q_i.
  4. *Stop.* This instruction stops the computation of the counter automaton and it can be assigned only to the final state q_f.

A transition of the counter automaton consists in updating/checking the value of a counter according to an instruction of one of types above and by changing the current state to another one. The computation starts in state q_0 and with all counters equal to zero. A result of the computation of a counter automaton is the set of all values of the first counter $c_1 \in C$ when the computation halts in state $q_f \in Q$.

It is known that non-deterministic counter automata generate all recursively enumerable sets of non-negative natural numbers starting from empty counters.

A P system with symport/antiport (symport) is a construct

$$\Pi = (O, \mu, w_1, \ldots, w_k, E, R_1, \ldots, R_k, i_0),$$

where:

1. O is a finite alphabet of symbols called objects,
2. μ is a membrane structure consisting of m membranes that are labelled in a one-to-one manner by $1, 2, \ldots, k$.
3. $w_i \in O^*$, for each $1 \leq i \leq k$ is a *finite* multiset (*i.e.*, multiset where elements are present in a finite number of copies) of objects associated with the region i (delimited by membrane i),
4. $E \subseteq O$ is the set of objects that appear in the environment in an infinite number of copies,
5. R_i, for each $1 \leq i \leq k$, is a finite set of symport/antiport rules associated with the region i and which have the forms (x, in), (y, out), $(y, out; x, in)$, where $x, y \in O^*$ (for symport P systems R_i contains only rules of the forms (x, in), (y, out)),
6. i_0 is the label of an elementary membrane of μ that identifies the output region.

A symport/antiport (symport) P system is defined as a computational device consisting of a set of k hierarchically nested membranes that identify k distinct regions (the membrane structure μ), where to each region i there are assigned a multiset of objects w_i and a finite set of symport/antiport (symport) rules R_i, $1 \leq i \leq k$. A rule $(x, in) \in R_i$ permits to objects specified by x to be moved into region i from the immediately outer region. Notice that for P systems with symport the rules in the skin membrane of the form (x, in), where $x \in E^*$, are forbidden (they directly lead to endless computations). A rule $(x, out) \in R_i$ permits to the multiset x to be moved from region i into the outer region. A rule $(y, out; x, in)$ permits to multisets y and x, which are situated in region i and the outer region of i respectively, to be exchanged. It is clear that a rule can be applied if and only if the multisets involved by it are present in the corresponding regions.

As usual, a computation in a symport/antiport (symport) P system is obtained by applying the rules in a non-deterministic maximally parallel manner. Specifically, in this variant, a computation is restricted to moving objects through membranes, since symport/antiport (symport) rules do not allow the system to modify the objects placed inside the regions. Initially, each region i contains the corresponding finite multiset w_i, whereas the environment contains only objects from E that appear in infinitely many copies.

A computation is successful if starting from the initial configuration it reaches a configuration where no rule can be applied. The result of a successful computation is a natural number that is obtained by counting the objects that are presented in region i_0. Given a P system Π, the set of natural numbers computed in this way by Π is denoted by $N(\Pi)$. If the multiplicity of each object is counted separately, then a vector of natural numbers is obtained, denoted by $Ps\Pi$, see [13].

We denote by $NOP_m(sym_r, anti_t)$ $(NOP_m(sym_r))$ the family of sets of natural numbers that are generated by a P system with symport/antiport (symport) having at most $m > 0$ membranes, symport rules of size at most $r \geq 0$, and antiport rules of size at most $t \geq 0$. The size of a symport rule (x, in) or (x, out) is given by $|x|$, while the size of an antiport rule $(y, out; x, in)$ is given by $max\{|x|, |y|\}$. We denote by NRE the family of recursively enumerable sets of natural numbers. If we replace numbers by vectors, then in the 3 notations of this paragraph N is replaced by Ps.

3   Main Results

Theorem 1. $NOP_3(sym_1, anti_1) = NRE$.

Proof. We prove this result by simulating a non-deterministic counter automaton $M = (Q, q_0, q_f, C, P)$ which starts with empty counters. We suppose that all instructions from P are labelled in a one-to-one manner with $\{1, \ldots, n\} = I$. Denote by I_+ $(I_+ \subseteq I)$ the set of labels of increment instructions, by I_- $(I_- \subseteq I)$ the set of labels of decrement instructions, and by $I_{=0}$ $(I_{=0} \subseteq I)$ the set of labels of zero test instructions.

We construct a P system Π with the membrane structure

$$[_1 [_2 [_3 \ ]_3]_2]_1,$$

and with the computations proceedings along three stages:

1. Preparation of the system for the computation.
2. The simulation of instructions of the counter automaton.
3. Terminating the computation.

We code the counter automaton as follows. At each moment (after stage one) region 1 holds the current state of the automaton, represented by a symbol $q_i \in Q$, region 2 keeps the value of all counters, represented by the number of occurrences of symbols $c_k \in C$. We simulate the instructions of the counter automaton and we use for this simulation the symbols $c_k \in C$, a_j, b_j, d_j, e_j, $j \in I$. During the first stage we bring from the environment an arbitrary number of symbols b_j into region 3, symbols d_j into region 2 and symbols c_k into region 1. We suppose that we have enough symbols in the corresponding membranes to perform the computation. We also use the following idea: we bring from the environment symbols c_k into region 1 all time during the computation. This process may be stopped only if all stages finish correctly. Otherwise, the computation will never stop.

We split our proof in several parts which depend on the logical separation of the behavior of the system. We will present rules and initial symbols for each part, but we remark that the system that we present is the union of all these parts.

We construct the P system Π as follows:

$$\Pi = (O, [_1 \, [_2 \, [_3 \,]_3 \,]_2 \,]_1, w_1, w_2, w_3, E, R_1, R_2, R_3, 3),$$
$$O = E \cup \{f_j \mid j \in I\} \cup \{m_1 \mid 1 \le i \le 5\}$$
$$\cup \{l_7, l_8, g_1, g_2, g_3, I_a, I_1, I_2, I_3, I_c, O_b, O_2, i, t, \#_0, \#_1, \#_2\},$$
$$E = \{a_j, b_j, d_j, e_j \mid j \in I\} \cup \{c_k \mid c_k \in C\}$$
$$\cup \{q_i \mid q_i \in Q\} \cup \{l_i \mid 1 \le i \le 6\},$$
$$w_1 = I_1 I_2 I_3 O_2 g_2 i l_7 l_8 \#_1 \#_2,$$
$$w_2 = I_c t m_1 m_2 \#_0,$$
$$w_3 = I_a O_b g_1 g_3 m_3 m_4 m_5 \prod_{j \in I} f_j,$$
$$R_i = R_{i,s} \cup R_{i,r} \cup R_{i,f} \cup R_{i,a}, \ 1 \le i \le 3.$$

The rules are given by phases: START (stage 1), RUN (stage 2), FIN (stage 3) and AUX.

AUX.

$$R_{1,a} = \{\mathbf{1a1} : (I_c, in), \ \mathbf{1a2} : (I_1, in)\} \cup \{\mathbf{1a3} : (I_c, out; c_k, in) \mid c_k \in C\}$$
$$\cup \{\mathbf{1a4} : (I_1, out; b_j, in) \mid j \in I\} \cup \{\mathbf{1a5} : (I_1, out; d_j, in) \mid j \in I_{=0}\}$$
$$\cup \{\mathbf{1a6} : (\#_0, in), \ \mathbf{1a7} : (\#_0, out)\},$$
$$R_{2,a} = \{\mathbf{2a1} : (O_b, out), \mathbf{2a2} : (I_a, in), \ \mathbf{2a3} : (I_2, in)\}$$
$$\cup \{\mathbf{2a4} : (b_j, out; O_b, in) \mid j \in I_-\} \cup \{\mathbf{2a5} : (I_a, out; a_j, in) \mid j \in I_+\}$$
$$\cup \{\mathbf{2a6} : (I_2, out; b_j, in) \mid j \in I\} \cup \{\mathbf{2a7} : (I_2, out; d_j, in) \mid j \in I_{=0}\},$$
$$R_{3,a} = \{\mathbf{3a1} : (O_2, out), \mathbf{3a2} : (I_3, in), \mathbf{3a3} : (I_3, out; c_1, in)\}$$
$$\cup \{\mathbf{3a4} : (x, out; O_2, in) \mid x \in \{I_1, I_2, g_2, l_1, l_2, l_3, l_7\}\}$$
$$\cup \{\mathbf{3a5} : (a_j, out; O_2, in) \mid j \in I\}$$
$$\cup \{\mathbf{3a6} : (\#_i, in), \ \mathbf{3a7} : (\#_i, out) \mid 1 \le i \le 2\}.$$

Symbols I_a, I_1, I_2, I_3, I_c bring symbols inside some membrane and return. Symbols O_1, O_b take symbols outside some membrane and return. Symbols $\#_0, \#_1, \#_2$ check for "invalid" computations.

START.

$$R_{1,s} = \{\mathbf{1s1} : (g_3, out; q_0, in)\},$$
$$R_{2,s} = \{\mathbf{2s1} : (I_2, out; \#_1, in), \ \mathbf{2s2} : (t, out; I_1, in), \ \mathbf{2s3} : (I_2, out; t, in)\}$$
$$\cup \{\mathbf{2s4} : (g_1, out; g_2, in), \ \mathbf{2s5} : (I_c, out; g_1, in), \ \mathbf{2s6} : (g_3, out; i, in)\},$$
$$R_{3,s} = \{\mathbf{3s1} : (b_j, in) \mid j \in I\} \cup \{\mathbf{3s2} : (g_1, out; I_1, in), \ \mathbf{3s3} : (g_3, out; g_2, in)\}$$
$$\cup \{\mathbf{3s4} : (I_1, out; I_2, in), \ \mathbf{3s5} : (O_b, out; I_1, in), \ \mathbf{3s6} : (I_a, out; i, in)\}.$$

Symbols I_1, I_2 bring from environment "sufficiently many" symbols d_j in region 2 and a "correct number of" symbols b_j in region 3 for the computation (rules 1a4,2a3,1a2,2a6,1a5,3s1,2a7). We illustrate this process in Figure 1.

The figures in this paper describe different stages of the evolution of the P system given in the corresponding theorem. For simplicity, we focus on explaining a particular stage and omit the objects that do not participate in the evolution at that time. Each rectangle represents a membrane, each variable represents a copy of an object in a corresponding membrane (symbols outside of the rectangle are in the environment). In each step, the symbols that will evolve (will be moved) are written in boldface. The labels of the applied rules are written above the $\Rightarrow$ symbol.

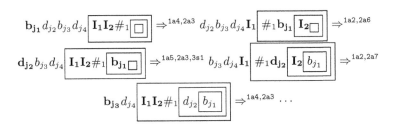

Fig. 1. Bringing objects b_j, d_j

Notice that I_2 cannot be idle, as it immediately leads to an infinite computation (rules 2s1,3a6,3a7), so d_j and b_j in region 1 must be moved to region 2 by I_2 (rules 2a6 and 2a7).

At some point, I_1 stops bringing symbols d_j, b_j. I_1 and I_2 are removed from their "pumping" positions, I_c is placed in region 1, where it can "pump" symbols c_k into the skin membrane, and q_0 is brought into region 1 to start the simulation of the register machine. In the meantime I_a reaches region 2 and O_b reaches region 1. Notice that both $(g_1, out; I_1, in)$ and $(O_b, out; I_1, in)$ from $R_{3,s}$ are applied, in either order (Figure 2).

RUN.

$$R_{1,r} = \{1\text{r}1 : (q_i, out; a_j, in),\ 1\text{r}2 : (b_j, out; q_l, in)$$
$$\mid (j : q_i \to q_l, c_k\gamma) \in P, \gamma \in \{+, -, = 0\}\}$$
$$\cup\ \{1\text{r}3 : (d_j, out; e_j, in) \mid (j : q_i \to q_l, c_k = 0) \in P\},$$
$$R_{2,r} = \{2\text{r}1 : (b_j, out; c_k, in) \mid (j : q_i \to q_l, c_k+) \in P\}\}$$
$$\cup\ \{2\text{r}2 : (c_k, out; a_j, in) \mid (j : q_i \to q_l, c_k-) \in P\}$$
$$\cup\ \{2\text{r}3 : (d_j, out; a_j, in),\ 2\text{r}4 : (c_k, out; e_j, in),$$
$$2\text{r}5 : (b_j, out; e_j, in) \mid (j : q_i \to q_l, c_k = 0) \in P\},$$
$$R_{3,r} = \{3\text{r}1 : (b_j, out; a_j, in) \mid (j : q_i \to q_l, c_k+) \in P\}$$
$$\cup\ \{3\text{r}2 : (b_j, out; a_j, in) \mid (j : q_i \to q_l, c_k-) \in P\}$$

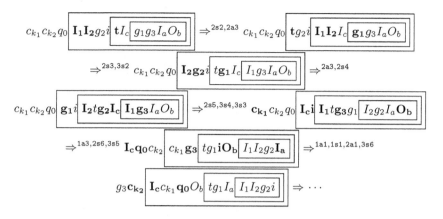

Fig. 2. Ending of the initialization (stage 1)

$$\cup \; \{\mathbf{3r3} : (f_j, out; a_j, in), \; \mathbf{3r4} : (b_j, out; f_j, in)$$
$$\mid (j : q_i \rightarrow q_l, c_k = 0) \in P\}.$$

While I_c is bringing symbols c_k into the skin membrane (rules $\mathbf{1a1}, \mathbf{1a3}$), instructions $(j : q_i \rightarrow q_l, c_k \gamma)$, $\gamma \in \{+, -, = 0\}$ of the register machine are simulated.
Increment instruction:

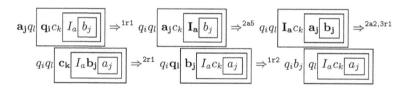

Fig. 3. q_i replaced by q_l, c_k moved into region 2

Decrement instruction:

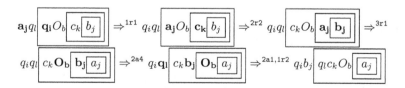

Fig. 4. q_i replaced by q_l, c_k removed from region 2

Checking for zero. q_i replaced by q_l if there is no c_k in region 2 (Figure 5), otherwise e_j exchanges with c_k and b_j remains in region 2 (Figure 6).

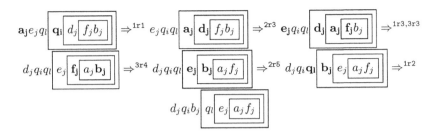

Fig. 5. Zero test instruction. There is no c_k in region 2

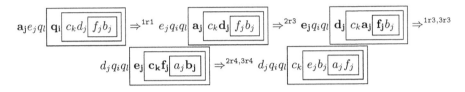

Fig. 6. Zero test instruction. There is c_k in region 2

FIN.

$$R_{1,f} = \{1\mathtt{f1} : (m_1, out; l_1, in), \ 1\mathtt{f2} : (\#_1, out; m_1, in), \ 1\mathtt{f3} : (m_2, out; l_2, in)\}$$
$$\cup \ \{1\mathtt{f4} : (m_3, out; l_3, in), \ 1\mathtt{f5} : (m_4, out; l_4, in), \ 1\mathtt{f6} : (l_4, out; l_5, in)\}$$
$$\cup \ \{1\mathtt{f7} : (m_5, out; l_6, in)\},$$
$$R_{2,f} = \{2\mathtt{f1} : (m_1, out; q_f, in), \ 2\mathtt{f2} : (q_f, out; l_7, in), \ 2\mathtt{f3} : (m_2, out; l_1, in)\}$$
$$\cup \ \{2\mathtt{f4} : (m_3, out; O_2, in), \ 2\mathtt{f5} : (m_4, out; I_3, in), \ 2\mathtt{f6} : (I_3, out; l_2, in)\}$$
$$\cup \ \{2\mathtt{f7} : (m_5, out; l_8, in), \ 2\mathtt{f8} : (l_8, out; I_c, in), \ 2\mathtt{f9} : (c_1, out; l_6, in)\}$$
$$\cup \ \{2\mathtt{fa} : (l_6, out; \#_2, in), \ 2\mathtt{fb} : (l_3, in), \ 2\mathtt{fc} : (\#_0, out, l_5, in)\}$$
$$\cup \ \{2\mathtt{fd} : (l_3, out, l_5, in)\},$$
$$R_{3,f} = \{3\mathtt{f1} : (m_3, out; l_7, in), \ 3\mathtt{f2} : (m_4, out; l_1, in), \ 3\mathtt{f3} : (m_5, out; l_2, in)\}$$
$$\cup \ \{3\mathtt{f4} : (b_j, out; l_3, in) \mid j \in I\}.$$

If a successful computation of the register machine is correctly simulated, then q_f will appear in region 1. $\#_1$ is removed from region 1, and a chain reaction is started, during which symbols l_i move inside the membrane structure, and symbols m_i move outside the membrane structure (Figure 7).

Now O_2 will pump outside the elementary membrane any symbol which stays there, except c_1 (rules **3a1**, **3a4**, **3a5**). m_4 will exchange with I_3 (rule **2f5**), and the latter will pump symbols c_1 into the elementary membrane (rules **3a2**, **3a3**), and eventually exchange with l_2 (rule **2f6**).

Object m_3 comes to the environment in exchange for l_3 (rule **1f4**), which goes to membrane 2 (rule **2fb**), and stays there if there is no object b_j in the elementary membrane (otherwise l_3 will exchange with b_j by rule **3f4**). m_4 comes to the environment in exchange for l_4 (rule **1f5**), which brings l_5 in the skin. l_5

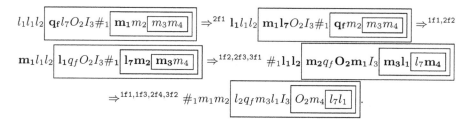

Fig. 7. Beginning of the termination (stage 3)

then exchanges with l_3 by rule **2fd**. Notice that presence of b_j in region 3 will force l_5 to move $\#_0$ in region 1 (rule **2fc**), leading to an infinite computation (rules **1a6**, **1a7**), as l_3 will be situated in region 3.

Finally (after I_3 returns to region 1 and l_2 comes in region 2 by rule **2f6**), l_2 moves m_5 into region 2 (rule **3f3**), and the latter exchanges with l_8 (rule **2f7**) and then with l_6 (rule **1f7**). At some point l_8 moves I_c into region 2 (rule **2f8**), to finish pumping objects c_k. As for l_6 in membrane 1, it guarantees that no more objects c_1 remain in membrane 2 (otherwise it moves $\#_2$ in membrane 2 (rules **2f9**, **2fa**), leading to an infinite computation (rule **3a6**, **3a7**)).

If the computation halts, then the elementary membrane will only contain objects c_1, in the multiplicity of the value of the first register of the register machine. Conversely, any computation of the register machine allows a correct simulation (from the construction). Thus, the class of P systems with symport and antiport of size 1 generate exactly all recursively enumerable sets of non-negative integers.   □

A "dual" class of systems $OP(sym_1, anty_1)$ is the class $OP(sym_2)$ where two objects are moved across the membrane in the same direction rather than in the opposite ones. We now prove a similar result for the other class.

Theorem 2. $NOP_3(sym_2) = NRE$.

Proof. As in the proof of Theorem 1 we simulate a non-deterministic counter automaton $M = (Q, q_0, q_f, C, P)$ which starts with empty counters. Again we suppose that all instructions from P are labelled in a one-to-one manner with $\{1, \ldots, n\} = I$, and I_+ ($I_+ \subseteq I$) is the set of labels of increment instructions, I_- ($I_- \subseteq I$) is the set of labels of decrement instructions, and $I_{=0}$ ($I_{=0} \subseteq I$) is the set of labels of zero test instructions.

We construct the P system Π_2 as follows:

$$\Pi_2 = (O, E, [_1 [_2 [_3]_3]_2]_1, w_1, w_2, w_3, R_1, R_2, R_3, 3),$$
$$O = E \cup \{d_j, e_j \mid j \in I\} \cup \{t_i \mid 0 \le i \le 10\}$$
$$\cup \{g_1, g_3, I_a, I_1, I_2, I_c, O_b, \#_1, \#_2\}$$
$$\cup \{q_i \mid q_i \in Q\},$$
$$E = \{a_j, b_j \mid j \in I\} \cup \{c_k \mid c_k \in C\} \cup \{l_i \mid 3 \le i \le 8\} \cup \{g_2\},$$

$$w_1 = t_0 t_1 t_2 t_3 t_4 I_1 I_2 I_a l_1 l_2 \#_1 \prod_{j \in I} e_j \prod_{q_i \in Q} q_i,$$

$$w_2 = t_5 t_6 t_7 t_8 t_9 t_{10} I_c g_3 s_1 m_2 \#_2 \prod_{j \in I} d_j,$$

$$w_3 = g_1 O_b s_2 m_1,$$

$$R_i = R_{i,s} \cup R_{i,r} \cup R_{i,m} \cup R_{i,c} \cup R_{i,f} \cup R_{i,a}, \ 1 \le i \le 3.$$

The functioning of this system may be split in three stages as it is done in Theorem 1.

We code the counter automaton as follows. At each moment (after stage one) the environment holds the current state of the automaton, represented by a symbol $q_i \in Q$, the membrane 2 holds the value of all counters, represented by the number of occurrences of symbols $c_k \in C$. We simulate the instructions of the counter automaton and we use for this simulation the symbols $c_k \in C$, $a_j, b_j, d_j, e_j, \ j \in I$. During the first stage we bring from environment in the membrane 3 an arbitrary number of symbols b_j. We suppose that we have enough symbols b_j in membrane 3 to perform the computation. We also use the following idea: we bring from environment to membrane 1 the symbols c_k all time during the computation. This process may be stopped only if all stages completed correctly. Otherwise, the computation will never stop.

We split our proof in several parts which depend on the logical separation of the behavior of the system. We will present rules and initial symbols for each part, but we remark that the system that we present is the union of all these parts.

The rules R_i are given by phases: START (stage 1); RUN (stage 2); MOVE, CLEANUP and FIN (stage 3), and AUX.

AUX.

$$R_{1,a} = \{1a1 : (I_c, out), \ 1a2 : (I_1, out)\} \cup \{1a3 : (I_c c_k, in) \mid c_k \in C\}$$
$$\cup \{1a4 : (I_1 b_j, in) \mid j \in I\} \cup \{1a5 : (\#_2, in), \ 1a6 : (\#_2, out)\},$$
$$R_{2,a} = \{2a1 : (O_b, in), \ 2a2 : (I_a, out), \ 2a3 : (I_2, out)\}$$
$$\cup \{2a4 : (O_b b_j, out) \mid j \in I_+\} \cup \{2a5 : (I_a a_j, in) \mid j \in I_-\}$$
$$\cup \{2a6 : (I_2 b_j, in) \mid j \in I\},$$
$$R_{3,a} = \{3a1 : (\#_1, in), \ 3a2 : (\#_1, out)\}$$
$$\cup \{3a3 : (s_i, in), \ 3a4 : (s_i, out) \mid 1 \le i \le 2\}.$$

Symbol I_1 brings symbols b_j inside membrane 1 and returns to the environment. Symbol I_c brings symbols c_k inside membrane 1 and returns to the environment. Symbol I_2 brings symbols b_j inside membrane 2 and returns to membrane 1. Symbol I_a brings symbols a_j inside membrane 2 and returns to membrane 1. Symbol O_b takes symbols b_j outside membrane 2 and returns. Symbols $\#_1, \#_2$ check for "invalid" computations. Symbols s_1, s_2 remember whether the derivation step is even or odd.

START.

$$R_{1,s} = \{\mathbf{1s1} : (g_1t_2, out), \ \mathbf{1s2} : (t_2g_2, in), \ \mathbf{1s3} : (g_3q_0, out)\},$$
$$R_{2,s} = \{\mathbf{2s1} : (t_0I_2, in), \ \mathbf{2s2} : (I_2\#_1, in), \ \mathbf{2s3} : (I_1t_1, in)\}$$
$$\cup \ \{\mathbf{2s4} : (g_1I_c, out), \ \mathbf{2s5} : (g_2t_3, in), \ \mathbf{2s6} : (t_3g_3, out)\},$$
$$R_{3,s} = \{\mathbf{3s1} : (b_j, in) \mid j \in I\} \cup \{\mathbf{3s2} : (I_2t_1, in), \ \mathbf{3s3} : (I_1t_7, in)\}$$
$$\cup \ \{\mathbf{3s4} : (t_7g_1, out), \ \mathbf{3s5} : (g_2t_{10}, in), \ \mathbf{3s6} : (t_{10}O_b, out)\}.$$

Symbols I_1, I_2 bring from environment a "correct number of" symbols b_j in region 3 for the computation (rules **1a2**, **1a4**, **2a6**, **2a3**, **3s1**) (see Figure 8). Notice that I_2 cannot be idle, as it immediately leads to infinite computation (rules **2s2**, **3a1**, **3a2**), so b_j in region 1 must be moved by I_2 by rule **2a6**.

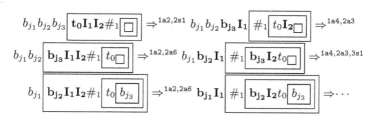

Fig. 8. Bringing objects b_j

At some point, I_1 stops bringing symbols b_j. I_1 and I_2 are removed from their "pumping" positions, I_c is placed in region 1, where it can "pump" symbols c_k into the skin membrane, and q_0 is brought into the environment to start the simulation of the register machine. In the meantime O_b reaches region 2 (Figure 9).

RUN.

$$R_{1,r} = \{\mathbf{1r1} : (q_ia_j, in), \ \mathbf{1r2} : (b_jq_l, out)$$
$$\mid (j : q_i \to q_l, c_k\gamma) \in P, \gamma \in \{+, -, = 0\}\}$$
$$R_{2,r} = \{\mathbf{2r1} : (a_jc_k, in) \mid (j : q_i \to q_l, c_k+) \in P\}$$
$$\cup \ \{\mathbf{2r2} : (b_jc_k, out) \mid (j : q_i \to q_l, c_k-) \in P\}$$
$$\cup \ \{\mathbf{2r3} : (a_je_j, in), \ \mathbf{2r4} : (e_jc_k, out),$$
$$\mathbf{2r5} : (e_jb_j, out) \mid (j : q_i \to q_l, c_k = 0) \in P\},$$
$$R_{3,r} = \{\mathbf{3r1} : (a_jd_j, in), \ \mathbf{3r2} : (d_jb_j, out)$$
$$\mid (j : q_i \to q_l, c_k\gamma) \in P, \gamma \in \{+, -, = 0\}\}.$$

While I_c is bringing symbols c_k into the skin membrane (rules **1a1**, **1a3**), instructions $(j : q_i \to q_l, c_k\gamma)$, $\gamma \in \{+, -, = 0\}$ of the register machine are simulated.

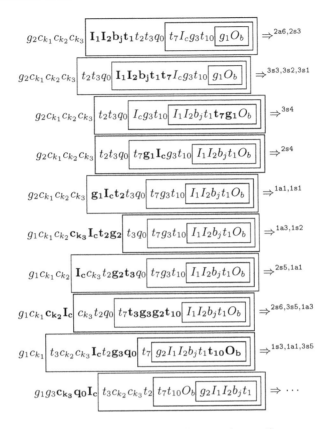

Fig. 9. End of the initialization (stage 1)

Increment instruction:
Decrement instruction:
Checking for zero. q_i replaced by q_l if there is no c_k in region 2 (Figure 12), otherwise e_j comes in region 1 with c_k and b_j remains in region 2 (Figure 13).

MOVE.

$R_{1,m} = \{1\mathbf{m}1 : (q_f l_3, in),\ 1\mathbf{m}2 : (m_1 t_4, out),\ 1\mathbf{m}3 : (t_4 l_4, in)\}$,
$R_{2,m} = \{2\mathbf{m}1 : (l_3 l_1, in),\ 2\mathbf{m}2 : (m_1 t_6, out),\ 2\mathbf{m}3 : (t_6 l_2, in),\ 2\mathbf{m}4 : (l_2 \# _2, out)\}$,
$R_{3,m} = \{3\mathbf{m}1 : (l_1 c_1, in),\ 3\mathbf{m}2 : (l_1, out),\ 3\mathbf{m}3 : (l_3 t_5, in)\}$
  $\cup \{3\mathbf{m}4 : (t_5 m_1, out),\ 3\mathbf{m}5 : (l_2 t_8, in)\} \cup \{3\mathbf{m}6 : (l_2 b_j, out) \mid j \in I\}$.

If a successful computation of the register machine is correctly simulated, then q_f will appear in region 1. A chain reaction is started, during which symbols l_i move inside the membrane structure, and symbols m_i move outside the membrane structure. Notice that q_f brings l_3 into region 1 (rule **1m1**), then l_3 brings l_1 into region 2 (**rule 2m1**), then l_1 moves objects c_1 from region 2 into region 3 by

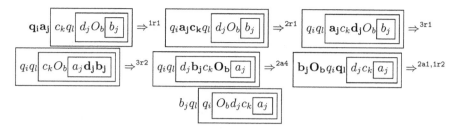

Fig. 10. q_i replaced by q_l, c_k moved into region 2

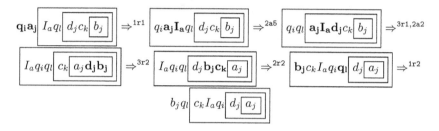

Fig. 11. q_i replaced by q_l, c_k removed from region 2

Fig. 12. Zero test instruction. There is no c_k in region 2

Fig. 13. Zero test instruction. There is c_k in region 2

rules 3m1 and 3m2. Also, the system verifies that no objects b_j are present in the inner region (otherwise l_2 would bring $\#_2$ in region 1 (rules 3m6, 2m4) and it immediately leads to infinite computation (rules 1a5,1a6)) and moves l_4 into the skin membrane, as shown below (Figure 14).

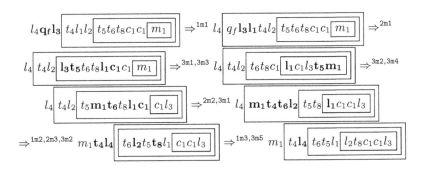

Fig. 14. Beginning of the termination (stage 3)

CLEANUP.

$$R_{1,c} = \{1c1 : (l_4s_1, out),\ 1c2 : (s_1l_5, in),\ 1c3 : (m_2\#_1, out)\}$$
$$\cup \{1c4 : (l_5s_2, out),\ 1c5 : (s_2l_7, in),\ 1c6 : (l_6s_2, in)\},$$
$$R_{2,c} = \{2c1 : (l_4, in),\ 2c2 : (l_4s_1, out),\ 2c3 : (l_5t_9, in)\}$$
$$\cup \{2c4 : (t_9m_2, out),\ 2c5 : (l_5s_2, out)\},$$
$$\cup \{2c6 : (l_4x, out) \mid x \in \{t_5, t_7, t_{10}\} \cup \{d_j \mid j \in I\}\},$$
$$R_{3,c} = \{3c1 : (l_5, in),\ 3c2 : (l_5s_2, out)\}$$
$$\cup \{3c3 : (l_5x, out) \mid x \in \{I_1, I_2, g_2, t_8, l_3\} \cup \{a_j \mid j \in I\}\}.$$

Objects d_j, $j \in I$ and t_5, t_7, t_{10} are removed from region 2, and then objects a_j, $j \in I$ and I_1, I_2, g_2, t_8, l_3 are removed from the inner region. Notice that l_4 only "meets" s_1 (and l_5 only "meets" s_2) after the corresponding cleanup is completed. Really, it is easily to see that object l_4 will be in region 2 after odd steps of computation. Symbol s_1 after odd steps of computation will be located in region 3 (rules 3a3, 3a4). Thus we cannot apply rule 2c2 and can apply rule 2c6 only, until all symbols t_5, t_7, t_{10} and d_j, $j \in I$ will be removed to region 1. After that symbol l_4 waits one step and together with symbol s_1 moves to region 1 and finally to the environment (rules 2c2 and 1c1).

So l_4 will be in the environment after even steps of computation and object l_5 will appear in region 3 after odd steps of computation (rules 1c2, 2c3 and 3c1). Notice that symbol s_2 can appear in region 3 after even steps of computation (rules 3a4, 3a3). Thus we cannot apply rule 3c2 and can apply rule 3c3 only, until all symbols I_1, I_2, g_2, t_8, l_3 and a_j, $j \in I$ will be removed to region 2. After that object l_5 moves to the environment together with symbol s_2 (rules 3c2, 2c5, 1c4) and object l_6 is brought in region 1 (rule 1c6). At that moment in membrane 3 among symbols c_1 there are only two "undesirable" symbols: t_1 and l_2.

FIN.

$$R_{1,f} = \{\mathbf{1f1} : (l_6t_1, out),\ \mathbf{1f2} : (t_1l_7, in),\ \mathbf{1f3} : (l_7l_2, out),\ \mathbf{1f4} : (l_2l_8, in)\},$$
$$R_{2,f} = \{\mathbf{2f1} : (l_6, in),\ \mathbf{2f2} : (l_6t_1, out),\ \mathbf{2f3} : (l_7, in)\}$$
$$\cup\ \{\mathbf{2f4} : (l_7l_2, out),\ \mathbf{2f5} : (l_8I_c, in)\},$$
$$R_{3,f} = \{\mathbf{3f1} : (l_6, in),\ \mathbf{3f2} : (l_6t_1, out),\ \mathbf{3f3} : (l_7, in),\ \mathbf{3f4} : (l_7l_2, out)\}.$$

Objects t_1 and l_2 are removed from the inner region, as shown below (Figure 15), and then l_8 moves I_c from region 1 into region 2 (rule **2f5**) so that the computation can halt.

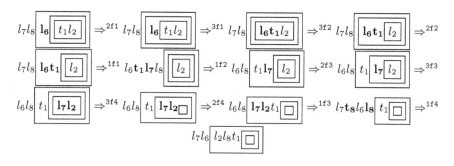

Fig. 15. End of the termination

If the computation halts, then the elementary membrane will only contain objects c_1, in the multiplicity of the value of the first register of the register machine. Conversely, any computation of the register machine allows a correct simulation (from the construction). Thus, the class of P systems with symport of weight 2 generate exactly all recursively enumerable sets of nonnegative integers.

□

4   Final Remarks

Both constructions can be easily modified to show $PsOP_3(sym_1, anti_1) = PsRE$ and $PsOP_3(sym_2) = PsRE$ by moving all output symbols c_k to the elementary membrane, as it is done for symbol c_1. In the proof of Theorem 1 we simply change rule **3a3**: $(I_3, out; c_1, in)$ by rules **3a3**: $(I_3, out; c_k, in)$ for all $c_k \in C$ and in the proof of Theorem 2 change rule **3m1**: (l_1c_1, in) by rules **3m1**: (l_1c_k, in) for all $c_k \in C$.

The questions what is the size of families of numbers computed by minimal symport/antiport (symport) P systems rules with 1 and 2 membranes is still open.

Program Check

P systems in both theorems were checked for errors by the third author using a modification of a program that simulates P systems, originally developed by the first author.

Acknowledgements. The first author is supported by the project TIC2002-04220-C03-02 of the Research Group on Mathematical Linguistics, Tarragona. All authors acknowledge the project IST-2001-32008 "MolCoNet" and the third and the fourth authors acknowledge also the Moldovan Research and Development Association (MRDA) and the U.S. Civilian Research and Development Foundation (CRDF), Award No. MM2-3034 for providing a challenging and fruitful framework for cooperation.

References

1. F. Bernardini, M. Gheorghe, On the Power of Minimal Symport/Antyport. *Preproceedings of Workshop on Membrane Computing, WMC-2003*, Tarragona, July 17–22, 2003, Technical Report No 28/03, RGML, Universitat Rovira i Virgili, Tarragona, 2003, 72–83.

2. F. Bernardini, A. Păun, Universality of Minimal Symport/Antiport: Five Membranes Suffice. *Membrane Computing. International Workshop WMC2003, Tarragona, Spain, Revised Papers*, LNCS **2933**, Springer-Verlag, 2004, 43–45.

3. R. Freund, M. Oswald, GP Systems with Forbidding Contexts. *Fundamenta Informaticae*, **49**, 1-3 (2002), 81–102.

4. R. Freund, A. Păun, Membrane Systems with Symport/Antiport: Universality Results. *Membrane Computing, International Workshop, WMC-CdeA 02, Curtea de Arges, Romania, Revised Papers*, LNCS **2597**, Springer-Verlag, 2003, 270–287.

5. P. Frisco, About P Systems with Symport/Antiport. *Proceedings of the Second Brainstorming Week on Membrane Computing*, TR 01/2004, RGNC, Sevilla University, 2004, 224–236.

6. P. Frisco, J.H. Hoogeboom, Simulating Counter Automata by P Systems with Symport/Antypot. *Membrane Computing, International Workshop, WMC-CdeA 02, Curtea de Arges, Romania,*,Revised Papers. LNCS **2597**, Springer-Verlag, 2003, 288–301.

7. L. Kari, C. Martin-Vide, A. Păun, On the universality of P systems with Minimal Symport/Antiport Rules. *Aspects of Molecular Computing*, LNCS **2950**, Springer-Verlag, 2004, 254–265.

8. M. Margenstern, V. Rogozhin, Y. Rogozhin, S. Verlan, About P Systems with Minimal Symport/Antiport Rules and Four Membranes. *Pre-Proceedings of Fifth Workshop on Membrane Computing, WMC5, Milano-Bicocca, Italy*, 2004, 283–294.

9. C. Martin-Vide, A. Păun, Gh. Păun, On the Power of P systems with Symport and Antiport rules. *Journal of Universal Computer Science*, **8** (2002), 295–305.

10. M.L. Minsky, *Finite and Infinite Machines*. Prentice Hall, Englewood Cliffs, New Jersey, 1967.

11. A. Păun, Gh. Păun, The Power of Communication: P systems with Symport/Antiport. *New Generation Computing*, **20** (2002), 295–305.

12. Gh. Păun, Computing with Membranes. *Journal of Computer and Systems Sciences*, **61** (2000), 108–143.
13. Gh. Păun, *Membrane Computing. An Introduction.* Springer-Verlag, 2002.
14. G. Vaszil, On the size of P systems with minimal symport/antiport. *Pre-Proceedings of Fifth Workshop on Membrane Computing, WMC5, Milano-Bicocca, Italy,* 2004, 422–431.
15. The P systems web page. http://psystems.disco.unimib.it/.

Ultimately Confluent Rewriting Systems. Parallel Multiset–Rewriting with Permitting or Forbidding Contexts

Artiom Alhazov[1,2], and Dragoş Sburlan[3,4]

[1] Research Group on Mathematical Linguistics,
Rovira i Virgili University, Spain
artiome.alhazov@estudiants.urv.es
[2] Institute of Mathematics and Computer Science,
Academy of Sciences of Moldova, Moldova
[3] Department of Informatics and Numerical Methods,
Ovidius University of Constantza, Romania
dsburlan@univ-ovidius.ro
[4] Department of Computer Science and Artificial Intelligence,
University of Sevilla, Spain

Abstract. The aim of this paper is to study the power of parallel multiset-rewriting systems with permitting or forbidding context (or P systems with *non-cooperative rules* with *promoters* or *inhibitors*). The main results obtained are those if we use promoters or inhibitors of weight two, then the systems are computational universal.

Moreover, both constructions satisfy a special property we define: they are *ultimately confluent*. This means that if the system allows at least one halting computation, then their final configurations are reachable from any reachable configuration. The other property both constructions satisfy is that a system allowing at least one halting computation will halt with probability 1.

1 Introduction

The computational model of membrane computing inspired from the functioning of living cells and formalized through P systems proved to be of a special interest for the scientific community, especially when the weakest forms of cooperation are studied. Activating and prohibiting reactions of various substances (molecules) present in cells is modeled in the P system framework by means of promoters/inhibitors (acting at the level of rules) which enforce/forbid the execution of certain rules. When no mechanism for inhibiting the massive parallel characteristic of a P system exists, a deterministic computation is harder to obtain, especially when non semi-linear languages not belonging to $ET0L$ are studied.

Usually in computer science theory we are interested to solve problems in a predictable time. In general, this is a reasonable request if it actually can be

G. Mauri et al. (Eds.): WMC5 2004, LNCS 3365, pp. 178–189, 2005.

done (usually by having a deterministic or a restricted form of nondeterministic computation). However, sometimes it may happen that we are not able to compute the time complexity of the problem to solve. In this case we would like, at least for a particular problem, to have the result in the limit (you may think of this as a semi-algorithm: the time complexity does not count, and the system gives the correct answer when it halts, or never halts if the correct answer does not exist). This bring us to the scope of the current work.

We assume the reader to be familiar with the fundamentals of membrane computing, see `http://psystems.disco.unimib.it` for the bibliography of the domain. The basic model we study is the transitional P systems with promoted/inhibited non-cooperative rules.

2   Deterministic and Confluent Rewriting

For a rewriting system RS, we write $C \Rightarrow C'$ if the system allows a direct transition from an instantaneous description C to an instantaneous description C' (C' is then called a next instantaneous description of C). The relation $\Rightarrow^*$ is a reflexive and transitive closure of $\Rightarrow$. For any rewriting system, we use the word *configuration* to mean any instantaneous description C, reachable from the starting one.

Definition 1. *A configuration of a rewriting system is called* halting *if no rules of the system can be applied to it.*

In this paper we will only talk about the rewriting systems, producing the result at halting.

Definition 2. *A rewriting system is called* deterministic *if for every accessible non-halting configuration C the next configuration is unique.*

Definition 3. *A rewriting system is called* confluent *if either all the computations are non-halting, or there exists a configuration C_h, such that all the computations halt in C_h.*

Notice that if, starting at some configuration C, all the computations halt, then there exists $m \geq 0$, such that all the computations starting from C halt in at most m steps.

We will now introduce a weaker definition of a property of systems, with the computations "unavoidably leading" to the same result, but not necessarily bounded by the number of steps.

Definition 4. *A rewriting system is* ultimately confluent *if there exists such a halting configuration C_h, that for any configuration C we have $C \Rightarrow^* C_h$.*

This property implies two facts:

1. the halting configuration is unique (C_h),
2. C_h is reachable from any configuration.

From now on we will only consider rewriting systems producing result at halting. Think of the graph of all reachable configurations (the arc from configuration C to configuration C' means that C can derive C' in one step). The graph may be infinite. The node is called *final* if it has out-degree 0.

The system is *deterministic* if all nodes have out-degree at most one (hence, there is at most one final node). The system is *confluent* if either there are no final nodes, or the final node is unique, and in that case the graph is finite and does not contain cycles. The *ultimately confluent* system may contain cycles, but either all nodes are non-final, or there is a final node reachable from any configuration. See Figure 1 in Section 6 for an example of such graph.

Example: Consider a rewriting system with the initial configuration S and rewriting rules:

$$S \rightarrow SA$$
$$A \rightarrow \lambda$$
$$S \rightarrow a.$$

Note that the system is not deterministic, and one can choose to apply the first rule an unbounded number of times, but from any configuration it is possible to arrive to the halting one $C_h = a$ by erasing all symbols A and applying the second rule (this is equally true no matter if the system is sequential, concurrent or maximally parallel).

3   Preliminaries

We will denote by V^* the set of all words (finite sequences) of elements of an alphabet (a finite set) V, we will represent the empty word by λ. In this paper we will represent an arbitrary multiset $M = \{(a, n_a) \mid a \in V\}$ by a word $w = \prod_{a \in V} a^{n_a}$ or its permutation, i.e., multiplicity n_a of some symbol a in a multiset M can be represented by number $|w|_a$ of its occurrences in a word w.

If the alphabet is linearly ordered ($V = \{a_j \mid 1 \leq j \leq N\}$), then the Parikh vector of a word is $\Psi_V(w) = (|w|_{a_1} \cdots |w|_{a_N})$. Then, for a language $L \subseteq V^*$ and a language family FL, $Ps(L) = \{\Psi_V(w) \mid w \in L\}$ and $PsFL = \{Ps(L) \mid L \in FL\}$. For instance, the family of recursively enumerable languages is denoted by RE and the family of recursively enumerable sets of vectors of nonnegative integers is denoted by $PsRE$.

3.1   Notations: P Systems

A non-coperative rule with promoters of weight at most k is a rule of the form $a \rightarrow y|_p$, where $a \in V$, $y \in V^*$, $p \in V^*$, $|p| \leq k$. If $p = \lambda$, we write the rule as $a \rightarrow y$. The use of inhibitor p is denoted as $a \rightarrow y|_{\neg p}$.

Let us recall some notations related to the power of P systems. By $r\alpha_c OtP_m(f)$ we denote the family of languages ($\alpha = L$), vector sets ($\alpha = Ps$) or number sets ($\alpha = N$), which are generated (c is omitted) or accepted (with internal input, $c = a$) by P systems with symbol-objects, restricted to satisfy property r (omitted if none), with at most m membranes with the list of features f.

The features considered in the paper are *ncoo* (with non-cooperative object rewriting rules), *pro*$_2$ (with promoters of weight at most 2) or *inh*$_2$ (with inhibitors of weight at most 2). The P systems can be restricted to be deterministic ($r = D$). We also introduce the classes of confluent ($r = C$) and ultimately confluent ($r = U$) P systems.

In this paper we study classes: $PsOP_1(ncoo, pro_2)$, $UPs_aOP_1(ncoo, pro_2)$, $PsOP_1(ncoo, inh_2)$ and $UPs_aOP_1(ncoo, inh_2)$.

3.2   Register Machines

An n-register machine is a construct $M = (n, P, i, h)$ where:

- n is the number of registers;
- P is a set of labeled instructions of the form $(j : op(r), k, l)$ where $op(r)$ is an operation on register r of M; symbols j, k, l belong to the set of labels associated in a one-to-one manner with instructions of P;
- i is the initial label;
- h is the final label.

The instructions allowed by an n-register machine are:

- $(e : inc(r), f, z)$ – add one to the contents of register r and proceed to instruction f or to instruction z ($f = z$ for the deterministic variant);
- $(e : dec(r), f, z)$ – jump to register z if the register r is null; otherwise subtract one from register r and jump to instruction labeled f.
- $(h : halt)$ – finish the computation. This is a unique instruction with label h.

If a register machine $M = (n, P, i, h)$, starting from the instruction labeled i with all registers being empty, stops by halting with value n_j in every register j, $1 \le j \le k$ and the contents of registers $k+1, \cdots, n$ being empty, then it generates a vector $(n_1, \cdots, n_k) \in \mathbb{N}^k$. Any recursively enumerable numeric vector set can be generated by a register machine.

A register machine $M = (n, P, i, h)$ accepts a vector $(n_1, \cdots, n_k) \in \mathbb{N}^k$ iff, starting from the instruction labeled i, with register j having value n_j for $1 \le j \le k$, and the contents of registers $k + 1, \cdots, n$ being empty, the machine stops by the *halt* instruction with all registers being empty. According with Proposition 1, *deterministic* register machines can accept the family of all recursively enumerable sets of numeric vectors.

Proposition 1. *For any partial recursive function $f : \mathbb{N}^\alpha \to \mathbb{N}^\beta$ there exists a deterministic $(max\{\alpha, \beta\} + 2)$–register machine M computing f in such a way that, when starting with $(n_1, \cdots, n_\alpha \in \mathbb{N}^\alpha$ in registers 1 to α, M has computed $f(n_1, \cdots n_{alpha}) = (r_1, \cdots r_\beta)$ if it halts in the final label h with registers 1 to β containing r_1 to r_β (and with all other registers being empty); if the final label cannot be reached, $f(n_1, \cdots, n_\alpha)$ remains undefined.*

4   Ultimately Confluent Universality

The following theorem shows the computational universality of P systems with object rewriting context-free rules and promoters. The system we propose simulates the moves of a register machine.

Even if the simulated machine is deterministic, because in our system we do not prevent a way to control the nondeterminism, the method used is to reestablish a previous configuration if the computation went in the "wrong way".

The system may not stop even if there is a halting computation and the total number of reachable configurations is finite. This is due to the nondeterminism and is the price paid to avoid the use of cooperative (or catalytic) rules which may inhibit the parallelism of the system. However, considering a fair computation, an endless simulation of a finite computation has probability zero. In this way the notion of algorithm (in the framework of total functions) makes sense because the solution is ultimately confluent and the system will stop with probability 1 if the simulated register machine stops.

Theorem 1. $UPs_aOP_1(ncoo, pro_2) = PsRE$.

Proof. To prove this assertion we simulate a n–register machine $M = (n, P, i, h)$. The contents of register j is denoted in our simulation by the multiplicity of the object a_j.

Formally we define the P system $\Pi = (O, [_1]_1, e_i, R_1, 1)$, where

$$O = \{a_j \mid 1 \leq j \leq n\} \cup \{h, x, y, k_0, k_1, k_2, k_3, k_4\}$$
$$\cup \{e \mid (e : inc(j), f) \in P\} \cup \{e, e_0, e_1, e_2, e_3, e_4 \mid (e : dec(j), f, z) \in P\},$$

with input $\prod_{1 \leq j \leq n} a_j{}^{n_j}$, and R_1 is defined as follows:

For each $(e : inc(j), f) \in P$, R_1 contains the rule $e \rightarrow a_j f$.

For each $(e : dec(j), f, z) \in P$, like to produce $fa_j{}^{n-1}$ in case that $n \geq 1$, or z if $n = 0$. To achieve this, we will add to R_1 the following set of rules: R_1 contains the rules given in the table below (for clarity, the rules are structured according to the order of application and different cases that may occur).

Step & Case	Rules		
1ABCD	$e \rightarrow e_0 k_0$		
2ABCD	$k_0 \rightarrow k_1$		
2BCD	$e_0 \rightarrow e_1\|_{a_j}$		
3ABCD	$k_1 \rightarrow \lambda$		
3A	$e_0 \rightarrow z\|_{k_1}$		
3BCD	$e_1 \rightarrow e_2 k_2$	$a_j \rightarrow x\|_{e_1}$	$a_j \rightarrow y\|_{e_1}$
4BCD	$k_2 \rightarrow k_3$		
4B	$e_2 \rightarrow e_4\|_{yy}$		
5B	$x \rightarrow a_j\|_{e_4}$	$y \rightarrow a_j\|_{e_4}$	$k_3 \rightarrow \lambda\|_{e_4}$ $e_4 \rightarrow e_1$
5CD	$k_3 \rightarrow k_4\|_{e_2}$		
5D	$e_2 \rightarrow e_3\|_{k_3 y}$		
6CD	$k_4 \rightarrow \lambda$		
6C	$x \rightarrow a_j\|_{e_2 k_4}$ $e_2 \rightarrow e_1 k_1\|_{k_4}$		
6D	$x \rightarrow a_j\|_{e_3}$	$e_3 \rightarrow f$	$y \rightarrow \lambda\|_{e_3}$

For a better understanding, below is the table of configurations structured with respect to the computational steps and cases. Also, the rules that can be applied on actual multiset are specified.

	Case A	Case B	Case C	Case D
t_1	e $e \to e_0 k_0$	e, a_j^m $e \to e_0 k_0$	e, a_j^m $e \to e_0 k_0$	e, a_j^m $e \to e_0 k_0$
t_2	e_0, k_0 $k_0 \to k_1$	$e_0, k_0, a_j^m, m \geq 1$ $k_0 \to k_1$ $e_0 \to e_1\|_{a_j}$	$e_0, k_0, a_j^m, m \geq 1$ $k_0 \to k_1$ $e_0 \to e_1\|_{a_j}$	$e_0, k_0, a_j^m, m \geq 1$ $k_0 \to k_1$ $e_0 \to e_1\|_{a_j}$
t_3	e_0, k_1 $e_0 \to z\|_{k_1}$ $k_1 \to \lambda$	$e_1, k_1, a_j^m, m \geq 1$ $k_1 \to \lambda$ $e_1 \to e_2 k_2$ $a_j \to x\|_{e_1}$ $a_j \to y\|_{e_1}$	$e_1, k_1, a_j^m, m \geq 1$ $k_1 \to \lambda$ $e_1 \to e_2 k_2$ $a_j \to x\|_{e_1}$ $a_j \to y\|_{e_1}$	$e_1, k_1, a_j^m, m \geq 1$ $k_1 \to \lambda$ $e_1 \to e_2 k_2$ $a_j \to x\|_{e_1}$ $a_j \to y\|_{e_1}$
t_4	z ready for next instruction	$e_2, k_2, x^r, y^p, r \geq 0, p \geq 2$ $k_2 \to k_3$ $e_2 \to e_4\|_{yy}$	e_2, k_2, x^m $k_2 \to k_3$	e_2, k_2, x^{m-1}, y $k_2 \to k_3$
t_5		$e_4, k_3, x^r, y^p, r \geq 0, p \geq 2$ $x \to a_j\|_{e_4}$ $y \to a_j\|_{e_4}$ $k_3 \to \lambda\|_{e_4}$ $e_4 \to e_1 k_1$	e_2, k_3, x^m $k_3 \to k_4\|_{e_2}$	e_2, k_3, x^{m-1}, y $k_3 \to k_4\|_{e_2}$ $e_2 \to e_3\|_{k_3 y}$
t_6		$e_1, k_1, a_j^m, m \geq 1$ like t_3	e_2, k_4, x^m $x \to a_j\|_{e_2 k_4}$ $e_2 \to e_1 k_1\|_{k_4}$ $k_4 \to \lambda$	e_3, k_4, x^{m-1}, y $k_4 \to \lambda$ $x \to a_j\|_{e_3}$ $e_3 \to f$ $y \to \lambda\|_{e_3}$
t_7			$e_1, k_1, a_j^m, m \geq 1$ like t_3	a_j^{m-1}, f ready for next instruction

Before we start explaining the simulation of the subtraction instruction, let us give a glance to the main idea of the algorithm. We start the computation by checking if the register j is empty or not (i.e., we check if there exists a symbol a_j). In case is empty we can generate the label of the new instruction to be applied, namely z, therefore we can execute a new instruction of the program (*Case A*). Otherwise (there exists at least one symbol a_j), in a nondeterministic way, we produce $x^{m-n} y^n$ from a^m. Now, if $n \neq 1$, then we reestablish the branching configuration by changing back the objects x and y to objects a (*Cases B, C*); therefore the process can start again. This process will last up to the moment when, after splitting the objects a into objects x and y, we will have only one object y. Then, we can continue the computation by deleting the object y and changing back the remaining $m - 1$ objects x into objects a. Also, we produce a new object (say f) which represent the label of the new instruction to be executed (*Case D*). In this way, we have correctly simulated the decrement scheme.

We start the computation having inside the region the object i representing the initial label which indicate the first instruction to be executed and $\prod_{1 \leq j \leq n} a_j{}^{n_j}$ representing the initial contents of registers.

More rigorously, let us see what happens during the computation step by step. Initially it is checked if the register j is empty. This is done by first generating objects e_0 and k_0 when rule $e \rightarrow e_0 k_0$ is applied. In the second step, the object e_0 will be transformed into e_1 iff in the region there exists at least one object a.

In case there is no object a, only rule $k_0 \rightarrow k_1$ is applied. Next, object k_1 will act as a promoter for rule $e_0 \rightarrow z|_{k_1}$ and, in the same time, will be deleted by rule $k_1 \rightarrow \lambda$.

If in the region there exists at least one object a, rules $k_0 \rightarrow k_1$ and $e_0 \rightarrow e_1|_a$ are executed simultaneously in the second step of computation. Now, rule $e_0 \rightarrow z|_{k_1}$ cannot be executed anymore because object e_0 was already transformed into e_1 in the previous computational step. Therefore, if in the region exists an object e_1, we know for sure that in the region is also at least one object a. As a consequence, in the same step, rules $a \rightarrow x$ or/and $a \rightarrow y$ are applied. Due to nondeterminism and because of the maximally parallel mode of functioning of the P systems, all objects a present in the region will be transformed into objects x and/or y.

In the same time, object e_1, which descends from object e, will be transformed into e_2 and k_2 (object k_2 represents a counter which is useful to reestablish the branching configuration if the computation did not work "well"). Now, the computation can split in three possible directions (the number of rules $a_j \rightarrow y|_{e_1}$ is zero, one or more). Let us consider the first case when we have inside the region objects x^{m-n} and y^n such that $m - n \geq 0$, $n \geq 2$ and also objects e_2 and k_2.

Since $n \geq 2$, the rules to be applied in the second step are $k_2 \rightarrow k_3$ and $e_2 \rightarrow e_4|_{yy}$. Next, the branching configuration is restored by the rules: $x \rightarrow a|_{e_4}$, $y \rightarrow a|_{e_4}$, $k_3 \rightarrow \lambda|_{e_4}$, $e_4 \rightarrow e_1$. Recall that promoters can react in the same time with the rules that they promote and also, because of the maximally parallel manner of applying the rules, we successfully restore the branching configuration.

Let us consider the second case, when, in a similar fashion as before, we will have after two computational steps the multiset $e_0, k_0, a^m, m \geq 1$. Then, instead of executing both rules $a \rightarrow x|_{e_1}$ and $a \rightarrow y|_{e_1}$, only one of them is executed, say $a \rightarrow x|_{e_1}$. Therefore, the new configuration is e_2, k_2, x^m and the rule to be applied is $k_2 \rightarrow k_3$. Now, since there exists the object e_2 (which in the previous case is transformed in forth step because there exists two objects y) the rule $k_3 \rightarrow k_4$ is applied. Once we have the object k_4 we can restore as before the branching configuration because we know for sure that the rules $a \rightarrow x|_{e_1}$ and $a \rightarrow y|_{e_1}$ where not applied in a "proper" order.

The third case that may occur represents a successful computation. Recall that the difference between this case and the previous ones occurs after applying the rules $a \rightarrow x$ and $a \rightarrow y$ when we will have the objects x^{n-1} and y. The computation is the same as in the third case up to the fifth step, when, in addition, the rule $e_2 \rightarrow e_4|_{k_3 y}$ is applied. After this, inside the region we will have the objects: x^{m-1}, y, k_4 and e_3. The presence of the object e_3 will drive the computation in the "right" way. The rules that will be applied are as follows: $k_4 \rightarrow \lambda$, $x \rightarrow a|_{e_3}$, $e_3 \rightarrow f$, $y \rightarrow \lambda|_{e_3}$, $e_3 \rightarrow f$. In this way, starting from the objects e, a^m we have successfully computed f, a^{m-1}. The object f is useful to indicate that the subtraction instruction was successfully applied and to point out the new instruction to be executed.

The simulation of the register machine will continue until the halting instruction is reached (if the simulated machine halts). So, the P system halts on some input iff the simulated register machine accepts the corresponding vector.

In conclusion, we have shown that $UPs_aOP_1(ncoo, pro_2) \supseteq PsRE$. By Turing-Church thesis we have the reverse inclusion. Consequently, we have proved that $UPs_aOP_1(ncoo, pro_2) = PsRE$. $\qquad\square$

A non-deterministic register machine can be simulated in a very similar way: addition $(e : inc(j), f_1, f_2) \in P$ would correspond to rules $e \rightarrow a_j f_1$, $e \rightarrow a_j f_2$ $\in R_1$. Based on the proof above, the following corollary holds.

Corollary 1. $PsOP_1(ncoo, pro_2) = PsRE$.

Moreover, the membrane contents in the halting configurations correspond to the value of the partial recursive function computed by the simulated register machine, together with its final label (a "witness" that the computation is finished).

In case we consider P systems with object rewriting context-free rules and inhibitors, the following results stand.

Theorem 2. $UPs_aOP_1(ncoo, inh_2) = PsRE$.

Proof. Consider a register machine $M = (n, P, i, h)$. We define the P system

$$\Pi = (O, [_1]_1, w_1, R_1, 1), \text{ where}$$
$$O = \{a_j, x_j, y_j, x'_j, y'_j, k_j, k'_j \mid 1 \leq j \leq n\} \cup \{e \mid (e : add(j), f) \in P\}$$
$$\cup \{e, e_0, e_1, e_2 \mid (e : sub(j), f, z) \in P\} \cup \{c, c'\},$$
$$w_1 = e_i c\gamma, \ \gamma = k_1 \cdots k_j,$$

and the system receives the input multiset $\{(a_j, n_j) \mid 1 \leq j \leq n\}$. R_1 is defined as follows (we will use notation $\gamma_j = k_1 \cdots k_{j-1} k_{j+1} \cdots k_n$ and $\gamma'_j = k'_1 \cdots k'_{j-1} k'_{j+1} \cdots k'_n$):

- for each register j, $1 \leq j \leq n$, we add to R_1 the rules:
  $$k'_j \rightarrow k_j, \qquad\qquad k_j \rightarrow \lambda;$$
- for each instruction $(e : add(j), f) \in P$, we add to R_1 a rule:
  $$e \rightarrow f a_j c\gamma;$$
- for each instruction $(e : sub(j), f, z) \in P$, we add to R_1 the rules:

$e \to e_0 c \gamma c' \gamma'_j,$

$e_0 \to z k_j |_{\neg a_j},$

$e_0 \to e_1 c \gamma c' \gamma'_j |_{\neg k_j}, a_j \to x_j |_{\neg k_j}, \quad a_j \to y_j |_{\neg k_j},$

$e_1 \to e_0 |_{\neg y_j}, \qquad x_j \to a_j |_{\neg y_j},$

$e_1 \to e_2 c \gamma c' \gamma'_j |_{\neg k_j}, x_j \to x'_j |_{\neg k_j}, \quad y_j \to y'_j |_{\neg k_j},$

$e_2 \to f k_j |_{\neg y'_j y'_j}, \quad x'_j \to a_j |_{\neg y'_j y'_j}, y'_j \to \lambda |_{\neg y'_j y'_j},$

$e_2 \to e_0 c \gamma_j |_{\neg k_j}, \quad x'_j \to a_j |_{\neg k_j}, y'_j \to a_j |_{\neg k_j};$

- we also add to R_1 the rules:

$c' \to c, \qquad\qquad c \to \lambda, \qquad\qquad e_h \to \gamma,$

$a_j \to A_j |_{\neg c}, 1 \le j \le n.$

The four cases corresponding to subtract instruction (register is zero, register is nonzero and rule $a_j \to y_j |_{\neg k_j}$ is applied $0, 1, \ge 2$ times) are illustrated by the table below. For simplicity, symbols $a_{j'}, k_j, k'_{j'}, j' \ne j$ and c, c' are skipped and the subscript j is omitted for symbols $a_j, k_j, x_j, y_j, x'_j, y'_j$.

Simulation of register machine decrement instruction

	Case A	Case B	Case C	Case D
t_1	ek	$ea^n k$	$ea^n k$	$ea^n k$
	$e \to e_0 k$	$e \to e_0 k$	$e \to e_0 k$	$e \to e_0 k$
	$k \to \lambda$	$k \to \lambda$	$k \to \lambda$	$k \to \lambda$
t_2	$e_0 k$	$e_0 k a^n$	$e_0 k, a^n$	$e_0 k a^n$
	$e_0 \to zk|_{\neg a}$	$k \to \lambda$	$k \to \lambda$	$k \to \lambda$
	$k \to \lambda$			
t_3	zk	$e_0 a^n$	$e_0 a^n$	$e_0 a^n$
	ready for	$e_0 \to e_1 k|_{\neg k}$	$e_0 \to e_1 k|_{\neg k}$	$e_0 \to e_1 k|_{\neg k}$
	next	$a \to x|_{\neg k}$	$a \to x|_{\neg k}$	$a \to x|_{\neg k}$
	instruction		$a \to y|_{\neg k}$	$a \to y|_{\neg k}$
t_4		$e_1 k x^n$	$e_1 k x^m y^p$	$e_1 k x^{n-1} y$
		$x \to a|_{\neg y}$	$k \to \lambda$	$k \to \lambda$
		$e_1 \to e_0|_{\neg y}$		
		$k \to \lambda$		
t_5		$e_0 a^n$	$e_1 x^m y^p$	$e_1 x^{n-1} y$
		like t_3	$x \to x'|_{\neg k}$	$x \to x'|_{\neg k}$
			$y \to y'|_{\neg k}$	$y \to y'|_{\neg k}$
			$e_1 \to e_2 k|_{\neg k}$	$e_1 \to e_2 k|_{\neg k}$
t_6			$e_2 x'^m y'^p k$	$e_2 x'^{n-1} y' k$
			$k \to \lambda$	$e_2 \to f k|_{\neg y' y'}$
				$y' \to \lambda|_{\neg y' y'}$
				$x' \to a|_{\neg y' y'}$
				$k \to \lambda$
t_7			$e_2 x'^m y'^p$	$fa^{n-1} k$
			$x' \to a|_{\neg k}$	ready for
			$y' \to a|_{\neg k}$	next
			$e_2 \to e_0|_{\neg k}$	instruction
t_8			$e_0 a^n$	
			like t_3	

This construction is somewhat similar to that of Theorem 1. The intuitive idea behind this proof is the following: instead of using some rule $a \to y|_p$, the "complement" q is generated (such that q is absent if and only if p is present), and then $a \to y|_{\neg q}$ is used.

Let us explain what happens to the objects a_j. It is clear that one copy of a_j is created during the simulation of the addition instruction. To each register j we associate a symbol k_j which is always present (deleted and recreated) in the system except the halting configuration and the following three situations that may happen during the simulation of decrementing register j:

- The system determines that the value of register j is not zero (step t_3, cases B,C,D of the table). The rule $e_0 \to zk_j|_{\neg a_j}$ was not applicable at the previous step, so a_j is re-written into x_j and/or y_j.
- The system determines that at least one object y_j was produced (step t_5, cases C,D). The rule $e_1 \to ek_j|_{\neg y_j}$ was not applicable at the previous step, so objects x_j and y_j are primed.
- The system determines that at least two objects y_j' were produced (step t_7, case C). The rule $e_2 \to fk_j|_{\neg y_j' y_j'}$ was not applicable at the previous step, so objects x_j' and y_j' are re-wriiten into a_j.

In the last step of the derivation, objects k_j are present, but c is absent, so objects a_j are re-written to A_j ("terminal symbols" in case we are interested in the final result) In all cases except these four, objects a_j do not evolve: each step either k_j is produced from some object e, e_0, e_1, e_2 during simulation of the register machine instruction with label e (any addition, decrementing register j step t_1, step t_2 case A, step t_3, step t_4 case B, step t_5, step t_6 case D, step t_7), or k_j is produced from k_j' (decrementing register other than j, step t_2 cases B,C,D, step t_4 cases C,D, step t_6 case C).

As for object e representing the label of the currently simulated instruction, in case of addition it is replaced with the label f of the next instruction, in case of subtraction case A simulates the zero-test, changing e to f, case B represents an attempt to subtract zero, returning to the configuration of step t_3, case C represents an attempt to subtract more than one, also returning to the configuration of step t_3, and case D represents subtracting one, changing e to f. The label e_h of the halt instruction is erased, and the final configuration only has objects A_j, each in the multiplicity representing the value of the corresponding register j, at the time when the register machine halts.

In conclusion, we have shown that $UPs_aOP_1(ncoo, inh_2) \supseteq PsRE$. By Turing-Church thesis we have the reverse inclusion. Consequently, we have proved that $UPs_aOP_1(ncoo, inh_2) = PsRE$. □

A non-deterministic register machine can be simulated in a very similar way: addition $(e : inc(j), f_1, f_2) \in P$ would correspond to rules $e \to f_1 a_j c\gamma$, $e \to f_2 a_j c\gamma \in R_1$. Based on the proof above, the following corollary holds.

Corollary 2. $PsOP_1(ncoo, inh_2) = PsRE$.

5   Concluding Remarks

We have introduced the concept of ultimately confluent rewriting systems – an "weaker" definition of confluent systems, with the computations "unavoidably leading" to the same result, but not necessarily bounded by the number of steps. In this respect we stated that ultimately confluent rewriting systems are systems whose computations have an unique halting configuration if it exists, reachable from any configuration. We have investigated two computational models: parallel multiset-rewriting systems with permitting context and with forbidding context; they represents particular cases of P systems with promoters / inhibitors, were the hierarchical tree structure of regions is reduced to one. For these models we studied both accepting and generative cases and we proved their computational universality by simulating register machines. In the accepting cases we proved that the constructed systems are ultimately confluent.

define $M \subseteq N$ iff $\forall i \geq 0 : M(a_i) \leq N(a_i)$. Analogously, the sum of two multisets $Z = M + N$ is defined by $Z(a_i) = M(a_i) + N(a_i)$ for $i \geq 0$; the difference of two multisets $Z = M \setminus N$ is defined by $Z(a_i) = max\{0, M(a_i) - N(a_i)\}$ for $i \geq 0$. Also, the operations $Z = M \cap N$ and $Z = M \cup N$ are defined as $Z = min\{M(a_i), N(a_i)\}, i \geq 0$ and $Z = max\{M(a_i), N(a_i)\}, i \geq 0$, respectively.

Acknowledgements. The first author is supported by the project TIC2002-04220-C03-02 of the Research Group on Mathematical Linguistics, Tarragona. The first author acknowledges IST-2001-32008 project "MolCoNet" and also the Moldovan Research and Development Association (MRDA) and the U.S. Civilian Research and Development Foundation (CRDF), Award No. MM2-3034.

The work of the second author was due to a doctoral grant from AECI, Spanish Ministry of Foreign Affairs.

References

1. P. Bottoni, C. Martín-Vide, Gh. Păun, G. Rozenberg, Membrane Systems with Promoters/Inhibitors, *Acta Informatica* 38, 10, 2002, 695–720.
2. M. Ionescu, D. Sburlan, On P Systems with Promoters/Inhibitors, *JUCS*, 10, 5, 2004, 581–599.
3. Gh. Păun, *Computing with Membranes: An Introduction.* Springer, Berlin, 2002.
4. G. Rozenberg, A. Salomaa, Eds., *Handbook of Formal Languages*, Springer-Verlag, Berlin, 1997.
5. D. Sburlan, New Results on P Systems with Multiset Promoted/Inhibited Rules, PAMM 2004, Balaton-Almady, Hungary.

6   Appendix: Example

Consider a register machine $G = (3, z, h, P)$ (with registers a, b, c) and instruction set P

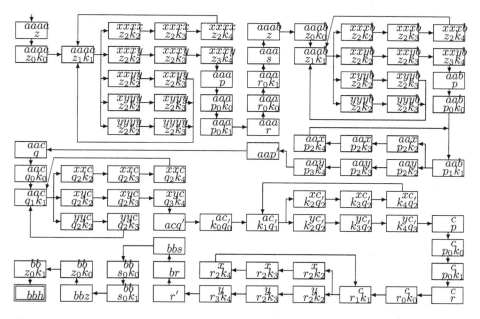

Fig. 1. The graph of reachable configurations of a P system simulating register machine G in the ultimately confluent way, recognizing $aaaa$

$$(z : dec(a), p, h), (p : dec(b), p', r), (p' : inc(c), q), (q : dec(a), q', f),$$
$$(q' : dec(a), p, f), (r : dec(c), r', s), (r' : inc(b), r), (s : inc(b),\ \ z),$$
$$(f : dec(a), f, f), (h :\ \ halt\ \ \ \ ).$$

accepting the number set $M = \{n^2 \mid n \geq 0\}$.

The idea of the machine is to repeat subtracting $2 \cdot value(b) + 1$ (i.e., 1, 3, 5, etc.) from register a, while incrementing b. Register c is used as an intermediary for subtraction, and then b is restored from c. Below is a derivation, accepting 4:

$$(4, 0, 0, z) \Rightarrow (3, 0, 0, p) \Rightarrow (3, 0, 0, r) \Rightarrow (3, 0, 0, s) \Rightarrow (3, 1, 0, z) \Rightarrow (2, 1, 0, p) \Rightarrow$$
$$(2, 0, 0, p') \Rightarrow (2, 0, 1, q) \Rightarrow (1, 0, 1, q') \Rightarrow (0, 0, 1, p) \Rightarrow (0, 0, 1, r) \Rightarrow (0, 0, 0, r') \Rightarrow$$
$$(0, 1, 0, r) \Rightarrow (0, 2, 0, s) \Rightarrow (0, 2, 0, z) \Rightarrow (0, 2, 0, h).$$

Thus, the machine stops if and only if the input number is a perfect square, and in that case the register b will contain the square root of the number, other registers containing zero.

To illustrate both the concept of ultimate confluence and the universality proof, we present Figure 1 representing the graph of configurations of the P system simulating G, reachable from $[_1 aaaaz]_1$. This graph happens to be finite, it contains cycles and a single final node. The final node is reachable from any node.

Unstable P Systems: Applications to Linguistics*

Gemma Bel Enguix

Research Group on Mathematical Linguistics,
Rovira i Virgili University,
Pl. Imperial Tàrraco, 1, 43005 Tarragona, Spain
and
Department of Computer Science, University of Milan-Bicocca,
Via Bicocca degli Arcimboldi 8, 20126 Milan, Italy
gbe@astor.urv.es

Abstract. The paper explores the possibility of predicting the evolution
of P systems by means of features like stability and internal relationship
between membranes. The idea of general rules governing the evolution
of the system is developed. The result can be applied to societies and
language contact, especially to sociolinguistics. In this respect, the paper
opens a new line of mathematical treatment for sociolinguistics.

1 Introduction

Membrane systems, introduced by [7], are a powerful and increasingly spread
model of computation. Their flexibility and intuitive functioning makes them
very suitable for applications, not only to computer science, but also for computing *real life events*, like interaction between societies, or language evolution.

In the present paper, systems without external rules are considered, which
evolve because their configuration is not stable. In fact, any natural system which
is unstable evolves until it gets the stability. Elucidating which configurations are
stable is, thus, one of the aims of the paper, in order to model the computation
of a given system. Another important matter is to establish the predictability of
the evolution, that is, whether changes in systems are made in a deterministic
way or not. Evolutionary principles for membrane systems are very similar to
the ones given by Darwin for explaining biological evolution. It can be said that
dominant and stronger symbols will spread faster. Defining which locations are
dominant or which symbols are stronger will be another of the purposes of our
research.

From the linguistic point of view, languages always evolve in contact with
other languages, like membranes change their configuration in contact with other

---

* This research has been supported by Marie Curie Fellowship of the European Community programme *Human Potential (IHP)* under contract number HPMF-CT-
2002-01582.

G. Mauri et al. (Eds.): WMC5 2004, LNCS 3365, pp. 190–209, 2005.

membranes. As we have seen in other papers ([1] and [2]), languages in societies can be modelled by membranes and the elements involving inside them. The evolution of languages is also continuous because of the instability of their systems and the contact with other languages. In this sense, we think the rules given for P systems can be also valid for modelling evolution of languages in contact with other languages and different human groups, what is called, in human sciences, sociolinguistics. Some of the most well-known linguistic phenomena caused by social influences, like bilingualism, monolingualism, and bipart-lingualism, can be tackled with the same methods unstable P systems are approached.

The present paper introduces the study of a membrane system in a given state, deciding about its stability, trying to establish if it is possible to predict the development of the computation, and applying the results to the study of interaction between languages in societies.

In the next section, we will establish some mathematical properties of P systems, and the way the evolution is done with no specific rules for any membrane. In Section 3, an example is introduced, whereas in Section 4 the same method will be applied for the definition of some basic concepts of sociolinguistcs. Finally, we give in Section 5 some suggestions for future researches of linguistic description by means of membrane systems.

2   Definitions and Basic Concepts

The basic concepts introduced in the present section describe the structure of a P system and explain how the properties described above induce the evolution of objects in the system. These concepts are gathered in the following topics:

- Structural features of a P system (of its membrane structure).
- Relationship between membranes.
- Spreading depth and wideness of a symbol in a system.
- Edges and paths.
- Generation and replication of symbols.
- Densities of symbols.
- Working of replication in the system.
- Stability and evolution

Structural Features

1. The *degree of a system* is the number of membranes of its membrane structure μ. It is denoted by $degree(\mu)$.

2. The *depth* of a membrane M in a membrane structure μ, denoted by $depth_m u(M)$, is the number of parental membranes of M, plus one.

3. The set of all membranes in the system with the same depth constitutes a *level*. The level of a membrane M in a membrane structure μ, denoted by $lv_\mu(M)$, is equal to $depth_\mu(M) - 1$; this is the number of parental membranes of M.

4. No symbol exists in level 0.

5. The *system/membrane structure depth*, denoted by $depth(\mu)$, is the maximal depth of membranes belonging to μ.

6. The *system/membrane structure wideness*, denoted by $w(\mu)$, is the number of membranes M in μ such that $depth_\mu(M) = 2$.

7. The deepest level in the membrane structure is denoted by $dl(\mu)$, and it is also the number of levels μ has.

8. $degree(depth(n))$ is the number of membranes in the system whose depth is n.

9. $degree(level(n))$ is the number of membranes in the system which are in level n.

Relationships Between Membranes

10. *Nesting.* Given two membranes M_1, M_2, we say that M_2 is nested in M_1 when it is inside M_1. The outer membrane M_1 is called *parent membrane* and the inner membrane M_2 is called *nested membrane*. This relation is denoted by $M_2 \subset M_1$. The notation $\subset M_1$ refers to the set of all membranes nested in M_1.

11. *The degree of nesting* refers to the number of membranes between the nested one and the parent one. The degree of nesting is obtained by subtracting the depth of the parent membrane M_p from the depth of the nested membrane M_n. That is, $deg(M_n \subset M_p) = depth(M_n) - depth(M_p)$.

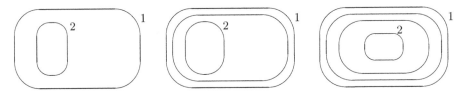

Fig. 1. $M_2 \subset M_1$ with degree 1, 2 and 3

12. *Sibling.* Two membranes M_n, M_m are related by sibling, if

  i. they are adjacent or nested in adjacent membranes, and
  ii. they have the same depth.

Sibling is denoted $M_n \approx M_m$. In the membrane structure $[_0 \ [_1 \ [_2 \ ]_2 \ ]_1 \ [_3 \ [_4 \ ]_4 \ ]_3 \ ]_0$, $M_1 \approx M_3$ and $M_2 \approx M_4$ (Figure 2). The notation $\approx M_n$ refers to the set of sibling membranes for M_n.

13. *The degree of sibling* refers to the proximity of two membranes related by sibling. For obtaining the degree of sibling, we proceed as follows:

– Two membranes $M_n \approx M_m$ are sibling of degree 0 when they have the same direct parent membrane.

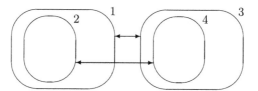

Fig. 2. Sibling

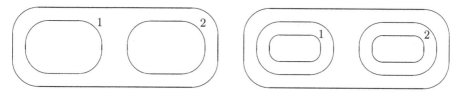

Fig. 3. $M_1 \approx M_2$ with degree 0 and 1

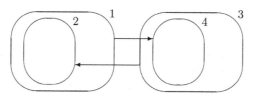

Fig. 4. Command

- For two sibling membranes $M_n \approx M_m$, which are not of degree 0, we obtain the degree of sibling by subtracting the depth of M_n, M_m (they are the same by definition) from the depth of M_i, M_j, where M_i, M_j are two membranes such that $M_i \approx M_j$ with degree 0, and $M_n \subset M_i$, $M_m \subset M_j$.

14. *Command.* Given two membranes M_n, M_m, we say that M_n commands M_m iff:

i. they are not nested,
ii. both are nested in a membrane M_j,
iii. $deg(M_n \subset M_j) = 1$, $deg(M_m \subset M_j) > 1$.

The command is denoted $M_n \triangleleft M_m$. In the system $[_0 \, [_1 \, [_2 \,]_2 \,]_1 \, [_3 \, [_4 \,]_4 \,]_3 \,]_0$ from Figure 4, $M_1 \triangleleft M_4$ and $M_3 \triangleleft M_2$. The notation $\triangleright M_n$ refers to all membranes commanded by M_n.

15. *The degree of command* is the depth of the commanded membrane with respect to the commander one. For obtaining the degree of command, we subtract the depth of the commander membrane from the depth of the commanded membrane. That is, $deg(M_n \triangleleft M_p) = depth(M_p) - depth(M_n)$.

16. A *terminal nesting membrane* is a membrane that does not contain any nested membrane.

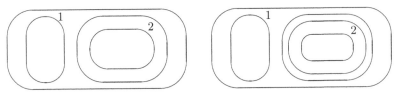

Fig. 5. $M_1 \lhd M_2$ with degree 1 and 2

17. A *terminal commanded membrane* is a membrane that cannot command any other membrane. The skin membrane is not terminal in command even if it cannot command.

18. A *terminal sibling membrane* is a membrane that does not have any sibling membrane, except the skin membrane.

19. A *terminal membrane* is a membrane which is terminal with respect of nesting, sibling, and command.

Spreading Depth and Wideness

20. The *spreading wideness* of an element x in a system is the number of membranes in the system where the symbol x is present. We denote it by $\mu sw(x)$. When $\mu sw(x) = degree(\mu)$, it is said that the spreading is *complete* and the symbol is present in every membrane of the system.

21. The *spreading wideness in level n of a symbol x* is the number of membranes in level n where the symbol is located. If i is the total number of membranes in level n in the system, the spreading wideness is represented by $sw(x)$ *in level n over i*. If $sw(x) = i$ in a given level, then the spreading wideness is said to be *full* in that level.

22. The *spreading depth* of a symbol x (denoted $\mu sd(x)$) is the level of the deepest membrane where the symbol is placed.

23. The *continued spreading depth* of a symbol x is the deepest level n in the system so that from level 1 to n we have $sw(x) \neq 0$. It is denoted by $csd(x)$.

24. The *full spreading depth* is the deepest level n of the system where a symbol x has the property that from level 1 to n, $sw(x)$ is *full*. It is denoted by $fsd(x)$.

25. When the *full spreading depth* for a symbol x is $depth(\mu) - 1$, then the spreading is called *complete*. If the spreading is complete, then a copy of x is present in every membrane of the system.

Edges and Paths

26. *Edges* are ways to connect two membranes in a system, considering the relations of *nesting*, *sibling*, and *command*. There are three types of edges:

- *Nesting edge.* It links two membranes related by nesting of degree 1.
- *Sibling edge.* It links two membranes related by sibling of degree 0.
- *Command edge.* It links two membranes related by command of degree 1.

A connection between two membranes which are not related by nesting, sibling or command is not an edge.

27. A *path* is a set of connected edges. It is a graph where membranes are vertices with or without symbol-objects.

28. Every vertex in a path has degree 2, except for two of them, called initial and terminal, which have degree 1.

29. The most external membrane in a path which is a vertex of degree 1 is called *initial vertex*. The deepest membrane in a path which is a vertex of degree 1 is called *terminal vertex*.

30. If we label the vertices in a path with $v_1, v_2, ..., v_n$, where v_1 is the initial vertex and v_n the terminal one, then they must observe the following condition $lv(v_1) \geq lv(v_2) \geq ... \geq lv(v_n)$.

31. The *degree of a path* is the number of edges it has.

32. It may exist a path with just one edge. It is called a *minimal path*.

33. A path with more than one edge is called a *multiple path*.

34. If every edge of a multiple path belongs to the same type, then the path is called *monotonic*.

35. If not every edge of a multiple path belongs to the same type, then the path is called *complex*.

36. There are three types of monotonic paths:

- A *nesting path* is a path where every edge is a nesting one.
- A *sibling path* is a path where every edge is a sibling one.
- A *command path* is a path where every edge is a command one.

37. When the initial vertex of a monotonic path is in level 1 and the terminal one is in a terminal membrane with level > 1, then it is called a *complete path*.

38. There are two types of complete paths:

- A *nesting complete path* is one going from a level 1 membrane to a nested terminal membrane.
- A *command complete path* is one going from a level 1 membrane to a command terminal membrane.

39. A path connecting every sibling membrane of degree 0 is called a *ring*.

Replication and Generation

40. In linguistics, as well as in genetics, two steps are necessary for a symbol to spread: 1) generation, 2) replication. Generation happens only once, whereas replication can be applied an arbitrary number of times.

41. An element can be generated anywhere in the system. In this paper we do not deal with mechanisms of generation.

42. The *primary occurrence* of a symbol in a system is the one which does not exist by replication, but by generation.

43. If a system has just one copy of an element, then such a symbol is called *unitary*. A unitary symbol is considered to be *primary*.

44. A primary occurrence of a symbol can be calculated in a system. It is the initial node of a spreading route.

45. When in a ring the primary occurrence cannot be calculated, this is, by convention, the vertex (membrane) labelled with the lowest number.

46. A *spreading route* is a path where every membrane (vertex) has a copy of the same symbol.

47. A *spreading route* must be maximal, that is, must connect as many membranes as possible.

48. A replicated symbol of the system may configure several spreading routes.

49. If two spreading routes of the same symbol share at least one node, then they are *connected*.

50. If a route for a replicated symbol in a system does not share any node with the other spreading routes of the same symbol, then this is a *disconnected* spreading route.

51. If no path representing a spreading route can be drawn from an element, then it is an *isolated symbol*.

52. If a spreading route is a minimal path, then it is a *minimal spreading route*. This is called *simple replication*.

53. If a spreading route is a multiple path, then it is a *multiple spreading route* and the process is called *multiple replication*.

54. If a multiple spreading route is a monotonic path, then it is a *monotonic route* and the process is called *monotonic replication*.

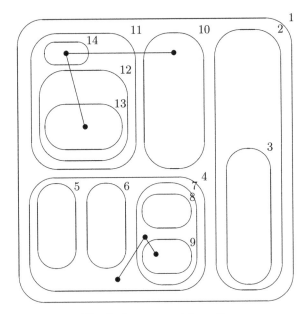

Fig. 6. Some complete paths

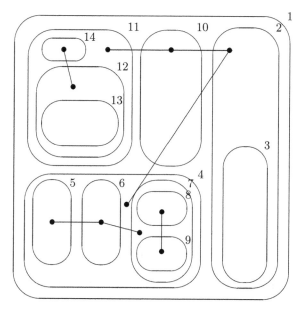

Fig. 7. Rings in a system

55. If a multiple route is a complex path, then it is a *complex route* and the process is called *complex replication*.

56. When a monotonic route is a nesting path, the route is called *nesting spreading route*. When a nested spreading is a complete path, it is called *complete nesting spreading route*.

57. When a monotonic route is a command path, the route is called *command spreading route*. When a nested spreading is a complete path, it is called *complete command spreading route*.

58. When a monotonic route is a sibling path, the route is called *sibling spreading route*. When a nested spreading is a complete ring, it is called *ring spreading route*.

59. The union of all spreading routes of a symbol forms a *spreading tree*. The parental node is the primary element.

Density

60. The *density* of a symbol x in a *membrane* M_n is the number of copies this symbol has in the membrane. It is denoted by $dens(x, M_n)$.

61. The *density* of a symbol x *in a level* n of the system is the average of the density of the symbol in every membrane of the level. It is denoted by $dens(x)$ *in level* n.

62. The *deepest density* of a symbol x is the density of this symbol in the deepest level of the system. It is denoted by $ddens(x)$.

63. The *maximal density* of a symbol x is the highest density of the symbol in the system. It is denoted by $max\ dens(x)$.

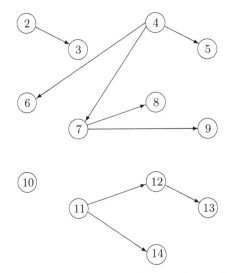

Fig. 8. Digraph representing nesting complete paths for Figure 7

64. The *minimal density* of a symbol x is the lowest density of the symbol in the system. It is denoted by $min\ dens(x)$.

65. The *maximal level density* of a symbol x, denoted by $max\ ldens(x)$, is the maximal density of the element in the levels of the system.

66. The *minimal level density* of a symbol x, denoted by $min\ ldens(x)$, is the minimal density of the element in the levels of the system.

67. *Over-representation*

- A symbol x is over-represented in a membrane M_n if $dens(x, M_n) > 1$.
- A symbol x is over-represented in a level n for a number i of membranes if:
  i) $sw(x)$ *in level n over* $i = i$, and ii) $dens(x)$ *in level n* > 1.
- A symbol x is over-represented in a complete nesting path if: i) $dens(x) \geq 1$ in every membrane of the path, and ii) at least in one membrane $dens(x) > 1$.
- A symbol x is over-represented in a complete command path if: i) $dens(x) \geq 1$ in every membrane of the path, and ii) at least in one membrane $dens(x) > 1$.
- A symbol x is over-represented in a ring, if: i) $dens(x) \geq 1$ in every membrane, and ii) at least in one membrane $dens(x) > 1$.
- A symbol x is over-represented in a spreading route if at least in one membrane we have $dens(x) > 1$.

Working of the System

68. In every path of the computation, only one element of each membrane can be replicated. The symbol replicated is the one with the highest density in that membrane. Just one copy of the maximal density symbol is created by a membrane in one step.

69. If the highest density is shared by two or more elements, then the membrane does not replicate any symbol.

70. The copy of a replicated symbol spreads to any membrane linked by an edge with the membrane where the symbol is.

71. When a terminal nesting membrane is also a terminal sibling membrane, then copies of symbols remain in the same membrane.

72. Computation proceeds in parallel.

73. Spreading goes from higher to lower levels, except for the case of rule 74.

74. *Rule of saturation.* When an element is present in every membrane nested with degree 1 in a membrane M_m, then it is expanded to M_m, provided that there is no copy of this symbol in M_m. The application of the expansion rule is immediate and it is applied just once. It does not take a step in the computation.

75. The goal of every symbol is to reach a *complete μsw*, that is, to be present in every membrane. When this happens, the system is said to be *oversaturated* by this element.

76. When an element over-saturates the system and it has the higher density in every membrane, the system stops evolving.

Stability and Evolution

77. A system is said to be stable when it is in one the following cases:

- No symbol is present in the system.
- The same symbol has the higher density in every membrane of the system. This is the last step of over-saturation.
- No symbol in any membrane of the system has higher density than the others. This is the situation of complete balance between elements.

78. A stable system does not evolve.

79. The situation of stability or complete balance can be reached in a system by the following mechanisms:

- By generation. Elements are generated in a situation of complete balance.
- When the symbols of the system are two symbols x and y located in sibling terminal membranes with no another sibling membrane, and the number of symbols x in a membrane is equal to the number of symbols y in the other one and vice versa. This is shown in Figure 9.

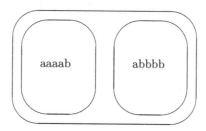

Fig. 9. Configuration in which stability will be reached

2.1   Predicting Oversaturation

From the main statements and definitions given above, we think it is possible to predict which element will be the most spread after n steps, and which of the elements will oversaturate that system. However, that prediction is an experimental stochastic process made by approximation. All that can be taken as a starting point is that there are situations that favour some elements to reach a complete spreading before the others. They are the following:

1. Spreading goes to the more shallow levels to the deepest ones, except for the case of saturation.
2. In general, a symbol located in the shallowest levels spreads in a easier way than a symbol located in the deeper levels.
3. For a symbol, to be alone in a membrane assures that it can be replicated.
4. To get high densities is even more important than to be very spread. A high density has two advantages:
   - it makes easier the replication,
   - it blocks the spreading of the other elements.
5. Rings are paths which help to make a double movement of expansion:
   - an external expansion by saturation,
   - the common inner expansion.
6. To get rings in deep nesting terminal membranes allows just one movement by saturation, but the symbols get blocked and they cannot spread.

Keeping these considerations in mind, we establish some advantageous situations for a symbol to get the oversaturation.

1. If a symbol is located, in a given state, in every nesting terminal path, then it will get a complete spread in one step. Recall that the application of rule of saturation does not depend of the density and that it is immediate. By replication, the probabilities this configuration to take place are very low, but when it happens it is direct.
2. A ring or fsw in level 1 with over-representation gives advantage to a symbol.

From here, we will try to give a formula for calculating the *spreading capacity* of a symbol x, which will be denoted by $\sigma(x)$, as follows:

$$\sigma(x) = \sum_{i=1}^{dl(\mu)-1} \frac{dens(x) \ in \ lev \ i}{i} + \frac{sw(x) \ in \ dl(\mu)}{degree \ (dl(\mu))}.$$

Usually, the symbol with the highest σ in the state we look at the system, will be the one to get the oversaturation.

Obviously, the formula is valid only for unstable systems.

3   An Example

For applying the concepts we have defined and for checking the validity of the formula we have introduced in order to predict the final state of the system – or, better, to predict which of the elements will get first a complete spread – we consider an example constructed randomly. It is the one shown in Figure 10.

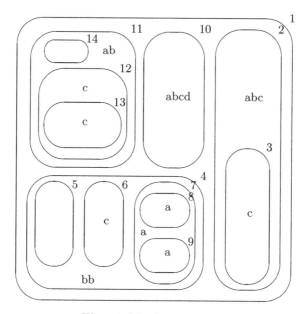

Fig. 10. Membrane system

Looking at the system, its main features can be described as follows.

System Features:

- $degree(\mu) = 14$
- $depth(\mu) = 4$
- $w(\mu) = 4$.
- $depth(M_2, M_4, M_{10}, M_{11}) = 2$, so that $M_2 \cup M_4 \cup M_{10} \cup M_{11}$ is the configuration level 1.
- $depth(M_3, M_5, M_6, M_7, M_{12}, M_{14}) = 3$, so that $M_3 \cup M_5 \cup M_6 \cup M_7 \cup M_{12} \cup M_{14}$ are in level 2.
- $depth(M_8, M_9, M_{13}) = 4$, so that $M_8 \cup M_9 \cup M_{13}$ belong to level 3.
- $dl(\mu) = 3$.
- Terminal nesting membranes: $M_3, M_5, M_6, M_8, M_9, M_{10}, M_{13}, M_{14}$.
- Terminal command membranes: $M_3, M_7, M_8, M_9, M_{12}, M_{13}$.
- Terminal sibling membranes: M_3, M_{13}.
- Terminal membranes: M_3, M_{13}

Spreading Depth and Wideness:

1. Spreading wideness:

   – $\mu sw(a)$ in $\mu = 5$
   – $\mu sw(b)$ in $\mu = 4$
   – $\mu sw(c)$ in $\mu = 4$
   – $\mu sw(d)$ in $\mu = 1$

2. Spreading wideness in levels:

   – For symbol a:
     • $sw(a)$ in $level$ 1 $over$ 4 $=$ 3.
     • $sw(a)$ in $level$ 2 $over$ 5 $=$ 0.
     • $sw(a)$ in $level$ 3 $over$ 3 $=$ 2.
   – For symbol b:
     • $sw(b)$ in $level$ 1 $over$ 4 $=$ 4: Full.
     • $sw(b)$ in $level$ 2 $over$ 5 $=$ 0.
     • $sw(b)$ in $level$ 3 $over$ 3 $=$ 0.
   – For symbol c:
     • $sw(c)$ in $level$ 1 $over$ 4 $=$ 1.
     • $sw(c)$ in $level$ 2 $over$ 5 $=$ 2.
     • $sw(c)$ in $level$ 3 $over$ 3 $=$ 1.
   – For symbol d:
     • $sw(d)$ in $level$ 1 $over$ 4 $=$ 1.
     • $sw(d)$ in $level$ 2 $over$ 5 $=$ 0.
     • $sw(d)$ in $level$ 3 $over$ 3 $=$ 0.

3. Spreading depth:

For symbol a	For symbol b	For symbol c	For symbol d
$\mu sd(a) = 3$	$\mu sd(b) = 1$	$\mu sd(c) = 3$	$\mu sd(d) = 1$
$csd(a) = 1$	$csd(b) = 1$	$csd(c) = 3$	$csd(d) = 1$
$fsd(a) = 0$	$fsd(b) = 1$	$fsd(c) = 0$	$fsd(d) = 0$

Nesting Complete Paths:

$13 \subset 12 \subset 11$; $14 \subset 11$; $3 \subset 2$; $9 \subset 7 \subset 4$; $8 \subset 7 \subset 4$; $6 \subset 4$; $5 \subset 4$

Rings:

$2 \approx 4 \approx 10 \approx 11$: level 1
$12 \approx 14$: level 2
$5 \approx 6 \approx 7$: level 2
$8 \approx 9$: level 3

Command Complete Paths:

$2 \vartriangleleft 5 \vartriangleleft 8$; $2 \vartriangleleft 5 \vartriangleleft 9$; $2 \vartriangleleft 6 \vartriangleleft 8$; $2 \vartriangleleft 6 \vartriangleleft 9$; $2 \vartriangleleft 14 \vartriangleleft 13$; $2 \vartriangleleft 12$
$4 \vartriangleleft 3$; $4 \vartriangleleft 14 \vartriangleleft 13$
$10 \vartriangleleft 3$; $10 \vartriangleleft 5 \vartriangleleft 8$; $10 \vartriangleleft 5 \vartriangleleft 9$; $10 \vartriangleleft 6 \vartriangleleft 8$; $10 \vartriangleleft 6 \vartriangleleft 9$; $10 \vartriangleleft 14 \vartriangleleft 13$; $10 \vartriangleleft 12$
$11 \vartriangleleft 3$; $11 \vartriangleleft 5 \vartriangleleft 8$; $11 \vartriangleleft 5 \vartriangleleft 9$; $11 \vartriangleleft 6 \vartriangleleft 8$; $11 \vartriangleleft 6 \vartriangleleft 9$

Spreading Routes:

- For a:
  - Route 1: $a_{10} \approx a_{11} \approx a_2 \vartriangleleft a_7 \supset a_8 \approx a_9$: multiple complex spreading route.
  - There is no tree.
  - Primary occurrence: a_{10}.
- For b:
  - $b_2 \approx b_4 \approx b_{10} \approx b_{11}$.
  - Ring in level 1.
  - Over-representation.
- For c:
  - Route 1: $c_2 \approx c_{10}$: simple sibling spreading.
  - Route 2: $c_2 \supset c_3$: simple nesting spreading.
  - Route 3: $c_{10} \vartriangleleft c_6$: simple command spreading.
  - Route 4: $c_{10} \vartriangleleft c_{12} \supset c_{13}$: multiple complex spreading.
  - These routes are connected forming a tree: $(c_3 \subset c_2) \approx (c_{10}(\vartriangleleft c_6, \vartriangleleft c_{12} \supset c_{13}))$.
  - Primary element is c_2.
- For d: it is an isolated element.

Densities:

In membranes

- $dens(a_{3,4,5,6,12,13,14}) = 0$
- $dens(a_{2,7,8,9,10,11}) = 1$
- $dens(b_{3,5,6,7,8,9,12,13,14}) = 0$
- $dens(b_{2,10,11}) = 1$
- $dens(b_4) = 2$
- $dens(c_{2,4,5,7,8,9,11,12,14}) = 0$
- $dens(c_{2,3,6,10,12,13}) = 1$
- $dens(d_{10}) = 1$
- $dens(d_{\mu-10}) = 0$

Maximal and minimal densities

Maximal	Minimal
$max\ dens(a) = 1$	$min\ dens(a) = 0$
$max\ dens(b) = 2$	$min\ dens(b) = 0$
$max\ dens(c) = 1$	$min\ dens(c) = 0$
$max\ dens(d) = 1$	$min\ dens(d) = 0$

In levels

Level 1	Level 2	Level 3
$dens(a) = 0.75$	$dens(a) = 0.16$	$dens(a) = ddens(a) = 0.6$
$dens(b) = 1.25$	$dens(b) = 0$	$dens(b) = ddens(b) = 0$
$dens(c) = 0.5$	$dens(c) = 0.5$	$dens(c) = ddens(c) = 0.3$
$dens(d) = 0.25$	$dens(d) = 0$	$dens(d) = ddens(d) = 0$

Maximal and minimal level densities

Maximal	Minimal
$max\ ldens(a) = 0.75$	$min\ ldens(a) = 0.16$
$max\ ldens(b) = 1.75$	$min\ ldens(b) = 0$
$max\ ldens(c) = 0.5$	$min\ ldens(c) = 0.3$
$max\ ldens(d) = 0.25$	$min\ ldens(d) = 0$

3.1   Development of the Computation

Before starting the computation, we try to predict the result, by appling the formula in 2.1. We have:

$$\sigma(a) = dens(a)\ in\ level\ 1 + \frac{dens(a)\ in\ level\ 2}{2} + \frac{sw(a)\ in\ level\ 3}{degree\ (level(3))} = 0.75 + 0.08 + 0.375$$
$$= 1.205$$

$$\sigma(b) = dens(b)\ in\ level\ 1 + \frac{dens(b)\ in\ level\ 2}{2} + \frac{sw(b)\ in\ level\ 3}{degree\ (level(3))} = 1.25 + 0 + 0.25 = 1.5$$

$$\sigma(c) = dens(c)\ in\ level\ 1 + \frac{dens(c)\ in\ level\ 2}{2} + \frac{sw(c)\ in\ level\ 3}{degree\ (level(3))} = 0.5 + 0.25 + 0.5 =$$
$$1.25$$

$$\sigma(d) = dens(d)\ in\ level\ 1 + \frac{dens(d)\ in\ level\ 2}{2} + \frac{sw(d)\ in\ level\ 3}{degree\ (level(3))} = 0.125 + 0 + 0.25$$
$$= 0.375$$

Our prediction is, then, that b will get the oversaturation, that is, it is going to be spread in the whole system while the other symbols will become probably blocked. Nevertheless this is only the most probable scenario. We do not know if the system is deterministic, what means that there could exist a game consisting in trying to find a way to block b.

Step 1. In the initial configuration, symbol a only has the possibility to replicate in the membranes nested in 4. But 8 and 9 are a closed ring. They just exchange elements between them. However, a_7 has a powerful location. It can extend to the sibling membranes, and then, by saturation, to the higher. It starts, in this step, going to the sibling membrane M_5.

The situation of b is the best. It can just reply in M_4, but it can choose where to be replied and it will be the more represented symbol in the membranes where it can go. Let us choose to go to M_{10}.

c is the symbol which can be replicated more times this step. But it is placed in two terminal nesting and sibling membranes. They cannot send the symbol to any other membrane. So, c_{13} and c_3 will replicate in the same place, without a possibility of expansion. Their replication is junk reproduction. The situation in M_6 and M_{12} is different, because c can be expanded to sibling membranes. If c_{12} goes to M_{14}, then, by saturation, the symbol is also extended to M_{11}. c_6 has to go to M_5 or M_7 knowing that a will be probably there, but it has not other options. Symbol d cannot reply. The configuration after the first step is shown in Figure 11.

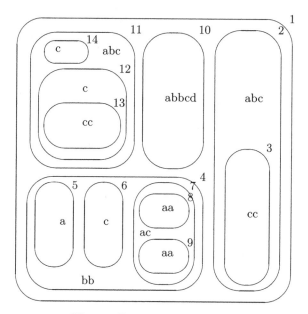

Fig. 11. First step of evolution

Step 2. In Figure 11, we see that a_7 has been blocked by c, so it cannot replicate. Terminal membranes M_8 and M_9 keep exchanging elements. On the other hand, a_5 can be extended to a_6, and, by saturation, to a_4. At the same time, b can choose again what to do, because its position with the higher density in two membranes of level 1 allows it to move by nesting, sibling or command. In this case, b_4 can be expanded to M_{14} and b_{10} to M_{12}, and then, by saturation, it also goes to M_{11}. As for c, it continues replicating at M_{13} and M_3, and M_{14}, M_{12} exchange elements. c_6 is expanded to M_5, and from here to M_4.

The configuration resulting from the second step of the computation is shown in Figure 12.

Step 3. At this moment, a is completely blocked, except for the ring $M_8 \approx M_9$. c is alive in $\subset M_{11}$, but nowhere else in the system. But b can be replicated in three level-one membranes. If it is able to block c, it will be able to expand

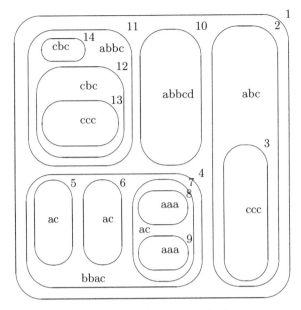

Fig. 12. Second step of evolution

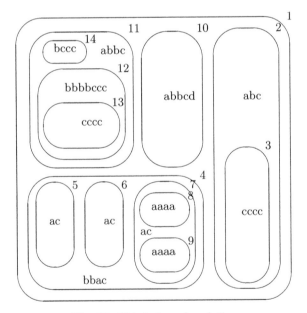

Fig. 13. Third step of evolution

anywhere with no problem. For doing that, it is necessary to concentrate every replicated symbol of *b* in the same membrane. Figure 13 shows the result of such movements.

The third step is not the last in the evolution of the system, but is the last interesting one. c can send an element to other membranes, but even so it gets blocked. During the following steps b will replicate and take every membrane of the system, as it was already predicted.

4   Some Sociolinguistic Concepts

With the concepts introduced above it is possible to describe linguistic situations in societies. The most intuitive sociolinguistic concepts that can be approached are *bilingualism* or *multilingualism, ambilingualism, bipart-lingualism,* and *language substitution.* Bilingualism refers to the situation of a society where two languages are used. Ambilingualism refers to societies in which two languages are equally used, with no functional distribution. Bipart-lingualism refers to the situation in which more than one language can be heard in a small area, but the large majority of speakers are monolingual. Finally, language substitution is the process in which a language starts to be spoken in a community instead of another one.

Applying the same concepts to membrane systems, some definitions are obtained that explain sociolinguistics in terms of membrane terminology. They are the following:

1. *Membrane bilingualism and n-lingualism* refer to the existence of two or more symbols in the same membrane. These phenomena can be symmetrical or asymmetrical and model bilingualism and multilingualism, respectively.

2. *Membrane symmetrical bilingualism* is defined as the situation of stability in a membrane with two different symbols. Consequently, in that membrane, both symbols have the same density. *Membrane symmetrical n-lingualism*, however, includes only one of the possible configurations of stability in a membrane with more than two symbols, the one in which every element has the same density.

3. *Membrane asymmetrical bilingualism* is defined as the existence of two symbols with different densities in the same membrane. *Membrane asymmetrical n-lingualism* is modelled by the existence of more than two symbols in a membrane, with at least two different densities.

It is easy to see that symmetrical bilingualism and n-lingualism are parallel to *ambilingualism*, in which languages have the same status in a territory. Theoretically, the situation is stable. If no external influence occurs, the membrane will remain with the same configuration. Asymmetrical bilingualism and n-lingualism are related with *bipart-lingualism*. This kind of bilingualism is clearly non-stable, and does not last for a long time.

The same sociolinguistic concepts that have been applied to membranes, have to be explained with regard to the entire system as well, giving rise to the following definitions:

1. A system is *monolingual* when it has just one symbol, *bilingual* when it has two symbols, and *n-lingual* when it has n symbols.

2. A *bilingual or n-lingual system* is *symmetrical* when it is stable, that is, when every membrane in the system is stable.

3. A *bilingual or n-lingual system* is *asymmetrical* when there is at least one membrane that is not stable.

Combining the definitios that correspond to membranes and systems, it can be deduced that there are three possible scenarios for bi- and n-lingualism in a society or membrane system:

- It is symmetrical in a symmetrical system. In this case, the system does not evolve and n-lingualism will be perpetuated.
- It is symmetrical in an asymmetrical system. In this case, the symmetry will be transformed in asymmetry after a number of steps of the computation.
- It is asymmetrical. The membrane will be transformed in a monolingual membrane, after a number of steps of the computation. This is related to *language substitution*, which is defined here as the last step of bilingualism.

Therefore it can be inferred that bi- or n-lingualism is an unstable situation most of the times. It is stable only in a symmetrical membrane in a symmetrical system. But in the real world that situation is hypothetical and it cannot exist. Therefore, the way from bilingualism to bipar-lingualism and from here to linguistic substitution is a continuous one. Moreover, whereas bilingualism usually evolves to language substitution, the contrary process is very unusual, since it is quite complicate to reach the stability in a system by replication. This idea is explained in the statement 79 of Section 2.

From the ideas explained in the paper, two important conclusions can be extracted about social systems, thanks to the theory provided by membrane systems: a) "social" or "linguistic" systems are unstable by definition, and b) societies tend to be mono-lingual, mono-memetical.

Finally, it seems to be possible to predict the final state of every symbol of the system by analyzing a given configuration of the computation. Knowing whether the future for a word, structure, slang, or language is the spread or the death is an important goal for sociolinguistics, that can be calculated by formal and simple methods in the framework of membrane systems.

5   Suggestions for Future Research

The present paper is an initial attempt to describe the mechanisms of evolution in membrane systems, mechanisms which are provided by their internal instability and structural configuration. The topic has been just introduced, and a further treatment should be done to improve the method and formalization. The development of the theory has as a final goal the application to sociolinguistics, an aim that has been only pointed out in this paper. In the near future, the tools proposed here must be improved and applied to more realistic situations. The interest of the future research is especially focused in the following matters:

- To investigate the mathematical properties of social and linguistic evolution.
- To apply P systems to the study of spreading of ideas, art, etc.
- To define linguistic membrane systems with fuzzy membranes, according to the composition of societies and languages.

References

1. G. Bel Enguix, Preliminaries about Some Possible Applications of P Systems in Linguistics. In *Membrane Computing. Workshop on Membrane Computing, WMC 2002, Curtea de Arges, Romania. Revised Papers, Lecture Notes in Computer Science* 2597, Springer-Verlag, Berlin, 2003, 74–89.
2. G. Bel Enguix, M.D. Jiménez-López, Linguistic P Systems and Applications. In G. Ciobanu, Gh. Păun, M.J. Pérez-Jiménez, eds., *Applications of Membrane Computing. Achievements and Perspectives*, Springer-Verlag, Berlin, 2005, to appear.
3. C.S. Calude, Gh. Păun, *Computing with Cells and Atoms*. Taylor and Francis, London, 2001.
4. W. Croft,*Explaining Language Change. An Evolutionary Approach*. Longman, Singapore, 2000.
5. M.D. Jiménez-López, *Using Grammar Systems*. GRLMC Report, Rovira i Virgili University, Tarragona, 2002.
6. A.M.S. McMahon, *Understanding Language Change*. Cambridge University Press, 1996.
7. Gh. Păun, Computing with Membranes. *Journal of Computer and System Sciences*, 61 (2000), 108–143.
8. Gh. Păun, *Membrane Computing. An Introduction*. Springer-Verlag, Berlin, 2002.
9. The P Systems Web Page: `http://psystems.disco.unimib.it`

A P System Description
of the Sodium-Potassium Pump[*]

Daniela Besozzi[1] and Gabriel Ciobanu[2]

[1]Università degli Studi di Milano,
Dipartimento di Informatica e Comunicazionem,
Via Comelico 39, 20135 Milano, Italy
besozzi@dico.unimi.it
[2]Romanian Academy, Institute of Computer Science,
Iaşi, Romania
gabriel@iit.tuiasi.ro

Abstract. The sodium-potassium pump is a fundamental transmembrane protein present in all animal cells. The functioning of the pump is described and analyzed in the formal framework of P systems, considered here as tools for modelling a bio-cellular process. New features such as variable membrane labelling, activation conditions for rules, membrane bilayer and specific communication rules are defined, to the aim of providing a more appropriate description of the pump. A Sevilla carpet of the sodium-potassium pump is given, as a starting point to identify the pumps as the processors able to execute the rules of a high-level P system in a maximal parallel and nondeterministic manner, activated and controlled by steady-state concentrations. Some related topics for further research are proposed.

1   Introduction

Cell membranes are crucial to the life of the cell. Defining the boundary of the living cells, membranes have various functions and participate in many essential cell activities including barrier functions, transmembrane signaling and intercellular recognition. The sodium-potassium exchange pump [15] is a transmembrane transport protein in the plasma membrane that establishes and maintains the appropriate internal concentrations of sodium (Na^+) and potassium ions (K^+) in cells. By using the energy from the hydrolysis of ATP molecules, the pump transports three Na^+ outside the cell, in exchange for two K^+ that are taken inside the cell, against their concentration gradients. This exchange is an important physiologic process and it is critical in maintaining the osmotic balance of the cell, the resting membrane potential of most tissues, and the excitable properties of muscle and nerve cells.

---

[*] Work partially supported by contribution of the EU commission under The Fifth Framework Programme, project "MolCoNet" IST-2001-32008.

G. Mauri et al. (Eds.): WMC5 2004, LNCS 3365, pp. 210–223, 2005.

In this paper we model the movement of ions and the conformational transformations of the sodium-potassium pump in the framework of P systems, hence using discrete mathematics instead of partial differential equations. A similar approach was used, for instance, in [3, 4] to model the activity of mechanosensitive channels in prokaryotic cells, and in [10] to describe the phenomenon of leukocyte selective recruitment in immune system.

P systems, or *membrane systems*, are formal systems with roots in the theory of formal languages. They look at the phenomena occurring inside the cell as computing processes. Initially proposed in [17], they are inspired by the architecture of the living cells, and the way biological substances are both modified and moved among internal organelles. In a P system, each compartment (an organelle inside the cell) can be seen as a computing unit, having its own data and its local program (molecular substances and biochemical reactions), and all compartments considered as a whole (the cell) can be seen as an "unconventional" computing device. In particular, each compartment is delimited and separated from the rest by a membrane; the whole computing unit is formally characterized by a membrane structure, where membranes can be hierarchically placed inside a unique external membrane delimiting the entire cell. All membranes are semi-permeable barriers, which either allow some substances to move inwards or outwards and consequently change their location in the membrane structure, or block the movement of some other substances. The biological substances and reactions are represented by means of objects and evolution rules. Objects are usually symbols or strings over a given alphabet, evolution rules are given as rewriting rules with target indications, thus describing both the transformation and the communication of objects. Further notions on P systems, their use as computing devices, and an updated bibliography can be found in [18] and at http://psystems.disco.unimib.it.

The paper is structured as follows. In Section 2 we recall some basic notions from P system area, in Section 3 we present the Post–Albers scheme for the activity of the sodium-potassium pump with occluded states, which will be then modelled in Section 4. We introduce new features such as variable membrane labelling, the activation conditions for evolution rules, the notion of membrane bilayer and new specific communication rules. In Section 5 we present a Sevilla carpet of the sodium-potassium pump, and propose to look at a cell as a P system having its transport carriers (pumps) as the processors able to execute the rules in a maximal parallel and nondeterministic manner. We conclude with some remarks and directions for future research.

2   Membrane Systems Prerequisites

A multiset (over a given alphabet V) is a map $M : V \to \mathbf{N}$, where $M(a)$ is the multiplicity of any symbol $a \in V$ in the multiset M and $\mathbf{N}$ is the set of natural numbers. If the set V is finite, e.g., $V = \{a_1, \ldots, a_n\}$, then the multiset M can be explicitly represented by the string $w = (M(a_1) \cdot a_1)(M(a_2) \cdot a_2) \ldots (M(a_n) \cdot a_n)$, with $M(a_i) \neq 0$ for all $i = 1, \ldots, n$, and by all its possible permutations.

Some basic operations may be defined for multisets. Let $M_1, M_2 : V \to \mathbf{N}$ be two multisets. We say that M_1 is included in M_2, and we denote it by $M_1 \subseteq M_2$, if $M_1(a) \leq M_2(a)$ for all $a \in V$. The inclusion is strict, $M_1 \subset M_2$, if $M_1 \subseteq M_2$ and $M_1 \neq M_2$. The union of M_1 and M_2 is the multiset $M_1 \cup M_2 : V \to \mathbf{N}$ defined by $(M_1 \cup M_2)(a) = M_1(a) + M_2(a)$ for all $a \in V$. The difference is the multiset $M_1 \setminus M_2 : V \to \mathbf{N}$ defined by $(M_1 \setminus M_2)(a) = M_1(a) - M_2(a)$ for all $a \in V$. Obviously, $M_1 \setminus M_2$ is defined only when M_2 is included in M_1.

The notion of multiset is widely used in P systems to describe the objects present in the membrane structure. We briefly recall that a *membrane structure* consists of a set of membranes hierarchically embedded in a unique membrane, called the *skin membrane*. The membrane structure is identified with a string of correctly matching square parentheses, placed in a unique pair of matching parentheses; each pair of matching parentheses corresponds to a membrane. Each membrane identifies a region, delimited by it and the membranes (if any) immediately inside it. Usually, a unique label is univocally associated to each membrane. For instance, the string $[_0 \, [_1 \,]_1 \, [_2 \,]_2 \,]_0$ identifies a membrane structure consisting of three membranes; the skin membrane is labelled with the number 0, the other two membranes are placed inside the skin at the same hierarchical level and are labelled with the numbers 1 and 2.

An *object* can be a symbol or a string over a specified finite alphabet V; *multisets* of objects are usually considered in order to describe the presence of multiple copies of any given object. In the following, we will only consider multisets of objects, and we will use their representation as strings. Objects are modified by means of *evolution rules*, which are rewriting rules with an associated target indication (*tar*, in short) of the form *here, out, in*. For multisets of objects, a rewriting rule can have the form $u \to v$, where u, v are string representations of multisets over V, with the objects from v having associated targets, thus appearing in the form (a, tar). The target indication determines the region where the object is communicated after the application of the rule: if $tar = here$, then the object remains in the same region; if $tar = out$, then the object exits from the region where it was placed; if $tar = in$, then the object nondeterministically enters one of the membranes immediately inside the region where the rule is applied, if any inner region exists (otherwise the rule cannot be applied).

In Section 4 the notion of membrane structure and the modalities of communication will be refined in order to give a more appropriate model for the sodium-potassium pump.

3   Sodium-Potassium Exchange Pump

The sodium-potassium pump (briefly, Na-K pump) is a primary active transport system driven by a cell membrane ATPase carrying sodium ions outside and potassium ions inside the cell. Many animated representations of the pump are available on the web, one can be found at `http://arbl.cvmbs.colostate.edu/` `hbooks/molecules/sodium_pump.html`.

Table 1. The Post–Albers cycle with occluded states

$$+ 3Na^+_{cyt} \rightleftharpoons E_1 \cdot ATP \cdot 3Na^+ \tag{1}$$

$$E_1 \cdot ATP \cdot 3Na^+ \rightleftharpoons E_1 \sim P \cdot (3Na^+)_{occ} + ADP \tag{2}$$

$$E_1 \sim P \cdot (3Na^+)_{occ} \rightleftharpoons E_2 \sim P \cdot 2Na^+ + Na^+_{ext} \tag{3}$$

$$E_2 \sim P \cdot 2Na^+ \rightleftharpoons E_2 \sim P + 2Na^+_{ext} \tag{4}$$

$$E_2 \sim P + 2K^+_{ext} \rightleftharpoons E_2 \sim P \cdot 2K^+ \tag{5}$$

$$E_2 \sim P \cdot 2K^+ \rightleftharpoons E_2 \cdot (2K^+)_{occ} + P_i \tag{6}$$

$$E_2 \cdot (2K^+)_{occ} + ATP \rightleftharpoons E_1 \cdot ATP \cdot 2K^+ \tag{7}$$

$$E_1 \cdot ATP \cdot 2K^+ \rightleftharpoons E_1 \cdot ATP + 2K^+_{cyt} \tag{8}$$

The description given in Table 1 is known as the Post-Albers cycle with occluded states. According to it, the sodium-potassium pump has essentially two conformations, namely E_1 and E_2 (both may be phosphorylated or dephosphorylated), which correspond to the mutually exclusive states in which the pump exposes ion binding sites alternatively on the intracellular (E_1) and extracellular (E_2) sides of the membrane. Ion transport is mediated by transitions between these conformations. During the translocation across cell membrane, there exist conformations in which the transported ions are occluded (trapped within the protein) before being released to the other side, and thus unable to be in contact with the surrounding media [11].

Remark 1. In Table 1, $A + B$ means that A and B are present together (e.g., in a test tube). $A \cdot B$ means that A and B are bound to each other noncovalently. $E_2 \sim P$ indicates that the phosphoryl group is covalently bound to E_2. P_i is the inorganic phosphate group (i means inorganic). $\rightleftharpoons$ indicates that the process can go either way, i.e., it can proceed reversibly.

In Figure 1 we give a graphical representation of the conformations and the functioning of the pump: Na^+ ions are pictured as small squares, K^+ ions as small circle; for simplicity, neither ATP molecules nor phospates are represented.

Let us consider an initial state, following the release of K^+ ions to the cytosol (Figure 1, left middle), where the pump is in the conformation E_1, and it is associated with ATP (we describe it as $E_1 \cdot ATP$ in Table 1). Its cation binding sites are empty and open to the intracellular space. In this situation, the affinity is high for Na^+ and low for K^+. Consequently, three Na^+ ions binds to the intracellular cation sites; this corresponds to the first equation of Table 1 and to the left up corner of Figure 1.

The binding of sodium catalyzes a phosphorylation of the pump by the previously bound ATP: the γ phosphate of ATP is transferred to the aspartate residue of the pump structure. The new conformation of the pump is described as $E_1 \sim P$ in Table 1. During this process, Na^+ ions are occluded (Figure 1, up middle, and Table 1, equation (2)). Thereafter the pump undergoes a conformational change to the E_2^P state and loses its affinity for Na^+. The Na^+ ions are

$E_1 \cdot ATP \cdot 3Na$ $E_1^P \cdot (3Na)$ $E_2^P \cdot 2Na$

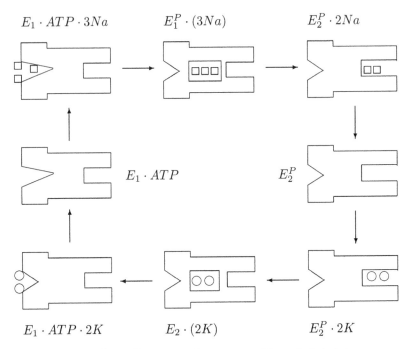

$E_1 \cdot ATP$ E_2^P

$E_1 \cdot ATP \cdot 2K$ $E_2 \cdot (2K)$ $E_2^P \cdot 2K$

Fig. 1. The sodium–potassium pump with occluded states

subsequently released; first one Na$^+$ ion is released during the conformational change from E_1^P to E_2^P when the cation binding sites are oriented toward the extracellular side (Figure 1, right up, and Table 1, equation (3)). The pump is in the E_2^P state, and the affinity for Na$^+$ ions is very low; the two remaining Na$^+$ ions are released into the extracellular medium (Figure 1, right middle, and Table 1, equation (4)). The binding sites now have a high affinity for K$^+$. Two external K$^+$ ions can bind; this corresponds to equation (5) of Table 1, and to the right down corner of Figure 1. The binding of K$^+$ at the outer surface induces the dephosphorylation of the E_2^P conformation, which turns to E_2. The release of the inorganic phosphate P_i into the intracellular medium is accompanied by the occlusion of the K$^+$ ions (equation (6)). De-occlusion of K$^+$ ions to the intracellular space is then catalyzed by ATP (equations (7) in Table 1 and Figure 1, left down corner): the pump returns to the conformation which has high affinity for sodium ions (namely, E_1) and still presents the binding with ATP. The affinity for K$^+$ ions reduces and they are released into the intracellular medium (equations (8) in Table 1). The pump protein is now ready to initiate a new cycle from the active conformation $E_1 \cdot ATP$ (Figure 1, left middle).

A detailed description of the overall functioning of the pump, as well as some graphical representations, can be found in [11, 12].

Na-K pump is under the control of many regulatory mechanisms and pathways. For instance, the intracellular concentrations of ions determine the maximal activity of the pump: whenever cellular Na$^+$ rises, the pump works more rapidly to expel the excess of Na^+, thus lowering its concentration to a steady-state value [14].

Regarding the relationship between the kinetic parameters of the transport process and the efficiency of the pump, we can mention that the rate constants of competing steps (that would decrease the efficiency) are quite small. This ensures that the binding and the release of substrate occur at the proper point in the cycle. For example, the reaction $E_1 \cdot ATP \Leftrightarrow E_1 \sim P + ADP$ of equation (2) is slower than the reaction of equation (1). As a consequence, E_1 has enough time to bind sodium ions before undergoing the transition to E_2. Similar relationships among rate constants ensure that ions are released from the enzyme before they come back to the side at which they were initially bound. In other words, the slow rate constants channel the enzyme along a reaction path in which the hydrolysis of ATP is tightly coupled to the transport process.

For further notions about Na-K pump, the interested reader can consult the reviews [11, 12, 14, 19], or more general books [1, 16].

4   Modelling Na–K Pump with Membrane Systems

Since Na–K pump is a transmembrane protein associated with the phospholipid bilayer of the plasma membrane, it suffices to consider a membrane structure consisting of the skin membrane only. However, in order to formally describe the pump with a high resemblance to its biological structure and functioning, we have to introduce a notation for the cellular lipid bilayer. To this aim, we use two symbols of type "|" which, placed next to the couple of square parentheses denoting a membrane, characterize a further intermediate region: the *skin membrane with bilayer* will be denoted as $[| \ |]$. The skin membrane with bilayer characterizes now three distinct spaces, precisely the extracellular environment (in short, *Env*), the lipid bilayer of the membrane (*Bilayer*), and the cytoplasm of the cell (*Reg*):

$$Env \ [Bilayer| \ Reg \ |Bilayer] \ Env.$$

In the following we will use only the semibracket notation for membranes, as introduced in [2].

The conformations of the pump are described by means of labels attached to the membrane, that is $[|_l$, with $l \in L, L = \{E_1 \cdot ATP, E_1^P, E_2, E_2^P\}$. We point out that, since we want to model the functioning of the pump during its transport activity, we will consider the conformation E_1 only in the case the binding of an ATP molecule (which triggers the process) has already occurred, and we describe this situation with label $E_1 \cdot ATP$. The labels E_1^P, E_2^P correspond to the phosphorylated conformations of the pump with high affinity for sodium and potassium ions, respectively, while E_2 correspond to the dephosphorylated conformation with high affinity for potassium ions, as already described in Section 3. For the description of occluded states, we consider a subset L_{occ} of L, namely $L_{occ} = \{E_1^P, E_2\}$, where the first label denotes the occluded conformation for sodium ions, the second the occluded conformation for potassium ions.

The alphabet of objects is $V = \{Na, K, ATP, ADP, P\}$, where symbols naturally represent the substances present in the cell and involved in the functioning of the pump. We consider also a second alphabet, $V_{occ} = \{\overline{Na}, \overline{K}\}$, to denote only those substances (sodium and potassium ions) which, at some time, are occluded within the pump, that is inside the bilayer region. The occlusion of these substances is expressed by means of overlined symbols, which will be present in a configuration if and only if the label of the membrane corresponds, at that time, to an occluded conformation of the pump.

Note the appearance of the symbols ATP and P in both the alphabet V and the label set L; the meaning of this aspect will be explained in the sequel.

In the initial configuration we assume that the multiset inside the region consists of n sodium symbols, m potassium symbols and s molecules of ATP, that is $M_{Reg} = \{nNa, mK, sATP\}$, the multiset in the environment is $M_{Env} = \{n'Na, m'K\}$, for some integers $n, n', m, m', s \geq 0$, while $M_{Bilayer}$ is empty.

We denote by $R_{Na} = \frac{n'}{n}$ and $R_K = \frac{m'}{m}$ the ratios of occurrences of sodium and potassium ions, respectively, outside and inside the membrane. These values are used to describe the starting time for the functioning of the pump. Indeed, in real cells it is known that the cytoplasmic concentration of sodium is very lower with respect to the external concentration, while the opposite holds for potassium concentration.[1] Whenever such natural conditions vary, e.g., when the intracellular concentration of Na^+ or extracellular concentration of K^+ rise above the steady-state values, the Na–K pumps in the plasma membrane try to re-establish the right physiological conditions. Hence, we assume that the activation of the pump is triggered by a change in the values of the ratios evaluated at the current step. Specifically, we define two *threshold conditions*, $R_{Na} \leq k_1$ and $R_K \geq k_2$ (for some fixed *threshold values* $k_1, k_2 \in \mathbf{R}$, corresponding to the ratios at steady-state concentrations), such that the pump will not be activated if they are not satisfied. Otherwise, the pump starts its functioning.

In the model of the pump, a generic evolution rule has the form

$$M_{Env} \; [M_{Bilayer}|_l \; M_{Reg} \xrightarrow{C} M'_{Env} \; [M'_{Bilayer}|_{l'} \; M'_{Reg},$$

where C is a (possibly null) threshold condition associated to the rule, $l, l' \in L$ and $M'_{Env}, M'_{Bilayer}, M'_{Reg}$ are multisets obtained from $M_{Env}, M_{Bilayer}, M_{Reg}$ by the application of the basic operations defined in Section 2.

The modification of objects happens only for symbols ATP and, in a different way, for Na and K. In the cell, the Na-K pump is autophosphorylated by the hydrolysis of one molecule of ATP, which produces one molecule of ADP (released free in the cell) and one inorganic phosphate group (covalently bounded to the pump). Hence, the transformation of the object ATP will involve the use of membrane labels that, as said before, correspond to conformations of the pump.

---

[1] For instance, a concentration of 145mM of sodium and 4mM of potassium can be found outside the cell, while 12mM of sodium and 139mM of potassium can be found inside (data taken from [16]).

On the other side, the objects Na, K only change their status (that is, occluded or not) during the functioning of the pump, thus we will only allow to transform each Na (K, respectively) into its corresponding occluded symbol $\overline{Na}$ ($\overline{K}$, respectively) and viceversa on condition that, in that step, the current membrane label belongs to L_{occ}. Precisely, we can have the following two situations:

$$[x|_l \rightarrow [y|_{l'}$$

when $l \in L, l' \in L_{occ}$ and, if $x \in \{Na\}^+$ then $y \in \{\overline{Na}\}^+$ (in this case, $l' = E_1^P$), if $x \in \{K\}^+$ then $y \in \{\overline{K}\}^+$ (in this case, $l' = E_2$), or

$$[x|_{l'} \rightarrow [y|_l$$

when $l \in L, l' \in L_{occ}$ and, if $x \in \{\overline{Na}\}^+$ then $y \in \{Na\}^+$ (in this case, $l' = E_1^P$), if $x \in \{\overline{K}\}^+$ then $y \in \{K\}^+$ (in this case, $l' = E_2$).

We also define two new types of evolution rules, which are needed only for the communication of objects, but not for their modification.

1. A *binding rule* has the form

$$b_{out,within} : x \; [|_l \rightarrow [x'|_{l'} \quad \text{or} \quad b_{in,within} : [|_l \; x \rightarrow [x'|_{l'}$$

   for some $x, x' \in V^+$ and $l, l' \in L$ (both not necessarily distinct).
   The application of a binding rule of the type $b_{out,within}$ ($b_{in,within}$) causes the movement of a multiset x from the environment (region) into the bilayer.
2. An *unbinding rule* has the form

$$u_{within,in} : [x|_l \rightarrow [|_{l'} \; x' \quad \text{or} \quad u_{within,out} : [x|_l \rightarrow x' \; [|_{l'}$$

   for some $x, x' \in V^+$ and $l, l' \in L$ (both not necessarily distinct).
   The application of an unbinding rule of the type $u_{within,in}$ ($u_{within,out}$) causes the movement of a multiset x from the bilayer into the region (environment).

The communication of objects happens when an unbinding rule is used after a binding rule (not necessarily in consecutive steps). For instance, if we first use a rule of the type $b_{out,within}$ and then we use a rule of the type $u_{within,in}$, then we have the passage of some objects from the outer environment into the internal region, while using first $b_{in,within}$ and then $u_{within,out}$ causes the passage of some objects from the internal region to the outer environment. In contrast to the usual and direct communication with target indication in P systems, here the passage of objects happens by means of the interplay of two rules and this corresponds to the presence of an intermediate region.

Remark 2. We stress here the fact that this kind of communication could be defined in another analogous way, namely using classical evolution rules with a new target indication of the type *within*, which would cause an object to pass from the environment or from the internal region directly into the bilayer. Anyway, this kind of mechanism would not be enough to model the Na–K pump, since in this case it is important to consider also the current label of the membrane and let the rule (possibly) modify it too. Indeed, in this system the membrane plays a fundamental role, since it represents (a part of) the cellular pump we are modelling and not only a separator for different regions. This is in line with the ideas expressed in [2] where rules are associated with membranes, instead of being only defined inside the regions.

Given all the necessary definitions, the functioning of the Na–K pump with occluded states can be now described by means of the following rules:

$$r_1 : \ [\ |_{E_1 \cdot ATP} \ 3Na \ \xrightarrow{(R_{Na} \leq k_1) \wedge (R_K \geq k_2)} \ [3Na|_{E_1 \cdot ATP}$$
$$r_2 : \ [3Na|_{E_1 \cdot ATP} \longrightarrow [3\overline{Na}|_{E_1^P} \ ADP$$
$$r_3 : \ [3\overline{Na}|_{E_1^P} \longrightarrow Na \ [2Na|_{E_2^P}$$
$$r_4 : \ [2Na|_{E_2^P} \longrightarrow 2Na \ [\ |_{E_2^P}$$
$$r_5 : \ 2K \ [\ |_{E_2^P} \longrightarrow [2K|_{E_2^P}$$
$$r_6 : \ [2K|_{E_2^P} \longrightarrow [2\overline{K}|_{E_2} \ P$$
$$r_7 : \ [2\overline{K}|_{E_2} \ ATP \longrightarrow [2K|_{E_1 \cdot ATP}$$
$$r_8 : \ [2K|_{E_1 \cdot ATP} \longrightarrow [\ |_{E_1 \cdot ATP} \ 2K$$

The application and meaning of rules is as follows. If threshold conditions in rule r_1 are both satisfied, the pump is in conformation $E_1 \cdot ATP$ and (at least) three Na symbols are present inside the internal region, then the pump is activated and three sodium ions are bound to the bilayer. Note that they are still not occluded within the bilayer, since the current membrane label is not in the alphabet L_{occ}.

Rule r_2 corresponds to the autophosphorylation of the pump: ATP is transformed into ADP with the (mute) production of one copy of the object P. Accordingly, the conformation of the pump is changed from $E_1 \cdot ATP$ into the phosphorylated form E_1^P. As mentioned above, the object P now becomes part of the membrane label, hence it undergoes a "structural modification" by passing from being an element of the alphabet V to being a component of the membrane labels in the set L. We believe that, instead of considering P as a free object, it is more appropriate to use the chosen formal description (rather than using, instead of rule r_2, the couple of rules $[3Na|_{E_1 \cdot ATP} \longrightarrow [3Na|_{E_1} \ ADP \ P$, and then $[3Na|_{E_1} \ P \longrightarrow [3\overline{Na}|_{E_1^P})$ since, actually, the phosphate directly intervene in the structural conformation of the pump (which is formally described here by means of membrane labels). The right-hand side of rule r_2 denotes the occlusion of sodium ions, that is possible because the membrane label is in L_{occ}.

In the system configuration $[3\overline{Na}|_{E_1^P}$, rule r_3 can be applied: the conformation of the pump changes from E_1^P to E_2^P, the sodium ions becomes de-occluded and are exposed to the extracellular side of the protein, where one of them is immediately released free in the environment. This is exactly an unbinding rule of the form $u_{within,out}$ which, applied after the binding rule r_1 (of the form $b_{in,within}$) allows the communication of objects from the region to the environment. Rule r_4 describes the unbinding of the remaining two sodium ions.

When the system configuration is $[|_{E_2^P}$, no objects are present in the bilayer and at least two copies of the object K are present in the environment, then rule r_5 can be applied: two potassium ions are bound within the bilayer and the pump conformation remains unchanged. By releasing into the region the phosphate P attached to the pump (expressed with the label E_2^P), the conformation turns to the occluded state E_2 and the objects K are transformed into their corresponding occluded objects $\overline{K}$ (rule r_6).

As reported in [11, 12], de-occlusion and successive release of K$^+$ ions is catalyzed by the binding of ATP to the pump. Hence, if at least one ATP symbol is present inside the region at this current step, its binding to the pump causes the membrane label to change from E_2 to $E_1 \cdot ATP$, and the occluded $\overline{K}$ symbols to pass to a non-occluded state (rule r_7). Note that, similarly to the structural modification of the symbol P, in rule r_7 there is a passage of the symbol ATP from being a component of M_{Reg} to being part of the membrane label.

Finally, by applying the unbinding rule r_8, two K symbols are released inside the region. An activation cycle of the pump is thus finished. The pump is in conformation $E_1 \cdot ATP$, the bilayer is empty and the simulation of pump activity can start again from rule r_1. The thresholds conditions must be evaluated again according to the current multisets and subsequent activation cycles might occur.

5   Sevilla Carpets and Pumps Systems

Sevilla carpets are introduced in [8] as a generalization of the control word of a Chomsky grammar, in order to describe computations in a P system. A Sevilla carpet is a table considering time on its horizontal axis, and the rules of a P system along its vertical axis; for each rule, this table contains a certain information at each computation step. We provide the Sevilla carpet of the Na–K pump where, at each computation step, it is specified whether a certain rule is used or not. We consider an initial configuration given by the following input values: 136 Na$^+$ ions and 10 K$^+$ ions in the environment, together with 21 Na$^+$ ions, 130 K$^+$ ions and 9 ATP energy units in the cytoplasmic region. These values correspond to the external and internal concentrations. As it was mentioned, the Na–K pump is activated in order to re-establish the physiological steady-state values, namely a concentration of 145mM of sodium and 4mM of potassium outside the cell, together with 12mM of sodium and 139mM of potassium inside (according to [16]).

We have a carpet with eight rules, and three iterations. It is easy to note that the pump has a deterministic behaviour provided by a clear sequence of rules, each rule being triggered by the successful execution of the previous one. Therefore the pump follows the same sequence of rules in each iteration, exhibiting a sequential behaviour. This sequential behaviour is also emphasized by the biological experiments [13].

Membrane Rule	Iteration 1	Iteration 2	Iteration 3
1	10000000	10000000	10000000
2	01000000	01000000	01000000
3	00100000	00100000	00100000
4	00010000	00010000	00010000
5	00001000	00001000	00001000
6	00000100	00000100	00000100
7	00000010	00000010	00000010
8	00000001	00000001	00000001
Env: 136Na, 10K	139Na, 8K	142Na, 6K	145Na, 4K
Reg: 21Na,130K,9ATP	18Na,132K,8ATP	15Na,134K,7ATP	12Na,136K,6ATP

Since we are in the framework of the bio-inspired approach of the membrane computing, and since parallelism is an important feature, it is normal to wonder where is this parallelism when we discuss about the biological membranes. And how this parallelism is actually activated and controlled. Considering a *hierarchical* organization and description of a biological cell, we can identify the various pumps as the processors able to execute the rules of a membrane in a maximal parallel and nondeterministic manner (see also [5]), where the activation of the pumps is triggered by concentration gradients conditions (in Section 4 we have defined specific threshold conditions corresponding to the ratios at steady-state concentrations). A final result is obtained when a stable state is reached. For the previous example, considering a certain number of Na–K pumps (say 10), as well as other pumps of a cell, the Sevilla carpet corresponding to the high-level computation of a general P system where pumps are seen as primitive constructions is given below. Here we emphasize only the communication of Na^+ and K^+ ions, as well as the consumption of ATP molecules (see the last lines of the table).

Pumps	Activation	Distribution
Na-K pumps	3 activations	0010100001
Ca pumps	0 activations	000000
Glucose-Na pumps	0 activations	0000000
other pumps	0 activations	00000000000
Env	136Na, 10K	145Na, 4K
Reg	21Na, 130K, 9ATP	12Na, 136K, 6ATP

It is easy to note the parallel execution of three pumps competing in this case for Na^+ and K^+ ions, as well as the nondeterministic choice of their activations represented in the Sevilla carpet by the distribution 0010100001 saying that the Na-K pumps 3, 5 and 10 of the given 10 pumps were activated.

We stress the fact that this is just an attempt to consider a cell as a P system working with pumps as processors of the rules. Undoubtedly, it is far from being a real description, since in such a case many biological factors should be considered as well. A strong and well motivated hint for future research is thus established.

6   Conclusion and Future Work

In this section we briefly present some possible extensions of the model and future investigations.

In [7], the Na–K pump was described by using the process algebra π-calculus. In [6], the transfer mechanisms were described step by step, and software tools of verification were also applied. This means that it would be possible to verify properties of the described systems by using a computer program, and the use of the verification software as a substitute for expensive lab experiments. A similar development for P systems would be a very useful achievement.

The P system proposed in this paper presents similar features with P automata (see [9]), where the membranes are only allowed to communicate with each other, and objects are never modified during a computation, but only exchanged among regions, or consumed from the environment through the skin membrane. As a future extension of our work, the model of the sodium-potassium pump can be translated into its corresponding P automaton (with the appropriate type of objects communication), and then its computational power could be investigate. In this way, we think we could establish a deeper theoretical link between the theory of formal languages and the (present description of a) biological transmembrane protein.

From the biological point of view, it is known that the drug *ouabain* (and other similar cardiac glycosides) is a specific inhibitor of the pump; it competes with K^+ ions for the same binding site (in conformation E_2^P) on the extracellular side of the pump [1]. Many animal cells swell, and often burst, when they are treated with ouabain. The occurrence of ouabain can be modelled by adding a new object o to the alphabet V, and by considering the rule

$$o\ [\ |_{E_2^P} \longrightarrow [o|_{E_2^P},$$

which could be (nondeterministically) chosen instead of the rule r_5 given in Section 4. The functioning of the pump would then be blocked, since no other rule can be further applied. It would be worthwhile to study, from a biological perspective, the consequences of pump inhibition, also due to changes in intracellular pH (via the exchange system of sodium and hydrogen) or calcium (via the exchange system of sodium and calcium), and the dynamics governing the interactions among the pump and other proteins. Considering different behaviors of the pump, in presence of specific chemicals, could open interesting scenarios of research.

Finally, it would be interesting to extend P systems with some stochastic features able to characterize the molecular interactions involving the dynamic efficiency of the pump and other quantitative aspects (e.g., kinetics rates, energy, pump failures). Regarding the sodium-potassium pump, the whole transport process can have failures, and the pump can fail to transport Na^+ out in exchange for K^+ that are taken in. For example, as already mentioned in Section 3, due to the lower rate constant for the reaction $E_1 \cdot ATP \Leftrightarrow E_1 \sim P + ADP$, E_1 has enough time to bind sodium before undergoing the transition to E_2. However, the reaction $E_1 \cdot ATP \Leftrightarrow E_1 \sim P + ADP$ can work sometime before the sodium ions bind to the pump; this occurs quite rarely compared to the usual activity of the pump. Mainly, ATP is working faster than the sodium ions, and the pump changes its conformation (from open inside to open outside) without the sodium ions. This simple biological example motivates the study of stochastic aspects related to the P system proposed here. Therefore, in order to have a more realistic description of the pump, we could give a probabilistic model and add some probability distributions to rules, in a similar way they were attached to the pump actions in [7]. In this way, it could also be possible to model the quantitative behavior of a P system.

References

1. B. Alberts, A. Johnson, J. Lewis, M. Raff, K. Roberts, P. Walter. *Molecular Biology of the Cell.*, 4th edition, Garland Science, New York, 2002.
2. F. Bernardini, V. Manca. P systems with boundary rules, in Gh. Păun, G. Rozenberg, A. Salomaa, C. Zandron (Eds.): *Membrane Computing. WMC-CdeA 2002*, LNCS 2597, Springer, Berlin, 2003, 107–118.
3. D. Besozzi, I.I. Ardelean, G. Mauri. The potential of P systems for modelling the activity of mechanosensitive channels in E. coli, *Pre-Proc. Workshop on Membrane Computing*, Rovira i Virgili University TR 28, 2003, 84–102.
4. D. Besozzi. *Computational and Modelling Power of P Systems*, PhD Thesis, University of Milano, 2003.
5. G. Ciobanu. Pumps systems of membranes, *Proc. 2nd Brainstorming Week on Membrane Computing*, University of Seville, 2004, 130–134.
6. G. Ciobanu. Software verification of the biomolecular systems, in *Modelling in Molecular Biology*, Natural Computing Series, Springer, 2004, 40–59.
7. G. Ciobanu, V. Ciubotariu, B. Tanasă. A pi-calculus model of the Na pump, *Genome Informatics*, Universal Academy Press, Tokyo, 2002, 469–472.
8. G. Ciobanu, Gh. Păun, Gh. Ştefănescu. Sevilla Carpets Associated with P Systems, *Tech. Report 26*, Rovira i Virgili University, 2003, 135–140. To appear in *New Generation Computing*, Springer, 2004.
9. E. Csuhaj-Varjú, G. Vaszil. P automata or purely communicating accepting P systems, in Gh. Păun, G. Rozenberg, A. Salomaa, C. Zandron (Eds.): *Membrane Computing. WMC-CdeA 2002*, LNCS 2597, Springer, Berlin, 2003, 219–233.
10. G. Franco, V. Manca. A membrane system for the leukocyte selective recruitment, in C. Martín-Vide, G. Mauri, Gh. Păun, G. Rozenberg, A. Salomaa (Eds.): *Membrane Computing. WMC 2003*, LNCS 2933, Springer, Berlin, 2004, 181–190.
11. H.G. Glitsch. Electrophysiology of the sodium-potassium-ATPase in cardiac cells, *Physiological Reviews*, 81, 4 (2001), 1791–1826.
12. I.M. Glynn. A hundred years of sodium pumping, *Annu. Rev. Physiol.*, 64 (2002), 1–18.
13. M. Holmgren, J. Wagg, F. Bezanilla, R.F. Rakowski, P. de Weer, D.C. Gadsby. Three distinct and sequential steps in the release of sodium ions by the Na/K-ATPase, *Nature*, 403 (2000), 898–901.
14. J.H. Kaplan. Biochemistry of Na,K-ATPase, *Annu. Rev. Biochem.*, 71 (2002), 511–535.
15. J.B. Lingrel, T. Kuntzweiler. Na$^+$,K$^+$-ATPase, *Journal of Biological Chemistry*, 269 ,31 (1994), 19659–19662.

16. H. Lodish, A. Berk, S.L. Zipursky, P. Matsudaira, D. Baltimore, J. Darnell. *Molecular Cell Biology*, 4th edition, W.H. Freeman and Co., New York, 2000.
17. Gh. Păun. Computing with membranes, *Journal of Computer and System Sciences*, 61 1 (2000), 108–143.
18. Gh. Păun. *Membrane Computing. An Introduction*, Springer, Berlin, 2002.
19. A.G. Therien, R. Blostein. Mechanisms of sodium pump regulation, *Am. J. Physiol. Cell Physiol.*, 279 (2000), C541–C566.

Inhibiting/De-inhibiting Rules in P Systems

Matteo Cavaliere[1], Mihai Ionescu[2], and Tseren-Onolt Ishdorj[2]

[1] Department of Computer Science and Artificial Intelligence,
University of Sevilla,
Av. Reina Mercedes s/n, 41012, Sevilla, Spain
martew@inwind.it
[2] Research Group on Mathematical Linguistics,
Rovira i Virgili University,
Pl. Imperial Tàrraco 1, 43005, Tarragona, Spain
mi@fll.urv.es,
tserenonolt.ishdorj@estudiants.urv.es

Abstract. We introduce in the P systems area a mechanism, inspired from neural-cell behavior, which controls computations by inhibiting and de-inhibiting evolution rules. We investigate the computational power of this mechanism in both generative and accepting P systems. In particular, we prove that universality can be obtained by using one catalyst. If we use only non-cooperative rules and one membrane, then we can obtain at least the family of Parikh images of the languages generated by ET0L systems. Several research proposals are also suggested.

1 Introduction

P systems represent a class of distributed/parallel computing devices whose functioning is inspired from the behavior of living cells. Chemical compounds are processed in a massive parallel manner inside a compartmental structure of membranes that control the exchanges of substances between the regions they delimit. The reactions that take place inside such a biological structure can be formally described by multiset processing rules.

In biology it is known that many reactions in the cell are catalyzed by the presence of associated enzymes. On the other hand, in bacteria, the enzymes (proteins) can be activated/inactivated during the cellular process (in other words, an inactivated enzyme is not able to catalyze the corresponding reaction). For instance, in cells, there are chemical reactions promoted/inhibited by the presence/absence of certain chemicals which are not directly implied in the reactions. A formalization of this fact has been done in [5] where P systems with promoters/inhibitors have been introduced and investigated.

Another possibility is to consider biological signals processed by living cells. Signals can arise from inside the cell or from the external environment and the correct answer to certain signals is essential for bacteria to survive in a certain environment. P systems based on this mechanism have been investigated in [3].

G. Mauri et al. (Eds.): WMC5 2004, LNCS 3365, pp. 224–238, 2005.

Again inspired from cell-biology, P systems with creation of evolution rules during the computation have been investigated in [4].

Recently P systems using operations inspired by the functioning of neural cells have been introduced and investigated in [1] and [7].

In this paper we continue the investigation of models of P systems using features imported from neural-cells functioning. In particular we introduce the ability for an evolution rule to inhibit or to de-inhibit, during the computation, other rules present in the systems.

Before introducing the formal definition of the proposed mechanism let us briefly recall the biological background of neural-cells. For more details about neural biology we refer to the classical book [16].

The basic unit of transmission in the nervous system is a cell called neuron. The neuron is not an homogeneous unit but is (potentially) divided in many sub-integrative units, each one with the ability of mediating a local synaptic output to another cell or to another part of the same cell.

Neurons are considered to have three main parts: a soma, the central part of the cell where the genetic material is present and life functions take place; a dendrite tree, the branches of the cell where impulses come in; an axon, the branch of the neuron over which the impulse (or signal) is propagated.

The branches present at the end of the axons are called terminal trees. An axon can be equipped with a structure composed by special sheaths. These sheaths are involved in molecular and structural modifications of axons needed to propagate impulse signals rapidly over long distance. There is a gap between neighboring myelinated regions that is know as the node of Ranvier, which contains channels for impulse generation. When the transmitting impulses reach the node of Ranvier, they cause the change in polarization of the membrane. The change in potential can be *excitatory* (moving the potential toward the threshold) or *inhibitory* (moving the potential away from the threshold).

The impulse transmission through a neuron follows this path: from dendrite to soma to axon to terminal tree to synapse. If different impulses reach at the same time a certain node, it might happen that the combined effects of the excitatory and inhibitory signals may cancel each other out. Once the threshold of the membrane potential is reached, an impulse is propagated along the neuron or to the next neuron.

It is possible to introduce this mechanism in the P systems area by using evolution rules equipped with the ability to send excitatory/inhibitory signals.

An inhibited rule is formally written as $r : \neg(u \to v)$, and the meaning is that the rule cannot be applied, more precisely, u cannot evolve to v. An evolution rule can de-inhibit an inhibited rule allowing it to be applied. To this aim, we also consider rules of the form $r : u \to v\langle r_1 \cdots r_k \rangle$, which say that, when the rule is applied, u evolves into v and the rules $r_1, \cdots, r_k$ are inhibited or de-inhibited according to their previous states.

We introduce a class of P systems using inhibiting/de-inhibiting rules and we explore the computational power of the class considering catalytic and non-cooperative inhibiting/de-inhibiting rules. In particular, we prove that universality can be obtained (in the generative and accepting cases) by using only one catalyst. If we use only non-cooperative rules, then the systems can generate at least the family of Parikh images of the languages generated by ET0L systems.

2   Preliminaries

We recall the main elements of formal language theory used in the paper; for more information the reader can consult [15].

First, some basic notations. O^* denote the set of all strings over the alphabet O. For $a \in O$ and $x \in O^*$ we denote by $|x|_a$ the number of occurrences of a in x. Then, for $O = \{a_1, \cdots, a_n\}$, the *Parikh mapping* associated with O is the mapping on O^* defined by $\Psi_O(x) = (|x|_{a_1}, \cdots, |x|_{a_n})$, for each $x \in O^*$. The family of recursively enumerable languages is denoted by RE and the family of Parikh images of recursively enumerable languages languages is denoted by $PsRE$ (this is the family of all recursively enumerable sets of vectors of natural numbers). The families of languages generated by context-free and context-sensitive grammars are denoted by CF and CS, respectively. The family of Parikh images of languages generated by context-free grammars is denoted by $PsCF$.

The multisets over a given finite support (alphabet) are represented by strings of symbols. The order of symbols does not matter, because the number of copies of an object in a multiset is given by the number of occurrences of the corresponding symbol in the string. Clearly, using strings is only one of many ways to specify multisets.

2.1   Matrix Grammars

We recall here the notion of matrix grammar because we will use in the paper the characterization of recursively enumerable languages by means of *matrix grammars with appearance checking*.

Such a grammar is a construct $G = (N, T, S, M, F)$, where N, T are disjoint alphabets, $S \in N$, M is a finite set of sequences of the form $(A_1 \to x_1, \ldots, A_n \to x_n)$, $n \geq 1$, of context-free rules over $N \cup T$ (with $A_i \in N, x_i \in (N \cup T)^*, 1 \leq i \leq n$), and F is a set of occurrences of rules in M (N is the nonterminal alphabet, T is the terminal alphabet, S is the axiom, while the elements of M are called matrices).

For $w, z \in (N \cup T)^*$ we write $w \Longrightarrow z$ if there is a matrix $(A_1 \to x_1, \ldots, A_n \to x_n)$ in M and the strings $w_i \in (N \cup T)^*, 1 \leq i \leq n+1$, such that $w = w_1, z = w_{n+1}$, and, for all $1 \leq i \leq n$, either $w_i = w_i' A_i w_i'', w_{i+1} = w_i' x_i w_i''$, for some $w_i', w_i'' \in (N \cup T)^*$, or $w_i = w_{i+1}$, A_i does not appear in w_i, and the rule $A_i \to x_i$ appears in F. (The rules of a matrix are applied in order, possibly skipping the rules in F if they cannot be applied – therefore we say that these rules are applied in the *appearance checking* mode.) If the set F is empty, then the grammar is said to be without appearance checking.

The language generated by G is defined by $L(G) = \{w \in T^* \mid S \Longrightarrow^* w\}$. The family of languages generated by matrix grammars with appearance checking is denoted by MAT_{ac}. It is known, [6], that $MAT_{ac} = RE$.

A matrix grammar $G = (N, T, S, M, F)$ is said to be in the *binary normal form* if $N = N_1 \cup N_2 \cup \{S, \#\}$, with these three sets mutually disjoint, and the matrices in M are in one of the following types:

1. $(S \to XA)$, with $X \in N_1, A \in N_2$,
2. $(X \to Y, A \to x)$, with $X, Y \in N_1, A \in N_2, x \in (N_2 \cup T)^*, |x| \leq 2$,
3. $(X \to Y, A \to \#)$, with $X, Y \in N_1, A \in N_2$,
4. $(X \to \lambda, A \to x)$, with $X \in N_1, A \in N_2$, and $x \in T^*, |x| \leq 2$.

Moreover, there is only one matrix of type 1 (that is why one uses to write it in the form $(S \to X_{init} A_{init})$, in order to fix the symbols X, A present in it), and F consists exactly of all rules $A \to \#$ appearing in matrices of type 3; $\#$ is a trap-symbol, because once introduced, it is never removed. A matrix of type 4 is used only once, in the last step of a derivation.

For each matrix grammar there is an equivalent matrix grammar in the binary normal form. Details can be found in [6].

2.2 Register Machines

We will also use in our paper register machines that is why we shortly recall here this notion (the reader can find more details in [9]). A register machine runs a program consisting of labelled instructions of several simple types. Several variants of register machines were shown to be computationally universal.

A *n-register machine* is a construct $M = (n, P, l_0, l_h)$, where:

- n is the number of registers,
- P is a set of labeled instructions of the form $l_i : (op(r), l_j, l_k)$, where $op(r)$ is an operation on register r of M, and l_i, l_j, l_k are labels from the set $lab(M)$ (that is the set of labels associated to the the instructions, in a one-to-one manner),
- l_0 is the label of the initial instruction, and
- l_h is the label of the halting instruction.

The machine is capable of the following instructions:

$(add(r), l_j, l_k)$: Add one to the content of register r and proceed, in a non-deterministic way, to instruction with label l_j or to instruction with label l_k; in the deterministic variants usually considered in the literature we demand $l_j = l_k$.

$(sub(r), l_j, l_k)$: If register r is not empty, then subtract one from its contents and go to instruction with label l_j, otherwise proceed to instruction with label l_k.

$halt$: This instruction stops the machine; it can only be assigned to the final label l_h.

A deterministic n-register machine can analyze an input $(n_1, ..., n_\alpha) \in \mathbf{N}^\alpha$, introduced in registers 1 to α, which is accepted if and only if the register machine finally stops by the halt instruction with all its registers being empty (this last requirement is not necessary). If the machine does not halt, then the analysis was not successful.

It is known (see [9]) that deterministic register machines accept exactly the family of Turing computable sets of vectors of natural numbers.

A non-deterministic n-register machine can be used also as a generating device, in the following way. A register machine generates a vector $(n_1, \cdots, n_\alpha) \in \mathbf{N}^\alpha$ when it starts from the instruction labeled l_0 with all registers being empty and stops by halting with value n_j in register j, $1 \leq j \leq \alpha$, and the contents of registers $\alpha + 1, \cdots, n$ being empty.

In this way, register machines can generate the family of Turing computable sets of natural numbers.

2.3   Lindenmayer Systems

An ET0L system is a construct $G = (\Sigma, T, H, w)$, where the components fulfill the following requirements: Σ is the alphabet; $T \subseteq \Sigma$ is the terminal alphabet; H is a finite set of of finite substitutions (tables) $H = \{h_1, h_2, \cdots, h_t\}$ (t is the number of tables); each $h_i \in H$ can be represented by a list of context-free rules $A \to x$, such that $A \in \Sigma$ and $x \in \Sigma^*$ (this list for h_i should satisfy that each symbol of Σ appears as the left side of some rule in h_i, $1 \leq i \leq t$); $w \in \Sigma^*$ is the axiom.

G defines a derivation relation $\Rightarrow$ by $x \Rightarrow y$ iff $y \in h_i(x)$, for some $1 \leq i \leq t$, where h_i is interpreted as substitution mapping.

The language generated by G is $L(G) = \{z \in T^* \mid w \Longrightarrow^* z\}$.

$ET0L$ denotes the family of languages generated by ET0L systems and $PsET0L$ the family of Parikh images of languages in $ET0L$.

The following inclusions are of interest for what follows:

$$CF \subset ET0L \subset CS \subset RE.$$

Moreover it is known that for each $L \in ET0L$, there exists an ET0L system G', with only 2 tables, such that $L = L(G')$ (see [15]).

We also need to present the following normal form for ET0L systems (for the proof we refer to [2]).

Lemma 1. (Normal form)
For each $L \in ET0L$ there is an extended tabled Lindenmayer system $G = (\Sigma, T, H, w)$ with 2 tables ($H = \{h_1, h_2\}$) generating L, such that, for each $a \in T$ if $(a \to \alpha) \in h_1 \cup h_2$, then $\alpha = a$. A production of the kind $a \to a, a \in T$, is called trivial.

In what follows we suppose the reader familiar with the main concepts and results of the P systems area, as, for instance, presented in [12].

3 Inhibiting/De-inhibiting Rules in P Systems

A P system *with inhibiting/de-inhibiting rules* (in short, an ID P system), of degree $m \geq 1$, is a construct

$$\Pi = (O, C, H, \mu, w_1, \ldots, w_m, R_1, \cdots, R_m, i_0),$$

where:

- O is the alphabet of *objects*;
- $C \subseteq O$ is the set of catalysts;
- To each rule in $R = R_1 \cup R_2 \cup \cdots \cup R_m$ is associated an unique label; the set of all labels is $H = \{r_1, \cdots, r_k\}$;
- μ is a *membrane structure*, consisting of m membranes, labeled $1, 2, \cdots, m$;
- $w_1, \ldots, w_m$ are strings over O, describing the *multisets of objects* placed in the m regions of μ at the beginning of the computation;
- $R_i, 1 \leq i \leq m$, is a finite set of *developmental rules*, associated with region i. The rules in R_i are non-cooperative, $r_j : \neg(a \rightarrow w)\langle S \rangle$, $r_j : a \rightarrow w\langle S \rangle$; catalytic, $r_j : \neg(ca \rightarrow cw)\langle S \rangle$, $r_j : ca \rightarrow cw\langle S \rangle$, where $r_j \in H$, $a \in O - C$, $w \in ((O - C) \times TAR)^*$, $c \in C$, $TAR = \{out, here\} \cup \{in_j \mid 1 \leq j \leq m\}$; if the target indication is not present, then it is intended to be *here*; S is a string that represents a subset of H;
- i_0 is the output region (0 is used to indicate the environment).

A configuration of an ID P system is described by using the m-tuple of multisets of objects present in the m regions of the system. With each region a finite number of objects is associated together with a finite number of rules. The m-tuple $(w_1, w_2, \cdots, w_m)$ describes the initial configuration of the system. Some of the rules are initially inhibited (if the symbol $\neg$ is written immediately before the rule). A transition between two configurations is governed by the application in a non-deterministic and maximally parallel way of the rules that are not inhibited.

When a rule $r_j : a \rightarrow w\langle S \rangle$ (or $r_j : ca \rightarrow cw\langle S \rangle$) is applied then the object a is rewritten with the objects in w (as in standard P systems) and each rule with label in S is de-inhibited (if it was inhibited) or inhibited (if it was de-inhibited); if a rule is inhibited and de-inhibited in the same step, then the choice is made in a non-deterministic way. For simplicity each symbol of S is called *switch*.

A sequence of configurations is called a *computation*. The system continues the application of the rules in a maximally parallel way until there remain no applicable rules in any region of the system; in this case the system has reached an *halting configuration* and the computation halts.

The output of a halting computation is the vector of numbers representing the multiplicities of objects present in the output region in the halting configuration.

If we collect all the vectors generated by Π considering any halting computation then we get the set of vectors of natural numbers generated by Π denoted by $Ps(\Pi)$.

We use the notation

$$PsIDP_m(\alpha), \alpha \in \{ncoo\} \cup \{cat_k \mid k \geq 0\},$$

to denote the family of sets of vectors of natural numbers generated by ID P systems with at most m membranes, evolution rules that can be non-cooperative ($ncoo$), or catalytic (cat_k), using at most k catalysts (as usual, $*$ indicates that the corresponding number is not bounded).

A system Π as above can be also used in the accepting mode in the following way. Given a vector v of natural numbers, let be x a string over the alphabet O such that $\Psi_O(x) = v$; the occurrences of objects corresponding to the multiset described by the string x are inserted in a specified region and the vector v is accepted by the system Π if and only if the computation halts. We denote by $Ps_a(\Pi)$ the set of all vectors of natural numbers accepted by the system Π.

We use the notation

$$PsID_aP_m(\alpha), \alpha \in \{ncoo\} \cup \{cat_k \mid k \geq 0\},$$

to denote the family of sets of vectors of natural numbers accepted by ID P systems with at most m membranes, evolution rules that can be non-cooperative ($ncoo$), or catalytic (cat_k), using at most k catalysts.

In what follows, for an arbitrary set of rules R of Π, we indicate with $Lab_\Pi(R)$ the set of labels associated to the rules in R.

4   An Example

We now illustrate the working of an ID P system by using an example that shows how powerful the simple mechanism of inhibiting/de-inhibiting rules can be.

Let us consider an ID P system of degree 1,

$$\Pi = (\{A, a\}, \emptyset, \{r_1, r_2, r_3\}, [\ ]_1, A, R_1, 1),$$

where:

$$R_1 = \{r_1 : A \to AA, \quad r_2 : A \to AA\langle r_1 r_2 r_3\rangle, \quad r_3 : \neg(A \to a)\}.$$

When the computation starts, the rules r_1 or r_2 can be applied but the rule r_3 cannot be applied because it is inhibited. We use the rule r_1 $m-1$ times and at step m we apply the rule r_2 (together with rule r_1). Then we produce 2^m copies of the object A and, at the same time, the rules r_1 and r_2 are inhibited and they cannot be used anymore; moreover, the rule r_3 is de-inhibited and all the As are changed to as in the next step. Therefore we have used non-cooperative inhibiting/de-inhibiting rules to obtain the Parikh image of $\{a^{2^m} \mid m \geq 1\}$ which is not in $PsCF$.

5   Using One Catalyst: Two Universality Results

In this section we prove the universality of ID P systems using catalytic rules (with only one catalyst) and one membrane. The first universality result deals with generative systems and is obtained by simulating matrix grammars with appearance checking. The second universality result is about accepting systems and it is proved by simulating deterministic register machines.

5.1   Universality for the Generative Case

Theorem 1. $PsIDP_1(cat_1) = PsRE$.

Proof. Consider a matrix grammar $G = (N, T, S, M, F)$ with appearance checking, in the binary normal form, hence with $N = N_1 \cup N_2 \cup \{S, \#\}$ as introduced in Section 2.1. Assume that all matrices are labeled in an injective manner with $m_i, 1 \leq i \leq n$, and each terminal matrix $(X \to \lambda, A \to x)$ is replaced by $(X \to f, A \to x)$, where f is a new symbol. We define the set of rules $R_\# = \{X \to \# \mid X \in N_1 \cup N_2\}$.

We construct the P system of degree 1,

$$\Pi = (O, C, H, \mu, w_1, R_1, i_0), \text{where:}$$
$$O = N_1 \cup T \cup N_2 \cup \{p, p', p'', \overline{p'}, \overline{p''}, c, d, d', d'', d''', f, \#\},$$
$$C = \{c\},$$
$$H = \{r_i \mid 1 \leq i \leq 13\} \cup \{r_{2,i}, r_{3,i}, r_{8,i}, r_{9,i}, r_{12,i} \mid 1 \leq i \leq n\}$$
$$\cup \{r_4', r_5', r_6'\} \cup Lab_\Pi(R_\#),$$
$$\mu = [\ ]_1,$$
$$w_1 = cpX_{init}A_{init},$$
$$i_0 = 0,$$

and the set R_1 is constructed in the following way

- The simulation of a matrix of type 2, $m_i : (X_i \to Y_i, A_i \to x_i)$, with $X_i \in N_1, Y_i \in N_1, A_i \in N_2, x_i \in (N_2 \cup T)^*, |x_i| \leq 2$, is done by using the following rules added to the set R_1:

$r_1 : p \to p'p''\langle r_{2,i}r_{3,i}\rangle$,
$r_{2,i} : \neg(X_i \to Y_i)\langle r_5'r_5r_{2,i}\rangle$,
$r_{3,i} : \neg(cA_i \to cx_id')\langle r_6'r_6r_{3,i}\rangle$,
$r_2 : d' \to d$,
$r_3 : d \to p\langle r_5'r_6'\rangle$,
$r_4 : p' \to \overline{p'}$,
$r_4' : p'' \to \overline{p''}$,
$r_5 : \neg(\overline{p'} \to \lambda)\langle r_5r_5'\rangle$,
$r_6 : \neg(\overline{p''} \to \lambda)\langle r_6r_6'\rangle$,
$r_5' : \overline{p'} \to \#$,
$r_6' : \overline{p''} \to \#$.

The idea is the following one. The rule r_1 chooses the matrix i to apply and this is made by the simultaneous de-inhibition of rules $r_{2,i}$ and $r_{3,i}$ (all other rules of other matrices remains inhibited). The execution of both $r_{2,i}$ and $r_{3,i}$ inhibits the rules r_5' and r_6' that are used to trash the computation in the case the matrix chosen is not correctly applied. If the matrix is applied in the correct way (both the rules are executed), then d is changed to p and the process can be iterated (the original configuration of inhibited / de-inhibited rules is re-established).

- The simulation of a matrix of type 3, $m_i : (X_i \rightarrow Y_i, A_i \rightarrow \#)$, with $X_i, Y_i \in N_1$ and $A_i \in N_2$, is done by using the following rules, added to the set of rules R_1:

$r_7 : p \rightarrow p' \langle r_{8,i} r_{9,i} \rangle$,
$r_{8,i} : \neg(X_i \rightarrow Y_i d'') \langle r_5' r_5 r_{8,i} r_{9,i} \rangle$,
$r_{9,i} : \neg(A_i \rightarrow \#)$,
$r_8 : p' \rightarrow \overline{p'}$,
$r_9 : d'' \rightarrow d'''$,
$r_{10} : d''' \rightarrow p$.

The idea of the simulation of this kind of matrix is the following one. The rule r_7 de-inhibits the rules corresponding to the matrix i to be simulated. If the first rule is not applied, then the rule r_5' is not inhibited and then the computation never halts (the application of the second rule is skipped without any problem if the symbol A_i is not present).

- The simulation of a terminal matrix $m_i : (X_i \rightarrow f, A_i \rightarrow x_i)$, with $X_i \in N_1$, $A_i \in N_2$, and $x_i \in T^*, |x_i| \leq 2$, is done using the following rules (added to the set R_1):

$r_{11} : p \rightarrow \lambda < u >$,
$r_{12,i} : \neg(cA_i \rightarrow cx_i) \langle r_{12,i} \rangle$,
$R_{11} = \{\neg(X \rightarrow \#) \mid X \in N_1 \cup N_2\}$,
where u is a string representing the set $Lab_\Pi(R_\#) \cup \{r_{12,i}\}$.

These rules are used to simulate a terminal matrix and then to halt the computation. In fact, p is deleted and the rule $r_{12,i}$ is executed; the rules in R_{11} are de-inhibited and they guarantee that, when the computation halts, only terminal objects are present.

R_1 also contains the following rules:

$r_{12} : a \rightarrow (a, out)$,
$r_{13} : \# \rightarrow \#$.

The result of the computation is collected in the environment; from the above explanation it follows that the set of vectors generated by Π is exactly the Parikh image of $L(G)$.   □

5.2   Universality for the Accepting Case

The following theorem illustrates the computational universality (in their *accepting* variant) of P systems with non-cooperative inhibiting/de-inhibiting rules. The system we use in the proof simulates the computation of a deterministic register machine. We can notice that, differently from the previous proof, the switches are used only by non-cooperative rules.

Theorem 2. $PsID_aP_1(cat_1) = PsRE$.

Proof. In order to prove this assertion we will simulate an n–register machine $M = (n, P, l_0, l_h)$. At each time during the computation, the current content of register r is represented by the multiplicity of the object a_r.

Formally, we define the P system of degree 1, as follows

$\Pi = (O, C, H, \mu, w_1, R_1, i_0)$, where:

$O = \{a_r \mid 1 \le r \le n\}$
$\quad \cup \{A_{i_r}, S_{i_r}, S'_{i_r}, S''_{i_r}, S'''_{i_r}, F_{i_r}, e_i, e'_i \mid 1 \le r \le n, 1 \le i \le lab(M)\} \cup \{p, c, l_h\}$
$\quad \cup \{l_i \mid l_i : (add(r), l_j, l_j) \in P\}$
$\quad \cup \{l_i \mid l_i : (sub(r), l_j, l_k) \in P\}$,

$C = \{c\}$,

$H = \{r_{ji} \mid 1 \le j \le 15, 1 \le i \le lab(M)\}$,

$\mu = [\ ]_1$,

$w_1 = cl_0 a_1^{k_1} \cdots a_i^{k_i} \cdots a_n^{k_n}$, with $k_i \ge 0, 1 \le i \le n$,

$i_0 = 0$,

and R_1 is defined as follows:

- for each instruction $l_i : (add(r), l_j, l_j) \in P$, we add to R_1 the rules:
  $r_{1i} : l_i \to A_{j_r}$,
  $r_{2i} : A_{j_r} \to a_r e_j$,
  $r_{3i} : e_j \to l_j$,
- for each instruction $l_i : (sub(r), l_j, l_k) \in P$, we add to R_1 the rules:
  $r_{4i} : l_i \to e_j S_{j_r}$,
  $r_{5i} : e_j \to e'_j$,
  $r_{6i} : S_{j_r} \to S'_{j_r} \langle r_{7i} \rangle$,
  $r_{7i} : \neg(ca_r \to cF_{j_r})$,
  $r_{8i} : S'_{j_r} \to S''_{j_r}$,
  $r_{9i} : F_{j_r} \to \lambda \langle r_{7i} r_{12i} \rangle$,
  $r_{10i} : S''_{j_r} \to S'''_{j_r}$,
  $r_{11i} : S'''_{j_r} \to \langle r_{13i} \rangle$,
  $r_{12i} : \neg(e'_j \to l_j p) \langle r_{12i} \rangle$,
  $r_{13i} : \neg(e'_j \to l_k) \langle r_{13i} r_{7i} \rangle$,
  $r_{14i} : p \to \lambda \langle r_{13i} \rangle$,
  $r_{15i} : l_h \to \lambda$.

The constructed system works in the following way. Initially the P system starts the computation having in its input region the objects $a_1^{k_1}, \cdots, a_n^{k_n}$ and the label l_0 of the first instruction of the register machine we want to simulate. The vector $(k_1, \cdots, k_n)$ represents the vector that has to be accepted by our P system.

The P system starts the computation by simulating the first instruction of the register machine program. Let us suppose that the current instruction to be executed is of type $l_i : (add(r), l_j, l_j) \in P$. Then, the rule $l_i \rightarrow A_{j_r}$ is executed. The object A_{j_r} indicates that the number of objects a_r has to be incremented. This will be realized, in the following step, by the evolution rule $A_{j_r} \rightarrow a_r e_j$. Next rule r_{3i} is executed and the operation allows our P system to further simulate the next instruction of the register machine indicated by label l_j.

If a subtraction instruction $l_i : (sub(r), l_j, l_k) \in P$ has to be simulated, then the rule $l_i \rightarrow e_j S_{j_r}$ is executed. In the following step the object S_{j_r} is used to de-inhibit rule r_{7i}, and to produce object S_{j_r}' by using the rule r_{6i}, while the object e_j evolves into e_j'.

In the next step, if the number of objects a_r in register r is greater than 0, then the execution of the de-inhibited rule $ca_r \rightarrow cF_{j_r}$ decreases the number of objects a_r by 1, and produces object F_{j_r} for the next step.

We have used the catalyst c in order to inhibit the parallelism (because more copies of a_r might be present in the region).

Meanwhile, the object S_{j_r}' evolves into S_{j_r}'' by using the r_{8i}.

When the rule r_{9i} is executed the rule r_{7i} is inhibited and this guarantees that r_{7i} is applied only once; the rule r_{12i} is de-inhibited by the execution of the rule r_{9i}.

The execution of the rule r_{12i} generates the label l_j of the next register machine instruction (it is executed only once because the rule is inhibited by itself).

In the other case (i.e., if there is no object a_r in region), the rule $ca_r \rightarrow cF_{j_r}$ cannot be executed, therefore the object F_{j_r} is not produced and rule r_{9i} cannot be applied.

On the other hand, object S_{j_r}'' evolves into S_{j_r}''' by the execution of rule r_{10i} and at the next step S_{j_r}''' de-inhibits rule r_{13i}, so e_j' evolves to label l_k (notice that the object e_j' still appears, because rule r_{12i} has not been applied in the previous steps); rule r_{13i} must also inhibit rule r_{7i} that has been previously de-inhibited by rule r_{6i}.

In the next step the rule r_{14i} is executed and then the rule r_{13i} is inhibited.

When the label of the next register machine instruction has been generated the entire process can be iterated.

The simulation stops (and then the input is accepted) when label l_h (which stands for *halt* instruction) is generated. From the above explanation follows that the set of vectors of natural numbers accepted by the system Π is the same as the machine M. □

Remark. The previous proof can be adapted to prove the universality also in the case of the generating variant. The only things to modify in Π are the following ones: we add to R_1 the set of rules $R_{16} = \{\neg(a_r \to (a_r, out)) \mid 1 \le r \le n\}$; we remove $a_1^{k_1} \cdots a_n^{k_n}$ from w_1 (in the generating case, at the beginning, the registers are empty); we delete the rule r_{15i} and we add the rule $r_{15i} : l_h \to \lambda\langle u\rangle$, where u is a string that represents the set $Lab_\Pi(\{a_r \to (a_r, out) \mid 1 \le r \le n\})$.

In this way, at the end of a successful computation (when the *halt* instruction is reached) the terminals corresponding to $a_r, 1 \le r \le n$, are sent outside.

6   Using Non-cooperative Rules and One Switch

In this section we show how ID P systems, using non-cooperative rules, are able to generate (at least) the family of Parikh images of languages in ET0L. The proof is made by simulating an ET0L system by using a very restricted ID P system with at most one switch for each evolution rule.

Theorem 3. $PsIDP_1(ncoo) \supseteq PsET0L$.

Proof. Given an extended tabled Lindenmayer system $G = (\Sigma, T, H, w)$ with 2 tables ($H = \{h_1, h_2\}$) in the normal form described in Section 2.3 generating L, we construct an ID P system Π generating the Parikh image of L (we remove the trivial productions from h_1 and h_2). Let us denote $N = \Sigma - T$. Suppose that $N = \{X_1, X_2, \cdots, X_k\}$. To each rule we need to associate a label; the labels for the productions present in h_1 are $l_1^1, l_2^1, \cdots, l_{m'}^1$ (this means that in h_1 there are m' productions) and the labels for the productions present in h_2 are $l_1^2, l_2^2, \cdots, l_{m''}^2$ (in h_2 there are m'' productions); in the continuation below we use the productions $X_1 \to \#, X_2 \to \#, \cdots, X_k \to \#$ and their labels are $l_{X_1}^\#, l_{X_2}^\#, \cdots, l_{X_k}^\#$, respectively; we also use the productions $X_1' \to X_1, X_2' \to X_2, \cdots, X_k' \to X_k$ and their labels are $l_{X_1}, l_{X_2}, \cdots, l_{X_k}$, respectively.

We use the morphism h defined by $h(x) = x'$, for each $x \in N$. We denote $N' = \{h(x) \mid x \in N\}$.

We take
$$\Pi = (O, C, H, \mu, w_1, R_1, i_0),$$
where:

$$O = \Sigma \cup N' \cup \{T, T^1, T^2, T^3, T_1^1, T_2^1, \cdots, T_{m'}^1, T_1^2, T_2^2, \cdots, T_{m''}^2,$$
$$T^{1'}, T^{1''}, T^{1'''}, S_1^1, S_2^1, \cdots, S_{m'}^1, T_{X_1}, T_{X_2}, \cdots, T_{X_k},$$
$$T^{2'}, T^{2''}, T^{2'''}, S_1^2, S_2^2 \cdots, S_{m''}^2, X, T_{x_1}, T_{x_2}, \cdots, T_{x_k}, \#\},$$

$$C = \emptyset,$$

$$H = \{l_1^1, l_2^1, \cdots, l_{m'}^1, l_1^2, l_2^2, \cdots, l_{m''}^2, l_{X_1}, l_{X_2}, \cdots, l_{X_k}, l_{X_1}^\#, l_{X_2}^\#, \cdots, l_{X_k}^\#\},$$

$$\mu = [\ ]_1,$$

$$R_1 = \{T^{1''} \to T^{1'''}, \quad T^{1'''} \to S_1^1 S_2^1 \cdots S_{m'}^1 X_1 X_2 \cdots X_k X\}$$
$$\cup \{T^{2''} \to T^{2'''}, \quad T^{2'''} \to S_1^2 S_2^2 \cdots S_{m''}^2 X_1 X_2 \cdots X_k X\}$$
$$\cup R_1^0 \cup R_1^1 \cup R_1^2 \cup R_1^3 \cup R_1^4 \cup R_1^5 \cup R_1^6 \cup R_1^7 \cup \overline{R_1^1}$$
$$\cup \overline{R_1^2} \cup \overline{R_1^3} \cup \overline{R_1^4} \cup S^1 \cup S^2,$$

where:

$$R_1^0 = \{T \to T^1, \; T \to T^2, \; T \to T^3\},$$

$$R_1^1 = \{T^1 \to T_1^1 T_2^1 \cdots T_{m'}^1 T^{1'}\},$$

$$R_1^2 = \{T_1^1 \to \lambda \langle l_1^1 \rangle, \; T_2^1 \to \lambda \langle l_2^1 \rangle, \cdots, \; T_{m'}^1 \to \lambda \langle l_{m'}^1 \rangle, \; T^{1'} \to T^{1''}\},$$

$$R_1^3 = \{\neg(u_1 \to h(v_1)), \; \neg(u_2 \to h(v_2)), \cdots, \; \neg(u_{m'} \to h(v_{m'})) \mid$$
$$\{u_1 \to v_1, \; u_2 \to v_2, \cdots, \; u_{m'} \to v_{m'}\} \in h_1\},$$

$$R_1^4 = \{S_1^1 \to \lambda \langle l_1^1 \rangle, \; S_2^1 \to \lambda \langle l_2^1 \rangle, \cdots, \; S_{m'}^1 \to \lambda \langle l_{m'}^1 \rangle\},$$

$$R_1^5 = \{X_1 \to \lambda \langle l_{X_1} \rangle, \; X_2 \to \lambda \langle l_{X_2} \rangle, \cdots, \; X_k \to \lambda \langle l_{X_k} \rangle\},$$

$$R_1^6 = \{X \to X' T_{X_1} T_{X_2} \cdots T_{X_k}, \; X' \to T, \; T_{X_1} \to \lambda \langle l_{X_1} \rangle,$$
$$T_{X_2} \to \lambda \langle l_{X_2} \rangle, \cdots, \; T_{X_k} \to \lambda \langle l_{X_k} \rangle\},$$

$$R_1^7 = \{\neg(X_i' \to X_i) \mid X_i \in N\},$$

$$\overline{R}_1^1 = \{T^2 \to T_1^2 T_2^2 \cdots T_{m''}^2 T^{2'}\},$$

$$\overline{R}_1^2 = \{T_1^2 \to \lambda \langle l_1^2 \rangle, \; T_2^2 \to \lambda \langle l_2^2 \rangle, \cdots, \; T_{m''}^2 \to \lambda \langle l_{m''}^2 \rangle, \; T^{2'} \to T^{2''}\},$$

$$\overline{R}_1^3 = \{\neg(u_1' \to h(v_1')), \; \neg(u_2' \to h(v_2')), \cdots, \; \neg(u_{m''}' \to h(v_{m''}))$$
$$\mid \{u_1' \to v_1', \; u_2' \to v_2', \cdots, \; u_{m''}' \to v_{m''}'\} \in h_2\},$$

$$\overline{R}_1^4 = \{S_1^2 \to \lambda \langle l_1^2 \rangle, \cdots, \; S_{m''}^2 \to \lambda \langle l_{m''}^2 \rangle\},$$

$$S^1 = \{T^3 \to T_{X_1} T_{X_2} \cdots T_{X_k}, \; T_{X_1} \to \lambda \langle l_{X_1}^{\#} \rangle, \cdots, \; T_{X_k} \to \lambda \langle l_{X_k}^{\#} \rangle\},$$

$$S^2 = \{\neg(X_1 \to \#), \; \neg(X_2 \to \#), \cdots, \; \neg(X_k \to \#), \; \# \to \#\},$$

$$i_0 = 1.$$

The system Π works in the following way. In region 1 the derivations of the ET0L system G are simulated. At the beginning of the computation, in region 1, only the objects corresponding to the axiom w of G and the object T are present. Initially the symbol-object T is changed in T^1, or T^2 or T^3 using the rule presents in R_1^0. The application of this rule corresponds to the choice of the table to simulate (T^1 or T^2) or to the halting of the computation (T^3).

We discuss more in details the case when T is changed in T^1 and then the first table, h_1, of G has to be simulated (the simulation of the second table, h_2, is done in a similar way).

After T has been changed to T^1 the only rule that can be applied is the one in R_1^1 that produces the objects $T_1^1 T_2^1 \cdots T_{m'}^1 T^{1'}$.

In the next step the rules in R_1^2 are applied: the objects $T_1^1 T_2^1 \cdots T_{m'}^1$ are deleted and at the same time the rules with labels $l_1^1, l_2^1, \cdots, l_{m'}^1$ present in R_1^3 (that are the rules of the first table h_1) are de-inhibited (initially, they are inhibited). Moreover the object $T^{1'}$ is changed into $T^{1''}$.

Therefore, in the next step the rules of table h_1, previously de-inhibited, are executed in region 1. The objects corresponding to nonterminals of G are rewritten according to the rules in h_1 and then objects with primes are produced. In the same step the object $T^{1''}$ is rewritten into $T^{1'''}$.

In the next step the rule $T^{1'''} \to S_1^1 S_2^1 \cdots S_{m'}^1 X_1 X_2 \cdots X_k X$ is executed. The objects produced by this rule are used to activate the rules needed to delete the primes from the produced nonterminals, to inhibit the rules of table h_1 and to produce again the object T needed to iterate the entire process. In fact, in the next step, the object X is changed to X', the rules in R_1^4 and the rules in R_1^5 are executed. The rules in R_1^4 are used to inhibit the rules in h_1 previously de-inhibited and used. The rules in R_1^5 are used to de-inhibit the rules with labels $l_{X_1}, l_{X_2}, \cdots, l_{X_k}$ present in R_1^7 and that are used to delete the primes from the nonterminals previously produced in region 1.

In the next step, the rules present in R_1^7 are applied, the primes are deleted, and, in the same step, the object X' is rewritten into T and then the entire process can be iterated.

The case when the object T is rewritten into T^2 is very similar; the difference is that, instead of using the rules in $R_1^1, R_1^2, R_1^3, R_1^4$ as previously described, the rules in $\overline{R_1^1}, \overline{R_1^2}, \overline{R_1^3}, \overline{R_1^4}$ are used in the same manner: in this way a derivation step by using the rules in h_2 can be simulated.

To halt the computation it is necessary to rewrite the object T into T^3. Once T^3 is produced, then the rule $T^3 \rightarrow T_{X_1} T_{X_2} \cdots T_{X_k}$ is used and, in the next step, the rules $T_{X_1} \rightarrow \lambda \langle l_{X_1}^\# \rangle$, $T_{X_2} \rightarrow \lambda \langle l_{X_2}^\# \rangle, \cdots$, $T_{X_k} \rightarrow \lambda \langle l_{X_k}^\# \rangle$ present in S^1 are used. In this way the rules present in S^2 are de-inhibited and they are applied if nonterminals are still present in region 1. In this way we guarantee that the computation halts if and only if only objects corresponding to terminals have been produced in region 1 and the system Π generates exactly the Parikh image of the language generated by the ET0L system G. Finally, we notice that the system Π uses at most one switch for each evolution rule.   □

7   Concluding Remarks and Open Problems

In this paper we have considered a mechanism used to control the computation in P systems by inhibiting/de-inhibiting the evolution rules. In general, this new mechanism can be associated also to other kinds of rules.

Many interesting problems have been left open: for instance, it would be useful to simulate the model proposed here by using existing P systems with promoters/inhibitors. Moreover, boolean circuits can be investigated by using the inhibiting/de-inhibiting rules like boolean switches ON/OFF.

On the other hand, the proposed mechanism seems very simple but enough powerful to get universality even with very simple ingredients (one catalyst, one membrane); we propose to use this mechanism also for other (restricted) models of P systems like the one with active membranes and with rule creation.

Finally we believe that the proposed mechanism might be used in neural-like P systems [14], that, like the inhibiting/de-inhibiting mechanism, are directly inspired from the neural-cell behavior.

Acknowledgments. The authors acknowledge the support of the IST-2001-32008 project "MolCoNet". The first and second authors were supported by FPU fellowship from the Spanish Ministry of Education, Culture and Sport. The third author acknowledges The State Training Fund of the Ministry of Science, Technology, Education and Culture of Mongolia.

References

1. A. Alhazov, T.O. Ishdorj, Membrane Operations in P Systems with Active Membranes, *Second Brainstorming Week on Membrane Computing, Technical Report 01/2004*, University of Seville, Seville, 2004, 37–44.
2. A. Alhazov, M. Cavaliere, Proton Pumping P Systems, *Membrane Computing* (C. Martín-Vide, G. Mauri, Gh. Păun, G. Rozenberg, A. Salomaa, eds.), LNCS 2933, Springer-Verlag, Berlin, 2004, 70–88.
3. I.I. Ardelean, M. Cavaliere, D. Sburlan, Computing Using Signals: From Cells to P Systems, *Second Brainstorming Week on Membrane Computing, Technical Report 01/2004*, University of Seville, Seville, 2004, 60–73, and *Soft Computing*, in press.
4. F. Arroyo, A.V. Baranda, J. Castellanos, Gh. Păun, Membrane Computing: The Power of (Rule) Creation, *Journal of Universal Computer Science*, 8, 3, 2002, 369–381.
5. P. Bottoni, C. Martín-Vide, Gh. Păun, G. Rozenberg, Membrane Systems with Promoters/Inhibitors, *Acta Informatica*, 38, 10, 2002, 695–720.
6. J. Dassow, Gh. Păun, *Regulated Rewriting in Formal Language Theory*, Springer-Verlag, Berlin, 1989.
7. M. Ionescu, T.-O. Ishdorj, Replicative-Distribution Rules in P Systems with Active Membranes, *Proc. of ICTAC2004, First International Colloquium on Theoretical Aspects of Computing*, Guiyang, China, 2004.
8. M. Ionescu, D. Sburlan, On P Systems with Promoters/Inhibitors, *Second Brainstorming Week on Membrane Computing, Technical Report 01/2004*, University of Seville, Seville, 2004, 264–280, and *Journal of Universal Computer Science*, 10, 5, 2004, 581–599.
9. M.L. Minsky, *Finite and Infinite Machines*, Prentice Hall, Englewood Cliffs, 1967.
10. L. Pan, A. Alhazov, T.-O Ishdorj, Further Remarks on P Systems with Active Membranes, Separation, Merging and Release Rules, *Soft Computing*, in press.
11. L. Pan, T.-O Ishdorj, P Systems with Active Membranes and Separation Rules, *Journal of Universal Computer Science*, 10, 5, 2004, 630–649.
12. Gh. Păun, *Membrane Computing: An Introduction*, Springer-Verlag, Berlin, 2002.
13. Gh. Păun, G. Rozenberg, A Guide to Membrane Computing, *Theoretical Computer Science*, 287, 1, 2002, 73–100.
14. J. Pazos, A. Rodriguez-Paton, A. Silva, Solving SAT in Linear Time with a Neural-Like Membrane System, *Proc. Conf. on Computational Methods in Neural Modeling* (J. Mira, J.R. Alvarez, eds.), LNCS 2686, Springer-Verlag, Berlin, 2003, 662–669.
15. G. Rozenberg, A. Salomaa, eds.: *Handbook of Formal Languages*, Springer-Verlag, Berlin, 1997.
16. G.M. Shepherd, *Neurobiology*, Oxford University Press, NY Oxford, 1994.

Time–Independent P Systems

Matteo Cavaliere[1] and Dragoş Sburlan[1,2]

[1] Department of Computer Science and Artificial Intelligence,
University of Sevilla,
Av. Reina Mercedes, 41012, Sevilla, Spain
`martew@inwind.it`
[2] Department of Informatics and Numerical Methods,
Ovidius University of Constantza,
124 Mamaia Bd., Constantza, Romania
`dsburlan@univ-ovidius.ro`

Abstract. We introduce a class of P systems called timed P systems where to each rule is associated an integer that represents the time needed by the rule (reaction) to be entirely executed. The idea comes from cell biology where chemical reactions take certain times to be executed. In this work we are interested in a special class of P systems, called time-free, working always in the same way (i.e., always producing the same result) independently from the values associated to the execution time of their rules.

Later we introduce a generalization of time-free P systems, namely clock-free P systems, where a time of execution is associated directly to each single application of the rules (in this case, different applications, even of the same rule, may take a different time to be executed). Several results are presented together with open problems and research proposals.

1 Introduction: Motivations

A standard feature of membrane computing is the fact that each rule is executed in exactly one time-unit; however, this mathematical feature, in general, does not have a counterpart in cell biology. Chemical reactions may take certain times to be executed. In many cases, different reactions with different times of execution are synchronized via biological signals that move across different areas present in the cell; some considerations on this topic can be found in [1] where a class of P systems that uses signals has been introduced. On the other hand, it is true that in a cell, when a reaction is applied, "almost" all the chemicals that can be subject of the reaction are transformed, in a parallel manner.

In cell biology, the execution time of a chemical reaction might be difficult to know precisely and usually such a parameter is very sensitive to environmental factors that might be hard to control. For instance, a certain reaction whose execution time depends on the medium temperature will behave differently even in the same cell region because the propagation of heat is not uniform in non-homogeneous mediums.

G. Mauri et al. (Eds.): WMC5 2004, LNCS 3365, pp. 239–258, 2005.
© Springer-Verlag Berlin Heidelberg 2005

Therefore, we believe that it is extremely interesting to construct systems that work in the way we expect, independently from the values associated to the execution times of the rules.

For this reason we introduce here the concept of *time-independent* P systems. Informally, a *time-independent* P system is a P system that produces always the same result, independently from the execution times of the rules.

Starting from these considerations, we initially define and investigate a model of P systems where to each rule r is associated a certain positive integer value $e(r)$ that indicates the execution time.

A P system that generates (or accepts) the same family of vectors of natural numbers, independently from the value assigned to the execution time of each rule r, is called *time-free*.

In this way, a time-free P system can be considered stable against environmental factors that might influence the execution times of the rules. If the execution times associated to the rules have to satisfy certain conditions, then the system is called *partially time-free* (the mathematical formalization of this kind of systems is not treated in this paper).

Later we will consider another possible model of time-independent P systems. We will investigate P systems where each application of a rule r has associated a certain finite positive integer value that indicates its execution time. In this respect, we define a class of P systems, called *clock-free* P systems, that produces the results independently from the times associated to the applications of the rules.

In this paper, we carry out only a preliminary investigation of these models of computation. Several results are presented, considering the use of cooperative or non-cooperative rules, the absence of signal-promoters/promoters and the use of a priority relation. Several open problems are also presented. In what follows we suppose the reader familiar with the main concepts and results of the P systems area. We start by directly introducing the class of systems we investigate in this paper.

2   Time-Free P Systems: Definition

Definition 1. *A P system Π of degree $m \geq 1$, with signal-promoters and bi-stable catalysts is a construct*

$$\Pi = (V, C, D, \mu, w_1, \ldots, w_m, R_1, \ldots, R_m, R'_1, \ldots, R'_m, i_0),$$

where:
- *V is the alphabet of Π; its elements are called objects;*
- *$C \subseteq V$ is the set of bi-stable catalysts; each bi-stable catalyst c is an object that can be in two states, c and $\bar{c}$ (if for a bi-stable catalyst c the two states are coincident, then c is a catalyst);*
- *$D \subseteq V$ is the set of signal-promoters;*
- *μ is a membrane structure consisting of m membranes labeled $1, 2, \cdots, m$;*

- w_i, $1 \le i \le m$, specifies the multiset of objects present in the corresponding region i at the beginning of a computation;
- R_i, $1 \le i \le m$, are finite sets of evolution rules over V associated with regions $1, 2, \ldots, m$ of μ; there are rules of two types, non-cooperative, that are of the form $a \to v$ where a is an object from $V \setminus (C \cup D)$ and v is a string over $\{a_{here}, a_{out} \mid a \in V \setminus (C \cup D)\} \cup \{a_{in_j} \mid a \in V \setminus (C \cup D), 1 \le j \le m\}$, and catalytic rules (using bi-stable catalysts) of the forms $ca \to cv, ca \to \bar{c}v, \bar{c}a \to \bar{c}v$ and $\bar{c}a \to cv$, where a is an object from $V \setminus (C \cup D)$, v is a string over $\{a_{here}, a_{out} \mid a \in V \setminus (C \cup D)\} \cup \{a_{in_j} \mid a \in V \setminus (C \cup D), 1 \le j \le m\}$, and $c \in C$;
- R'_i, $1 \le i \le m$, are finite sets of signaling-rules over D associated with regions $1, 2, \ldots, m$ of μ; the signaling-rules are of the form $a \to v|_z$ or $ca \to cv|_z$, where a is an object from $V \setminus (C \cup D)$, v is a string over $V \setminus (C \cup D)$, z is a string representing a subset of $\{(p, here), (p, out) \mid p \in D\} \cup \{(p, in_j) \mid p \in D, 1 \le j \le m\}$, and $c \in C$;
- i_0 is a number between 0 and m and specifies the output region of Π (0 represents the environment).

Given a computable mapping

$$e : R_1 \cup \cdots \cup R_m \cup R'_1 \cup \cdots \cup R'_m \longrightarrow \mathbb{N},$$

and a system Π as defined above, it is possible to construct a *timed P system* $\Pi(e) = (V, C, D, \mu, w_1, \ldots, w_m, R_1, \ldots, R_m, R'_1, \ldots, R'_m, i_0, e)$ working in the following way.

We suppose to have an external clock (that does not have any influence on the system) that marks time-units of equal length, starting from time 0.

To each region of the system is associated a finite number of objects (among them, signal-promoters and catalysts) and a finite number of evolution rules and of signaling-rules.

At each time, in the regions of the system we have together rules in execution and rules not in execution. At each time, all the rules that can be applied (started) in each region, must be applied.

If a rule $r \in R_i \cup R'_i, 1 \le i \le m$, is applied, then all objects that can be processed by the rule have to evolve by this rule.

To apply an evolution rule $u \to v$ or $u \to v|_z$ in a region i means to remove the multiset of objects identified by u from region i, and to add the objects specified by the multiset v, into the regions specified by the target indications associated to each object in v.

Signaling rules are evolution rules, promoted by the signal-promoters specified in the string z (signal-promoters work like standard promoters but they can only be moved and not created, see [1]).

In the case of a signaling-rule $u \to v|_z$, also the signal-promoters specified by z are moved to the regions according to their target indications. In every region the signal-promoters are present in the *set sense*, i.e., we cannot have more than one copy of the same signal-promoter in one region.

When a rule r (either evolution or signaling) is started at time j, then its execution terminates at time $j + e(r)$ (the objects produced as well as the signal-promoters moved by the rule can be used starting from the time $j + e(r) + 1$).

If two rules start at the same time, then possible conflicts for using the occurrences of objects are solved assigning the occurrences in a non-deterministic way. The rules are applied in the maximally parallel manner as usually defined in the P systems framework.

Notice that, when a rule r is started, the occurrences of objects used by this rule are not available for other rules during the entire execution of r.

Using signal-promoters, two situations can cause conflicts.

If (at least one of) the signal-promoters that activates a rule r is moved out from the region where r is present before rule r is terminated, then the execution of r cannot continue and then the entire computation is trashed.

On the other hand, if two or more signaling-rules, promoted by the same signal-promoters but with different targets terminate their execution at the same time, then also in this case the computation is trashed (a conflict over the destination of promoters is present). However, in the paper these conflicts will never appear.

The computation stops when no rule can be applied in any region and there are no rules in execution (the systems has reached a *halting configuration*).

The output of a halting computation is the vector of numbers representing the multiplicities of objects present in the output region in the halting configuration.

Collecting all the vectors obtained, for any possible halting computation, we get the set $Ps(\Pi(e))$ of vectors of natural numbers generated by the system $\Pi(e)$.

We also investigate systems using a priority relation in the *strong* sense (as described in [8], Section 3.4.2).

In a timed system, a rule $r_1 \in R_i$ can be started if there is no rule $r_2 \in R_i$, for $1 \leq i \leq m$, which can also be started at the same time or that is already in execution and $r_2 > r_1$. If a rule r_2 with a higher priority with respect to r_1 is applied or is already in execution and it terminates at time j, then r_1 can be started only at time $j + 1$. Notice that, when we say that a rule can be started, this means that there are the necessary occurrences of symbol-objects (without considering the presence/absence of signal-promoters needed to activate the rule).

For shortness, in what follows, a P system not using signal-promoters (i.e., the set D is empty) is called basic.

A P system $\Pi = (V, C, D, \mu, w_1, \ldots, w_m, R_1, \ldots, R_m, R'_1, \ldots, R'_m, i_0)$ is *time-free* if and only if every timed system in the set

$$\{\Pi(e) \mid e : R \longrightarrow \mathbb{N}, e \text{ computable}\},$$

where $R = R_1 \cup \cdots \cup R_m \cup R'_1 \cup \cdots \cup R'_m$, produces the same set of vectors of natural numbers.

We use the notation

$$PsP_m(\alpha, j, free, pri), \alpha \in \{ncoo, coo\} \cup \{2cat_k, cat_k \mid k \geq 0\},$$

to denote the family of sets of vectors of natural numbers generated by *time-free* P systems with at most m membranes, at most j signal-promoters, evolution rules and signaling-rules that can be non-cooperative (*ncoo*), or catalytic ($cat_k/2cat_k$), using at most k catalysts/k bi-stable catalysts (as usual, $*$ is used if the corresponding number of membranes, signal-promoters or catalysts/bistable catalysts is not known), and priority (the parameter j is 0 if the system is basic).

3 Time-Free P Systems: An Example

We present a simple example of a time-free P system using two membranes, one signal-promoter, and non-cooperative rules that generates the Parikh image of the language $\{a^{2^n} \mid n \geq 0\}$. From this example, it is clear how signal-promoters are useful to synchronize rules with different execution times.

We consider the system

$$\Pi = (V, C, D, \mu, w_1, w_2, R_1, R_2, R'_1, R'_2, i_0),$$

where:

$$V = \{a, b, p\};$$
$$C = \emptyset;$$
$$D = \{p\};$$
$$\mu = [_1 [_2]_2]_1;$$
$$w_1 = bp;$$
$$w_2 = a;$$
$$R_1 = \emptyset;$$
$$R_2 = \emptyset;$$
$$R'_1 = \{b \rightarrow b|_{(p,in_2)}, \ b \rightarrow b|_{(p,out)}\};$$
$$R'_2 = \{a \rightarrow aa|_{(p,out)}\};$$
$$i_0 = 2.$$

The rule $a \rightarrow aa|_{(p,out)}$ is activated by the signal-promoter p which is present at the beginning of the computation in region 1. The rule is applied an arbitrary number of times in the maximally parallel way. Every time the signal-promoter p is sent to region 1 and one of the rules present in that region is applied. If rule $b \rightarrow b|_{(p,in_2)}$ is applied, then the process can be iterated. In case the rule $b \rightarrow b|_{(p,out)}$ is applied, then the signal-promoter is sent to the environment and the computation halts with a number of objects in the output region that is a power of 2. It is easy to see that the system generates the set $\{2^n \mid n \geq 0\}$ independently from the execution times of the rules and, therefore, the system Π is time-free.

4   Time-Free P Systems Using Non-cooperative Rules and Signal-Promoters

We generalize what presented in the previous section by investigating the class of time-free P systems using non-cooperative evolution rules and signal-promoters.

Before presenting the result of this section, we recall the *Indian parallel grammar* definition (for more details we refer the reader to [3] and [4]).

An Indian parallel grammar is a context-free grammar $G = (N, T, S, P)$, where at each step of the derivation every occurrence of one letter is rewritten using the same production. That is, the derivations are defined in the following way: for $x \in (N \cup T)^+$, and $y \in (N \cup T)^*$ we write $x \Rightarrow y$ if and only if $x = x_1 A x_2 A \cdots x_n A x_{n+1}$, $A \in N$, $x_i \in ((N \cup T) \setminus A)^*$, $1 \le i \le n + 1$, $y = x_1 w x_2 w \cdots x_n w x_{n+1}$, and $A \to w \in P$.

The language generated by G is $L(G) = \{w \in T^* \mid S \Rightarrow^* w\}$, where $\Rightarrow^*$ denotes the reflexive and transitive closure of $\Rightarrow$.

The family of languages generated by Indian parallel grammars is denoted by *IPG*.

Using only non-cooperative rules, signal-promoters, and two regions it is possible to generate at least the family of Parikh images of languages in *IPG* (denoted by *PsIPG*), as shown by the following theorem.

Theorem 1. $PsIPG \subseteq PsP_2(ncoo, *, free)$.

Proof. Given an Indian parallel grammar $G = (N, T, S, P)$, we suppose that to each rule $r \in P$ an unique label $l(r)$ has been associated. The set of the labels associated to the rules in P is denoted by $Lab(P) = \{r_1, r_2, \cdots, r_k\}$.

We construct the following P system simulating G:

$$\Pi = (V, C, D, \mu, w_1, w_2, R_1, R_2, R'_1, R'_2, i_0),$$

where:

$V = N \cup T \cup D \cup \{Q', T, T', Z, \#\} \cup \{T_r \mid r \in Lab(P)\};$

$C = \emptyset;$

$D = Lab(P) \cup \{s', s\};$

$\mu = [_1 \, [_2 \,]_2 \,]_1;$

$w_1 = ZT sr_1 r_2 \cdots r_k;$

$w_2 = Ss'Q;$

$R_1 = \{Z \to Z\};$

$R_2 = \{\# \to \#\};$

$R'_1 = \{Z \to \lambda|_{(s', here)}, \; T \to T'|_{(s, in_2)}\}$
$\quad \cup \{T \to T_r|_{(r, in_2)}, \; T_r \to T|_{(r, here)} \mid r \in Lab(P)\};$

$R'_2 = \{X \to w|_{(r, out)} \mid X \to w \in P \text{ and } r = l(X \to w)\}$
$\quad \cup \{X \to \#|_{(s, here)} \mid X \in N\} \cup \{Q' \to \lambda|_{(s', out)}, \; Q \to Q'|_{(s, here)}\};$

$i_0 = 2.$

The system works in the following way. In region 2 (the output region) the rules of grammar G are simulated. In region 1 the application of one of the rules in the set $\{T \to T_r|_{(r,in_2)} \mid r \in Lab(P)\}$ selects the rule of the grammar G to be activated (and, if possible, applied) in region 2, by sending the corresponding signal-promoter $r \in Lab(P)$. When an activated rule $X \to w|_{(r,out)}$ is applied in region 2, the signal-promoter r is sent back to region 1. Therefore the simulation of another rule can be made.

To stop the computation it is necessary to halt the rule $Z \to Z$ present in region 1. To do this, the rule $T \to T'|_{(s,in_2)}$ must be used in region 1. When $T \to T'|_{(s,in_2)}$ is executed, the signal-promoter s will arrive in region 2, checking that all symbol-objects present are terminals (by activating the rules $X \to \#|_{(s,here)}$, $X \in N$). Moreover, the rules $Q' \to \lambda|_{(s',out)}$, $Q \to Q'|_{(s,here)}$ will send to region 1 the signal-promoter s' necessary to delete Z and then to stop the computation. Therefore, the computation halts when $Z \to \lambda|_{(s',here)}$ is applied if and only if all terminals have been obtained in the output region. This means that the system Π generates exactly the Parikh image of $L(G)$. From the description above it is clear that the system is time-free because it generates the Parikh image $L(G)$ independently from the execution times of the rules. $\square$

5   Time-Free P Systems Using Non-cooperative Rules and Priority

If the system is basic and, like in Section 4, only non-cooperative rules are used, then it seems harder to synchronize the applications of the rules in the regions of the system.

This section is dedicated to a (brief) investigation concerning basic time-free P systems and "partially" time-free P systems using only non-cooperative rules and priorities.

It is easy to see that, for basic time-free P systems, the following result is true:

$$PsCF \subseteq PsP_1(ncoo, 0, free).$$

In fact, given a context-free grammar $G = (N, T, S, P)$ we can construct the following P system simulating G:

$$\Pi = (V, C, D, \mu, w_1, R_1, R'_1, i_0),$$

where:

$$V = N \cup T;$$
$$C = \emptyset;$$
$$D = \emptyset;$$
$$\mu = [_1 \ ]_1;$$
$$w_1 = S;$$

$$R_1 = P \cup \{A \rightarrow A \mid A \in N\};$$
$$R'_1 = \emptyset;$$
$$i_0 = 1.$$

Clearly, the system Π generates exactly the Parikh image of $L(G)$ and this is true independently from the execution times of the rules.

It seems natural to ask what we gain if we use use a priority relation in the strong sense as introduced earlier. This problem seems particularly interesting because standard P systems (i.e., where the execution time of each rule is fixed as one step) using symbol-objects, non-cooperative rules and priority in the strong sense can generate at least the Parikh image of the languages generated by ET0L systems (see Theorem 3.4.4 in [8]).

The following example shows that basic time-free P systems, using priority and non-cooperative rules, can generate the Parikh image of non-semilinear languages. Notice that in this case the P system constructed is not time-free but only "partially" time-free: this means that, because the system generates always the same result, the time-mapping e cannot be arbitrary but it must fulfill some conditions. We use the term "partially time-free" in an informal way and the exact mathematical formalization of partially time-free systems is left as open problem.

Example 1. We take the following basic partially time-free P system Π:

$$\Pi = (V, C, D, \mu, w_1, R_1, R'_1, i_0, e),$$

where:

$V = \{A, T, T_1, T_2, a, T_3\};$

$C = \emptyset;$

$D = \emptyset;$

$\mu = [_1\ ]_1;$

$w_1 = TA;$

$R_1 = \{r_1 : T \rightarrow T_1,\ \ r'_1 : T \rightarrow T_2,\ \ r_2 : A \rightarrow A'A',\ \ r_3 : A \rightarrow a\}$
$\quad \cup \{r_4 : T_1 \rightarrow T'_1,\ \ r_5 : T_2 \rightarrow T'_2,\ \ r_6 : T'_1 \rightarrow T,\ \ r_7 : T'_2 \rightarrow T_3,\ \ r_8 : A' \rightarrow A\};$

$R'_1 = \emptyset;$

$i_0 = 1;$

$\quad\ \ r_1 > \{r_2, r_3\},\ \ r'_1 > \{r_2, r_3\},\ \ r_4 > r_3,\ \ r_5 > r_2,\ \ r_3 > r_7,\ \ r_6 < r_2;$
$\quad\ \ e(r_6) = e(r_8),\ \ e(r_2) > e(r_4),\ \ e(r_3) > e(r_5).$

The system works in the following way. At the beginning of the computation only objects A and T are present in region 1.

Because of the priority relations $r_1 > \{r_2, r_3\}, r'_1 > \{r_2, r_3\}$, the rules that can be applied are only r_1 and r'_1. The application of one of the two rules corresponds to the choice of rule r_2 or r_3. In fact, if T is changed to T_1 (the other choice is similar), then, because of priority $r_4 > r3$, rule $r_2 : A \to A'A'$ is applied while rule $A \to a$ is blocked. Rules r_4 and r_2 are executed in parallel. Because of the time condition $e(r_2) > e(r_4)$, rule r_4 terminates before rule r_2. When rule r_4 ends, rule r_6 might be applied, but, because of the priority $r_6 < r_2$, rule r_6 has to wait the end of r_2 (still in execution) in order to be applied.

When r_2 ends, rules r_6 and r_8 are applied in parallel and they terminate at the same time (because of the time condition $e(r_6) = e(r_8)$). Therefore, T is obtained again, all the objects A' are changed into A and the process can be iterated.

Hence, at the end of any halting computation, region 1 contains a number of objects a that is a power of 2. Then the set of numbers generated by Π, using an arbitrary mapping e that fulfills the indicated conditions, is $\{2^n \mid n \in \mathbb{N}\}$.

It seems difficult to avoid the conditions imposed on the time-mapping e and then to make the system Π time-free. This fact suggests us the following *open problem*: is it possible to generate non-semilinear sets of numbers with basic time-free P systems using non-cooperative rules and priority?

6   Time-Free P Systems Using Catalysts and Signal-Promoters

In Section 4 and 5 we have investigated systems (basic or not) using only non-cooperative rules. Now we show that, using one catalyst together with signal-promoters, is possible to synchronize the execution of the evolution rules in a way to simulate sequential grammar devices, even if the P system considered is time-free.

In particular, in this section we show how to simulate programmed grammars; we recall that a context-free *programmed grammar* with appearance checking (a.c.) is a construct $G = (N, T, P, S)$, where N, T, S are the set of non-terminals, the set of terminals, and the start symbol respectively, and P is a finite set of rules of the form $(b : A \to x, E, F)$, where b is a label, $A \to x$ is a context-free rule over $N \cup T$, and E, F are two sets of labels of rules of G (E is called the *success field* and F the *failure field* of the rule). A rule $(b : A \to x, E, F)$ is applied as follows: if A is present in the sentential form, then the rule is used and the next rule to be applied is chosen from those with the label in E, otherwise, the sentential form remains unchanged and we choose the next rule from the rules labelled by some element of F, and try to apply it. If no failure field is given for any of the rules, then we obtain a programmed grammar without appearance checking.

We denote $Lab(P) = \{b \mid (b : A \to x, E, F) \in P\}$.

A context-free programmed grammar with a.c. can be also written in the form $G = (N, T, S, R, \sigma, \varphi)$, where N, T, S are defined as before, R is a set of context-free rules and σ and φ are mappings from R to the power set of R; $\sigma(p)$ is the success field of the rule p (this means that a rule in $\sigma(p)$ must be used after successfully applying the rule p), and $\varphi(p)$ is the failure field (this means that a rule from $\varphi(p)$ must be considered when p cannot be applied).

Sometimes both definitions are joined, and this will be done also below: we consider a context-free programmed grammar with a.c. as a construct $G = (N, T, P, S)$, as defined before, where each production in P is of the kind $(b : A \rightarrow x, \sigma(b), \varphi(b))$ ($\sigma(b)$ is the success field of the rule (with label) b and $\varphi(b)$ is the failure field of the rule (with label) b).

In the following theorem we show how a time-free P system can simulate a programmed grammar without appearance checking by using one catalyst, two membranes, and an unbounded number of signal-promoters. We know from [3] that such grammars generate non-semilinear languages, hence whose Parikh image is not in $PsCF$. The family of languages generated by programmed grammars with λ rules and without appearance checking is denoted by PR and the set of Parikh images of languages in PR is denoted by $PsPR$.

Theorem 2. $PsPR \subseteq PsP_2(cat_1, *, free)$.

Proof. Consider the programmed grammar $G = (N, T, P, S)$ without appearance checking. We denote by $l(S)$ the set of labels of rules of the form $(k : S \rightarrow x, \sigma(k)) \in P$. We add to P the triple $(0 : U \rightarrow S, \sigma(0))$ with $\sigma(0) = l(S)$, where U is a new non-terminal. We denote by G' the obtained grammar (N', T, P', U), where $N' = N \cup \{U\}$. Clearly, $L(G) = L(G')$ and each derivation in G' starts with the rule with label 0. We suppose $Lab(P') = \{i_1, i_2, \cdots, i_k\}$.

We construct the P system

$$\Pi = (V, C, D, \mu, w_1, w_2, R_1, R_2, R'_1, R'_2, i_0),$$

where:

$V = N' \cup T \cup D \cup \{A^i, \underline{A}^i \mid i \in Lab(P')\} \cup \{A^{-1}, \#, Z, B, B_2, c\};$

$C = \{c\};$

$D = \{s, s'\} \cup Lab(P');$

$\mu = [_1 [_2]_2]_1;$

$w_1 = ZsA^{-1}i_1i_2\cdots i_k;$

$w_2 = BUcs';$

$R_1 = \{Z \rightarrow Z\} \cup \{a \rightarrow a_{out} \mid a \in T\};$

$R_2 = \{a \rightarrow a_{out} \mid a \in T\};$

$R'_1 = \{A^j \rightarrow \lambda|_{(s,in)} \mid j \in Lab(P')\}$

$\qquad \cup \{A^j \rightarrow \underline{A}^i|_{(i,in)} \mid i \in \sigma(j)\} \cup \{A^{-1} \rightarrow \underline{A}^0|_{(0,in)}\}$

$\qquad \cup \{\underline{A}^i \rightarrow A^i|_{(i,here)} \mid i \in Lab(P')\} \cup \{Z \rightarrow \lambda|_{(s',here)}\};$

$R'_2 = \{cX \rightarrow cw|_{(i,out)} \mid (i : X \rightarrow w, \sigma(i)) \in P'\}$

$\qquad \cup \{B \rightarrow B_2|_{(s,here)}, B_2 \rightarrow \lambda|_{(s',out)}\} \cup \{X \rightarrow \#|_{(s,here)} \mid X \in N\};$

$i_0 = 0.$

The constructed system simulates the programmed grammar G' in the following way. The rules $cX \rightarrow cw|_{(i,out)}$, $(i : X \rightarrow w, \sigma(i)) \in P'$, present in region

2 simulate the context-free rules of G'. The rules present in region 1 are used to select the rules in region 2, following the order defined by the labels in the success field of G'. In the initial configuration, in region 2 is present the object U that is the axiom of G'. In region 1 is present the symbol-object A^j indicating that the last rule of G' simulated in region 2 has been the one with label j (at the beginning of the computation the object A^{-1} is present in region 1). The object A^j is changed to $\underline{A}^i$ using one of the rules in the set $A^j \rightarrow \underline{A}^i|_{(i,in)}$, $i \in \sigma(j)$. When this rule is terminated the signal-promoter i is sent to region 2. This signal-promoter activates the rule $cX \rightarrow cw|_{(i,out)}$, $(i : X \rightarrow w, \sigma(i)) \in P'$; this means that the rule of the grammar G' with label i can be simulated in region 2. Suppose the activated rule $cX \rightarrow cw|_{(i,out)}$ can be applied (i.e., object X is present in region 2; the case when the rule cannot be applied will be discussed later).

When the execution of the rule $cX \rightarrow cw|_{(i,out)}$ is terminated, the signal-promoter i is sent back to region 1. The presence of the signal-promoter in region 1 activates the rule $\underline{A}^i \rightarrow A^i$; therefore, the object A^i is obtained and the process can be iterated.

To halt the computation it is necessary to stop the evolution rule $Z \rightarrow Z$ that runs in region 1. The only way to stop this rule is to delete the object Z by using the rule $Z \rightarrow \lambda|_{(s',here)}$ present in region 1. Therefore, it is necessary to introduce in region 1 the signal-promoter s'. This can be done only by using one of the rules present in the set $\{A^j \rightarrow \lambda|_{(s,in)} \mid j \in Lab(P')\}$ and then sending the signal-promoter to region 2. This signal-promoter activates in region 2 the rules to send s' to region 1 (and then to delete the Z) and the rules $X \rightarrow \#|_{(s,here)}$, $X \in N$ present in region 2. Therefore, the computation will halt if and only if all terminals are present in region 2. Then, the system Π generates exactly the Parikh image of the language generated by grammar G'. Because in each step a single application of a rule is started or is in execution (except for the rules used to delete the Z in the final phase) then it is clear that the output of the constructed system is independent from the execution times of the rules. $\square$

7   Universality of Time-Free P Systems

In this section, we prove the universality of time-free P systems. We show that it is possible to get universality for the basic model by using bi-stable catalysts and priority; on the other hand, it is also possible to get universality by using catalysts, signal-promoters, and priority.

In Theorem 3.4.6 from [8] it is shown that by using bi-stable catalysts, targets, and strong priority, the family of sets of numbers computed by *non-synchronized P systems* is exactly the family of recursively enumerable sets of natural numbers (non-synchronized P systems are introduced in [8], see Section 3.4.5, and they are P systems with symbol-objects where in each region is present a rule $a \rightarrow a$ for each symbol a in the alphabet).

Looking to the proof of Theorem 3.4.6 in [8] we can notice that the evolution rules of the constructed system are executed sequentially, that is, never more than one single application of an evolution rule running at a certain time (this is true because of the use of the bi-stable catalysts and of the priority).

In this way the same proof works also for basic P systems, independently from the duration of the evolution rules. Therefore:

Theorem 3. $PsRE = PsP_2(2cat_*, 0, free, pri)$.

On the other hand, as we can see in the next theorem, a basic time-free P system with bi-stable catalysts, strong priority and a membrane structure of the form $\mu = [_1 [_2 \cdots [_m]_m \cdots]_2]_1$ can be simulated by a time-free P system using only catalysts, strong priority, signal-promoters and (at most) $m+1$ membranes.

Theorem 4. $PsRE = PsP_3(cat_*, *, free, pri)$.

Proof. To prove the theorem we show how a basic time-free P system

$$\Pi_1 = (V_1, C_1, \emptyset, [_1 [_2 \cdots [_m]_m \cdots]_2]_1, w_{1,1}, w_{1,2}, \cdots, w_{1,m},$$
$$R_{1,1}, R_{1,2}, \cdots, R_{1,m}, \emptyset, \emptyset, \cdots, \emptyset, i_0),$$

using bi-stable catalysts, m membranes and strong priority can be simulated by a time-free P system

$$\Pi_2 = (V_2, C_2, D_2, [_0 [_1 [_2 \cdots [_m]_m \cdots]_2]_1]_0, w_{2,0}, w_{2,1}, w_{2,2}, \cdots, w_{2,m},$$
$$R_{2,0}, R_{2,1}, R_{2,2}, \cdots, R_{2,m}, R'_{2,0}, R'_{2,1}, R'_{2,2}, \cdots, R'_{2,m}, i_0),$$

using catalysts, $m + 1$ membranes, signal-promoters, and strong priority (both systems Π_1, Π_2 are written according to the notation given in Definition 1). Without loss of generality, we suppose that each occurrence of the bi-stable catalysts present in the regions of Π_1 is named differently. We suppose that the set of bi-stable catalysts used in Π_1 is $C_1 = \{c_1, c_2, \cdots, c_h\}$.

We construct the system Π_2 in the following way.

Suppose $j \in \{1, 2, \cdots, h\}$. For each rule $r^{1,1}_{i\langle a \to w \rangle} : \overline{c_j} a \to c_j w$ that is present in $R_{1,i}$ we add to $R'_{2,i}$ the signaling-rule $r^{2,1}_{i\langle a \to w \rangle} : c_j a \to c_j w|_{(\overline{p_j}, out)}$ and we add to the set $R'_{2,i-1}$ the signaling-rules $X_j \to X''_j|_{(\overline{p_j}, here)}$ and $X''_j \to X'''_j|_{(p_j, in)}$.

In a similar way, for each rule $r^{1,2}_{i\langle a \to w \rangle} : c_j a \to \overline{c_j} w$ that is present in $R_{1,i}$ we add the signaling-rule $r^{2,2}_{i\langle a \to w \rangle} : c_j a \to c_j w|_{(p_j, out)}$ to $R'_{2,i}$, and to the set $R'_{2,i-1}$ the signaling-rules $X'''_j \to X_j|_{(p_j, here)}$ and $X'_j \to X_j|_{(\overline{p_j}, in)}$.

For each rule $r^{1,3}_{i\langle a \to w \rangle} : \overline{c_j} a \to \overline{c_j} w$ that is present in $R_{1,i}$ we add the signaling-rule $r^{2,3}_{i\langle a \to w \rangle} : c_j a \to c_j w|_{(\overline{p_j}, here)}$ to $R'_{2,i}$; for each rule $r^{1,4}_{i\langle a \to w \rangle} : c_j a \to c_j w$ presents in $R_{1,i}$ we add the rule $r^{2,4}_{i\langle a \to w \rangle} : c_j a \to c_j w|_{(p_j, here)}$ to the set $R'_{2,i}$.

For each non-cooperative rule $r^{1,0}_{i\langle X \to w \rangle} : X \to w$ that is present in $R_{1,i}$ we add the non-cooperative rule $r^{2,0}_{i\langle X \to w \rangle} : X \to w$ to the set $R_{2,i}$.

We take the alphabet $V_2 = V_1 \cup \{X_i, X_i'', X_i', X_i''' \mid 1 \le i \le h\}$ and the set of signal-promoters as $D_2 = \{p_i, \overline{p_i} \mid 1 \le i \le h\}$. The set of catalysts C_2 is exactly the set C_1 except the fact that objects in C_2 are used as catalysts and not as bi-stable catalysts.

We maintain the priority for the corresponding rules: if in the system Π_1, rule $r_{i\langle u' \to w'\rangle}^{1,k}$ has priority over rule $r_{i\langle u'' \to w''\rangle}^{1,k}$, then in Π_2, rule $r_{i\langle u' \to w'\rangle}^{2,k}$ has priority over the rule $r_{i\langle u'' \to w''\rangle}^{2,k}$, $1 \le i \le m, 0 \le k \le 4$.

Finally we construct $w_{2,l}$, for $0 \le l \le m$, in the following way. We add to $w_{2,l}$ all the objects $x \in V_1 \setminus C_1$ present in $w_{1,l}$ (by definition, $w_{2,0} = \lambda$). If $w_{1,l}$ contains $c_{j'}$, for some $j' \in \{1, 2, \cdots, h\}$, then we add $p_{j'}$ and $c_{j'}$ to $w_{2,l}$; if $w_{1,l}$ contains $\overline{c_{j'}}$ for some $j' \in \{1, 2, \cdots, h\}$, then we add $\overline{p_{j'}}$ and $c_{j'}$ to $w_{2,l}$; if $w_{1,l+1}$ contains $\overline{c_{j'}}$, for some $j' \in \{1, 2, \cdots, h\}$, then we add $X_{j'}$ to $w_{2,l}$; if $w_{1,l+1}$ contains $c_{j'}$, for some $j' \in \{1, 2, \cdots, h\}$, then we add $X_{j'}'''$ to $w_{2,l}$.

The main idea of the proof is that the "change of state" of a bi-stable catalyst present in region i of Π_1 is simulated by an exchange of signal-promoters between region i and the surrounding region $i - 1$ of Π_2.

For instance (in all other cases the situation is similar), the execution of the rule $r_{i\langle a \to w\rangle}^{1,1} : \overline{c_j}a \to c_j w$ present in region i of Π_1, for some $j \in \{1, 2, \cdots, h\}$, is simulated in Π_2 in the following way. First, rule $c_j a \to c_j w|_{(\overline{p_j}, out)}$ is executed in region i; at the end of its execution the signal-promoter $\overline{p_j}$ is sent out to the surrounding region $i - 1$. There, both rules $X_j \to X_j''|_{(\overline{p_j}, here)}$ and $X_j'' \to X_j'''|_{(p_j, in)}$ are executed sequentially and they send inside region i the signal-promoter p_j. In region i of Π_2, the presence of signal-promoter p_j activates now all (and only) the rules that are catalyzed by c_j in region i of Π_1; in this way the simulation of the execution of rule $r_{i\langle a \to w\rangle}^{1,1} : \overline{c_j}a \to c_j w$ in Π has been completely simulated (the obtained object X_j''' in region $i - 1$ stores the information that the bi-stable catalyst c_j has been switched to state c_j).

The execution of rule $r_{i\langle a \to w\rangle}^{1,2} : c_j a \to \overline{c_j}w$ present in region i of Π_1 is simulated in Π_2 in the following way. First the rule $r_{i\langle a \to w\rangle}^{2,2} : c_j a \to c_j w|_{(p_j, out)}$ in $R_{2,i}'$ of Π_2 is executed; at the end of its execution the signal-promoter p_j is sent out to the surrounding region $i - 1$. There, both rules $X_j''' \to X_j'|_{(p_j, here)}$ and $X_j' \to X_j|_{(\overline{p_j}, in)}$ are executed and the signal-promoter $\overline{p_j}$ is sent to region i. In region i of Π_2, the presence of signal-promoter $\overline{p_j}$ activates now all (and only) the rules that are catalyzed by $\overline{c_j}$ in region i of Π_1; in this way the simulation of the execution of rule $r_{i\langle a \to w\rangle}^{1,2} : c_j a \to \overline{c_j}w$ has been completely simulated (the object X_j obtained in region $i - 1$ stores the information that the bi-stable catalyst c_j has been switched to state $\overline{c_j}$).

From the way we construct Π_2 and because Π_1 is time-free, then also Π_2 is time-free; moreover they generate the same set of vectors of natural numbers. Therefore, because of Theorem 3, the statement is true.   □

8   Clock-Free P Systems

In this section we propose a second variant of time-independent P systems, slightly different from the previously considered time-free P systems: in this case, the execution time is associated directly to the applications of the rules. In particular, we consider the class of clock-free P systems producing the result independently from the times associated to the applications of rules.

Definition 2. *A* clock-free P system *(in short, a P^c system) of degree $m \geq 1$, with catalysts and promoters is a construct*

$$\Pi = (V, C, P, \mu, w_1, \ldots, w_m, R_1, \ldots, R_m, i_0),$$

where:
- *V is an alphabet; its elements are called objects;*
- *$C \subseteq V$ is a distinguished subset of the alphabet, called the set of catalysts;*
- *$P \subseteq V$ is a distinguished subset of the alphabet, called the set of promoters;*
- *μ is a membrane structure consisting of m membranes labeled $1, 2, \ldots, m$;*
- *w_i, $1 \leq i \leq m$, specify the multiset of objects present in the corresponding regions at the beginning of the computation;*
- *R_i, $1 \leq i \leq m$, are finite sets of evolution rules over V associated with regions $1, 2, \ldots, m$ of μ; we have non-cooperative rules, of the form $a \to v$, where a is an object from $V \setminus C$ and v is a string over $\{a_{here}, a_{out} \mid a \in V \setminus C\} \cup \{a_{in_j} \mid a \in V \setminus C, 1 \leq j \leq m\}$; catalytic rules $ca \to cv$, where a is an object from $V \setminus C$ and v is a string over $\{a_{here}, a_{out} \mid a \in V \setminus C\} \cup \{a_{in_j} \mid a \in V \setminus C, 1 \leq j \leq m\}$ and $c \in C$; promoted rules $a \to v|_t$ and $ca \to cv|_t$, with $t \in P$, $c \in C$, a is an object from $V \setminus C$, and v is a string over $\{a_{here}, a_{out} \mid a \in V \setminus C\} \cup \{a_{in_j} \mid a \in V \setminus C, 1 \leq j \leq m\}$ (when there is no ambiguity on the target, then the target in_j is simply written as in);*
- *$i_0 \in \{0, 1, \cdots, m\}$ specifies the output region of Π (0 indicates the environment).*

The computation starts from the initial configuration. The rules by which the objects evolve are chosen in a non-deterministic manner and applied in a maximally parallel manner.

A promoted rule $u \to v|_a \in R_i$ is active only in the presence of object a in region i (notice that promoters themselves can evolve according to some rules; see [2]).

Each application of a rule has an execution time that is an arbitrary positive integer number. Different applications (even of the same rule) may have different execution times. All objects produced by a rule are used (if they can be) in the same time as soon as they appear.

The system will stop in an *halting computation* if and only if reaches an halting configuration, where there is neither rule applicable in any region, nor rules that are in execution.

The output of an halting computation is the vector of numbers representing the multiplicities of objects present in the output region in the halting configuration.

Collecting all the vectors obtained, for any possible halting computation, we get the set $Ps(\Pi)$ of vectors of natural numbers generated by the system Π. We use the notation:

$$PsP_m^c(\alpha, proR), \alpha \in \{ncoo, coo\} \cup \{cat_k \mid k \geq 0\},$$

to denote the family of sets of vectors of natural numbers generated by clock-free P systems, having at most m membranes, evolution rules that can be non-cooperative ($ncoo$), cooperative (coo), or catalytic (cat_k), using at most k catalysts, and promoters ($proR$) at the level of rules.

9   Clock-Free P Systems: An Example

The following example shows how a clock-free P system can generate the Parikh image of $\{A^{2^n}c \mid n \geq 0\}$. The example anticipates the universality result given in the next section. Notice that, in case of clock-free P systems, applications of the same rule might have associated different execution times; therefore the approach used in the Example presented in Section 3 cannot be used anymore.

Example 2. Let us consider the clock-free P system

$$\Pi = (V, C, P, \mu, w_1, R_1, i_0 = 1),$$

where:

$$
\begin{aligned}
V &= \{A, S, S_1, S_2, \overline{S_1}, \overline{S_2}, T, F, c\}; \\
C &= \{c\}; \\
P &= \{S_1, \overline{S_1}, F, \overline{F}, A, B, T_1, \overline{T_1}\}; \\
\mu &= [_1\ ]_1; \\
w_1 &= ASc; \\
R_1 &= \{S \to S_1,\ \ S \to \lambda,\ \ cA \to cBBF|_{S_1}\} \\
&\cup \{S_1 \to S_2T|_F,\ \ F \to \lambda|_{S_1},\ \ S_2 \to S_1|_A\} \\
&\cup \{cT \to cT_1,\ \ S_2 \to \overline{S_1}|_{T_1},\ \ T_1 \to \lambda\} \\
&\cup \{cB \to cA\overline{F}|_{\overline{S_1}},\ \ \overline{S_1} \to \overline{S_2}\overline{T}|_{\overline{F}},\ \ \overline{F} \to \lambda|_{\overline{S_1}}\} \\
&\cup \{\overline{S_2} \to \overline{S_1}|_B,\ \ c\overline{T} \to c\overline{T_1},\ \ \overline{S_2} \to S|_{\overline{T_1}},\ \ \overline{T_1} \to \lambda\}.
\end{aligned}
$$

Here is how the system performs the computation. Rules $S \to S_1$, $S \to \lambda$ represent a selector, i.e., they decide whether the generation should stop or continue. In the case generation should continue ($S \to S_1$ is applied) then, after the appearance of object S_1, the rule $cA \to cBBF|_{S_1}$ is executed. It will take an arbitrary time (but finite) up to the moment when objects B and F appear simultaneously. In that moment, rules $S_1 \to S_2T|_F$, $F \to \lambda|_{S_1}$ can be applied and will be started simultaneously. We have the following situation: object F

will be eventually deleted so it will not count in further computations; objects S_2 and T appear synchronously. After this, rule $cT \to cT_1$ is started; however we do not know if the rule starts in the same time with rule $S_2 \to S_1|_A$ (because we do not know if all objects A were already rewritten). The usage of catalyst c by rule $cT \to cT_1$ assures us that rule $cA \to cBBF|_{S_1}$ cannot be executed before rule $cT \to cT_1$ ends (this guarantees that no other object T is produced before rule $cT \to cT_1$ ends).

If there still exist objects A, then object S_1 is generated (by rule $S_2 \to S_1|_A$) and object T_1 will be eventually deleted.

Otherwise, object $\overline{S_1}$ is generated and we can start the transformation of all the Bs into As (with a quite similar construction).

In case the process should stop, the object S is deleted ($S \to \lambda$ is executed), the transformation of objects A into B is not repeated and the computation ends having in the output region the Parikh image of $\{A^{2^n}c \mid n \geq 1\}$.

As final remark, one can observe that without the parallelism involved while executing the rules $S \to S_2T|_F$ and $F \to \lambda|_{S_1}$ the system presented is sequential; therefore the constructed system is clock-free.

10   Universality of Clock-Free P Systems

Here, we present a universality result concerning clock-free P systems using promoters at the level of rules and one catalyst. The proof is based on the simulation of register machines.

We will give some notions regarding register machines and their computational power (see [7]).

An n-register machine is a construct $M = (n, \mathcal{P}, l_0, l_h)$ where n is the number of registers (each register stores an arbitrary natural number); $\mathcal{P}$ (the *program* of the machine) is a finite set of labeled instructions of the form $(l_1 : op(r), l_2, l_3)$ where $op(r)$ is an operation on the register r of M, $l_1, l_2, l_3 \in Lab(\mathcal{P})$ (where $Lab(\mathcal{P})$ denotes the set of labels of the instructions from $\mathcal{P}$); l_0 is the initial label; l_h is the final label.

The operations allowed by an n-register machine are:

- $(l_1 : \text{ADD}(r), l_2, l_3)$ – increment the value stored into register r and nondeterministically proceed to instruction labeled l_2 or to instruction labeled l_3;
- $(l_1 : \text{SUB}(r), l_2, l_3)$ – jump to instruction labeled l_3 if the register r is empty; otherwise subtract one from the value stored into register r and jump to instruction labeled l_2;
- $(l_h : \text{HALT})$ – halts the computation (there is an unique halting instruction).

A register machine generates a vector of numbers in the following manner: we start with all registers being empty, and the computation starts with the instruction labelled by l_0 ; if the computation reaches the instruction $(l_h : \text{HALT})$ (that is, it halts), then the vector generated by the computation is $(j_1, \cdots, j_n)$, where j_r, $1 \leq r \leq n$ is the value stored into register r. The set of all vectors of numbers generated in this way by M, considering any halting computation, is denoted by $Ps(M)$.

It is known (see [7]) that nondeterministic register machines generate the family $PsRE$, of Turing computable set of vectors of natural numbers.

Now, we can state the following:

Theorem 5. $PsRE = PsP_2^c(cat_1, proR)$.

Proof. In order to prove this assertion we will simulate a n–register machine $M = (n, \mathcal{P}, l_0, l_h)$.

Formally, we define the P system

$$\Pi = (V, C, P, [_1 [_2]_2]_1, w_1 = \emptyset, w_2, R_1 = \emptyset, R_2, i_0 = 1),$$

where:

$$V = \{a_r, A_r, S_r \mid 1 \leq r \leq n\} \cup \{E, T, F, F_1, F_2, c\} \cup \{l, \bar{l} \mid l \in Lab(\mathcal{P})\};$$
$$C = \{c\};$$
$$P = \{a_r, A_r, S_r \mid 1 \leq r \leq n\} \cup \{E, T, F_1, F_2, h\};$$
$$w_2 = cl_0;$$

R_2 is defined as follows:

- for each instruction $(l_1 : ADD(r), l_2, l_3) \in \mathcal{P}$, we add to R_2 the rules:
$l_1 \rightarrow \bar{l_1} A_r,$
$c \rightarrow ca_r E|_{A_r},$
$A_r \rightarrow \lambda,$
$\bar{l_1} \rightarrow l_2|_E,$
$\bar{l_1} \rightarrow l_3|_E,$
$E \rightarrow \lambda;$

- for each instruction $(l_1 : SUB(r), l_2, l_3) \in \mathcal{P}$, we add to R_2 the rules:

$l_1 \rightarrow \bar{l_1} S_r T F,$	$S_r \rightarrow \lambda,$
$ca_r \rightarrow cE\|S_r,$	$\bar{l_1} \rightarrow l_2\|_E,$
$T \rightarrow \lambda\|_{a_r},$	$\bar{l_1} \rightarrow l_3\|_{F_2},$
$T \rightarrow \lambda\|_{F_2},$	$E \rightarrow \lambda\|_{F_1},$
$F \rightarrow F_1,$	$F_1 \rightarrow F_2\|_T,$
$F_1 \rightarrow \lambda\|_E,$	$F_2 \rightarrow \lambda.$

- for instruction $(l_h : HALT)$ we add to R_2 the rules:

$a_1 \rightarrow a_{1_{out}}|_{l_h},$
$\cdots$

$a_k \rightarrow a_{k_{out}}|_{l_h},$
$l_h \rightarrow \lambda.$

Before we start analyzing the work of Π, let us recall the followings. Objects l_1, l_2, l_3 correspond to the register machine instruction labels l_1, l_2 and l_3 respectively; the multiplicity of object a_r represents the value stored in register r; object A_r represents the incrementation command (it corresponds to the ADD operation in the register machine definition); object S_r represents the subtraction command (it correspond to SUB operation in the register machine definition).

Here is how the simulation of the register machine increment instruction $(l_1 : \text{ADD}(r), l_2, l_3) \in \mathcal{P}$ works.

Suppose that the current configuration of the region 2 of Π is represented by the multiset $ca_1^{n_1} \cdots a_r^{n_r} \cdots a_k^{n_k} l_1$. Obviously, only rule $l_1 \to \overline{l_1} A_r$ can be applied. After a while a the systems reaches a configuration represented by the multiset $ca_1^{n_1} \cdots a_k^{n_k} \overline{l_1} A_r$; therefore the rules to be further applied are $c \to ca_r E|_{A_r}$ and $A_r \to \lambda$. Both rules are started at the same time.

Object A_r will be deleted so we do not have to worry when this will actually happen. After some time, objects a_r and E will appear simultaneously; then, the configuration of the region 2 of Π will be the one represented by the multiset $ca_1^{n_1} \cdots a_r^{n_r+1} \cdots a_k^{n_k} \overline{l_1} E$. Next, the rules to be executed simultaneously will be $\overline{l_1} \to l_2|_E$ or $\overline{l_1} \to l_3|_E$, and $E \to \lambda$. Because we have obtained the next instruction label and moreover we deleted useless objects, we have correctly simulated the register machine increment instruction.

Suppose that the current configuration of the system is given by the multiset $ca_1^{n_1} \cdots a_r^{n_r} \cdots a_k^{n_k} l_1$. As it can be seen, only the rule $l_1 \to \overline{l_1} S_r T F$ can be applied. This means that after a while we will have the multiset $ca_1^{n_1} \cdots a_j^{n_j} \cdots a_k^{n_k} \overline{l_1} S_r T F$ (recall that objects $\overline{l_1}$, S_r, T, and F have appeared simultaneously since they were produced from the "same" object l_1). Next, the rules $ca \to cE|_{S_r}$, $T \to \lambda|_{a_r}$, $F \to F_1$, and $S_r \to \lambda$, will start their execution in the same time. However, we do not know if the objects E and F_1 will appear simultaneously. If object F_1 appears before object E it cannot be rewritten by rule $F_1 \to F_2|_T$ because object T is missing (object T is involved in rule $T \to \lambda|_{a_r}$); only rule $F_1 \to \lambda|_E$ could be further applied, but only after object E has appeared. If object E appears into region, then the following rules are applied $F_1 \to \lambda|_E$, $\overline{l_1} \to l_2|_E$, $E \to \lambda|_{F_1}$.

In this way, the next instruction label l_2 is generated and the simulation can continue. We do not need to know when objects F_1 and E will be removed since they cannot be involved in other rules.

Now, suppose that current configuration of the system is represented by the multiset $ca_1^{n_1} \cdots a_{r-1}^{n_{r-1}} a_{r+1}^{n_{r+1}} \cdots a_k^{n_k} l_1$. As above, only the rule $l_1 \to \overline{l_1} S_r T F$ can be applied. This means that after a while we will have the multiset $c\overline{l_1} S_r T F a_1^{n_1} \cdots a_{j-1}^{n_{j-1}} a_{j+1}^{n_{j+1}} \cdots a_k^{n_k}$.

Next, the rules $F \to F_1$, $D_a \to \lambda$ will start their execution simultaneously. Once the object F_1 has appeared the rule to be further applied is $F_1 \to F_2|_T$.

If object F_2 has appeared, then the system will execute the rules $T \to \lambda|_{F_2}$, $F_2 \to \lambda$, $\overline{l_1} \to l_2|_{F_2}$.

After some time the next instruction label will be generated and the computation can continue. Finally, if object l_h is generated then all the following rules are executed $a_1 \rightarrow a_{1_{out}}|_{l_h}, \cdots, a_k \rightarrow a_{k_{out}}|_{l_h}, l_h \rightarrow \lambda$. The reason for sending all objects a_r, $1 \leq r \leq n$, into region 1 is because we do not want to consider in the halting configuration the catalyst c.

In conclusion, we have shown that: $PsP_2^c(cat_1, proR) \supseteq PsRE$. By invoking Turing-Church thesis we have the reverse inclusion. Consequently, we have proved that $PsP_2^c(cat_1, proR) = PsRE$. Notice that the same proof works also for time-free P systems.   □

11 Concluding Remarks

We have introduced the concept of time-independent P systems that are systems producing the same result independently from the execution time of the rules. In this respect we have investigated two models.

First we have introduced a class of P systems called timed P systems where to each rule is associated a time of execution according to a time-mapping e. Further, we have introduced and investigated time-free P systems that are systems always producing the same result independently of the time-mapping e used.

We have shown that time-free P systems using one catalyst and an unbounded number of signal-promoters can generate the Parikh image of the languages generated by Indian parallel grammars. Adding the ability to use priority (in the strong sense) then time-free P systems become universal (the result has been obtained simulating non-synchronized P systems that are known to be universal when using bi-stable catalysts and priority, [8]).

Unfortunately, not much has been found regarding time-free P systems not using signal-promoters (such restricted model has been called basic). We have shown that basic (partially) time-free P systems, using only non-cooperative rules and priority, can generate non-semilinear set of vectors of natural numbers. The result has been obtained only by introducing certain conditions over the time of executions of the rules (from here the name partially time-free). We do not know if it is possible to get the same result for basic time-free P systems.

On the other hand, we think it might be useful to formalize the model of partially time-free P systems and to investigate classes of partially time-free P systems.

It is also possible to add other parameters to construct a P system "more realistic"; for instance, it would be very interesting to associate to each rule a time of delay that indicates the time to wait before a rule is started. This might model the fact that, sometime, chemical rules are not started immediately, even in the presence of the necessary chemicals.

The second model investigated in the paper is a generalization of the first one in what concerns the execution time of a rule: while in the first model the time is associated to the rule, in the second one the time is associated to each application of a rule.

In this respect, we have considered P systems that are independent from the time associated with the applications of the rules and we have called them as clock-free P systems. We have shown that clock-free P systems using one catalyst and promoters are computational universal.

We conclude with the belief that many interesting problems and results can be found in these lines of research.

Acknowledgements. The work of the first author was supported by the FPU-MEC doctoral fellowship. The work of the second author was possible due to a doctoral fellowship from AECI, Spanish Ministry of Foreign Affairs.

References

1. I.I. Ardelean, M. Cavaliere, D. Sburlan, Computing Using Signals: From Cells To P Systems, *Technical Report 01/2004 of RGNC, Brainstorming Week on Membrane Computing*, University of Sevilla, 2004, and *Soft Computing*, to appear.
2. P. Bottoni, C. Martín-Vide, Gh. Păun, G. Rozenberg, Membrane Systems with Promoters/Inhibitors, *Acta Informatica* 38, 10 (2002), 695–720.
3. J. Dassow, Gh. Păun, *Regulated Rewriting in Formal Language Theory*, Springer-Verlag, Berlin, 1989.
4. H. Fernau, Parallel Grammars: A Phenomenology, *Grammars*, 6, 1 (2003), 25–87.
5. M. Ionescu, D. Sburlan, On P Systems with Promoters/Inhibitors, *JUCS*, 10, 5 (2004), 581–599.
6. J.E. Hopcroft, J.D. Ullman, *Introduction to Automata Theory, Languages, and Computation*, Addison-Wesley, 1979.
7. M.L. Minsky, *Finite and Infinite Machines*, Prentice Hall, Englewood Cliffs, 1967.
8. Gh. Păun, *Membrane Computing – An Introduction*, Springer-Verlag, Berlin, 2002.

On Two-Dimensional Mesh Networks and Their Simulation with P Systems

Rodica Ceterchi[1] and Mario J. Pérez–Jiménez[2]

[1] Faculty of Mathematics and Computer Science, University of Bucharest,
Academiei 14, 010014 Bucharest, Romania
rc@funinf.cs.unibuc.ro
[2] Research Group on Natural Computing,
Department of Computer Science and Artificial Intelligence,
University of Sevilla,
Avda. Reina Mercedes s/n, 41012 Sevilla, Spain
Mario.Perez@cs.us.es

Abstract. We analize in this paper the possibility of simulating the parallel architecture **SIMD-MC**^{2}, also known as the two-dimensional mesh, with P systems with dynamic communication graphs. We illustrate this simulation for an algorithm which computes the sum of given integers. Next, we show how to extend the formalism to the reduction problem.

1 Introduction

P systems are powerful computational devices, with a high degree of parallelism, whose functioning is inspired by biological processes at the level of the cells, and of their membranes ([6], [7]). Among these processes, communication plays an important role (see [5]).

We have started in previous work ([2], and [3]) to analyze the possibility of simulating (classical) parallel architectures with P systems. A parallel machine consists of a large number of processors (each one having an arithmetic logic unit with registers and a private memory) able to solve problems in a cooperative way. The "cooperation" (sharing of data among processors) is accomplished via a specific communication network which characterizes the architecture.

We have considered in [2], and [3], the case of the *shuffle–exchange* architecture. In the present paper we deal with a different type of architecture, the *two–dimensional mesh*, in which the processors are placed in the vertices of a 2D-lattice in the plane, and communication is possible only between adjacent processors.

In the course of this study, a new type of P systems has emerged: P systems with *dynamic communication graphs* of specific types. They are in a way similar to tissue-like P systems, the connections between elementary membranes being described by graph structures, but they have a dynamic behavior: the underlying graph structures change in time. Moreover, rules, which are generally associated

G. Mauri et al. (Eds.): WMC5 2004, LNCS 3365, pp. 259–277, 2005.
© Springer-Verlag Berlin Heidelberg 2005

to regions inside membranes, are in this new version associated to underlying graphs. This new formalism covers both the simulation of internal processing, modelled by symbol rewriting rules, and the communication of data, modelled by symport/antiport rules.

The paper is organized as follows. Section 2 describes briefly the 2D-mesh parallel architecture. In Section 3 we introduce the P systems *with dynamic communication of 2D-mesh type*, the tools with which we accomplish the desired simulation. Section 4 illustrates an application of the 2D-mesh architecture to an algorithm for computing the sum of a set of integers, and contains a proof of its correctness. In Section 5 we discuss several simulations of the sum algorithm with P systems with dynamic communication of 2D-mesh type. In the next two sections we give some indications on how to extend the formalism to solve a general reduction problem.

2   The 2D-Mesh Architecture

Recall that a parallel machine consists of a large number of processors (each one having an arithmetic logic unit with registers and a private memory) able to solve problems in a cooperative way; that is, the machine is capable of executing several instructions in the same time unit.

According to Flynn's classification of computers (see [4]), a form of synchronous parallelism is called **SIMD** (Single–Instruction–Multiple–Data). A **SIMD** machine consists of a set of identical processors capable of simultaneously performing the same instruction issued by a central control unit, on different sets of data, and in a synchronous manner: each processor executing an instruction in parallel must be allowed to finish before the execution of the next instruction starts.

Several different methods of connecting processors in a parallel computer have been proposed. Quinn [8], quoting Ullman [9], mentions six important processor organizations, among which the **mesh network**. In a mesh network the processors are arranged into a q-dimensional lattice, and communication is allowed only between neighboring nodes, hence interior nodes communicate with $2q$ other processors. A **SIMD** machine in which the processors may communicate with each other via a mesh-connected network of dimension q is called in [8] a **SIMD-MC**^{q} machine.

We deal in this paper with **SIMD-MC**^{2} machines, i.e., a set of processors working according to the **SIMD** paradigm, and able to communicate (share) data among them according to a two–dimensional lattice architecture, which we will call in the sequel the **2D-mesh architecture**.

In general, in a given parallel architecture, we say that two processors are *adjacent* if they are directly connected. The *distance* between a pair of processors in a given architecture is the smallest length of a path between the processors. The *diameter* of an architecture is defined as the largest distance between any processors in the network. The *two–dimensional mesh* architecture provides a network with a large number of communication links connected to each processor, permitting to reduce the diameter of the network.

In general, we consider a *two–dimensional mesh–connected* parallel computer as a SIMD machine consisting of $n \times m$ identical processors, $P_{11}, \ldots, P_{nm}$, placed in the nodes of a 2D-lattice, or, equivalently, arranged in a 2D array.

Each processor has a local memory consisting of a number of registers, and it can perform a number of operations on data stored in these registers.

The communication between processors (mainly transmission of values of local variables) can take place only according to the 2D-lattice structure of the underlying network. Thus the processor placed in row i and column j, is denoted by $P_{i,j}$, (or P_{ij}) with $1 \leq i \leq n$ and $1 \leq j \leq m$. If $P_{i,j}$ is an interior node, i.e., $i \neq 1$, $j \neq 1$, $i \neq n$, $j \neq m$, then $P_{i,j}$ has four neighbors: $P_{i-1,j}$ and, $P_{i+1,j}$ on the same column, j, and $P_{i,j-1}$, $P_{i,j+1}$ on the same row, i. The rows $i = 1$ and $i = n$ are the *boundary rows*, and columns $j = 1$ and $j = m$ are the *boundary columns*. The nodes at the intersection of a boundary row and a boundary column have each one precisely two neighbors, and the rest of the boundary nodes have three neighbors.

3   P Systems with Dynamic Communication Graphs of 2D-Mesh Type

The model we develop here for the simulation of the 2D-mesh architecture is along the same general lines as the model proposed for the shuffle-exchange networks in [2] and [3], with some differences which arise inherently from the differences in the two parallel architectures in question.

We have a **SIMD-MC^2** machine, composed of $n \times m$ processors, denoted P_{ij}, with $1 \leq i \leq n$, $1 \leq j \leq m$, organized in a 2D-mesh architecture. To each processor P_{ij} we will associate a membrane, which we will still denote P_{ij}. Similarly to tissue-like P systems, we will have a collection of elementary membranes, connected by certain graphs, at certain moments of their evolution in time. The graphs we will consider will be sub-graphs of the total graph of the 2D-mesh network, also sub-graphs of the identity graph of the 2D-mesh network, as we will explain in the sequel.

The *contents* of each processor P_{ij} will be codified in its associated membrane with symbol objects. The alphabet of symbols used, V, will depend on the contents of the processors we are simulating (see the applications in the following sections). If each processor has to contain say r variables with positive integer values, they can be in principle codified with an alphabet with r letters. In the case of the applications illustrated further, we will have to represent at most two integer variables. Their simulation with P systems will use accordingly an alphabet with two (or four) symbols.

Basically, we have to model:

– *Patterns of specific internal processing* in each processor: these will be modelled by symbol rewriting rules.
– *Patterns of communication* between processors.

Recall that in the 2D-mesh architecture the communication between processors takes place along edges which connect two neighboring processors. As

we have done in general for parallel architectures, and, in particular, for the
perfect–shuffle architecture in previous work (see [2], [3]), we will speak of the
(underlying) *communication graph* associated to a given architecture: the *vertices* of the graph are the processors, and the *edges* (oriented or not) are the
network connections characteristic of the architecture. In the case of the 2D-
mesh, the underlying communication graph is composed of all edges between
neighboring nodes. We will call it the *total graph*, and we distinguish between
horizontal edges and *vertical edges*. We use the following notation:

$$G_{total} = G_h \cup G_v = \bigcup_{i=1}^{n} G_{i*} \cup \bigcup_{j=1}^{m} G_{*j},$$

where

$$G_{i*} = \{((i,j),(i,j+1)) \mid 1 \le j \le m-1\}, \text{ for all } 1 \le i \le n,$$

$$G_{*j} = \{((i,j),(i+1,j)) \mid 1 \le i \le n-1\}, \text{ for all } 1 \le j \le m.$$

G_{i*} is the set of all horizontal edges on line i, with $1 \le i \le n$, and G_{*j} is the
set of all vertical edges on column j, for $1 \le j \le m$.

For every particular algorithm implemented on a 2D-mesh network of processors, not all edges of the communication graph are used simultaneously for
transmitting values of local variables, as we will see in the illustrations which
follow. For this reason we will speak of the total *virtual* communication graph,
and of *active sub-graphs* of G_{total}, composed of sets of edges along which actual
communication takes place, in parallel, at certain steps of a given algorithm.

For modelling the internal processing steps, in order to have unity of notation,
we will associate the rules to the *identity* graph: the set of vertices is composed
of all processors/membranes, the set of edges is defined as

$$Id = \{((i,j),(i,j)) \mid 1 \le i \le n, 1 \le j \le m\}.$$

If an internal processing occurs only in a subset of the processors/membranes,
then we will consider the respective *active sub-graphs* of Id. For instance, if internal processing occurs only for processors/membranes on line i, we will associate
it with the active sub-graph

$$Id_{i*} = \{((i,j),(i,j)) \mid 1 \le j \le m\}.$$

Similarly, if an internal processing occurs only for processors/membranes on
column j, we will associate it with the active sub-graph

$$Id_{*j} = \{((i,j),(i,j)) \mid 1 \le i \le n\}.$$

The P systems which we consider in the sequel, for modelling the 2D-mesh
architecture, similarly to those considered in [2] and [3], depart from the classical
P systems in two respects:

- The connections between individual membranes of a P system, μ, which was a tree-like structure of membranes (see [6]), and which in tissue-like P systems becomes a graph structure, is now, a *sequence of graphs*.
- The rules of a P system, usually associated to *membranes*, will now be associated to *communication graphs* between membranes.

  (a) We simulate the internal computations performed by a subset of processors by the action of symbol or object rewriting rules, at work simultaneously inside the corresponding subset of membranes. We will associate such rules to the corresponding active subsets of Id.

  (b) We simulate the exchange of data performed by the processors with communication rules (symport/antiport rules) between membranes. The communication rules will be associated to the active sub-graphs of G_{total}.

We will consider the edges to have an *orientation* which gives meaning to the *in* and *out* of the symport/antiport rules: *out* means travelling in the sense of the edge's orientation, *in* means travelling in the opposite sense. Thus, rules such as (a, out), (a, in) function along an oriented edge in the same way they would function if they were attached to the source vertex of the edge.

As in [2] and [3] (with slight modifications), we will use pairs $[graph, rules]$ to describe the evolution of a P system which simulates the behavior of a given algorithm, in the 2D-mesh architecture.

For every particular architecture, its underlying network structure imposes restrictions on the set $Graphs$ to which the first member of a pair $[graph, rules]$ can belong. For the 2D-mesh architecture $Graphs$ is either a subset of G_{total}, or a subset of Id.

The set $Rules$, of all symbol/object rewriting rules which simulate internal computations performed by the individual processors, will depend on the particular algorithm, used to solve a particular problem, within the framework of a given architecture.

We model *deterministic algorithms*, each *iterative step* of such an algorithm will be modelled by *a finite sequence of pairs* $[graph, rules]$ (sometimes each pair simulating the effect of "an instruction", but not necessarily). The entire execution of such an algorithm will be modelled by a sequence of pairs $[graph, rules]$, denoted in the sequel by R_μ.

A P system which simulates a particular algorithm in the 2D-mesh architecture will thus be a construct

$$\Pi = (V, P_{11}, \cdots, P_{nm}, R_\mu),$$

where $P_{11}, \cdots, P_{nm}$ are elementary membranes, V is an alphabet of symbols used to codify the contents of the membranes, and R_μ is a finite sequence of pairs $[graph, rules]$, such that: (i) if $graph \subset Id$, then its rules are rewriting rules; (ii) if $graph \subset G_{total}$, then its rules are communication rules. We will call such a system a *P system with dynamic communication of 2D-mesh type*.

The P system starts in an initial configuration, with its elementary membranes $P_{11}, \cdots, P_{nm}$ simulating the initial configuration of the corresponding processors. Each application of an element $[graph, rules] \in R_\mu$ to a configuration consists of considering the (active) graph $graph$ and applying the rules $rules$ associated to it: (i) if $graph \subset Id$, the corresponding rewriting rules are applied in the membranes which are vertices of $graph$; (ii) if $graph \subset G_{total}$, the corresponding symport/antiport rules are applied along the edges of $graph$. This leads to the next configuration. The final configuration is obtained after the application of the entire sequence R_μ.

Note that the general presentation of a P system with dynamic communication graph which simulates a given (arbitrary) parallel architecture based on communication networks (denote it by X) is the same: it specifies an alphabet of symbols used to codify the contents of membranes, a finite set of elementary membranes, and, finally, a finite sequence R_μ of pairs $[graph, rules]$. The specifics of each architecture X impose certain particular forms for the sets $Graphs$ to which the first member of a pair $[graph, rules]$ can belong, and for the pairing $[graph, rules]$. Further, the specifics of each architecture, and sometimes of an algorithm implemented on it, govern the *structure* of the entire sequence R_μ.

Denote by $Graphs(X)$ the active graphs associated to the architecture X. For $X =$ perfect shuffle SIMD $=$ **PS-SIMD** we have (see [2], [3]):

$$Graphs(\textbf{PS-SIMD}) = \{G_s, G_e, G_{Id}\},$$

and the conditions for pairs are:

1. (i) if $graph = G_{Id}$, then its rules are rewriting rules;
2. (ii) if $graph \in \{G_s, G_e\}$, i.e., $graph$ is either of type *shuffle* or of type *exchange*, then its rules are communication rules.

For $X =$ 2D-mesh SIMD $=$ **SIMD-MC^2** we have:

$$Graphs(\textbf{SIMD-MC}^2) = \mathcal{P}(G_{total}) \cup \mathcal{P}(Id),$$

and the conditions for pairs are:

1. (i) if $graph \subset Id$, then its rules are rewriting rules;
2. (ii) if $graph \subset G_{total}$, then its rules are communication rules.

As for the differences in the structure of the sequence R_μ, in the case of the perfect shuffle architecture R_μ was periodic, while in the case of the 2D-mesh architecture it is not necessarily so, as we will see in the example illustrated in the next section.

4   The Sum on the 2D-Mesh

We compute the sum of n integer numbers $a_{11}, a_{12}, \ldots, a_{ll}$, where $n = l^2$, using the 2D-Mesh architecture, each integer held in one processor.

We have $n = l^2$ processors P_{ij} $(1 \le i, j \le l)$ that possess two local variables: x_{ij} (initialized by a_{ij}) and t_{ij} (initialized by 0).

The following procedure computes the sum $a_{11} + a_{12} + \cdots + a_{ll}$.

```
procedure sum2D-MESH(a11, a12, ··· , all)
begin
    for all i, j where 1 ≤ i, j ≤ l do
        xij ← aij;  tij ← 0
    endfor
    for j ← l − 1 downto 1 do
        for all i where 1 ≤ i ≤ l do
            tij ⇐ xi(j+1)
            xij ← xij + tij
        endfor
    endfor
    for i ← l − 1 downto 1 do
        ti1 ⇐ xi+1,1
        xi1 ← xi1 + ti1
    endfor
end
```

where $t_{ij} \Leftarrow x_{i(j+1)}$ means that processor $P_{i,(j+1)}$ links by the mesh with processor P_{ij} and communicates the value of variable x, and processor P_{ij} puts it in variable t.

In order to prove the correctness of this algorithm we reformulate in detail what is happening in each processor throughout the execution. We denote by x_{ij}^r and t_{ij}^r the corresponding values of the local variables of processor P_{ij} after step r of the execution.

The above algorithm can now be reformulated in the following, more detailed, manner:

```
procedure sum2D-MESH(a11, a12, ··· , all)
begin
    for all i, j where 1 ≤ i, j ≤ l do
        x⁰ij ← aij;  t⁰ij ← 0
    endfor
    for j ← l − 1 downto 1 do
        for all i where 1 ≤ i ≤ l do
            tl−jij ⇐ xl−j−1i(j+1)
            xl−jij ← x⁰ij + tl−jij
        endfor
    endfor
    for i ← l − 1 downto 1 do
        t2l−i−1i1 ⇐ x2l−i−2i+1,1
        x2l−i−1i1 ← xl−1i1 + t2l−i−1i1
    endfor
end
```

Theorem 1. *The formula* $\theta(j) \equiv \forall i \ (1 \le i \le l \longrightarrow x_{ij}^{l-1} = \sum\limits_{s=j}^{l} a_{is})$ *is an invari-*

ant of the loop "for $j \leftarrow l - 1$ downto 1 do" *of the procedure* $\text{sum}_{2D-\text{MESH}}$.

Proof. By descendant induction on j.

– For $j = l - 1$ we have, for each i such that $1 \le i \le l$:

$$
\begin{aligned}
x_{i,l-1}^{l-1} = x_{i,l-1}^{1} &= x_{i,l-1}^{0} + t_{i,l-1}^{1} \\
&= x_{i,l-1}^{0} + x_{i,l}^{0} \\
&= a_{i,l-1} + a_{i,l} \\
&= \sum_{s=l-1}^{l} a_{is}
\end{aligned}
$$

– Let $j > 1$ and suppose that the formula $\theta(j)$ is true. Let us prove that the formula $\theta(j-1)$ is also true.
  For each i such that $1 \le i \le l$ we have:

$$
\begin{aligned}
x_{i,j-1}^{l-(j-1)} &= x_{i,j-1}^{0} + t_{i,j-1}^{l-(j-1)} \\
&= x_{i,j-1}^{0} + x_{i,j}^{l-j} \\
&\overset{i.h.}{=} a_{i,j-1} + \sum_{s=j}^{l} a_{is} \\
&= \sum_{s=j-1}^{l} a_{is}
\end{aligned}
$$

$\square$

Theorem 2. *The formula* $\varphi(i) \equiv x_{i1}^{2l-i-1} = \sum\limits_{r=i}^{l}\sum\limits_{s=j}^{l} a_{rs}$ *is an invariant of the*

loop "for $i \leftarrow l - 1$ downto 1 do" *of procedure* $\text{sum}_{2D-\text{MESH}}$.

Proof. By descendant induction on i.

– For $i = l - 1$ we have:

$$
\begin{aligned}
x_{i,1}^{2l-i-1} = x_{l-1,1}^{2l-(l-1)-1} &= x_{l-1,1}^{l-1} + t_{l-1,1}^{2l-(l-1)-1} \\
&= x_{l-1,1}^{l-1} + x_{l,l}^{l-1} \\
&= \sum_{s=1}^{l} a_{l-1,s} + \sum_{s=1}^{l} a_{l,s} \\
&= \sum_{r=l-1}^{l}\sum_{s=l-1}^{l} a_{rs}
\end{aligned}
$$

– Let $i > 1$ and suppose that the formula $\varphi(i)$ is true. Let us prove that the formula $\varphi(i-1)$ is also true.

For each i such that $1 \le i \le l$ we have:

$$
\begin{aligned}
x_{i-1,1}^{2l-(i-1)-1} &= x_{i-1,1}^{l-1} + t_{i-1,1}^{2l-(i-1)-1} \\
&= x_{i-1,1}^{l-1} + x_{i,1}^{2l-i-1} \\
&\overset{Th.1+i.h.}{=} \sum_{s=1}^{l} a_{i-1,1} + \sum_{r=i}^{l}\sum_{s=j}^{l} a_{rs} \\
&= \sum_{r=i-1}^{l}\sum_{s=j}^{l} a_{rs}
\end{aligned}
$$

$\square$

Corollary 1. *At the end of the execution of procedure* $\mathsf{sum_{2D-MESH}}$*, the variable* x *of processor* P_{11} *contains the value of the sum* $a_{11} + \cdots + a_{ll}$.

Proof. At the end of execution the formula $\varphi(1)$ is true; that is, it is verified that:

$$
x_{11}^{2l-1-1} = \sum_{r=1}^{l}\sum_{s=j}^{l} a_{rs} = a_{11} + a_{12} + \cdots + a_{ll}.
$$

Recall that x_{11}^{2l-1-1} is the content of the processor P_{11} at the end of the execution.

$\square$

Let us note that the above algorithm, although formulated for a square 2D-mesh, works in the same way on a rectangular mesh, of dimensions $n \times m$, and only slight changes are necessary in the proofs of the corresponding correctness results.

The following procedure computes the sum $a_{11} + a_{12} + \cdots + a_{nm}$.

```
procedure sum2D-MESH(a11, a12, · · · , anm)
begin
    for all i,j where 1 ≤ i ≤ n,1 ≤ j ≤ m do
        xij ← aij; tij ← 0
    endfor
    for j ← m − 1 downto 1 do
        for all i where 1 ≤ i ≤ n do
            tij ⇐ xi(j+1)
            xij ← xij + tij
        endfor
    endfor
    for i ← n − 1 downto 1 do
        til ⇐ xi+1,1
        xil ← xil + til
    endfor
end
```

Its running time, measured in number of iterative steps, is $(n-1)+(m-1)$.

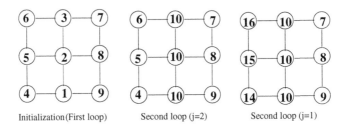

Initialization(First loop)   Second loop (j=2)   Second loop (j=1)

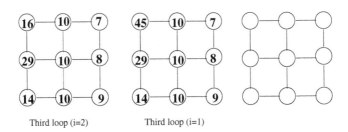

Third loop (i=2)   Third loop (i=1)

Fig. 1. The sum on a 2D-mesh

Remark: Note that, in the above procedures, the sequence

$$t_{ij} \Leftarrow x_{i(j+1)}$$
$$x_{ij} \leftarrow x_{ij} + t_{ij}$$

can be replaced by

$$t_{i(j+1)} \leftarrow x_{i(j+1)}$$
$$t_{ij} \Leftarrow t_{i(j+1)}$$
$$x_{ij} \leftarrow x_{ij} + t_{ij}$$

and the sequence

$$t_{i1} \Leftarrow x_{i+1,1}$$
$$x_{i1} \leftarrow x_{i1} + t_{i1}$$

by

$$t_{i+1,1} \leftarrow x_{i+1,1}$$
$$t_{i1} \Leftarrow t_{i+1,1}$$
$$x_{i1} \leftarrow x_{i1} + t_{i1}.$$

The difference is that, instead of communicating directly the value of $x_{i(j+1)}$ to the variable t_{ij} through a mesh connection between P_{ij} and $P_{i(j+1)}$, we first copy in $P_{i(j+1)}$ the value of $x_{i(j+1)}$ into the auxiliary variable $t_{i(j+1)}$, and we use the mesh connections to transmit values of only the auxiliary corresponding variables t. This is an important aspect for the simulations which follow.

In Figure 1 the functioning of the sum algorithm on a 3×3 2D-mesh is illustrated, from the initial configuration (after initialization), through the subsequent ones – each obtained after an iterative step, to the last one (after the fourth iterative step), in which the sum is obtained in processor P_{11}.

5   Simulation of the Sum

We present a simulation of the sum algorithm on 2D-mesh using P systems with dynamic communication graphs of the 2D-mesh type. Actually, as we will see, we will have three possible simulations, depending on the input data, and the requirements we impose on the "memory" of membranes P_{ij}, with $ij \neq 11$, which can be considered auxiliary in the process of summation.

As already stated in Section 3, each processor will be simulated by a membrane, and we keep the same labels for membranes as for processors.

Thus, each membrane P_{ij}, for $1 \leq i \leq n$, $1 \leq j \leq m$, will have to have distinct representations for its two internal variables, x_{ij} and t_{ij} (when both are necessary). Let us denote by $|x|$ the positive part of any integer x. We codify the integer values of the local variables x_{ij} and t_{ij}, in the following manner:

- Let a and $\bar{a}$ be the symbols to codify the integer content of the x_{ij} variable of every membrane P_{ij}. Symbol a is used to represent the positive units, and $\bar{a}$ for the negative ones. Suppose x_{ij} has integer value a_{ij}: if a_{ij} is positive, it will be codified as $a^{a_{ij}}$, if a_{ij} is negative, it will be codified as $\bar{a}^{|a_{ij}|}$.
- Let b and $\bar{b}$ be the symbols to codify the integer content of the t_{ij} variable of every membrane P_{ij}, b for positive units, and $\bar{b}$ for negative ones. They are used in the same fashion as a and $\bar{a}$ are used to codify x_{ij}, described above.

If the data are arbitrary integers, the contents of the processors will be codified with symbol objects over the alphabet $V = \{a, \bar{a}, b, \bar{b}\}$. If the data are always positive integers, the contents of the processors can be codified with symbol objects over the smaller alphabet $V = \{a, b\}$.

Let us illustrate how addition of two integers can be performed using two (adjacent) membranes: consider P_x and P_y two membranes, each containing an integer, x, and respectively y, codified as a^z, for $z \geq 0$ and/or as $\bar{a}^z$ for $z < 0$, $z \in \{x, y\}$. Suppose both integers are positive, thus the initial configuration is $P_x : a^x$, and $P_y : a^y$.

Suppose moreover that we are interested in obtaining the result of the addition in P_x, and that we are not interested if we loose the original initial value of P_y. Then, using an active edge (P_y, P_x) together with the symport rule (a, out), i.e., the pair $[(P_y, P_x), (a, out)]$ accomplishes our desired objective: precisely y occurrences of a travel "along" the edge, and we will have $x + y$ occurrences of a in P_x.

If our integers are arbitrary, i.e., we can have any of the four combinations of initial configurations, P_x : either a^x or $\bar{a}^x$, P_y : either a^y or $\bar{a}^y$, if we are interested in obtaining the result of the addition in P_x, and we are not interested if we loose the original initial value of P_y, then, we can use an active edge (P_y, P_x) together with the symport rules $\{(a, out), (\bar{a}, out)\}$, i.e., the pair $[(P_y, P_x), \{(a, out), (\bar{a}, out)\}]$, followed by $[Id_{P_x}, (a\bar{a} \longrightarrow \lambda)]$. The last internal rewriting step taking place in P_x ensures us that the addition is correctly performed, positive and negative units annihilate themselves in pairs.

If we do wish to keep however also the contents of P_y, additional rewriting steps are necessary, and the use of symbols $\{b, \bar{b}\}$ becomes apparent. The sequence

$$[Id_{P_y}, \{a \longrightarrow ab, \bar{a} \longrightarrow \bar{a}\bar{b}\}], [(P_y, P_x), \{(b, out), (\bar{b}, out)\}],$$

$$[Id, \{b \longrightarrow a, \bar{b} \longrightarrow \bar{a}, a\bar{a} \longrightarrow \lambda\}],$$

accomplishes the task of having $x + y$ represented in P_x and y still in P_y: by the first set, the a's, respectively $\bar{a}$'s, in P_y are duplicated also as b's, respectively $\bar{b}$'s; by the second set of rules all the b's, respectively $\bar{b}$'s, get from P_y into P_x; by the third set, the b's, respectively $\bar{b}$'s in P_x get rewritten as a's, respectively $\bar{a}$'s, and the rule $a\bar{a} \longrightarrow \lambda$ ensures the proper addition of positive and negative units, if it is necessary. The result of adding $x + y$ is represented as a^{x+y} or $\bar{a}^{|x+y|}$ in P_x; in P_y we have the same content as before, since all b's, or $\bar{b}$'s have travelled by the second rule into P_x, and thus none of the rules of the third set are applicable in P_y.

Let us go back now to our system of membranes P_{ij}, for $1 \le i \le n, 1 \le j \le m$, seen as the nodes of a (virtual) 2D-lattice of dimension $n \times m$.

Suppose, for the sake of simplicity, that we deal only with positive integers, and that we are only interested in obtaining the result of the addition $a_{11} + \cdots + a_{nm}$ in membrane P_{11}, loosing the initial and intermediate values in all the other membranes.

For our system of membranes and the problem stated above we will have:

- *The initial configuration:* for $1 \le i \le n, 1 \le j \le m$, every membrane P_{ij} contains $a^{a_{ij}}$, and no b's.
- *The sequence of horizontal subgraphs:* For the first $m - 1$ iterative steps, we will consider, at each step $j = m-1, \cdots, 1$, the subgraphs $\{((i, j+1), (i, j)) \mid 1 \le i \le n\}$ composed of all horizontal edges connecting column $j + 1$ to column j, and we consider them oriented edges. Along each such edge, we have to perform the addition of variables $x_{i(j+1)}$ and x_{ij}, and put the result in x_{ij}. If we are not interested in preserving the values (initial or intermediate) of every processor (with the exception of processor P_{11} which collects the final result), we can simply use the rule (a, out) along each such (oriented) edge. Along each edge $((i, j + 1), (i, j))$, $x_{i(j+1)}$ occurrences of symbol a will travel into membrane P_{ij} where they will increase the number of a's, so that it will be precisely $x_{i(j+1)} + x_{ij}$ (and the codification for variable $x_{i(j+1)}$ in processor $P_{i(j+1)}$ is lost).
- *The sequence of vertical subgraphs:* For the last $n - 1$ iterative steps, we will consider, at each step $i = n - 1, \cdots, 1$, the subgraph $(((i + 1), 1), (i, 1))$ composed of an oriented vertical edge connecting on column 1 line $i + 1$ to line i. Along each such edge, we have to perform again the addition of variables $x_{(i+1)1}$ and x_{i1}, and put the result in x_{i1}. Again, we can use the rule (a, out) along each such (oriented) edge.

Note that we have used an alphabet of only one symbol, $\{a\}$, and that there are no internal computation steps in the form of rewriting taking place in any subset of membranes.

Theorem 3. *Consider the P system with dynamic communication of 2D-mesh type*

$$\Pi_1 = (\{a\}, \{P_{ij} \mid 1 \le i \le n, 1 \le j \le m\}, R_{\mu 1}),$$

where $R_{\mu 1}$ is the following sequence of pairs [graph, rules]:

$$R_{\mu 1} = \{[\{((i, j+1), (i, j)) \mid 1 \le i \le n\}, (a, out)], \ j = m-1, \cdots, 1,$$

$$[(((i+1), 1), (i, 1)), (a, out)], \ i = n-1, \cdots, 1\}.$$

Then, starting from the initial configuration $\{P_{ij} : a^{a_{ij}} \mid 1 \le i \le n, 1 \le j \le m\}$, where all a_{ij} are positive integers, the application of the sequence $R_{\mu 1}$ will lead to the final configuration $P_{11} : a^S$, where $S = a_{11} + \cdots + a_{nm}$, and $P_{ij} : \emptyset$ for all $ij \ne 11$.

Let us consider now the case in which we have to sum arbitrary integers, and suppose that we do not wish to keep the initial or intermediate contents of any other membrane but P_{11}. We will have:

- *The initial configuration:* for $1 \le i \le n$, $1 \le j \le m$, for $a_{ij} \ge 0$ every membrane P_{ij} contains $a^{a_{ij}}$, and for $a_{ij} < 0$ every membrane P_{ij} contains $\bar{a}^{|a_{ij}|}$.
- *The sequence of horizontal subgraphs – communication followed by internal computations:* For the first $m - 1$ iterative steps, we will consider, at each step $j = m - 1, \cdots, 1$, the subgraphs $\{((i, j+1), (i, j)) \mid 1 \le i \le n\}$ composed of all horizontal edges connecting column $j + 1$ to column j, and we consider them oriented edges. To each such edge we associate the symport rules $\{(a, out), (\bar{a}, out)\}$ which ensure that either positive or negative units, depending on the case, travel all into membrane P_{ij}. (The codification for the value $a_{i(j+1)}$ in membrane $P_{i(j+1)}$ is lost). In order to ensure proper addition of integers with different signs on column j, we will use an internal computation step modelled as $[Id_{*j}, a\bar{a} \longrightarrow \lambda]$, where Id_{*j} is the subgraph of the identity graph associated to column j.
  The sequence $[graph, rules]$ which models this stage will thus be

$$R_h^j = [\{((i, j+1), (i, j)) \mid 1 \le i \le n\}, \{(a, out), (\bar{a}, out)\}], [Id_{*j}, a\bar{a} \longrightarrow \lambda],$$

  for $j = m - 1, \cdots, 1$.
- *The sequence of vertical subgraphs – communication followed by internal computations:* For the last $n - 1$ iterative steps, we consider, at each step $i = n - 1, \cdots, 1$, the subgraph $((i + 1, 1), (i, 1))$ composed of an oriented vertical edge connecting on column 1 line $i + 1$ to line i. Along each such edge, we use the rules $\{(a, out), (\bar{a}, out)\}$. After such a communication step, we have an internal computation step, which we model with $[Id_{i*}, a\bar{a} \longrightarrow \lambda]$, where Id_{i*} is the subgraph of the identity graph associated to line i. (We could have used only the subgraph Id_{i1}.)
  The sequence $[graph, rules]$ which models this stage will thus be

$$R_v^i = [\{((i + 1, 1), (i, 1))\}, \{(a, out), (\bar{a}, out)\}], [Id_{i*}, a\bar{a} \longrightarrow \lambda],$$

  for $i = n - 1, \cdots, 1$.

Theorem 4. *Consider the P system with dynamic communication of 2D-mesh type*

$$\Pi_2 = (\{a, \bar{a}\}, \{P_{ij} \mid 1 \leq i \leq n, 1 \leq j \leq m\}, R_{\mu 2}),$$

where $R_{\mu 2}$ is the following sequence of pairs [graph, rules]:

$$R_{\mu 2} = R_h{}^{m-1} \cdots R_h{}^{j} \cdots R_h{}^{1} \cdot R_v{}^{n-1} \cdots R_v{}^{i} \cdots R_v{}^{1}.$$

Then, starting from the initial configuration $\{P_{ij} : a^{a_{ij}} \mid 1 \leq i \leq n, 1 \leq j \leq m, a_{ij} \geq 0\}$, and $\{P_{ij} : \bar{a}^{|a_{ij}|} \mid 1 \leq i \leq n, 1 \leq j \leq m, a_{ij} < 0\}$, where all a_{ij} are arbitrary integers, the application of the sequence $R_{\mu 2}$ will lead to the final configuration $P_{11} : a^S$, where $S = a_{11} + \cdots + a_{nm}$, and $P_{ij} : \emptyset$ for all $ij \neq 11$.

Consider now the most general case: we have to sum arbitrary integers, and we do not wish to destroy the contents of any membrane when it links by mesh to another membrane and transmits the value of a variable. We will use for transmission only the auxiliary variables t_{ij}, codified over the set of symbols $\{b, \bar{b}\}$. Some more internal processing in the form of rewriting will be necessary, both before, and after the communication step. (Note that in the previous versions, we did not have to simulate in our membranes the auxiliary variables t.) The simulation which follows resembles the modified version of the algorithm as in the Remark of Section 4.

We will have:

- *The initial configuration:* for $1 \leq i \leq n$, $1 \leq j \leq m$, for $a_{ij} \geq 0$ every membrane P_{ij} contains $a^{a_{ij}}$, and for $a_{ij} < 0$ every membrane P_{ij} contains $\bar{a}^{|a_{ij}|}$. There are neither b's, nor $\bar{b}$'s (the t variables are all initialized to 0).
- *The sequence of horizontal subgraphs – communication and internal computations:*

Consider the sequence [graph, rules]:

$$R_h{}^{j} = [Id_{*(j+1)}, \{a \longrightarrow ab, \bar{a} \longrightarrow \bar{a}\bar{b}\}],$$

$$[\{((i, j+1), (i, j)) \mid 1 \leq i \leq n\}, \{(b, out), (\bar{b}, out)\}],$$

$$[Id_{*j}, \{b \longrightarrow a, \bar{b} \longrightarrow \bar{a}, a\bar{a} \longrightarrow \lambda\}],$$

for $j = m-1, \cdots, 1$. Each sequence $R_h{}^{j}$ simulates the j iterative step of the first part of the algorithm. By the first set, in column $j + 1$ simultaneous rewriting take place, simulating copying the contents of variable $x_{i(j+1)}$ into $t_{i(j+1)}$. By the second set, the b's (respectively $\bar{b}$'s) travel along the active horizontal edges of the mesh, from column $j + 1$ to column j on each line i. By the third set, another internal computation takes place, in column j, simulating the addition of the auxiliary variable t_{ij} to a_{ij} and putting the result in a_{ij}. (Again, the t_{ij}'s will be zero.)

The sequence obtained by catenation

$$R_h = R_h{}^{m-1} \cdots R_h{}^{j} \cdots R_h{}^{1}$$

simulates the sequential execution of the first $m - 1$ iterative steps of the sum algorithm.

- *The sequence of vertical subgraphs – communication and internal computations:*
  Consider for each $i = n - 1, \cdots, 1$, the sequence $[graph, rules]$:

$$R_v{}^i = [Id_{(i+1)1}, \{a \longrightarrow ab, \bar{a} \longrightarrow \bar{a}\bar{b}\}],$$

$$[\{((i + 1, 1), (i, 1))\}, \{(b, out), (\bar{b}, out)\}],$$

$$[Id_{i*}, \{b \longrightarrow a, \bar{b} \longrightarrow \bar{a}, a\bar{a} \longrightarrow \lambda\}].$$

It functions in a similar way to the sequences associated to the horizontal subgraph. By catenation we obtain the sequence

$$R_v = R_v{}^{n-1} \cdots R_v{}^i \cdots R_v{}^1$$

which simulates the last $n - 1$ iterative steps of the algorithm.

Theorem 5. *Consider the set $\{a_{ij} \mid 1 \le i \le n, 1 \le j \le m\}$ of arbitrary integers, and consider the P system with dynamic communication of 2D-mesh type*

$$\Pi_3 = (\{a, \bar{a}, b, \bar{b}\}, \{P_{ij} \mid 1 \le i \le n, 1 \le j \le m\}, R_{\mu 3}),$$

where $R_{\mu 3}$ is the following sequence of pairs $[graph, rules]$:

$$R_{\mu 3} = R_h \cdot R_v = R_h{}^{m-1} \cdots R_h{}^j \cdots R_h{}^1 \cdot R_v{}^{n-1} \cdots R_v{}^i \cdots R_v{}^1,$$

with $R_h{}^j$ and $R_v{}^i$ as defined previously.
  Then, starting from the initial configuration $\{P_{ij} : a^{a_{ij}} \mid 1 \le i \le n, 1 \le j \le m, a_{ij} \ge 0\}$, and $\{P_{ij} : \bar{a}^{|a_{ij}|} \mid 1 \le i \le n, 1 \le j \le m, a_{ij} < 0\}$, the application of the sequence $R_{\mu 3}$ will lead to a final configuration in which $P_{11} : a^S$, where $S = a_{11} + \cdots + a_{nm}$, and $P_{ij} :\ne \emptyset$ for all $ij \ne 11$ (with the possible exception of those containing integer 0).

We end this section with some remarks on the three versions of simulations we have proposed. We believe that discussing them, versus the parallel algorithm implemented on the 2D-mesh in Section 4, illustrates similarities and differences between "communication" and "internal computations" as understood, on one hand in parallel architectures, and on the other hand, in their simulation with P systems.

First, let us note that the third version, in Theorem 5, can be considered a complete simulation of the algorithm in Section 4, in the sense that each membrane P_{ij}, even with $ij \ne 11$, will have, in a codified form, the same content as processor P_{ij}.

If we concentrate only on the result, i.e., on membrane P_{11} which must finally contain the sum, we note that, in the simulation with P systems, we can almost obtain it with only "communication" rules: rewriting is necessary only in Theorem 4, and only because the input data may contain integers with different signs. Moreover, both "communication" and "internal computations" steps in the parallel architecture, were modelled with "communication-only" rules in the P systems simulation (the case of Theorem 3). In the first two simulations, Theorem 3 and Theorem 4, there was no need to even represent the auxiliary variable t, a local memory essential for the functioning of the parallel algorithm. This implies that the notion of "communication" in P systems is stronger than the corresponding notion in classical parallel models, of course, at the cost of "local memory loss".

6   The Reduction on the 2D-Mesh Architecture

Let $(A, *, 0)$ be a commutative monoid, i.e., A is a set, $*$ is a binary associative and commutative operation over A, and 0 is the neutral element of $*$.

Let $a_0, \ldots, a_{k-1}$ be elements of this set. The *reduction* (see [8], Section 2.3.1) is the process of computing $a_0 * \cdots * a_{k-1}$.

The 2D-mesh architecture can be used to solve the reduction problem. Let us suppose that the total number of elements is $k = (2m + 1) \times (2n + 1)$. Consider $k = (2m + 1) \times (2n + 1)$ processors connected by a 2D-mesh network. The nodes of the network will be labelled by pairs (i, j) (or simply ij), with i the row index, $-m \leq i \leq m$, and with j the column index, $-n \leq j \leq n$. The set of elements to which we want to apply the reduction is

$$\{a_{(-m)(-n)}, \ldots, a_{(-m)(n)}, \ldots, a_{00}, \ldots, a_{m(-n)}, \ldots, a_{mn}\}.$$

Processor P_{ij}, with label ij, $-m \leq i \leq m$, $-n \leq j \leq n$, possesses two local variables: x_{ij} (initialized by a_{ij}) and t_{ij} (initialized by 0).

The following procedure computes

$$a_{(-m)(-n)} * \cdots * a_{(-m)(n)} * \cdots * a_{00} * \cdots * a_{m(-n)} * \cdots * a_{mn},$$

and puts the result in processor P_{00}:

```
procedure reduction₂D-MESH(a(−m)(−n), . . . , a₀₀, . . . , aₘₙ)
begin
    for all i, j where −m ≤ i ≤ m, −n ≤ j ≤ n, do
        xᵢⱼ ← aᵢⱼ; tᵢⱼ ← 0
    endfor
    for j ← n − 1 downto 0 do
        for all i where −m ≤ i ≤ m do
            tᵢⱼ ⇐ xᵢ(ⱼ₊₁)
            xᵢⱼ ← xᵢⱼ * tᵢⱼ
        endfor
    endfor
    for j ← −n + 1 to 0 do
        for all i where −m ≤ i ≤ m do
            tᵢⱼ ⇐ xᵢ(ⱼ₋₁)
            xᵢⱼ ← xᵢⱼ * tᵢⱼ
```

```
      endfor
    endfor
    for i ← m − 1 downto 0 do
        t_{i0} ⇐ x_{i+1,0}
        x_{i0} ← x_{i0} * t_{i0}
    endfor
    for i ← −m + 1 to 0 do
        t_{i0} ⇐ x_{i−1,0}
        x_{i0} ← x_{i0} * t_{i0}
    endfor
end
```

The second and fourth **for** loops are iterative steps, one responsible for performing the $*$ operation on columns from n to 0, the other for performing the $*$ operation on rows from m to 0, similarly to the algorithm for sum in section 4.

However, this algorithm has some improvement over the one in section 4. The third **for** loop is the "mirror image" of the second one: a sequence of iterative steps, performing the $*$ operation on columns, this time from $-n$ to 0. Note that the execution of iterative step j in the second loop can be done in parallel with the execution of iterative step $-j$ of the third loop. Similarly, the fifth **for** loop is the "mirror image" of the fourth one: a sequence of iterative steps, performing the $*$ operation on rows, this time from $-m$ to 0. Note that the execution of iterative step i in the fourth loop can be done in parallel with the execution of iterative step $-i$ of the fifth loop.

This ensures that the running time of this algorithm, (if we apply the parallelism mentioned above), measured in iterative steps is $(2m + 2n)/2$, i.e., this algorithm takes $\sqrt{k}/2$ steps, compared with $\sqrt{k}$ steps required by the previous algorithm for sum. The simulation which follows makes use of this enhanced parallelism.

7 Simulation of the Reduction

In order to simulate the algorithm for reduction presented in section 6 with P systems with dynamic communication of 2D-mesh type, we have to work under the following supplementary assumptions:

1. The elements a_{ij} on which the operation $*$ is performed can be codified inside each membrane P_{ij} over a finite alphabet, say V_x; the alphabet will be used to codify all values of variable x_{ij}, both initial and intermediate;
2. Using the same codification, the values of local variables t_{ij} are codified inside each membrane P_{ij} over a finite alphabet, say V_t;
3. V_x and V_t are in bijective correspondence: to each $a \in V_x$ there corresponds a symbol $a' \in V_t$;
4. There exists a set of symbol rewriting rules on $V_x \cup V_t$, denoted r_*, which simulates performing the operation $x_{ij} * t_{ij}$ inside each membrane P_{ij}; the value of the result $x_{ij} * t_{ij}$ is codified over V_x as the new value of x_{ij}.

Under these assumptions, the rest of the model follows the general lines of the models for sum in Section 5. Copying the value of x_{ij} into t_{ij} is done by the set of symbol rewriting rules $\{a \longrightarrow aa' \mid a \in V_x\}$. Since the codifications for x's and t's are the same, the effect is the desired one. Transfer of values for t's over the appropriate edges can be accomplished with the set of symport rules $\{(a', out) \mid a' \in V_t\}$. Finally, the set r_* will compute $x_{ij} * t_{ij}$ and put the result in x_{ij}.

We construct now the sequences of pairs $[graph, rules]$ which simulate the iterative steps of the reduction algorithm. To simplify the notation we write all i instead of $-m \leq i \leq m$.

For each $j = n, \ldots, 1$ (the horizontal steps), we take

$$R_h{}^j = [Id_{*j} \cup Id_{*(-j)}, \{a \longrightarrow aa' \mid a \in V_x\}],$$

$$[\{((i,j), (i, j-1)) \mid \text{all } i\} \cup \{((i, -j), (i, -j+1)) \mid \text{all } i\}, \{(a', out) \mid a' \in V_t\}],$$

$$[Id_{*(j-1)} \cup Id_{*(-j+1)}, r_*].$$

For each $i = m, \ldots, 1$ (the vertical steps on column 0), we take

$$R_v{}^i = [Id_{i0} \cup Id_{(-i)0}, \{a \longrightarrow aa' \mid a \in V_x\}],$$

$$[\{((i,0), (i-1,0))\} \cup \{((-i,0), (-i+1,0))\}, \{(a', out) \mid a' \in V_t\}],$$

$$[Id_{i0} \cup Id_{(-i)0}, r_*].$$

Let $(A, *, 0)$ be a commutative monoid, and consider the following set of elements of A:

$$\{a_{(-m)(-n)}, \ldots, a_{(-m)(n)}, \ldots, a_{00}, \ldots, a_{m(-n)}, \ldots, a_{mn}\}.$$

Assume that every element of A can be codified over an alphabet V_x, and that there exists a set of rewriting rules r_* which simulates performing operation $*$ on two elements of A, one codified over V_x, the other over V_t, and the result of the computation is again codified over V_x. Consider the P system with dynamic communication of 2D-mesh type

$$\Pi_* = (V_x \cup V_t, \{P_{ij} \mid -m \leq i \leq m, -n \leq j \leq n\}, R_{\mu *}),$$

where $R_{\mu *}$ is the sequence of pairs $[graph, rules]$:

$$R_{\mu *} = R_h{}^n \cdots R_h{}^j \cdots R_h{}^1 \cdot R_v{}^m \cdots R_v{}^i \cdots R_v{}^1,$$

with $R_h{}^j$ and $R_v{}^i$ as defined previously.

Then, starting from an initial configuration in which each membrane P_{ij} contains a codification of the value a_{ij} over V_x, for all $-m \leq i \leq m, -n \leq j \leq n$, the application of the sequence $R_{\mu *}$ will lead to a final configuration in which P_{00} contains a codification of $S \in A$, where

$$S = a_{(-m)(-n)} * \cdots * a_{(-m)(n)} * \cdots * a_{00} * \cdots * a_{m(-n)} * \cdots * a_{mn}.$$

8 Conclusions

We have analyzed in this paper the possibility of simulating the parallel architecture known as the 2D-mesh with a new version of P systems, P systems with dynamic communication graphs.

In Section 3 a comparison is made between dynamic communication graphs of 2D-mesh type, introduced here, and dynamic communication graphs of shuffle–exchange type, introduced in previous work. We believe this illustrates the power of this new version of P systems as tools for formalizing other network architectures as well.

We have illustrated the proposed simulation with the particular algorithm for computing the sum of a given set of integers. Discussing several possible simulations of the sum algorithm has given us the opportunity to compare "communication" as understood in P systems, and communication in classical parallel architectures.

We have further presented an algorithm to solve the reduction problem implemented on a 2D-mesh, and discussed its simulation with P systems with dynamic communication graphs, simulation possible under some supplementary assumptions.

References

1. R. Ceterchi, C. Martín–Vide, P Systems with Communication for Static Sorting. In M. Cavaliere, C. Martín–Vide and Gh. Păun (eds.), *Proceedings of the Brainstorming Week on Membrane Computing*, Report GRLMC 26/03, 2003, 101–117.
2. R. Ceterchi, M.J. Pérez–Jiménez, Simulating Shuffle–Exchange Networks with P Systems. In Gh. Păun, A. Riscos–Núñez, F. Sancho–Caparrini and A. Romero–Jiménez (eds.), *Proceedings of the Second Brainstorming Week on Membrane Computing*, Report RGNC 01/04, 2004, 117–129.
3. R. Ceterchi, M.J. Pérez–Jiménez, A Perfect Shuffle Algorithm for Reduction Processes and its Simulation with P Systems. In I. Dzitac, T. Maghiar, C. Popescu (eds.), *Proceedings of the International Conference on Computers and Communications ICCC 2004, May 27-29, 2004, Baile Felix Spa – Oradea, Romania*, Editura Univ. Oradea, 2004, 92–97.
4. M.J. Flynn, Very High-Speed Computing Systems, *Proceedings of the IEEE* 54, 12 (1966), 1901–1909.
5. A. Păun, Gh. Păun, The Power of Communication: P Systems with Symport/Antiport. *New Generation Computers*, 20, 3 (2002), 295–306.
6. Gh. Păun, Computing with Membranes. *Journal of Computer and System Sciences*, 61, 1 (2000), 108–143, and *Turku Center for CS-TUCS Report* No. 208, 1998.
7. Gh. Păun, *Membrane Computing. An Introduction*, Springer-Verlag, Berlin, 2002.
8. M.J. Quinn, *Parallel Computing. Theory and Practice*, McGraw–Hill Series in Computer Science, 1994.
9. J.D. Ullman, *Computational Aspects of VLSI*, Computer Science Press, Rockville, MD, 1984.

Exploring Computation Trees
Associated with P Systems

Andrés Cordón-Franco, Miguel A. Gutiérrez-Naranjo,
Mario J. Pérez-Jiménez, and Agustín Riscos-Núñez

Research Group on Natural Computing,
Department of Computer Science and Artificial Intelligence,
University of Sevilla,
Avda. Reina Mercedes s/n, 41012 Sevilla, Spain
{acordon, magutier, marper, ariscosn}@us.es

Abstract. Usually, the evolution of a P system generates a computation tree too large to be efficiently handled with present–day computers; moreover, different branches in this tree may differ significantly from a computational complexity point of view, that is, for the amount of time and storage necessary to reach a result. In this paper we propose a first approach to outline a strategy for selecting a suitable branch, in some sense, of the computation tree associated with a P system. To this end, we introduce the key notion of the *dependency graph* of a P system.

1 Introduction

The evolution of a non-deterministic computational device usually gives rise to a computation tree with several branches, potentially infinite. Moreover, even in the case of finite computation trees, the amount of information is often too big to be efficiently handled with present-day computers. This is why it is convenient to look for good strategies for exploring such computation trees.

In this paper, we address one of these non-deterministic computational devices: P systems (see [2, 3] or visit [4]). Our goal is to enrich the simulation of the evolution of a P system with a new component, usually called *strategy* or *search plan*, that *controls* the rules to be applied in each cellular step, in order to select a branch of the computation tree with a low (if possible, minimal) cost.

The ideal situation would be to have a mapping h^* assigning to each node n of a computation tree a number $h^*(n)$ which measures the minimum length of a path from node n to a leaf (that is, to a halting configuration). Then, the strategy would consist on selecting at each non-deterministic step of the computation a node corresponding to the least value of h^*. However, the drawback is the high computational cost of such a mapping.

In a more realistic situation, we look for a computable mapping being an *efficient estimation* of h^*, that will be referred to as a *heuristic function* or *evaluation function*.

The paper is organized as follows. In Section 2 we describe the P system variant used in this paper. Section 3 introduces the key notion of the *dependency*

G. Mauri et al. (Eds.): WMC5 2004, LNCS 3365, pp. 278–286, 2005.

graph of a P system. Based upon this notion, in Section 4 we present a mapping h, which helps us to search for a short branch in the computation tree of a P system. We also prove that this mapping is, indeed, a heuristic function. Finally, in Section 5 we develop an illustrative example and we finish with some final remarks.

2   P Systems with a Fixed Number of Membranes

Let us now briefly introduce the P system variant we shall work with in this paper. We shall only use evolution and communication rules and we shall avoid division or dissolution rules; so, the number of membranes (indeed, the whole membrane structure) remains unchanged during the evolution of the system.

P systems will be represented as tuples $\Pi = (\Gamma, H, \mu, w_1, \ldots, w_q, R)$, where:

- Γ is a finite alphabet (the working alphabet) whose elements are called objects.
- H is a finite set of labels for membranes.
- μ is a tree-like membrane structure of degree q, one-to-one labelled by the set H.
- $w_1, \ldots, w_q$ are multisets over Γ describing the multisets of objects initially placed in membranes from μ.
- R is a finite set of developmental rules of the following forms:
  1. $[a \rightarrow v]_l$, where $a \in \Gamma$, $v \in \Gamma^*$ *(object evolution rules)*.
     Internal rule: an object a can evolve to a multiset v inside a membrane labelled by l.
  2. $[a]_l \rightarrow [\ ]_l\, b$, where $a, b \in \Gamma$ *(send-out communication rules)*.
     An object a can get out of a membrane labelled by l, possibly transformed in a new object b.
  3. $a[\ ]_l \rightarrow [b]_l$, where $a, b \in \Gamma$ *(send-in communication rules)*.
     An object a can get into a membrane labelled by l, possibly transformed in a new object b.

Note that cooperation is not allowed, and priority or electrical charges are not considered either. Besides, let us observe that the rules of the system are associated with labels (e.g., the rule $[a \rightarrow v]_l$ is associated with the label $l \in H$).

The rules are applied according to the following principles. Object evolution rules are applied in a maximal parallel way (that is, all objects which can evolve by such rules must do it), while communication rules are used sequentially, in the sense that one membrane can be used by at most one rule of this type at one step.

Concerning the interaction with the user, we shall consider that the results of the computations are collected outside the system (note that objects can leave the system during the evolution, provided that *send-out* rules are applied in the skin membrane). In order to be able to handle this external output of the computations in a formal way, we add a new region to the membrane structure, called *environment*. In this way, the information about the contents of the environment can be included in the configurations of the system.

3   Dependency Graphs

Roughly speaking, transitions in P systems are performed by rules in which the occurrence of an element a_0 in a membrane m_0 produces the apparition of the element a_1 in a membrane m_1. In a certain sense, one can consider a dependency between the pair (a_0, m_0) and the pair (a_1, m_1). This dependency is not based on the initial configuration but on the set of rules of the P system.

More formally, the rules in the P system model presented above can be re-formulated as follows:

$$(a_0, m_1) \rightarrow (a_1, m_2)(a_2, m_2) \ldots (a_n, m_2)$$

The occurrence of the element a_0 in membrane m_1 triggers the rule and produces the apparition of the multiset $a_1 a_2 \ldots a_n$ into membrane m_2.

Obviously, if $m_1 \neq m_2$, then we have a communication rule. In this case, n must be equal to 1 and both membranes must be adjacent (one membrane is the father of the other one). If m_1 is the father of m_2, then we have a send-in communication rule, and if the opposite holds, then we have a send-out communication rule. On the other hand, if $m_1 = m_2$, then we have an *evolution* rule.

The pair (a_0, m_1) stands for the *left side* of the rule and the multiset of pairs $(a_1, m_2)(a_2, m_2) \ldots (a_n, m_2)$ stands for the *right side* of the rule.

Next, we define the *dependency graph* of a P system based on this new representation of the rules.

Definition 1. *The dependency graph of a P system Π is a pair $G_\Pi = (V_\Pi, E_\Pi)$ such that V_Π is the set of all the pairs (z, m), where z is a symbol of the alphabet of Π and m is a label of a membrane (or env for the environment), and E_Π is the set of all ordered pairs (arcs) of elements of V_Π, $((z_1, m_1), (z_2, m_2))$, such that (z_1, m_1) is the left side of a rule and (z_2, m_2) belongs to the right side of that rule.*

The distance between two nodes of the dependency graph is defined as usual.

Definition 2. *A path of length n from a vertex x to a vertex y in a directed graph $G = (V, E)$ is a finite sequence $v_0, v_1, \ldots, v_n$ of vertices such that $v_0 = x$, $v_n = y$, and $(v_i, v_{i+1}) \in E$ for $i = 0, \ldots, n - 1$. The sequence of vertices with a single vertex is also considered a path. If there is a path γ from x to y, we say that y is reachable from x (via γ). The distance between two vertices v_1 and v_2, $d(v_1, v_2)$, is the length of the shortest path from v_1 to v_2, or infinite, if v_2 is not reachable from v_1.*

We illustrate the definition of dependency graph with an example. Let us consider the next toy P system, with alphabet $\Gamma = \{a, b, c, d, v, w, z, yes\}$, membrane structure $\mu = [\,[\,]_e\,]_s$ and set of rules:

Rule 1: $[\,a \to zb\,]_e$ **Rule 6:** $[\,a\,]_s \to [\,]_s\, yes$
Rule 2: $[\,a\,]_e \to [\,]_e\, a$ **Rule 7:** $[\,z\,]_e \to [\,]_e\, a$
Rule 3: $[\,b\,]_e \to [\,]_e\, c$ **Rule 8:** $z\,[\,]_e \to [\,d\,]_e$
Rule 4: $[\,a \to z^2v\,]_s$ **Rule 9:** $[\,v \to w\,]_s$
Rule 5: $[\,z\,]_s \to [\,]_s\, z$ **Rule 10:** $[\,w\,]_s \to [\,]_s\, yes$

In order to construct the corresponding dependency graph, we have to consider the set of regions that are determined by the membrane structure of the P system. Since the elements can be sent out of the system (rules **5**, **6** and **10**), we have to consider three regions: $\{e, s, env\}$. Then, with the new representation, the rules can be rewritten as follows:

Rule 1: $(a, e) \to (z, e)(b, e)$ **Rule 6:** $(a, s) \to (yes, env)$
Rule 2: $(a, e) \to (a, s)$ **Rule 7:** $(z, e) \to (a, s)$
Rule 3: $(b, e) \to (c, s)$ **Rule 8:** $(z, s) \to (d, e)$
Rule 4: $(a, s) \to (z, s)^2(v, s)$ **Rule 9:** $(v, s) \to (w, s)$
Rule 5: $(z, s) \to (z, env)$ **Rule 10:** $(w, s) \to (yes, env)$

Therefore, the dependency graph of Π, $G_\Pi = (V_\Pi, E_\Pi)$, is defined by the following sets:

$$V_\Pi = \left\{ \begin{array}{l} (a, e),\ (b, e),\ (c, e),\ (d, e),\ (v, e),\ (w, e),\ (z, e),\ (yes, e), \\ (a, s),\ (b, s),\ (c, s),\ (d, s),\ (v, s),\ (w, s),\ (z, s),\ (yes, s), \\ (a, env),\ (b, env),\ (c, env),\ (d, env), \\ (v, env),\ (w, env),\ (z, env),\ (yes, env) \end{array} \right\},$$

$$E_\Pi = \left\{ \begin{array}{l} ((a, e), (z, e)),\ ((a, e), (b, e)),\ ((a, e), (a, s)), \\ ((a, s), (z, s)),\ ((a, s), (v, s)),\ ((a, s), (yes, env)), \\ ((b, e), (c, s)), \\ ((z, e), (a, s)),\ ((z, s), (z, env)),\ ((z, s), (d, e)), \\ ((v, s), (w, s)), \\ ((w, s), (yes, env)) \end{array} \right\}.$$

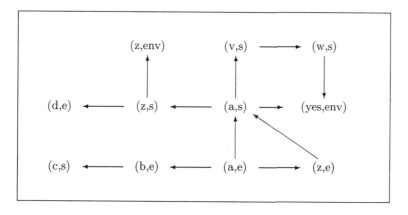

Fig. 1. The dependency graph

The set V_{Π} of vertices has 24 elements, but 13 of them are isolated: only 11 vertices occur in some arc. Figure 1 shows the connected vertices of the graph. Note that the dependency graph only depends on the membrane structure and on the set of rules of the P system, and not on the elements of the membranes at the initial configuration. This example will be further studied in Section 5.

4   Heuristics

The simulation of a P system with current computers is a quite complex task. P systems are intrinsically non-deterministic computational devices and therefore their computation trees are difficult to store and handle with one-processor (or a bounded number of processors) computers. A possible way to overtake this shortcoming is to follow only one branch of the associated computation tree in each run of the simulator. Choosing which branch must be explored is not an easy decision, as different branches may differ significantly from a computational complexity point of view.

In order to select the best branch of the computation tree, the ideal situation would be to have a mapping h^* assigning to every node a number which indicates the minimum length of a path from this node to a leaf. Unfortunately, such a mapping usually has a high computational cost.

In a more realistic situation, we look for a mapping h being an *efficient estimation* of h^*, in the following sense:

- h assigns to each node n of a computation tree a number $h(n)$ verifying $h(n) \leq h^*(n)$; and
- the value $h(n)$ can be calculated with a *low* computational cost.

Then, $h(n)$ is a real-valued function over the nodes that, in some cases, provides a lower bound of the number of cellular steps needed to reach a halting configuration from node n. Such a mapping h will be referred to as a *heuristic function* or *evaluation function*. The aim of this section is to present a heuristic function h based on the notion of dependency graph of a P system.

In general, given a configuration of a non-deterministic P system, there exist several essentially different halting configurations which can be reached. However, in this first approach to the use of heuristics, we shall only consider a family of P system that behaves *well* in the following sense. Despite of the non-determinism, every computation of a P system in the family halts (i.e., there are no infinite branches in the computation tree) and, starting from a given initial configuration, all computations send out to the environment the same answer, just at the last step.

Consequently, when simulating such a P system, no matter which branch of the associated computation tree we follow, we will get the same answer, but the computational cost measured as the number of steps in the computation may vary widely. Hence, it is interesting to define a heuristic function measuring, in some sense, how far a given configuration is from a halting configuration in the computation tree.

In order to define such a heuristic mapping, we introduce the concept of *L-configuration of a P system*. As above, we codify the information as ordered pairs *(element, membrane)*.

Definition 3. *An* L-configuration, *LC*, *associated with a given configuration, C, is a multiset of pairs (z, m) such that, for every object z of the alphabet and for every membrane m, the multiplicity of z in m in the configuration C is equal to the multiplicity of the pair (z, m) in LC.*

Next we define a mapping h which helps to select a good branch in each choice point of the computation tree associated with a P system.

Definition 4. *Let Π be a P system. Let LC be an L-configuration of Π, and z the object sent out to the environment at the end of the computation. The heuristic function h is defined as*

$$h(LC) = \min\{\, d(v, (z, env)) \mid v \in LC\}$$

where d is the distance in the dependency graph.

We finish this section with a theorem which states that the mapping h verifies the required property.

Theorem 1. *Let h^* be a function mapping a configuration C onto the number of steps of the shortest path in the computation tree from C to a halting configuration. For each configuration C, we have $h(LC) \leq h^*(C)$, where LC is the L-configuration associated with C.*

Proof. The basic idea of the proof is that the *transition* between two adjacent vertices in the dependency graph needs at least one evolution step of the P system. Keeping this in mind, the proof is quite natural.

We will reason by *reductio ad absurdum*. Suppose that there exists a configuration C_0 such that $h^*(C_0) < h(LC_0)$ and let C^* be a halting configuration such that from C_0 to C^* there are $h^*(C_0)$ evolution steps. Let z be the element sent out in the last step of the computation. Since C^* is a halting configuration, (z, env) belongs to the L-configuration LC^* and

$$h^*(C_0) < h(LC_0) = \min\{\, d(v, (z, env)) \mid v \in LC_0\}$$

In particular, for all $v \in LC_0$ such that (z, env) is reachable from v, $h^*(C_0)$ is less than the length of the shortest path from v to (z, env) in the dependency graph. That is, the distance from any element of the L-configuration LC_0 to (z, env) is larger than the number of computation steps of the P system from C_0 to a halting configuration.

But this is impossible since, as remarked above, the transition between two adjacent vertices in the dependency graph needs at least one computation step of the P system. $\square$

5   Example

To illustrate the definition of the heuristic function h, we consider again the example described in Section 3. Figure 2 shows the computation tree associated with the evolution of this P system. In the first step of the computation two new configurations are possible. We use the function h to select one of them in order to reach a halting configuration in the minimum number of steps.

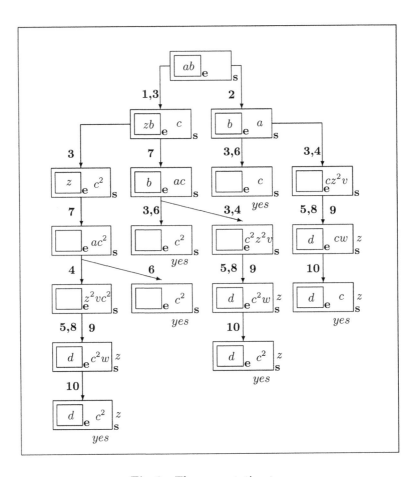

Fig. 2. The computation tree

The two possible configurations to proceed with are:

$$C_1 \equiv [\,[\,zb\,]_e\,c\,]_s, \quad \text{by applying rules } \mathbf{1} \text{ and } \mathbf{3},$$
$$C_2 \equiv [\,[\,b\,]_e\,a\,]_s, \quad \text{by applying rule } \mathbf{2}.$$

The information of these configurations can be represented by their associated L-configurations:

$$LC_1 = \{(z, e), (b, e), (c, s)\},$$
$$LC_2 = \{(b, e), (a, s)\}.$$

In this example, the halting configurations are characterized by sending the object yes to the environment; that is, a configuration is a halting one if and only if (yes, env) is an element of its associated L-configuration. In order to decide which branch we must follow in the computation tree, we compute $h(LC_i)$, for $i = 1, 2$:

$$h(LC_1) = \min\{\, d(v, (yes, env)) \mid v \in LC_1\}$$
$$= d((z, e), (yes, env))$$
$$= 2,$$

$$h(LC_2) = \min\{\, d(v, (yes, env)) \mid v \in LC_2\}$$
$$= d((a, s), (yes, env))$$
$$= 1.$$

We have $h(LC_2) < h(LC_1)$, so, according to the heuristic h, we should follow the computation from the configuration C_2 to reach a halting configuration. Figure 2 shows the whole computation tree and it can be checked that, in the next evolution step, a halting configuration is reached from C_2 and this is the shortest path from the initial configuration to a halting one.

If we consider the subtree dominated by the configuration $C_1 \equiv [\, [\, zb\,]_e\, c\,]_s$, that is, if we consider C_1 as initial configuration, the function h can help to find the shortest computation. As Figure 2 shows, starting from C_1 two new configurations are possible:

$$C_{11} \equiv [\, [\, z\,]_e\, c^2\,]_s, \text{ by applying rule } \mathbf{3},$$
$$C_{12} \equiv [\, [\, b\,]_e\, ac\,]_s, \text{ by applying rule } \mathbf{7}.$$

Their associated L-configurations are:

$$LC_{11} = \{(z, e), (c, s), (c, s))\},$$
$$LC_{12} = \{(b, e), (a, s), (c, s)\}.$$

In order to decide which branch we must follow in the computation tree, we compute $h(LC_{1i})$ for $i = 1, 2$:

$$h(LC_{11}) = \min\{\, d(v, (yes, env)) \mid v \in LC_{11}\}$$
$$= d((z, e), (yes, env))$$
$$= 2,$$

$$h(LC_{12}) = \min\{\, d(v, (yes, env)) \mid v \in LC_{12}\}$$
$$= d((a, s), (yes, env))$$
$$= 1.$$

So, we should follow C_{12} to obtain the shortest computation. In fact, starting from C_{12}, a halting configuration is reached in the next step.

6   Conclusions and Further Research

In this paper we have presented a first approach towards an *efficient strategy* for searching in the computation tree associated with the evolution of a P system. Our aim is to select a branch with a low computational cost, measured as the number of steps needed to reach a halting configuration.

We propose a heuristic function h being an estimation of this computational cost, based on the notion of *dependency graph* of a P system.

We have illustrated the use of this heuristic function with an example belonging to a special family of P systems that, in a specific sense, "behaves well". Nonetheless, the search plan proposed here can be generalized, in a rather natural way, to other (less restrictive) variants of P system. In particular, extending the notion of *dependency graph* to P systems where the number of membranes can vary during the evolution (e.g., P systems with active membranes) seems to be a very promising question.

Another interesting topic is to study the transformation of configurations as a pre-computation phase, when the system itself is built. In this framework several important topics appear, such as the edit-distance between configurations, normal forms, reachability, etc.

Acknowledgement

The support for this research through the project TIC2002-04220-C03-01 of the Ministerio de Ciencia y Tecnología of Spain, cofinanced by FEDER funds, is gratefully acknowledged.

References

1. A. Cordón-Franco, M.A. Gutiérrez-Naranjo, M.J. Pérez-Jiménez, A. Riscos-Núñez, Weak metrics on configurations of a P system. In Gh. Păun, A. Riscos-Núñez, A. Romero-Jiménez, and F. Sancho-Caparrini, (eds.), *Proceedings of the Second Brainstorming Week on Membrane Computing*, Report RGNC 01/04, University of Sevilla, 2004, 139–151.

2. Gh. Păun, Computing with membranes, *Journal of Computer and System Sciences*, **61**, 1 (2000), 108–143.

3. Gh. Păun, *Membrane Computing. An introduction*. Springer-Verlag, 2002.

4. http://psystems.disco.unimib.it/

Approximating Non-discrete P Systems

Andrés Cordón-Franco and Fernando Sancho-Caparrini

Dpt. Computer Science and Artificial Intelligence,
E.T.S.Ingeniería Informática,
University of Seville, Spain
{acordon, fsancho}@us.es

Abstract. The main goal of this paper is to propose some geometric approaches to the computations of non-discrete P systems. The behavior of this kind of P systems is similar to that of classic systems, with the difference that the contents of the membranes are represented by non-discrete multisets (the multiplicities can be non-integers) and, consequently, also the number of applications of a rule in a transition step can be non-integer.

1   Introduction

Usual variants of P systems have only a finite number of options in every step of their computations and, in consequence, an associated computation tree is defined for them (see [5] or [6] for a formal definition of these concepts). In this way, irrespectively whether they are non-deterministic or probabilistic P systems [3], we obtain a discrete space (possibly infinite) of computations where the system evolves.

Here we will work with a variant which can evolve in every step in a non-discrete number of possibilities. For that, we will not use discrete multisets, but an extension of them where the multiplicity of the objects can be any positive real number.

The inspiration of this variant comes from the fact that, in vitro, we can control neither the application of the rules nor the exact number of objects in every membrane, but we deal with an approximate number of applications. If we allow to work with the concentrations of the objects in the membranes instead of the exact number of objects that are involved in the reactions, then we must deal with a non-integer number of applications of the rules. In this way, the multiplicity of an object will not reflect the exact number of identical copies of it in a membrane, but its concentration in the solution (a similar idea was firstly used in [2] in order to simulate de photosynthesis process by membrane devices).

Once we have an idea about what non-integer multiplicity can mean, and we establish non-discrete multisets as a theoretical tool to handle this idea (Section 2), we define and formalize in Section 3 non-discrete P systems. Such systems can contain a non-discrete multiset of objects in every membrane, and evolve by applying a non-integer amount of times every rule (of course, always under the assumption that there are objects enough for such an application).

G. Mauri et al. (Eds.): WMC5 2004, LNCS 3365, pp. 287–295, 2005.

In Section 4 we define the space of *extremal transitions* as the set of transitions consuming the maximal amount of objects in the usual sense of maximality (we cannot apply more rules simultaneously), and we study some simple geometric properties of them.

Section 5 is devoted to the study of some approximating properties on the computations of non-discrete P systems. For that, we define some distances in the set of multisets and transitions, and establish some bounds in the evolution of the system.

Finally, the paper closes with some conclusions and possible future work in the environment of non-discrete P systems.

2   Non-discrete Multisets

As it was proceeded also in [2], we can define a generalization of multisets by using non integer multiplicities in the following way.

Definition 1. *Let V be a finite alphabet. A* non-discrete multiset *(ND-multiset) over V is an application, $w : V \to \mathbb{R}^+$. We denote by $NDM(V)$ the set of non-discrete multisets over V.*

In a similar way to multisets, we can define the *support* of an ND-multiset $(supp(w))$, as well as the usual operations between them:

1. Addition: $(w_1 + w_2)(a) = w_1(a) + w_2(a)$.
2. Subtraction: $(w_1 - w_2)(a) = w_1(a) - w_2(a)$ (it is not an inner operation).
3. Arithmetic subtraction: $(w_1 \boxminus w_2)(a) = \max\{w_1(a) - w_2(a), 0\}$.
4. External product by real numbers: $(n \cdot w)(a) = n \cdot w(a)$.

and the usual relations:

1. $w_1 \subseteq w_2 \ (w_1 \leq w_2) \iff \forall a \in V(w_1(a) \leq w_2(a))$ (provides a partial order in $NDM(V)$).
2. $w_1 \neq w_2 \iff \exists a \in V(w_1(a) \neq w_2(a))$.

Finally, $\mathbf{0}$ stands for the empty ND-multiset $(\forall a \in V \ (\mathbf{0}(a) = 0))$.

3   Non-discrete P Systems

Now we formalize the variant of P systems that makes use of ND-multisets. In this variant we allow neither the use of dissolutions nor active membranes (creation, duplication, charges, etc.), but we include in it the (now) *classic* transition P systems (where we can transform and move objects between adjacent membranes) and the communication ones (where we only can move objects taking into account the elements inside and immediately outside of the membrane).

In order to do that, we define the *ball* of a membrane as the set of membranes adjacent with it (and itself).

Definition 2. *Let μ be a membrane structure (a directed tree). For every node of μ, x, the ball of x in μ is the set $B_\mu(x) = \{y \in \mu \mid x \to y \vee y \to x \vee y = x\}$ (usually, we write $B(x)$ instead of $B_\mu(x)$).*

In this context, a rule over a membrane structure is a pair of applications, indicating the objects consumed and the objects created, respectively, in every membrane. We say that a rule is associated with a membrane x, if the only membranes affected by the application of the rule are those adjacent to x.

Definition 3. *A rule over a membrane structure μ is an application $r : \mu \to NDM(V) \times NDM(V)$ (we will denote $r = (r_1, r_2)$).*
We say that the rule r is associated with $x \in \mu$ if the following condition holds:

$$\forall y \notin B(x) \ (r(y) = (\mathbf{0}, \mathbf{0})).$$

Example 1.
Let us consider the membrane structure $\mu = [_1 \ [_2 \ ]_2 \ [_3 \ ]_3 \ ]_1$, the alphabet $V = \{a, b, c, d\}$, and the following two rules, r (transition rule) and s (communicating rule), associated with membranes 2 and 3, respectively, written in the usual form:

$$r : ab \to c(d, out),$$
$$s : (ab, in; cd, out).$$

These rules are expressed in our system as:

$$r_1(1) = \mathbf{0}, \ r_1(2) = ab, \ r_1(3) = \mathbf{0},$$
$$r_2(1) = d, \ r_2(2) = c, \ r_2(3) = \mathbf{0},$$

and

$$s_1(1) = ab, \ s_1(2) = \mathbf{0}, \ s_1(3) = cd,$$
$$s_2(1) = cd, \ s_2(2) = \mathbf{0}, \ s_2(3) = ab.$$

(We use here the standard notation for multisets: $w \in NDM(V)$ will be represented by $a^{w(a)} b^{w(b)} c^{w(c)} d^{w(d)}$).

Note 1.
This representation of rules is useful not only in order to unify transition and communicating rules, but it also allows the generalization of this kind of rules from tree-like membrane structures to general graphs (or indeed hypergraphs, where the set of hyperedges are not pairs, but general subsets of vertices). For example, in a structure with 3 membranes, we can consider the following rule, r, that is not associated with any membrane, unless we extend the concept of membrane structure to capture more complex graphs:

$$r_1(1) = a, \ r_1(2) = b, \ r_1(3) = c,$$
$$r_2(1) = c, \ r_2(2) = a, \ r_2(3) = b.$$

Indeed, if dissolution is not allowed, then the relations between membranes are determined by the rules.

We define a non-discrete P system as a membrane structure with a set of rules over it.

Definition 4. *A non-discrete P system over an alphabet V is a pair $\Pi = (\mu, R)$, where μ is a membrane structure, and R is a finite set of rules over μ.*

A *cell* is defined by assigning an ND-multiset to every membrane of the structure.

Definition 5. *A cell for Π is an application $C : \mu \to NDM(V)$. The set of cells for Π will be denoted by $Cell(\Pi)$.*

Starting from a cell, a *transition* is a non-discrete application of the rules in a parallel manner. In this way, we can also see the transitions as ND-multisets over the set of rules, where the multiplicity of every rule indicates the number of times that the a rule is applied.

Definition 6. *Let $\Pi = (\mu, R)$ be a non-discrete P system, and let C be a cell for Π. A transition for C is a non-discrete multiset over R, $T \in NDM(R)$, such that for every $x \in \mu$*

$$\sum_{r \in R} T(r) \cdot r_1(x) \subseteq C(x).$$

We will denote by $Tr(C)$ the set of transitions for C.

Now, the formalization of the application of the rules according to one selected transition can be given.

Definition 7. *Let Π be a non-discrete P system, C be a cell for Π, and $T \in Tr(C)$. The cell obtained from C by the application of T is the cell $C' = T(C)$, such that for every $x \in \mu$:*

$$C'(x) = C(x) + \sum_{r \in R} T(r) \cdot r_2(x) - \sum_{r \in R} T(r) \cdot r_1(x).$$

If we give an enumeration $\{x_1, \ldots, x_j\}$ of the nodes of μ, and an enumeration $\{r^1, \ldots, r^N\}$ of the rules of R, then we can write a transition in the following matricial form:

$$[C'_1, \ldots, C'_j] = [C_1, \ldots, C_j] + [T_1, \ldots, T_N] \cdot \begin{bmatrix} r_2^1(x_1) - r_1^1(x_1) & \cdots & r_2^1(x_j) - r_1^1(x_j) \\ \vdots & \ddots & \vdots \\ r_2^N(x_1) - r_1^N(x_1) & \cdots & r_2^N(x_j) - r_1^N(x_j) \end{bmatrix},$$

where, C_i, C'_i, T_i stand for $C(x_i)$, $C'(x_i)$, $T(r_j)$, respectively.

This matrix form can be briefly written as

$$T(C)(x) = C(x) + T \cdot (R_2 - R_1)(x), \quad \forall x \in \mu,$$

and

$$T(C) = C + T \cdot (R_2 - R_1).$$

4   Extremal Transitions

The set of *extremal transitions* is the set of transitions consuming the maximal amount of objects, in the following sense.

Definition 8. *The set of* extremal transitions *for C is the set of maximal points of $Tr(C)$ (regarding the partial order defined in $NDM(R)$), that is,*

$$ExTr(C) = \{T \in Tr(C) :| \forall\, T' \in Tr(C)\ (T' \neq T \rightarrow \neg(T' \geq T))\}.$$

In other words, if we apply an extremal transition, then we cannot simultaneously apply further rules over the remaining objects.

As a difference with the discrete case, in the non-discrete one we obtain that the set of transitions has good geometrical properties.

Proposition 1. *Let Π be a non-discrete P system. For every cell C for Π we obtain that its set of transitions, $Tr(C)$, is a convex and compact set.*

Proof.
Let C be a cell for Π. To see that $Tr(C)$ is a convex set, let $T, T' \in Tr(C)$ be two transitions for C, and let $p \in [0, 1]$. We prove that $p \cdot T + (1-p) \cdot T' \in Tr(C)$. It is direct to check that, for all $r \in R$, $p \cdot T(r) + (1-p) \cdot T(r) \in \mathbb{R}^+$ holds.
Let $x \in \mu$. Then,

$$\sum_{r \in R} (p \cdot T(r) + (1-p) \cdot T'(r)) \cdot r_1(x) =$$

$$= p \cdot \sum_{r \in R} T(r) \cdot r_1(x) + (1-p) \cdot \sum_{r \in R} T'(r) \cdot r_1(x) \subseteq$$

$$\subseteq p \cdot C(x) + (1-p) \cdot C(x) = C(x).$$

Finally, it is easy to prove that $Tr(C)$ is compact, because it is a closed and bounded subset of some Euclidean space $\mathbb{R}^k$.   □

The previous result is not true for $ExTr(C)$, that is, it is possible that this set will not be convex. Of course, $Extr(C)$ is a compact set.

Example 2.
Given the rules $r : ab \rightarrow b$ and $s : a^2c \rightarrow b$ in a membrane, if the content of this membrane in a configuration is a^2bc, it is clear that, in the discrete case, we can apply the rules in a maximal parallel manner in two ways: $\{(1, 0), (0, 1)\}$. But, if we allow a non-integer number of applications of the rules, then we obtain the following set of transitions (each of them producing different computations in the evolution of the P system):

$$Ap = \{(\alpha_1, \alpha_2) \mid \alpha_1 + 2\alpha_2 \leq 2,\ \alpha_1 \leq 1,\ \alpha_2 \leq 1, \alpha_1, \alpha_2 \in \mathbb{R}^+\}.$$

In Fig. 1 the obtained sets of transitions, Tr, and extremal transitions, $ExTr$, are represented.

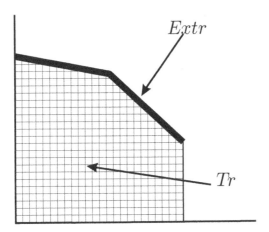

Fig. 1. Sets of transitions and extremal transitions

5   Geometric Aspects of Non-discrete P Systems

In this section we present some metrics in order to prove that, in case of finite computations (but not only in these ones), we can confine ourselves to the study of non-discrete P systems where the multiplicities and the number of applications are rational numbers.

We can consider that all above objects (non-discrete multisets, cells, transitions, sets of transitions, etc.) are subsets or applications in finite-dimensional Euclidean spaces, so all the metrics we define here will be the usual ones.

Lemma 1. *The following mappings are metrics (in the corresponding spaces):*

1. $d_{NDM(V)} : NDM(V) \times NDM(V) \longrightarrow \mathbb{R}^+$, *defined by*

$$d_{NDM(V)}(w_1, w_2) = \max\{|w_1(a) - w_2(a)| \mid a \in V\},$$

2. $d_C : Cell(C) \times Cell(C) \longrightarrow \mathbb{R}^+$, *defined by*

$$d_C(C, C') = \max\{d_{NDM(V)}(C(x), C'(x)) \mid x \in \mu\}.$$

We denote by d_{Tr} the restriction of $d_{NDM(R)}$ to Tr.

By using this metric we can define something like a continuity in the application of the transitions. We can *control* the evolution of the system by taking *near* transitions.

Lemma 2. *Let Π be a non-discrete P system. There exist $N, K > 0$ (only depending on Π) such that for every cell C for Π and $T, T' \in Tr(C)$, if $d_{Tr}(T, T') < \varepsilon$, then*

$$d_C(T(C), T'(C)) < KN\,\varepsilon.$$

Proof.

We take $N = card(R)$. Because R is a finite set, there exists $K > 0$ such that:

$$\forall r \in R \ \forall a \in V \ (r_1(x)(a) \leq K \ \wedge \ r_2(x)(a) \leq K).$$

Let $x \in \mu$ and $a \in V$; we have

$$|T(C)(x)(a) - T'(C)(x)(a)| = |\sum_{r \in R}(T(r) - T'(r)) \cdot (r_2(x)(a) - r_1(x)(a))| \leq$$

$$\leq \sum_{r \in R}|T(r) - T'(r)| \cdot |r_2(x)(a) - r_1(x)(a)| < KN \ \varepsilon$$

From here we obtain $d_C(T(C), T'(C)) < KN \ \varepsilon.$ □

Moreover, we can prove something similar considering two different cells.

Lemma 3. *Let Π be a non-discrete P system, C, C' be two cells for Π, and T, T' be two transitions for C and C', respectively. Then*

$$d_C(T(C), T'(C')) \leq d_C(C, C') + KN \cdot d_{Tr}(T, T').$$

Proof.

Let $x \in \mu$, and $a \in V$. We have

$$|T(C)(x)(a) - T'(C')(x)(a)| =$$

$$= |C(x)(a) + \sum_{r \in R}T(r)(r_2(x) - r_1(x))(a) -$$

$$-C'(x)(a) - \sum_{r \in R}T'(r)(r_2(x) - r_1(x))(a)| \leq$$

$$\leq |C(x)(a) - C'(x)(a)| + |\sum_{r \in R}(T(r) - T'(r))(r_2(x) - r_1(x))(a)| \leq$$

$$\leq |C(x)(a) - C'(x)(a)| + \sum_{r \in R}|T(r) - T'(r)| \cdot |(r_2(x) - r_1(x))(a)| \leq$$

$$\leq d_C(C, C') + KN \cdot d_{Tr}(T, T')$$ □

We can go further and consider a metric between the sets of transitions.

Definition 9. *Let Π be a non-discrete P system, C, C' be two cells for Π. We define*

$$d(Tr(C), Tr(C')) = \max\{d(T, Tr(C')) \mid T \in Tr(C)\},$$

where $d(T, Tr(C')) = \min\{d_{Tr}(T, T') \mid T' \in Tr(C')\}.$

Proposition 2. *In this context, the application Tr is continuous. That is,*

$$\forall \varepsilon > 0 \ \exists \delta > 0 \ (d_C(C, C') < \delta \rightarrow d(Tr(C), Tr(C')) < \varepsilon).$$

Proof. This result has a very technical proof, whose main idea is to consider the continuous dependence of the transitions on the content of the cells.   □

The combination of the previous two results allows us to obtain a general approximating procedure in the evolution of a non-discrete P system.

Until now, what we can do is to approximate one step (and, of course, a finite computation) of the evolution of a non-discrete P system by another one where the transitions verify the condition of not being "too far" form the original ones, and obtaining a *similar* final cell (in content). Of course, since the set of transitions are convex, this fact can be used in order to approximate computations by using only rational applications of rules. But, can we do the same if we consider only extremal transitions? The answer to this question is, in general, negative; nevertheless, if we add some (computationally usual) restrictions in our P systems, we can give an affirmative answer.

Note 2. If we restrict:

- the rules, to be applications $r : \mu \rightarrow NDM_{\mathbb{Q}}(V) \times NDM_{\mathbb{Q}}(V)$, where $NDM_{\mathbb{Q}}(V)$ stands for non-discrete multisets where only rational values are considered,
- and we start from a *rational* cell (that is, $\forall\, x \in \mu\ \forall\, a \in V\ (C(x)(a) \in \mathbb{Q})$),

then we can make approximations of extremal transitions by means of extremal transitions where all the values are rational. That is,

$$\forall\, \varepsilon > 0\ \forall\, T \in ExTr(C)\ \exists\, T' \in Extr(C) \cap \mathbb{Q}^N\ (d_{Tr}(T, T') < \varepsilon).$$

Of course, the application of a rational extremal transition over a rational cell provides a rational cell, so we can iterate this procedure along finite computations and obtain an approximation of the computation by means of using only rational numbers.

6   Conclusions

This work is intended as an attempt to provide a new variant of P systems where only some approximate behaviors of the real reactions inside the cell are known. This approach is currently used in the development of probabilistic software tools allowing the user to work with concentrations of the reactants, not with the exact number of each of them, trying to be nearer of the real case in laboratory.

But, also, this variant can provide new problems related with some other topics. As an example, from the case we have studied here we can observe that the procedure to obtain new cells by the application of the transitions have some similarities with *iterated functions*, and maybe some results from this topic can be applied here. Moreover, if we consider a probability function associated with the space of transitions, we come into the world of *iterated random functions*, where a lot of interesting results were obtained in the last years. We can also obtain a new kind of probabilistic non-discrete P systems where the probabilistic measure is defined over a continuous domain.

About the relationship between these P systems and the classical ones, one question arises: how can we simulate/approximate the functioning of these devices by means of classical P systems?

Of course, of a high interest can be the study of these devices as dynamical systems. Can they have a chaotical behavior (in the sense that two near cells produce very different evolution, not only in content, but in the irrespective orbits of the transitions)? If we model some parts of the cell with these P systems, will we obtain that the life of the cell is in the edge of this chaos? The study of complex systems and their relations with living organizations is now starting, and maybe P systems can provide a new mathematical tool to attack and understand this kind of problems [1].

Acknowledgment

The support for this research through the project TIC2002-04220-C03-01 of the Ministerio de Ciencia y Tecnología of Spain, cofinanced by FEDER funds, is gratefully acknowledged.

References

1. A.L. Barabási, Z. N. Oltvai. Network biology: Understanding the cell's functional organization, *Nature Review Genetics*, **5**, 2 (2004), 101–13.
2. T.Y. Nishida. Simulations of photosynthesis by a K-Subset transforming system with membranes, *Fundamenta Informaticae*, **49**, 1 (2002), 249–259.
3. A. Obtulowicz, Gh. Păun. (In search of) Probabilistic P systems, *BioSystems*, **70**, 2 (2003), 107–121.
4. Gh. Păun. Computing with membranes, *Journal of Computer and System Sciences*, **61**, 1 (2000), 108–143.
5. Gh. Păun. *Membrane Computing. An Introduction*, Springer-Verlag, Berlin, 2002.
6. M.J. Pérez-Jiménez, F. Sancho-Caparrini. A formalization of basic P systems, *Fundamenta Informaticae*, 49, 1–3 (2002), 261–272.

Reducing the Size of Extended Gemmating P Systems*

Erzsébet Csuhaj-Varjú and György Vaszil

Computer and Automation Research Institute,
Hungarian Academy of Sciences,
Kende utca 13-17, 1111 Budapest, Hungary
{csuhaj, vaszil}@sztaki.hu

Abstract. We improve some results concerning the size of P systems with gemmation of mobile membranes. We show that systems with meta-priority relations and without (in/out) communication rules generate any recursively enumerable language with three membranes, thus we present an optimal result on the necessary number of membranes to obtain computational completeness. In the case of gemmating P systems with only pre-dynamical rules, we prove that four membranes are sufficient to generate any recursively enumerable language.

1   Introduction

Membrane systems, or P systems were introduced in [6] as distributed parallel computing devices of a biochemical type. The model is inspired by the functioning of the living cell: it consists of a membrane structure composed of several cell-membranes, hierarchically embedded in a membrane called the skin membrane. The membranes delimit regions and contain objects which evolve according to given evolution rules associated to the regions. Computations of the system are performed by the parallel and non-deterministic evolution of the contents of the membranes.

For a detailed introduction to the area of P systems, the interested reader is referred to the monograph [7]. A survey and an up-to-date bibliography of the field with an amount of additional information can be found at the web address http://psystems.disco.unimib.it.

In this paper we consider P systems with gemmation of mobile membranes or gemmating P systems, introduced in [3], which represent membrane systems with a new kind of communication.

The biological background of this new model can be summarized as follows: The cellular membranes are selectively permeable to small substances as, for example, water and gases, but not to bigger substances as proteins. These bigger substances are communicated among the cells by means of vesicles, encased on

---

* Research supported in part by the Hungarian Scientific Research Fund "OTKA" Grants No. T 042529 and F 037567 and the project "MolCoNet" IST-2001-32008.

their cytosolic face by a specific protein which causes their budding from the membrane. When the vesicle fuses with its target membrane, the carried proteins are introduced inside it, where they can undergo different chemical reactions. For more details see [8, 10]. This process can be modelled by so-called mobile membranes, that is, we can consider some objects in the original membrane to be transported by means of small membranes to a target membrane.

Gemmating P systems are with simple membrane structures, where the skin membrane contains only elementary membranes with string objects which correspond to proteins or any other structured bigger substances. These strings evolve according to operations with biochemical motivations, namely mutation, replication and splitting. The mutation in this case corresponds to the application of a context-free rule. Any membrane is provided with a set of classical evolution rules, that is, rules representing the previously mentioned operations and a set of so-called pre-dynamical rules, which are rules defining the gemmation of the mobile membranes. There is a meta-priority relation defined between the set of classical evolution rules and the set of pre-dynamical rules which is needed to simulate the completion of the maturation path of an object. A pre-dynamical rule is a particular variant of an evolution rule which also indicates the membrane where the string must be communicated. After a pre-dynamical rule is used, the modified string object is transported into the target membrane, and from then it will evolve according to the rules of this membrane. This procedure corresponds to the gemmation and the fusion of the mobile membrane. In particular, the output of the system is due to the fusion of a mobile membrane with the skin membrane: this process causes the release of the objects outside the system and simulates the biological process of exocytosis.

In [2, 3] the computational power of P systems with gemmation of mobile membranes was examined. It was shown that these systems are as powerful as the Turing machines, in the case of extended systems (where a terminal set of objects is distinguished) with eight membranes [2] or with nine membranes if only pre-dynamical rules are allowed. These bounds were improved to five and six, respectively, in [1].

We continue the study of this area and show that extended systems with meta-priority relations but no (in/out) communication rules generate any recursively enumerable language with at most three membranes. We also show that these P systems with two membranes determine the class of context-free languages, thus the previous result gives an optimal size bound for these variants of membrane systems to obtain computational completeness. We also prove that gemmating P systems with only pre-dynamical rules and with four membranes generate any recursively enumerable language. This latter result can also be found in [4], obtained at the same time but independently from our one and using another technique for proving the statement. Gemmating P systems with only pre-dynamical rules and with two membranes determine the class of finite languages, while having three membranes they define a language class which properly contains the class of regular languages.

2 Preliminaries and Definitions

We first recall the notions and the notations we use. For more on the basic notions of formal language theory refer to [9]. Let V be an alphabet, let V^* be the set of all words over V, and let $V^+ = V^* - \{\varepsilon\}$, where ε denotes the empty word. The mirror image, or the reverse of a word $x \in V^*$ is denoted by x^R, the set of natural numbers is denoted by $\mathbb{N}$. We denote by FIN, REG, CF, and RE the class of finite, regular, context-free, and recursively enumerable languages, respectively. RE is the class accepted by Turing machines or generated by phrase structure grammars.

Now we present the notion of an Extended Post Correspondence (or EPC in short) from [5] and then define a set of context-free rewriting rules which can be derived from any such EPC and which will be used in the proofs of the results.

Definition 1. Let $\Sigma = \{a_1, \dots, a_n\}$, $1 \le n$, be an alphabet. An *Extended Post Correspondence* (an EPC) is a pair

$$E = (\{(u_1, v_1), \dots, (u_m, v_m)\}, (z_{a_1}, \dots, z_{a_n})),$$

where $u_i, v_i, z_{a_j} \in \{0,1\}^*$, $1 \le i \le m$, $1 \le j \le n$. The *language represented by* E, denoted by $L(E)$, is the following:

$$L(E) = \{x_1 \dots x_r \in \Sigma^* \mid \text{there are } i_1, \dots i_s \in \{1, \dots, m\}, s \ge 1,$$
$$\text{such that } u_{i_1} \dots u_{i_s} z_{x_1} \dots z_{x_r} = v_{i_1} \dots v_{i_s}\}.$$

It is known (see [5]) that for each recursively enumerable language L there exists an EPC E such that $L(E) = L$.

Definition 2. Let E be an EPC as above, and let g, h be two mappings $g, h : \{0,1\} \to \{A, B, C\}^*$ defined as $g(0) = AB$, $h(0) = C$, $g(1) = A$, $h(1) = BC$. Let us define a set P_E of rewriting rules containing the productions

$$\begin{aligned}
S &\to g(u_i) S h(v_i^R), \quad 1 \le i \le m, \\
S &\to S', \\
S' &\to g(z_a) S' a, \qquad a \in \Sigma, \\
S' &\to \varepsilon,
\end{aligned}$$

constructed according to the EPC E.

Let us now observe the sentential forms that these rules generate. Starting from the symbol S, the rules of P_E generate strings of the form

$$g(u_{i_1} \dots u_{i_s} z_{x_1} \dots z_{x_r}) \, x_r \dots x_1 \, h((v_{i_1} \dots v_{i_s})^R),$$

where if $u_{i_1} \dots u_{i_s} z_{x_1} \dots z_{x_r} = v_{i_1} \dots v_{i_s}$, then $x_1 \dots x_r \in L(E)$, as above.

Let $u = u_{i_1} \dots u_{i_s}$, $v = v_{i_1} \dots v_{i_s}$, and $z_w = z_{x_1} \dots z_{x_r}$, for some $w = x_1 \dots x_r \in L(E)$. If $u z_w = v$, then the following properties must hold: The string $g(u z_w)$ either starts with AB or with AA, and $h(v^R)$ either ends with BC

or with CC. Furthermore, if $g(uz_w)$ starts with AB, then $h(v^R)$ ends with CC, if $g(uz_w)$ starts with AA, then $h(v^R)$ ends with BC.

Based on these properties we might use the following procedure to produce any recursively enumerable language $L = L(E)$ for some EPC E.

Definition 3. Take an EPC E with $L = L(E)$, and construct the rule set P_E as above. The procedure $PROC_E$ consists of the instructions as follows.

Starting with the symbol S, use the rules of P_E to generate a string of the form $\alpha = g(uz_w)\, w^R\, h(v^R)$, u, z_w, v as above. Execute the following instructions on α.

1. Obtain α' by cutting an A from the left end of α.

2. Obtain α'' by cutting a C from the right end of α'.

3. Obtain α''' by cutting a B either from the left end or from the right end of α''.

4. If $\alpha''' = x_r \ldots x_1$, the reverse of $w = x_1 \ldots x_r$, then $w \in L$, otherwise start again with executing the first instruction on α'''.

If at some point cutting the symbols from the ends of the string is not possible in the order required by the instructions above, then we might stop the procedure without any explicit conclusion. However, it is ensured that for each $w \in L$ there exists at least one α of the form above which leads us to the result of $w \in L$, thus, the procedure above produces all words belonging to $L(E)$.

Now we present the basic notions of membrane computing and then also define P systems with gemmation of mobile membranes. The interested reader may find more detailed information on the theory of P systems in the monograph [7].

Let U be a set of of objects, called the *universe*. A multiset is a pair $M = (V, f)$, where $V \subseteq U$ and $f : U \to \mathbb{N}$ is a mapping which assigns to each object from V its multiplicity, and $f(a) = 0$ for $a \notin V$. The support of $M = (V, f)$ is the set $supp(M) = \{a \in V \mid f(a) \geq 1\}$. If $supp(M)$ is a finite set, then M is called a finite multiset. The set of all finite multisets over the set V is denoted by V°.

We say that $a \in M = (V, f)$ if $a \in supp(M)$, furthermore, $M_1 = (V_1, f_1) \subseteq M_2 = (V_2, f_2)$ if $supp(M_1) \subseteq supp(M_2)$ and for all $a \in V_1$, $f_1(a) \leq f_2(a)$. The union of two multisets is defined as $(M_1 \cup M_2) = (V_1 \cup V_2, f')$ where for all $a \in V_1 \cup V_2$, $f'(a) = f_1(a) + f_2(a)$, the difference is defined for $M_2 \subseteq M_1$ as $(M_1 - M_2) = (V_1, f'')$ where $f''(a) = f_1(a) - f_2(a)$ for all $a \in V_1$, and the intersection of two multisets is $(M_1 \cap M_2) = (V_1 \cap V_2, f''')$ where for $a \in V_1 \cap V_2$, $f'''(a) = min(f_1(a), f_2(a))$. We say that M is empty, denoted by ϵ, if its support is empty, $supp(M) = \emptyset$. When giving the elements $x_1, \ldots, x_n$ of a multiset M, we use double brackets as $M = \{\{x_1, \ldots, x_n\}\}$ to distinguish from the notation used for sets.

A P system is a structure of hierarchically embedded membranes, each having a label and enclosing a region containing a multiset of objects and possibly other membranes. The out-most membrane is unique and it is called the skin membrane. The membrane structure is denoted by a sequence of matching parentheses where the matching pairs have the same label as the membranes they represent. If $x \in \{[_i,]_i \mid 1 \leq i \leq n\}^*$ is such a string of matching parentheses of length $2n$, denoting a structure where membrane i contains membrane j, then $x = x_1 \, [_i \, x_2 \, [_j \, x_3 \,]_j \, x_4 \,]_i \, x_5$ for some $x_k \in \{[_l,]_l \mid 1 \leq l \leq n, \, l \neq i, j\}^*$, $1 \leq k \leq 5$. If membrane i contains membrane j, and there is no other membrane, k, such that k contains j and i contains k (x_2 and x_4 above are strings of matching parentheses themselves), then we say that membrane i is the parent membrane of j, denoted by $i = parent(j)$, and at the same time, membrane j is one of the child membranes of i.

By the contents of a region associated to a given membrane, we mean the multiset of objects which can be found inside the corresponding membrane but outside of all of its child membranes. The evolution of the contents of the regions of a P system is described by rules associated to the regions. Applying the rules synchronously in each region, the system performs a computation by passing from one configuration to another one.

By [2], gemmating P systems use only membrane structures of depth 2. The skin membrane will be always labelled with the number 0, while the inner membranes will be labelled with the numbers $1, \ldots, n$.

Gemmating P systems work with string-objects and use evolution rules which are able to multiply the number of the strings. There are three types of rules defined with biochemical inspiration: mutation, replication, and splitting of a string. In this paper we use only mutation rules without in/out communication which are context free rules of the form $a \to u$, where $a \in V$ and $u \in V^*$, V being the alphabet of the string objects.

With each region $i = 0, 1, \ldots, n$ we associate two distinct sets of rules:

- A set C_i of classical evolution rules, that is, a set of mutation rules of the above form, and

- a set D_i of pre-dynamical evolution rules, that is, a set of mutation rules of the form $a \to u$, with $a \in V$, such that given a string $w_1 = w'_1 a$ (or $w_1 = a w'_1$) we obtain $w_2 = w'_1 u$ ($w_2 = u w'_1$, respectively), where $u = u' @_j$ ($u = @_j u'$, respectively) with $w'_1, u'_1 \in V^*$. The letter @ is a special symbol not in V and $j \in \{0, 1, \ldots, n\}, j \neq i$.

Pre-dynamical rules may introduce the special symbol $@_j$ only at the ends of the string. We will always consider the set D_0 as an empty set, that is no pre-dynamical rule will ever be defined for the skin membrane. When a symbol $@_j$ appears in some string w present in a membrane i, for $j \neq i$, then inside the P system two sequential and dynamical communication processes take place. We say that a mobile membrane carries the string w from the originating membrane i to the target membrane j.

To keep the construction closer to the functioning of real cells, we define a meta-priority relation between the rules of set C_i and D_i, for all $i = 1, \ldots, n$, by which all applicable classical rules in C_i must be used before any applicable pre-dynamical rule in D_i. We remark that we do not define any priority relation between rules in the set C_i neither between rules in the set D_i.

Definition 4. An extended P system Π with gemmation of mobile membranes of degree $n + 1$, $n \geq 0$, is

$$\Pi = (V, T, \mu, I_0, \ldots, I_n, (C_0, D_0), (C_1, D_1), \ldots, (C_n, D_n)),$$

where:

- V is an alphabet not containing the symbols $@_0, @_1, \ldots, @_n$,
- $T \subseteq V$ is the output (terminal) alphabet,
- $\mu = [_0 [_1]_1 [_2]_2 \cdots [_{n-1}]_{n-1} [_n]_n]_0$ is a membrane structure of depth 2 and degree $n + 1$,
- I_i, $1 \leq i \leq n$, are finite multisets over V^+,
- (C_i, D_i), $0 \leq i \leq n$, are sets of classical evolution rules and sets of pre-dynamical evolution rules, respectively. The set C_i has a meta-priority over D_i as far as the application of all of its rules is concerned. The set D_0 is empty.

An extended gemmating P system works as follows. The regions are processed simultaneously, that is, in every step, inside each region, all the strings which can be the subject of an evolution rule are simultaneously rewritten. The rules to be applied can be nondeterministically chosen among all the applicable rules in accordance with the meta-priority relation defined over the set of classical rules and the set of pre-dynamical rules. This means that no pre-dynamical rule $d \in D_i$ can be applied if there exists at least one classical rule $c \in C_i$ which is applicable. At each step of a computation a string can be rewritten by one rule only. The strings resulting after the application of a rule can remain inside the membrane where they are placed, or can be communicated by mobile membranes to the regions specified by the target indications $@_i$, $0 \leq i \leq n$.

At any given moment, the membrane structure together with all multi-sets of objects associated with the regions defined by the membrane structure form the configuration of the system. However, since we do not consider split-ting/recombination rules, the processing of each string is independent of the other strings present in the regions. This means that instead of simultaneously keeping track of every multiset of objects that can be found in the regions of the system, we might consider the strings traveling through the regions of the membrane structure independently of the contents of the region.

Definition 5. Let $[w]_i$ denote a string over V present in region i, $1 \leq i \leq n$. We say that

- $[w]_i$ directly derives $[w']_i$ by a classical evolution rule, denoted as $[w]_i \Rightarrow [w']_i$ if $w = w_1 a w_2$, $w' = w_1 u w_2$, and $a \rightarrow u \in C_i$, or

- [w]$_i$ directly derives [w']$_j$ by a pre-dynamical rule, denoted as [w]$_i$ $\Rightarrow$ [w']$_j$ if $w = a_1 \ldots a_m$, $a_k \to u \notin C_i$ for any k, $1 \leq k \leq m$, and any $u \in V^*$, but $w = w_1 a$ (or $w = a w_1$) and $w' = w_1 u$ ($w' = u w_1$, respectively), for some $a \to u@_j \in D_i$ ($a \to @_j u \in D_i$, respectively).

A sequence of transitions forms a computation. A computation halts when there is no rule which can be applied to any string in the current configuration. The output of the P system Π (or the language of Π) is the set of strings over T expelled from the system during a halting computation, that is, the set of strings sent to region 0 during the computation. Non-halting computations provide no output.

Definition 6. Let Π be an extended gemmating P system of degree $n + 1$, for $n \geq 0$, as above. The language generated by Π is the set of strings

$$L(\Pi) = \{ w' \in T^* \mid w \in I_i \text{ and } [\, w\,]_i \Rightarrow^* [\, w'\,]_0 \text{ during a halting}$$
$$\text{computation of } \Pi,\ 1 \leq i \leq n \},$$

where $\Rightarrow^*$ denotes the reflexive and transitive closure of $\Rightarrow$.

Let $EGemP_n(MPri, n(in/out))$ and $EGemP_n(Dyn)$ denote the class of languages generated by extended gemmating P systems of degree n with meta-priority but without the use of in/out communication rules, and the class of languages generated by systems degree n with pre-dynamical rules only, respectively.

3   The Size of Extended Gemmating P Systems

We first show that extended gemmating P systems with meta-priority relations but no (in/out) communication rules generate any recursively enumerable language with at most three membranes. Since these P systems with two membranes determine the class of context-free languages, the obtained result gives an optimal size bound for these variants of membrane systems to obtain computational completeness.

Theorem 1. $EGemP_3(MPri, n(in/out)) = RE$.

Proof. Our proof is based on the procedure outlined in Definition 3,. Let $L \subseteq \Sigma^*$, let E be an Extended Post Correspondence as above with $L^R = L(E)$, and let P_E be the set of rewriting rules based on the EPC E as described above.
Let $\Pi = (V, \Sigma, \mu, I_0, I_1, I_2, (\emptyset, \emptyset), (C_1, D_1), (C_2, D_2))$ where $I_0 = I_2 = \epsilon$, and

$$V = \Sigma \cup \{S, S', A, B, C, C', C'', C''', T, T'\},$$
$$\mu = [_0\ [_1\ ]_1\ [_2\ ]_2\ ]_0,$$
$$I_1 = \{\{S\}\},$$
$$C_1 = P_E \cup \{C \to C', C'' \to C''', T \to T'\},$$

$$D_1 = \{A \rightarrow @_2 T, C''' \rightarrow @_2\},$$
$$C_2 = \{C' \rightarrow C'', T' \rightarrow \varepsilon, C''' \rightarrow C\},$$
$$D_2 = \{B \rightarrow @_0, B \rightarrow @_1, T \rightarrow @_1 T'\}.$$

This system works as follows. Starting with the start symbol S in I_1, the rules of P_E and $C \rightarrow C'$ generate a string of the form $uzwv$, $uz \in \{A, B\}^*$, $w \in \Sigma^*$, $v \in \{B, C'\}^*$ where if uz and v can be deleted using the instructions of the procedure $PROC_E$ in the previous section (with cutting C' instead of C in step 2), then $w \in L$.

Now, using the pre-dynamical rules of D_1, an A on the left end of $uzwv$ is changed to T, and the result is sent to region 2. Here the rules of C_2 rewrite every C' to C''. The result is sent back to region 1 by the pre-dynamical rules of D_2 and at the same time either a B is cut off the right end of the string, or the T on the left end is changed to T'. (If $B \rightarrow @_0$ is used, then the computation produces no result, since the nonterminal T is still present in the string sent out of the system.) In the first case, when T is not changed to T', the rules $T \rightarrow T$ of C_1 lead the computation to an infinite loop. In the second case, all C'' is rewritten to C''' and the result is sent back to region 2 after cutting off a C''' from the right end. Now T' is erased, all C''' is changed to C, and the result is sent back to region 1 by cutting off a B from the left or right end of the string, or sent out of the system by $B \rightarrow @_0$. If the string is sent out and it is terminal, then it is the reverse of some $w \in L^R = L(E)$, thus it is an element of $(L^R)^R = L$. If it is not sent out, then the system continues in the same way by cutting symbols off the ends of the string as long as it either enters an infinite loop, or sends out a non-terminal string, or produces a result by sending out a terminal word.

These steps execute instructions of the procedure $PROC_E$ described in the previous section, so our statement is proved.   □

In order to demonstrate that the above result is optimal, we note that

$$EGemP_2(MPri, n(in/out)) = CF.$$

Certainly, in this case, the only membrane which is able to modify the string is membrane 1. Furthermore, a word can be sent out to membrane 0 only if no mutation (context-free) rule of membrane 1 can be applied to it. Then, it is easy to see that for any context-free grammar $G = (N, T, P, S)$, where N is the set of nonterminals, T is the set of terminals, P is the set of productions, and S is the start symbol, the language $L(G)$ of G can be generated by the extended gemmating P system Π, with meta-priority relations but no (in/out) communication rules and with two membranes, where membrane 1 is defined by $I_1 = \{S\}$, $C_1 = P$, and $D_1 = \{a \rightarrow @_0 \mid a \in T\}$. If the empty word is in $L(G)$, then we add the rule $S \rightarrow @_0$ to D_1. The fact, that no more than a context-free language can be obtained by these systems is obvious.

Now we prove that gemmating P systems with only pre-dynamical rules and with four membranes generate any recursively enumerable language. These variants of P systems with two membranes determine the class of finite languages, while having three membranes they define a language class which properly contains the class of regular languages.

Theorem 2. $EGemP_4(Dyn) = RE$.

Proof. Let $L \subseteq \Sigma^*$ where $\Sigma = \{a_1, \ldots, a_n\}$, let E be an Extended Post Correspondence as above with $L^R = L(E)$, and let P_E be the set of rewriting rules based on the EPC E as described above. Let the rules of P_E be denoted as

$$P_E = \{S \to \alpha_i S \beta_i, \ S \to S', \ S' \to \gamma_j S' a_j, \ S' \to \varepsilon \mid 1 \le i \le m, 1 \le j \le n\},$$

where $\alpha_i = g(u_i)$, $\beta_i = h(v_i^R)$, $\gamma_j = g(z_{a_j})$ for some pair (u_i, v_i), $1 \le i \le m$, and z_{a_j}, $a_j \in \Sigma$, $1 \le j \le n$, of the EPC E with mappings g, h as above.

Let $\Pi = (V, \Sigma, \mu, I_0, I_1, I_2, I_3, D_0, D_1, D_2, D_3)$, where $I_0 = I_2 = I_3 = \epsilon$, $D_0 = \emptyset$, and

$$
\begin{aligned}
V &= \Sigma \cup \{S_1, S_2, S_1', S_2', \bar{S}_1, X, \bar{X}, A, B, C, \$\}, \\
\mu &= [_0 \ [_1 \ ]_1 \ [_2 \ ]_2 \ [_3 \ ]_3 \ ]_0, \\
I_1 &= \{\{S_1 \gamma_i a_i S_2 \mid 1 \le i \le n\}\} \\
&\quad \cup I_1' \text{ where } I_1' = \{\{\$\}\} \text{ if } \varepsilon \in L, \text{ otherwise } I_1' = \epsilon, \\
D_1 &= \{S_1' \to @_2 \bar{S}_1 X^{2i} S_1' \alpha_i, \ S_2' \to \beta_i S_2' \bar{X}^{2i} @_3, \ S_1 \to @_2 S_1', \\
&\quad S_1 \to @_2 \bar{S}_1 X^{2m+2j} S_1 \gamma_j, \ S_2 \to a_j S_2 \bar{X}^{2m+2j} @_3, \\
&\quad S_1' \to @_2 \bar{S}_1, \ S_2' \to @_2, \ B \to @_2, \ B \to @_0, \ S_2' \to @_0 \\
&\quad \$ \to @_0 \mid 1 \le i \le m, \ 1 \le j \le n\}, \\
D_2 &= \{\bar{S}_1 \to @_1, \ S_2 \to S_2' @_3, \ \bar{X} \to @_3, \ A \to @_3\}, \\
D_3 &= \{X \to @_2, \ S_1 \to @_1 S_1, \ S_1' \to @_1 S_1', \ C \to @_1\}.
\end{aligned}
$$

This system works by executing the procedure $PROC_E$ described in the previous section. First, a string of the form $uzwv$, $uz \in \{A, B\}^*$, $w \in \Sigma^+$, $v \in \{B, C\}^*$ is created where if uz and v can be deleted using the instructions of $PROC_E$, then $w \in L$. The empty word is treated separately, if $\varepsilon \in L$, then it is generated by the rule $\$ \to @_0$.

The work of the system starts in region 1 with words of the form $S_1 \gamma_i a_i S_2$, $1 \le i \le n$. Let $S_1 \gamma a S_2$ denote one of these strings and let us follow its possible route through the regions of Π. If the rule for S_2 is applied first, then there is no terminal word produced from this string, since

$$[\ S_1 \gamma a S_2 \ ]_1 \Rightarrow [\ S_1 \gamma a a_i S_2 \bar{X}^{2m+2i} \ ]_3 \Rightarrow [\ S_1 \gamma a a_i S_2 \bar{X}^{2m+2i} \ ]_1 \Rightarrow$$

1. $[\ \bar{S}_1 X^{2m+2j} S_1 \gamma_j \gamma a a_i S_2 \bar{X}^{2m+2i} \ ]_2 \Rightarrow$

   (a) $[\ X^{2m+2j} S_1 \gamma_j \gamma a a_i S_2 \bar{X}^{2m+2i} \ ]_1$

   (b) $[\ \bar{S}_1 X^{2m+2j} S_1 \gamma_j \gamma a a_i S_2 \bar{X}^{2m+2i-1} \ ]_3$

2. $[\ S_1' \gamma a a_i S_2 \bar{X}^{2m+2i} \ ]_2 \Rightarrow [\ S_1' \gamma a a_i S_2 \bar{X}^{2m+2i-1} \ ]_3 \Rightarrow$
   $[\ S_1' \gamma a a_i S_2 \bar{X}^{2m+2i-1} \ ]_1 \Rightarrow [\ \bar{S}_1 x \gamma a a_i S_2 \bar{X}^{2m+2i-1} \ ]_2 \Rightarrow$

(a) $[\ x\gamma a a_i S_2 \bar{X}^{2m+2i-1}\ ]_1$

(b) $[\ \bar{S}_1 x\gamma a a_i S_2 \bar{X}^{2m+2i-2}\ ]_3$ where $x = \varepsilon$ or $x = X^{2j} S'_1 \alpha_j$,

thus, one of the rules for S_1 has to be applied. (Note that γ either starts with an A or $\gamma = \varepsilon$, so no rule can be applied to the string of point 2.(a) in region 1. even if $x = \varepsilon$.) Let us assume first that the rule $S_1 \to @_2 \bar{S}_1 X^{2m+2i} S_1 \gamma_i$ is used.

$[\ S_1 \gamma a S_2\ ]_1 \Rightarrow [\ \bar{S}_1 X^{2m+2i} S_1 \gamma_i \gamma a S_2\ ]_2 \Rightarrow$

1. $[\ \bar{S}_1 X^{2m+2i} S_1 \gamma_i \gamma a S'_2\ ]_3$

2. $[\ X^{2m+2i} S_1 \gamma_i \gamma a S_2\ ]_1 \Rightarrow [\ X^{2m+2i} S_1 \gamma_i \gamma a a_j S_2 \bar{X}^{2m+2j}\ ]_3 \Rightarrow$
   $[\ X^{2m+2i-1} S_1 \gamma_i \gamma a a_j S_2 \bar{X}^{2m+2j}\ ]_2 \Rightarrow$
   $[\ X^{2m+2i-1} S_1 \gamma_i \gamma a a_j S_2 \bar{X}^{2m+2j-1}\ ]_3 \Rightarrow \ldots \Rightarrow$

   (a) $[\ X^{2i-2j} S_1 \gamma_i \gamma a a_j S_2\ ]_3 \Rightarrow [\ X^{2i-2j-1} S_1 \gamma_i \gamma a a_j S_2\ ]_2 \Rightarrow$
      $[\ X^{2i-2j-1} S_1 \gamma_i \gamma a a_j S'_2\ ]_3 \Rightarrow [\ X^{2i-2j-2} S_1 \gamma_i \gamma a a_j S'_2\ ]_2$

   (b) $[\ S_1 \gamma_i \gamma a a_j S_2 \bar{X}^{2j-2i}\ ]_3 \Rightarrow [\ S_1 \gamma_i \gamma a a_j S_2 \bar{X}^{2j-2i}\ ]_1 \Rightarrow$

      i. $[\ \bar{S}_1 X^{2m+2k} S_1 \gamma_k \gamma_i \gamma a a_j S_2 \bar{X}^{2j-2i}\ ]_2 \Rightarrow$

         A. $[\ X^{2m+2k} S_1 \gamma_k \gamma_i \gamma a a_j S_2 \bar{X}^{2j-2i}\ ]_1$

         B. $[\ \bar{S}_1 X^{2m+2k} S_1 \gamma_k \gamma_i \gamma a a_j S_2 \bar{X}^{2j-2i-1}\ ]_3$

      ii. $[\ S'_1 \gamma_i \gamma a a_j S_2 \bar{X}^{2j-2i}\ ]_2 \Rightarrow [\ S'_1 \gamma_i \gamma a a_j S_2 \bar{X}^{2j-2i-1}\ ]_3 \Rightarrow$
         $[\ S'_1 \gamma_i \gamma a a_j S_2 \bar{X}^{2j-2i-1}\ ]_1 \Rightarrow [\ \bar{S}_1 x\gamma_i \gamma a a_j S_2 \bar{X}^{2j-2i-1}\ ]_2 \Rightarrow$

         A. $[\ x\gamma_i \gamma a a_j S_2 \bar{X}^{2j-2i-1}\ ]_1$

         B. $[\ \bar{S}_1 x\gamma_i \gamma a a_j S_2 \bar{X}^{2j-2i-2}\ ]_3$ where $x = \varepsilon$ or $x = X^{2k} S'_1 \alpha_k$,

   (c) $[\ S_1 \gamma_i \gamma a a_j S_2\ ]_3 \Rightarrow [\ S_1 \gamma_i \gamma a a_j S_2\ ]_1$ (if $i = j$)

The system cannot produce any terminal word from the strings of the above cases except case 2.(c) where we have a word of the form $S_1 \gamma_i \gamma_j a_j a_i S_2$ for $S' \to \gamma_i S' a_i$ and $S' \to \gamma_j S' a_j$, rules of P_E associated to the EPC E, $1 \le i, j \le n$, $a_i, a_j \in \Sigma$. The system may continue by appending corresponding strings and terminal symbols to the left and right ends of the sentential form in the same way as above, producing strings of the form $S_1 \gamma_{i_1} \ldots \gamma_{i_j} a_{i_j} \ldots a_{i_1} S_2$, or it may choose to apply the rule $S_1 \to @_2 S'_1$, in which case we get

$[\ S_1 \gamma w S_2\ ]_1 \Rightarrow [\ S'_1 \gamma w S_2\ ]_2 \Rightarrow [\ S'_1 \gamma w S'_2\ ]_3 \Rightarrow [\ S'_1 \gamma w S'_2\ ]_1$

where $\gamma \in \{A, B\}^*$, $w \in \Sigma^+$.

We obtain a word of the same form if at the beginning of the work of the system, the rule $S_1 \to @_2 S'_1$ is applied on an initial sentential form $S_1 \gamma_i a_i S_2$ in region 1 as

$[\ S_1 \gamma_i a_i S_2\ ]_1 \Rightarrow [\ S'_1 \gamma_i a_i S_2\ ]_2 \Rightarrow [\ S'_1 \gamma_i a_i S'_2\ ]_3 \Rightarrow [\ S'_1 \gamma_i a_i S'_2\ ]_1,$

so we may continue by assuming that we have a string of the form $S'_1 \gamma w S'_2$ with γ, w as above in region 1.

If one of the rules for S'_2 are applied, then the derivation stops without producing a terminal word as

$$[S'_1 \gamma w S'_2]_1 \Rightarrow [S'_1 \gamma w]_2, \text{ or } [S'_1 \gamma w S'_2]_1 \Rightarrow [S'_1 \gamma w]_0,$$

or as

$$[S'_1 \gamma w S'_2]_1 \Rightarrow [S'_1 \gamma w \beta_i S'_2 \bar{X}^{2i}]_3 \Rightarrow [S'_1 \gamma w \beta_i S'_2 \bar{X}^{2i}]_1 \Rightarrow [\bar{S}_1 x \gamma w \beta_i S'_2 \bar{X}^{2i}]_2 \Rightarrow$$

1. $[x \gamma w \beta_i S'_2 \bar{X}^{2i}]_1$

2. $[\bar{S}_1 x \gamma w \beta_i S'_2 \bar{X}^{2i-1}]_3$ where $x = \varepsilon$, or $x = X^{2j} S'_1 \alpha_j$,

thus, one of the rules for S'_1 has to be applied. (Note that either the first symbol of γ is an A, or γ is empty, so even if $x = \varepsilon$, no rule can be applied to the sentential form of point 1. in region 1.)

If the rule $S'_1 \to @_2 \bar{S}_1$ is used we have the following possibilities.

$$[S'_1 \gamma w S'_2]_1 \Rightarrow [\bar{S}_1 \gamma w S'_2]_2 \Rightarrow [\gamma w S'_2]_1 \Rightarrow$$

1. $[\gamma w \beta_i S'_2 \bar{X}^{2i}]_3$

2. $[\gamma w]_2 \Rightarrow [\gamma' w]_3$ where $\gamma = A\gamma'$

3. $[\gamma w]_0$, so if $\gamma = \varepsilon$, then $w \in L$.

The strings of cases 1. and 2. cannot produce any terminal words, in case 3., if $\gamma = \varepsilon$, then w, the corresponding terminal word is correctly output by the system.

If the rule $S'_1 \to @_2 \bar{S}_1 X^{2i} S'_1 \alpha_i$ is applied, we have

$$[S'_1 \gamma w S'_2]_1 \Rightarrow [\bar{S}_1 X^{2i} S'_1 \alpha_i \gamma w S'_2]_2 \Rightarrow [X^{2i} S'_1 \alpha_i \gamma w S'_2]_1 \Rightarrow$$

1. $[X^{2i} S'_1 \alpha_i \gamma w]_0$

2. $[X^{2i} S'_1 \alpha_i \gamma w]_2$

3. $[X^{2i} S'_1 \alpha_i \gamma w \beta_j S'_2 \bar{X}^{2j}]_3 \Rightarrow [X^{2i-1} S'_1 \alpha_i \gamma w \beta_j S'_2 \bar{X}^{2j}]_2 \Rightarrow$
   $[X^{2i-1} S'_1 \alpha_i \gamma w \beta_j S'_2 \bar{X}^{2j-1}]_3 \Rightarrow \ldots \Rightarrow$

   (a) $[X^{2i-2j} S'_1 \alpha_i \gamma w \beta_j S'_2]_3 \Rightarrow [X^{2i-2j-1} S'_1 \alpha_i \gamma w \beta_j S'_2]_2$

   (b) $[S'_1 \alpha_i \gamma w \beta_j S'_2 \bar{X}^{2j-2i}]_3 \Rightarrow [S'_1 \alpha_i \gamma w \beta_j S'_2 \bar{X}^{2j-2i}]_1 \Rightarrow$
   $[\bar{S}_1 x \alpha_i \gamma w \beta_j S'_2 \bar{X}^{2j-2i}]_2 \Rightarrow$

      i. $[x \alpha_i \gamma w \beta_j S'_2 \bar{X}^{2j-2i}]_1$

      ii. $[\bar{S}_1 x \alpha_i \gamma w \beta_j S'_2 \bar{X}^{2j-2i-1}]_3$ where $x = \varepsilon$, or $x = X^{2k} S'_1 \alpha_k$

   (c) $[S'_1 \alpha_i \gamma w \beta_j S'_2]_3 \Rightarrow [S'_1 \alpha_i \gamma w \beta_j S'_2]_1$ (if $i = j$)

(Note that either the first symbol of $\alpha_i \gamma$ is an A, or $\alpha_i \gamma$ is empty, so even if $x = \varepsilon$, no rule can be applied to the sentential form of point 3.(b)i. in region 1.) Thus, the system produced a string of the form $S'_1 \alpha_i \gamma w \beta_i S'_2$ for some rule $S \to \alpha_i S \beta_i$, $1 \le i \le m$, of P_E associated to E. It may continue to add corresponding string pairs to the two ends of the string as above producing a string of the form $S_1'\alpha\gamma w\beta S_2'$, $\alpha, \gamma \in \{A, B\}^*$, $\beta \in \{B, C\}^*$, $w \in \Sigma^+$, or it may choose to apply the rule $S_1' \to @_2 \bar{S}_1$.

$$[\, S_1'\alpha\gamma w\beta S_2' \,]_1 \Rightarrow [\, \bar{S}_1\alpha\gamma w\beta S_2' \,]_2 \Rightarrow [\, \alpha\gamma w\beta S_2' \,]_1 \Rightarrow$$

1. $[\, \alpha\gamma w\beta\beta_i S_2' \bar{X}^{2i} \,]_3$

2. $[\, \alpha\gamma w\beta \,]_0$

3. $[\, \alpha\gamma w\beta \,]_2$

No terminal string is produced in case 1. In case 2., if $\alpha\gamma = \beta = \varepsilon$, then w is correctly output by the system. In case 3., the execution of the erasing instructions of $PROC_E$ may start. First an A is erased in region 2 and the string is sent to region 3, where a C is erased. These must have been on the left and right ends of the string, respectively. Now a B is erased in region 1 from one of the two ends of the string and it is either sent out of the system or the erasing process might continue in region 2.

From these considerations we see that Π correctly simulates $PROC_E$, thus our statement is proved.   □

Before closing the section, we add some remarks about the question of the optimality of the above result. We can immediately see that gemmating P systems with only pre-dynamical rules and two membranes determine the class of finite languages, thus

$$EGemP_2(Dyn) = FIN.$$

Certainly, any finite language $L = \{w_1, \ldots, w_n\}$, where $w_i \in T^*$, for some alphabet T and $1 \le i \le n$, can be obtained with a system where $I_1 = \{S\}$ and $D_1 = \{S \to w_i@_0 \mid 1 \le i \le n\}$. The fact that membrane 1 is able to send out only a finite number of words is obvious.

Moreover,

$$REG \subset EGemP_3(Dyn).$$

In this case, only membrane 1 and membrane 2 are able to modify the strings they have, by appending words to its left-end and/or to its right-end. The language of the system is determined by the interplay of these two membranes. Now, suppose that $G = (N, T, P, S)$, is a regular grammar with productions of the form $A \to aB$ and $A \to a$, where A, B are nonterminals and a is a terminal symbol. Then, the gemmating P system with $I_1 = \{S\}$, $I_2 = \emptyset$, $D_1 = \{A \to A'@_2\}$, and $D_2 = \{A' \to aB@_1 \mid A \to aB \in P\} \cup \{A' \to a@_0\}$ determines $L(G)$, the language of G. For the gemmating P system with $I_1 = \{AB\}$, $I_2 = \emptyset$, $D_1 = \{B \to bB@_2, B \to b@_2\}$, and $D_2 = \{A \to @_1 Aa, A \to a@_0\}$, we obtain the language $L = \{a^n b^n \mid n \ge 1\}$, which is a linear non-regular language. It is an open question how large computational power can be obtained with gemmating P systems with only pre-dynamical rules and three membranes.

4   Conclusion

In this paper we showed that extended gemmating P systems with even a minimal configuration, with three membranes, are as powerful as Turing machines. Since these constructions with 2 membranes can determine only the context-free language class, the obtained result is optimal. The result is interesting, since the size of the distributed architectures in molecular computing usually represents a separator between the class of regular languages and the class of recursively enumerable languages. In addition to this statement, we also proved that gemmating P systems with only pre-dynamical rules and with four membranes are computationally complete tools as well. These constructs with two membranes determine the class of finite languages, and with three membranes they are more powerful than the regular grammars.

References

1. D. Besozzi, E. Csuhaj-Varjú, G. Mauri, C. Zandron. Size and power of extending gemmating P systems. In: Gh. Păun, A. Riscos-Núñez, A. Romero-Jiménez, F. Sancho-Caparrini (eds.), *Proc. Second Brainstorming Week on Membrane Computing, Sevilla. 2-7 February 2004*, TR 01/2004, Research Group on Natural Computing, University of Sevilla, 2004, 92–101.
2. D. Besozzi, G. Mauri, Gh. Păun, C. Zandron. Gemmating P systems: collapsing hierarchies. *Theoretical Computer Science*, 296 (2):253–267, 2003.
3. D. Besozzi, C. Zandron, G. Mauri, N. Sabadini. P systems with gemmation of mobile membranes. In: A. Restivo, S. Ronchi Della Rocca, L. Roversi (eds.), *Proceedings of the 7th Italian Conference of Theoretical Computer Science 2001*, volume 2202 of *Lecture Notes in Computer Science*, Springer-Verlag, Berlin, 2001, 136–153.
4. R. Freund, A. Păun, M. Oswald. Gemmating P systems are computationally complete with four membranes. In: L. Ilie, D. Wotschke (eds.), *Descriptional Complexity of Formal Systems. London, Canada, 26-28 July, 2004*. Department of Computer Science, University of Western Ontario, Report no. 619, 2004, 191–203.
5. V. Geffert. Context-free-like forms for the phrase structure grammars. In: M.P. Chytil, L. Janiga, V. Koubek (eds.), *Mathematical Foundations of Computer Science 1988, 13th Symposium Carlsbad, Czechoslovakia, August 29 - September 2, 1988. Proceedings*, volume 324 of *Lecture Notes in Computer Science*, Springer-Verlag, 1988, 309–317.
6. Gh. Păun. Computing with membranes. *Journal of Computer and System Sciences*, 61 (1):108–143, 2000. (See also as *Turku Center for Computer Science Report no. 208*, 1998, www.tucs.fi).
7. Gh. Păun. *Membrane Computing. An Introduction*, Springer-Verlag, Berlin, 2002.
8. J.E. Rothman, L. Orci. Budding vesicles in cells. *Scientific American*, 274 (3):70–75, 1996.
9. G. Rozenberg, A. Salomaa (eds.). *Handbook of Formal Languages*, Springer-Verlag, Berlin, 1997.
10. D. Voet, J.G. Voet. *Biochemistry*, John Wiley and Sons Inc., 1995.

P Systems Generating Trees

Rudolf Freund[1], Marion Oswald[1], and Andrei Păun[2]

[1] Faculty of Informatics, Vienna University of Technology,
Favoritenstr. 9, A-1040 Wien, Austria
{rudi, marion}@emcc.at
[2] Department of Computer Science, Louisiana Tech University, Ruston
PO Box 10348, Louisiana, LA-71272 USA
apaun@latech.edu

Abstract. We consider P systems with active membranes, but without polarizations, yet with using membrane division and membrane generation, but as the result of a halting computation we do not take the terminal string generated in a designated output membrane, instead we consider the resulting tree representing the membrane structure of the final configuration as its result. We show that each recursively enumerable tree language can be obtained in that way generated by P systems with active membranes working on strings.

1 Introduction

In [11] membrane systems (then called P systems) were introduced as bio-inspired computing devices that work in a parallel and distributed way (see [13] for a comprehensive overview and [9] for actual developments in the area).

One main feature of membrane systems (P systems) is their membrane structure. So far, P systems have usually been considered as devices for generating or accepting multisets of symbol objects or string objects to be found in a designated output membrane in the final configuration of a halting configuration. In this paper we now consider the membrane structure itself as the result of a successful computation, i.e., we obtain a set of trees being computed as the membrane structures in the final configurations of halting computations.

P systems with active membranes were introduced (e.g., see [13]; for variants solving NP complete problems, e.g., see [7], [10], [14]) with rules for

(a) rewriting multisets;
(b) introducing objects into membranes;
(c) sending objects out of membranes;
(d) dissolving membranes;
(e) dividing elementary membranes;
(f) dividing non-elementary membranes.

All these rules were associated with membranes not only having a specific label, but also having assigned an electrical charge (also called polarization),

G. Mauri et al. (Eds.): WMC5 2004, LNCS 3365, pp. 309–319, 2005.
© Springer-Verlag Berlin Heidelberg 2005

which could be $+$, 0, and $-$. The rules of the forms (b) and (c) involving membranes could change the polarization(s) of the involved membrane(s), but never changed the label(s) of the membranes.

For generating tree languages, in this paper we use a special variant of P systems with active membranes with rules especially including division of elementary membranes, but without changing polarizations, which in fact means that we simply may forget the polarizations of membranes; moreover, we also use membrane generation rules as introduced in [4]. In contrast to the original model, where P systems with active membranes were working on symbol objects, in this paper (as in [4]) we consider P systems with active membranes working on string objects.

The rest of the paper is organized as follows: In the following section, we first recall some basic definitions from the theory of formal languages, give the definitions of deterministic register machines and then recall the most important results concerning the (universal) computational power of these devices. In the third section, we specify P systems with active membranes working on string objects; as we shall show as the main result of this paper, the model of P systems we chose to use allows us to generate each recursively enumerable tree language by interpreting the membrane structure of final configurations in halting computations as tree objects. A short summary and an outlook to future research conclude the paper.

2   Preliminaries

Before proceeding to a formal description of P systems, we first fix some basic notations in this section. For more notions as well as basic results from the theory of formal languages, the reader is referred to [1], [6], and [15].

For an alphabet V, by V^* we denote the free monoid generated by V under the operation of concatenation; the *empty string* is denoted by λ, and $V^* - \{\lambda\}$ is denoted by V^+. Any subset of V^+ is called a λ-*free (string) language*. Moreover, by $\mathbf{N}$ we denote the set of positive integers (or natural numbers). The family of λ-free recursively enumerable languages is denoted by RE, the family of sets of λ-free recursively enumerable languages over a one-letter alphabet by NRE (in fact, this family corresponds to the set of recursively enumerable sets of natural numbers $PsRE$, the family of Parikh sets of the languages in NRE).

A *(string) grammar* is a quadruple $G = (V_N, V_T, P, A)$, where V_N and V_T are finite sets of *nonterminal* and *terminal symbols*, and $V_N \cap V_T = \emptyset$, P is a finite set of *productions* $\alpha \to \beta$ with $\alpha \in V^+$ and $\beta \in V^*$, where $V = V^+ \cup V^*$, and $A \in V_N$ is the *axiom*. For $x, y \in V^*$ we say that y *is directly derivable* from x in G, denoted by $x \Rightarrow_G y$, if and only if for some $\alpha \to \beta$ in P and $u, v \in V^*$ we get $x = u\alpha v$ and $y = u\beta v$. Denoting the reflexive and transitive closure of the derivation relation $\Rightarrow_G$ by $\Rightarrow_G^*$, the *language generated by G* is $L(G) = \{w \in V_T^* \mid A \Rightarrow_G^* w\}$. A production $\alpha \to \beta$ is called *context-free* if $\alpha \in V_N$. If G contains only context-free rules it is called a *context-free grammar*. A context-free grammar is said to be in *Chomsky normal form*, if it contains only rules of the form $A \to BC$ and $A \to a$ where $A, B, C \in V_N$ and $a \in V_T$ (a context-free grammar in Chomsky normal form usually is also assumed to be *reduced,* which means that every non-terminal symbol $A \in V_N$ can be reached from the start symbol S, i.e., $S \Rightarrow_G^* uAv$ for some $u, v \in (V_N \cup V_T)^*$, and that from every non-terminal symbol $A \in V_N$ we can derive a terminal word, i.e., $A \Rightarrow_G^* w$ for some $w \in V_T^*$).

A *deterministic register machine* is a construct $M = (n, R, l_0, l_h)$, where n is the number of registers, R is a finite set of instructions injectively labelled with elements from a given set $lab(M)$, l_0 is the initial/start label, and l_h is the final label.

The instructions are of the following forms:

- $l_1 : (add(r), l_2)$
  Add 1 to the contents of register r and proceed to the instruction (labelled with) l_2. (We say that we have an ADD instruction.)
- $l_1 : (sub(r), l_2, l_3)$
  If register r is not empty, then subtract 1 from its contents and go to instruction l_2, otherwise proceed to instruction l_3. (We say that we have a SUB instruction.)
- $l_h : halt$
  Stop the machine. The final label l_h is only assigned to this instruction.

A register machine M is said to accept a natural number n if and only if, starting with the instruction with label l_0 and with register one containing the number n and all other registers containing the number 0, the machine stops (it reaches the instruction $l_h : halt$) with all registers containing the number 0.

The register machines are known to be computationally universal, equal in power to deterministic Turing machines (e.g., see [8]): they accept exactly the sets of natural numbers which can be accepted by Turing machines, that is, the family $PsRE$. Even more specifically, register machines can accept string languages $L \subseteq T^*$ accepted by Turing machines (i.e., the family RE) in the following way: For each $w \in T^*$ the register machine accepts the number $2^{g_{z+1}(w)}$ if and only if the string w is accepted by the Turing machine, where $g_{z+1}(w)$ is the numerical z-ary encoding of w at base $z + 1$, z being the number of symbols in T (e.g., see [2], [3], [5]).

Without loss of generality, in the proofs of the following section we will assume that in each SUB instruction $l_1 : (sub(r), l_2, l_3)$ the labels l_1, l_2, l_3 are mutually distinct: For instance, to achieve this goal, we replace each SUB instruction $l_1 : (sub(r), l_2, l_3)$ by the instruction $l_1 : (sub(r), l_2', l_3'')$ and add the instructions $l_2' : (add(n + 1), l_2'''), l_2''' : (sub(n + 1), l_2, l_2'), l_3'' : (add(n + 1), l_3^{iv}), l_3^{iv} : (sub(n+1), l_3, l_3'')$, where $n + 1$ is a new register (this can be the same for all SUB instructions we start from), and all primed labels are distinct and different from the initial labels.

3   P Systems with Active Membranes and String Objects as Tree Generating Devices

A *P system with active membranes and string objects* (for sake of simplicity, we often will refer to such a device as a *P system* in the following) is a construct

$$\Pi = (V, T, H, \mu, w_1, \ldots, w_m, R),$$

where: $m \geq 1$; V is an alphabet (the *total alphabet* of the system); $T \subseteq V$ (the *terminal* alphabet); H is a finite set of *labels* for membranes (in the following we will always label the skin membrane by 0); μ is a *membrane structure*, consisting of m membranes (represented by matching pairs of brackets), labelled with elements of H; $w_1, \ldots, w_m$ are finite multisets of words over V (describing the *initial objects in the membranes* placed in the m regions of μ); R is a finite set of *rules*, of the following forms:

(sa) $[A]_h \longrightarrow [v]_{h'}$, where $A \in V$, $v \in V^*$, $h, h' \in H$ (a letter A is rewritten into v in a membrane labelled with h thereby changing its label to h');

(sb) $A[\ ]_h \longrightarrow [v]_{h'}$, where $A \in V$, $v \in V^*$, $h, h' \in H$ (a letter A is rewritten into v and then the resulting word is sent into a membrane labelled with h thereby changing its label to h'),

(sc) $[A]_h \rightarrow v[\ ]_{h'}$, where $A \in V$, $v \in V^*$, $h, h' \in H$ (an object A is rewritten into v and then the resulting string is sent out of the membrane labelled with h thereby changing its label to h'),

(sd) $[A]_h \rightarrow v$, where $A \in V$, $v \in V^*$, $h \in H$ (an object A is rewritten into v at the same time dissolving the surrounding membrane labelled with h),

(se) $[A]_h \rightarrow [v]_{h'}[v']_{h''}$, where $A \in V$, $v, v' \in V^*$, $h, h', h'' \in H$ (2-division rule for elementary membranes; in reaction with an object, the membrane is divided into two membranes with, possibly, different labels; the word containing the letter A specified in the rule is replaced in the corresponding words in the two new membranes by possibly new substrings v, v'; at the same time, all the objects except for the word containing the letter A that started the membrane division are duplicated into the two new membranes),

(sg) $[A]_h \longrightarrow [[v]_{h''}]_{h'}$, where $A \in V$, $v \in V^*$, $h, h', h'' \in H$ (a letter A in a membrane labelled with h, by changing its label to h', is rewritten into v and then the resulting word is sent into a newly generated inner membrane labelled with h'').

We refer to [12], [13], and [14] for a more precise definition of the way originally P systems with active membranes were supposed to work; here we only informally describe the way of passing from one configuration of the system to the next one. The difference between the original model and our proposed model mainly lies in the fact that we work on strings rather than with symbols (therefore, the types of rules carry the additional marking s); moreover, in describing the membrane structure as well as the rules we only label the right-hand brackets of the matching pairs.

The rules are applied in a maximally parallel manner, yet with the following restrictions: The rules are applied "from bottom up", in one step, starting with the rules of the innermost region and, then, going up level by level until the region of the skin membrane is reached. In each region, all strings which can evolve using a rule of the forms (sa), (sb), (sc), (sg) can and have to evolve if they do not change the label of the surrounding/involved membrane, yet (at most) only one string (afterwards!) may take a rule changing the label of the surrounding/involved membrane or dissolve it or divide it, i.e., rules of type (sa), (sb), (sc), (sg) can be used in parallel as long as they do not change the label of the membrane they affect. At most one rule of type (se) can be applied to one selected string after the evolution of all other strings in the membrane region not changing the membrane label or dissolving the membrane; if a membrane with label h is divided by a rule of type (se), which involves a word containing letter A, then all other words in membrane h are copied into each of the resulting membranes.

The rules associated with a membrane labelled with h are used for all copies of this membrane; it does not matter whether the membrane is an initial one or it was obtained by membrane division or membrane generation. The skin membrane can never divide (nor dissolve). By (sx_0), $x \in \{a, b, c, d, e, g\}$, we denote the types of rules corresponding to (sx), if the rules do not change the labels of the involved membranes (i.e., in any case we have $h = h'$).

In this paper, as the result of a halting computation (no rule can be used in the last configuration) we consider the tree represented by the membrane structure of the final configuration: the skin membrane represents the root of the tree and is always labelled by 0 (remember that the skin membrane cannot be divided); if a membrane labelled by i is enclosed by a membrane labelled by j, in the tree the edge from the corresponding node representing this membrane labelled by j to the corresponding node representing this membrane labelled by i gets the label i. In what concerns the labels of nodes, we might consider several variants: First, we could neglect the contents of the membrane regions and thus consider trees without node labels. Yet in the following, we shall consider trees having labels at the nodes, too; hence, in the final configuration the contents of each membrane region has to be a singleton $a \in T$ which then is taken as the label of the corresponding node representing this membrane (if this condition is not fulfilled, this final configuration does not contribute to the tree language).

By $L(\Pi)$ we denote the tree language generated as described above by a P system Π. If a computation goes forever, then it does not contribute to the set $L(\Pi)$.

Now let D be a non-empty subset of $\{sx, sx_0 \mid x \in \{a, b, c, d, e, g\}\}$. Then, by $LPT(D)$ we denote the family of tree languages generated by P systems with active membranes and string objects as defined above using only rules of types from D.

Example 1. Consider a context-free grammar in Chomsky normal form $G = (V_N, V_T, P, A)$. Then we construct a P system

$$\Pi = (V_N \cup V_T, V_T, H, [\,]_0, S, R)$$

with the following rules in R:

- $[S]_0 \to [a]_0$
  for $S \to a \in P$, $a \in V_T$;
- $[S]_0 \to [[S']_1]_0$, $[S']_1 \to [B]_1 [C]_2$
  for $S \to BC \in P$, $B, C \in V_N$;
- $[A]_h \to [[A']_1]_h$, $[A']_1 \to [B]_1 [C]_2$
  for $h \in \{1, 2\}$, $A \to BC \in P$, $A, B, C \in V_N$;
- $[A]_h \to [a]_h$
  for $h \in \{1, 2\}$, $A \to a \in P$, $A \in V_N$, $a \in V_T$.

As we can assume G to be reduced, termination of a computation in Π already means that we obtain the resulting membrane structure in the final configuration as our terminal tree result. Obviously, the trees we obtain are the derivation trees of G.

Now let TRE denote the family of recursively enumerable tree languages over finite alphabets of labels for nodes and edges. Then, as the main result of this paper, we can show the following theorem:

Theorem 1. *Each recursively enumerable tree language over finite alphabets of labels for nodes and edges can be generated by a P system, more specifically,*

$$LPT\left(\{sb_0, sc_0, sd_0, se_0, sg_0\}\right) = TRE.$$

Proof (Sketch). We only sketch the proof for the inclusion

$$LPT\left(\{sb_0, sc_0, sd_0, se_0, sg_0\}\right) \supseteq TRE,$$

i.e., given a tree language L_t (over the alphabet T for the labels of the nodes and the alphabet $\{j \mid 1 \leq j \leq k\}$ for the labels of the edges) we describe the main ingredients of a P system

$$\Pi = (V, T, H, [\,]_0, X_0, R)$$

such that $L_t = L(\Pi)$. Let N denote the set of non-terminal symbols in Π, i.e., $N = V - T$. The skin membrane is always labelled by 0, hence $H \supseteq \{j \mid 0 \leq j \leq k\}$. The additional labels as well as non-terminal symbols will become obvious from the description of the rules in R given below.

The main idea of the proof now is to generate the membrane structure corresponding to an arbitrary tree over T and $\{j \mid 1 \leq j \leq k\}$ and in parallel to encode the tree in a single word just by encoding the corresponding rules taken in the P system for the generation of the membrane (=tree) structure, which can be done in the following way: For each rule in Π relevant for the generation of the membrane structure we take a specific symbol (only finitely many symbols are needed as we shall see later in the construction given below); now let all these symbols form the set E with cardinality z, then each element from E can be identified by a number between 1 and z. Hence, we can encode a sequence of these rules not only by a word w, but also by the number $g_{z+1}(w)$ at base $z+1$, i.e., applying the next rule can be codified by multiplying the current number by $z + 1$ and then adding the value for the applied rule.

For the given tree language L_t, by definition, there exists a deterministic Turing machine $M_T(L_t)$ accepting the code $c(s)$ of a tree s if and only if $s \in L_t$. Obviously, from this Turing machine $M_T(L_t)$ one can construct a Turing machine $M'_T(L_t)$ which accepts the code w (which may be different from $c(s)$) of a tree s as described above representing the generation of the membrane structure corresponding to s if and only if $s \in L_t$. As already mentioned in the preceding section, for the Turing machine $M'_T(L_t)$ there exists a register machine $M_R(L_t)$ that for each w accepts the number $2^{g_{z+1}(w)}$ if and only if the string w is accepted by the Turing machine $M'_T(L_t)$. Here and in the register machine programs described below we take advantage of the constructions elaborated, e.g., in [2], [3], [5], and therefore omit the annoying details of these constructions; in contrast, we only show how (sequences of) ADD instructions and SUB instructions of a register machine can be simulated in the P system Π.

We now start the description of the rules needed in the generation phase:

- $[X_0]_0 \to [[X'_0]_{C_a}]_0$ for $a \in T$;

  $[X'_0]_{C_a} \to [X''_0]_{C_a} \left[X_A E_1^{g_{z+1}(a)} \right]_C$ for $a \in T$;

  E_1 is the symbol used for representing the contents of register one of the register machine $M_R(L_t)$, i.e., the number of symbols E_1 in the current string corresponds with the value stored in register one in that moment of the simulation; $X_A E_1^{g_{z+1}(a)}$ now starts the acceptance check for a tree consisting only of the root labelled with a (the acceptance phase will be described in more detail below).

- $[X''_0]_{C_a} \to a$ for $a \in T$;

  this rule as desired yields the label a for the root represented by the skin membrane labelled by 0.

- $[X'_0]_{C_a} \to [X''_0]_{C_a} \left[X_G E_1^{g_{z+1}(a)} \right]_h$ for $a \in T$, $1 \le h \le k$;

  $[X_G]_h \to [aD]_h [\langle X'_G, h, a, h' \rangle]_{h'}$ for $a \in T$, $1 \le h \le k$, $2 \le h' \le k+1$, $h < h'$;

  At a specific level of the tree, the children of a node are generated by the rules given above in an ordered manner (according to the number assigned to the edges).

  $\langle X'_G, h, a, h' \rangle$ stands for a "subroutine" which simply multiplies the current number of symbols E_1 by $z + 1$ and adds the number that encodes the generation of a new membrane labelled by h' from the membrane labelled by h (which now will get the node label a); it ends up with the control symbol X_G; in fact, as already mentioned above, this is a simple register machine program we are not going to describe in more detail, as we will

show later how (sequences of) ADD instructions and SUB instructions of a
register machine can be simulated.

- $[X_G]_{k+1} \to \tilde{X}_A;$

at some point we may end the generation phase and go to start the acceptance check; for this purpose we move the single word containing all
information and now carrying the control symbol $\tilde{X}_A$ to the skin membrane
by using the following rules:

- $\left[\tilde{X}_A\right]_h \to \tilde{X}_A\,[\;]_h$ for $1 \le h \le k;$

$\left[\tilde{X}_A\right]_0 \to [[X_A]_C]_0\,;$

with $\tilde{X}_A$ we now start the checking phase which first from n symbols E_1
computes 2^n symbols E_1 (which again is a simple register machine program)
and then simulates the actions of the Turing machine $M_T'\,(L_t)$ by simulating
the register machine $M_R\,(L_t)$. This procedure will end up with the final control symbol X_{halt} (corresponding to the final label of the register machine)
if and only if the generated membrane structure corresponds with a tree in
L_t; in the positive case, we halt after having applied the rule

- $[X_{halt}]_C \to \lambda,$

otherwise we end up in an infinite loop.

- $[X_G]_{k+1} \to \tilde{X}_G;$

the control symbol $\tilde{X}_G$ allows us to move the string containing all necessary information to other membranes already generated and to produce new
membranes in them.

- $\left[\tilde{X}_G\right]_h \to \left\langle \tilde{X}_G, h, out \right\rangle [\;]_h\,,$

$\tilde{X}_G\,[\;]_h \to \left[\left\langle \tilde{X}_G, h, in \right\rangle\right]_h$ for $1 \le h \le k;$

the "subroutines" $\left\langle \tilde{X}_G, h, out \right\rangle$ and $\left\langle \tilde{X}_G, h, in \right\rangle$, respectively, multiply the
current number of symbols E_1 by $z+1$ and add the number that encode these
movements (of the string carrying all information encoded in the number of
symbols E_1) out of/ into a membrane labelled by h; they both end up with
the control symbol $\tilde{X}_G$ again.

The control symbol X_G can only be regained to generate new children:

- $\tilde{X}_G\,[\;]_h \to \left[\tilde{X}_G'\right]_h$ for $1 \le h \le k;$

$\left[\tilde{X}_G'\right]_h \to \left[\left[\left\langle \tilde{X}_G', h, h' \right\rangle\right]_{h'}\right]_h$ for $1 \le h, h' \le k;$

the "subroutine" $\left\langle \tilde{X}_G', h, h' \right\rangle$ multiplies the current number of symbols E_1
by $z+1$ and adds the number that encodes this movement into a membrane
labelled by h and the generation of a new membrane labelled with h' inside;
it ends up with the control symbol X_G, which then allows for the generation
of other children by using the rules

$[X_G]_h \to [aD]_h\,[\langle X_G', h, a, h'\rangle]_{h'}$ for $a \in T$, $1 \le h \le k$, $2 \le h' \le k+1$, $h < h'$,
already listed above. In contrast to the first use of these rules for the children
of the root, the string with aD now also contains a lot of non-terminal
symbols E_1. In general, for removing all non-terminal symbols from a string
carrying the control symbol D we use the following rules:

- $[D]_h \to [[D]_D]_h$ for $h \in \{j \mid 1 \le j \le k\} \cup \{C\}$,
  $[A]_D \to \lambda$ for $A \in N$;

  in that way, all non-terminal symbols (including D) can be eliminated; if D is eliminated before all other non-terminal symbols have been eliminated from the string, we are forced to enter an infinite loop according to the following rules:

- $[A]_h \to [[\#]_D]_h$ for $A \in N$, $h \in \{j \mid 1 \le j \le k + 1\} \cup \{C\}$,
  $[\#]_D \to \#$,
  $[\#]_h \to [[\#]_D]_h$ for $h \in \{j \mid 1 \le j \le k + 1\} \cup \{C\}$.

  The occurrence of the trap symbol $\#$ prohibits halting.

  It now only remains to show how ADD instructions and SUB instructions can be simulated:

- The ADD instruction $X_1 : (add\,(r_i)\,, X_2)$ incrementing register i of $M_R\,(L_t)$ can be simulated by the rules
  $[X_1]_h \to [[X_1'E_i]_I]_h$ for $h \in \{j \mid 1 \le j \le k + 1\} \cup \{C\}$,
  $[X_1']_I \to X_2$,

  where the number of symbols E_i corresponds with the value stored in register i.

- Decrementing register i of $M_R\,(L_t)$ by the SUB instruction $X_1 : (sub\,(r_i)\,, X_2, X_3)$ is accomplished by the rules
  $[X_1]_h \to [[X_2]_{E_i}]_h$ for $h \in \{j \mid 1 \le j \le k + 1\} \cup \{C\}$,
  $[E_i]_{E_i} \to \lambda$,
  $[X_2]_{E_i} \to \#$.

  The rule $[X_2]_{E_i} \to \#$ introduces the trap symbol $\#$ (which will lead to a non-halting computation) only if decrementing is not possible, i.e., there is no symbol E_i in the current string, otherwise we proceed correctly with the control symbol X_2.

  The other case, where we assume that register i contains zero, i.e., no symbol E_i occurs in the current string, is settled by the following rules:
  $[X_1]_h \to \left[[X_3']_{E_i'}\right]_h$ for $h \in \{j \mid 1 \le j \le k + 1\} \cup \{C\}$;
  $[X_3']_{E_i'} \to [X_3]_{E_i'}\,[E_i']_{E_i'}$,
  $[X_3]_{E_i'} \to X_3$;

  the first copy now containing X_3 assumes the choice was correct, whereas the second copy of the string carrying the symbol E_i' in membrane E_i' now checks for the occurrence of E_i; in the positive case the introduction of the trap symbol $\#$ leads to an infinite computation, otherwise the second copy is completely erased:
  $[B]_{E_i'} \to \lambda\,[\,]_{E_i'}$ for $B \in N - \{E_i\}$,
  $E_i'\,[\,]_{E_i'} \to [E_i']_{E_i'}$,
  $[E_i']_{E_i'} \to \lambda$.

  If the string after the application of the rule $[E_i']_{E_i'} \to \lambda$ is not yet empty (which for sure is the case if at least one symbol E_i originally was present), then the trap symbol $\#$ will be introduced.

In total, we have shown how we can generate an arbitrary membrane structure and in parallel compute its code for the acceptance check carried out by simulating the register machine representing the given tree language. We get a halting computation if and only if the register machine halts, i.e., if and only if it accepts the code of the tree represented by the generated membrane structure. This observation completes the proof.   □

As can be seen from the construction of the proof given above, a halting computation fulfills all conditions for interpreting the final configuration as a tree over the node alphabet T and the edge alphabet $\{1, ..., k\}$, which provides an even stronger result than that stated in the theorem, because the additional condition for being able to interpret the membrane structure of the final configuration as a (node-labelled) tree, i.e., that the contents of each membrane region has to be a singleton $a \in T$, need not be taken into account.

4   Summary and Future Research

We have shown that P systems can also be used for generating (representations of) any recursively enumerating tree language by taking the tree representing the membrane structure of the final configuration as the result of a halting computation. In this paper we took the model of P systems with active membranes (but without using polarizations) working on string objects for obtaining this result for tree languages. By allowing for membrane deletion we could avoid changing labels.

Future investigations will focus on variants of P systems with active membranes using other restricted types of rules, even with using polarizations or changing labels; moreover, we shall consider various models of P systems working with symbol objects and investigate their computational power with respect to generating or accepting tree languages.

Acknowledgements

This paper was partly initiated in the friendly and inspiring atmosphere of the Brainstorming Week on Membrane Computing taking place at Seville in the first week of February 2004, where the first author could take advantage of the fruitful discussions with several participants. The first two authors acknowledge IST-2001-32008 project "MolCoNet".

References

1. J. Dassow, Gh. Păun, *Regulated Rewriting in Formal Language Theory*. Springer-Verlag, Berlin, 1989.
2. R. Freund, C. Martin-Vide, Gh. Păun, From regulated rewriting to computing with membranes: collapsing hierarchies. *Theoretical Computer Science*, **312** (2004), 143–188.

3. R. Freund, M. Oswald, GP systems with forbidding context. *Fundamenta Informaticae*, **49**, 1-3 (2002), 81–102.
4. R. Freund, A. Păun, P systems with active membranes and without polarizations. *Soft Computing* (to appear).
5. R. Freund, Gh. Păun, On the number of non-terminal symbols in graph-controlled, programmed and matrix grammars. In: M. Margenstern, Yu. Rogozhin, eds.: *Proc. MCU 2001*, Chişinău, 2001, LNCS 2055, Springer-Verlag, Berlin, 2001, 214–225.
6. J. Hopcroft, J. Ulmann, *Introduction to Automata Theory, Languages, and Computation*. Addison-Wesley, Reading, Mass., 1979.
7. S.N. Krishna, R. Rama, A variant of P systems with active membranes: solving NP-complete problems. *Romanian J. of Information Science and Technology*, **2**, 4 (1999), 357–367.
8. M.L. Minsky, *Computation: Finite and Infinite Machines*. Prentice Hall, Englewood Cliffs, New Jersey, USA, 1967.
9. The P Systems Web Page: `http://psystems.disco.unimib.it/`
10. A. Păun, On P systems with active membranes. *Proc. of the First International Conference on Unconventional Models of Computation* (UMC2K). In: I. Antoniou, C.S. Calude, M.J. Dinneen, eds.: Discrete Mathematics and Theoretical Computer Science, Springer-Verlag, Brussels, Belgium (2000) 187–201
11. Gh. Păun, Computing with membranes. *Journal of Computer and System Sciences*, **61**, 1 (2000), 108–143, and TUCS Research Report 208 (1998) (`http://www.tucs.fi`).
12. Gh. Păun, P systems with active membranes: attacking NP complete problems. *Journal of Automata, Languages and Combinatorics*, **6**, 1 (2001), 75–90.
13. Gh. Păun, *Membrane Computing: An Introduction*. Springer-Verlag, Berlin, 2002.
14. Gh. Păun, Y. Suzuki, H. Tanaka, T. Yokomori, On the power of membrane division in P systems. *Publ. Math Debrecen*, 62 (2004).
15. G. Rozenberg, A. Salomaa, eds., *Handbook of Formal Languages*. Springer-Verlag, Berlin, 1997.

On Descriptive Complexity of P Systems

Miguel A. Gutiérrez-Naranjo, Mario J. Pérez-Jiménez,
and Agustin Riscos-Núñez

Research Group on Natural Computing,
Department of Computer Science and Artificial Intelligence,
University of Sevilla,
Avda. Reina Mercedes s/n, 41012 Sevilla, Spain
{magutier, marper, ariscosn}@us.es

Abstract. In this paper we address the problem of describing the complexity of the evolution of a P system. This issue is is specially hard in the case of P systems with active membranes, where the number of steps of a computation is not sufficient to evaluate the complexity. Sevilla carpets were introduced in [1], and they describe the space-time complexity of P systems. Based on them, we define some new parameters which can be used to compare evolutions of P systems. To illustrate this, we also include two different cellular solutions to the Subset Sum problem and compare them via these new parameters.

1 Introduction

The evolution of a P system is a complex process where (possibly) a large number of symbol-objects, membranes and rules are involved. In the case of P systems with active membranes, the problem of describing the complexity of the computational process becomes specially hard. In this case, elementary membranes can divide into two new membranes and, due to the parallelism intrinsic to P systems, an exponential number of membranes can be obtained in polynomial time. This feature makes P systems with active membranes a powerful tool to attack NP-complete problems and, indeed, several efficient solutions to this type of problems have been presented (see, e.g., [4, 9, 10, 11] or [12]). These solutions are proposed in the framework of *recognizer P systems with external output*, and they present significant similarities among them. The basic idea in these designs is the creation of an exponential number of membranes (*workspace*) in polynomial time and the use of each membrane as an independent computational device. All membranes evolve *in parallel* and the computation has a polynomial cost in time. The process ends with a final stage (with polynomial cost) that checks the answers of these devices and sends an output to the environment.

The complexity in *time* (the number of cellular steps) of these solutions is polynomial, but it is clear that the time is not the unique variable that we need to consider in order to evaluate the complexity of the process. Ciobanu, Păun and Ştefănescu presented in [1] a new way to describe the complexity of a computation in a P system. The so-called *Sevilla carpet* is an extension of the

G. Mauri et al. (Eds.): WMC5 2004, LNCS 3365, pp. 320–330, 2005.

notion of Szilard language from grammars to the case when several rules are used at the same time.

In this paper we make use of Sevilla carpets to describe the computations of P systems that solve the Subset Sum problem. Two families of recognizer P systems have been designed that need a polynomial time to send an output to the environment. We present their corresponding Sevilla carpets in order to compare them, and then some ideas to improve the design of P systems for solving other new problems are proposed.

The paper is organized as follows. In Section 2 we first give some preliminary notions about *recognizer P systems* and a polynomial complexity class on P systems is defined. Section 3 presents the Sevilla carpets and some new parameters related with them are introduced in Section 4. Finally, we use these parameters to compare two solutions of the Subset Sum problem.

2   Preliminaries

Roughly speaking, a P system consists of a cell-like membrane structure, in the compartments of which one places multisets of objects which evolve according to given rules in a synchronous non-deterministic maximally parallel manner.

Definition 1. *A P system with input is a tuple* (Π, Σ, i_Π)*, where:* Π *is a P system, with working alphabet* Γ*, with* p *membranes labelled by* $1, \ldots, p$*, and initial multisets* $\mathcal{M}_1, \ldots, \mathcal{M}_p$ *associated with them;* Σ *is an (input) alphabet strictly contained in* Γ*; the initial multisets are over* $\Gamma - \Sigma$*; finally,* i_Π *is the label of a distinguished (input) membrane.*

The computations of a P system with input a multiset m over Σ, are defined in a natural way. The only novelty is that the initial configuration must be the initial configuration of the system to which the input multiset m is added to the multiset from region i_Π.

Definition 2. *Let* (Π, Σ, i_Π) *be a P system with input. Let* Γ *be the working alphabet of* Π*,* μ *the membrane structure and* $\mathcal{M}_1, \ldots, \mathcal{M}_p$ *the initial multisets of* Π*. Let* m *be a multiset over* Σ*. The initial configuration of* (Π, Σ, i_Π) *with input* m *is* $(\mu, \mathcal{M}_1, \ldots, \mathcal{M}_{i_\Pi} \cup m, \ldots, \mathcal{M}_p)$*.*

In the case of P systems with input and with external output, the concept of computation is as standard in membrane computing, with a minor difference which will be explained below. We consider that it is not possible to observe the internal processes inside the P system and we can only know if the computation has halted via some distinguished objects sent out of the skin. We can formalize these ideas in the following way.

2.1   Recognizer P Systems

Recall that a decision problem X is a pair (I_X, θ_X) such that I_X is a language over a finite alphabet (whose elements are called *instances*) and θ_X is a total boolean function over I_X.

In order to solve decision problems we need P systems with input such that all halting computations starting from an initial configuration with a given input multiset (encoding an instance of the problem) produce the same output. The systems of this type will be called *recognizer* P systems.

Definition 3. *A recognizer P system is a P system with input,* (Π, Σ, i_Π), *and with external output such that:*

1. *The working alphabet contains two distinguished elements YES, NO.*
2. *All computations halt.*
3. *If $\mathcal{C}$ is a computation of Π, then either object YES or object NO (but not both) must have been released into the environment, and only in the last step of the computation. We say that $\mathcal{C}$ is an accepting computation (respectively, rejecting computation) if the object YES (respectively, NO) appears in the environment associated with the corresponding halting configuration of $\mathcal{C}$.*

The above definitions are stated in a general way, but in this paper P systems with active membranes will be used. We refer to [8] (see chapter 7) for a detailed definition of evolution rules, transition steps, configurations and computations in this model.

We denote by $\mathcal{AM}$ the class of all recognizer P systems with active membranes.

2.2   The Computational Complexity Class PMC$_\mathcal{F}$

The first results about "solvability" of **NP**–complete problems in polynomial time (even linear) by cellular computing systems with membranes were obtained using variants of P systems that lack an input membrane (see e.g. [7] or [14]). Thus, the constructive proofs of such results need to design one system for each instance of the problem.

If we wanted to perform such a solution of some decision problem in a laboratory, we will find a drawback on this approach: a system constructed to solve a concrete instance is useless when trying to solve another instance. This shortcoming can be easily overtaken if we consider a P system with input. Then, a system could solve different instances of the problem, provided that the corresponding input multisets are introduced in the input membrane.

Instead of looking for a single system that solves a problem, we prefer designing a *family* of P systems such that each element decides all the instances of "equivalent size", in certain sense.

Definition 4. *Let $\mathcal{F}$ be a class of recognizer P systems. We say that a decision problem $X = (I_X, \theta_X)$ is solvable in polynomial time by a family $\Pi = (\Pi(n))_{n \in \mathbf{N}^+}$ of type $\mathcal{F}$, and we denote this by $X \in \mathbf{PMC}_\mathcal{F}$, if the following is true:*

- *The family Π is polynomially uniform by Turing machines; that is, there exists a deterministic Turing machine constructing $\Pi(n)$ from $n \in \mathbf{N}^+$ in polynomial time.*

- *There exists a pair (g, h) of polynomial-time computable functions $g : L \rightarrow \bigcup_{n \in \mathbf{N}^+} I_{\Pi(n)}$ and $h : L \rightarrow \mathbf{N}^+$ such that for every $u \in L$ we have $g(u) \in I_{\Pi(h(u))}$, and*
  - *The family $\mathbf{\Pi}$ is polynomially bounded with regard to (g, h); that is, there exists a polynomial function p, such that for each $u \in I_X$ every computation of $\Pi(h(u))$ with input $g(u)$ is halting and, moreover, it performs at most $p(|u|)$ steps.*
  - *The family $\mathbf{\Pi}$ is sound, with regard to (X, g, h); that is, for each $u \in I_X$ it is verified that if there exists an accepting computation of $\Pi(h(u))$ with input $g(u)$, then $\theta_X(u) = 1$.*
  - *The family $\mathbf{\Pi}$ is complete, with regard to (X, g, h); that is, for each $u \in I_X$ it is verified that if $\theta_X(u) = 1$, then every computation of $\Pi(h(u))$ with input $g(u)$ is an accepting one.*

In the above definition we have imposed every P system $\Pi(n)$ to be *confluent*, in the following sense: every computation with the *same* input produces the *same* output. From the dfinition, one can easily prove that the class $\mathbf{PMC}_{\mathcal{F}}$ is closed under polynomial–time reduction and complement.

3   Sevilla Carpets

Sevilla carpets were presented in [1] as an extension of the Szilard language, which consists of all strings of rule labels describing correct derivations in a given grammar (see, e.g., [5, 6] or [13]). The Szilard language is usually defined for grammars in the Chomsky hierarchy where only a single rule is used in each derivation step, so a derivation can be represented as the string of the labels of the rules used in the derivation (the labelling is supposed to be one-to-one). Sevilla carpets are a Szilard-way to describe a computation in a P system. The main difference is that now a multiset of rules can be used in each evolution step of a P system. In [1] a bidimensional writing is proposed to describe a computation of a P system. The (Sevilla) carpet associated with a computation of a P system is a table with the time on the horizontal axis and the rules explicitly mentioned along the vertical axis; then, for each rule, in each step, a piece of information is given. Depending on the amount of information given to describe the evolution, Ciobanu, Păun, and Ştefănescu propose five variants for the Sevilla carpets:

1. Specifying in each time unit for each membrane whether at least one rule was used in its region or not.
2. Specifying in each time unit for each rule whether it was used or not.
3. Mentioning in each time unit the number of applications of each rule; this is 0 when the rule is not used and can be arbitrarily large when the rules are dealing with arbitrarily large multisets.
4. We can also distinguish three cases: that a rule cannot be used, that a rule can be used but it is not because of the nondeterministic choice, and that a rule is actually used.

5. A further possibility is to assign a cost to each rule, and to multiply the number of times a rule is used with its cost.

They also propose two parameters (*weight* and *surface*) to study Sevilla carpets. In this paper we popose two new parameters (*height* and *average weight*) that will be described in the next section.

4   Parameters for the Descriptive Complexity

Many times we are not interested only in the number of cellular steps of the computation, but also in other types of resources required to perform the computation. Especially if we want to implement *in silico* a P system, we need to be careful with the number of times that a rule is applied, maybe with the number of membranes and/or the number of objects present in a given configuration.

In order to describe the complexity of the computation, the following parameters are proposed:

- **Weight:** It is defined in [1] as the sum of all the elements in the carpet, i.e., as the total number of applications of rules along the computation. The application of a rule has a cost and the weight measures the total cost of the computation.
- **Surface:** This is the multiplication of the number of steps by the total number of the rules used by the P system. It can be considered as the *potential size* of the computation. From a computational point of view we are not only interested in P systems which halt in a small number of steps, but in P systems which use a small amount of resources. The *surface* measures the resources used in the design of the P system. Graphically, it represents the surface where the Sevilla carpet lies on.
- **Height:** This is the maximum number of applications of any rule in a step along the computation. Graphically, it represents the highest point reached by the Sevilla carpet.
- **Average Weight:** It is calculated by dividing the *weight* to the *surface* of the Sevilla carpet. This concept provides a relation between both parameters, and gives an indication on how the P system exploits its massive parallelism.

5   Comparing Two Solutions to the Subset Sum Problem

The Subset Sum problem is the following one: *Given a finite set A, a weight function, $w : A \to \mathbf{N}$, and a constant $k \in \mathbf{N}$, determine whether or not there exists a subset $B \subseteq A$ such that $w(B) = k$.*

We will use a tuple $(n, (w_1, \ldots, w_n), k)$ to represent an instance of the problem, where n stands for the size of $A = \{a_1, \ldots, a_n\}$, $w_i = w(a_i)$, and k is the constant given as input for the problem.

We propose here two solutions to this problem based on a brute force algorithm implemented in the framework of P systems with active membranes. The idea of the design is better understood if we divide the solution to the problem into several stages:

- *Generation stage*: for every subset of A, a membrane is generated via membrane division.
- *Weight calculation stage*: in each membrane the weight of the associated subset is calculated. This stage will take place in parallel with the previous one.
- *Checking stage*: in each membrane it is checked whether or not the weight of its associated subset is exactly k. This stage cannot start in a membrane before the previous ones are over in that membrane.
- *Output stage*: when the previous stage has been completed in all membranes, the system sends out the answer to the environment.

First Design

Next we present a family of recognizer P systems solving Subset Sum, according to Definition 4. This family can be found in [9].

First, we consider a polynomial–time computable and bijective function from $\mathbf{N}^2$ onto $\mathbf{N}$ (for example, $\langle x, y \rangle = ((x+y)(x+y+1)/2)+y$). For each $(n, k) \in \mathbf{N}^2$ we consider the P system $(\Pi_1(\langle n, k \rangle), \Sigma(n, k), i(n, k))$, where the input alphabet is $\Sigma(n, k) = \{x_1, \ldots, x_n\}$, the input membrane is $i(n, k) = e$ and $\Pi_1(\langle n, k \rangle) = (\Gamma(n, k), \{e, s\}, \mu, \mathcal{M}_e, \mathcal{M}_s, R)$ is defined as follows:

- Alphabet: $\Gamma(n, k) = \Sigma(n, k) \cup \{\bar{a}_0, \bar{a}, a_0, a, d_+, e_0, \ldots, e_n, q, q_0, \ldots, q_{2k+1},$
$$z_0, \ldots, z_{2n+2k+2}, Yes, \overline{no}, No, \#\}.$$

- membrane structure: $\mu = [\ [\ ]_e\ ]_s$.
- Initial multisets: $\mathcal{M}_s = z_0$; $\mathcal{M}_e = e_0 \bar{a}^k$.
- The set R of evolution rules consists of the following rules:

(a) $[e_i]_e^0 \rightarrow [q]_e^- [e_i]_e^+$, for $i = 0, \ldots, n$.
$[e_i]_e^+ \rightarrow [e_{i+1}]_e^0 [e_{i+1}]_e^+$, for $i = 0, \ldots, n-1$.

(b) $[x_0 \rightarrow \bar{a}_0]_e^0$; $\quad [x_0 \rightarrow \lambda]_e^+$; $\quad [x_i \rightarrow x_{i-1}]_e^+$, for $i = 1, \ldots, n$.

(c) $[q \rightarrow q_0]_e^-$; $\quad [\bar{a}_0 \rightarrow a_0]_e^-$; $\quad [\bar{a} \rightarrow a]_e^-$.

(d) $[a_0]_e^- \rightarrow [\ ]_e^0 \#$; $\quad [a]_e^0 \rightarrow [\ ]_e^- \#$.

(e) $[q_{2j} \rightarrow q_{2j+1}]_e^-$, for $j = 0, \ldots, k$.
$[q_{2j+1} \rightarrow q_{2j+2}]_e^0$, for $j = 0, \ldots, k-1$.

(f) $[q_{2k+1}]_e^- \rightarrow [\ ]_e^0 Yes$; $\quad [q_{2k+1}]_e^0 \rightarrow [\ ]_e^0 \#$.
$[q_{2j+1}]_e^- \rightarrow [\ ]_e^- \#$, for $j = 0, \ldots, k-1$.

(g) $[z_i \rightarrow z_{i+1}]_s^0$, for $i = 0, \ldots, 2n + 2k + 1$; $\quad [z_{2n+2k+2} \rightarrow d_+ \overline{no}]_s^0$.

(h) $[d_+]_s^0 \rightarrow [\ ]_s^+ d_+$; $\quad [\overline{no} \rightarrow No]_s^+$; $\quad [Yes]_s^+ \rightarrow [\ ]_s^0 Yes$; $\quad [No]_s^+ \rightarrow [\ ]_s^0 No$.

Let us recall that the instance $u = (n, (w_1, \ldots, w_n), k)$ is processed by the P system $\Pi_1(\langle n, k \rangle)$ with input the multiset $x_1^{w_1} x_2^{w_2} \ldots x_n^{w_n}$.

This design depends on the two constants that are given as input in the problem: n and k. It consists on $5n + 5k + 18$ evolution rules, and if an apropriate input multiset is introduced inside membrane e before starting the computation, the system will stop and output an answer in $2n + 2k + 6$ steps (if the answer is *No*) or in $2n + 2k + 5$ steps (if the answer is *Yes*).

According to Definition 4 and using the above family of P systems, we can prove that, *Subset Sum* $\in \mathbf{PMC}_{\mathcal{AM}}$ (see [9], for details).

Second Design

Next we present a new family of recognizer P systems solving Subset Sum, inspired in the previous one. Some modifications are made following the design presented in [3].

For each $n \in \mathbf{N}$ we consider the P system $(\Pi_2(n), \Sigma(n), i(n))$, where the input alphabet is $\Sigma(n) = \{x_1, \ldots, x_n\}$, the input membrane is $i(n) = e$ and $\Pi_2(n) = (\Gamma(n), \{e, r, s\}, \mu, \mathcal{M}_e, \mathcal{M}_r, \mathcal{M}_s, R)$ is defined as follows:

- Alphabet: $\Gamma(n) = \Sigma(n) \cup \{\bar{a}_0, \bar{a}, a_0, a, c, d_0, d_1, d_2, e_0, \ldots, e_n, g, \bar{g}, \hat{g}, h_0, h_1,$
$$q, q_0, q_1, q_2, q_3, Yes, No, \overline{no}, z_0, \ldots, z_{2n+1}, \# \}.$$

- Membrane structure: $\mu = [\, [\,]_e \,]_s$.
- Initial multisets: $\mathcal{M}_s = z_0$; $\mathcal{M}_e = e_0 g \bar{a}^k$; $\mathcal{M}_r = h_0 b$.
- The set R of evolution rules consists of the following rules:

(a) $[e_i]_e^0 \rightarrow [q]_e^- [e_i]_e^+$, for $i = 0, \ldots, n$.
  $[e_i]_e^+ \rightarrow [e_{i+1}]_e^0 [e_{i+1}]_e^+$, for $i = 0, \ldots, n - 1$.

(b) $[x_0 \rightarrow \bar{a}_0]_e^0$; $[x_0 \rightarrow \lambda]_e^+$; $[x_i \rightarrow x_{i-1}]_e^+$, for $i = 1, \ldots, n$.

(c) $[q \rightarrow q_0]_e^-$; $[\bar{a}_0 \rightarrow a_0]_e^-$; $[\bar{a} \rightarrow a]_e^-$.
  $[g]_e^- \rightarrow [\,]_e^- \bar{g}$.

  $[e_n]_e^+ \rightarrow \#$.
  $[\bar{a}_0 \rightarrow \lambda]_s^0$; $[\bar{a} \rightarrow \lambda]_s^0$; $[g \rightarrow \lambda]_s^0$.
  $[a \rightarrow \lambda]_e^+$; $[a_0 \rightarrow \lambda]_e^+$.

(d) $[a_0]_e^- \rightarrow [\,]_e^0 \#$; $[a]_e^0 \rightarrow [\,]_e^- \#$.

(e) $[q_0 \rightarrow q_1]_e^-$; $[q_1 \rightarrow q_0]_e^0$.
  $[q_0]_e^0 \rightarrow [\,]_e^+ \overline{no}$.
  $[q_1 \rightarrow q_2 c]_e^-$; $[q_2 \rightarrow q_3]_e^0$; $[c]_e^- \rightarrow [\,]_e^0 k$.

(f) $[q_3]_e^0 \rightarrow [\,]_e^+ Yes$; $[q_3]_e^- \rightarrow [\,]_e^+ \overline{no}$.

(g) $[z_i \rightarrow z_{i+1}]_s^0$, for $i = 0, \ldots, 2n$; $[z_{2n+1} \rightarrow d_0 d_1]_s^0$.
  $d_0[\,]_r^0 \rightarrow [d_0]_r^-$; $[d_1]_s^0 \rightarrow [\,]_s^+ d_1$.

(det) $[h_0 \rightarrow h_1]_r^-$, $[h_1 \rightarrow h_0]_r^+$,
  $[b]_r^- \rightarrow [\,]_r^+ b$, $\hat{g}[\,]_r^+ \rightarrow [\hat{g}]_r^-$,
  $b[\,]_r^- \rightarrow [b]_r^+$, $[\hat{g}]_r^+ \rightarrow [\,]_r^- \hat{g}$,
  $[h_0]_r^+ \rightarrow [\,]_r^+ d_2$, $[d_2]_s^+ \rightarrow [\,]_s^- d_2$.

(h) $[\overline{no} \rightarrow No]_s^-$; $[Yes]_s^- \rightarrow [\,]_s^0 Yes$; $[No]_s^- \rightarrow [\,]_s^0 No$.

In this solution the instance $u = (n, (w_1, \ldots, w_n), k)$ is processed by the P system $\Pi_2(n)$ with input the multiset $x_1^{w_1} x_2^{w_2} \ldots x_n^{w_n}$.

The above design depends only on one of the constants that are given as input in the problem: n. It is quite similar to the previous one, the difference lies in the checking stage and the answer stage. In this case we avoid the use of counters that require knowing the constant k.

The number of evolution rules is $5n + 41$, and the number of steps of the computation depends on the concrete instance that we need to solve, but it is linearly bounded.

Descriptive Complexity

We present some detailed statistics about the previous designs, trying to compare them on a more general basis than just looking the number of steps that the computation performs. Following this scheme, we present the Sevilla carpets associated with the computations of the two different solutions to the Subset Sum problem working on the same instance: $u = (5, (3, 5, 3, 2, 5), 9)$. That is, $n = 5$, $k = 9$, and the list of weights is $w_1 = 3, w_2 = 5, w_3 = 3, w_4 = 2, w_5 = 5$. The input multiset is then: $x_1^3 x_2^5 x_3^3 x_4^2 x_5^5$.

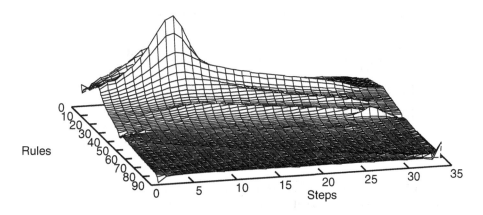

Fig. 1. Sevilla carpet for solution 1

The P system $\Pi_1(\langle 5, 9 \rangle)$ has 88 evolution rules, and all of them are applied with the exception of the rules: $[q_{19}]_e^- \to [\ ]_e^0 Yes$, $[q_3]_e^- \to [\ ]_e^- \#$, $[q_9]_e^- \to [\ ]_e^- \#$ and $[Yes]_s^- \to [\ ]_s^0 Yes$. The P system $\Pi_1(5, 9)$ stops at step 33 and sends an object No to the environment.

The weight of the Sevilla carpet (the total number of rule applications along the computation) is 2179, and its height (the maximal number of times that a rule is applied in one evolution step) is 82 and it is reached at Step 9 by the rule $[\bar{a}_0 \to a_0]_e^-$. The surface of the Sevilla carpet is 2904, and its average weight is 0.749656

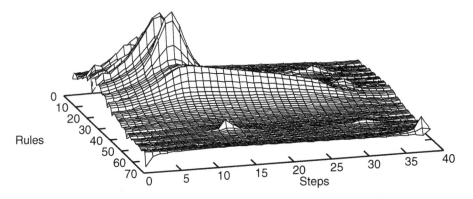

Fig. 2. Sevilla carpet for solution 2

The P system $\Pi_2(5)$ has 65 evolution rules, and all of them are applied with the exception of the rules: $[q_3]_e^0 \to [\ ]_e^+ Yes$ and $[Yes]_s^- \to [\ ]_s^0 Yes$. The P system $\Pi_2(5)$ stops at step 38 and sends an object No to the environment.

The weight of the Sevilla carpet is 3368, and its height is 108, this height is reached at Step 10 by the rule $[\bar{a}_0 \to \lambda]_s^0$. The surface of the Sevilla carpet is 2470, and its average weight is 1.36275

The following table shows the parameters of both solutions:

	Solution 1	Solution 2
Rules	88	65
Steps	33	38
Surface	2904	2470
Weight	2179	3368
Height	82	108
Average Weight	0.749656	1.36275

If we consider the number of steps as a complexity measure to compare both designs, then we conclude that the first solution is *better* than the second one (although not asymptotically), since it needs less steps.

Moreover, concerning the weight of the Sevilla carpet, solution 1 is again *better* than solution 2, because it uses less resources during the computation. However, the fact that the average weight of solution 2 is larger than the average weight of solution 1 can be interpreted by saying that the second design makes a better use of the parallelism in P systems (the computation is more *intense*).

We would like to remark that these are not asymptotical comparisons, as we focus only on the data corresponding to one instance. Indeed, due to the exponential number of membranes created during the generation stage, we believe that considering another instance with a greater size will stress the differences between the design based only on n and the other one, based on both n and k. The bound on the size of the intances that can be studied is imposed by the necessity to use a P systems simulator to obtain the detailed description of the computation: number of rules, number of cellular steps, and number of times that the rules are applied in each step. The simulator we are using (presented in [2]) is written in Prolog, and it runs on a sequential conventional computer.

6   Final Comments and Future Work

This paper illustrates the necessity of a deeper study of parameters which describe the complexity of P systems as computational devices. In order to analyze this complexity we use the Sevilla carpets. We also define two new parameters which provide us with a more detailed description of the evolution of a P system.

A more detailed study of the differences between the computations of the two solutions discussed here is to be done, in order to extract some conclusions about the usefullness and/or the interest of these new complexity parameters that can be used to evaluate the design of cellular solutions to problems.

In the example illustrated in the previous section, the second design solves the same instance in 5 additional cellular steps, but the number of rules is much lower. Can we decrease more the number of rules and keep a linear bound on the number of steps? Is it worth it?

In the near future, we plan to carry out descriptive complexity studies of other variants of P systems, maybe giving rise to new significant parameters. We would like also to improve the graphical treatment of Sevilla carpets, designing a software able to go directly from the description of the computation provided by our P systems simulator to the picture of the carpet.

Acknowledgement

The support for this research through the project TIC2002-04220-C03-01 of the Ministerio de Ciencia y Tecnología of Spain, cofinanced by FEDER funds, is gratefully acknowledged.

References

1. G. Ciobanu, Gh. Păun, Gh. Ştefănescu, Sevilla carpets associated with P systems. In M. Cavaliere, C. Martín–Vide and Gh. Păun (eds.), *Proceedings of the Brainstorming Week on Membrane Computing*, Tarragona, Spain, 2003, Report RGML 26/03, 135–140.
2. C. Cordón-Franco, M.A. Gutiérrez-Naranjo, M.J. Pérez-Jiménez, F. Sancho-Caparrini, A Prolog simulator for deterministic P systems with active membranes. *New Generation Computing*, **22** (4), 2004, 349–363.
3. M.A. Gutiérrez-Naranjo, M.J. Pérez-Jiménez, A. Riscos-Núñez, Towards a programming language in cellular computing. *Proceedings of the 11th Workshop on Logic, Language, Information and Computation* (WoLLIC'2004), July 19-22, 2004, 1-16 Campus de Univ. Paris 12, Paris, France. A preliminary version in Gh. Păun, A. Riscos, A. Romero, F. Sancho (eds.) *Proceedings of the Second Brainstorming Week on Membrane Computing*, Report RGNC 01/04, 2004, 247–257.

4. M.A. Gutiérrez-Naranjo, M.J. Pérez-Jiménez, A. Riscos-Núñez, A fast P system for finding a balanced 2-partition. *Soft Computing.* Springer. To appear.

5. E.Mäkinen, *A Bibliography on Szilard Languages.* Dept. of Computer and Information Sciences, University of Tampere, `http://www.cs.uta.fi/reports/pdf/Szilard.pdf`

6. A. Mateescu, A. Salomaa, Aspects of classical language theory. In G. Rozenberg and A. Salomaa (eds.), *Handbook of Formal Languages* (vol. 1), Springer-Verlag, Berlin Heidelberg, 1997.

7. Gh. Păun, P systems with active membranes: Attacking NP complete problems. *Journal of Automata, Languages and Combinatorics,* **6**(1), 2001, 75–90.

8. Gh. Păun, *Membrane Computing. An Introduction.* Springer-Verlag, Berlin, 2002.

9. M.J. Pérez-Jiménez, A. Riscos-Núñez, Solving the Subset Sum problem by active membranes. *New Generation Computing,* to appear.

10. M.J. Pérez-Jiménez, A. Riscos-Núñez, A linear solution for the Knapsack problem using active membranes. In C. Martín-Vide, G. Mauri, Gh. Păun, G. Rozenberg and A. Salomaa (eds.), *Membrane Computing. Lecture Notes in Computer Science,* **2933**, 2004, 250–268.

11. M.J. Pérez-Jiménez, A. Romero-Jiménez, F. Sancho-Caparrini, A polynomial complexity class in P systems using membrane division. In E. Csuhaj–Varjú, C. Kintala, D. Wotschke, and Gy. Vaszyl (eds.), *Proceedings of the 5th Workshop on Descriptional Complexity of Formal Systems,* Budapest, Hungary, 2003, 284–294.

12. M.J. Pérez-Jiménez, A. Romero-Jiménez, F. Sancho-Caparrini, Solving VALIDITY problem by active membranes with input. In M. Cavaliere, C. Martín-Vide, and Gh. Păun (eds), *Proceedings of the Brainstorming Week on Membrane Computing,* Tarragona, Spain, 2003, Report RGML 26/03, 279–290.

13. A. Salomaa, *Formal Languages.* Academic Press, New York, 1973.

14. C. Zandron, *A Model for Molecular Computing: Membrane Systems.* Ph.D. Thesis, Università degli Studi di Milano, 2001.

P Systems with Symport/Antiport: The Traces of RBCs

Shankara Narayanan Krishna

Department of Computer Science and Engineering,
Indian Institute of Technology, Bombay
Powai, Mumbai, 400 076 India
krishnas@cse.iitb.ac.in

Abstract. This paper is inspired from two directions: (1) finding out the minimum number of membranes required for proving universality with minimal symport/antiport, and (2) the functionality of red blood corpuscles and how it can be translated in the membrane computing scenario. We are motivated by (2) and try to solve (1) using (2). Red blood corpuscles (RBCs) are the basic elements of all kinds of cells. RBCs are present in all the membranes of mammals. They get replaced periodically. They do not evolve or divide like usual cells; they are just carriers of oxygen and hence are communicating agents in a cell. This being the case, symport/antiport rules are the most suitable control structures to model their activity. We exploit the properties of RBCs in order to impose a natural restriction on the traces of objects; we consider a class of P systems where the objects represent RBCs and symport/antiport rules are used for communication. We prove a universality result with two membranes using symport/antiport rules of weight one, thus giving a solution for the number of membranes required for minimal symport/antiport in the RBC setting.

1   Introduction

In recent years, observations of cells and of their biochemical processes have been of inspiration for the creation of theoretical computational devices. One of the most recent attempts in this direction has been to look at the structure of cells as a set of nested compartments delimited by membranes. Each of the membranes are composed of chemicals and interact with the chemicals swimming in the aqueous solution from the compartments. The objects (chemicals) in the compartments can evolve, interact with other chemicals, and pass to other membranes. Membrane systems (P systems) were introduced in [11].

One of the most elegant variants of P systems was introduced in [10] under the name of membrane systems with symport/antiport. This variant models the synchronized movement of chemicals present in a cell: specific groups of objects may pass together through a membrane either in the same or in opposite directions. The former case is referred to as symport and the latter as antiport.

G. Mauri et al. (Eds.): WMC5 2004, LNCS 3365, pp. 331–343, 2005.

There is no modification to any of the objects, communication is the only driving power of these systems.

Various variants of symport/antiport have been considered in [1], [2], [6], [8] and [9]. In [1] the authors show that passing at most one object per time can generate any recursively enumerable set of numbers using nine membranes; this was improved in [6] to six membranes, which was further improved to five membranes in [2] and to four in [4] and [7]. The most recent improved result is given in [12], where universality is obtained in three membranes.

In this paper, we consider P systems having symport/antiport rules motivated by the movement and regeneration of red blood corpuscles (RBC) in the membranes of mammals. We prove universality of such systems in two membranes using symport/antiport rules of weight one. We give a brief overview of RBCs and their functions and the motivation for considering them in Section 2. In Section 3, we map the functionality of RBCs in the membrane computing scenario, imposing a natural restriction on the movement of objects. We give the formal definition of the class of systems investigated here, and prove a universality result in Section 4.

2   Red Blood Corpuscles (RBC)

Red blood corpuscles (RBC) are the basic elements of all kinds of cells. They are composed of a colorless stroma filled in with semi fluid hemoglobin and other matters. The RBC (also called erythrocytes) make up 44% of the volume of the blood. The rest of the blood are the white cells (1%) and the plasma. The RBC are the small (7/1000 mm diameter) cells in the blood that contain the red pigment, hemoglobin, and carry oxygen around the body.

The RBC are made in the marrow of the flat bones and the blood contains 5 million of them in each cc of blood. The RBC flow through the arteries, veins and capillaries. After an average life of 100-120 days, during which they incur substantial damage, RBCs are broken down and removed by the spleen. The broken up RBCs are taken by the tissues of the body. About 25×10^{10} corpuscles are replaced daily, a turnover rate of 2.5 million per second. Both damaged and normal but "worn-out" erythrocytes are removed from the vascular system by macrophages, which are found primarily in the liver, spleen, and bone marrow. Breakdown products of hemoglobin are used in the formation of bile (bilirubin), and iron is conserved and used in new red cell production. The production rate of RBCs depend on environmental conditions; at high altitudes, shortage of oxygen stimulates the body to produce more erythroprotein (EPO) that stimulates the production of more RBC. We refer to the period of time after which new RBCs are produced (100-120 days) replacing worn-out ones as 'period of replacement'. An organism dies when it is not capable of producing new RBCs within the period of replacement.

The main functions of RBC include:

- Transport oxygen in the blood from the lungs to all the cells and tissues of the body.

– Assist with the transport of carbon (IV) oxide from the tissues to the lungs.
– Regulating the acid-base balance of the blood, preventing large changes in pH.
– Assist when a blood clot is formed.

2.1   Motivation

We are mainly motivated by the following facts about RBC [13]:

(a) RBCs are carriers of oxygen from the lungs to the cells of the body and carbon dioxide back to the lungs.
(b) The production of new RBCs occur periodically, or RBCs are replenished (replaced) periodically.
(c) An organism dies when it is not capable of producing new RBCs.

3   RBCs in the Membrane Computing Scenario

In this section, we try to model the functionality of RBCs in the membrane computing setting. We first discuss some terminology used in this paper. Let μ be a membrane structure and let i be a membrane of μ.

A symport rule associated with membrane i is of the form (a, in), specifying that the object a *enters* the region of membrane i coming from the surrounding region (from the environment, in the case when i is the skin membrane), or of the form (a, out), saying that the object a *exits* from membrane i. An antiport rule associated with membrane i is of the form $(a, out; b, in)$ and says that at the same time a exits membrane i and b enters it.

3.1   Modelling RBCs in P Systems

In the following, we consider P systems with multisets of objects. The multisets of objects represent RBCs. Let μ denote the membrane structure.

In view of 2.1 (a), since RBCs are agents of communication from the lungs to all other cells and back, and do not evolve, we do not use any evolution rules for the objects but only symport/antiport rules. We next model the way the objects move. Since the movement of RBCs happens between the lungs and other cells in the body, the movement of objects in our systems should also be between a specific membrane (say l) and other membranes, where the membrane labeled l is supposed to represent the lungs. The specific membrane l should be one that is innermost.

In view of 2.1 (b), the objects in the P system should be replaced by new ones periodically. This is done by assuming that the environment has arbitrarily many copies of each object, and periodically using an antiport rule $(b, out; a, in)$ in the skin membrane, thereby replacing an object b by an object a. The period of replacement (denotes how often objects are replaced) p is a finite integer in an interval $[min, max]$ where min and max are numbers obtained from the system under consideration.

We now model the movement of objects in the system based on the following facts of RBCs:

F1 An RBC carries carbondioxide from a number of cells/tissues to the lungs, and then carries oxygen back possibly to a number of cells/tissues, after which it gets replaced.

Since the multisets of objects in our systems represent RBCs, their movement should also be in concurrence to the movement of RBCs. The movement of an object in a membrane $j \neq l$ in the initial configuration should be in the order as given below:

1. It can pass through possibly all membranes in μ other than l once (entry once + exit once).
2. It enters l once.
3. It exits l and can again pass through possibly all membranes other than l in μ once (entry once + exit once).
4. It gets replaced.

F2 An RBC carries oxygen from the lungs to a number of cells/tissues, and gets replaced.

The movement of an object in l in the initial configuration should be as follows:

1. It leaves l, and passes through possibly all membranes in μ other than l once (entry once + exit once).
2. It gets replaced.

Since every object is replaced periodically, and replacements happen in the skin membrane, after a few steps of computation (when all objects in the initial configuration are replaced), the movement of every new object will be as in F1. Note also that the skin membrane has not been included in the restrictions F1 1,3 and F2 1 since an exit from the skin corresponds to replacement and entry into the skin corresponds to a new object.

Consider a system of depth $k \geq 1$. Let the skin membrane have $j+1$ children, labeled $c_1, c_2, \ldots, c_{j+1}$. Let the specified membrane l be a descendant of c_{j+1}. Let n_i denote the number of children each c_i has, $1 \leq i \leq j + 1$. Consider an object in any membrane $i \neq l$ of the system in the initial configuration. The movement of such an object should be from i to l and back to some n (n can be the skin) before getting replaced. Similarly, the movement of an object of w_l should be toward the skin membrane, after possibly passing through all other membranes. The minimum number of symport/antiport rules required so that an object executes conditions F1 or F2 is clearly $min = k - 1$. This is so, since an object in w_l can come straight to the skin and get replaced. The maximum number of symport/antiport rules required for satisfying F1 or F2 is

$$max = 2(2j + 1) + 2(k - 2)[2(n_1 + \ldots n_j) + 2(n_{j+1} - 1) + 1].$$

To see this, consider a system of the above description, such that all of $c_1, \ldots, c_{j+1}$ have a descendant at depth k and a new object in the skin membrane. Note that an object in any membrane other than the skin in the initial configuration will not require max rules to do the same. Thus, an object can be replaced if it has been part of at least min symport/antiport rules or if it has been part of at most max symport/antiport rules. Thus, we say that for the above system, the period p is a finite integer in the interval $[min, max]$.

Before going into further details, let us examine an example. Consider the system of depth 4,

$$[_0\ c\ [_1\ [_2\ [_3\ dc\ ]_3\ ]_2\ ]_1\ [_4\ [_5\ ]_5\ ]_4\ [_6\ [_7\ ]_7\ ]_6\ ]_0$$

The system contains the objects c, d in membrane 3 and c in the skin. Here, $l = 3$. Let

$$R_3 = \{(c, out),\ (c, in),\ (d, out; b, in)\},$$
$$R_2 = \{(c, out),\ (c, in),\ (b, in),\ (d, out)\},$$
$$R_1 = \{(c, out),\ (c, in),\ (b, in),\ (d, out)\},$$
$$R_0 = \{(c, out; b, in),\ (d, out; e, in)\},$$
$$R_4 = R_5 = R_6 = R_7 = \{(c, in),\ (c, out)\}.$$

The applicable rules are $(c, out) \in R_3$ to the object c in w_3, and $(c, in) \in R_2$ (or R_4, R_6) to the object c in the skin. Note that the rule $(c, out; b, in)$ in the skin is not applicable to the copy of c in the skin during the first step of computation since it has not yet visited membrane 3. The following are steps of a valid computation:

0. $[_0\ c\ [_1\ [_2\ [_3\ dc\ ]_3\ ]_2\ ]_1\ [_4\ [_5\ ]_5\ ]_4\ [_6\ [_7\ ]_7\ ]_6\ ]_0,$
1. $[_0\ [_1\ [_2\ c\ [_3\ d\ ]_3\ ]_2\ ]_1\ [_4\ c\ [_5\ ]_5\ ]_4\ [_6\ [_7\ ]_7\ ]_6\ ]_0,$
2. $[_0\ [_1\ c\ [_2\ [_3\ d\ ]_3\ ]_2\ ]_1\ [_4\ [_5\ c\ ]_5\ ]_4\ [_6\ [_7\ ]_7\ ]_6\ ]_0,$
3. $[_0\ c\ [_1\ [_2\ [_3\ d\ ]_3\ ]_2\ ]_1\ [_4\ c\ [_5\ ]_5\ ]_4\ [_6\ [_7\ ]_7\ ]_6\ ]_0,$
4. $[_0\ b\ [_1\ [_2\ [_3\ d\ ]_3\ ]_2\ ]_1\ c\ [_4\ [_5\ ]_5\ ]_4\ [_6\ [_7\ ]_7\ ]_6\ ]_0,$
5. $[_0\ [_1\ bc\ [_2\ [_3\ d\ ]_3\ ]_2\ ]_1\ [_4\ [_5\ ]_5\ ]_4\ [_6\ [_7\ ]_7\ ]_6\ ]_0,$
6. $[_0\ [_1\ [_2\ bc\ [_3\ d\ ]_3\ ]_2\ ]_1\ [_4\ [_5\ ]_5\ ]_4\ [_6\ [_7\ ]_7\ ]_6\ ]_0,$
7. $[_0\ [_1\ [_2\ d\ [_3\ bc\ ]_3\ ]_2\ ]_1\ [_4\ [_5\ ]_5\ ]_4\ [_6\ [_7\ ]_7\ ]_6\ ]_0,$
8. $[_0\ [_1\ d\ [_2\ c\ [_3\ b\ ]_3\ ]_2\ ]_1\ [_4\ [_5\ ]_5\ ]_4\ [_6\ [_7\ ]_7\ ]_6\ ]_0,$
9. $[_0\ d\ [_1\ c\ [_2\ [_3\ b\ ]_3\ ]_2\ ]_1\ [_4\ [_5\ ]_5\ ]_4\ [_6\ [_7\ ]_7\ ]_6\ ]_0,$
10. $[_0\ ec\ [_1\ [_2\ [_3\ b\ ]_3\ ]_2\ ]_1\ [_4\ [_5\ ]_5\ ]_4\ [_6\ [_7\ ]_7\ ]_6\ ]_0,$
11. $[_0\ eb\ [_1\ [_2\ [_3\ b\ ]_3\ ]_2\ ]_1\ [_4\ [_5\ ]_5\ ]_4\ [_6\ [_7\ ]_7\ ]_6\ ]_0.$

Here, the object c in the skin was replaced during the 11th rule which used it. Consider a structure like $[_0\ c\ [_1\ [_2\ [_3\ dc\ ]_3\ ]_2\ ]_1\ [_4\ [_5\ [_8\ ]_8\ ]_5\ ]_4\ [_6\ [_7\ [_9\ ]_9\ ]_7\ ]_6\ ]_0$ with $R_8 = R_9 = R_7 = R_6 = R_5 = R_4$ and $R_i, 1 \le i \le 7$ as above, and $j + 1 = 3, c_3 = 1, c_2 = 4, c_3 = 6, l = 3, n_1 = n_2 = n_3 = 1$. If the object c of w_0 had visited all of 4,5,6,7,8 and 9 before visiting membrane 3 and had visited all of them again, it would have been replaced in the 31st rule it takes part in, i.e., after being part of $2(2.2 + 1) + 2.2[2(1 + 1) + 2(1 - 1) + 1] = 30$ rules. Also, note from the above that the object c of w_3 can be replaced during the use of the 4th rule. Hence, the period for the above system lies in $[3, 30]$.

In view of 2.1(c), a computation stops when objects in the system are not replaced periodically; this amounts to saying that there are no more applicable rules in the system after a point of time.

With all the above concepts, we propose a type of P systems having RBC-like objects. Since we are interested in the output of a P system, the result of a computation consists of the number of objects present in a specified membrane after the computation stops.

3.2   Traces of RBCs

In this section, we use the concept of traces of objects introduced in [5]. The trace of an object in our systems is a sequence of moves the object makes in the system before getting replaced. In other words, the trace of an object is a string made up of the labels of the membranes the object visited before getting replaced. For example, consider the membrane structure $[_1 \ b \ [_2 \ c \ ]_2 \ [_3 \ a \ ]_3 \ ]_1$ with $w_1 = \{b\}, w_2 = \{c\}, w_3 = \{a\}, E = \{newa\}$. If there are rules $(a, out; b, in)$ in R_3, $(a, in; c, out)$ and (a, out) in R_2, and $(a, out; newa, in)$ in R_1, then traces of a are 31, 3121.

This idea is very useful for representing the path chosen by an object in our systems, because an object moves along a special trajectory satisfying F1 or F2. Consider the membrane structure $[_1 \ [_5 \ [_2 \ [_3 \ ]_3 \ ]_2 \ [_4 \ ]_4 \ ]_5 \ [_6 \ [_7 \ ]_7 \ [_8 \ ]_8 \ ]_6 \ ]_1$. Let o be a new object in the skin and let 3 be the special membrane l. Then some of the possible traces of o (as per F1) are 1676154523254516761, 1523251, 15452325451, 154523251, 1676861523251. Observe that the first three traces are palindromes. If the trace of a new object is a palindrome, it means that the object visits exactly those membranes it visited before visiting l (or replenishes oxygen to those cells from which it carried carbon dioxide to the lungs).

Now let us consider the trace of an object in a membrane other than the skin during the initial configuration. Let a be an object of w_7. Then the possible traces of a (as per F1) include 761523251, 7686154523251, 7686154523251686761. Let us now consider the trace of an object in l (here 3) in the initial configuration. 3251, 3254541, 32516761, 3251676861 are some of the possible traces. All these are in accordance with F2.

Since every object is replaced periodically by new ones, after a point of time we need to bother about the traces of new objects only. The traces of new objects start with the label of the skin membrane. We enforce the following rules for the traces of objects in our systems:

(a) All traces end with the label of the skin; they contain exactly one occurrence of the label l of the special membrane.
(b) All traces must satisfy F1 or F2.

These are called *rules of traces of RBCs*. Note that an object may have an incomplete trace due to unavailability of rules. In such cases, the trace should be a proper prefix of one of the traces satisfying (a) and (b).

3.3   Formal Definition

A P system with RBC-like objects is a construct

$$\Pi = (V, \mu, w_1, \ldots, w_m, E, R_1, \ldots, R_m, i_0, l, k, p),$$

where:

1. V is the alphabet of objects;
2. μ is the membrane structure with m membranes;
3. $w_1, \ldots, w_m$ are strings over V representing multisets of objects initially present in the regions of the system;
4. $E \subseteq V$ is the set of objects present in the environment in arbitrarily many copies;
5. $R_1, \ldots, R_m$ are finite sets of rules for regions $1, 2, \ldots, m$ of the form $(x, out; y, in)$, for $x, y \in V^*$ with $xy \neq \lambda$; if one of x, y is empty, we have a symport rule, when both x, y are non-empty, we have an antiport rule;
6. i_0 is an elementary membrane of μ (output membrane);
7. l is a specific elementary membrane; k is the depth of μ;
8. p is a finite integer (in $[min, max]$ called *period*, where min and max are as computed in Section 3.1).

Symport/antiport rules are applied as usual in a non-deterministic maximally parallel manner but obeying the rules of traces of RBC's for each object. A sequence of transitions between configurations constitutes a computation; a computation is successful if it halts; i.e., if it reaches a configuration wherein no rules can be applied to any of the available objects, following the rules of traces.

The result of a successful computation is the number of objects present in the membrane labeled i_0 in the halting configuration. A computation which never halts has no result. The set of all numbers computed by Π is denoted by $N(\Pi)$. The family of all sets $N(\Pi)$, computed by systems Π of degree at most m, depth at most k using symport/antiport rules of weight at most q, r is denoted by $NRBC_{m,k}(sym_q, anti_r)$.e

Before going into universality results, we will examine an example. Consider the system

$$\Pi = (\{B, C, a, b, m, n, o\}, [_1 \ [_2[_3 \ ]_3 \ ]_2 \ ]_1, \{a\}, \emptyset,$$
$$\{C\}, \{a, b, n, m, o, B\}, R_1, R_2, R_3, 3, 3, p),$$

with $p \in [2, 4]$ and the following sets of rules:

$R_1 = \{(C, out; b, in), (C, out; B, in), (a, out; aan, in), (n, out; m, in)\}$
$\quad \cup \{(n, out; o, in), (m, out), (b, out)\}$
$R_2 = \{(C, out), (a, in), (n, in), (b, in), (b, out), (a, out), (m, in), (m, out), (n, out)\}$
$R_3 = \{(C, out), (a, in), (n, in), (m, in), (b, out), (n, out), (m, out),$
$\quad (m, in; aa, out), (b, in; a, out)\}.$

To begin with, the rules (C, out) of R_3 and (a, in) of R_2 are applied. Note that the rule $(a, out; aan, in)$ of R_1 is not applicable initially to the object a in w_1. At the end of two steps, a reaches 3 and C goes out bringing in either b or B. If b comes in, then the computation continues. If B enters, then the system halts with a in membrane 3. Assuming b has entered, b can enter membrane 3 pulling

a out. Subsequently, b exits the system, and a is replaced by aan. The symbols a, n reach membrane 3, after which n comes out to the skin. If n is replaced by m, the computation continues, but if n is replaced by o, the system halts. The output of a halting computation is $\{2^n \mid n \geq 0\}$. The traces of objects are as follows: $C : 321, b : 12321, n : 12321, m : 12321$. B and o have no rules, and so they have no traces. The trace of the objects a present in the system after a halting configuration is 123, since there are no rules to pull a out when the system halts. The traces of objects a in all configurations previous to the halting configuration is 12321.

4   Universality

In the following proof of computational universality, we use the characterization of recursively enumerable languages by means of *matrix grammars with appearance checking*. Such a grammar is a construct $G = (N, T, S, M, F)$ where N, T are disjoint alphabets, $S \in N$, M is a finite set of sequences of the form $(A_1 \to x_1, \ldots, A_n \to x_n), n \geq 1$, of context-free rules over $N \cup T$ (with $A_i \in N, x_i \in (N \cup T)^*$), and F is a set of occurrences of rules in M (N is the non-terminal alphabet, T is the terminal alphabet, S is the start symbol, while the elements of M are called matrices).

For $w, z \in (N \cup T)^*$, we write $w \Rightarrow z$ if there is a matrix $(A_1 \to x_1, \ldots, A_n \to x_n)$ in M and the strings $w_i \in (N \cup T)^*, 1 \leq i \leq n + 1$, such that $w = w_1, z = w_{n+1}$, and for all $1 \leq i \leq n$, either $w_i = w_i' A_i w_i''$, $w_{i+1} = w_i' x_i w_i''$, for some $w_i', w_i'' \in (N \cup T)^*$, or $w_i = w_{i+1}$, A_i does not appear in w_i, and the rule $A_i \to x_i$ appears in F. (The rules of a matrix are applied in order, skipping the rules in F that cannot be applied.)

The language generated by G is defined by $L(G) = \{w \in T^* \mid S \Rightarrow^* w\}$. The family of languages of this form is denoted by MAT_{ac}. It is known that $MAT_{ac} = RE$ [3].

The following normal form theorem was given in [9].

A matrix grammar with appearance checking $G = (N, T, S, M, F)$ is said to be in Z-binary normal form if $N = N_1 \cup N_2 \cup \{S, Z, \dagger\}$, with these three sets mutually disjoint, and the matrices in M are in one of the following forms:

1. $(S \to XA)$, with $X \in N_1, A \in N_2$,
2. $(X \to Y, A \to x)$, with $X, Y \in N_1, A \in N_2, x \in (N_2 \cup T)^*, |x| \leq 2$,
3. $(X \to Y, A \to \dagger)$, with $X \in N_1, Y \in N_1 \cup \{Z\}, A \in N_2$,
4. $(Z \to \lambda)$.

Moreover, there is only one matrix of type 1, F consists exactly of all rules $A \to \dagger$ appearing in matrices of type 3 and if a sentential form generated by G contains the symbol Z, then the string will be of the form $Zw, w \in (T \cup \{\dagger\})^*$.

Theorem 1. $NRE = NRBCP_{2,2}(sym_1, anti_1)$.

Proof. We only have to prove the inclusion $\subseteq$. For that purpose, let us consider a matrix grammar with appearance checking $G = (N, T, S, M, F)$ in the Z-binary normal form. Since we deal with the length of the strings, it is enough to consider $T = \{a\}$. Let there be $n+2$ matrices in M, injectively labeled $m_0, m_1, \ldots, m_{n+1}$, with $m_0 : (S \rightarrow X_0 A_0)$ being the initial one; the next k matrices $m_i : (X \rightarrow Y, A \rightarrow x)$, $1 \leq i \leq k$, of type 2 without appearance checking, and the next $n - k$ matrices of type 3, $m_i : (X \rightarrow Y, A \rightarrow \dagger), k + 1 \leq i \leq n$. Finally we have $m_{n+1} : (Z \rightarrow \lambda)$. We say $X \rightarrow Y, A \rightarrow x \in m_i$ or $X \rightarrow Y, A \rightarrow \dagger \in m_i$ if $m_i : (X \rightarrow Y, A \rightarrow x)$ or $(X \rightarrow Y, A \rightarrow \dagger)$ is a matrix in G for some i, respectively. We construct the P system of degree 2e , depth 2, having RBC like objects and symport/antiport rules of weight 1

$$\Pi = (V, [_1 [_2]_2]_1, w_1, w_2, E, R_1, R_2, 2, 2, p),$$

$$V = N_1 \cup N_2 \cup \{A_i', X_j', T_j, S_j \mid A \in N_2, X \in N_1, 1 \leq i \leq n, k+1 \leq j \leq n\}$$
$$\cup \{j \mid 1 \leq j \leq n\},$$
$$w_1 = \{X_0, a', \kappa\} \cup \{j, A_j', S_i, T_i \mid 1 \leq j \leq n, k+1 \leq i \leq n\},$$
$$w_2 = \{A_0\} \cup \{X_i' \mid k+1 \leq i \leq n\},$$
$$E = \{\langle \alpha\beta \rangle, \langle \gamma \rangle, C_i, Y_j, Z, e, L_q, \dagger, X_l', T_l, S_l \mid \alpha \in \{B_j, a\}, \beta \in \{C_i, a, e\},$$
$$\gamma \in \{C_i, a, e, Y_j, Z\}, B, C \in N_2, \ X, Y, Z \in N_1, 1 \leq i, j, \leq n,$$
$$k+1 \leq l \leq n, \ k+2 \leq q \leq n\},$$

p is an integer in the interval $[1,2]$ (every object which has communicated for one or two steps obeying the rules of traces will be replaced), and the rules as defined below.

The work of the P system is divided into 3 phases.

(1) Simulation of matrices $m_i : (X \rightarrow Y, A \rightarrow x)$

The following rules are introduced in R_1

1. $\{(A_i, out; \langle \alpha\beta \rangle, in), (A_i, out; \langle e \rangle, in) \mid \alpha \in \{B_j, a\}, \beta \in \{C_r, a, e\},$
   $A, B, C \in N_2,$ for $A \rightarrow BC \in m_i,$ or $A \rightarrow aC \in m_i,$ or
   $A \rightarrow Ba \in m_i,$ or $A \rightarrow aa \in m_i,$ or $A \rightarrow B \in m_i,$ or $A \rightarrow a \in m_i$
   or $A \rightarrow \lambda \in m_i, 0 \leq i \leq k, 1 \leq j, r \leq n,$ and $B \rightarrow x \in m_j$ or
   $B \rightarrow \dagger \in m_j,$ and $C \rightarrow y \in m_r$ or $C \rightarrow \dagger \in m_r\},$

5. $\{(\langle \alpha\beta \rangle, out); (\langle \beta \rangle, in) \mid \alpha \in \{B_j, a\}, \beta \in \{C_r, a, e\}, B, C \in N_2,$
   $1 \leq j, r \leq n\},$

7. $\{(B_j', out; B_j, in) \mid 1 \leq j \leq n\} \cup \{(a', out; a, in)\},$

9. $\{(X_i, out; \langle Y_j \rangle, in) \mid X \rightarrow Y \in m_i, \ X, Y \in N_1,$
   $1 \leq i \leq k, 1 \leq j \leq n,$ and $Y \rightarrow Y' \in m_j, Y' \in N_1\}$
   $\cup \{(X_i, out; \langle Z \rangle, in) \mid X, Z \in N_1, 1 \leq i \leq k$ and $X \rightarrow Z \in m_i\}$

11. $\{(j, out; B_j', in) \mid 1 \leq j \leq n\} \cup \{(\kappa, out; a', in)\}$

13. $\{(\langle \alpha \rangle, out); (\alpha, in) \mid \alpha \in \{a, C_r, e\}, 1 \leq r \leq n\} \cup \{(e, out)\}$

14. $\{(j, in) \mid 1 \le j \le n\} \cup \{(\kappa, in)\}$

16. $\{(\langle Y_j \rangle, out; Y_j, in) \mid 1 \le j \le n\} \cup \{(\langle Z \rangle, out; Z, in)\}$,

and the following rules are introduced in R_2:

2. $\{(X_i, in; A_i, out) \mid X \in N_1, A \in N_2, 0 \le i \le k\}$

3. $\{(\langle \alpha\beta \rangle, in) \mid \alpha \in \{B_j, a\}, \beta \in \{C_r, a, e\}, 1 \le j, r \le n\}$

4. $\{(\langle \alpha\beta \rangle, out); (\alpha', in), \mid \alpha \in \{B_j, a\}, \beta \in \{C_r, a, e\}, 1 \le j, r \le n\}$

6. $\{(B'_j, out; j, in) \mid 1 \le j \le n\} \cup \{(a', out; \kappa, in)\}$

8. $\{(\langle \alpha \rangle, in; X_i, out) \mid \alpha \in \{C_r, a, e\}, C \in N_2, X \in N_1, \ 0 \le i \le k,$
   $1 \le r \le n\}$

10. $\{(B_j, in; j, out) \mid 1 \le j \le n\} \cup \{(a, in; \kappa, out)\}$

12. $\{(\langle \alpha \rangle, out); (\langle \beta \rangle, in) \mid \ \alpha \in \{C_r, a, e\}, \beta \in \{Y_j, Z\}, C \in N_2, Y, Z \in N_1,$
   $1 \le r, j \le n\}$

15. $\{(\alpha, in; \langle \beta \rangle, out) \mid \alpha \in \{C_r, a, e\}, \beta \in \{Y_j, Z\}, 1 \le r, j \le n\}$
   $\cup \{(e, out)\}$

In the initial configuration, the symbol X_0 is in the skin and the corresponding A_0 in the special membrane l (here $l=2$). To start the computation, rule 2 of R_2 is used which brings out A_0 to the skin. This is followed by rule 1 of R_1 bringing in one of the symbols $\langle B_j C_r \rangle, \langle a C_r \rangle, \langle C_r a \rangle, \langle aa \rangle$ etc. as the case may be. Rules 3,4 follow next. The symbol B'_j or a' enters membrane 2 by rule 4. Iinally, $\langle B_j C_r \rangle$ (or $\langle a C_r \rangle, \langle C_r a \rangle, \langle aa \rangle$) leaves the skin using rule 5, bringing in another symbol $\langle C_r \rangle$ or $\langle a \rangle$. Rule 6 is applied in parallel with rule 5, pushing out B'_j or a' from membrane 2. The symbol j which keeps track of the indices of matrices enters membrane 2 instead. Next, rules 7 and 8 are applied in parallel, pushing out $X_i, 0 \le i \le k$, from membrane 2, and obtaining the symbol $B_j, 1 \le j \le n$, from the environment. The symbol X_i then gets its corresponding symbol of N_1 from E in the form $\langle Y_j \rangle$ and the symbol B_j enters membrane 2 respectively by rules 9 and 10. Rules 11 and 12 follow next in parallel, getting back B'_j and getting $\langle C_r \rangle$ out of membrane 2. Rules 13 and 14 follow in parallel, getting C_r from E getting back j to the skin. We have now completed simulating the rule $A \rightarrow BC$ of $m_i, 0 \le i \le k$. What needs to be completed now is the simulation of $X \rightarrow Y$. To this end, rule 15 is used, bringing out $\langle Y_j \rangle$. Rule 16 now sends this symbol out, getting Y_j, to start the next round of simulation.

(2) Simulation of matrices $m_i : (X \rightarrow Y, A \rightarrow \dagger)$

We introduce in R_1 the rules:

3. $\{(X'_l, out; X'_l, in) \mid k+1 \le l \le n\}$,

5. $\{(X_l, out; Y_q, in) \mid X, Y \in N_1$ and $X \rightarrow Y \in m_l, \ k+1 \le l \le n,$
   $1 \le q \le n$ and $Y \rightarrow Y' \in m_q, Y' \in N_1\}$
   $\cup \{(X_l, out; Z, in) \mid X, Z \in N_1$ and $X \rightarrow Z \in m_l, \ k+1 \le l \le n\}$,

7. $\{(T_l, in; T_l, out) \mid k+1 \leq l \leq n\}$,

9. $\{(A_l, out; \dagger, in) \mid k+1 \leq l \leq n\}$,

10. $\{(S_l, in; S_l, out) \mid k+1 \leq l \leq n\}$,

12. $\{(\dagger, in; \dagger, out)\}$,

and in R_2 the rules:

1. $\{(X_l, in; X_l', out) \mid k+1 \leq l \leq n\}$,

2. $\{(X_l, out; T_l, in) \mid k+1 \leq l \leq n\}$,

4. $\{(X_l', in; A_l, out) \mid k+1 \leq l \leq n \text{ and } A \rightarrow \dagger \in m_l\}$,

6. $\{(S_l, in; T_l, out) \mid k+1 \leq l \leq n\}$,

8. $\{(X_l', in; S_l, out) \mid k+1 \leq l \leq n\}$,

11. $\{(\dagger, in), (\dagger, out)\}$.

The simulation of type 3 matrices is initiated by rule 1 of R_2. The symbol X_l, $k+1 \leq l \leq n$ enters membrane 2, while X_l' comes out. This is followed by rules 2 and 3 in parallel. Rule 3 has to be applied here for X_l' to preserve the rules of traces. Rules 5,6 and 4 (if applicable) follow next in parallel. Rules 7, 8 (if not rule 4 in the previous step) and 9 (if rule 4 in the previous step) are the next set of possible rules. Assuming we applied rules 5,6 simultaneously and then rules 7 and 8, we can successfully start another simulation. But if rules 4 and 9 were applied, the system will never halt, because rules 11 and 12 can be applied forever, cyclically.

(3) Termination:

We introduce the rules:

3. $\{(Z, out; L_{k+2}, in)\}$,

6. $\{(L_i, out; L_{i+1}, in) \mid k+2 \leq i \leq n-1\}$

in R_1, and the rules:

1. $\{(Z, in; X_{k+1}', out)\}$,

2. $\{(Z, out)\}$,

4. $\{(L_i, in; X_i', out) \mid k+2 \leq i \leq n\}$,

5. $\{(L_i, out) \mid k+2 \leq i \leq n\}$,

in R_2.

Once the symbol Z appears, we can be sure that the remaining symbols computed are over $T \cup \{\dagger\}$. Assuming that there is no $\dagger$ present (otherwise the computation never stops), we need to eliminate all the X_l', $k+1 \leq l \leq n$, from membrane 2, the output membrane. Rule 1 is used first getting out X_{k+1}' from membrane 2. This is followed by rules 2 and 3, obtaining the symbol L_{k+2} from E. Rule 4 is applied to get the next symbol from membrane 2. Rules 5, 6 then ensure that the contents of membrane 2 at the end of a halting computation is $L(G)$. Observe that all objects other than a have complete traces in a halting configuration. The traces of all new objects introduced other then a is 121 and the trace of objects of w_2 is 21. The trace of the a's is 12.   □

Corollary 1. $NFIN \subseteq NRBCP_{1,1}(sym_1, anti_0) = NRBCP_{1,1}(sym_0, anti_1) = NRBCP_{1,1}(sym_1, anti_1) = NRBCP_{2,2}(sym_1, anti_0) = NRBCP_{2,2}(sym_0, snti_1) \subset NRBCP_{2,2}(sym_1, anti_1) = NRE.$

Remark 1. The above universality result also supports the known fact that there is no interaction between RBCs (except when agglutination occurs) [17]. Hence, symport/antiport rules of weight one are sufficient to model their activity.

References

1. F. Bernadini, M. Gheorghe, On the power of minimal symport/antiport. *Pre-proceedings of Workshop on Membrane Computing, WMC2003*, Tarragona, Spain, July 2003, GRLMC Report 28/03, 72–83.
2. F. Bernadini, A. Păun, Symport/antiport: Five membranes suffices. *Membrane Computing. Intern. Workshop, WMC2003, Tarragona, Lecture Notes in Computer Science* 2933, Springer-Verlag, Berlin, 2004, 43–54.
3. J. Dassow, G. Păun, *Regulated Rewriting in Formal Language Theory.* Springer-Verlag, Berlin, 1990.
4. P. Frisco, About P systems with symport/antiport. *Second Brainstorming Week on Membrane Computing*, Sevilla, Spain, Feb. 2004, RGNC Res. Rep. 01/2004, 224–236.
5. Ionescu M., Martin-Vide C, Păun G., P systems with symport/antiport rules: The traces of objects. *Grammars*, 5, 2 (2002), 65–79.
6. L. Kari, C. Martin-Vide, A. Păun, Universality of P systems with minimal symport/antiport rules. In *Aspects of Molecular Computing: Essays Dedicated to Tom Head on the Occasion of his 70th Birthday, Lecture Notes in Computer Science* 2950, Springer-Verlag, Berlin, 2004, 254–265.
7. M. Margenstern, V. Rogozhin, Y. Rogozhin, S. Verlan, About P systems with minimal symport/antiport rules and four membranes. *Pre-proceedings of Workshop on Membrane Computing, WMC5*, Milan, Italy, June 2004, 283–294.
8. C. Martin-Vide, A. Păun, G. Păun, On the power of P systems with symport rules. *Journal of Universal Computer Science*, 8 (2002), 317–331.
9. C. Martin-Vide, A. Păun, G. Păun, G. Rozenberg, Membrane systems with coupled transport: universality and normal forms. *Fundamenta Informaticae*, 49 (2002), 1–15.
10. A. Păun, G. Păun, The power of communication: P systems with symport/antiport. *New Generation Computing*, 20, 3 (2002), 295–306.
11. G. Păun, Computing with membranes. *Journal of Computer and System Sciences*, 61, 1 (2000), 108–143.
12. G. Vaszil, On the size of P systems with minimal symport/antiport. *Pre-proceedings of Workshop on Membrane Computing, WMC5*, Milan, Italy, June 2004, 422–431.

13. http://www.earthlife.net/mammals/blood.html
14. http://www.botany.uwc.ac.za/sci_ed/grade10/mammal/blood.htm
15. http://www.link.med.ed.ac.uk/RIDU/BLOOD.pdf
16. http://www.starsandseas.com/SAS%20Physiology/Blood.htm
17. http://nobelprize.org/medicine/educational/landsteiner/readmore.html

Conservative Computations in Energy–Based P Systems

Alberto Leporati, Claudio Zandron, and Giancarlo Mauri

Dipartimento di Informatica, Sistemistica e Comunicazione,
Università degli Studi di Milano – Bicocca,
Via Bicocca degli Arcimboldi 8, 20126 Milano, Italy
{leporati, zandron, mauri}@disco.unimib.it

Abstract. Energy–based P systems have been recently introduced as P systems in which the amount of energy consumed and/or manipulated during computations is taken into account. In this paper we consider *conservative computations* performed by energy–based P systems, that is, computations for which the amount of energy entering the system is the same as the amount of energy leaving it. We show that conservative computations naturally allow to define an NP–hard optimization problem, here referred to as MIN STORAGE, and a corresponding NP–complete decision problem, CONSCOMP. Finally, we present a polynomial time 2–approximation algorithm for MIN STORAGE.

1 Preliminaries

P systems (also called *membrane systems*) were introduced in [16] as a new class of distributed and parallel computing devices, inspired by the structure and functioning of living cells. The basic model consists of a hierarchical structure composed by several membranes, embedded into a main membrane called the *skin*. Membranes divide the Euclidean space into *regions*, that contain some *objects* (represented by symbols of an alphabet) and *evolution rules*. Using these rules, the objects may evolve and/or move from a region to a neighboring one. The rules are applied in a nondeterministic and maximally parallel way: all the objects that may evolve are forced to evolve. A *computation* starts from an initial configuration of the system and terminates when no evolution rule can be applied. The result of a computation is the multiset of objects contained into an *output membrane* or emitted from the skin of the system.

In what follows we assume the reader is already familiar with the basic notions and the terminology underlying P systems. For details, and a systematic introduction on the subject, we refer the reader to [18]. The latest information about P systems can be found in [22].

Energy–based P systems have been introduced in [13] as P systems in which the amount of energy manipulated and/or consumed during computations is taken into account. A given amount of energy is associated to each object of the system. Moreover, instances of a special symbol e are used to denote free

G. Mauri et al. (Eds.): WMC5 2004, LNCS 3365, pp. 344–358, 2005.
© Springer-Verlag Berlin Heidelberg 2005

energy units occurring into the regions of the system. These energy units can be used to transform objects, using appropriate rules. The rules are defined according to conservativeness considerations: for each rule of the system, the amount of energy occurring on the left side is the same as the amount of energy occurring on the right side. An object can always be transformed into another object having the same energy. On the other hand, if the transformed object has a different energy then the required (resp., exceeding) free energy units are taken from (resp., released to) the region where the rule is applied. We assume that the application of rules consumes no energy. This means, in particular, that objects can be moved (without altering them) between the regions of the system without energy consumption. A special case of energy–based P systems are *conservative* P systems, where the amount of energy entering the system with the input values is completely returned with the output values at the end of the computation, and no free energy units enter or leave the system during the computation.

Formally, an energy–based P system (of degree $m \geq 1$) is a construct

$$\Pi = (A, \varepsilon, \mu, e, w_1, \ldots, w_m, R_1, \ldots, R_m, i_{\mathrm{in}}, i_{\mathrm{out}}),$$

where:

- A is an alphabet; its elements are called *objects*;
- $\varepsilon : A \to \mathbb{N}$ is a linear mapping that associates to each object $a \in A$ the value $\varepsilon(a)$ (also denoted by ε_a), which can be thought of as the "energy value of a". If $\varepsilon(a) = \ell$, we also say that object a *embeds* ℓ units of energy. Precisely, if $A = \{a_1, a_2, \ldots, a_d\}$ then for all $i \in \{1, 2, \ldots, d\}$ it holds $\varepsilon(a_i) = \varepsilon(a_1) + (i-1)\delta$ for an appropriate integer value $\delta > 0$. Hence, the energy values considered in the system are equispaced by the quantity δ. By adding "dummy" symbols into the alphabet (that is, symbols which never appear in the system during the computations), we can always assume $\delta = 1$ without loss of generality;
- μ is a hierarchical membrane structure consisting of m membranes. For the sake of clarity, we will label membranes with mnemonic identifiers which recall their function;
- $e \notin A$ is a special symbol that denotes one *free energy* unit, that is, one unit of energy which is not embedded into any object;
- w_i, for all $i \in \{1, \ldots, m\}$, specify the multisets (over $A \cup \{e\}$) of objects initially present in region i;
- R_i, for all $i \in \{1, \ldots, m\}$, is a finite set of evolution rules over A associated with region i. Only rules of the following types are allowed:

$$ae^k \to (b, p) \ , \qquad a \to (b, p)e^k \ , \qquad e \to (e, p)$$

where $a, b \in A$, $p \in \{\mathrm{here}, \mathrm{in}(name), \mathrm{out}\}$ and k is a non negative integer;
- i_{in} is an integer between 1 and m and specifies the input membrane of Π;
- i_{out} is an integer between 0 and m and specifies the output membrane of Π. If $i_{\mathrm{out}} = 0$, then the environment is used for the output, that is, the output value is the multiset of objects (over A) emitted from the skin.

A special attention is due to the definition of rules. The meaning of rule $ae^k \to (b, p)$, with $a, b \in A$, $p \in \{here, in(name), out\}$, and k a positive integer number, is the following: the object a, in presence of k free energy units, is allowed to be transformed into object b. If $p = here$ then the new object b remains in the same region; if $p = out$ then b leaves the current membrane. Finally, if $p = in(name)$ then b enters into the membrane labelled with $name$, which must be a child of the current membrane in the membrane hierarchy.

The meaning of rule $a \to (b, p)e^k$, when k is a positive integer number, is analogous. The object a is allowed to be transformed into object b by releasing k units of free energy. As above, the new object b may optionally move one level up or down into the membrane hierarchy. The k free energy units can now be used by another rule to produce "more energetic" objects from "less energetic" ones.

When $k = 0$ the rule $ae^k \to (b, p)$ is written as $a \to (a, p)$, and simply moves (if $p \neq here$) the object a upward or downward into the membrane hierarchy, without acquiring nor releasing any free energy unit. Analogously, rules $e \to (e, p)$ simply move (if $p \neq here$) one unit of free energy upward or downward into the membrane hierarchy.

A further constraint is that each rule must be "conservative", in the sense that the amount of energy occurring on the left side of the rule must be the same as the amount of energy which occurs on the right side.

With a little abuse of notation, when the pair (x, p), with $x \in A \cup \{e\}$ and $p \in \{here, in(name), out\}$, appears into a rule we will write x_p. Also, if $p = in(name)$ and no confusion arises we will usually write just the name of the membrane. Moreover, instead of writing e^k we will sometimes explicitly write k instances of e. It is also understood that the position of e^k (that is, on the left or on the right of the symbol of A) either into the left or into the right side of a rule is uninfluent. Finally, when the position p of an object which occurs in the right side of a rule is "here" we will omit to write it.

Example 1. Let us assume $A = \{a, b, c, d\}$, where the objects have energy values $\varepsilon_a = 1$, $\varepsilon_b = 2$, $\varepsilon_c = 3$ and $\varepsilon_d = 4$. Then the application of the rule $be^2 \to (d, out)$ (also written as $bee \to d_{out}$) transforms an instance of the object b into an instance of the object d, provided that two free energy units are available, and makes the new object d exit from the current membrane.

On the other hand, the application of the rule $c \to (a, here)e^2$ (also written as $c \to aee$) transforms an instance of the object c into an instance of the object a and releases two free energy units into the region which contains the rule.

Let us also note that in case of necessity (for example, during proofs) we can safely assume that for each rule at most one instance of e cooperates with a symbol of the alphabet. In fact, any rule of the kind $a \to (b, p)e^k$, with $a, b \in A$ and $p \in \{here, in(name), out\}$, involving k instances of e, can be decomposed as follows:

$$a \rightarrow (b_1, \text{here})e$$
$$b_1 \rightarrow (b_2, \text{here})e$$

$$\vdots$$

$$b_{k-2} \rightarrow (b_{k-1}, \text{here})e$$
$$b_{k-1} \rightarrow (b, p)e$$

by adding to the alphabet the *new* symbols $b_1, \ldots, b_{k-1}$. An analogous observation holds for rules of the kind $ae^k \rightarrow (b, p)$.

A possible extension of the model, which is nevertheless uninfluent with respect to the problems considered in this paper, is to allow the use of constructor and destructor rules. A *constructor rule* is a rule of the kind $e^k \rightarrow (a, p)$, where $a \in A$, $\varepsilon_a = k$, $p \in \{\text{here}, \text{in}(name), \text{out}\}$ and k is a positive integer. Informally, a constructor rule for an object $a \in A$ is a rule which uses ε_a free energy units to build the object a. In other words, we allow transformations from "pure" energy to system objects. Analogously, a *destructor rule* is a rule of the kind $a \rightarrow e^k$, where $a \in A$ and $\varepsilon_a = k$ (a positive integer). Hence, a destructor rule for an object $a \in A$ is a rule which transforms the object a into ε_a units of free energy.

A *configuration* of Π is the tuple $(M_1, \ldots, M_m)$ of multisets (over $A \cup \{e\}$) of objects contained in each region of the system. $(w_1, \ldots, w_m)$ is called the *initial configuration*. For two configurations $(M_1, \ldots, M_m)$, $(M'_1, \ldots, M'_m)$ of Π we write $(M_1, \ldots, M_m) \Rightarrow (M'_1, \ldots, M'_m)$ to denote a *transition* from $(M_1, \ldots, M_m)$ to $(M'_1, \ldots, M'_m)$. The reflexive and transitive closure of $\Rightarrow$ is denoted by $\Rightarrow^*$. A *final configuration* is a configuration where no rule can be applied.

A *computation* is a sequence of transitions between configurations of Π, starting from the initial configuration. A computation is *successful* if and only if it reaches a final configuration or, in other words, it *halts*. It is understood that the multiset (over A, that is, not considering free energy units) of objects which occur in $w_{i_{in}}$ are the *input values* for the computation. Analogously, the multiset (over A) of objects occurring in the output membrane (or emitted from the skin if $i_{out} = 0$) in the final configuration is the *output* of the computation. A non–halting computation produces no output.

If $\mathcal{M}$ denotes the set of all possible multisets over A then we can define the *function* $G : \mathcal{M} \rightarrow 2^{\mathcal{M}} \cup \{\perp\}$ *computed by* Π as the (partial) function that to each multiset $M \in \mathcal{M}$ associates the set $G(M)$ of possible multisets which can be produced in output by Π when given M in input. If the computation does not halt then $G(M) = \perp$. Here we stress that, for a halting computation, only one of the multisets in $G(M)$ is nondeterministically produced in output. With an abuse of notation, for any fixed computation we denote also this multiset by $G(M)$.

Since energy is an additive quantity, it is natural to define the *energy of a multiset* M, denoted by $E(M)$, as the sum of the amounts of energy associated to each instance of the objects which occur into M. Analogously, the *energy of a configuration* $\mathcal{C} = (M_1, \ldots, M_m)$, denoted by $E(\mathcal{C})$, is the sum of the amounts of energy associated to each multiset which occurs into the configuration: $E(\mathcal{C}) = \sum_{i=1}^{m} E(M_i)$. A *conservative energy–based P system* can thus be defined as an energy–based P system such that for every possible computation all configurations have the same amount of energy. Moreover, in a conservative P system it is required that the amount of energy entering the system with the input multiset M is entirely returned with the output multiset $G(M)$ at the end of the computation. Let us note that conservativeness is here defined as a mathematical notion; namely, it is *not* required that the entire energy used to perform the computations is preserved or that the computing device is a *physical* conservative system (an ideal but unrealistic situation). In particular, we do not consider the energy needed to supply the computing device.

In [14] we have shown that energy–based P systems are able to simulate any reversible circuit made of Fredkin gates. Since families $\{FC_n\}_{n\in\mathbb{N}}$ of reversible Fredkin circuits are able to compute any family $\{f_n\}_{n\in\mathbb{N}}$ of boolean functions, (families of) energy–based P systems constitute a *universal* model of computation. The simulating P systems considered in [14] are *self–reversible*, meaning that the same system is able to perform both "forward" and "backward" computations, that is, to compute the output values corresponding to any given input values, and vice versa. An interesting aspect of the simulations presented in [14] is that the simulating P systems are also *conservative*: the amount of energy present into the system during computations is constant. Hence it is possible to perform universal computations using only self–reversible and conservative P systems.

This is by no means the first time that energy is considered when dealing with P systems. The energy balancing of processes in a cell was first investigated in [21] and then in [5]. There the energies of all rules to be used in a given step in a membrane are summed up; if the total amount of energies is positive [21] or within a given range [5], then this multiset of rules can be applied if it is maximal with this property. Energy and associations between energy and information have also been considered in [1, 7, 8, 9].

The paper is organized as follows. In Section 2 we define conservative computations for energy–based P systems. Moreover, we introduce the NP–hard optimization problem MIN STORAGE and its corresponding NP–complete decision version, CONSCOMP. In Section 3 a 2–approximation algorithm for MIN STORAGE is presented. Section 4 proposes conservative languages with some directions for future research. Finally, Section 5 concludes the paper.

2   Conservative Computations

As stated above, in a conservative energy–based P system the amount of energy entering the system with the input values is completely returned with the output values at the end of the computation. This means, in particular, that if some free energy units are present in the initial configuration $(w_1, \ldots, w_m)$ of a computation then these energy units will occur also in the final configuration. Once the output values have been removed from the output membrane (or, alternatively, once they have been expelled from the skin), this amount of free energy units can be used to perform another computation.

This situation suggests the following scenario. Assume that we have a sequence $S_{in} = \langle M_1, M_2, \ldots, M_k \rangle$ of multisets (over A) to be used as input values for an energy–based P system Π. Moreover, assume that we already know that Π will produce the multisets $G(M_1), \ldots, G(M_k)$ when given in input $M_1, \ldots, M_k$, where $G(M_i) \neq \bot$ for all $i \in \{1, 2, \ldots, k\}$. Let $E(M_1), \ldots, E(M_k)$ and $E(G(M_1)), \ldots, E(G(M_k))$ be the energies associated with the input and output multisets, respectively, and let us consider the quantities $e_i = E(M_i) - E(G(M_i))$, for all $i \in \{1, 2, \ldots, k\}$. As told above, we may assume without loss of generality that all e_i's are integer values. We say that the computation of the output sequence $S_{out} = \langle G(M_1), \ldots, G(M_k) \rangle$, obtained starting from S_{in}, is *conservative* if the following condition holds:

$$\sum_{i=1}^{k} e_i = \sum_{i=1}^{k} E(M_i) - \sum_{i=1}^{k} E(G(M_i)) = 0$$

This condition formalizes the requirement that the total energy provided by *all* input multisets of S_{in} is used to build all the output multisets of S_{out}. If no additional energy, in the form of free energy units, is supplied during the computation of S_{out} then this condition formalizes also the requirement that the energy entering the system during the computation is equal to the energy leaving it. Of course it may happen that $e_i > 0$ or $e_i < 0$ for some $i \in \{1, 2, \ldots, k\}$. In the former case some free energy units remain into the system after producing $G(M_i)$. These energy units can be used during the computation of subsequent output multisets $G(M_{i+1}), \ldots, G(M_k)$. Hence the P system Π acts as an *accumulator* of energy. Notice that in every conceivable physical realization of a P system there is a bound on the maximum amount C of energy units (both free and embedded into objects) which can be stored into the system. We call C the *capacity* of the system.

If the output multisets $G(M_1), G(M_2), \ldots, G(M_k)$ of S_{out} are computed exactly in this order then, assuming that the system Π starts with zero internal energy, it is easily seen that $st_1 := e_1$, $st_2 := e_1 + e_2$, $\ldots$, $st_k := e_1 + e_2 + \ldots + e_k$ is the *sequence of the amounts of energy stored* into the system during the computation of S_{out}. Notice that $st_k = 0$ for conservative computations, so the amount of energy stored into the system at the end of the computation is zero.

In some cases the order with which the output multisets of S_{out} are computed does not matter. We can thus introduce the following problem: Given an input sequence $\langle M_1, \ldots, M_k \rangle$ and the corresponding output sequence $\langle G(M_1), \ldots, G(M_k) \rangle$, is there a permutation $\pi \in S_k$ (the symmetrical group of order k) such that the computation of $G(M_{\pi(1)}), \ldots, G(M_{\pi(k)})$ can be performed by an energy–based P system having a predefined capacity C? This is a decision problem, whose formal statement follows. (Note that we do not actually need to know the multisets $M_1, \ldots, M_k$ and $G(M_1), \ldots, G(M_k)$: all we need are the values $e_i = E(M_i) - E(G(M_i))$, for $i \in \{1, 2, \ldots, k\}$.)

Let $\mathcal{E} = \langle e_1, e_2, \ldots, e_k \rangle$ be a finite sequence of integer numbers. For a fixed $i \in \{1, 2, \ldots, k\}$, the *i-th prefix sum of* $\mathcal{E}$ is the value $\sum_{j=1}^{i} e_j$. Let C be a positive integer; we say that $\mathcal{E}$ is C–feasible if for each $i \in \{1, 2, \ldots, k\}$ the i-th prefix sum of $\mathcal{E}$ is in the closed interval $[0, C]$.

Problem 1. NAME: CONSCOMP.

- INSTANCE: a set $\mathcal{E} = \{e_1, e_2, \ldots, e_k\}$ of integer numbers such that $e_1 + e_2 + \ldots + e_k = 0$, and an integer number $C > 0$.
- QUESTION: is there a permutation $\pi \in S_k$ (the symmetric group of order k) such that the sequence $e_{\pi(1)}, e_{\pi(2)}, \ldots, e_{\pi(k)}$ is C–feasible? □

The fact that the resulting sequence $e_{\pi(1)}, e_{\pi(2)}, \ldots, e_{\pi(k)}$ is C–feasible can be explicitly written as:

$$0 \leq \sum_{j=1}^{i} e_{\pi(j)} \leq C \qquad \forall i \in \{1, 2, \ldots, k\} \qquad (1)$$

The CONSCOMP problem can be obviously solved by trying every possible permutation π from S_k. However, this procedure requires an exponential time with respect to k, the length of the input sequence. A natural question is whether it is possible to give the correct answer in polynomial time. With the following theorem we show that the CONSCOMP problem is NP–complete, and hence it is very unlikely that a polynomial time algorithm exists that solves it. The proof of this theorem was originally published in [4].

Theorem 1. CONSCOMP *is* NP–*complete.*

Proof. CONSCOMP is clearly in NP, since a permutation $\pi \in S_k$ has linear length and verifying whether π is a solution can be done in polynomial time. In order to conclude that CONSCOMP is NP–complete, let us show a polynomial reduction from PARTITION, which is a well known NP–complete problem [10, page 47]. Let $A = \{a_1, a_2, \ldots, a_k\}$ be a set of positive integer numbers, and let $m = \sum_{i=1}^{k} a_i$. The set A is a positive instance of PARTITION if and only if there exists a set $A' \subseteq A$ such that $\sum_{a \in A'} a = \frac{m}{2}$. If m is odd then A is certainly a negative instance, and we can associate it to any negative instance of CONSCOMP. On the other hand, if m is even then we build the corresponding instance $(\mathcal{E}, C)$ of CONSCOMP by putting $C = \frac{m}{2}$ and $\mathcal{E} = \{e_1, e_2, \ldots, e_k, e_{k+1}, e_{k+2}\}$, where $e_i = -a_i$ for all $i \in \{1, 2, \ldots, k\}$ and $e_{k+1} = e_{k+2} = \frac{m}{2}$. It is immediately seen that this construction can be performed in polynomial time.

We claim that A is a positive instance of PARTITION if and only if $(\mathcal{E}, C)$ is a positive instance of CONSCOMP. In fact, let us assume that A is a positive instance of PARTITION. Then there exists a set $A' \subseteq A$ such that $\sum_{a \in A'} a = \frac{m}{2}$, and the corresponding negative elements of $\mathcal{E}$ constitute a subset $\mathcal{E}'$ such that $\sum_{e \in \mathcal{E}'} e = -\frac{m}{2}$. We build a permutation $\pi \in S_k$ by selecting first the element e_{k+1} followed by the elements of $\mathcal{E}'$ (chosen with any order), and then e_{k+2} followed by the remaining elements of $\mathcal{E}$. It is immediately seen that π satisfies the inequalities stated in (1), and hence $(\mathcal{E}, C)$ is a positive instance of CONSCOMP. Conversely, let us assume that $(\mathcal{E}, C)$ is a positive instance of CONSCOMP. Then there exists a permutation $\pi \in S_k$ that satisfies the inequalities stated in (1). Since the first chosen element cannot be negative, it must necessarily be $\frac{m}{2}$. Moreover, since $C = \frac{m}{2}$, the second $\frac{m}{2}$ can be chosen if and only if the energy stored into the system is zero, that is, if and only if there exists a set $\mathcal{E}' \subseteq \mathcal{E}$ of negative elements whose sum is equal to $-\frac{m}{2}$. The opposites of these elements constitute a set $A' \subseteq A$ such that $\sum_{a \in A'} a = \frac{m}{2}$, and thus we can conclude that A is a positive instance of PARTITION.

The CONSCOMP problem naturally leads to the formulation of the following optimization problem.

Problem 2. NAME: MIN STORAGE.

- INSTANCE: a set $\mathcal{E} = \{e_1, e_2, \ldots, e_k\}$ of integer numbers such that $e_1 + e_2 + \ldots + e_k = 0$.
- SOLUTION: a permutation $\pi \in S_k$ such that $\sum_{j=1}^{i} e_{\pi(j)} \geq 0$ for each $i \in \{1, 2, \ldots, k\}$.
- MEASURE: $\max_{1 \leq i \leq k} \sum_{j=1}^{i} e_{\pi(j)}$.   □

Informally, the output of MIN STORAGE is the minimum value of C for which there exists a permutation $\pi \in S_k$ such that the sequence $e_{\pi(1)}, e_{\pi(2)}, \ldots, e_{\pi(k)}$ is C–feasible. Notice that a trivial upper bound for the value of C is:

$$\sum_{i \in \{1, 2, \ldots, k\} \,:\, e_i > 0} e_i = \frac{1}{2} \sum_{i=1}^{k} |e_i|$$

while a trivial lower bound is $\max_{1 \leq i \leq k} |e_i|$.

It is immediately seen that MIN STORAGE is in the class NPO [2, page 27]. In fact, checking whether some given integers $e_1, e_2, \ldots, e_k$ sum up to zero can be trivially done in polynomial time; each feasible solution has linear length and besides it can be verified in polynomial time whether a given permutation $\pi \in S_k$ is a feasible solution; finally, the measure function can be computed in polynomial time. Since the underlying decision problem CONSCOMP is NP–complete, we can immediately conclude that MIN STORAGE is NP–hard [2, page 30]. As with the CONSCOMP decision problem, this means that it is very unlikely that a polynomial time algorithm exists that gives the correct solution to every instance of MIN STORAGE.

If we drop the requirement $e_1 + e_2 + \ldots + e_k = 0$ in the instances of CONSCOMP and MIN STORAGE we obtain the following problems.

Problem 3. NAME: CONSCOMP II.

- INSTANCE: a set $\mathcal{E} = \{e_1, e_2, \ldots, e_k\}$ of integer numbers, and an integer number $C > 0$.
- QUESTION: is there a permutation $\pi \in S_k$ such that the sequence $e_{\pi(1)}, e_{\pi(2)}, \ldots, e_{\pi(k)}$ is C–feasible?   □

Problem 4. NAME: MIN STORAGE II.

- INSTANCE: a set $\mathcal{E} = \{e_1, e_2, \ldots, e_k\}$ of integer numbers.
- SOLUTION: a permutation $\pi \in S_k$ such that $\sum_{j=1}^{i} e_{\pi(j)} \geq 0$ for each $i \in \{1, 2, \ldots, k\}$.
- MEASURE: $\max_{1 \leq i \leq k} \sum_{j=1}^{i} e_{\pi(j)}$.   □

Notice that it may happen that, for some instance $\mathcal{E}$, the set of feasible solutions of MIN STORAGE II is empty. In such a case, we put the solution equal to 0 by definition.

CONSCOMP II is obviously NP–complete, by the restriction property [10, page 63], since it contains CONSCOMP as a particular case. Notice that interesting instances of CONSCOMP II are obtained only for values $e_1, e_2, \ldots, e_k$ taken from the interval $[-C, C]$ of integers. In fact, if $e_i \notin [-C, C] \cap \mathbb{Z}$ for some $i \in \{1, 2, \ldots, k\}$ (a situation which can be verified in linear time) then the instance does not admit a solution. Since CONSCOMP II is the decision version of MIN STORAGE II, and it is NP–complete, MIN STORAGE II is NP–hard. Also for this problem, if the set of feasible solutions is not empty then a trivial upper bound for the value of the optimal solution is $\sum_{i \in \{1, 2, \ldots, k\} \, : \, e_i > 0} e_i$, while a trivial lower bound is $\max_{1 \leq i \leq k} |e_i|$.

We conclude this section by observing that a different interpretation of CONSCOMP II and MIN STORAGE II can be given without reference to conservativeness and conservative computations. Let us consider a merchant whose business involves k cities. When the merchant arrives to the i-th city he either buys or sells some good. If he sells, he earns an amount e_i of money; if he buys, he spends an amount e_i of money. Hence we can associate to each city a positive integer earning $e_i > 0$ or a "negative earning" (that is, an expense) $e_i < 0$. The CONSCOMP II problem can thus be seen as the formalization of the following problem: Given a wallet that may contain a maximum amount C of money, is the merchant able to make a tour of all cities (as in the TSP problem) without going out of money or earning too much? We call this interpretation of CONSCOMP II the TRAVELING MERCHANT problem. Analogously, MIN STORAGE II can be seen as the formalization of the problem which asks what is the minimum capacity of the wallet that allows the merchant to perform a tour of all cities. An appropriate name for this interpretation of MIN STORAGE II seems to be MIN WALLET.

3   Approximating MIN STORAGE

Since the MIN STORAGE problem is NP–hard, a natural question is how well its optimal solutions can be approximated in polynomial time. Precisely, we ask ourselves whether there exists a PTAS (Polynomial Time Approximation Scheme) or even an FPTAS (Fully Polynomial Time Approximation Scheme) for MIN STORAGE.

The fact that PARTITION can be thought of as a particular case of the SUBSET SUM problem (indeed, a direct polynomial reduction from SUBSET SUM to CONsCOMP can be trivially derived from the proof of Theorem 1) could suggest that a modification to the standard FPTAS for SUBSET SUM [12] could lead to an FPTAS for MIN STORAGE. However, differently from SUBSET SUM, CONSCOMP is NP–complete in the strong sense (and hence MIN STORAGE is NP–hard in the strong sense), as it is easily proved in the following. Let us consider the 3–PARTITION problem [10, page 224].

Problem 5. NAME: 3–PARTITION.

- INSTANCE: Set A of $3m$ elements, a bound $B \in \mathbb{Z}^+$, and a size $s(a) \in \mathbb{Z}^+$ for each $a \in A$ such that $B/4 < s(a) < B/2$ and such that $\sum_{a \in A} s(a) = mB$.
- QUESTION: Can A be partitioned into m disjoint sets $A_1, A_2, \ldots, A_m$ such that, for $1 \leq i \leq m$, $\sum_{a \in A_i} s(a) = B$ (note that each A_i must therefore contain exactly three elements from A)?   □

The 3–PARTITION problem is NP–complete in the strong sense [10, page 224]. A simple modification to the proof of Theorem 1 allows to build an explicit polynomial reduction from 3–PARTITION to CONSCOMP, thus proving that also CONSCOMP is strongly NP–complete. As it is well known [2, page 116] this fact prevents the existence of an FPTAS for MIN STORAGE. Hence the next natural question is whether there exists a PTAS for MIN STORAGE. This possibility is still under investigation.

Here we show that MIN STORAGE is in the class APX of problems which admit a constant factor polynomial time approximation algorithm. Let us consider the following algorithm.

APPROX MIN STORAGE($\{e_1, e_2, \ldots, e_k\}$)

```
M ← max_{1≤i≤k} |e_i|
E_p = E_n = ∅
for i ← 1 to k
    do if e_i ≥ 0
        then E_p = E_p ∪ {e_i}
        else E_n = E_n ∪ {e_i}
max ← st ← 0
while E_p ≠ ∅
    do if st < M
        then x ← an element of E_p
            st ← st + x
            if st > max then max ← st
            E_p = E_p \ {x}
        else x ← an element of E_n
            st ← st + x
            E_n = E_n \ {x}
return max
```

The algorithm works as follows. The variable M is set to $\max_{1\le i\le k}|e_i|$, which is a theoretical lower bound for the optimal solution. While scanning the elements of the instance in order to compute M, we can divide them into negative (E_n) and non negative (E_p) elements. The elements which are equal to 0 are uninfluent to the solution of the problem, and can be put either in E_n or in E_p; in the pseudo–code above we have put them all into E_p. The variable st records the energy which is currently stored into the system. The idea is to make this variable assume values only from the interval $[0, 2M]$ (actually, from the interval $[0, 2M - 1]$). The variable max, which contains the value returned at the end of the computation, records the maximum of the values assumed by st into the subinterval $[M, 2M]$. Since the optimal solution cannot be less than M, this strategy allows the algorithm to return a value which is by a factor at most 2 greater than the optimal solution.

Notice that at the end of the execution only some elements of E_n will not be chosen. Since $\sum_{i=1}^{k} e_i = 0$, these elements will lead st to 0 and they will not affect the returned result. If we are required to build a permutation $\pi \in S_k$ that corresponds to the solution found by the algorithm then it suffices to store the elements into an array as they are selected; the remaining elements from E_n can be chosen in any order to fill the final portion of the array.

A direct inspection of the pseudo–code reveals that the time complexity of the algorithm is linear with respect to k, the length of the input sequence.

Proposition 1. APPROX MIN STORAGE *is a 2–approximation algorithm for* MIN STORAGE.

Proof. We have to prove that, for any instance $\mathcal{E}$ of MIN STORAGE, the algorithm 2-APPROX MIN STORAGE always returns a solution $sol(\mathcal{E})$ which is at most the double of the optimal solution $opt(\mathcal{E})$:

$$sol(\mathcal{E}) \le 2 \cdot opt(\mathcal{E})$$

First of all we note that the value of st is always non negative. In fact, when the execution starts the value of st is set equal to 0. In the subsequent steps the algorithm chooses a negative element of $\mathcal{E}$ if and only if $st \ge M$. Since the absolute values of all negative elements are not greater than M, at the next iteration the value of st will remain non negative.

On the other hand, the value of st is always less than $2M$. In fact, the algorithm chooses a positive element of $\mathcal{E}$ if and only if $st < M$. Since the chosen element cannot be greater than M, the resulting value of st remains less than $2M$.

The value returned by APPROX MIN STORAGE is the maximum value comprised between M and $2M - 1$ assumed by the variable st. Since $opt(\mathcal{E}) \ge M$ and $sol(\mathcal{E}) < 2M$, we can conclude that $sol(\mathcal{E}) < 2M \le 2 \cdot opt(\mathcal{E})$.

4   Conservative Languages

As a direction for future work we propose to study the properties of *conservative languages*, which can be defined as follows. For a fixed integer $C > 0$, we first define the alphabet $\Sigma_C = \mathbb{Z} \cap [-C, C]$ whose $2C + 1$ elements are the integers from the interval $[-C, C]$. Moreover, let Σ_C^k be the set of strings of length k composed by symbols taken from Σ_C.

Definition 1. *For any integer $k \geq 1$, the language* $\mathrm{CONS}_C(k)$ *is the following set of strings:*

$$\mathrm{CONS}_C(k) = \left\{ w = \sigma_1 \sigma_2 \cdots \sigma_k \in \Sigma_C^k : 0 \leq \sum_{j=1}^{i} \sigma_j \leq C \right.$$
$$\left. \text{for all } i \in \{1, 2, \ldots, k\}, \text{ and } \sum_{i=1}^{k} \sigma_i = 0 \right\}$$

Moreover, we define the languages $\mathrm{CONS}_C = \bigcup_{k \geq 1} \mathrm{CONS}_C(k)$ *and* $\mathrm{CONS} = \bigcup_{C \geq 1} \mathrm{CONS}_C$.

Depending upon the need it may be appropriate to include or not the empty string λ in CONS_C. Since the addition of zeroes in a given string w does not change the values of its prefix sums we can immediately conclude that for all $k \geq 1$ the language $\mathrm{CONS}_C(k+1)$ contains an isomorphic image of $\mathrm{CONS}_C(k)$. It is also immediate to see that the languages CONS_C form the following (infinite) hierarchy:

$$\mathrm{CONS}_1 \subset \mathrm{CONS}_2 \subset \ldots \subset \mathrm{CONS}_C \subset \ldots$$

In fact, for any fixed positive integer C let $w_C = C, -C$ be the string formed by the juxtaposition of the symbols C and $-C$. Then clearly $w_C \in \mathrm{CONS}_C \setminus \mathrm{CONS}_{C-1}$ for all integers $C > 1$.

Let us now consider the following problems.

Problem 6. Given a positive integer C, and $\sigma_1, \sigma_2, \ldots, \sigma_k \in \Sigma_C$ such that $\sum_{i=1}^{k} \sigma_i = 0$, can we form a word $w \in \mathrm{CONS}_C(k)$ by taking each σ_i exactly once?   □

The formalization of this problem is $\mathrm{CONSCOMP}$, and hence it is NP–complete in the strong sense.

Problem 7. Given $\sigma_1, \sigma_2, \ldots, \sigma_k \in \Sigma_C$ such that $\sum_{i=1}^{k} \sigma_i = 0$, what is the minimum value of C such that there exists $w \in \mathrm{CONS}_C(k)$, obtained by taking each σ_i exactly once?   □

The formalization of this problem is MIN STORAGE, and hence it is NP–hard in the strong sense. A new interesting problem is the following.

Problem 8. Given a positive integer C, and $\sigma_1, \sigma_2, \ldots, \sigma_k \in \Sigma_C$, what is the *longest* word $w \in \Sigma_C^\ell$, with $0 \leq \ell \leq k$, that can be formed by picking each σ_i at *most* once, such that $w \in \mathrm{CONS}_C$?   □

Formally, this problem can be stated as follows.

Problem 9. NAME: MAX STRING LENGTH.

- INSTANCE: a set $\{e_1, e_2, \ldots, e_k\}$ of integer numbers, and an integer number $C > 0$.
- SOLUTION: a permutation $\pi \in S_k$.
- MEASURE: $\max\limits_{0 \le i \le k} \left\{ i \,\middle|\, 0 \le \sum_{j=1}^{r} e_{\pi(j)} \le C \text{ for all } r \in \{1, \ldots, i\}, \text{ and } \sum_{j=1}^{i} e_{\pi(j)} = 0 \right\}.$ □

It is immediate to see that MAX STRING LENGTH is in NPO. In fact, each feasible solution has linear length, and the measure function can be computed in polynomial time.

The decision version of this optimization problem asks whether, given a set $\{e_1, e_2, \ldots, e_k\}$ of integer numbers, a positive integer number C, and a non negative integer number L, there exists a permutation $\pi \in S_k$ such that:

$$\max_{0 \le i \le k} \left\{ i \,\middle|\, 0 \le \sum_{j=1}^{r} e_{\pi(j)} \le C \text{ for all } r \in \{1, \ldots, i\}, \text{ and } \sum_{j=1}^{i} e_{\pi(j)} = 0 \right\} \ge L$$

This decision problem, that we name STRING LENGTH, is clearly NP–complete in the strong sense. In fact, let $(\mathcal{E} = \{e_1, \ldots, e_k\}, C)$ be an instance of CONSCOMP. We build the corresponding instance of STRING LENGTH by putting $L = k$. Then, a solution to this last problem immediately corresponds to a solution of CONSCOMP. As a consequence, we can conclude that the optimization problem MAX STRING LENGTH is NP–hard in the strong sense.

As for the computational power of energy–based P systems we propose the introduction of languages which can be generated using a bounded (fixed, logarithmic, polynomial, etc.) amount of energy or capacity, and the subsequent investigation of the properties of these languages. Another possibility is to define *families* $\{P_n\}_{n \in \mathbb{N}}$ of energy–based P systems, where P_n uses n units of energy. Then, we can define the language generated by $\{P_n\}_{n \in \mathbb{N}}$ as $\bigcup_{n \in \mathbb{N}} L_n$, where L_n is the language generated by P_n. This approach is reminiscent of circuit complexity [23]. Moreover, having defined both an input and an output membrane, we can view energy–based P systems as devices which map multisets into multisets, as we have done in this paper. With respect to this point of view, instead of asking what multisets can be generated by the system we can ask what mappings can be realized by imposing different bounds on the amount of resources that the system is allowed to use.

5   Conclusions and Directions for Future Work

We have introduced the notion of conservative computations for energy–based P systems, as computations in which the initial energy of the system is the same as the energy at the end of the computation.

We have shown that conservative computations naturally allow to define MIN STORAGE, a new NP–hard optimization problem, and CONSCOMP, its associated decision problem. Being CONSCOMP NP–complete in the strong sense, the existence of an FPTAS for MIN STORAGE is prevented. The existence of a PTAS is still under investigation. We have also presented a 2–approximation algorithm for MIN STORAGE, thus proving that the problem is in the complexity class APX.

Finally, we have introduced conservative languages. As a main direction for future work, we advocate the study of the language–theoretic and complexity–related features of these languages.

References

1. G. Alford. Membrane Systems with Heat Control. In *Pre–Proceedings of the Workshop on Membrane Computing*, Curtea de Arges, Romania, August 2002. Available at: *http://psystems.disco.unimib.it/*
2. G. Ausiello, P. Crescenzi, G. Gambosi, V. Kann, A. Marchetti–Spaccamela, M. Protasi. *Complexity and Approximation. Combinatorial Optimization Problems and Their Approximability Properties.* Springer–Verlag, 1999.
3. J. Castellanos, G. Păun, A. Rodriguez–Paton. P Systems with Worm-Objects. In *IEEE 7th International Conference on String Processing and Information Retrieval*, SPIRE 2000, La Coruna, Spain, 2000, pp. 64–74. See also CDMTCS Technical Report 123, University of Auckland, 2000. Available at: *http://www.cs.auckland.ac.nz/CDMTCS*
4. G. Cattaneo, G. Della Vedova, A. Leporati, R. Leporini. Towards a Theory of Conservative Computing. Accepted on *International Journal of Theoretical Physics.* Preprint available at *http://arxiv.org/abs/quant-ph/0211085*, November 2002.
5. R. Freund. Energy–Controlled P Systems. In *Membrane Computing*, Proceedings of the International Workshop WMC–CdeA 2002, Curtea de Arges, Romania, August 2002, Lecture Notes in Computer Science 2597, Springer, 2002, pp. 247–260.
6. R. Freund, A. Leporati, M. Oswald, C. Zandron. Sequential P Systems with Unit Rules and Energy. In *Machines, Computation and Universality* (MCU 2004), Saint–Petersburg, Russia, September 21–26, 2004. To appear in Lecture Notes in Computer Science.
7. P. Frisco. The Conformon–P Systems: A Molecular and Cell Biology–Inspired Computability Model. *Theoretical Computer Science*, 312:295–319, 2004.
8. P. Frisco, S. Ji. Info–Energy P Systems. In *Proceedings of DNA 8, Eighth International Meeting on DNA Based Computers*, Hokkaido University, Japan, June 2002.
9. P. Frisco, S. Ji. Towards a Hierarchy of Conformons–P Systems. In *Membrane Computing*, Proceedings of the International Workshop WMC–CdeA 2002, Curtea de Arges, Romania, August 2002, Lecture Notes in Computer Science 2597, Springer, 2002, pp. 302–318.
10. M.R. Garey, D.S. Johnson. *Computers and Intractability. A Guide to the Theory on NP–Completeness.* W. H. Freeman and Company, 1979.
11. G.V. Gens, E.V. Levner. Computational Complexity of Approximation Algorithms for Combinatorial Problems. *Proceedings of the 8th International Symposium on Mathematical Foundations of Computer Science*, Lecture Notes in Computer Science 74, Springer–Verlag, Berlin, 1979, pp. 292–300.
12. O.H. Ibarra, C.E. Kim. Fast Approximation Algorithms for the Knapsack and Sum of Subset Problems. *Journal of the ACM*, **22**, 1975, pp. 463–468.
13. A. Leporati, C. Zandron, G. Mauri. Simulating the Fredkin Gate with Energy-based P Systems. In [19], pp. 292–308.

14. A. Leporati, C. Zandron, G. Mauri. Universal families of Reversible P Systems. In *Machines, Computation and Universality* (MCU 2004), Saint–Petersburg, Russia, September 21–26, 2004. To appear in Lecture Notes in Computer Science.

15. G. Mauri, A. Leporati. On the Computational Complexity of Conservative Computing. In *Proceedings of the 28th International Symposium on Mathematical Foundations of Computer Science* (MFCS 2003), Lecture Notes in Computer Science 2747, Springer–Verlag Heidelberg, 2003, pp. 92–112.

16. G. Păun. Computing with Membranes. *Journal of Computer and System Sciences*, Vol. 1, No. 61, 2000, pp. 108–143. See also Turku Centre for Computer Science — TUCS Report No. 208, 1998. Available at: *http://www.tucs.fi/Publications/techreports/TR208.php*

17. G. Păun. Computing with Membranes. An Introduction. *Bulletin of the EATCS*, 67:139–152, February 1999.

18. G. Păun. *Membrane Computing. An Introduction.* Springer–Verlag, Berlin, 2002.

19. G. Păun, A. Riscos Nuñez, A. Romero Jiménez, F. Sancho Caparrini (Eds.). *Proceedings of Second Brainstorming Week on Membrane Computing*, Seville, Spain, February 2–7, 2004. Department of Computer Sciences and Artificial Intelligence, University of Seville TR 01/2004.

20. G. Păun, G. Rozenberg. A Guide to Membrane Computing. *Theoretical Computer Science*, Vol. 287, No. 1, 2002, pp. 73–100.

21. G. Păun, Y. Suzuki, H. Tanaka. P Systems with Energy Accounting. *International Journal Computer Math.*, Vol. 78, No. 3, 2001, pp. 343–364.

22. The P systems Web page: `http://psystems.disco.unimib.it/`

23. H. Vollmer. *Introduction to Circuit Complexity: A Uniform Approach.* Springer–Verlag, 1999.

General Multi-fuzzy Sets and Fuzzy Membrane Systems

Adam Obtułowicz

Institute of Mathematics,
Polish Academy of Sciences,
Śniadeckich 8, P.O. Box 21, 00-956 Warsaw, Poland
adamo@impan.gov.pl

Abstract. We propose a certain fuzzification of membrane systems and their evolution rules which is motivated by some practical applications, where the strength (or weakness causing uncertainty) of an occurrence of an object in a system is determined not only by the number of occurring copies of that object but also by the quality of these copies.

1 Introduction

In [12], A. Syropoulos introduced the concept of a fuzzy P system, as a fuzzy set-theoretic counterpart of P systems introduced by Gh. Păunin [9] (see also the book [10]).

In the present paper we propose another approach to the fuzzification of P systems, which is motivated by some practical applications in biochemistry and medical sciences, where a strength (or weakness causing uncertainty) of an occurrence of an object in a system is determined not only by the number of occurring copies of that object, but also by the quality of occurring copies.

The approach is aimed to provide:

- classification of processes generated by systems with respect to evolution rules transforming systems in the steps of processes,
- computer simulations of processes generated by the application of evolution rules,
- analysis of evolution rules to simplify them (by idealization) for efficient computer simulation of processes,
- all concerning improvement of simulation methods discussed in medical sciences [6].

In Section 2 we describe a new interpretation of general multi-fuzzy sets, different from that discussed in [4] and [12], which respects the strength of occurrence of objects in a system determined by the number and quality of occurring copies of these objects. Then, in Sections 3, 4, we discuss some algebra of general multi-fuzzy sets focusing on their sum and their various subtractions used to describe an idea of an evolution rule of a general fuzzy membrane system

G. Mauri et al. (Eds.): WMC5 2004, LNCS 3365, pp. 359–372, 2005.

introduced in Section 5. We show in Section 6 that general multi-fuzzy sets may unify various approaches to the occurrence of an object in a system.

The practical applications of the proposed approach will be reported in forth-coming papers concerning examples from biochemistry and medical sciences.

The author thanks Dr. J. Andrzej Pomykała for useful remarks and discussions.

2   Multisets, Fuzzy Sets, and General Multi-fuzzy Sets

In this section we recall the known concepts of multisets [2], fuzzy sets [1], [5], and general multi-fuzzy sets [4], [12]. We also present some new and practical interpretations of general multi-fuzzy sets.

Multisets over a set $\mathcal{O}$, called sometimes *Boolean multisets* over a set $\mathcal{O}$ or bags in [14], are functions $M : \mathcal{O} \to \mathbb{N}$ valued in the set $\mathbb{N}$ of natural numbers, where $\mathcal{O}$ is a set of objects, and the value $M(x)$ is the number of copies of an object $x \in \mathcal{O}$ which (currently) occur in a system or its part. Thus multisets describe resources of copies of objects of $\mathcal{O}$. Characteristic functions of subsets of $\mathcal{O}$ are among multisets over $\mathcal{O}$. We write $\mathbb{N}^{\mathcal{O}}$ to denote the set of multisets over $\mathcal{O}$.

The usual orderings $<, \leq$ on $\mathbb{N}$, the usual operation $+$ of addition (sum) of natural numbers, and subtraction $\dot{-}$ of natural numbers given by

$$m \dot{-} n = \begin{cases} m - n & \text{if } m \geq n, \\ 0 & \text{otherwise,} \end{cases}$$

induce the orderings $<, \leq$, and the operations of addition (sum) $+$ and subtraction $\dot{-}$ of multisets which are defined *componentwise* by

$M_1 < M_2 \ [M_1 \leq M_2]$ iff $M_1(x) < M_2(x) \ [M_1(x) \leq M_2(x)]$ for all $x \in \mathcal{O}$,

$(M_1 + M_2)(x) = M_1(x) + M_2(x)$,

$(M_1 \dot{-} M_2)(x) = M_1(x) \dot{-} M_2(x)$,

for all $x \in \mathcal{O}$ and for all multisets M_1, M_2 over $\mathcal{O}$. We write 0 to denote that multiset M over $\mathcal{O}$ which is defined by

$$M(x) = 0 \text{ for all } x \in \mathcal{O}.$$

Fuzzy sets over a set $\mathcal{O}$ are functions $f : \mathcal{O} \to [0,1]$ valued in the unit interval $[0,1]$ of real numbers, where $\mathcal{O}$ is a set of *objects* and the value $f(x)$ is the degree of membership of an object $x \in \mathcal{O}$ in f.

Characteristic functions of subsets of $\mathcal{O}$ are among fuzzy sets over $\mathcal{O}$. The usual orderings $<, \leq$ of real numbers, and infima, suprema of finite sets of natural numbers in $[0,1]$ determine the orderings $<, \leq$ and the operations of union $\cup$ and intersection $\cap$ of fuzzy sets which are defined *pointwise* by

$f_1 < f_2 \ [f_1 \leq f_2]$ iff $f_1(x) < f_2(x) \ [f_1(x) \leq f_2(x)]$ for all $x \in \mathcal{O}$,

$(f_1 \cup f_2)(x) = \sup\{f_1(x), f_2(x)\}$,

$(f_1 \cap f_2)(x) = \inf\{f_1(x), f_2(x)\}$,

for all $x \in \mathcal{O}$ and for all fuzzy sets f_1, f_2 over $\mathcal{O}$. We write $[0, 1]^{\mathcal{O}}$ to denote the set of fuzzy sets over $\mathcal{O}$ and we write 0 to denote that fuzzy set f over $\mathcal{O}$ which is defined by $f(x) = 0$ for all $x \in \mathcal{O}$.

General multi-fuzzy sets over a set $\mathcal{O}$ are functions $M : \mathcal{O} \times \mathbb{N} \to [0, 1]$ or, equivalently, functions $\mathcal{M} : \mathcal{O} \to [0, 1]^{\mathbb{N}}$, where $\mathcal{O}$ is a set of objects, $[0, 1]$ is a unit interval of real numbers, $[0, 1]^{\mathbb{N}}$ is the set of fuzzy sets of natural numbers, and the value $M(x, n)$ or $\mathcal{M}(x)(n)$ is the degree of certainty that n copies of an object $x \in \mathcal{O}$ occur in a system or its part. Since $[0, 1]^{\mathbb{N}}$ is the set of fuzzy sets, the already defined orderings $<, \leq$, and operations of union and intersection of fuzzy sets of natural numbers induce the corresponding orderings and operations of general multi-fuzzy sets which are defined componentwise in a similar way as in the case of multisets.

We propose another interpretation of general multi-fuzzy sets which is motivated by some practical applications.

Since for a Boolean multiset $M : \mathcal{O} \to \mathbb{N}$ and an object $x \in \mathcal{O}$ the characteristic function of the segment $\{i \in \mathbb{N} \,|\, 0 \leq i < M(x)\}$ is among the fuzzy sets of natural numbers and elements of this segment serve for numbering $M(x)$ copies of x such that a natural number i with $i < M(x)$ is identified with the i-th copy of x, for a general multi-fuzzy set $\mathcal{M}$ over $\mathcal{O}$ and an object $x \in \mathcal{O}$ one can treat the fuzzy set $\mathcal{M}(x)$ of natural numbers such that $\mathcal{M}(x)(i)$ is the degree of membership of i-th copy of x in $\mathcal{M}(x)$. One may claim here $\mathcal{M}(x)$ to be a fuzzy set theoretic counterpart of a Boolean segment of natural numbers (i.e., the set $\{i \in \mathbb{N} \,|\, 0 \leq i < n\}$ for $n \in \mathbb{N}$) in an obvious way.

We propose the following definition of fuzzy segments of natural numbers to be claimed fuzzy set theoretic counterparts of Boolean segments of natural numbers.

By a *fuzzy segment* of natural numbers we mean a fuzzy set $f : \mathbb{N} \to [0, 1]$ of natural numbers for which the following conditions hold:

(1) $m < n$ implies $f(m) \geq f(n)$ for all natural numbers m, n (*comonotonicity*),
(2) $f(k) = 0$ for some natural number k.

If $f = \mathcal{M}(x)$ for a general multi-fuzzy set $\mathcal{M}$, then condition (1) ensures that there is no other (preference) relation between copies of x in f than that determined by their degree of membership in f, and conditions (1) with (2) provide that there is only a finite number of copies of x with the degree of membership greater than 0.

The following practical meaning can be given to the values $\mathcal{M}(x)(i)$ of a general multi-fuzzy set $\mathcal{M}$, where the values $\mathcal{M}(x)$ are fuzzy segments of natural numbers. If lifetime(x) is the average time of life of an object x and t_i is the current time counted from the birth (or emergence) of i-th copy of x, one can identify $\mathcal{M}(x)(i)$ with the number

$$1 \dot{-} \frac{t_i}{\text{lifetime}(x)}$$

which is the degree of freshness of the i-th copy of x, where subtraction $\dot{-}$ of real numbers greater than or equal to 0 is defined in an analogous way as already defined subtraction of natural numbers. Hence the value $\mathcal{M}(x)(i)$ near 0 means that i-th copy of x tends to decay caused by aging and $\mathcal{M}(x)(i) = 0$ means the decay of the i-th copy of x. Therefore $\mathcal{M}(x)$ describes the current freshness of copies of x occurring in a system, where this freshness is specified by the values $\mathcal{M}(x)(i)$.

The above practical meaning of the values $\mathcal{M}(x)(i)$ was suggested to the author by the discussion of fuzzy timed Petri nets in [11] and by the lecture [15].

There are other possibilities of assigning a practical meaning to the values $\mathcal{M}(x)(i)$ of a general multi-fuzzy set $\mathcal{M}$ over $\mathcal{O}$ with $\mathcal{M}(x)$ being fuzzy segments of natural numbers; for instance, $\mathcal{M}(x)(i)$ can be a relative amount of energy carried by the i-th copy of x.

Thus, a general multi-fuzzy set $\mathcal{M}$ over $\mathcal{O}$ with values $\mathcal{M}(x)$ being fuzzy segments of natural numbers can describe the strength of occurrences of objects which is determined by the quality of currently occurring copies of objects.

In the next two sections we describe some useful properties of fuzzy segments of natural numbers.

3   Properties of Fuzzy Segments of Natural Numbers

In this section we describe some properties of fuzzy segments of natural numbers.

One can represent fuzzy segments of natural numbers by *finite multisets* over $(0, 1]$ which are defined to be such that $\{\alpha \in (0, 1] \,|\, M(\alpha) > 0\}$ is a finite set, where $(0, 1]$ is a left open unit interval of real numbers, i.e., $(0, 1] = \{x \in \mathbb{R} \,|\, 0 < x \leq 1\}$ for $\mathbb{R}$ denoting the set of real numbers. Let $\mathrm{SGM}(\mathbb{N}, [0, 1])$ denote the set of fuzzy segments of natural numbers and let $\mathrm{FIN}((0, 1], \mathbb{N})$ denote the set of finite multisets over $(0, 1]$. Finite multisets over $(0, 1]$ are more or less explicitly discussed in [4] and [13].

A representation of fuzzy segments of natural numbers by finite multisets over $(0, 1]$ is provided by a mapping $(-)^{\S} : \mathrm{SGM}(\mathbb{N}, [0, 1]) \to \mathrm{FIN}((0, 1], \mathbb{N})$ defined in the following way for every fuzzy segment f of natural numbers:

$$(f)^{\S}(\alpha) \text{ is the number of elements of the set } \{i \in \mathbb{N} \,|\, f(i) = \alpha\}$$

for all $\alpha \in (0, 1]$.

Proposition 1. *The mapping* $(-)^{\S}$ *is a bijection whose inverse*

$$(-)^{-\S} : \mathrm{FIN}((0, 1], \mathbb{N}) \to \mathrm{SGM}(\mathbb{N}, [0, 1])$$

is defined in the following way for every finite multiset M over $(0, 1]$:

- *if $\{\alpha \in (0, 1] \,|\, M(\alpha) > 0\}$ is empty, then $(M)^{-\S}(n) = 0$ for all natural numbers n,*
- *if $\{\alpha \in (0, 1] \,|\, M(\alpha) > 0\}$ is nonempty, then its elements form a finite decreasing string $\alpha_0 > \ldots > \alpha_{k-1}$ of real numbers for k equal to the number of elements of $\{\alpha \in (0, 1] \,|\, M(\alpha) > 0\}$ and one defines*

$$(M)^{-\S}(i) = \begin{cases} \alpha_0 & \textit{if } 0 \le i \le M(\alpha_0), \\ \alpha_j & \textit{if } \sum_{m=0}^{j-1} M(\alpha_m) \le i < \sum_{m=0}^{j} M(\alpha_m) \textit{ and } 0 < j < k, \\ 0 & \textit{otherwise.} \end{cases}$$

Proof. We prove that $((f)^\S)^{-\S} = f$ and $((M)^{-\S})^\S = M$ in an immediate way by using the definitions of $(-)^\S$ and $(-)^{-\S}$. □

Therefore the mappings $(-)^\S$ and $(-)^{-\S}$ provide a representation of fuzzy segments of natural numbers by finite multisets over $(0, 1]$.

Thus one simply defines the sum $+$ of fuzzy segments f, g of natural numbers by

$$f + g = ((f)^\S + (g)^\S)^{-\S},$$

where $+$ standing in the right hand side of the above equation is the sum of Boolean multisets already defined.

Lemma 1. *For two finite multisets M_1, M_2 over $(0, 1]$ the inequality $M_1 \le M_2$ implies the inequality $(M_1)^{-\S} \le (M_2)^{-\S}$.*

Proof. We prove the lemma by induction on the number of the elements of the set $\{\alpha \in (0, 1] \,|\, M_1(\alpha) > 0\}$. □

There are simple examples showing that $(M_1)^{-\S} \le (M_2)^{-\S}$ does not imply $M_1 \le M_2$.

By analogy with the sum of fuzzy segments of natural numbers one defines the subtraction $\dotdiv$ of fuzzy segments f, g of natural numbers by

$$f \dotdiv g = ((f)^\S \dotdiv (g)^\S)^{-\S},$$

where $\dotdiv$ standing in the right hand side of the above equation is the subtraction of Boolean multisets already defined.

For a fuzzy segment f of natural numbers we define

$$\text{size}(f) = \min\{i \in \mathbb{N} \,|\, f(i) = 0\}.$$

Lemma 2. *For all fuzzy segments f, g of natural numbers the inequality $(f)^\S \ge (g)^\S$ implies the following conditions:*

(a) $\text{size}(f \dotdiv g) = \text{size}(f) - \text{size}(g)$,
(b) $(f \dotdiv g) + g = f$.

Proof. The lemma is an immediate consequence of the definitions of $+$ and $\dotdiv$ of fuzzy segments. □

We use the following property of subtraction of fuzzy segments of natural numbers.

For a fuzzy segment f of natural numbers and an integer $k \geq -1$ we define a fuzzy segment $f \upharpoonright k$ of natural numbers by

$$(f \upharpoonright k)(i) = \begin{cases} f(i) & \text{if } 0 \leq i \leq k, \\ 0 & \text{if } k = -1 \text{ and } i \geq 0, \\ 0 & \text{if } i > k > -1. \end{cases}$$

Lemma 3. *For all fuzzy segments f of natural numbers and all integers $k \geq -1$ the following condition holds:*

$$\bigl(f \doteq (f \upharpoonright k)\bigr)(i) = f(i + k + 1) \quad \text{for every } i \in \mathbb{N}.$$

Proof. The lemma is an immediate consequence of the definitions of the subtraction of fuzzy segments and $f \upharpoonright k$.   □

Since in general $f \geq g$ does not imply $(f)^\S \geq (g)^\S$ for fuzzy segments f and g of natural numbers, it remains to discuss the possibilities of defining the subtraction in such a way to respect the pointwise defined ordering $\leq$ of fuzzy segments of natural numbers, so that a counterpart of Lemma 2 with $(f)^\S \geq (g)^\S$ replaced by $f \geq g$ would hold. We discuss some of these possibilities in the next section.

4   Subtracting Fuzzy Segments with Respect to Their Pointwise Defined Ordering $\leq$

For two fuzzy segments f, g of natural numbers with $f \geq g$ we say that a finite multiset M over $(0, 1]$ is a *subtractive choice multiset* with respect to $f \geq g$ if the following conditions hold:

(i) $M \leq (f)^\S$,
(ii) $g \leq (M)^{-\S}$,
(iii) $\operatorname{size}\bigl((M)^{-\S}\bigr) = \operatorname{size}(g)$.

A subtractive choice multiset M with respect to $f \geq g > 0$ represents the chosen numbers of copies of real numbers in $(0, 1]$ to be deleted (subtracted) from $(f)^\S$ providing (ii) and (iii).

Thus, for two fuzzy segments f, g of natural numbers with $f \geq g$ and subtractive choice multiset M with respect to $f \geq g$ we define the *subtraction of f and g determined by M* to be that fuzzy segment $f \,\$_M\, g$ of natural numbers which is given by

$$f \,\$_M\, g = f \doteq (M)^{-\S}.$$

Lemma 4. *For every subtractive choice multiset M with respect to $f \geq g$ the following conditions hold:*

(a') $\operatorname{size}(f \,\$_M\, g) = \operatorname{size}(f) - \operatorname{size}(g)$,
(b') $(f \,\$_M\, g) + (M)^{-\S} = f$.

Proof. The lemma is a consequence of Lemma 2 and the definition of $f \mathbin{\$_M} g$. □

For two fuzzy segments f, g of natural numbers with $f \geq g > 0$ we define

$$\Phi_{f,g} = \{(M)^{-\S} \mid M \text{ is a subtractive choice multiset with respect to } f \geq g\}.$$

We show that $\Phi_{f,g}$ has the greatest element and the smallest element with respect to pointwise ordering $\leq$ of fuzzy segments of natural numbers.

Proposition 2. *Let f, g be two fuzzy segments of natural numbers with $f \geq g > 0$. Then $f \restriction (\mathrm{size}(g) - 1)$ is the greatest element in the set $\Phi_{f,g}$ with respect to pointwise defined ordering of fuzzy segments of natural numbers.*

Proof. Since by Lemma 1 $(h)^{\S} \leq (h')^{\S}$ implies $h \leq h' \restriction (\mathrm{size}(h) - 1)$ for all fuzzy segments h and h', we obtain by Lemma 1 and conditions (i), (iii) the following inequality

$$(M)^{-\S} \leq f \restriction (\mathrm{size}(g) - 1)$$

for all subtractive choice multisets M with respect to $f \geq g > 0$. Therefore $f \restriction (\mathrm{size}(g) - 1)$ is the greatest element in $\Phi_{f,g}$ with respect to pointwise defined ordering $\leq$ of fuzzy segments of natural numbers. □

A fuzzy segment g of natural numbers is called a *threshold fuzzy segment* if the set $\{g(i) \mid i \in \mathbb{N} \text{ and } 0 \leq i < \mathrm{size}(g)\}$ has at most one element which we call *threshold value* of g.

Proposition 3. *Let f, g be two fuzzy segments with $f \geq g > 0$ such that g is a threshold fuzzy segment. Then $\left(f \mathbin{\dot{-}} (f \restriction c)\right) \restriction (\mathrm{size}(g) - 1)$ is the smallest element in $\Phi_{f,g}$ with respect to the pointwise defined ordering $\leq$ of fuzzy segments of natural numbers, where*

$$c = \max\left(\{j \in \mathbb{N} \mid f \mathbin{\dot{-}} (f \restriction j) \geq g\} \cup \{-1\}\right).$$

Proof. For $c = -1$ we have $\Phi_{f,g} = \{f \restriction (\mathrm{size}(g) - 1)\}$, hence the proposition is true. For $c \geq 0$ let $\left(f \mathbin{\dot{-}} (f \restriction c)\right) \restriction (\mathrm{size}(g) - 1)$ be denoted by f^*. We show that the negation of the inequality

$(+)$ $\hspace{4cm} f^* \leq (M)^{-\S}$

leads to a contradiction for a subtractive choice multiset M with respect to $f \geq g > 0$. Since the negation of $(+)$ means that

$$f^*(j) > (M)^{-\S}(j) \text{ for some } j \text{ with } 0 \leq j < \mathrm{size}(g),$$

we obtain by (i) and (ii) holding for M and by comonotonicity of $(M)^{-\S}$ that the following strong inequality holds

$$\sum_{x \in D(j)} M(x) < \sum_{x \in D(j)} (f^*)^{\S}(x)$$

for $D(j) = \{x \in (0,1] \mid x \leq (M)^{-\S}(j)$ and $0 < \max\{M(x), (f^*)^\S(x)\}\}$ and for some natural number j with $0 \leq j < \text{size}(g) - 1$. Hence condition (iii) does not hold for M. Therefore the negation of the inequality $(+)$ leads to a contradiction. Thus f^* is the smallest element in $\Phi_{f,g}$ with respect to pointwise defined ordering $\leq$ of fuzzy segments of natural numbers.   □

A generalization of Proposition 3 to arbitrary fuzzy segments f, g of natural numbers with $f \geq g > 0$ requires more considerations.

For two fuzzy segments $f \geq g > 0$ of natural numbers we define:

$$\text{caliber}(f, g) = \max\big(\{j \in \mathbb{N} \mid f \overset{\cdot}{-} (f \restriction j) \geq g\} \cup \{-1\}\big),$$

$$\text{cocaliber}(f, g) = \min\Big(\{k \in \mathbb{N} \mid g \overset{\cdot}{-} (g \restriction k) > 0 \text{ and }$$

$$\text{caliber}\big(f \overset{\cdot}{-} (f \restriction (\text{caliber}(f, g) + k + 1)), g \overset{\cdot}{-} (g \restriction k)\big) \geq 0\}$$

$$\cup \big\{\text{size}(g) - 1\big\}\Big).$$

The procedure $\pi_{f,g}$ described by the diagram below is aimed to compute the smallest element in the set $\Phi_{f,g}$ with respect to pointwise defined ordering $\leq$ of fuzzy segments of natural numbers.

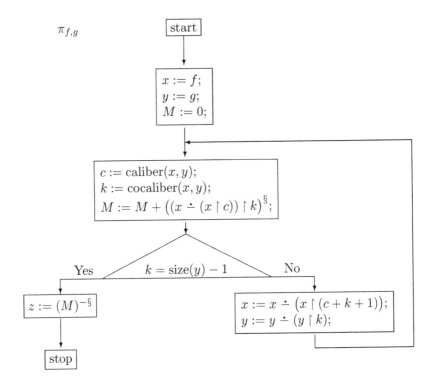

Theorem 1. *For all fuzzy segments $f \geq g > 0$ of natural numbers the fuzzy segment z resulting from the procedure $\pi_{f,g}$ is the smallest element in the set $\Phi_{f,g}$ with respect to the pointwise defined ordering of fuzzy segments of natural numbers.*

Proof. One proves the theorem by induction on the number n of elements of the set $\{g(i) \mid i \in \mathbb{N} \text{ and } g(i) > 0\}$. For the case $n = 1$ the proof is analogous to the proof of Proposition 3. $\square$

For two fuzzy segments f, g of natural numbers with $f \geq g$ we define the *high subtraction* $f \, \$^{\top} g$ of $f \geq g$ and the *low subtraction* $f \, \$^{\perp} g$ of $f \geq g$ by

$$f \, \$^{\top} g = f \, \$_M \, g \quad \text{for} \quad (M)^{-\S} = f \upharpoonright (\text{size}(g) - 1)$$

and

$$f \, \$^{\perp} g = \begin{cases} f & \text{if size}(g) = 0, \\ f \, \$_{\mathbf{z}} \, g & \text{otherwise,} \end{cases}$$

where $(\mathbf{Z})^{-\S}$ is the smallest element in $\Phi_{f,g}$ with respect to the pointwise defined ordering $\leq$ of fuzzy segments or, equivalently, $(\mathbf{Z})^{-\S}$ is equal to the result of the procedure $\pi_{f,g}$.

Let $\mathcal{M}$ and $\mathcal{M}'$ be two general multi-fuzzy sets over $\mathcal{O}$ whose values $\mathcal{M}(x)$ and $\mathcal{M}'(x)$ are fuzzy segments of natural numbers and let $\mathcal{M} \geq \mathcal{M}'$, i.e., $\mathcal{M}(x) \geq \mathcal{M}'(x)$ for all $x \in \mathcal{O}$. Thus for a function $\delta : \mathcal{O} \rightarrow \{\perp, \top\}$ one defines the subtraction $\mathcal{M} \, \$^{\delta} \, \mathcal{M}'$ of $\mathcal{M} \geq \mathcal{M}'$ to be a general multi-fuzzy set defined componentwise by

$$(\mathcal{M} \, \$^{\delta} \, \mathcal{M}')(x) = \mathcal{M}(x) \, \$^{\delta(x)} \, \mathcal{M}'(x) \quad \text{for all } x \in \mathcal{O}.$$

According to the interpretation (given in Section 2) of general multi-fuzzy sets $\mathcal{M}$ with values $\mathcal{M}(x)$ being fuzzy segments of natural numbers we explain the subtraction $\mathcal{M} \, \$^{\delta} \, \mathcal{M}'$ of $\mathcal{M} \geq \mathcal{M}'$ in the following way.

If $\delta(x) = \top$ and $\text{size}(\mathcal{M}(x)) > \text{size}(\mathcal{M}'(x)) > 0$, the value $(\mathcal{M} \, \$^{\delta} \, \mathcal{M}')(x) = \mathcal{M}(x) \, \$^{\top} \, \mathcal{M}'(x)$ is the result of deleting from $\mathcal{M}(x)$ the number $\text{size}(\mathcal{M}'(x))$ of those copies of x which are of relatively high degree of membership in $\mathcal{M}(x)$, meaning that their degrees $\mathcal{M}(x)(i)$ of membership are not smaller than $\mathcal{M}(x)(\text{size}(\mathcal{M}'(x)) - 1)$.

If $\delta(x) = \perp$ and $\text{size}(\mathcal{M}(x)) > \text{size}(\mathcal{M}'(x)) > 0$, the value $(\mathcal{M} \, \$^{\delta} \, \mathcal{M}')(x) = \mathcal{M}(x) \, \$^{\perp} \, \mathcal{M}'(x)$ is the result of deleting from $\mathcal{M}(x)$ the number $\text{size}(\mathcal{M}'(x))$ of those copies of x which are of relatively low degree of membership in $\mathcal{M}(x)$, meaning that they form the smallest fuzzy segment z in $\Phi_{\mathcal{M}(x), \mathcal{M}'(x)}$, i.e., z is the smallest fuzzy segment such that $\text{size}(z) = \text{size}(\mathcal{M}'(x))$ and $z \geq \mathcal{M}'(x)$.

5   General Fuzzy P Systems and Their Evolution Rules

In this section we introduce the concept of a general fuzzy membrane system and then present some evolution rules of general fuzzy membrane systems.

We recall according to [8] and [10] that a *(Boolean) membrane system* S is given by the following data:

- a finite non-empty set $\mathbb{B}_S$ of balls of finite diameters greater than 0 (in the Euclidean space E^n for $n \geq 1$) such that the frontiers of the balls contained in $\mathbb{B}_S$ are pairwise disjoint sets, and there exists the greatest ball b_0 in $\mathbb{B}_S$ with respect to the inclusion relation $\subseteq$; the balls contained in $\mathbb{B}_S$ are called *membranes* of S and $\mathbb{B}_S$ is called the *underlying set of membranes* of S;
- three functions $l_S : \mathbb{B}_S \to L_S$, $e_S : \mathbb{B}_S \to \{-, 0, +\}$, and $\mathcal{M}_S : \mathcal{O}_S \to N^{\mathcal{O}_S}$, where L_S is the *set of labels* of S, l_S is called the *labelling function* of S, e_S is called the *electric charge function* of S, and $\mathcal{M}_S$, called the *object distribution function* of S, is a function whose values $\mathcal{M}_S(m)$ are Boolean multiset over $\mathcal{O}_S$ for $\mathcal{O}_S$ called the *set of objects* of S.

The value $l_S(m)$ is the label assigned to a membrane m of S, $e_S(m)$ is the electric charge of a membrane m of S, and the value $\mathcal{M}_S(m)$ is a Boolean multiset M whose values $M(x)$ are the numbers of copies of $x \in \mathcal{O}_S$ contained in the *region of the membrane* m of S which is the space between the frontier of m and the frontiers of those membranes of S which are immediate subsets of m.

A *general fuzzy membrane system* S is defined in an analogous way as a Boolean membrane system except the object distribution function $\mathcal{M}_S$ of S is such that the values $\mathcal{M}_S(m)$ for $m \in \mathbb{B}_S$ are those general multi-fuzzy sets M over $\mathcal{O}_S$ whose values $M(x)$ are fuzzy segments of natural numbers.

We consider evolution rules of general fuzzy membrane systems which are expressions of the form

$$(*) \qquad\qquad [_h\mathcal{N} \to \delta, \varepsilon, \mathcal{N}']_h^\alpha,$$

where $\mathcal{N}, \mathcal{N}'$ are general multi-fuzzy sets over a set $\mathcal{O}$ (or some presentations of them) whose values $\mathcal{N}(x), \mathcal{N}'(x)$ are fuzzy segments of natural numbers ($x \in \mathcal{O}$), h is a label in a set L of labels, $\alpha \in \{-, 0, +\}$, δ is a function defined on $\mathcal{O}$ and valued in $\{\perp, \top\}$, and $\varepsilon \in [0, 1]$. We assume that $\mathcal{N}'(x)(i) = 1$ for all natural numbers i with $0 \leq i < \text{size}(\mathcal{N}'(x))$ and for $\mathcal{N}'(x) > 0$. The evolution rules of the form $(*)$ have common features with some evolution rules in [8] and [10].

For a general fuzzy membrane system S and an evolution rule R of the form $(*)$ with $\mathcal{O} = \mathcal{O}_S$ and $L = L_S$ we say that this rule R *can be applied to a membrane m of S* if the following conditions hold:

- $l_S(m) = h$ and $e_S(m) = \alpha$,
- for $M = \mathcal{M}_S(m)$ we have $M \geq \mathcal{N}$, i.e., $M(x) \geq \mathcal{N}(x)$ for all objects x of S, where $\geq$ occurring in the last inequality is the pointwise defined ordering of fuzzy segments of natural numbers.

The *result of the application* of R to a membrane m of S, whenever R can be applied to m, is a general fuzzy membrane system S' which is the same as S except

$$(**) \qquad\qquad \mathcal{M}_{S'}(m) = ((\mathcal{M}_S(m)\,\$^\delta\,\mathcal{N}) \div \varepsilon) + \mathcal{N}',$$

where for a general multi-fuzzy set $\mathcal{M}$ over $\mathcal{O}$ and $\varepsilon \in [0,1]$ we define $(\mathcal{M} \div \varepsilon)(x)(i) = \mathcal{M}(x)(i) \mathbin{\dot{-}} \varepsilon$ for all objects $x \in \mathcal{O}$ and natural numbers $i \in \mathbb{N}$. Here ε is meant to be an average expense of time (or energy, etc.) consumed during the application of the rule.

Other evolution rules of general fuzzy membrane systems will be discussed in the forthcoming papers about practical applications of the approach proposed in the present paper.

An application of an evolution rule of the form $(*)$ to a membrane of a general fuzzy membrane system and the result of this application can be explained from the point of view of practical applications in the following way.

An emergence of new high quality (fresh) copies (presented by $\mathcal{N}'$ in $(*)$) in the region of a membrane causes the deletion from this region of the old copies forming those segments above the segments presented by $\mathcal{N}$ in $(*)$ (i.e., those segments $\geq \mathcal{N}(x)$ for objects $x \in \mathcal{O}_S$) which according to the function δ in $(*)$ are relatively high or relatively low (see the explanation of $\mathcal{M} \, \$^\delta \, \mathcal{M}'$ given in Section 4). An emergence of new copies of objects can be understood here in two ways such that new copies have been introduced (may be from outside) to eliminate (to delete) some old copies or new copies have been generated by consuming (deleting) some old copies. The first of the above meanings of emergence of new copies has been suggested by [15], namely, one can treat new copies as copies of some enzymes introduced to a system by some medicine aimed to eliminate simultaneously the old copies of enzymes according to the general multi-fuzzy set $\mathcal{N}$ and the function δ in $(*)$.

6   Rational Fuzzy Segments

Very often an occurrence of an object in a system is determined by some quantity corresponding to some attribute of objects, like size, volume, weight, etc., where that quantity is measured in units and unit fractions of some scale (which sometimes is not decimal) and expressed by a rational number. Concerning medical applications, such a quantity may correspond to a dosage of some medicine which is measured in fractions of some unit. The occurrence of objects in a system described above can be modelled by real-valued multisets [3] (see also [7]), where scales and fraction systems are not specified.

We show in this section that fuzzy segments themselves can be used to represent rational numbers (based on various fraction systems like binary, ternary, and decimal fraction systems, etc.) which provides that for a general multi-fuzzy set $\mathcal{M}$ with the value $\mathcal{M}(x)$ representing a rational number for some object x the rational number represented by $\mathcal{M}(x)$ can be interpreted as a quantity corresponding to some attribute of x which determines an occurrence of x in a system. Therefore, generalized multi-fuzzy sets may unify various treatments of an occurrence of objects in a system, where an occurrence of some object is determined by the numbers of its copies and simultaneously an occurrence of some other object is determined by quantities corresponding to some attributes of the object and expressed by rational numbers.

For every rational number $n \geq 2$, every non-negative rational number $q = d_0 + r$, with its *total part* d_0 being a natural number and its *n-ary fraction* $r < 1$ determined by a string $d_1 \ldots d_k$ of natural numbers d_j with $0 \leq d_j < n$ for $1 \leq j \leq k$ such that

$$q = \sum_{j=1}^{k} n^{-j} \cdot d_j,$$

can be *represented* in a unique way by a fuzzy segment f_q defined by

$$f_q(i) = \begin{cases} 1 & \text{if } 0 \leq i < d_0 \text{ and } d_0 > 0, \\ n^{-(m+1)} & \text{if } \sum_{j=0}^{m} d_j \leq i < \sum_{j=1}^{m+1} d_j, \ d_{m+1} > 0, \text{ and } 0 \leq m < k, \\ 0 & \text{otherwise.} \end{cases}$$

Here for $n = 2$, $n = 3$, and $n = 10$, the n-ary fraction is read binary, ternary, decimal fraction, respectively.

All fuzzy segments $f_q > 0$ representing non-negative rational numbers $q = d_0 + r$ with n-ary fractions r can be characterized in the following way for a given natural number $n \geq 2$.

For a fuzzy segment f we define the j-th *critical point* of f to be a natural number n such that

- $f(n+1) < f(n)$,
- the set $\{m \in \mathbb{N} \mid f(m+1) < f(m) \text{ and } m < n\}$ has $j - 1$ elements.

For a fuzzy segment f with $k > 0$ critical points, we define for a natural number m with $0 < m \leq k$

$$\Delta_m = \begin{cases} i_1 + 1 & \text{if } m = 1 \text{ and } i_1 \text{ is the first critical point of } f, \\ i_m - i_{m-1} & \text{if } m > 1 \text{ and } i_{m-1}, i_m \text{ are } m - 1\text{-th and } m\text{-th critical} \\ & \text{points of } f, \text{ respectively,} \end{cases}$$

and then for a natural number j with $0 < j \leq k$

$$\int_j f = \sum_{j \leq m \leq k} \Delta_m \cdot f(i_m),$$

where i_m denotes the m-th critical point of f.

Theorem 2 (Characterization of Fuzzy Segments Representing Rational Numbers). *For a natural number $n \geq 2$ and the set $\mathbb{D} = \{n^{-m} \mid m \in \mathbb{N}\}$ of basic fractions, all fuzzy segments $f > 0$ representing rational numbers $q = d_0 + r$ with n-ary fractions r satisfy the following conditions:*

(Q_1) $\{f(i) \mid i \in \mathbb{N}\} \subseteq \mathbb{D} \cup \{0, 1\} \subseteq [0, 1]$,
(Q_2) *if the number of critical points of f is $k \geq 1$, then for every natural number j with $1 \leq j \leq k$ if i_j is the j-th critical point of f, then*

$$f(i_j) = \sup\{d \in \mathbb{D} \cup \{1\} \mid 0 < d \leq 1 \text{ and } \int_j f \geq d\} \text{ and}$$

$$\Delta_j = \max\{m \in \mathbb{N} \mid m > 0 \text{ and } \int_j f \geq f(i_j) \cdot m\}.$$

If a fuzzy segment $f > 0$ satisfies conditions (Q_1)–(Q_2) for $\mathbb{D} = \{n^{-m} \mid m \in \mathbb{N}\}$ with $n \geq 2$, then $f = f_q$ for $q = \int_1 f$.

Proof. One proves the theorem by induction on the number of critical points of f. $\square$

The conditions (Q_1), (Q_2) give rise to the following generalization of the representation of rational numbers by fuzzy segments.

For a set $\mathbb{D} \subseteq [0,1]$ we say that a fuzzy segment is a $\mathbb{D}$-*segment* if the conditions (Q_1) and (Q_2) hold for f. Then we say that a $\mathbb{D}$-segment *represents* a number q if $q = \int_1 f$. The uniqueness of representation of numbers by $\mathbb{D}$-segments is provided by the following theorem.

Theorem 3 (Uniqueness of Representation). *For an arbitrary set $\mathbb{D} \subseteq [0,1]$ and for all $\mathbb{D}$-fuzzy segments f, g, if $\int_1 f = \int_1 g$, then $f = g$.*

Proof. We prove the theorem by induction on $n = \max\{\mathrm{size}(f), \mathrm{size}(g)\}$. We use in the proof the property that if f is a $\mathbb{D}$-segment, then $f \mathbin{\dot{-}} (f \restriction k)$ is a $\mathbb{D}$-segment for $k \geq 0$. $\square$

We say that a set $\mathbb{D}$ of basic fractions with $\mathbb{D} \subseteq [0,1]$ is an *additive* [*subtractive*] set if for all $\mathbb{D}$-segments f, g there exists a $\mathbb{D}$-segment h such that $\int_1 h = \int_1 f + \int_1 g$ [$\int_1 h = \int_1 f \mathbin{\dot{-}} \int_1 g$]. The sets $\{(n)^{-m} \mid m \in \mathbb{N}\}$ $(n \in \mathbb{N}$ with $n \geq 2)$ are examples of additive and subtractive sets.

By Theorem 3, for an additive and subtractive set $\mathbb{D}$ of basic fractions one defines for two segments f, g their sum $f \oplus g$ and their subtraction $f \ominus g$ to be the unique $\mathbb{D}$-segments h and h', respectively, such that

$$\int_1 h = \int_1 f + \int_1 g \quad \text{and} \quad \int_1 h' = \int_1 f \mathbin{\dot{-}} \int_1 g.$$

Therefore, one can generalize the evolution rules of the form $(*)$ in Section 5 and their interpretation to the case where δ is a function defined on the sets $O_{\mathcal{S}}$ of objects of a general fuzzy membrane system $\mathcal{S}$ and valued in the set $\{\bot, \top\} \cup \mathrm{BF}_{\mathcal{S}}$ for $\mathrm{BF}_{\mathcal{S}}$ denoting the set of additive and subtractive sets of basic fractions considered for $\mathcal{S}$. Here the value $\delta(x) \in \mathrm{BF}_{\mathcal{S}}$ means that an occurrence of an object x in a system $\mathcal{S}$ is determined by a quantity corresponding to some attribute of x and measured in the scale with basic fractions belonging to $\mathbb{D} = \delta(x)$; the value $\delta(x) \in \{\bot, \top\}$ means that an occurrence of an object x in $\mathcal{S}$ is determined by the numbers of copies of x of different quality. For δ with values $\delta(x) \in \mathrm{BF}_{\mathcal{S}}$ for some objects x of $\mathcal{S}$, an evolution rule itself, the application conditions of a rule, and the result of the application of a rule are defined in an analogous way as in Section 5 except the following modifications. For x with $\delta(x) \in \mathrm{BF}_{\mathcal{S}}$ one imposes that:

- the general multi-fuzzy sets $\mathcal{N}, \mathcal{N}'$ occurring in $(*)$ in Section 5 should be such that their values $\mathcal{N}(x)$ and $\mathcal{N}'(x)$ are $\delta(x)$-segments,

– in the definition that a rule can be applied to a membrane m of $\mathcal{S}$ the general multi-fuzzy set $\mathcal{M} = \mathcal{M}_\mathcal{S}(m)$ should be such that $\mathcal{M}(x)$ is a $\delta(x)$-segment and the inequality $\mathcal{M}(x) \geq \mathcal{N}(x)$ should mean that $\int_1 f \geq \int_1 g$ for $f = \mathcal{M}(x)$ and $g = \mathcal{N}(x)$,

– in the formula $(**)$ defining in Section 5 the result of an application of a rule to a membrane of a system, the subtraction $\$^{\delta(x)}$ should be $\ominus$ and $+$ should be meant as $\oplus$ for the values at x of the corresponding general multi-fuzzy sets which occur in the formula.

Thus fuzzy segments representing (rational) numbers may unify various treatments of an occurrence of objects in systems for the case of evolution rules and their application.

References

1. H. Bandemer and S. Gottwald, *Fuzzy Sets, Fuzzy Logic, Fuzzy Methods with Applications*, New York 1995.
2. W.D. Blizard, The development of multiset theory, *Notre Dame Journal of Formal Logic*, 30 (1989), 36–66.
3. W.D. Blizard, Real-valued multisets and fuzzy sets, *Fuzzy Sets and Systems*, 33 (1989), 23–37.
4. J. Casasnovas and R. Rosselló, Scalar and fuzzy cardinalities of crisp and fuzzy multisets, submitted, 2004.
5. R. Lowen, *Fuzzy Set Theory, Basic Concepts, Techniques and Bibliography*, Dordrecht 1996.
6. *Meeting of the Society in Europe for Simulation Applied to Medicine (SESAM)*, 10–11 May 2002, Santander, Spain, Abstracts, *European Journal of Anaesthesiology*, 20, No. 10 (October 2003), 836–850.
7. T.Y. Nishida, Simulations of photosynthesis by a K-subset transforming system with membranes, *Fundamenta Informaticae*, 49, 1–3 (2002), 249–259.
8. A. Obtułowicz, On P systems with active membranes solving the integer factorization problem in a polynomial time, in: *Multisets Processing* (C. S. Calude et al., eds.), LNCS vol. 2235, Berlin, 2001, 267–285.
9. Gh. Păun, Computing with Membranes. *Journal of Computer and System Sciences*, 61, 1 (2000), 108–143.
10. Gh. Păun, *Membrane Computing. An Introduction*, Berlin 2002.
11. W. Pudrycz and H. Camargo, Fuzzy timed Petri nets, *Fuzzy Sets and Systems*, 140 (2003), 301–330.
12. A. Syropoulos, *Fuzzifying P systems*, manuscript, 2003.
13. M. Wygralak, *Vaguely Defined Objects*, Dordrecht 1996.
14. R.R. Yager, On the theory of bags, *International Journal of General Systems*, 13 (1986), 23–37.
15. M. Żylicz, *Cancer-like transformations, a challenge for biochemists, computer scientists and mathematicians*, lecture given at the Institute of Mathematics of Polish Academy of Sciences, Warsaw, March 2004.

Trading Polarization for Bi-stable Catalysts in P Systems with Active Membranes

Mario J. Pérez-Jiménez and Francisco José Romero-Campero

Research Group on Natural Computing,
Department of Computer Science and Artificial Intelligence,
University of Sevilla,
Avda. Reina Mercedes s/n, 41012 Sevilla, Spain
{Mario.Perez, Francisco-Jose.Romero}@cs.us.es

Abstract. In the last time, several efforts have been made in order to remove polarizations of membranes from P systems with active membranes; the present paper is a contribution in this respect. In order to compensate the loss of power represented by avoiding polarizations, we use bi-stable catalysts. Polarizationless systems with active membranes which use bi-stable catalysts are proven to be computationally complete and able to solve efficiently NP-complete problems. In this paper we present a solution to SAT in linear time. In order to illustrate the presented solution, we also provide a simulation with CLIPS.

1   Introduction

In membrane computing, P systems with active membranes are specially suitable to solve efficiently NP-complete problems, because of the fact that they provide membrane division, inspired from cell division. By using this operation, one can create an exponential number of membranes (working space) in linear time; in this way, we trade space for time to solve NP-complete problems (this has been reported for SAT, VALIDITY, Subset Sum, Knapsack, etc.).

One important feature of P systems with active membranes is the polarization of membranes; each membrane has an "electrical charge", positive $(+)$, negative $(-)$ or neutral (0). However, the electrical charges are not very realistic from a biological point of view. Because of this, several efforts are being made in order to remove the polarizations without losing the universality and the efficiency.

This paper goes into this direction of research: we remove the polarization of the membranes but on the other hand we use bi-stable catalysts. This variant of P systems with active membranes is proven to be computationally complete and able to solve NP-complete problems like SAT in linear time.

The paper is organized as follows: Section 2 introduces bi-stable catalytic P systems with active membranes without charges as generating devices and as recognizer devices. In Section 3 the complexity classes for P systems are briefly recalled. Sections 4, 5, and 6 present a cellular solution in linear time to the SAT problem within the framework of this variant of P systems. In Section 7

G. Mauri et al. (Eds.): WMC5 2004, LNCS 3365, pp. 373–388, 2005.

the programming language CLIPS is used to exhibit a simulation of the designed solution in order to illustrate how it works. Conclusions are given in Section 8.

2   Bi-stable Catalytic P Systems with Active Membranes Without Polarizations

Definition 1. *A bi-stable catalytic P system with active membranes and without polarizations is a tuple*

$$\Pi = (\Gamma, K, H, \mu, \mathcal{M}_1, \ldots, \mathcal{M}_p, R),$$

where:

1. $p \geq 1$ *is the initial degree of the system;*
2. Γ *is the alphabet of symbol-objects;*
3. K *is a subset of Γ, $K \subseteq \Gamma$, such that if $c \in K$ then $\bar{c} \in K$ (the elements of K are called bi-stable catalysts);*
4. H *is a finite set of labels for membranes;*
5. μ *is a membrane structure consisting of p membranes labelled (not necessarily in a one-to-one manner) with elements of H;*
6. $\mathcal{M}_1, \ldots, \mathcal{M}_p$ *are strings over Γ, describing the initial multisets of objects associated with the regions of μ;*
7. R *is a finite set of evolution rules, of the following forms:*

   (a) $[\, a \to \omega \,]_h$, *for $h \in H$, $a \in \Gamma - K, \omega \in (\Gamma - K)^*$. This is an object evolution rule, associated with a membrane labelled with h but not directly involving the membrane.*

   (b) $[\, ca \to c\omega \,]_h$, $[\, ca \to \bar{c}\omega \,]_h$, $[\, \bar{c}a \to \bar{c}\omega \,]_h$, $[\, \bar{c}a \to c\omega \,]_h$, *for $h \in H$, $c \in K$ and $a \in \Gamma - K, \omega \in (\Gamma - K)^*$ (bi-stable catalytic evolution rules). Such a rule is an object evolution rule involving bi-stable catalysts, associated with a membrane labelled with h but not directly involving the membrane.*

   (c) $a[\ ]_h \to [\, b \,]_h$, *for $h \in H$, $a, b \in \Gamma - K$ ("send in" communication rules). An object from the region immediately outside a membrane labelled with h is introduced in this membrane, possibly transformed into another object.*

   (d) $[\, a \,]_h \to b[\ ]_h$, *for $h \in H$, $a, b \in \Gamma - K$ ("send out" communication rules). An object is sent out from membrane labelled with h to the region immediately outside, possibly transformed into another object.*

   (e) $[\, a \,]_h \to b$, *for $h \in H$, $a, b \in \Gamma - K$ (dissolving rules). A membrane labelled with h is dissolved in reaction with an object. The skin is never dissolved.*

   (f) $[\, a \,]_h \to [\, b \,]_h [\, c \,]_h$, *for $h \in H$, $a, b, c \in \Gamma - K$ (division rules for elementary membranes). An elementary membrane can be divided into two membranes with the same label, possibly transforming some objects.*

Note that, in contrast to [2], the bi-stable catalysts are not always flip-flop-ing from non-barred to barred versions and back, but also rules of the form $ca \to cw$

and $\bar{c}a \rightarrow \bar{c}w$ are allowed. The case when the catalysts appear only in rules of the form $ca \rightarrow \bar{c}w$ and $\bar{c}a \rightarrow cw$ is called *restricted*.

These rules are applied according to the following principles:

- All the rules are applied in parallel and in a maximal manner. In one step, one object of a membrane can be used by only one rule (chosen in a non deterministic way), but any object which can evolve by one rule of any form, should evolve.
- If a membrane is dissolved, its content (multiset and internal membranes) is left free in the surrounding region.
- If at the same time a membrane h is divided by a rule of type (e) and there are objects in this membrane which evolve by means of rules of type (a) and (b), then we suppose that first the evolution rules of types (a) and (b) are used, and then the division is produced. Of course, this process takes only one step.
- The rules associated with membranes labelled with h are used for all copies of this membrane. At one step, a membrane labelled with h can be the subject of *only one* rule of types (c)-(f).

2.1 Bi-stable Catalytic P Systems with Active Membranes Without Polarizations, as Generating Devices

As a generating device, the result (output) of a halting configuration of a bi-stable catalytic P system is the cardinality of the multiset associated with the environment in the last configuration. In these P systems a non halting computation yields no output.

Definition 2. *We denote by $N(\Pi)$ the set of all outputs of halting computations with respect to a bi-stable catalytic P system Π.*

Theorem 1. *Restricted bi-stable catalytic P systems with active membranes without polarization, using rules of type (b) and (d), are computationally complete.*

Proof. Let L be a recursively enumerable language. Let G be a matrix grammar with appearance checking such that $L(G) = L$. We can consider that $G = (N, \{a\}, S, M, F)$ is given in Z-binary normal form, in the standard notation. That is,

- $N = N_1 \cup N_2 \cup \{S, Z, \sharp\}$, with these three sets mutually disjoint.
- The matrices in M are in one of the following forms:
  1. $(S \rightarrow XA)$, where $X \in N_1, A \in N_2$,
  2. $(X \rightarrow Y, A \rightarrow x)$, where $X, Y \in N_1, A \in N_2, x \in (N_2 \cup T)^*, |x| \leq 2$,
  3. $(X \rightarrow Y, A \rightarrow \sharp)$, where $X \in N_1, Y \in N_1 \cup \{Z\}, A \in N_2$,
  4. $(Z \rightarrow \lambda)$.
- $F = \{A \rightarrow \sharp \mid \exists m \in M(m = (X \rightarrow Y, A \rightarrow \sharp))\}$.
  Moreover, if the special symbol Z appears in a sentential form w, then we have $w = Zw'$, with $w' \in (T \cup \{\sharp\})^*$ (that is, no nonterminal from N_2 is present).

- The matrices in M will be ordered as follows:

m_0 : $(S \to X_{init} A_{init})$, with $X_{init} \in N_1, A_{init} \in N_2$,

$\left.\begin{matrix} m_1 : \\ \vdots \\ m_k : \end{matrix}\right\}$ $(X \to \alpha, A \to x)$, with $x \in N_1, \alpha \in N_1 \cup \{\lambda\}, A \in N_2$,

$\left.\begin{matrix} m_{k+1} : \\ \vdots \\ m_n : \end{matrix}\right\}$ $\begin{matrix} (X \to Y, A \to \sharp). \\ (X \to Z, A \to \sharp) \end{matrix}$, with $X, Y \in N_1, A \in N_2$

m_{n+1} : $(Z \to \lambda)$

We construct the system

$$\Pi = (\Gamma, K, \{1\}, [\ ]_1, \mathcal{M}_1, R),$$

where:

- $\Gamma = N \cup K \cup \{a, \sharp\} \cup \{X', \overline{X}, \overline{X}' \mid X \in N_1\}$,
- $K = \{c_i, \overline{c}_i \mid 0 \le i \le n\}$,
- $\mathcal{M}_1 = \{X_{init}, A_{init}, E, c_0, c_1, \ldots, c_n\}$,
- The set R consists of the following rules:

(1.)

$$\left.\begin{matrix} [\ c_i X \to \overline{c}_i Y'\ ]_1 \\ [\ \overline{c}_i A \to c_i x\ ]_1 \\ [\ \overline{c}_i E \to c_i \sharp\ ]_1 \\ [\ c_0 Y' \to \overline{c}_0 Y\ ]_1 \\ [\ \overline{c}_0 Y' \to c_0 Y\ ]_1 \end{matrix}\right\} \quad \text{for each } m_i : (X \to Y, A \to x), \text{ with } 1 \le i \le k\ .$$

These rules simulate the matrices m_i, for $i = 1, \ldots, k$. When we have in the skin region a multiset containing X and there exists in M a matrix $m_i : (X \to Y, A \to x)$, the rule $[\ c_i X \to \overline{c}_i Y'\ ]_1$ is applicable. In order to simulate the second component of the grammar one of the rules $[\ c_0 Y' \to \overline{c}_0 Y\ ]_1$, $[\ \overline{c}_0 Y' \to c_0 Y\ ]_1$ (either c_0 or $\overline{c}_0$ is present, hence one of these rules can be used) provides a step in which if there exists an object A in the skin region, then the rule $[\ \overline{c}_i A \to c_i x\ ]_1$ can be applied; otherwise, if there is no such object, the rule $[\ \overline{c}_i E \to c_i \sharp\ ]_1$ produces the trap symbol $\sharp$ showing that we can not apply this matrix and so this is not a correct derivation.

(2.)

$$\left.\begin{matrix} [\ c_i X \to \overline{c}_i \overline{Y}'\ ]_1 \\ [\ c_0 \overline{Y}' \to \overline{c}_0 \overline{Y}\ ]_1 \\ [\ \overline{c}_0 \overline{Y}' \to c_0 \overline{Y}\ ]_1 \\ [\ \overline{c}_i A \to c_i \sharp\ ]_1 \\ [\ \overline{c}_i \overline{Y} \to c_i Y\ ]_1 \end{matrix}\right\} \quad \text{for each } m_i : (X \to Y, A \to \sharp), \text{ with } k + 1 \le i \le n$$

These rules simulate the matrices m_i, for $i = k+1, \ldots, n$. When we have in the skin region a multiset containing X and there exists in M a matrix $m_i : (X \to Y, A \to \sharp)$, the rule $[\, c_i X \to \overline{c}_i \overline{Y}' \,]_1$ is applicable. In order to simulate the second component of the grammar, one of the rules $[\, c_0 \overline{Y}' \to \overline{c}_0 \overline{Y} \,]_1, [\, \overline{c}_0 \overline{Y}' \to c_0 \overline{Y} \,]_1$ provides a step in which if there exists an object A in the skin region, the rule $[\, \overline{c}_i A \to c_i \sharp \,]_1$ is applied; otherwise, if there is no such object, then the rule $[\, \overline{c}_i \overline{Y} \to c_i Y \,]_1$ completes the simulation of this matrix.

(3.)

$$[\, a \,]_1 \to a [\,\,]_1, \quad [\, c_0 \sharp \to \overline{c_0 \sharp} \,]_1, \quad [\, \overline{c}_0 \sharp \to c_0 \sharp \,]_1,$$

The first of these two last rules, $[\, a \,]_1 \to a [\,\,]_1$, sends out to the environment the object a. In a halting configuration of the system the multiplicity of the object a in the environment represents the length of the word generated by G. If the computation of the system simulates a non terminal derivation in G, then the rules $[\, c_0 \sharp \to \overline{c}_0 \sharp \,]_1, [\, \overline{c}_0 \sharp \to c_0 \sharp \,]_1$ produce a non halting computation.

From the above remarks it is easy to prove that the equality $length(L(G)) = N(\Pi)$ holds, where $length(L(G))$ is the length set of the language $L(G)$, that is, $length(L(G)) = \{|u| \mid u \in L(G)\}$. $\square$

In the previous proof we do not actually use the fact that the membranes are *active* (for instance, we do not use membrane division); otherwise stated, the proof can be easily reformulated in terms of basic transition P systems, and this makes necessary the comparison of Theorem 1 with universality results known for such systems. First, the universality is known for systems with bi-stable catalysts already from [5], where, however, one uses two membranes (see also Theorem 3.4.7 from [2]; our results improves on this point, because we use only one membrane. Then, in [1] it is proven that two catalysts are sufficient to get universality in P systems without polarizations and without priorities, but the systems considered in [1] contain both catalytic and non-catalytic rules.

2.2 Recognizer Bi-stable Catalytic P Systems with Active Membranes Without Polarization

Definition 3. *A P system with input is a tuple (Π, Σ, i_Π), where Π is a P system, with working alphabet Γ, with p membranes labelled $1, \ldots, p$, and initial multisets $\mathcal{M}_1, \ldots, \mathcal{M}_p$ associated with them, Σ is an (input) alphabet strictly contained in Γ, the initial multisets are over $\Gamma - \Sigma$, and i_Π is the label of a distinguished (input) membrane.*

The computations of a P system with an input in the form of a multiset m over Σ are defined in a natural way; they start from a configuration which is obtained by adding the multiset m to the initial configuration of the system.

Definition 4. *Let (Π, Σ, i_Π) be a P system with input. Let Γ be the working alphabet of Π, μ the membrane structure and $\mathcal{M}_1, \ldots, \mathcal{M}_p$ the initial multisets* *of Π. Let m be a multiset over Σ. The* initial configuration *of (Π, Σ, i_Π) with input m is $(\mu, \mathcal{M}_1, \dots, \mathcal{M}_{i_\Pi} \cup m, \dots \mathcal{M}_p)$.*

In the case of P systems with input and with external output, the concept of computation is introduced in a similar way as for standard P systems – see [2] – but with a small change. We consider that it is not possible to observe the internal processes inside the P system and we can only know if the computation has halted via some distinguished objects sent out of the skin. We can formalize these ideas in the following way.

Definition 5. *A* recognizer bi-stable catalytic P system *is a P system with input, (Π, Σ, i_Π), and with external output such that:*

1. *Π is a bi-stable catalytic P system.*
2. *The working alphabet of Π contains two distinguished objects YES, NO.*
3. *All its computations halt.*
4. *If $\mathcal{C}$ is a computation of Π, then either the object YES or the object NO (but not both) is sent to the environment, and only in the last step of the computation.*

We say that $\mathcal{C}$ is an accepting computation (respectively, rejecting computation) if the object YES (respectively, NO) appears in the environment in the halting configuration of $\mathcal{C}$.

In what follows we will deal with recognizer bi-stable P systems with active membranes without polarizations. Let us denote by $\mathcal{BAM}$ the class of this variant of recognizer P systems.

3   The Complexity Class $\mathbf{PMC}_{\mathcal{F}}$

The first results about "solvability" of **NP**–complete problems in polynomial time (even linear) by cellular computing systems with membranes were obtained using variants of P systems that lack an input membrane. Thus, the constructive proofs of such results need to design one system for each instance of the problem.

This drawback can be easily avoided if we consider a P system with input. Then, the same system could solve different instances of the problem, provided that the corresponding input multisets are introduced in the input membrane.

Instead of looking for a single system that solves a problem, we prefer designing a family of P systems such that each element decides all the instances of "equivalent size" of the problem.

Definition 6. *Let $\mathcal{F}$ be a class of recognizer P systems. We say that a decision problem $X = (I_X, \theta_X)$ is solvable in polynomial time by a family $\Pi = (\Pi(n))_{n \in \mathbf{N}^+}$, of systems from $\mathcal{F}$, and we denote this by $X \in \mathbf{PMC}_{\mathcal{F}}$, if the following is true:*

- *The family Π is polynomially uniform by Turing machines; that is, there exists a deterministic Turing machine constructing $\Pi(n)$ from $n \in \mathbf{N}^+$ in polynomial time.*

- *There exists a pair (g, h) of polynomial-time computable functions $g : L \to \bigcup_{n \in \mathbb{N}^+} I_{\Pi(n)}$ and $h : L \to \mathbb{N}^+$ such that for every $u \in L$ we have $g(u) \in I_{\Pi(h(u))}$, and*
    - *the family $\mathbf{\Pi}$ is polynomially bounded with regard to (X, g, h); that is, there exists a polynomial function p, such that for each $u \in I_X$ every computation of $\Pi(h(u))$ with input $g(u)$ is halting and, moreover, it performs at most $p(|u|)$ steps;*
    - *the family $\mathbf{\Pi}$ is sound with regard to (X, g, h); that is, for each $u \in I_X$, if there exists an accepting computation of $\Pi(h(u))$ with input $g(u)$, then $\theta_X(u) = 1$;*
    - *the family $\mathbf{\Pi}$ is complete with regard to (X, g, h); that is, for each $u \in I_X$, if $\theta_X(u) = 1$, then every computation of $\Pi(h(u))$ with input $g(u)$ is an accepting one.*

In the above definition we have imposed to every P system $\Pi(n)$ to be *confluent*, in the following sense: every computation with the *same* input produces the *same* output.

The class $\mathbf{PMC}_{\mathcal{F}}$ is closed under polynomial–time reduction and complement, as proven, for instance, in [10].

4   Solving SAT in Linear Time

The SAT problem is the following one: *Given a boolean formula in conjunctive normal form (CNF), to determine whether or not it is satisfiable; that is, whether there exits an assignment to its variables on which it evaluates true.*

We will address the resolution of this problem via a brute force algorithm within the framework of recognizer bi-stable catalytic P systems with active membranes without charges. Our strategy will consist in:

- *Generation stage*: Using membrane division we generate all possible assignments associated with the formula.
- *Evaluation stage*: In each membrane we evaluate the formula on the assignment produced in that membrane.
- *Checking stage*: In each membrane we check wether or not the formula evaluates true on the assignment from that membrane.
- *Output stage*: Send to the environment the right answer according to the previous stage.

Let us consider the function $\langle \, , \, \rangle$ defined by $\langle n, m \rangle = ((n+m)(n+m+1)/2)+n$ for $\varphi = C_1 \wedge \cdots \wedge C_m$ a propositional formula in CNF and $Var(\varphi) = \{x_1, \ldots, x_n\}$. The function $\langle \, , \, \rangle$ is polynomial-time computable (it is primitive recursive and bijective from $\mathbb{N}^2$ onto $\mathbb{N}$). Also, the inverse function of $\langle \, , \, \rangle$ is polynomial. The family presented here is

$$\mathbf{\Pi} = \{ \, (\Pi(\langle n, m \rangle), \Sigma(n, m), i(n, m)) \mid (n, m) \in \mathbb{N}^2 \, \}.$$

For each element of the family, the input alphabet is

$$\Sigma(n, m) = \{x_{i,j}, \overline{x}_{i,j} \mid 1 \leq i \leq m, 1 \leq j \leq n\},$$

the input membrane is $i(n, m) = 2$, and the P system

$$\Pi(\langle n, m \rangle) = (\Gamma(n, m), K(n, m), \{1, 2\}, \mu, \mathcal{M}_1, \mathcal{M}_2, R)$$

is defined as follows:

- Bi-stable catalysts:

  $K(n, m) = \{t_j, \overline{t}_j, f_j, \overline{f}_j, s_i, \overline{s}_i, ans, \overline{ans} \mid 1 \leq i \leq m, 1 \leq j \leq n\}.$
- Working alphabet:

  $$\Gamma(n, m) = \Sigma(n, m) \cup K(n, m) \cup \{v_j, p_j, n_j \mid 1 \leq j \leq n\}$$
  $$\cup \{c_i, r_i \mid 1 \leq i \leq m\} \cup \{no_k \mid 1 \leq k \leq n + m + 3\}$$
  $$\cup \{\natural, yes, YES, NO\}.$$

- Membrane structure: $\mu = [_1 \, [_2 \,\,]_2 \,]_1$ (we will say that every membrane with label 2 is an *internal membrane*).

- Initial Multisets:

  $\mathcal{M}_1 = \{no_1, ans\},$
  $\mathcal{M}_2 = \{v_1, \ldots, v_n, \overline{t}_1, \ldots, \overline{t}_n, \overline{f}_1, \ldots, \overline{f}_n, \overline{s}_1, \ldots, \overline{s}_m, c_1\}.$

- The set R consists of the following rules:

  1. $[\, v_j \,]_2 \;\rightarrow\; [\, p_j \,]_2 \,[\, n_j \,]_2, \quad 1 \leq j \leq n.$

     The goal of these rules is to generate an internal membrane for each assignment to the variables of the formula. The new membrane where the object p_j appears represents the assignment where $x_j = true$ and the new membrane where the object n_j appears represents the assignment where $x_j = false$.

  2.
     $$\left.\begin{array}{l} [\, \overline{t}_j p_j \;\rightarrow\; t_j p_j \,]_2 \\ [\, t_j \, x_{ij} \;\rightarrow\; t_j \, r_i \,]_2 \\ [\, t_j \, \overline{x}_{ij} \;\rightarrow\; t_j \, \natural \,]_2 \end{array}\right\} \text{ for } 1 \leq i \leq m, \, 1 \leq j \leq n.$$

     The object p_j activates the catalyst t_j which "erases" the objects $\overline{x}_{i,j}$ (these objects represent the literals $\neg x_j$), but reacts with the objects $x_{i,j}$ (these objects represent the literals x_j) to produce the object r_i (this object indicates that the clause number i evaluates true on the assignment associated with the membrane).

  3.
     $$\left.\begin{array}{l} [\, \overline{f}_j n_j \;\rightarrow\; f_j n_j \,]_2 \\ [\, f_j \, \overline{x}_{ij} \;\rightarrow\; f_j \, r_i \,]_2 \\ [\, f_j \, x_{ij} \;\rightarrow\; f_j \, \natural \,]_2 \end{array}\right\} \text{ for } 1 \leq i \leq m, \, 1 \leq j \leq n.$$

The object n_j activates the catalyst f_j which "erases" the objects $x_{i,j}$ (these objects represent the literals x_j), but reacts with the objects $\overline{x}_{i,j}$ (these objects represent the literals $\neg x_j$) to produce the object r_i (this object indicates that the clause number i evaluates true on the assignment associated with the membrane).

4. $[\, \overline{s}_i r_i \;\to\; s_i r_i \,]_2$, for $1 \le i \le m$,
   $[\, s_i c_i \;\to\; s_i c_{i+1} \,]_2$, for $1 \le i \le m - 1$,
   $[\, s_m\, c_m \;\to\; s_m\, yes \,]_2$.

The objects c_i are counters which represent the number of clauses that evaluate true on the assignment associated with the internal membrane. So the object c_i, for $1 \le i \le m - 1$, reacts with the catalyst s_i, which is activated by the object r_i, to produce the object c_{i+1}, and the object c_m reacts with the object r_m to produce the object yes in order to show that every clause of the formula evaluates true on the assignment associated with the internal membrane.

5. $[\, yes \,]_2 \;\to\; yes\, [\;\,]_2$,
   $[\, ans\, yes \;\to\; \overline{ans} YES \,]_1$,
   $[\, YES \,]_1 \;\to\; YES\, [\;\,]_1$.

These rules produce and send the object YES to the environment.

6. $[\, no_i \;\to\; no_{i+1} \,]_1$, for $1 \le i \le n + 2m + 3$,
   $[\, ans\, no_{n+2m+4} \;\to\; \overline{ans} NO \,]_1$,
   $[\, NO \,]_1 \;\to\; NO\, [\;\,]_1$.

These rules produce and send out the object NO to the environment. Note that the object NO appears one step later than the object YES and that the catalyst ans get barred in the output stage in order to make sure that the system sends out the right answer.

5   An Overview of the Computation

First of all we must define a suitable pair (g, h) of polynomial-time computable functions (see Definition 6) associated with the SAT problem. Given a formula $\varphi = C_1 \wedge \ldots C_m$ in CNF such that $Var(\varphi) = \{x_1, \ldots, x_n\}$, we define $h(\varphi) = \langle n, m \rangle$ (recall the bijection mentioned in the previous section) and $g(\varphi) = \{x_{ij} \mid x_j \in C_i\} \cup \{\overline{x}_j \mid \neg x_j \in C_i\}$

Next we will informally describe how the recognizer bi-stable catalytic P system $\Pi(h(\varphi))$ with input $g(\varphi)$ works.

The computation starts with the *generation and evaluation stages*. These two stages take place in parallel following the rules from group 1 to 3. The generation of membranes is controlled by the objects v_j, for $1 \le j \le n$. When an object v_j is present in an internal membrane the rule in 1 is applicable and so the system produces two new membranes. In one of these two new membranes the object p_j appears encoding that in the assignment associated with the membrane we have $x_j = true$. In the other membrane the object n_j appears to show that in the assignment associated with this membrane we have $x_j = false$.

The *evaluation stage* takes place in a similar way in every internal membrane. The object p_j (respectively n_j) representing that $x_j = true$ (respectively $x_j = false$) in the assignment associated with the internal membrane, activates the bi-stable catalyst t_j (respectively f_j). The *active catalyst* t_j (respectively f_j) according to the rules in 2 (respectively 3) reacts with the objects x_{ij} and $\overline{x}_{ij}$ to produce the objects $\sharp$ and r_i. The objects r_i represent that the clause C_i evaluates true on the assignment associated with the membrane. These two stages take place in parallel and they take n steps of division, one step to activate the catalysts and m steps to evaluate each clause, that is, an overall of at most $n + m + 1$ steps.

The *checking stage* takes place according to the rules in 4. The object r_i activates the catalyst s_i which reacts with the object c_i for $1 \le i \le m - 1$ to produce the object c_{i+1}. The object c_i represents that the clauses $C_1, \ldots, C_{i-1}$ for $1 \le i \le m$, evaluate true on the assignment associated with the internal membrane. So, the catalyst s_m reacts with the object c_m to produce the object *yes*, in order to show that the whole formula evaluates true on the assignment associated with the internal membrane. As it can be seen, the *checking stage* takes one step to activate the catalysts and m steps to check that every clause evaluates true; that is, an overall of at most $m + 1$ steps.

In the output stage the rules in 4 and 5 are applied to send the correct answer to the environment. The answer YES is sent out following the rules in 5; the object *yes* is sent to the skin by the first rule, in the second rule the bi-stable catalyst *ans* reacts with the object *yes* to produce the object YES and *ans* remains barred from now on, and finally the object YES is sent out to the environment. On the other hand, following the first rule in 5, the object no_k waits $n + 2m + 4$ and, if no object *yes* has been sent to the skin, the bi-stable catalyst *ans* and no_{n+2m+4} react to produce the object NO which is sent out to the environment. Note that the object no_{n+2m+4} appears a step later than the object *yes* in order to be sure that the system sends out the right answer. Thus, the output stage takes at most 4 steps.

6   Required Resources

The presented family of recognizer bi-stable catalytic P systems solving the SAT is polynomially uniform by Turing machines. Note that the definition of the family is done in a recursive manner starting from a given instance, in particular, from the constants n and m. Furthermore, the required resources to build the element $\Pi(\langle n, m \rangle)$ of the family are the following:

- Size of the alphabet: $2nm + 8n + 5m + 9 \in O((max\{n, m\})^2)$.
- Number of membranes: $2 \in \Theta(1)$.
- $|\mathcal{M}_1| + |\mathcal{M}_2| = 3n + m + 3 \in O(n + m)$.

- Sum of the rules lengths: $32nm + 27n + 32m + 60 \in O((max\{n, m\})^2)$.

The number of steps in each stage in the worst case are the following:

1. *Generation and evaluation stage:* $n + m + 1$ steps.
2. *Checking stage:* $m + 1$ steps.
3. *Output stage:* 4 steps.

Therefore, the overall number of steps is $n + 2m + 6 \in O(max\{n, m\})$.
    From the above discussion we deduce the following results:

Theorem 2.

1. $SAT \in \mathbf{PMC}_{\mathcal{BAM}}$.
2. $\mathbf{NP} \subseteq \mathbf{PMC}_{\mathcal{BAM}}$, and $\mathbf{NP} \cup \mathbf{co} - \mathbf{NP} \subseteq \mathbf{PMC}_{\mathcal{BAM}}$.

Proof. In order to prove the theorem, it suffices to make the following remarks: the SAT problem is $\mathbf{NP}-$complete, $SAT \in \mathbf{PMC}_{\mathcal{BAM}}$ and the class $\mathbf{PMC}_{\mathcal{BAM}}$ is closed under polynomial-time reduction, and under complement.   □

7   A CLIPS Session with $\varphi = (\, x_1 \vee \neg x_2\,) \wedge (\, \neg x_1 \vee x_2\,)$

In this section we illustrate how the designed family of recognizer bi-stable catalytic P systems works by presenting a simulation with CLIPS for the instance $\varphi = (\, x_1 \vee \neg x_2\,) \wedge (\, \neg x_1 \vee x_2\,)$.

```
Configuration number: 1

[environment [multiset ]]
[skin      [children 3 4]
           [label 1] [multiset ans , no 2]]
[membrane
    [number 4] [children ] [father 1]
    [label 2]  [multiset v 1 , n 2 , t- 1 , t- 2 , f- 1 , f- 2 ,
                         s- 1 , s- 2 , c 1 ,
                         x 1 1 , -x 1 2 , -x 2 1 , x 2 2]]
[membrane
    [number 3] [children ] [father 1]
    [label 2] [multiset v 1 , p 2 , t- 1 , t- 2 , f- 1 , f- 2 ,
                        s- 1 , s- 2 , c 1 ,
                        x 1 1 , -x 1 2 , -x 2 1 , x 2 2]]
```

Here it can be seen how the generation stage takes place. In the presence of the object v_2 the system produces two new membranes. The membrane number 4, where the object n_2 appears, indicates that in the assignment associated with this membrane we have $x_2 = false$. The membrane number 3, where the object p_2 appears, indicates that in the assignment associated with this membrane we have $x_2 = true$.

```
Configuration number: 2

[environment [multiset ]]
[skin      [children 5 6 7 8]
           [label 1] [multiset ans , no 3]]
[membrane
    [number 8] [children ] [father 1]
    [label 2] [multiset n 1 , # , t- 1 , t- 2 , f- 1 , f 2 ,
                        s- 1 , s- 2 , c 1 ,
                        x 1 1 , -x 1 2 , -x 2 1 , x 2 2]]
[membrane
    [number 7] [children ] [father 1]
    [label 2] [multiset p 1 , # , t- 1 , t- 2 , f- 1 , f 2 ,
                        s- 1 , s- 2 , c 1 ,
                        x 1 1 , -x 1 2 , -x 2 1 , x 2 2]]
[membrane
    [number 6] [children ] [father 1]
    [label 2] [multiset n 1 , # , t- 1 , t 2 , f- 1 , f- 2 ,
                        s- 1 , s- 2 , c 1 ,
                        x 1 1 , -x 1 2 , -x 2 1 , x 2 2]]
[membrane
    [number 5] [children ] [father 1]
    [label 2] [multiset p 1 , # , t- 1 , t 2 , f- 1 , f- 2 ,
                        s- 1 , s- 2 , c 1 ,
                        x 1 1 , -x 1 2 , -x 2 1 , x 2 2]]


Configuration number: 3

[environment [multiset ]]
[skin      [children 5 6 7 8]
           [label 1] [multiset ans , no 4]]
[membrane
    [number 5] [children ] [father 1]
    [label 2] [multiset # , # , t 1 , t 2 , f- 1 , f- 2 ,
                        s- 1 , s- 2 , c 1 ,
                        x 1 1 , # , -x 2 1 , x 2 2]]
[membrane
    [number 7] [children ] [father 1]
    [label 2] [multiset # , # , t 1 , t- 2 , f- 1 , f 2 ,
                        s- 1 , s- 2 , c 1 ,
                        x 1 1 , r 1 , -x 2 1 , x 2 2]]
[membrane
    [number 6] [children ] [father 1]
    [label 2] [multiset # , # , t- 1 , t 2 , f 1 , f- 2 ,
                        s- 1 , s- 2 , c 1 ,
                        x 1 1 , -x 1 2 , -x 2 1 , r 2]]
[membrane
    [number 8] [children ] [father 1]
    [label 2] [multiset # , # , t- 1 , t- 2 , f 1 , f 2 ,
                        s- 1 , s- 2 , c 1 ,
```

```
                    x 1 1 , r 1 , -x 2 1 , x 2 2]]
```

Configuration number: 4

```
[environment [multiset ]]
[skin      [children 5 6 7 8]
           [label 1] [multiset ans , no 5]]
[membrane
    [number 7] [children ] [father 1]
    [label 2] [multiset # , # , t 1 , t- 2 , f- 1 , f 2 ,
                    s 1 , s- 2 , c 1 , # , r 1 , -x 2 1 , #]]
[membrane
    [number 5] [children ] [father 1]
    [label 2] [multiset # , # , t 1 , t 2 , f- 1 , f- 2 ,
                    s- 1 , s- 2 , c 1 , r 1 , # , -x 2 1 , r 2]]
[membrane
    [number 6] [children ] [father 1]
    [label 2] [multiset # , # , t- 1 , t 2 , f 1 , f- 2 ,
                    s- 1 , s 2 , c 1 , # , # , -x 2 1 , #]]
[membrane
    [number 8] [children ] [father 1]
    [label 2] [multiset # , # , t- 1 , t- 2 , f 1 , f 2 ,
                    s 1 , s- 2 , c 1 , x 1 1 , # , r 2 , #]]
```

   At the end of the generation and evaluation stage it can be seen that the assignment associated with the internal membranes are: $\{x_1 = false, x_2 = false\}$ with the membrane number 8, $\{x_1 = false, x_2 = true\}$ with the membrane number 6, $\{x_1 = true, x_2 = false\}$ with the membrane number 7, and $\{x_1 = true, x_2 = true\}$ with the membrane number 5.

Configuration number: 5

```
[environment [multiset ]]
[skin      [children 5 6 7 8]
           [label 1] [multiset ans , no 6]]
[membrane
    [number 5] [children ] [father 1]
    [label 2] [multiset # , # , t 1 , t 2 , f- 1 , f- 2 ,
                    s 1 , s 2 , c 1 , # , # , # , #]]
[membrane
    [number 7] [children ] [father 1]
    [label 2] [multiset # , # , t 1 , t- 2 , f- 1 , f 2 ,
                    s 1 , s- 2 , c 2 , # , r 1 , # , #]]
[membrane
    [number 6] [children ] [father 1]
    [label 2] [multiset # , # , t- 1 , t 2 , f 1 , f- 2 ,
                    s- 1 , s 2 , c 1 , # , # , r 2 , #]]
[membrane
    [number 8] [children ] [father 1]
    [label 2] [multiset # , # , t- 1 , t- 2 , f 1 , f 2 ,
                    s 1 , s 2 , c 2 , # , # , # , #]]
```

```
Configuration number: 6

[environment [multiset ]]
[skin      [children 5 6 7 8]
           [label 1] [multiset ans , no 7]]
[membrane
    [number 7] [children ] [father 1]
    [label 2] [multiset # , # , t 1 , t- 2 , f- 1 , f 2 ,
                         s 1 , s- 2 , c 2 , # , r 1 , # , #]]
[membrane
    [number 6] [children ] [father 1]
    [label 2] [multiset # , # , t- 1 , t 2 , f 1 , f- 2 ,
                         s- 1 , s 2 , c 1 , # , # , r 2 , #]]
[membrane
    [number 5] [children ] [father 1]
    [label 2] [multiset # , # , t 1 , t 2 , f- 1 , f- 2 ,
                         s 1 , s 2 , c 2 , # , # , # , #]]
[membrane
    [number 8] [children ] [father 1]
    [label 2] [multiset # , # , t- 1 , t- 2 , f 1 , f 2 ,
                         s 1 , s 2 , yes , # , # , # , #]]
```

As a result of the *checking stage* the object YES is produced and sent out to the environment in the output stage.

```
Configuration number: 7

[environment [multiset ]]
[skin      [children 5 6 7 8]
           [label 1] [multiset yes , ans , no 8]]
[membrane
    [number 7] [children ] [father 1]
    [label 2] [multiset # , # , t 1 , t- 2 , f- 1 , f 2 ,
                         s 1 , s- 2 , c 2 , # , r 1 , # , #]]
[membrane
    [number 6] [children ] [father 1]
    [label 2] [multiset # , # , t- 1 , t 2 , f 1 , f- 2 ,
                         s- 1 , s 2 , c 1 , # , # , r 2 , #]]
[membrane
    [number 5] [children ] [father 1]
    [label 2] [multiset # , # , t 1 , t 2 , f- 1 , f- 2 ,
                         s 1 , s 2 , yes , # , # , # , #]]
[membrane
    [number 8] [children ] [father 1]
    [label 2] [multiset # , # , t- 1 , t- 2 , f 1 , f 2 ,
                         s 1 , s 2 , # , # , # , #]]

Configuration number: 8

[environment [multiset ]]
```

```
[skin      [children 5 6 7 8]
           [label 1] [multiset yes , YES , ans- , no 9]]
[membrane
    [number 7] [children ] [father 1]
    [label 2] [multiset # , # , t 1 , t- 2 , f- 1 , f 2 ,
                         s 1 , s- 2 , c 2 , # , r 1 , # , #]]
[membrane
    [number 6] [children ] [father 1]
    [label 2] [multiset # , # , t- 1 , t 2 , f 1 , f- 2 ,
                         s- 1 , s 2 , c 1 , # , # , r 2 , #]]
[membrane
    [number 8] [children ] [father 1]
    [label 2] [multiset # , # , t- 1 , t- 2 , f 1 , f 2 ,
                         s 1 , s 2 , # , # , # , #]]
[membrane
    [number 5] [children ] [father 1]
    [label 2] [multiset # , # , t 1 , t 2 , f- 1 , f- 2 ,
                         s 1 , s 2 , # , # , # , #]]


Configuration number: 9

[environment [multiset YES]]
[skin      [children 5 6 7 8]
           [label 1] [multiset yes , ans- , no 10]]
[membrane
    [number 7] [children ] [father 1]
    [label 2] [multiset # , # , t 1 , t- 2 , f- 1 , f 2 ,
                         s 1 , s- 2 , c 2 , # , r 1 , # , #]]
[membrane
    [number 6] [children ] [father 1]
    [label 2] [multiset # , # , t- 1 , t 2 , f 1 , f- 2 ,
                         s- 1 , s 2 , c 1 , # , # , r 2 , #]]
[membrane
    [number 8] [children ] [father 1]
    [label 2] [multiset # , # , t- 1 , t- 2 , f 1 , f 2 ,
                         s 1 , s 2 , # , # , # , #]]
[membrane
    [number 5] [children ] [father 1]
    [label 2] [multiset # , # , t 1 , t 2 , f- 1 , f- 2 ,
                         s 1 , s 2 , # , # , # , #]]
```

The system has reached a halting configuration in the step number 9 and the element YES has been released into the environment.

8   Conclusions

In this paper we have presented a variant of P systems with active membrane in which we have traded polarization for bi-stable catalysts. We have proven that this variant is computationally complete and able to solve efficiently NP-complete problems like SAT.

Future projects are to design families of recognizer bi-stable catalytic P systems to solve numerical NP-complete problems like Knapsack and Tripartite Matching and to study the computational power and efficiency of P systems with active membranes without polarizations.

CLIPS has been shown to be a convenient programming language for simulating P systems and it was helpful to debug the design and to understand how the P systems from the family Π work.

Acknowledgement

This work is supported by the Ministerio de Ciencia y Tecnología of Spain, by the *Plan Nacional de I+D+I (2000–2003)* (TIC2002-04220-C03-01), cofinanced by FEDER funds, and by a FPI fellowship (of the second author) from the University of Seville.

References

1. R. Freund, L. Kari, M. Oswald, P. Sosik, Computationally universal P systems without priorities: Two catalysts suffice. *Theoretical Computer Sci.*, to appear.
2. Gh. Păun, *Membrane Computing. An Introduction*, Springer-Verlag, 2002.
3. Gh. Păun, Computing with membranes. *Journal of computer and Systems Sciences*, 61(1), 2000, 108–143.
4. Gh. Păun, M.J. Pérez-Jiménez, A. Riscos-Núñez, P systems with tables of rules. In: Gh. Păun, A. RiscosNúñez, A. Romero-Jiménez, F. Sancho-Caparrini, eds., *Proceedings of the Second Brainstorming Week on Membrane Computing*, Report RGNC 01/04, 2004, 366–380.
5. Gh. Păun, S. Yu, On synchronization in P systems. *Fundamenta Informaticae*, 38, 4 (1999), 397–410.
6. M.J. Pérez-Jiménez, A. Romero-Jiménez, F. Sancho-Caparrini, *Teoría de la Complejidad en modelos de computacion celular con membranas*, Ed. Kronos, Sevilla, 2002.
7. M.J. Pérez-Jiménez, A. Riscos-Núñez, Solving the Subset-Sum problem by active membranes. *New Generation Computing*, in press.
8. M.J. Pérez-Jiménez, A. Riscos-Núñez, A linear-time solution for the Knapsack problem using active membranes. *Lecture Notes in Computer Science*, 2933 (2004) 140–152.
9. M.J. Pérez-Jiménez, F.J. Romero-Campero, A CLIPS simulator for recognizer P systems with active membranes. In: Gh. Păun, A. Riscos-Núñez, A. Romero-Jiménez, F. Sancho-Caparrini, eds., *Proceedings of the Second Brainstorming Week on Membrane Computing*, Report RGNC 01/04, 2004, 387–413.
10. M.J. Pérez-Jiménez, A. Romero-Jiménez, F. Sancho-Caparrini, A polynomial complexity class in P systems using membrane division. In: E. Csuhaj-Varjú, C. Kintala, D. Wotschke, Gy. Vaszyl, eds., *Proceedings of the Fifth International Workshop on Descriptional Complexity of Formal Systems*, 2003, 284–294.

Modelling Dynamic Organization of Biology-Inspired Multi-agent Systems with Communicating X-Machines and Population P Systems

Ioanna Stamatopoulou[1], Marian Gheorghe[2], and Petros Kefalas[3]

[1] South-East European Research Center, Thessaloniki, Greece
istamatopoulou@seerc.info
[2] Department of Computer Science, University of Sheffield, UK
M.Gheorghe@dcs.shef.ac.uk
[3] Department of Computer Science, CITY College, Thessaloniki, Greece
kefalas@city.academic.gr

Abstract. Dynamic organization of multi-agent systems can be inspired by the way biological systems adapt to the evolution of their components. In this paper, we investigate how multi-agent systems can be formally modelled as well as how their configurations can be altered, thus affecting the communication between agents. We use two different formal methods, communicating X-machines and population P systems with active membranes, in order to model the case of flocking agents. Each method possesses different appealing characteristics which are examined through the modelling process.

1 Introduction

An agent is an encapsulated computing system that is situated in some environment and is capable of flexible, autonomous actions in order to meet its design objectives [14]. The extreme complexity of agent systems is due to substantial differences between the attributes of their components, high computational power required by the processes running within these components, huge volume of data manipulated by these processes and finally possibly extensive amount of communication in order to achieve coordination and collaboration. The use of a computational framework that is capable of modelling both the dynamic aspects (i.e., the continuous change of agents' states together with their communication) and the static aspects (i.e., the amount of knowledge and information available), will facilitate modelling and simulation of such complex systems.

The multi-agent paradigm can be further extended to include biology-inspired systems. Many biological processes seem to behave like multi-agent systems, as for example a colony of ants or bees, a flock of birds, cell tissues etc. [5]. The vast majority of computational biological models are based on an assumed, fixed system structure that is not realistic. The concept of growth, division,

G. Mauri et al. (Eds.): WMC5 2004, LNCS 3365, pp. 389–403, 2005.

and differentiation of individual components (agents) and the communication between them should be addressed in order to create a complete biological system which is based on rules that are linked to the underlying biological mechanisms allowing a dynamic evolution.

For example, consider the case of a flock of birds. Each bird has its own evolution rules that allow it to grow, reproduce and die over time or under other specific circumstances; other rules define the flying behaviour of the birds. The birds are arranged in some two- or three-dimensional space, and this layout implies the way birds interact with each others in the local neighbourhood. The structure of the flock, that is the arrangement of the flying birds, changes over time, thus imposing a change in their interactions.

In the last years attempts have been made to devise biology inspired computational models in the form of generative devices [19], [20], unconventional programming paradigms [2], bio-engines solving NP hard problems [1], adequate mechanisms to specify complex systems [11]. In this paper we have selected two formal methods, X-machines and population P systems, in order to develop multi-agent system models. Each of these methods possesses different appealing characteristics which will be examined through the modelling process.

The structure of this paper is as follows: Sections 2 and 3 present the theory regarding communicating X-machines and population P systems, respectively. Section 4 presents the actual models developed for an artificial case of agent flocking. Section 5 discusses some issues concerning the empirical comparison of the two models. Finally, Section 6 concludes the paper.

2   Communicating X-Machines

The X-machines formal method [6], [10] forms the basis for a specification language with a great potential to software engineers. It is rather intuitive while at the same time formal descriptions of data types and functions can be written in any known mathematical notation.

For modelling systems containing more than one agent, the X-machine components need to be extended with new features, such as hierarchical decomposition and communication. A communicating X-machine model consists of several X-machines that are able to exchange messages. This involves the modelling of the participating agents and the definition of the rules of their communication.

The complete model is a *communicating X-machine system* Z defined as a tuple

$$Z = ((C_i)_{i=1,\ldots,n}, CR),$$

where:

- C_i is the i-th communicating X-machine component, and
- CR is a relation defining the communication among the components, $CR \subseteq C \times C$ and $C = \{C_1, \ldots, C_n\}$. A tuple $(C_i, C_k) \in CR$ denotes that the X-machine component C_i can output a message to a corresponding input stream of the X-machine component C_k for any $i, k \in \{1, \ldots, n\}$, $i \neq k$.

A *communicating X-machine component* C_i is defined as a tuple [18]

$$C_i = (\Sigma_i, \Gamma_i, Q_i, M_i, \Phi C_i, F_i, q_{0_i}, m_{0_i}),$$

where:

- Σ_i and Γ_i are the input and output alphabets respectively.
- Q_i is the finite set of states.
- M_i is the (possibly) infinite set called memory.
- ΦC_i is a set of partial functions φ_i that map an input and a memory value to an output and a possibly different memory value, $\varphi_i : \Sigma_i \times M_i \to \Gamma_i \times M_i$. There are four different types of functions in ΦC_i (in all of the following it is assumed that $\sigma \in \Sigma_i$, $\gamma \in \Gamma_i$, $m, m' \in M_i$; $(\sigma)_j$ means that the input is provided by machine C_j whereas $(\gamma)_k$ denotes an outgoing message to machine C_k):
  - the functions that read the input from the standard input stream and write their output to the standard output stream:
    $$\varphi_i (\sigma, m) = (\gamma, m'),$$
  - the functions that read the input from a communication input stream and write their output to the standard output stream:
    $$\varphi_i ((\sigma)_j, m) = (\gamma, m'),$$
  - the functions that read the input from the standard input stream and write their output to a communication output stream:
    $$\varphi_i (\sigma, m) = ((\gamma)_k, m'),$$
  - the functions that read the input from a communication input stream and write their output to a communication output stream:
    $$\varphi_i ((\sigma)_j, m) = ((\gamma)_k, m').$$
- F_i is the next state partial function, $F_i : Q_i \times \Phi C_i \to Q_i$, which, given a state and a function from the type ΦC_i, determines the next state. F_i is often described as a state transition diagram.
- q_{0_i} and m_{0_i} are the initial state and initial memory respectively.

Graphically, on the state transition diagram we denote the acceptance of an input by a stream other than the standard one by a solid circle along with the name C_j of the communicating X-machine component that sends it. Similarly, a solid diamond with the name C_k denotes that an output is sent to the C_k communicating X-machine component. An abstract example of a communicating X-machine component is depicted in Fig. 1.

The above allows the definition of systems of a static configuration. However, most multi-agent systems are highly dynamic and this requires that their structure and the communication among the agents is constantly changing. For this to happen in a communicating X-machine model, the control has to be taken over by another system acting on a higher level. This controlling device can be modelled as a set of meta-rules that refer to the configuration of the system or as a meta-X-machine that will be able to apply a number of operators which will be affecting the structure of the communicating system [17].

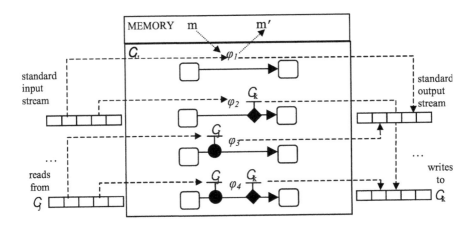

Fig. 1. An abstract example of a communicating X-machine with functions that receive inputs and send their output in any possible combination of source and destination streams

Attachment Operator

This operator is responsible for establishing the communication between an existing communicating X-machine component and a set of other existing components. Its definition is

$$\textbf{ATT}: \mathcal{C} \times \mathcal{Z} \rightarrow \mathcal{Z},$$

where $\mathcal{C}$ is the set of communicating X-machine components, and $\mathcal{Z}$ is the set of communicating X-machine systems. For an existing component $C \in \mathcal{C}$ and a communicating X-machine system Z (to which C belongs to) a new communicating X-machine system Z' will be built that has different communication channels. The components remain the same except that for each function φ of the component machine C the streams of the other components, if any, it receives inputs from or sends outputs to are specified. Similarly, the communicating functions of the other components, with which C establishes communication, become related to the streams of the component C so that input can be received or output can be sent to it. It is this kind of relationships between the component C and the other components that define how the whole system is to communicate as a collection of units cooperating through streams of data.

Detachment Operator

This operator is used in order to remove communication channels between an existing communicating X-machine component and a set of other existing components with which it currently communicates. Its definition is

$$\textbf{DET}: \mathcal{C} \times \mathcal{Z} \rightarrow \mathcal{Z},$$

where $\mathcal{C}$, $\mathcal{Z}$ are defined as previously. In this case all the relationships between the component C and its streams and the other components and their streams are broken down.

Generation Operator

A new communicating X-machine component is created and introduced into the system. If communication requests exist from other components, then communication channels are established. The definition of the operator is

$$\textbf{GEN}: \mathcal{C} \times \mathcal{Z} \to \mathcal{Z},$$

where $\mathcal{C}$, $\mathcal{Z}$ are defined as previously.

Destruction Operator

This operator is used for the removal of an existing communicating X-machine component from the system along with the channels that allow its communication with other components. The operator is written as

$$\textbf{DES}: \mathcal{C} \times \mathcal{Z} \to \mathcal{Z},$$

where $\mathcal{C}$, $\mathcal{Z}$ are defined as previously.

Conceptually, the meta-system could be considered to play the role of the environment to the actual communicating system. Because the meta-machine should be able to control the reconfiguration of the communicating system through the application of the above operators, it should possess the following information at all times:

- The communicating system $Z = ((C_1, \ldots, C_i, \ldots, C_n), CR)$.
- The current system state SZ of Z. SZ is defined as a set of tuples $SZ = \{sz \mid \exists C_i, 1 \le i \le n, \ sz = (q_c, M_c, \varphi_c)_i$, where q_c is the current state in which C_i is in, M_c is the current memory of C_i and φ_c is the last function that was applied in $C_i\}$.
- Definitions of all components that exist or may be added to the system. These definitions act as genetic codes (GC) for the system. GC is a set of tuples, $GC = \{\ldots(\Sigma, \Gamma, Q, M, \Phi, F, \Phi_{\mathrm{R}}, \Phi_{\mathrm{W}})_j, \ldots\}$ where the first six elements are as in the definition of the X-machine and the last two are the set of functions that may be involved in communication with other components (i.e., Φ_{R} includes the functions that may read from communicating streams and Φ_{W} the ones that may write to communicating streams).

Using the above information, the control device can generate a new component and attach it to the communicating machine Z, through the operator GEN, destruct an existing component of Z and rearrange the communication of the other components appropriately, through the operator DES, and add or remove channels of communication between a component and a communicating machine due to some system reconfigurations, through the operators ATT and DET.

3   Population P Systems with Active Cells

A natural generalization of the standard P system model (which is based on a hierarchical arrangement of membranes) can be obtained by considering P systems where the structure of the system is defined as an arbitrary graph. Each node in the graph represents a membrane, which gets assigned a multiset of objects and a set of rules for modifying these objects and communicating them alongside the edges of the graph [20]. These networks of communicating membranes are also known as population P systems because, from a biological point of view, they can be interpreted as an abstract model of bio-entities aggregated together in a more complex bio-unit. In this respect the model also addresses the case of various colonies of more complex organisms like ants, bees etc. These populations of individuals are usually far from being stable; mechanisms enabling new individuals to be introduced, to update the links between them or to remove some individuals play a fundamental role in the evolution of a biological system as a population of interacting components. The model of population P systems is augmented with an operation of cell division as a mechanism to introduce new cells in the system, and with an operation of cell death as a mechanism to remove cells from the system. As well as this, an operation of cell differentiation is considered that allows the type of the cells to be changed by varying in this way the sets of rules that can be used inside the cells. The above leads to a new model, the *population P system with active cells* which is defined as a construct [3]

$$\mathcal{P} = (V, K, \gamma, \alpha, w_\mathrm{E}, C_1, C_2, \ldots, C_n, R),$$

where:

- V is a finite alphabet of symbols called objects;
- K is a finite alphabet of symbols, which define different types for the cells;
- $\gamma = (\{1, 2, \ldots n\}, A)$, with $A \subseteq \{\{i, j\} \mid 1 \leq i \neq j \leq n\}$, is a finite undirected graph;
- α is a finite set of bond making rules $(t, x_1; x_2, p)$, with $x_1, x_2 \in V^*$, and $t, p \in K$;
- $w_\mathrm{E} \in V^*$ is a finite multiset of objects initially assigned to the environment;
- $C_i = (w_i, t_i)$, for each $1 \leq i \leq n$, with $w_i \in V^*$ a finite multiset of objects, and $t_i \in K$ the type of cell i;
- R is a finite set of rules dealing with:
  - communication,
  - object transformation,
  - cell differentiation,
  - cell division,
  - cell death.

Communication rules of the form $(a; b, in)_t$, $(a; b, enter)_t$, $(b, exit)_t$, for $a \in V \cup \{\lambda\}$, $b \in V$, $t \in K$, allow moving objects between neighbouring cells or a cell and the environment according to the cell type and the current bonds. The first rule means that in the presence of an object a inside a cell of type t an object b can be obtained from a neighbouring cell non-deterministically chosen. The second rule is similar to the first excepting that the object b is not obtained from a neighbouring cell but from the environment. Lastly, the third rule denotes that if an object b is present, then it can be expelled out to the environment.

Transformation rules of the form $(a \rightarrow b)_t$, for $a \in V$, $b \in V^+$, $t \in K$, have the meaning that an object a is replaced by an object b within a cell of type t.

Cell differentiation rules of the form $(a)_t \rightarrow (b)_p$, with $a, b \in V$, $t, p \in K$, denote that the consumption of an object a inside of a cell of type t changes the cell into one of type p. All existing objects remain the same apart from a which is replaced by b.

Cell division rules of the form $(a)_t \rightarrow (b)_t(c)_t$, with $a, b, c \in V$, $t \in K$, mean that a cell of type t containing an object a is divided into two cells of the same type. One of the new cells has a replaced by b while the other one replaced by c. All other objects of the initial cell appear in both new cells.

Cell death rules of the form $(a)_t \rightarrow \dagger$, with $a \in V$, $t \in K$, mean that an object a inside a cell of type t causes the removal of the cell from the system.

4   Case Study: Agent Flocking

The following example is a kind of biology-inspired multi-agent system that resembles bird flocking. Consider a set of agents that move inside a two-dimensional (for reasons of simplicity) plane. There exist three types of agents: (a) leaders, (b) donors, and (c) incubators with the following behaviours:

Agent type	Behaviours
Leader	(a) flies freely when there is available space (b) avoids other agents by turning to a different direction
Donor	(a) flies freely when there is available space (b) avoids other agents by turning to a different direction (c) follows a leader (d) signals to other agents (incubators) to reproduce
Incubator	(a) flies freely when there is available space (b) avoids other agents by turning to a different direction (c) follows a leader (d) accepts signals from other agents (donors) to reproduce

All agents know the current direction to which they move, their exact position in the plane, and have a perception radius (a range within which they can perceive other agents). Once a leader is sensed by donors or incubators, the leader is followed in whatever moves it performs. Once a donor senses an incubator, they mate and a new leader agent is generated. At the same time, the parent agents disappear. Two consecutive instances of the multi-agent system are depicted in Fig. 2.

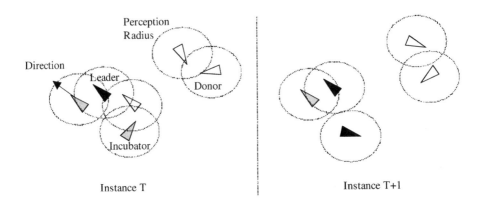

Fig. 2. Two consecutive instances of agent flocking

Modelling the system as either a communicating X-machine or a population P system with active membranes requires the modelling of individual agents (i.e., knowledge, states, behaviours etc.) on one hand, as well as the modelling of the dynamic configurations of the system since the communication between agents changes over time according to the rules of flocking. For example, the two consecutive instances of the system configurations that correspond to Fig. 2 are shown in Fig. 3. Leader L_1 communicates with I_1 and D_3 since I_1 and D_3 sense L_1 within their perception radius. The same happens between D_3 and I_2. In the next instance, I_2 and D_3 mate to produce a leader L_2 which is a totally independent new agent while I_2 and D_3 disappear.

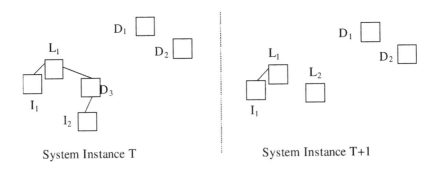

Fig. 3. Two consecutive instances of the communicating system

4.1   Communicating X-Machine Model for Agent Flocking

The system consists of the component X-machines shown in Fig. 4 of types Leader, Incubator, and Donor. In particular, it contains instances of those types

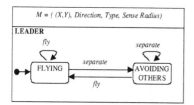

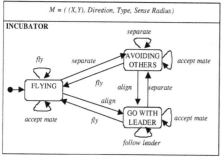

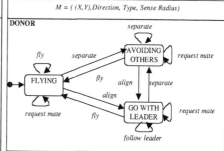

Fig. 4. The three X-machine types used in the example of the flocking agents

(for example, one Leader L_1, two Incubators I_1 and I_2 and three Donors D_1, D_2, D_3), which are connected according to the system requirements at various time instances (in our example in Fig. 3 the system at moments T and $T + 1$):

$$Flock = ((L_1, I_1, I_2, D_1, D_2, D_3), \{(L_1, I_1), (L_1, D_3), (D_3, I_2)\}).$$

The memory of these machines consists of a tuple containing the position *pos* of the agent, its direction *dir* and a sense radius *rad*. The input to all functions is a set of percepts that consists of tuples of the form *(type, direction, position)* describing the visible agents within the agent's sense radius. The output is a set of messages. The functions are defined in such a way that they model each particular behaviour associated with the agents. For example:

$fly(\emptyset, (pos, dir, rad)) =$
    $("flying", (pos', dir', rad))$ where
    $dir' = random(set\_of\_directions)$ and
    $pos' = determine\_pos(pos, dir)$

$separate(percepts, (pos, dir, rad)) =$
    $("changing\ direction", (pos', dir', rad))$ where
    $dir' = random(set\_of\_directions \setminus forbidden\_directions)$ and
    $forbidden\_directions = identify\_possible\_collisions(percepts, dir)$ and
    $pos' = determine\_pos(pos, dir)$

The communication functions of the X-machine components at moment T are partially shown in Fig. 5. L_1 sends its direction to I_1 and D_3, which receive it

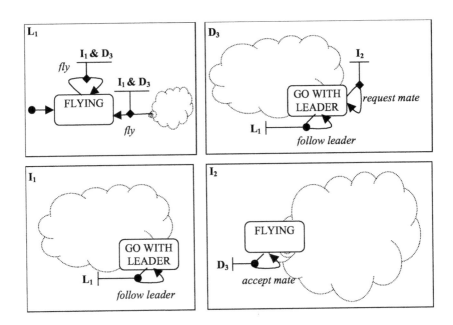

Fig. 5. Communication of the X-machines' functions at instance T

and follow the leader. D_3 sends a request to mate with I_2, which accepts it. For example, the functions become:

$fly_{L_1}(\emptyset, (pos, dir, rad)) =$
$\quad (\{(Leader, dir', pos')\}_{L_1 \& D_3}, (pos', dir', rad))$ where
$\quad dir' = random(set\_of\_directions)$ and
$\quad pos' = determine\_pos(pos, dir)$

$follow\_leader_{D_3}(\{(Leader, dir_l, pos_l)\}_{L_1}, (pos, dir, rad)) =$
$\quad (\text{"}following\ leader\text{"}, (pos', dir_l, rad))$ where
$\quad pos' = determine\_pos(pos, dir_l)$

Having a particular configuration of the system, we now need to show how the system state changes over time. For example in Fig. 3, consider the system at the instance moment T. I_2 and D_3, having sent messages to one another, activate the appropriate functions in order to reproduce. The meta-machine, by identifying this event into the system state, applies the operators DES for both I_2 and D_3 in order to destroy the two components, and then the operator GEN in order to generate a new component according to the existing genetic code.

$$\textbf{DES}\ (I_2, Flock) = Flock',$$

where:

$$Flock' = ((L_1, I_1, D_1, D_2, D_3), \{(L_1, I_1), (L_1, D_3)\}),$$

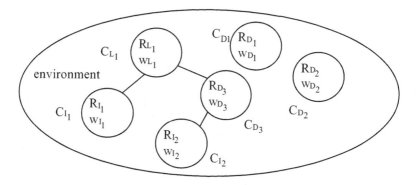

Fig. 6. An instance configuration of the population P system

$$\mathbf{DES}\ (D_3, Flock') = Flock'',$$

where:

$$Flock'' = ((L_1, I_1, D_1, D_2), \{(L_1, I_1)\}),$$

$$\mathbf{GEN}\ (L_2, Flock'') = Flock''',$$

where:

$$Flock''' = ((L_1, I_1, D_1, D_2, L_2), \{(L_1, I_1)\}).$$

4.2 A Population P System Model for Agent Flocking

In population P systems with active membranes agents can be modelled as cells of different types while the graph represents the communication channels between them. The bond making rules can be responsible for the system reconfiguration. Knowledge and attributes form objects within cells. The communication can be achieved through messages that are also objects. The rules associated with cells take care of transformation of objects, communication as well as differentiation, division and death. Let us examine all the above briefly (Fig. 6).

Leaders, donors, and incubators form the three different types of cells, $K = \{Leader, Donor, Incubator\}$.

The undirected graph is

$$\gamma = (\{L_1, I_1, I_2, D_1, D_2, D_3\}, \{\{I_1, L_1\}, \{L_1, D_3\}, \{D_3, I_2\}\}).$$

The agents are modelled as cells $\{C_{L_1}, C_{I_1}, C_{I_2}, C_{D_1}, C_{D_2}, C_{D_3}\}$, where:

$$C_{L_1} = (w_{L_1}, Leader),$$
$$C_{I_1} = (w_{I_1}, Incubator),$$
$$C_{I_2} = (w_{I_2}, Incubator),$$
$$C_{D_1} = (w_{D_1}, Donor),$$

$$C_{D_2} = (w_{D_2}, Donor),$$
$$C_{D_3} = (w_{D_3}, Donor)$$

.

All cells contain multisets of objects, which, modelling-wise, can be distinguished into two categories: objects that refer to knowledge and attributes (such as the position of agents, their direction etc.) and input or output messages (such as messages for reproduction sent by the donor etc.). For example, w_{L_1} contains the objects *pos*, *dir*, *rad* for position, direction and sense radius, respectively. Similarly, w_{D_1} contains the same symbols together with *seed* as a message to be sent to an incubator type cell.

The set of bond making rules α, contains rules that refer to when direct communication between cell types is achieved, which in this case is the distance between cells that must be within the sense radius. For example a bonding rule in α might be:

$$(Leader, pos_l ; pos_d \, rad_d, Donor),$$

when the leader in position pos_l is in the sense radius of the donor rad_d in position pos_d.

The set of rules R contains various types of rules. More analytically:

– **Communication rules**
   Those rules triggered when there is a direct communication between agents. For example, when a donor is within the sense radius of an incubator an edge is added due to the bonding rule and a *seed* is received by the incubator through the rule:
   $(\lambda ; seed, in)_{Incubator}$
   Another communication rule refers to the incoming percepts (stimuli) from the environment that trigger the agents' behaviours:
   $(\lambda ; stimuli_l, enter)_{Leader}$
   Finally, a communication rule would be responsible to export a copy of the current position and direction to the environment in order for the environment to prepare the next percepts:
   $(cpos \, cdir, exit)_{Donor}$
– **Transformation rules**
   These rules correspond to the behaviours of an agent type, i.e., *fly* and *separate* for the leader type cells. For example, *fly* is modelled by rules of the form:
   $(stimuli \, pos \, dir \rightarrow pos' \, dir')_{Leader}$
   where pos' and dir' are determined according to current *pos* and *dir* and the stimuli (percepts) received from the environment.
– **Cell division rules**
   These rules are used to divide a cell into two others of the same type. In our example this models agent birth; an incubator having received a seed is divided into two cells; one that will become a leader (the child—see cell differentiation rule below) and one that will die immediately afterwards:
   $(seed)_{Incubator} \rightarrow (toTransform)_{Incubator}(toDie)_{Incubator}$

- **Cell differentiation**

  These rules are used by agents in order to change their type. In our example, after having received a seed from a donor, one of the two cells into which an incubator is divided becomes a leader:

  $(toTransform)_{\text{Incubator}} \rightarrow (\lambda)_{\text{Leader}}$

- **Cell death**

  These rules are used to model an agent who is going to be removed from the system. In our example, an incubator that has just given birth ceases to exist:

  $(toDie)_{\text{Incubator}} \rightarrow \dagger$

According to the above model, the environment apart from containing the multiset of objects w_E which represent the stimuli for each of the agents, it should be able to process and update them, through a set of transformation rules. In addition, there should be other transformation rules to deal with various issues within the cell, e.g., keeping copies of objects that are going to be sent as messages to other cells or the environment, which, for the sake of simplicity, are not described.

5   Empirical Comparison of Models

This work has been an initial attempt to model a multi-agent system with dynamic configurations through two different methods, namely communicating X-machines and population P systems with active membranes. In the process of modelling we have identified a number of issues on which an empirical comparison between the two methods is based and that will be further investigated.

There are advantages to both methods, though at different modelling levels. X-machines appear to be a natural metaphor for the modelling of the internal behaviour of agents because they can naturally describe the internal states, transitions between them caused by stimuli and represent the data structures which form the knowledge of an agent. However a communicating X-machine model cannot by itself manage the required reconfiguration, which is a prominent property of biology-inspired multi-agent systems. As a result, an external device, in the form of a meta-X-machine, is necessary; this device possesses global control over the structure of the overall system. Control is achieved through meta-operations which change the way that components interact or function. Population P systems, on the other hand, possess a natural trait for capturing the behaviour of a community that is formed by individuals and how the structure of such a community may change over time, although when it comes to the modelling of an agent, population P systems are less straightforward in representing the internal states and behaviour of each individual.

Both methods have sound theoretical foundations and act as formal specification languages, this being the main advantage when viewing them as software engineering techniques. Towards this end, the X-machine Description Language (XMDL) [15] has been defined offering the ability of formally describing X-machine models and acting as an interchange tool for software engineers. XMDL also serves as a common basis for the development of tools, such as the X-System [9], that allow the syntactical check and automatic animation of the models. The latter is of great practical importance as it checks the properties of the system and provides an understanding of the behaviour of the system.

In addition to this practical aspect, X-machines have further techniques supporting the modelling activity such as formal verification of desired system properties [8], [7] and complete testing [12], [13]. Towards practical modelling, appropriate XML notation in order to define population P systems is currently under development and soon expected to be made available.

6   Conclusions and Further Work

We have attempted an empirical comparison between two formal methods, namely population P systems and communicating X-machines, based on a case study involving re-configurable systems. We specifically focused on biology-inspired multi-agent systems and presented the case study of bird flocking. Each method has its own advantages and limitations as far as the modelling of individual agents and the dynamic re-configuration of the whole system are concerned.

High in the list of priorities comes the need for tools that allow the animation of the created models, the lack of which is considered to be a major disadvantage in the field of formal methods. X-System, initially implemented for the animation of stand-alone X-machines has recently been extended so as to facilitate the animation of communicating models as well. Animation tools also exist for P systems [4].

Bearing in mind the above, one cannot easily choose one method instead of the other as they offer different and complementary advantages. These might prompt us to devise new hybrid methods that combine the features of each one. Effort has been put into modelling a P system as a communicating X-machine [16]. Further investigations regarding possible transformations between communicating X-machine models and population P system models would be useful in order to support both a formal theoretical comparison as well as the modelling activity by allowing us to take advantage of the positive traits of both methods.

References

1. Adleman, L.M. 1994. Molecular computation of solutions to combinatorial problems, *Science*, 226, 1021–1024.
2. Banatre, J.P., Le Metayer, D. 1990. The gamma model and its discipline of programming, *Science of Computer Programming*, 15, 55–77.
3. Bernardini, F., Gheorghe, M. 2004. Population P systems, *Journal of Universal Computer Science*, 10, 509–539.
4. Bianco, L., Fontana, F., Franco, G., Manca, V. 2004. P systems in bio systems. In Ciobanu, G., Păun, Gh., M.J. Pérez-Jiménez, eds. 2005. *Application of Membrane Computing*, submitted.

5. Dorigo, M., Maniezzo, V., Colorni, A. 1996. The Ant System: Optimisation by a colony of co-operating agents, *IEEE Transactions on Systems, Man and Cybernetics*, 26, 1–13.

6. Eilenberg, S. 1974. *Automata, Languages and Machines*, Academic Press.

7. Eleftherakis, G. 2003. *Formal Verification of X-Machine Models: Towards Formal Development of Computer-based Systems*, PhD Thesis, Department of Computer Science, University of Sheffield.

8. Eleftherakis, G., Kefalas, P. 2000. Model checking safety critical systems specified as X-machines, *Analele Universitatii Bucharest, Matematica-Informatica series*, 49, 59–70.

9. Eleftherakis, G., Kefalas, P., Sotiriadou, A. 2003. Formal modelling and verification of reactive agents for intelligent control. In *Proceedings of the 12th Intelligent System Applications to Power Systems Conference* (ISAP).

10. Holcombe, M. 1988. X-machines as a basis for dynamic system configuration, *Software Engineering Journal*, 3, 69–76.

11. Holcombe, M. 2001. Computational models of cells and tissues: Machines, agents and fungal infection, *Briefings in Bioinformatics*, 2, 271–278.

12. Holcombe, M., Ipate, F. 1998. *Correct Systems: Building a Business Process Solution*, Springer-Verlag, London, 1998.

13. Ipate, F., Holcombe, M. 1997. An integration testing method that is proved to find all faults, *International Journal of Computer Mathematics*, 63, 159–178.

14. Jennings, N.R. 2000. On agent-based software engineering, *Artificial Intelligence*, 117, 277–296.

15. Kapeti, E., Kefalas, P. 2000. A design language and tool for X-machines specification, In Fotiadis, D.I., Spyropoulos, S.D., eds. 2000. *Advances in Informatics*, World Scientific Publishing Company, 134–145.

16. Kefalas, P., Eleftherakis, G., Holcombe, M., Gheorghe, M. 2003. Simulation and verification of P systems through communicating X-machines, *BioSystems*, 70, 135–148.

17. Kefalas, P., Eleftherakis, G., Holcombe, M., Stamatopoulou, I. 2004. Formal modelling of the dynamic behaviour of biology-inspired agent-based systems, In Gheorghe, M. ed. 2004. *Molecular Computational Models: Unconventional Approaches*, Idea Publishing, Inc.

18. Kefalas, P., Eleftherakis, G., Kehris, E. 2003. Communicating X-machines: A practical approach for formal and modular specification of large systems, *Journal of Information and Software Technology*, 45, 269–280.

19. Păun, G. 2000. Computing with membranes, *Journal of Computer and System Sciences*, 61, 1, 108–143.

20. Păun, Gh. 2002. *Membrane Computing: An Introduction*, Springer-Verlag, Berlin.

On the Size of P Systems with Minimal Symport/Antiport*

György Vaszil

Computer and Automation Research Institute,
Hungarian Academy of Sciences,
Kende utca 13-17, 1111 Budapest, Hungary
vaszil@sztaki.hu

Abstract. We show that P systems with symport/antiport rules sending at most one object per direction generate any recursively enumerable set of natural numbers with three membranes. This improves the previously known best bound of four membranes.

1 Introduction

Membrane systems, or P systems were introduced in [9] as computing models inspired by the functioning of the living cell. Their main components are membrane structures consisting of membranes hierarchically embedded in the outermost skin membrane. Each membrane encloses a region containing a multiset of objects and possibly other membranes. Each region has an associated set of operators working on the objects contained by the region. These operators can be of different types, they can change the objects present in the regions or they can provide the possibility of transferring the objects from one region to another one. The evolution of the objects inside the membrane structure from an initial configuration to a somehow specified end configuration corresponds to a computation having a result which is derived from some properties of the specific end configuration. Several variants of the basic notion have been introduced and studied proving the power of the framework – see the monograph [10] for a summary of notions and results of the area.

One of the most interesting variants of the model was introduced in [8] called P systems with symport/antiport. In these systems the modification of the objects present in the regions is not possible, they may only move through the membranes from one region to another. The movement is described by communication rules called symport/antiport rules associated to the regions. A symport rule specifies a multiset of objects that might travel through a given membrane in a given direction, an antiport rule specifies two multisets of objects which might

* Research supported in part by the Hungarian Scientific Research Fund "OTKA" grant no. F037567, and by the EU commission under the project "MolCoNet" IST-2001-32008.

G. Mauri et al. (Eds.): WMC5 2004, LNCS 3365, pp. 404–413, 2005.

simultaneously travel through a given membrane in the opposite directions. The result can be read as the number of objects present inside a previously specified output membrane after the system reaches a halting configuration, that is, a configuration when no application of any rule in any region is possible.

P systems with symport/antiport were shown to be able to generate any recursively enumerable set of numbers already in [8]. This result was improved from the point of view of the number of necessary membranes and the complexity of communication rules in [5, 6, 7]. The study of minimal symport/antiport, when the multisets in the rules contain at most one object, started in [1] where it was shown that such systems with nine membranes generate any recursively enumerable set of numbers. Then the number of necessary membranes were decreased to six in [3], to five in [2], and then to four in [4].

In the present paper we continue to improve this result by showing that three membranes are sufficient to generate any recursively enumerable set of numbers with minimal symport/antiport.

2 Preliminaries and Definitions

We first recall the notions and the notations we use. The reader is assumed to be familiar with the basics of formal language theory; for details see [11]. Let V be an alphabet, let V^* be the set of all words over V, and let $V^+ = V^* - \{\varepsilon\}$ where ε denotes the empty word. The set of natural numbers is denoted by $\mathbb{N}$, the class of recursively enumerable sets of natural numbers is denoted by $\mathbb{N}RE$. With $\mathbb{N}_k RE$, for some $k \in \mathbb{N}$, we denote the class $\{k + L \mid L \in \mathbb{N}RE\}$ where $k + L = \{x + k \mid x \in L\}$.

Let U be a set of objects, called the *universe*. A multiset is a pair $M = (V, f)$, where $V \subseteq U$ and $f : V \to \mathbb{N}$ is a mapping which assigns to each object $a \in V$ its multiplicity, and $f(a) = 0$ for $a \notin V$. The support of $M = (V, f)$ is the set $supp(M) = \{a \in V \mid f(a) \geq 1\}$. If $supp(M)$ is a finite set, then M is called a finite multiset. The set of all finite multisets over the set V is denoted by V°.

The number of objects in a finite multiset $M = (V, f)$, the cardinality of M, is defined by $card(M) = \sum_{a \in V} f(a)$. We say that $a \in M = (V, f)$ if $a \in supp(M)$. $M_1 = (V_1, f_1) \subseteq M_2 = (V_2, f_2)$ if $supp(M_1) \subseteq supp(M_2)$ and for all $a \in V_1$, $f_1(a) \leq f_2(a)$. The union of two multisets is defined as $(M_1 \cup M_2) = (V_1 \cup V_2, f')$ where for all $a \in V_1 \cup V_2$, $f'(a) = f_1(a) + f_2(a)$. We say that M is empty, denoted by ϵ, if its support is empty, $supp(M) = \emptyset$. In the following we enumerate the not necessarily distinct elements $a_1, \ldots, a_n$ of a multiset as $M = \{\{a_1, \ldots, a_n\}\}$, by using double brackets to distinguish from the usual set notation.

A P system is a structure of hierarchically embedded membranes, each having a label and enclosing a region containing a multiset of objects and possibly other membranes. The out-most membrane which is unique and usually labelled with 1, is called the skin membrane. The membrane structure is denoted by a sequence of matching parentheses where the matching pairs have the same label as the membranes they represent. If $x \in \{[_i,]_i \mid 1 \leq i \leq n\}^*$ is such a string of matching parentheses of length $2n$, denoting a structure where membrane i

contains membrane j, then $x = x_1 \, [_i \, x_2 \, [_j \, x_3 \,]_j \, x_4 \,]_i \, x_5$ for some $x_k \in \{[_l,]_l \mid 1 \leq l \leq n, \; l \neq i, j\}^*$, $1 \leq k \leq 5$. If membrane i contains membrane j, and there is no other membrane, k, such that k contains j and i contains k (x_2 and x_4 above are strings of matching parentheses themselves), then we say that membrane i is the parent membrane of j. A membrane m is called elementary if it contains no membrane; in this case $x = x_1 \, [_m \,]_m \, x_2$.

The evolution of the contents of the regions of a P system is described by rules associated to the regions. Applying the rules synchronously in each region, the system performs a computation by passing from one configuration to another one. In the following we concentrate on communication rules called symport or antiport rules.

A symport rule is of the form (x, in) or (x, out), $x \in V^\circ$. If such a rule is present in a region i, then the objects of the multiset x must enter from the parent region or must leave to the parent region, respectively. An antiport rule is of the form $(x, in; y, out)$, $x, y \in V^\circ$. In this case, objects of x enter from the parent region and in the same step, objects of y leave to the parent region.

The rules are applied in the maximal parallel manner, that is, as many rules are applied in each region as possible. The end of the computation is defined by halting: A P system halts when no more rules can be applied in any of the regions, the result is the number of objects in an elementary membrane labelled as output.

Definition 1. A P system with symport/antiport of degree $n \geq 1$ is a construct

$$\Pi = (V, \mu, E, w_1, \ldots, w_n, R_1, \ldots, R_n, out),$$

where:

- V is an alphabet of objects,
- μ is a membrane structure of n membranes,
- $E \subseteq V$ is a set of objects (the ones which can be found in the environment in an arbitrary number of copies),
- $w_i \in V^\circ$, $1 \leq i \leq n$, are the initial contents of the n regions,
- R_i, $1 \leq i \leq n$, are the sets of symport/antiport rules associated to the regions,
- $out \in \{1, \ldots, n\}$ is the label of an elementary membrane, the output membrane.

To simplify the notations we denote symport and antiport rules as $(x, in; y, out)$, $x, y \in V^\circ$ where we also allow at most one of x, y to be the empty multiset. If $y = \epsilon$ or $x = \epsilon$, then the notation above denotes the symport rule (x, in) or (y, out), respectively.

The $n + 1$-tuple of finite multisets of objects present in finite number of copies in the environment and in the n regions of the P system Π describes a configuration of Π; $(\epsilon, w_1, \ldots, w_n) \in (V^\circ)^{n+1}$ is the initial configuration.

Definition 2. For a configuration $(u_0, \ldots, u_n)$, the P system may enter the new configuration $(u'_0, \ldots, u'_n)$, denoted as $(u_0, \ldots, u_n) \Rightarrow (u'_0, \ldots, u'_n)$, if there exist rules as follows.

For all $i, 1 \leq i \leq n$, there is a multiset of rules $P_i = \{\{r_{i,1}, \ldots, r_{i,m_i}\}\}$, where $r_{i,j} = (x_{i,j}, in; y_{i,j}, out) \in R_i$, satisfying the conditions below where x_i, y_i denote the multisets $\bigcup_{1 \leq j \leq m_i} x_{i,j}$ and $\bigcup_{1 \leq j \leq m_i} y_{i,j}$, respectively. Furthermore, there is no $r \in R_j$, for any j, $1 \leq j \leq n$, such that the rule multisets P_i' with $P_i' = P_i$ for $i \neq j$ and $P_j' = \{\{r\}\} \cup P_j$, also satisfy the conditions which are given as

$$x_1 = x_1' \cup x_1'' \text{ with } supp(x_1') \subseteq E, \ x_1'' \subseteq u_0, \text{ and}$$

$$\bigcup_{parent(j)=i} x_j \cup y_i \subseteq u_i, \text{ for } 1 \leq i \leq n.$$

Then the new configuration is obtained by

$$u_0' = u_0 - x_1'' \cup y_1, \text{ and}$$

$$u_i' = u_i \cup x_i - y_i \cup \bigcup_{parent(j)=i} y_j - \bigcup_{parent(j)=i} x_j, \text{ for } 1 \leq i \leq n.$$

The P system generates numbers as follows.

Definition 3. The set of natural numbers generated by a symport/antiport P system as above, $N(\Pi)$, is the following one:

$$N(\Pi) = \{x = card(u_{out}) \mid (\epsilon, w_1, \ldots, w_n) \Rightarrow^* (u_0, \ldots, u_n),$$

$$\text{where } (u_0, \ldots, u_n) \text{ is a halting configuration}\}$$

and $\Rightarrow^*$ denotes the reflexive and transitive closure of $\Rightarrow$.

Let $NOP_n(sym_r, anti_s)$ denote the class of sets of numbers generated by symport/antiport P systems of degree at most n where for all (x, in), (y, out), $(v, in; z, out) \in R_i$, $1 \leq i \leq n$, $card(x) \leq r$, $card(y) \leq r$, and $card(v) \leq s$, $card(z) \leq s$.

Before we proceed, we need the notion of a counter automaton which will be used in the proof of our result. In the context of numbers or languages over unary alphabets, it is possible to consider counter automata without an input tape but with an output counter. We present the definition in this form, as given in [4]; for more details see [4] and its references.

Definition 4. A counter automaton is a construct

$$M = (Q, C, R, q_0, f)$$

where Q is a set of states, $C = \{c_0, c_1, \ldots, c_n\}$ is a set of counters, c_0 being the output counter, R is a set of transitions of the form $(r \rightarrow s, X)$, for two states $r, s \in Q$, and an instruction $X \in \{i+, i-, e, (i = 0) \mid 0 \leq i \leq n\}$, $q_0 \in Q$ is the initial state, and $f \in Q$ is the final state.

If a transition $(r \rightarrow s, X)$ is an element of R, then the machine can pass from state r to state s executing X. If X is $i+$ or $i-$, then it instructs the machine to increase or decrease, respectively, the value of counter c_i by one, if it is e, then it instructs the machine to leave the counter values unchanged, if it is $i = 0$, then the transition from r to s is only possible by having zero as the contents of counter c_i.

Definition 5. The configuration of a counter automaton M is given by the $(n+2)$-tuple $(q, c_0, c_1, \ldots, c_n)$ where $q \in Q$ is a state, and $c_i \in \mathbb{N}$, $0 \leq i \leq n$, are the values stored in the counters, c_0 being the value of the output counter. The initial configuration is $(q_0, 0, 0, \ldots, 0)$, a final configuration is of the form $(f, c_0, c_1, \ldots, c_n)$ where f is the final state of M.

Given a configuration $(q, c_0, c_1, \ldots, c_n)$, the machine can pass to configuration $(q', c_0', c_1', \ldots, c_n')$, denoted as $(q, c_0, c_1, \ldots, c_n) \Rightarrow (q', c_0', c_1', \ldots, c_n')$, if $(q \rightarrow q', X) \in R$, and

- if $X = j+$, then $c_j' = c_j + 1$ and $c_i' = c_i$, $0 \leq i \leq n$, $i \neq j$,
- if $X = j-$, then $c_j' = c_j - 1$ and $c_i' = c_i$, $0 \leq i \leq n$, $i \neq j$,
- if $X = e$, then $c_i' = c_i$, $0 \leq i \leq n$,
- if $X = (j = 0)$, then $c_i' = c_i$, $0 \leq i \leq n$, and $c_j = 0$.

Let $\Rightarrow^*$ denote the reflexive and transitive closure of $\Rightarrow$.

A computation is a sequence of such transitions leading from the initial configuration to a final configuration, and its result can be read from the output counter.

Definition 6. The set of natural numbers generated by a counter automaton M as above is

$$N(M) = \{c_0 \in \mathbb{N} \mid (q_0, 0, 0, \ldots, 0) \Rightarrow^* (f, c_0, c_1, \ldots, c_n), \text{ where}$$
$$q_0 \text{ and } f \text{ are the initial and the final states, respectively}\}.$$

It is known that counter automata are able to generate any recursively enumerable set of numbers if they have two or more counters beside the output counter.

3   The Number of Membranes

In this section we show that P systems with minimal symport/antiport rules generate any recursively enumerable set of numbers with elements greater then five with three membranes. To do this, we will show how these systems simulate the computations of counter automata.

Theorem 1. $NOP_3(sym_1, anti_1) = \mathbb{N}_5 RE$.

Proof. Consider the counter automaton $M = (Q, C, R, q_0, f)$ with counters $C = \{c_0, c_1, \ldots, c_n\}$ as above, c_0 being the output counter, and let the transitions be uniquely labelled by elements of the set $lab(R)$. We construct a P system Π generating the language $L(\Pi) = \{x + 5 \mid x \in L(M)\}$ as follows. Let

$$\Pi = (V, \mu, E, w_1, w_2, w_3, R_1, R_2, R_3, 3),$$

where $\mu = [_1 \, [_2 \, [_3 \,]_3 \,]_2 \,]_1$, and

$$V = \{I_1, \bar{I}_1, I_2, I_3, I_4, I_5, \infty_1, \infty_2, \infty_3, \infty_4, C, f_1, f_1', f_2, f_2', \bar{f}_2, f_3, f_3', f_4\}$$
$$\cup \{t, t' \mid t \in lab(R)\} \cup \{c_i, 0_i \mid 0 \leq i \leq n\},$$
$$E = \{t, t' \mid t \in lab(R)\} \cup \{I_4, f_1, f_2, \bar{f}_2, f_3, f_4\} \cup \{c_i \mid 0 \leq i \leq n\}.$$

The initial region contents are

$$w_1 = \{\{I_1, \bar{I}_1, I_2, I_3, \infty_1, \infty_2, \infty_3, \infty_4, \infty_4, C\}\},$$
$$w_2 = \{\{\infty_1, \infty_2\}\} \cup \{\{0_i \mid 0 \le i \le n\}\}, \text{ and}$$
$$w_3 = \{\{I_5, f'_1, f'_2, f'_3, \infty_3\}\}.$$

The work of the P system can be divided into three phases:

- Initialization,
- simulation of the counter automaton, and
- termination.

In the *initialization phase* an arbitrary number of counter symbols $c_i, 0 \le i \le n$, are moved into region 1 and an arbitrary number of transition symbols t' for some $t \in lab(R)$ are moved into region 3.

In the *simulation phase* Π simulates M by modifying the number of counter symbols present in region 2 according to the counter contents of M as follows. First Π imports a transition symbol t_1 for a possible transition $t_1 : (q \to r, X) \in R$ of M into region 1. Then this symbol travels to region 2 and then to region 3 where it remains until the termination phase, and from where the primed version, t'_1, is released to region 2 moving to region 1 where it is sent out to the environment and at the same time an other transition symbol $t_2 \in lab(R)$ is imported for an other valid transition $t_2 : (r \to s, Y)$ of M. While these transition symbols travel through the system to region 3 and back, the modifications on the number of counter symbols in region 2 are realized. If $X = i-$, then a copy of c_i is removed from region 2 when t_1 enters this region from region 1. If $X = i+$, then a copy of c_i is imported from region 1 to region 2 when t'_1 moves from region 2 to region 1. For $X = (i = 0)$, through the aid of maximal parallel rule application, the system allows the above described movement of the transition symbols only in the case when region 2 does not contain any symbol c_i.

In the *termination phase*, the counter symbols corresponding to the output counter are moved to region three, then the possibly still present transition symbols of the form t, t' for some $t \in lab(R)$ are moved from region 3 to region 2. In case of an unsuccessful simulation, Π may never stop which is ensured by an infinite loop: A pair of ∞_1 symbols are present in region 1 and 2, together with the rule $(\infty_1, in; \infty_1, out)$ in region 2. This loop is "destroyed" only in the termination phase after a successful simulation allowing the computation to stop.

For the sake of easier readability we present the rules of Π in groups corresponding to these phases $R_i = R_i^{ini} \cup R_i^{sim} \cup R_i^{ter}$, $1 \le i \le 3$.

For j, $0 \le j \le n$, and $t \in lab(R)$,

$$(t', in; I_1, out), (I_1, in), (I_4, in; I_1, out), (c_j, in; \bar{I}_1, out), (\bar{I}_1, in) \in R_1^{ini},$$
$$(I_2, in), (t', in; I_2, out), (\infty_3, in; I_2, out), (I_3, in; \infty_2, out) \in R_2^{ini},$$
$$(I_3, in), (t', in; I_3, out) \in R_3^{ini}.$$

With the help of the initialization symbols $I_1, \bar{I}_1, I_2, I_3 \in w_1$, these rules import an arbitrary number of transition symbols t' with $t \in lab(R)$ into region 3 and counter symbols c_i, $0 \leq i \leq n$, into region 1. In the first step, I_1 and $\bar{I}_1$ are moved out of the system, I_2 and I_3 are moved to region 2. Since there will be other rules in region 1 for I_3, it is necessary to make sure that it is moved to region 2 by sending out the symbol ∞_2. If ∞_2 is not sent out, an infinite loop is formed which can not be later destroyed. By applying these rules in succession, the imported transition symbols are moved to region 3, the counter symbols remain in region 1. If for some reason, because of the application of some other rule, a transition symbol can not be moved to region 2 from region 1, then ∞_3 is moved into region 2 instead, creating an infinite loop. Another infinite loop involving the two ∞_1 objects keeps the system working until a correct simulation of a successful computation is finished, then it is removed, otherwise if the simulation does not follow the right track, the system will produce no result. These infinite loops need rules

$$(\infty_1, in; \infty_1, out), (\infty_2, in; \infty_2, out) \in R_2^{ini},$$
$$(\infty_3, in; \infty_3, out) \in R_3^{ini}.$$

If once in region 1, instead of a transition symbol, I_4 is imported, then the initialization phase is finished using the following rules.

$$(I_3, out) \in R_1^{ini}$$
$$(I_4, in; I_3, out), (I_1, in; I_4, out), (\infty_4, in; I_4, out), (\bar{I}_1, in; I_5, out) \in R_2^{ini}$$
$$(I_1, in; I_5, out), (I_2, in; I_1, out) \in R_3^{ini}$$

First, the symbol I_3 is moved out from region 2 to region 1 and at the same time I_4 is moved from region 1 to region 2. Then I_3 leaves the system, and I_4 is sent back to region 1 while moving I_1 to region 2. Since there are other rules for I_1 in region 1, an infinite loop is created with the ∞_4 symbols if in this step I_1 is not moved to region 2. Then I_1 is transferred to region 3, where it brings also I_2 to region 3, and releases I_5 which moves to region 1 while bringing $\bar{I}_1$ to region 2. The infinite loop needs the rule

$$(\infty_4, in; \infty_4, out) \in R_2^{ini}.$$

Thus, at the end of a successful initialization phase, the system ends up in a configuration where u_1, u_2, u_3 are the multisets contained by the three regions as

$$u_1 = \{\{c_{i_1}, \dots, c_{i_k} \mid i_j \in \{0, \dots, n\}, \ 1 \leq j \leq k\}\}$$
$$\cup \{\{I_4, I_5, \infty_2, \infty_2, \infty_3, \infty_4, \infty_4, \infty_1, C\}\},$$

$$u_2 = \{\{I_1, \bar{I}_1, \infty_1, 0_0, 0_1, \dots, 0_n\}\}, \text{ and}$$

$$u_3 = \{\{t_1', \dots, t_m' \mid t_j \in lab(R), \ 1 \leq j \leq m\}\}$$
$$\cup \{\{I_2, f_1', f_2', f_3', \infty_3\}\}.$$

The simulation of the counter automaton is realized with the following rules.

$$R_1^{sim} = \{(t_0, in; I_5, out), (t_2, in; t_1', out) \mid t_0, t_1, t_2 \in lab(R) \text{ with}$$
$$t_0 : (q_0 \to q, X), t_1 : (q \to r, Y), t_2 : (r \to s, Z) \text{ for some } X, Y, Z\},$$

$$R_2^{sim} = \{(t, in), (c_i, in; t', out) \mid t : (r \to s, i+) \in R\}$$
$$\cup \{(t, in; c_i, out), (t', out) \mid t : (r \to s, i-) \in R\}$$
$$\cup \{(t, in), (t', out) \mid t : (r \to s, e) \in R\}$$
$$\cup \{(t, in; 0_i, out), (0_i, in; c_i, out), (0_i, in; t', out) \mid t : (r \to s, i = 0) \in R\},$$

$$R_3^{sim} = \{(t, in; t', out) \mid t \in lab(R)\}.$$

First I_5 is sent out of the system and one transition symbol, denoting a transition from the initial state q_0 is imported, then the transition corresponding to the symbol is simulated. This is done by moving the transition symbol to the third region, exchanging it to its primed version, and moving the primed version back to region 1. While the transition symbol travels through the regions, it adds or subtracts a counter symbol to or from region 2 when necessary. If the instruction corresponding to the simulated transition is $i = 0$, then the above described movement of the transition symbol is only possible if there are no c_i counter symbols present in region 2.

If the system simulates a transition $t_f : (q \to f, X)$ to the final state f, it may enter the terminating phase. In this phase the following rules are used.

$$R_1^{ter} = \{(f_1, in; t_f', out), (\bar{f}_2, in; f_1', out), (\bar{f}_2, in; \bar{f}_2, out), (f_2, in; \bar{f}_2, out),$$
$$(f_3, in; f_2', out), (f_4, in; f_3', out)\},$$

$$R_2^{ter} = \{(f_1, in), (C, in; f_1', out), (f_2, in; 0_0, out), (0_0, in; c_0, out),$$
$$(0_0, in; f_2', out), (f_3, in; C, out), (f_3', out), (f_4, in; \infty_1, out)\},$$

$$R_3^{ter} = \{(f_1, in; f_1', out), (C, in), (C, out), (c_0, in; C, out), (f_2, in; f_2', out),$$
$$(f_3, in; f_3', out), (f_4, in; rs'out), (f_4, in; rs, out), (f_4, out)\}.$$

During the terminating phase, symbols f_1, f_2, f_3, and f_4 travel through the system, each performing a specific task. First, after a transition symbol t_f' is present in region 1, f_1 is imported into the system. It moves to region 3 where f_1' is released which moves to region 1 bringing C to region 2. The task of C is to move all c_0 counter symbols corresponding to the output counter to region 3. This may take several steps, so f_1' is exchanged with $\bar{f}_2$ in region 1, and $\bar{f}_2$ can move in and out of the system for an arbitrary amount of time. When $\bar{f}_2$ is exchanged with f_2, the termination process continues. The travel of f_2 is only possible if there is no c_0 present in region 2. In this case, after f_2' leaves the system, f_3 is imported. While f_3 moves through the system it removes C from region 2, so no further movement of possibly newly appearing c_0 will be allowed to region 3, then, when f_3' leaves the system, f_4 is introduced. When f_4 moves to region 2, it removes ∞_1, thus removes the infinite loop, and then it also removes the remaining transition symbols from region 3. When all of these symbols are out of region 3, the system stops working, having only the counter symbols plus five other symbols, f_1, f_2, f_3, ∞_3, and I_2 in region 3, the output region, thus producing a result $x \in \mathbb{N}$ for some $(x - 5) \in L(M)$.   □

4   Conclusion

We have shown how to simulate counter automata using P systems with minimal symport/antiport rules and three membranes, thus we have improved the previously known best result stating that four membranes are sufficient to reach this power. The optimality of our result is still to be demonstrated, but we conjecture that it cannot be further improved.

Acknowledgement. Thanks to Pierluigi Frisco for pointing out several faults in a previous version of this paper.

References

1. F. Bernardini, M. Gheorghe. On the power of minimal symport/antiport. In: *Workshop on Membrane Computing, WMC-2003, Tarragona, July 17-22, 2003*. Edited by A. Alhazov, C. Martín-Vide, Gh. Păun. Technical Report 28/03 of the Research Group on Mathematical Linguistics, Rovira i Virgili University, Tarragona, Spain, 2003, 72-83.
2. F. Bernardini, A. Păun. Universality of minimal symport/antiport: Five membranes suffice. In: *Membrane Computing. International Workshop WMC 2003, Tarragona, Spain, July 17-22, 2003. Revised Papers*. Volume 2933 of *Lecture Notes in Computer Science*, edited by C. Martín-Vide, G. Mauri, Gh. Păun, G. Rozenberg, A. Salomaa. Springer-Verlag, 2004, 43-54.
3. L. Kari, C. Martín-Vide, A. Păun. On the universality of P systems with minimal symport/antiport rules. In: *Aspects of Molecular Computing, Essays Dedicated to Tom Head on the Occasion of His 70th Birthday*. Volume 2950 of *Lecture Notes in Computer Science*, edited by N. Jonoska, Gh. Păun, G. Rozenberg. Springer-Verlag, 2004, 254-265.
4. P. Frisco. About P systems with symport/antiport. In: *Second Brainstorming Week in Membrane Computing. Sevilla, February 2-7, 2004*. Edited by Gh. Păun, A. Riscos-Núñez, A. Romero-Jiménez, F. Sancho-Caparrini. Technical Report 01/2004 of the Research Group in Natural Computing, University of Sevilla, Spain, 2004, 224-236.
5. P. Frisco, H. J. Hoogeboom. P systems with symport/antiport simulating counter automata. Submitted.
6. C. Martín-Vide, A. Păun, Gh. Păun. On the power of P systems with symport rules. *Journal of Universal Computer Science*, 8:317-331, 2002.
7. C. Martín-Vide, A. Păun, Gh. Păun, G. Rozenberg. Membrane systems with coupled transport. *Fundamenta Informaticae*, 49:1-15, 2002.

8. A. Păun, Gh. Păun. The power of communication: P systems with symport/anti-port. *New Generation Computing*, 20(3):295-306, 2002.
9. Gh. Păun. Computing with Membranes. *Journal of Computer and System Sciences*, 61(1):108-143, 2000.
10. Gh. Păun, *Membrane Computing. An Introduction.* Springer-Verlag, Berlin, 2002.
11. G. Rozenberg, A. Salomaa (eds.) *Handbook of Formal Languages.* Springer-Verlag, Berlin, 1997.

Author Index

Alhazov, Artiom   146, 161, 178
Andrei, Oana   126

Bel Enguix, Gemma   190
Besozzi, Daniela   210
Bianco, Luca   63

Cavaliere, Matteo   224, 239
Ceterchi, Rodica   259
Ciobanu, Gabriel   126, 210
Colson, Loïc   1
Cordón-Franco, Andrés   278, 287
Csuhaj-Varjú, Erzsébet   19, 296

Fontana, Federico   63
Freund, Rudolf   36, 146, 309

Gheorghe, Marian   389
Gutiérrez-Naranjo, Miguel A.   278, 320

Ionescu, Mihai   224
Ishdorj, Tseren-Onolt   224

Jonoska, Nataša   1

Kato, Norio   110
Kefalas, Petros   389
Krishna, Shankara Narayanan   331

Leporati, Alberto   344
Lucanu, Dorel   126

Manca, Vincenzo   63
Margenstern, Maurice   1, 161
Mauri, Giancarlo   344

Obtułowicz, Adam   359
Oswald, Marion   309

Păun, Andrei   309
Pérez-Jiménez, Mario J.   85, 259, 278, 320, 373

Riscos-Núñez, Agustín   278, 320
Rogozhin, Vladimir   161
Rogozhin, Yurii   161
Romero-Campero, Francisco José   373

Sancho-Caparrini, Fernando   287
Sburlan, Dragoş   178, 239
Stamatopoulou, Ioanna   389

Ueda, Kazunori   110

Vaszil, György   296, 404
Verlan, Sergey   161

Zandron, Claudio   344

Lecture Notes in Computer Science

For information about Vols. 1–3306

please contact your bookseller or Springer

Vol. 3418: U. Brandes, T. Erlebach (Eds.), Network Analysis. XII, 471 pages. 2005.

Vol. 3416: M. Böhlen, J. Gamper, W. Polasek, M.A. Wimmer (Eds.), E-Government: Towards Electronic Democracy. XIII, 311 pages. 2005. (Subseries LNAI).

Vol. 3412: X. Franch, D. Port (Eds.), COTS-Based Software Systems. XVI, 312 pages. 2005.

Vol. 3410: C.A. Coello Coello, A. Hernández Aguirre, E. Zitzler (Eds.), Evolutionary Multi-Criterion Optimization. XVI, 912 pages. 2005.

Vol. 3409: N. Guelfi, G. Reggio, A. Romanovsky (Eds.), Scientific Engineering of Distributed Java Applications. X, 127 pages. 2005.

Vol. 3406: A. Gelbukh (Ed.), Computational Linguistics and Intelligent Text Processing. XVII, 829 pages. 2005.

Vol. 3404: V. Diekert, B. Durand (Eds.), STACS 2005. XVI, 706 pages. 2005.

Vol. 3403: B. Ganter, R. Godin (Eds.), Formal Concept Analysis. XI, 419 pages. 2005. (Subseries LNAI).

Vol. 3401: Z. Li, L. Vulkov, J. Waśniewski (Eds.), Numerical Analysis and Its Applications. XIII, 630 pages. 2005.

Vol. 3398: D.-K. Baik (Ed.), Systems Modeling and Simulation: Theory and Applications. XIV, 733 pages. 2005. (Subseries LNAI).

Vol. 3397: T.G. Kim (Ed.), Artificial Intelligence and Simulation. XV, 711 pages. 2005. (Subseries LNAI).

Vol. 3396: R.M. van Eijk, M.-P. Huget, F. Dignum (Eds.), Advances in Agent Communication. X, 261 pages. 2005. (Subseries LNAI).

Vol. 3393: H.-J. Kreowski, U. Montanari, F. Orejas, G. Rozenberg, G. Taentzer (Eds.), Formal Methods in Software and Systems Modeling. XXVII, 413 pages. 2005.

Vol. 3391: C. Kim (Ed.), Information Networking. XVII, 936 pages. 2005.

Vol. 3388: J. Lagergren (Ed.), Comparative Genomics. VIII, 133 pages. 2005. (Subseries LNBI).

Vol. 3387: J. Cardoso, A. Sheth (Eds.), Semantic Web Services and Web Process Composition. VIII, 147 pages. 2005.

Vol. 3386: S. Vaudenay (Ed.), Public Key Cryptography - PKC 2005. IX, 436 pages. 2005.

Vol. 3385: R. Cousot (Ed.), Verification, Model Checking, and Abstract Interpretation. XII, 483 pages. 2005.

Vol. 3383: J. Pach (Ed.), Graph Drawing. XII, 536 pages. 2005.

Vol. 3382: J. Odell, P. Giorgini, J.P. Müller (Eds.), Agent-Oriented Software Engineering V. X, 239 pages. 2005.

Vol. 3381: P. Vojtáš, M. Bieliková, B. Charron-Bost, O. Sýkora (Eds.), SOFSEM 2005: Theory and Practice of Computer Science. XV, 448 pages. 2005.

Vol. 3379: M. Hemmje, C. Niederee, T. Risse (Eds.), From Integrated Publication and Information Systems to Information and Knowledge Environments. XXIV, 321 pages. 2005.

Vol. 3378: J. Kilian (Ed.), Theory of Cryptography. XII, 621 pages. 2005.

Vol. 3376: A. Menezes (Ed.), Topics in Cryptology – CT-RSA 2005. X, 385 pages. 2004.

Vol. 3375: M.A. Marsan, G. Bianchi, M. Listanti, M. Meo (Eds.), Quality of Service in Multiservice IP Networks. XIII, 656 pages. 2005.

Vol. 3374: D. Weyns, H.V.D. Parunak, F. Michel (Eds.), Environments for Multi-Agent Systems. X, 279 pages. 2005. (Subseries LNAI).

Vol. 3372: C. Bussler, V. Tannen, I. Fundulaki (Eds.), Semantic Web and Databases. X, 227 pages. 2005.

Vol. 3368: L. Paletta, J.K. Tsotsos, E. Rome, G.W. Humphreys (Eds.), Attention and Performance in Computational Vision. VIII, 231 pages. 2005.

Vol. 3366: I. Rahwan, P. Moraitis, C. Reed (Eds.), Argumentation in Multi-Agent Systems. XII, 263 pages. 2005. (Subseries LNAI).

Vol. 3365: G. Mauri, G. Păun, M.J. Pérez-Jiménez, G. Rozenberg, A. Salomaa (Eds.), Membrane Computing. IX, 415 pages. 2005.

Vol. 3363: T. Eiter, L. Libkin (Eds.), Database Theory - ICDT 2005. XI, 413 pages. 2004.

Vol. 3362: G. Barthe, L. Burdy, M. Huisman, J.-L. Lanet, T. Muntean (Eds.), Construction and Analysis of Safe, Secure, and Interoperable Smart Devices. IX, 257 pages. 2005.

Vol. 3361: S. Bengio, H. Bourlard (Eds.), Machine Learning for Multimodal Interaction. XII, 362 pages. 2005.

Vol. 3360: S. Spaccapietra, E. Bertino, S. Jajodia, R. King, D. McLeod, M.E. Orlowska, L. Strous (Eds.), Journal on Data Semantics II. XI, 223 pages. 2005.

Vol. 3359: G. Grieser, Y. Tanaka (Eds.), Intuitive Human Interfaces for Organizing and Accessing Intellectual Assets. XIV, 257 pages. 2005. (Subseries LNAI).

Vol. 3358: J. Cao, L.T. Yang, M. Guo, F. Lau (Eds.), Parallel and Distributed Processing and Applications. XXIV, 1058 pages. 2004.

Vol. 3357: H. Handschuh, M.A. Hasan (Eds.), Selected Areas in Cryptography. XI, 354 pages. 2004.

Vol. 3356: G. Das, V.P. Gulati (Eds.), Intelligent Information Technology. XII, 428 pages. 2004.

Vol. 3355: R. Murray-Smith, R. Shorten (Eds.), Switching and Learning in Feedback Systems. X, 343 pages. 2005.

Vol. 3353: J. Hromkovič, M. Nagl, B. Westfechtel (Eds.), Graph-Theoretic Concepts in Computer Science. XI, 404 pages. 2004.

Vol. 3352: C. Blundo, S. Cimato (Eds.), Security in Communication Networks. XI, 381 pages. 2005.

Vol. 3350: M. Hermenegildo, D. Cabeza (Eds.), Practical Aspects of Declarative Languages. VIII, 269 pages. 2005.

Vol. 3349: B.M. Chapman (Ed.), Shared Memory Parallel Programming with Open MP. X, 149 pages. 2005.

Vol. 3348: A. Canteaut, K. Viswanathan (Eds.), Progress in Cryptology - INDOCRYPT 2004. XIV, 431 pages. 2004.

Vol. 3347: R.K. Ghosh, H. Mohanty (Eds.), Distributed Computing and Internet Technology. XX, 472 pages. 2004.

Vol. 3346: R.H. Bordini, M. Dastani, J. Dix, A.E.F. Seghrouchni (Eds.), Programming Multi-Agent Systems. XIV, 249 pages. 2005. (Subseries LNAI).

Vol. 3345: Y. Cai (Ed.), Ambient Intelligence for Scientific Discovery. XII, 311 pages. 2005. (Subseries LNAI).

Vol. 3344: J. Malenfant, B.M. Østvold (Eds.), Object-Oriented Technology. ECOOP 2004 Workshop Reader. VIII, 215 pages. 2005.

Vol. 3342: E. Şahin, W.M. Spears (Eds.), Swarm Robotics. IX, 175 pages. 2005.

Vol. 3341: R. Fleischer, G. Trippen (Eds.), Algorithms and Computation. XVII, 935 pages. 2004.

Vol. 3340: C.S. Calude, E. Calude, M.J. Dinneen (Eds.), Developments in Language Theory. XI, 431 pages. 2004.

Vol. 3339: G.I. Webb, X. Yu (Eds.), AI 2004: Advances in Artificial Intelligence. XXII, 1272 pages. 2004. (Subseries LNAI).

Vol. 3338: S.Z. Li, J. Lai, T. Tan, G. Feng, Y. Wang (Eds.), Advances in Biometric Person Authentication. XVIII, 699 pages. 2004.

Vol. 3337: J.M. Barreiro, F. Martin-Sanchez, V. Maojo, F. Sanz (Eds.), Biological and Medical Data Analysis. XI, 508 pages. 2004.

Vol. 3336: D. Karagiannis, U. Reimer (Eds.), Practical Aspects of Knowledge Management. X, 523 pages. 2004. (Subseries LNAI).

Vol. 3335: M. Malek, M. Reitenspieß, J. Kaiser (Eds.), Service Availability. X, 213 pages. 2005.

Vol. 3334: Z. Chen, H. Chen, Q. Miao, Y. Fu, E. Fox, E.-p. Lim (Eds.), Digital Libraries: International Collaboration and Cross-Fertilization. XX, 690 pages. 2004.

Vol. 3333: K. Aizawa, Y. Nakamura, S. Satoh (Eds.), Advances in Multimedia Information Processing - PCM 2004, Part III. XXXV, 785 pages. 2004.

Vol. 3332: K. Aizawa, Y. Nakamura, S. Satoh (Eds.), Advances in Multimedia Information Processing - PCM 2004, Part II. XXXVI, 1051 pages. 2004.

Vol. 3331: K. Aizawa, Y. Nakamura, S. Satoh (Eds.), Advances in Multimedia Information Processing - PCM 2004, Part I. XXXVI, 667 pages. 2004.

Vol. 3330: J. Akiyama, E.T. Baskoro, M. Kano (Eds.), Combinatorial Geometry and Graph Theory. VIII, 227 pages. 2005.

Vol. 3329: P.J. Lee (Ed.), Advances in Cryptology - ASIACRYPT 2004. XVI, 546 pages. 2004.

Vol. 3328: K. Lodaya, M. Mahajan (Eds.), FSTTCS 2004: Foundations of Software Technology and Theoretical Computer Science. XVI, 532 pages. 2004.

Vol. 3327: Y. Shi, W. Xu, Z. Chen (Eds.), Data Mining and Knowledge Management. XIII, 263 pages. 2005. (Subseries LNAI).

Vol. 3326: A. Sen, N. Das, S.K. Das, B.P. Sinha (Eds.), Distributed Computing - IWDC 2004. XIX, 546 pages. 2004.

Vol. 3325: C.H. Lim, M. Yung (Eds.), Information Security Applications. XI, 472 pages. 2005.

Vol. 3323: G. Antoniou, H. Boley (Eds.), Rules and Rule Markup Languages for the Semantic Web. X, 215 pages. 2004.

Vol. 3322: R. Klette, J. Žunić (Eds.), Combinatorial Image Analysis. XII, 760 pages. 2004.

Vol. 3321: M.J. Maher (Ed.), Advances in Computer Science - ASIAN 2004. Higher-Level Decision Making. XII, 510 pages. 2004.

Vol. 3320: K.-M. Liew, H. Shen, S. See, W. Cai (Eds.), Parallel and Distributed Computing: Applications and Technologies. XXIV, 891 pages. 2004.

Vol. 3319: D. Amyot, A.W. Williams (Eds.), System Analysis and Modeling. XII, 301 pages. 2005.

Vol. 3318: E. Eskin, C. Workman (Eds.), Regulatory Genomics. VIII, 115 pages. 2005. (Subseries LNBI).

Vol. 3317: M. Domaratzki, A. Okhotin, K. Salomaa, S. Yu (Eds.), Implementation and Application of Automata. XII, 336 pages. 2005.

Vol. 3316: N.R. Pal, N.K. Kasabov, R.K. Mudi, S. Pal, S.K. Parui (Eds.), Neural Information Processing. XXX, 1368 pages. 2004.

Vol. 3315: C. Lemaître, C.A. Reyes, J.A. González (Eds.), Advances in Artificial Intelligence – IBERAMIA 2004. XX, 987 pages. 2004. (Subseries LNAI).

Vol. 3314: J. Zhang, J.-H. He, Y. Fu (Eds.), Computational and Information Science. XXIV, 1259 pages. 2004.

Vol. 3313: C. Castelluccia, H. Hartenstein, C. Paar, D. Westhoff (Eds.), Security in Ad-hoc and Sensor Networks. VIII, 231 pages. 2004.

Vol. 3312: A.J. Hu, A.K. Martin (Eds.), Formal Methods in Computer-Aided Design. XI, 445 pages. 2004.

Vol. 3311: V. Roca, F. Rousseau (Eds.), Interactive Multimedia and Next Generation Networks. XIII, 287 pages. 2004.

Vol. 3310: U.K. Wiil (Ed.), Computer Music Modeling and Retrieval. XI, 371 pages. 2005.

Vol. 3309: C.-H. Chi, K.-Y. Lam (Eds.), Content Computing. XII, 510 pages. 2004.

Vol. 3308: J. Davies, W. Schulte, M. Barnett (Eds.), Formal Methods and Software Engineering. XIII, 500 pages. 2004.

Vol. 3307: C. Bussler, S.-k. Hong, W. Jun, R. Kaschek, D.. Kinshuk, S. Krishnaswamy, S.W. Loke, D. Oberle, D. Richards, A. Sharma, Y. Sure, B. Thalheim (Eds.), Web Information Systems – WISE 2004 Workshops. XV, 277 pages. 2004.